Financial Management

An Introduction to Principles and Practice

Custom Edition

Lewellen | Halloran | Lanser

CENGAGE
Learning™

Australia • Brazil • Japan • Korea • Mexico • Singapore • Spain • United Kingdom • United States

Financial Management: An Introduction to Principles and Practice, Custom Edition

Lewellen | Halloran | Lanser

Executive Editors:
Michele Baird

Maureen Staudt

Michael Stranz

Project Development Manager:
Linda deStefano

Senior Marketing Coordinators:
Sara Mercurio

Lindsay Shapiro

Production/Manufacturing Manager:
Donna M. Brown

PreMedia Services Supervisor:
Rebecca A. Walker

Rights & Permissions Specialist:
Kalina Hintz

Cover Image:
Getty Images*

© 2005 Cengage Learning

For product information and technology assistance, contact us at
Cengage Learning Customer & Sales Support, 1-800-354-9706

For permission to use material from this text or product, submit all requests online at **cengage.com/permissions**
Further permissions questions can be emailed to
permissionrequest@cengage.com

ISBN-13: 978-0-324-33798-3

ISBN-10: 0-324-33798-1

Cengage Learning
5191 Natorp Boulevard
Mason, Ohio 45040
USA

Cengage Learning is a leading provider of customized learning solutions with office locations around the globe, including Singapore, the United Kingdom, Australia, Mexico, Brazil, and Japan. Locate your local office at:
international.cengage.com/region

Cengage Learning products are represented in Canada by Nelson Education, Ltd.

For your lifelong learning solutions, visit **custom.cengage.com**

Visit our corporate website at **cengage.com**

Printed in the United States of America

Custom Table of Contents

1	The Nature of Financial Management	2
2	The Accounting Environment: Financial Statements	25
3	The External Environment: The Financial System	60
5	Money, Time, and Value	128
6	Investment Value and Required Rates of Return	164
7	The Valuation of Securities	205
9	Capital Expenditures Decision Rules	262
10	Capitol Investment Cash Flows	302
14	Finacial Leverage	444
15	The Cost of Capitol and the Required Rate of Return	486
17	Working Capitol Policy	556
20	Management of Accounts Receivable and Inventory	616
21	Financial Planning and Corporate Growth	644
Appendix A	Financial Calculators Appendix	775
Appendix B	Answers to Selected Problems	783
Appendix C	Future Value and Present Value Tables	792
Appendix D	Answers to Self-Study Quizzes	798
Glossary		807
Index		816

The Nature of Financial Management

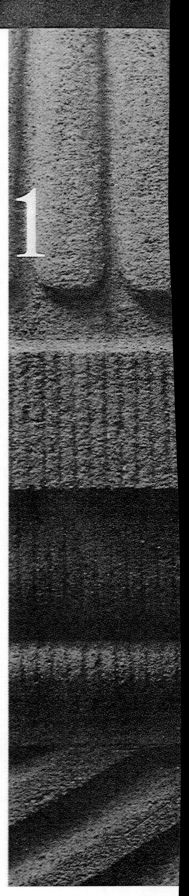

This text deals with financial decision-making within a business organization. Although financial decisions have always been important to a firm's owners and managers, the role of finance has grown in significance in recent years as the world economy and its financial markets have become increasingly interdependent. Hardly a month passes without the occurrence of some major financial event that affects the health and performance of both multinational and domestic companies. Within the last decade in particular, there have been substantial developments in the following areas, all of which are central to the management of a firm's finances:

1. Executive compensation
2. Corporate control
3. Accounting practices
4. Financial markets
5. Borrowing policies
6. Investment strategies
7. Corporate restructuring

Consider, as examples in each of these areas:

- In the United States in the mid-1990s, it was not unusual for the top executives of major corporations to receive annual compensation from their firms in amounts ranging from $5 million to $10 million per executive. In some cases, the amounts reached as much as $200 million for a single individual. Why were these payments deemed necessary? Were they a fair reflection of the efforts put forth by the executives for their firms' shareholders?

- Beginning in the late 1980s, companies started to adopt plans that allowed their stockholders to buy additional shares of stock in the company at a 50% discount from its market price if the company was the target of a takeover attempt from another firm. What was the intent of such plans? Do they benefit or harm the stockholders of the firms that adopt them?

- In 1999, a major American company announced that it was going to recognize a $1.5 billion loss in connection with the discontinuance of part of its operations and the layoff of a large number of employees who worked in those operations. On the day the announcement was made, the company's stock price rose by approximately 5% on the New York Stock Exchange. Why would the stock price climb in response to such apparent bad news? In general, what is the relationship between a firm's reported earnings and its stock price?

- In October 1987, stock prices in the United States fell by approximately 23% in a single day, and by nearly 30% in a five-day period. Losses to investors over the five days were estimated at $500 billion. Similar large declines took place in most other countries at the same time. In early 1992, stock prices in Japan fell by more than 25% in a three-week period. In October 1997, another round of stock price shocks occurred around the globe. U.S. stocks fell 7% in one day, while European markets fell by similar amounts. The declines on Asian markets were even sharper. What caused these sudden and dramatic changes? What do they tell us about the extent to which stock prices are accurate reflections of companies' earning power?

- Over a recent five-year period, approximately $400 billion of common stock was retired by U.S. corporations through stock buy-back plans and acquisitions of other companies. These retirements were financed largely by increases in corporate borrowing. But in the two years following, some $100 billion of new stock was issued to retire debt. Why would firms alter their financing strategies so substantially? What is the correct mix of debt and common stock capital for a firm to use in financing its operations?

- The EuroDisney theme park opened near Paris after a total in excess of $3 billion was spent to construct the park and its amusement attractions, over a four-year period. These expenditures occurred before even a single paying visitor to the park was expected to arrive. How were the park's owners able to obtain the funds needed for that investment, with no revenues being received? How could they justify making the expenditure, given the long time lag between the outlays and the potential revenues? How were they able to analyze the risks associated with the investment?

- During the 1990s, nearly 2,000 public corporations in the United States reverted to private ownership through a financial technique known as a "Leveraged Buyout" (LBO). This privatization movement began with relatively small firms but eventually extended to very large corporations as well. Why would a public corporation want to return to private ownership? How is an LBO financed? What effect does it typically have on a firm's stockholders?

In the chapters that follow, we shall examine these and other developments that have shaped the world of financial management in recent years. Our purpose will be not merely to describe those developments but to provide a conceptual model that will allow us to analyze their logic and significance for the owners and managers of firms. With that model, we can offer some answers to the questions that were just posed.

Our objective in this first chapter is to establish the central goal that should guide the decisions of a firm's managers, and to lay the groundwork for the discussion in subsequent chapters of how that goal can be attained. As you shall see, the major focus of our presentation will be on how financial decisions affect the *value* of the firm to its owners. Another way to put the point is to note that the concern of financial management is basically about "what things are worth." There are two key "things" in particular whose worth we shall deal with: the securities a firm issues to finance its operations, and the investments it makes in those operations. Both can be analyzed with the same fundamental valuation model.

Several characteristics of the text should be emphasized. First, although we do rely on a valuation model as the unifying theme for our discussion, that model—while powerful—is not a very complicated one. Its elements are relatively simple and relatively straightforward. Mathematical sophistication is not required either for its understanding or its use. Second, our focus is on the practical application of the model to actual business decisions. We shall offer numerous illustrations of such applications throughout the text. Finally, we shall examine financial decisions not only for firms that operate primarily in a single domestic marketplace, but also for firms doing business internationally. Chapters that address the international context are integrated into the presentation. Conveniently, the principles that apply to domestic financial decisions are also the ones that apply to international decisions. Only minor modifications are necessary. We hope in this process not simply to cover the topics that are relevant to managing the financial affairs of the modern business organization, but also to encourage you to think carefully and critically about those topics.

THE GOAL OF THE FIRM

Our discussion of financial management contains both descriptive and analytical elements. The *descriptive* elements deal with the nuts and bolts of financial management. Since this is a first course in the subject, you need to be exposed to the institutions involved in financial decision-making as well as to the terminology and techniques they employ. The *analytical* aspect of the text deals with the methods of evaluating proposed alternative courses of action to arrive at the best decision. In these discussions, we emphasize the **normative** elements of financial management: how decisions *should* be made rather than merely *how* they are made.

Normative A form of financial analysis that dictates how decisions should be made rather than merely describing how they are made.

In stressing a normative approach, we address a crucial question of financial management: When financial managers are faced with a number of alternative choices in one decision area, what rule should they use to determine the best alternative?

The answer is based on two key concepts: *agency* and *value maximization*. The theory of agency suggests that financial managers should base their decisions on the criterion that would be employed by the firm's owners. The concept of value maximization holds that it is the potential effect of a decision on the value of the firm that is the critical concern of the firm's owners. Let us examine these two concepts more closely.

Agency

Agency The principle that decisions should not be based on the needs and desires of the agents (corporate managers) but rather on the interests of those individuals whom the agents represent (shareholders).

In professionally managed firms, managers are indirectly hired by a firm's owners. Since the firm's managers have been entrusted with the owners' resources, they are obligated to act as agents of the owners. The guiding principle of **agency** is that decisions should not be based on the needs and desires of the agents but rather on the interests of those individuals whom the agents represent.

As an illustration of this principle, consider the case of a firm whose management is evaluating a proposal to build a new plant. The expansion would double the firm's manufacturing capacity and expand its market share. According to the concept of agency, potential benefits to the firm's managers in the form of increased firm size and market share, the prestige and power of a larger firm, or the additional intellectual challenges associated with expansion should be irrelevant to the ultimate decision. Only the benefits that will accrue to the firm's *owners* should be considered by the management team.

In actual practice, the managers of firms often seem to make decisions based on their own interests rather than on those of the firm's owners. These potential conflicts of interest between managers and owners are perhaps most visible in the area of executive compensation. Table 1-1 shows the 1997 total compensation of the chief executives of several large multinational firms. Critics of executive compensation argue that pay levels of this sort are inappropriate for at least two reasons. First, executive compensation in industry is inconsistent with that of other occupations. Namely, why should the Chairman of the Travelers Group have received salary and other compensation in 1997 of over $230 million when the President of the United States earned only $200,000? Second, critics contend that the pay received by chief executives is not very highly related to their firms' profitability. Firm *size* rather than profitability often seems to be the major determinant of compensation levels. Critics charge that a chief executive who maximizes firm size and therefore his or her salary, rather than value, is acting contrary to the economic interests of the firm's owners.

What gives rise to this **agency problem**, or conflict of interest, between a firm's owners and its managers? The answer is simple: managers do not own 100% of the firms for which they work. In fact, in the typical large corporation, managers own a very small portion of the outstanding shares of stock. As a result, the managers' share in the profits earned by their firms is also very small. The major compensation of most managers takes the direct form of salaries and bonus plans and the indirect form of executive benefits such as expansive offices, club memberships, company planes and cars, and personal staffs. The cost of this direct and indirect management compensation, of course, reduces profits available for the payment of dividends to stockholders. Thus, what managers gain through increased compensation necessarily comes at the immediate expense of a firm's owners.

Stockholders are not powerless in their attempts to deal with the agency problem, however. They have at their disposal both positive and negative incentives to persuade managers to act in the interest of owners. Among the most effective *negative* incentives is the threat of firing. Stockholders elect a Board of Directors

Agency Problem The conflict of interest between the welfare of a firm's owners and its managers due to the small ownership position of the managers.

The Compensation of Corporate Chief Executives in 1997		
		TABLE 1-1

Industry	Company	Chief Executive Compensation (in millions)
Insurance	Travelers Group	$230.5
Investment Banking	Morgan Stanley	50.1
Chemicals	Monsanto	49.3
Diversified	General Electric	39.8
Travel/Credit Cards	American Express	33.2
Pharmaceuticals	Bristol-Myers Squibb	29.2
Diversified	Allied-Signal	28.2

who, in turn, appoint a firm's managers. Managers who neglect the stockholders' interests can be replaced by the Board. They can also be replaced in the aftermath of a hostile takeover by another firm that buys the shares of disgruntled stockholders. Perhaps the most widely used *positive* incentive is to tie executive compensation to a firm's earnings performance. Many firms have compensation plans under which the annual bonuses that managers receive are set at a specified percentage of the year's profits. Others compensate their managers in the form of shares of the company's common stock, rather than simply cash payments, in order to induce managers to pay increased attention to decisions that favorably affect stock prices. Through such compensation schemes, the interests of managers and owners can be more closely aligned, and there is increasing emphasis in large companies on plans of this sort.

Agency Costs The expenses associated with stockholder efforts to monitor the actions of managers to minimize the agency problem.

Another widely used alternative for dealing with agency problems is the establishment of a complex organizational structure that involves close monitoring of managerial decisions. This type of structure usually limits the scope and dollar value of decisions that an individual manager can make independently. Decisions beyond these limits are subject to approval by superiors or management committees. This method of dealing with agency problems, however, involves both the out-of-pocket cost of additional employees and the opportunity cost of delayed management decisions. These **agency costs** are a necessary expense of monitoring managerial decisions.

Despite the practical difficulties with the concept of agency, it remains a useful decision guide in a normative sense. Since our objective is to describe and apply fundamental principles of financial management, *we stress theoretically correct decision-making methodologies that reflect the economic interests of a firm's owners.* In order to promote those interests, of course, financial managers must be able to *identify* them. The concept of value maximization is the key to understanding and satisfying owner economic interests.

Wealth Maximization and Value Maximization

The material welfare of individuals is measured in terms of their wealth, which consists of *real assets* such as houses, land, cars, gold, jewelry, and *financial assets* such as currency, bank accounts, stocks, and bonds. Clearly, the *economic* objective of an individual is to maximize wealth within legal and ethical constraints. In their role as agents, the goal of a firm's financial managers is to make decisions that are consistent with maximizing the wealth of the firm's owners. While an individual owner's wealth consists of the total value of numerous assets, financial managers' decisions can affect only that portion of owners' wealth that comprises their investment in the company. In the case of the corporation, then, the abstract objective of owner wealth maximization translates into the operational goal of maximizing the market price of the corporation's common stock—that is, **value maximization**.

Value Maximization The maximization of owners' wealth achieved by the maximization of the value of a firm's common stock.

Value maximization is not concerned with short-term day-to-day fluctuations in stock prices that accompany an active stock market. Market psychology, national economic conditions, and national and international news events seem to be the dominant determinants of daily stock price changes. The *long-term* level and trend in a firm's stock price, however, reflects the underlying economic performance of the company, which translates into earnings and the dividends received by its stockholders. Those are the elements that should be the major concern of the firm's managers, who can influence them on behalf of the firm's owners.

■ Ethics

ISSUES

DO GOLDEN PARACHUTES SERVE THE INTERESTS OF A FIRM'S OWNERS?

The potential conflict between the theoretical duty of managers to serve the economic interests of a firm's owners and the managers' practical incentive to pay attention to their own interests is highlighted by the existence of so-called golden parachute clauses in many executive compensation contracts. A golden parachute is a special employment agreement that promises a firm's key executives generous severance pay if they lose their jobs following a takeover of their firm by another company. The payments in many cases can amount to five to ten times the executives' normal annual salaries.

Executives who are covered by the plans argue that they are necessary to enable a firm to hire and retain competent managers who will want to be protected from arbitrary dismissal if their firm is acquired. Other supporters contend that managers will be more amenable to accepting a takeover offer from another firm that will benefit their firm's owners, if they are assured that they will not personally suffer in the process. Critics point out that the cost of the golden parachutes raises the cost of an acquisition to the acquiring firm, which must honor the severance payments. This may inhibit otherwise logical mergers. Other critics describe these severance payments as blatant attempts by managers to profit from corporate takeovers.

In principle, managers should be enthusiastic about mergers that will result in a high price being received by their firms' owners for their stock. In practice, they may be less enthusiastic if they think they will lose their jobs in the process. Thus, golden parachutes are an additional focused incentive—to induce managers to behave in the interest of shareholders.

Given value maximization as a goal, it remains to be seen whether a firm's financial management team can effectively utilize this goal as a guide in making decisions. Can the goal of value maximization be translated into an action plan that clearly and accurately indicates which decisions *will* maximize a firm's stock price?

Value Maximization as an Operating Criterion

In order to be useful, a goal statement must be translated into an operating criterion that: (1) accurately indicates the best of several alternative decisions; (2) is generally applicable to all types of decisions; and (3) is relatively simple to apply. To meet these requirements, the goal of value maximization requires that we establish a valuation model that a firm's managers can use to guide their decisions. Such a valuation model must have the following attributes:

- Be normative in nature
- Be able to be expressed mathematically
- Be reasonably realistic

Value maximization is definitely a *normative* guide. Our previous discussion of the role of managers as agents established that managers should attempt to maximize firm value. With value maximization as their criterion, managers can be certain that the stockholders will agree with decisions that are consistent with this goal.

The second attribute of a valuation model is that it must take a mathematical form. The long-term effects of a subjective, nonmathematical decision guide almost certainly will include serious disagreements among managers and stockholders, and inconsistent decisions. On the other hand, a mathematical model has the

http://

MCB University Press Ltd. developed a strategy for price, product development, and value maximization. Read about dealing with a shrinking budget, increased costs, and a quality product at

www.mcb.co.uk/serials.htm

advantages of being unambiguous and consistent. It is *unambiguous* because the laws of mathematics follow precise definitions. It is *consistent* because, once the mathematical relationship is stated, it can be used repeatedly without distortion. Later in this text, we will develop a mathematical model that can convert the cash flows associated with a proposed decision into their potential impact on the value of a firm to its stockholders.

The mathematical expression of the decision guide must also be reasonably realistic. Clearly, no manageable mathematical expression could incorporate all the variables necessary to produce an *ideally* realistic model. Our socioeconomic environment is too complex for that. Given the tremendous uncertainty inherent in predicting the future impact of today's decisions, any mathematical model is at best only a rough approximation of reality. A model must be realistic enough to produce credible results and sufficiently workable to be acceptable to financial managers. The valuation model developed in this text is realistic because it incorporates all of the attributes of a decision that determine its impact on firm value. Furthermore, it performs this analysis in a relatively simple and straightforward manner.

The relationship between the valuation model and owner wealth is summarized in Figure 1-1. The valuation model serves as the criterion used by financial managers in evaluating alternative investing and financing decisions that determine the firm's risk and return characteristics. This same model is used by investors to determine the value of the firm's stock and, ultimately, the wealth of the firm's owners. In order to accurately guide the decisions of financial managers, the valuation model depicted in Figure 1-1 must take into account the major factors that determine a firm's value. Although we will leave a detailed discussion of those factors for later chapters, we will briefly introduce them now.

Determinants of Value

Financial managers must know which variables affect the value of the firm if they are to maximize stock price and owner wealth successfully. Very simply, *firm value is a function of the size, timing, and riskiness of the returns expected to be gen-*

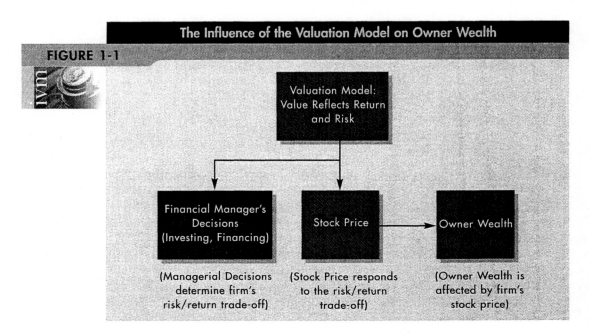

FIGURE 1-1

The Influence of the Valuation Model on Owner Wealth

Valuation Model: Value Reflects Return and Risk

Financial Manager's Decisions (Investing, Financing)

Stock Price

Owner Wealth

(Managerial Decisions determine firm's risk/return trade-off)

(Stock Price responds to the risk/return trade-off)

(Owner Wealth is affected by firm's stock price)

erated by future operations. In some special cases, an individual may invest funds in a firm in order to exercise direct control over its operations. For example, the major attraction of owning your own firm may be the power and independence associated with being your own boss. In the case of a large firm like IBM, on the other hand, the major motivation for its owners is the economic benefits or returns that are associated with owning its stock. It is the prospect of making money that entices individuals to buy IBM stock. Thus, the returns generated by IBM for its stockholders are what give value to its stock. More specifically, three major characteristics of those returns—their *size*, *timing*, and *riskiness*—determine the exact value of its shares to investors.

Since investors normally try to maximize their economic welfare, they prefer larger, more rapid, and more certain returns to smaller, less rapid, and less certain returns. As a result, the relationship between a firm's value and the size and timing of the returns that it generates for its owners is positive. *When the riskiness of returns is ignored, an increase in the size or an acceleration in the timing of returns expected by owners should increase the value of the firm.* Notice that we use the term "expected" in connection with these returns. The value of a firm in the present is determined by the returns that its owners anticipate will be generated by *future* operations. Past returns are irrelevant to current value.

The fact that a firm's current value is affected by investor forecasts of future returns means that the uncertainty of investors concerning their forecasts also affects firm value. Given a choice between two investments with identical forecasted returns, investors will normally set a lower value on the investment about whose return forecast they are more uncertain. For instance, most investors would pay less for a share of stock in a small unestablished computer manufacturer than they would for a share of stock in IBM if their forecasts of future earnings for both firms were identical. It is this investor uncertainty about the size or timing of forecasted returns on an investment that is referred to in finance as **risk**. The basic relationship between firm value and the riskiness of future returns is negative. *When the size and timing of returns is ignored, an increase in the riskiness of returns expected by owners decreases the value of the firm.*

In order to maximize firm value, financial managers should make those decisions that maximize anticipated returns and minimize their riskiness. In their attempt to do this, however, they encounter the basic dilemma of financial management: the **risk/return trade-off**. In practice, the relationship between anticipated returns and risk is typically positive. Those investments that promise the greatest and fastest returns also generally offer the greatest risk.

For example, the commitment of funds by Exxon Corporation to the exploration for petroleum in Alaska or the North Sea offers the potential for a much larger payoff than building additional service stations in the continental United States. It also offers the potential for no payoff at all. This is exactly what occurred when a group of oil companies, including British Petroleum, Mobil, Shell, Texaco, and Diamond Shamrock invested approximately $500 million in the Mukluk test well off the Alaska coast. The firms were forced to write off the investment as a *total loss* after the test well produced only salt water instead of the anticipated major oil discovery.

The firms that participated in this venture understood the risks they were taking. They simply felt that the size of the potential returns justified the uncertainty. In the words of one of the companies:

> "We have found that, from time to time, the unconventional action can generate the uncommon profit."

http://

Investorwords is an investing glossary Web site with more than 4,000 terms. Bookmark this site and check out the financial terms used in the business finance environment at

www.investorwords.com/s5.htm

Risk Investor uncertainty about the size or timing of the forecasted returns on an investment.

Risk/Return Trade-off The principle that financial decisions which increase a firm's anticipated returns also increase the riskiness of those returns. The trade-off involves the positive effect on firm value of larger expected returns versus the negative effect of greater uncertainty of returns.

From the point of view of the risk/return trade-off, the unconventional action can also generate the uncommon loss. Ironically, the uncommon loss can be suffered even when the search for oil is successful. This problem was dramatically demonstrated by the 1989 crash of the oil tanker *Exxon Valdez* in the Prince William Sound off the Alaskan coast, which resulted in the spilling of eleven million barrels of crude oil and unprecedented environmental damage. The cleanup costs borne by Exxon alone were estimated by the firm at over $2 billion.

The dilemma posed by the risk/return trade-off is summarized in Figure 1-2. If return could be increased while risk is held constant, value would rise. Value would fall if risk were increased while return is held constant. Typically, neither of these cases is possible in reality. Any action that increases return will usually also increase risk, with the result that the net effect on value is unknown. Later, we will describe the Investment Valuation Model (IVM), which will enable financial managers to measure the effect on firm value of a decision that alters *both* the expected size and riskiness of a firm's returns.

Value Maximization Versus Profit Maximization

While financial theory is based on the goal of value maximization, financial practice seems to stress a goal of profit maximization. Managers, stockholders, security analysts, and creditors continuously monitor and emphasize earnings in their evaluation of a firm's performance. This emphasis on profits stems largely from the accounting environment of firms that requires that they report performance in terms of profits and losses. Thus, profits have become the criterion, or benchmark, by which a firm's *performance* is evaluated. Financial theory, on the other hand, states that the criterion on which a firm's managers should base their *decisions* is not profits but firm value.

We will examine the potential conflict between the value decision criterion and the profit performance criterion in detail subsequently. At this point, however, it is important to discuss the difference between these two concepts. The basic flaw with the concept of profit maximization is that it is not sufficiently precise to serve as a useful operating criterion. *Profit maximization* is an appropriate decision criterion only where one ignores the *risk and timing* of anticipated returns. Under actual business conditions, the riskiness and timing of benefits is critically important.

Some simple examples will demonstrate the problems with profit maximization as a decision criterion. Assume that a firm is faced with a choice between the two investments shown in Table 1-2. Both investments are identical in terms of total profits over their expected life of five years. With profit maximization

The Risk/Return Trade-off

FIGURE 1-2

Effect of Action on Return and Risk	Effect of Action on Firm Value
Return up, Risk constant	Value up
Return constant, Risk up	Value down
Return up, Risk up	Value up or down
Return down, Risk down	Value up or down

The Effect of the Timing of Returns on an Investment

TABLE 1-2

Year	Profits from Investment A	Profits from Investment B
1	$ 100	$ 500
2	200	400
3	300	300
4	400	200
5	500	100
Total	$1,500	$1,500

as a decision criterion, therefore, the firm would be indifferent between investments A and B. In reality, however, Investment B would be preferable to Investment A due to the more rapid realization of its returns. The sooner the firm receives those returns, the sooner it can use them to make additional investments or to pay dividends to the firm's owners. The sooner the owners receive dividends, the sooner they can spend or reinvest the funds themselves. Thus, even by this simple comparison, Investment B is clearly more valuable than Investment A. The profit maximization criterion is inadequate because it ignores the timing of returns.

Table 1-3 contains data on two additional investments. Assume that in both cases the profits are expected to be realized at the end of one year. The returns from each investment, however, are uncertain because they depend on the state of the economy. Investment C's return is more uncertain than that on Investment D because it will be higher if the economy is good and lower if the economy is bad.

A firm's financial managers will be indifferent between these two investments if they use profit maximization as their decision criterion because the average of the three possible returns is $500 for both C and D. Since most owners dislike risk, however, Investment D should be more valuable to the firm than Investment C. Investment D is more valuable because it promises the same average return as Investment C with much less risk or uncertainty associated with the return. The low return in the case of a bad economy and the high return in the case of a good economy are much closer to the average or expected return in the case of Investment D than for Investment C. Once again, the profit maximization criterion fails to distinguish between two investments that should be unequal in value from the viewpoint of a firm's owners.

The Effect of the Timing of the Riskiness of Returns on an Investment

TABLE 1-3

State of the Economy	Profit from Investment C	Profit from Investment D
Bad	$ 0	$400
Normal	500	500
Good	1,000	600
Average Return	$ 500	$500

THE ROLE OF FINANCIAL MANAGERS

Our discussion of the goal of the firm began with the question: What criterion should financial managers use to guide their decisions? We have answered this question in terms of the concepts of agency and value maximization. As agents of a firm's owners, financial managers should make those decisions that will maximize the market value of their firms' stock. We can now raise a second question that logically follows from the first: what types of decisions do financial managers make in their attempt to maximize firm value? The answer to this question requires a closer look at the role of financial management in a firm.

The Role of Financial Management Within the Firm

Figure 1-3 portrays a typical organizational chart for a large manufacturing firm. The Board of Directors consists of a number of individuals elected by the owners to set strategy and oversee the operations of the firm. The President or Chief Executive Officer (CEO) is responsible for coordinating all management decisions. These decisions are made and implemented by vice presidents who specialize in the major functional areas: manufacturing, marketing, finance, and personnel.

The finance function in a large firm is frequently divided into two major components that are supervised by the Vice President of Finance: the *treasury* and the *control* functions. The Controller is typically the firm's chief accountant who is responsible for the preparation of financial statements and budgets. This individual also supervises the payment of bills, salaries, and taxes, and the collection of

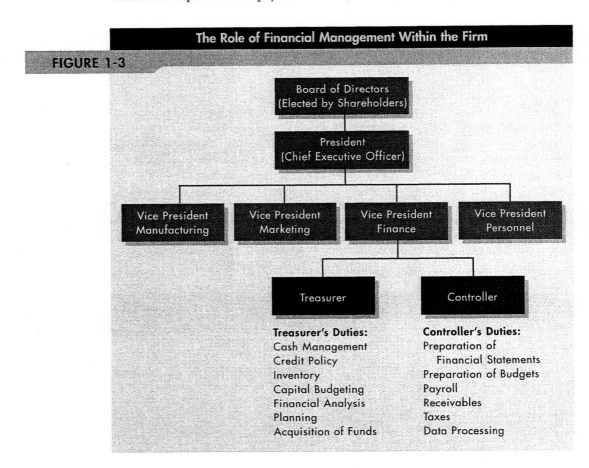

The Role of Financial Management Within the Firm

FIGURE 1-3

credit sales. Since his or her position requires a detailed knowledge of the firm's financial information system, the Controller may also supervise the firm's entire data processing system.

The Treasurer typically is assigned the task of analyzing the firm's financial statements and developing financial plans that will enable the firm to carry out its manufacturing and sales plans. Based on this financial analysis and planning, the Treasurer must obtain the financing required by operations and allocate these funds to various uses within the firm. Major areas of responsibility in this allocation process include determining the proper levels of cash, accounts receivable that arise from credit sales, and inventories. The Treasurer also supervises the capital allocation process that determines the quantity of funds committed to new plant and equipment.

Even after this brief discussion of the role of financial managers within the firm, it should be apparent that financial management is a vital and complex function that requires the efforts of numerous individuals throughout the firm. The three major financial executives depicted in Figure 1-3 maintain large staffs of specialists in accounting, financial analysis, and data processing. In addition, managers in the manufacturing and marketing areas are responsible for providing financial data and preliminary analyses that are used as input by the staffs of the Treasurer and the Controller. *The financial management function requires the cooperation of individuals throughout the firm.*

The Duties of Financial Managers

The major duties of financial managers are summarized in Figure 1-4. The basic responsibility of financial managers is to evaluate the financial implications of alternative courses of action and select those alternatives that will maximize the value of the firm to its owners. The figure indicates that this evaluation and selection process involves three important duties: financial planning, investing decisions, and financing decisions.

Financial Planning. From a financial management viewpoint, the management of the firm involves the planning of sources and uses of funds. Typical long-term planning involves decisions concerning new markets and products, plant expansion or contraction, and updating or replacing machinery and equipment. Short-term

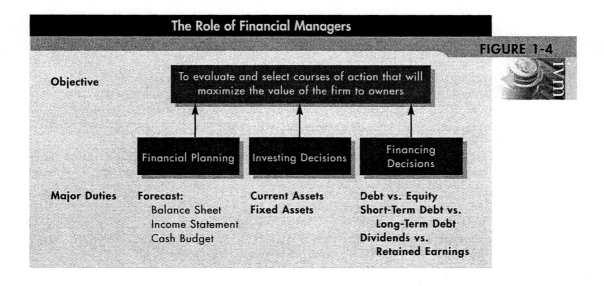

The Role of Financial Managers

FIGURE 1-4

Objective	To evaluate and select courses of action that will maximize the value of the firm to owners		
	Financial Planning	Investing Decisions	Financing Decisions
Major Duties	Forecast: Balance Sheet Income Statement Cash Budget	Current Assets Fixed Assets	Debt vs. Equity Short-Term Debt vs. Long-Term Debt Dividends vs. Retained Earnings

plans take the form of detailed cash budgets prepared on a quarterly, monthly, weekly, or even daily basis. The forecasted balance sheets, income statements, and cash budgets that are generated in the planning process summarize the anticipated financial effects of specific courses of action. In order to construct these financial statements, the financial management team must evaluate alternative decisions to invest in various types of assets such as inventories, plant, and equipment. They also have to evaluate alternative decisions regarding the method of financing these assets, such as through bank loans or the sale of stock.

Investing Decisions. An investment represents *the commitment of funds in the present in order to realize economic benefits in the future.* The investments that a firm has made are described by the current and fixed assets on its balance sheet. It is important to remember that the values in the asset accounts did not just "happen." They are planned and controlled with a specific objective: to maximize the value of the firm to its owners. The investing decisions regarding current and fixed assets are important because they can alter the risk/return trade-off and, hence, the value of a firm to its owners.

Financing Decisions. The funds that are invested in fixed and current assets must be acquired by retaining some of the cash generated by business operations and/or from sources outside the business. As a business grows, additional funds are needed to support expanding assets. A firm's financial managers must choose among many kinds of financing arrangements with different maturities, costs, and tax consequences. The choice among these alternatives has a significant impact on the owners in terms of risk and return. In making their financing decisions, financial managers face a number of key questions:

- Should the firm utilize debt or equity funds?
- If the firm uses debt funds, what is the optimal breakdown between long-term and short-term debt?
- If the firm uses equity funds, should the firm retain earnings or should it pay out earnings as dividends and sell new stock?

Although there are no universal answers to these questions, there *are* certain features of each financing alternative, which we can identify, that determine its impact on the firm's risk/return trade-off and value. In later chapters, we will make a detailed examination of the relationships among these financing decisions.

Up to this point, the discussion has centered on value maximization as the goal of financial managers and on the types of decisions that must be made to achieve that goal. In the chapters that follow, we shall go on to provide an in-depth analysis of these topics. Before beginning that analysis, however, we pause briefly to examine how the legal environment can influence managers' decisions. Specifically, we will look at the different legal forms of business organization.

FORMS OF BUSINESS ORGANIZATION

At first glance, the legal manner in which a firm is organized would not seem to affect financial managers. Since the owners select the form of ownership *prior* to hiring managers, this decision is typically not influenced by a firm's management. The form of ownership is a significant feature to both the owners and the managers, however, because it can affect the risk-return characteristics of a firm. The relationship between the form of ownership and a firm's value is summarized in Figure 1-5.

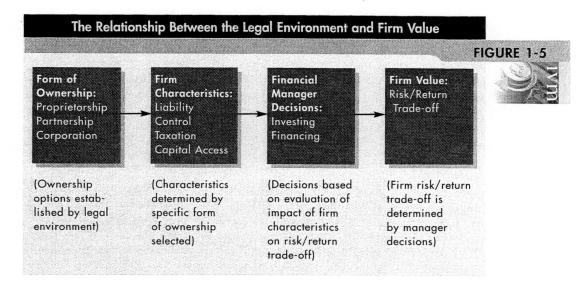

The Relationship Between the Legal Environment and Firm Value

FIGURE 1-5

| **Form of Ownership:** Proprietorship Partnership Corporation | → | **Firm Characteristics:** Liability Control Taxation Capital Access | → | **Financial Manager Decisions:** Investing Financing | → | **Firm Value:** Risk/Return Trade-off |

| (Ownership options established by legal environment) | (Characteristics determined by specific form of ownership selected) | (Decisions based on evaluation of impact of firm characteristics on risk/return trade-off) | (Firm risk/return trade-off is determined by manager decisions) |

The three major forms of ownership determine the liability, control, taxation, and capital access characteristics of a firm. These characteristics can influence financial managers' decisions which, in turn, determine the firm's risk/return trade-off and its value.

Sole Proprietorship

The least complicated way to organize a business is in the form of a sole proprietorship. A sole proprietorship is a firm that has a single owner who is also the major manager of the business. Since there usually is no registration fee or need for much legal help, organizational costs are minimal. There may be some license requirements depending on the locale and nature of the business. The owner/manager is in complete control and has freedom to manage as he or she sees fit. He or she is also personally entitled to all the profits and absorbs all the losses. All of the firm's revenues and expenses are subject to the tax code for individuals.

There is no legal distinction between the proprietor and the firm either in terms of activities or assets and liabilities. This fact has a number of important consequences. The foremost is the concept of **unlimited liability** of the owner. According to the law, personal assets and business assets have equal standing in satisfying legal claims against the firm. In addition, the ability of a proprietorship to obtain financing is limited to loans from financial institutions such as commercial banks and additional investment in the firm by its owner. Since a sole proprietorship can have only one owner, financing required by operations cannot be obtained by selling a share of the firm to new owners.

Partnership

A partnership is a contractual relationship in which two or more people combine their capital, skills, and knowledge to carry on a business. From a legal perspective, it is identical to a proprietorship except that there is more than one owner. While organizational costs are still minimal, there is the need to draw up a partnership agreement that specifies factors such as each partner's share of authority and earnings.

On the subject of owner liability, a distinction can be drawn between a general partnership and a limited partnership. In a **general partnership**, all owners have unlimited liability and accountability for the acts of any of the partners. In a **limited partnership**, the liability of the limited partners is restricted or limited

Unlimited Liability The liability that applies to both general partnerships and proprietorships whereby no legal distinction is made between personal and business activities or assets and liabilities.

General Partnership A contractual relationship in which two or more people combine their capital, skills, and knowledge to carry on a business and each party possesses unlimited liability.

Limited Partnership A form of business ownership in which the liability of one or more of the partners is legally limited to their initial investment in the firm. A limited partnership must have at least one general partner with unlimited liability.

to the funds that they have invested in the firm. There are certain restrictions, however, that the law typically places on limited partnerships. First, there must be at least one general partner with unlimited liability in each limited partnership. Second, limited partners are banned from actively taking part in the operations of the business. The advantage to a limited partnership is that investors can be attracted to the partnership as limited partners because of the lower risk associated with limited liability. The general partners, on the other hand, are able to maintain control over the firm's operations even though new owners are brought into the business.

Corporation

A corporation is an organization recognized by the law as an entity with rights, privileges, assets, and liabilities distinct from those of its owners. In fact, the primary characteristic of this form of ownership is that a *corporation is a legal entity that has an existence separate from that of its owners in the eyes of the law*. If the ownership of a corporation should completely change hands, the corporation's legal identity and existence remain unchanged.

As opposed to the unincorporated firm, organizational costs for a corporation can be significant. At the time of formation, the owners of the business file an application for incorporation. Upon approval, a charter is issued that establishes the corporation as a legal entity. In the United States, corporate charters are issued by individual state governments, and those governments specify the rules that apply to the firms they incorporate. In other countries, it is most often the national government that issues the charters and sets the rules.

The separate legal identity of a corporation and the distinction between a corporation and its owners give the incorporated firm a number of unique characteristics relative to proprietorships and partnerships:

- Limited liability of the owners
- Control of the firm
- Double taxation of earnings
- Access to capital

Limited Liability. Due to the legal separation of the owners and the corporation, the *liability of the owners* for the financial obligations of the firm is limited *to the amount of capital they have invested in the business*. This **limited liability** is an essential element of the corporate form of ownership, which allows individuals to invest in risky firms without exposing themselves to major losses in their personal wealth as a result of financial difficulties encountered by the business.

Limited Liability A form of liability that exists in corporations and limited partnerships whereby the liability of the owners for financial obligations of the firm is limited to the amount of capital they have invested in the business.

Control. Ownership of a corporation is divided into a number of shares represented by common stock certificates which are transferable between individuals. The corporation can exist indefinitely, as ownership of the shares passes from individual to individual. Shares of common stock give the right to control the corporation and to share in the firm's earnings. *Control is exercised through a Board of Directors elected by the shareholders.*

The role of the Board is to act as the representative of the stockholders in supervising the management of the firm. This role involves the establishment of broad goals and policies, and the appointment and evaluation of the senior managers of the firm, who are responsible for setting strategy and directing operations. The separation of the owners and the managers of a corporation makes it possible for individual investors to share in the returns generated by a firm without taking an active role in its operations. It can also lead to the agency problems discussed earlier in the chapter.

Double Taxation. An added dimension to the separation between the corporation and its owners is *taxes*. While the revenues and expenses of unincorporated businesses become part of the owners' personal tax calculations, *taxes are assessed against the corporation's earnings based on a separate corporate tax code*. The firm's stockholders receive cash payments out of these after-tax earnings in the form of dividends declared by the Board of Directors. The stockholders then must pay personal taxes on this dividend income. Since earnings that are paid out as dividends are subject to both corporate and personal taxes, stockholders are subject to **double taxation** on their investment. Although this double taxation of firm earnings is a distinct disadvantage, it reflects the risk/return trade-off of the corporate form of ownership. While corporate ownership reduces owner *risk* by offering limited liability, it also reduces owner *return* by increasing the total taxes levied against the firm's earnings. In some countries, however, corporations pay taxes at a lower rate on the portion of their earnings that are distributed as dividends than they do on the portion that is retained in the firm. This alleviates the burden of double taxation to some extent.

Double Taxation A system of taxation that applies to corporate income under which corporate taxes are assessed against the corporation's earnings and personal taxes are assessed against cash dividends paid to stockholders.

Access to Capital. A significant benefit that accrues from the characteristics of a corporation is its ability to attract additional investment. It is relatively easy even for a small corporation *to raise capital by selling additional shares of stock to current or new stockholders*. The small investment required per share of stock, and the ease with which stockholders can resell these shares to other investors, make common stock an attractive investment. The ability to raise equity capital is critical in a modern economy that favors firms of massive size.

Figure 1-6 summarizes our discussion of the features of each form of business ownership. While the number of corporations is relatively small, their importance in terms of overall economic activity is overwhelming. Given the advantages of limited liability and ready access to equity capital, it is no surprise that the corporation is the dominant form of business ownership. For example, although corporations accounted for only 20% of all businesses in the United States in 1999, they generated more than 90% of all business revenues.

Not-for-Profit Organizations

There is a further class of organizations that can reasonably be described as "businesses," but for which the major motivation is not producing earnings for the business itself. These include such not-for-profit entities as community hospitals, community water and electric systems, and cooperatives, which are set up to provide goods and services to their members at cost. Typically, these entities are organized as corporations in order to take advantage of the limited-liability feature of the corporate form.

Profit maximization clearly does not apply as a meaningful decision criterion for organizations of this sort. The question would be whether one can logically apply a *value* maximization test to the decisions that must be made by the organizations' managers. We would argue that it is possible to do so, in a number of important areas.

Most not-for-profit firms will, for example, be required to make decisions involving expenditures on buildings, equipment, computer systems, and other assets to support their operations. They will also often have to decide between alternative locations, sizes, and types of these investments. A sensible decision rule for the managers would be to choose the alternatives that minimize long-run operating costs. These would be the choices that would make the not-for-profit firm most *valuable* to the community or the membership group it serves.

http://

The following Web site has links to resources for non-profit management: centers, organizations, news, resource catalogs, and newsletters:

www.uwm.edu/~mbarndt/lnonprft.htm

Characteristics of the Forms of Business Ownership

SUMMARY FIGURE 1-6

	Organizational Requirements	Owner's Liability	Management and Control	Taxation	Availability of Owner Capital
Sole Proprietorship	Licenses may be required.	Unlimited.	Complete freedom to manage.	Subject to tax code for individuals.	Limited to single owner's ability to invest capital.
Partnership	Licenses may be required. Partnership agreement necessary.	General Partner —Unlimited. Limited Partner —Limited.	Control shared by general partners.	Subject to tax code for individuals.	Limited to partners' ability to invest capital. Somewhat easier for limited partnerships.
Corporation	Application for charter necessary. Compliance with regulations. License may be required.	Limited to the amount invested.	Control through an elected Board of Directors. Managed by appointed officers.	Double Taxation: Firm earnings subject to corporate tax code. Stockholder dividends subject to personal tax code.	Ready access to capital through sales of new stock.

The investment choices available will typically differ in the initial outlays required and in the timing, size, and degree of uncertainty of expected future operating costs. These are exactly the kinds of differences that a valuation model is designed to be able to analyze. There are other areas, such as cash management and credit policies, where cost minimization will be an issue and where a valuation model can also be used to develop decision rules for the not-for-profit organization. The principles we shall discuss, therefore, are not restricted to decisions made only by profit-seeking enterprises.

THE LEGAL, SOCIAL, AND ETHICAL ENVIRONMENT OF THE FIRM

We have stated that the fundamental objective of financial managers' decisions should be to maximize the value of the firm to its owners. This does not mean, of course, that *every* action that could be taken to achieve that objective is desirable or appropriate. All financial decisions should be constrained not only by the legal requirements of the jurisdiction in which the firm operates, but also by society's ethical standards.

Thus, an investment in a plant facility to produce a particular product might promise a high return for shareholders. If the consequences of the production process were to release toxic chemicals into the nearby community's water supply over time, or to expose production workers to long-term health problems from the same chemicals, the investment becomes unacceptable by a legitimately broader test of merit, even though in the short run it might increase the firm's stock price. A company's managers have responsibilities to shareholders, as we have emphasized. They also, however, have responsibilities to the larger community in which the company resides. *In that respect, managers have the same obligations to conduct themselves as good citizens in their corporate decision-making roles as they do to conduct themselves as good citizens in their personal activities.*

We state this obvious point early in our discussion only because it often seems

■ Ethics

ISSUES

OUTSIDE DIRECTORS SPEAK UP FOR SHAREHOLDERS

Corporate Boards of Directors have traditionally consisted of "inside" directors from the company's senior management ranks, and "outside" directors who are not company employees but who are distinguished professionals from other occupations—such as senior corporate executives from other firms, lawyers, bankers, consultants, and university faculty. The outside directors' role is to provide a diversity of viewpoints and to monitor the performance of company management for the firm's stockholders. In the United States, the majority of Board members are outside directors.

The process of electing those outsiders, however, has been criticized as deficient in producing Boards who are objective in their assessment of management and truly representative of shareholder interests. In most cases, outside director candidates are selected by the firm's management and presented to shareholders for their automatic approval. The selection of such candidates is often based on existing personal relationships with management. Consequently, there has been a tendency for Board members merely to endorse management's decisions rather than to evaluate those decisions critically. Moreover, it is seldom the case that a Board will act to remove senior management even when the firm's earnings performance has been lackluster.

A result of this inaction has been an increasing sensitivity on the part of both shareholders and regulators to the need for more vigorous oversight of management's decisions and performance by corporate directors, and more accountability on the part of those directors. Outside directors have had lawsuits filed against them for alleged negligence in fulfilling their responsibilities, and shareholder rights and legal remedies have been steadily strengthened over time.

The responses of firms' management and Boards to these pressures have been extensive. It is common now for Boards to have a number of standing committees comprised predominantly of outside directors who address particular aspects of corporate operations. Audit committees verify the integrity of firms' accounting practices. Compensation committees decide on the types and amounts of senior executive pay and benefits. Executive committees directly monitor management performance. Perhaps most importantly, nominating committees recruit outside directors. Boards of many firms meet monthly to fulfill these responsibilities, and they have become much less inclined to take management's viewpoint as a matter of course. In 1992, for example, the outside directors of General Motors Corporation—the largest U.S. auto manufacturer—insisted on a realignment of the firm's top management and forced the resignation of its chief executive because of the firm's poor earnings record. A move like that would have been virtually unheard-of in a major corporation even a few years previously.

to be ignored in finance texts that stress the principle of value maximization. We do not mean to downgrade that principle, but we do want to stress that there are some equally obvious limits to its application. Some of those limits are legal, and the potential negative economic consequences of legal actions against the firm in response to management decisions clearly do not serve the ultimate cause of value maximization for shareholders. Other limits are just as important, however, even if legality is not an issue. This is the reason why individual businesses and industry trade associations develop written guidelines for ethical behavior. These guidelines are intended to extend the constraints on management decisions beyond the narrow scope of laws.

Even the most carefully constructed guidelines, however, cannot cover every contingency. As a result, a firm's managers must often look to commonly accepted societal values and customs for ethical guidance. Unfortunately, the trade-off between ethics and economics is much less subject to formal analysis than is the trade-off between financial risk and financial return. Nonetheless, in our examination of economic issues, we shall regularly refer to ethical issues as well.

■ Ethics

ISSUES

WHAT ARE THE ETHICAL ISSUES?

In our discussion of the financial manager's job, we have stressed his or her role as an agent of the shareholders. Yet there are a number of other interested parties associated with a firm whose welfare is affected by management decisions. These "stakeholders" include employers, customers, suppliers, and the general community at large. All too often, conflicts of interest arise among the various stakeholders or between the self-interest of the managers and that of these stakeholders.

The types of situations in which these conflicts can occur in the practice of financial management are numerous. Earlier in the chapter, we discussed the agency problem of conflicts between the manager's self-interest and the economic welfare of the shareholders. For instance, managers may favor expansion of the firm, which will increase their compensation or prestige but which will not necessarily maximize the stock price. A similar conflict can arise from the problem of asymmetric information in which managers have knowledge of adverse information that is not publicly known. Since the information may threaten management's compensation and jobs, the managers may decide to withhold it from shareholders. Conflicts between the interests of shareholders and employees arise from decisions to lay off employees or terminate pension benefits following a merger. Decisions to change a firm's capital structure may involve trade-offs between the welfare of shareholders and that of creditors.

Business ethics can provide an orderly framework for evaluating the moral implications of a policy decision. The guidelines developed within this framework represent social values that call for restraining self-interest and balancing the interests of the various stakeholders in a firm.

SUMMARY

In this chapter, we have discussed the role of the financial managers of a firm. In fulfilling their role, these managers perform three major functions: financial planning, the analysis of investment decisions, and the analysis of financing decisions. Financial planning involves forecasting the anticipated results of operating plans and translating them into balance sheets, income statements, and cash budgets. Investing decisions deal with the uses of funds as they are committed to current and fixed assets. Financing decisions determine the sources of funds employed by the firm: the combination of debt and equity that is obtained, and the choice of paying out earnings as dividends or retaining them in the firm.

The goal of financial managers in performing these functions is to maximize the wealth of the firm's owners. In the context of corporate finance, this means maximizing the market price of the firm's stock. The application of that criterion often causes managers to confront a critical dilemma—the trade-off between risk and return. A firm's value is positively related to the size and speed of realization of its returns, but negatively related to the riskiness of those returns. Thus, simultaneous increases in size and riskiness have an ambiguous effect on value. We also discussed the distinction between profit maximization and value maximization as decision criteria. Profit maximization is an imprecise guide to decision-making because it does not take into account the timing and riskiness of returns from investments.

While managers *should* act in the best interests of the firm's owners in making financial decisions, there are reasons to believe that in practice this will not always be the case. That is what is referred to as the "agency" problem. Among the solutions to this problem are to establish compensation plans which link the payments managers receive to the earnings or stock price performance of the firm, and to have effective monitoring of managers' actions by Boards of Directors who represent shareholder interests.

The legal aspects of the form of a firm's ownership have important implications not only for the owners but also for the investing and financing decisions of the managers. We described the characteristics of the major forms of ownership: sole proprietorship, partnership, and corporation. The key attributes of the corporation include limited owner liability, indirect owner control, the double taxation of earnings, and expanded access to sources of capital. Because corporations account for the great majority of economic activity in most countries, the financial management of corporations will be the primary focus of our discussion in this text.

CONTENT QUESTIONS

1. Name and define the three main duties of financial managers.
2. Define an investment.
3. Explain the difference between a normative statement and a descriptive statement.
4. What is the responsibility of financial managers as the agents of the firm's owners?
5. Why does an agency problem arise between the managers and the owners of a firm?
6. What are the three major determinants of value?
7. Why is profit maximization not useful as an operating criterion for financial decisions?
8. What are the principal differences between incorporated and unincorporated businesses?
9. What is the most frequent trade-off that managers confront in attempting to make correct financial decisions?
10. How do stockholders exercise control of the corporations they own?

CONCEPT QUESTIONS

1. Ethics   The Coca-Cola Corporation announced that it would reward its top executive with shares of company stock whose value was estimated at $81 million. Is this level of compensation consistent with the manager's role as an agent of the stockholders? Under what conditions would you consider this compensation appropriate? Under what conditions would you consider it excessive?
2. IVM   Nonfinancial managers and critics of firms sometimes argue that the use of value maximization as a decision criterion forces managers to ignore important intangible, nonquantifiable factors that cannot be readily analyzed in a value maximization framework. Can you identify specific examples of such factors? How should such factors be evaluated by a manager whose decision criterion is value maximization?
3. Ethics   Critics of the corporate form of ownership sometimes argue that managers do not reliably act as agents of stockholders because they are appointed by Boards of Directors who are, in turn, nominated for the Boards by managers. The critics see a dangerous conflict of interest in this system, which works to the detriment of the stockholder. Do you agree with this viewpoint? If so, what do you think can be done to protect shareholders' interests?

4. IVM   Large corporations are frequently called upon to make substantial contributions to charities, cultural groups, and other not-for-profit organizations. While these contributions are tax-deductible expenses, they still reduce after-tax profits. Are such contributions appropriate for firms that employ the value maximization decision criterion? How should a financial manager decide how much of a firm's resources to commit to such philanthropic uses?

INTERNET EXERCISE

You are curious about company performance and executive compensation. Check out the most current compensation of five Fortune 500 executives and the performance of their companies. The Time Warner home page showcases several business magazines including *Fortune*. You can link to *Fortune*, the Fortune 500 list, and a Company Snapshot to check out company performance including earnings per share and the percentage change from the previous year. Using the pathfinder search, you can search for (executive compensation). You will come up with enough sources of executive compensation to complete the assignment.
www.pathfinder.com

APPENDIX: CORPORATE TAXES

It is impossible in a beginning text in financial management to provide a full discussion of the manner in which corporate income is taxed. The problem of doing so is compounded by the fact that the tax laws are revised frequently, both in the United States and in other countries. There are some major features of the corporate tax code with which it is important to be generally familiar, however, even if one does not intend to become a tax expert. Taxes, like any other cost of doing business, have an obvious impact on managers' efforts to maximize shareholder wealth.

In the United States, corporations pay taxes at increasing rates as their annual income increases. This has been the case for many years. As of the late 1990s, the applicable federal income tax schedule was as follows:

Annual Income		Marginal Tax Rate
First	$ 50,000	15%
Next	25,000	25%
Next	25,000	34%
Next	235,000	39%
Next	9,665,000	34%
Next	5,000,000	35%
Next	3,333,333	38%
Over	18,333,333	35%

Thus, a corporation whose annual income was $335,000 would have a total federal income tax bill amounting to:

$$
\begin{array}{lll}
(0.15)(\$\ 50,000) & = & \$\ 7,500 \\
(0.25)(\$\ 25,000) & = & 6,250 \\
(0.34)(\$\ 25,000) & = & 8,500 \\
(0.39)(\$235,000) & = & \underline{91,650} \\
& & \$113,900
\end{array}
$$

for an overall effective tax rate of ($113,900)/($335,000) or 34%. Notice that the effect of the high 39% tax rate on income between $100,000 and $335,000 is to "recapture" the benefit of the low 15% and 25% tax rates on income up to $75,000. Those low rates are designed to ease the tax burden on small corporations. At income levels of $335,000 and above, therefore, 34% is both the *average* and the *marginal* federal corporate tax rate. A similar recapture occurs when income above $15,000,000 is taxed at 38%, which increases the average and marginal tax rates to 35%. Since many state governments also impose taxes on corporate income, the effective combined tax rate for U.S. companies is often close to 40%. We shall, in most of our examples in this text, use a 40% rate as our estimate.

Over the years, the top marginal corporate tax rates in other countries have varied widely. There has, however, been a trend toward lowering those rates—with the United States leading this move during the decade of the 1980s. A representative current sampling would be:

Country	Top Marginal Tax Rate
Germany	42%*
Japan	38%*
Canada	38%
Spain	35%
Mexico	35%
Korea	34%
France	33%
United Kingdom	33%
Singapore	31%
Brazil	30%
Argentina	20%
Hong Kong	18%
Bahamas	0%
Bermuda	0%
Cayman Islands	0%

*Reduced to approximately 30% on income distributed to shareholders as dividends

Multinational corporations will often attempt to "locate" a portion of their world-wide income in countries like the Bahamas, Bermuda, or the Cayman Islands in order to minimize their total tax bills. We shall discuss the mechanisms for doing this in a later chapter.

The tax treatment of gains and losses also varies widely. These items of income arise when an operating asset—such as a building or a piece of equipment—is sold by the firm at a price either higher or lower than its depreciated book cost. In the United States, these gains and losses are taxed at the same rate as ordinary operating income. In other countries, there may be a special lower rate that applies. In some cases, such gains and losses are entirely free from taxation, both for corporations and individuals.

Direct out-of-pocket operating expenditures for wages, salaries, employee medical and retirement benefits, purchased materials, and energy costs are deductible items in computing taxable income in all countries. The same is true of interest costs on borrowed funds. The major category of "indirect" deductible expense is depreciation on fixed assets. Expenditures on buildings and equipment are generally not fully deductible in the year in which they are made but are allocated out as expenses over a series of years following the expenditure. Thus, there can be a substantial difference between the timing of the *cash* outlay for a fixed asset and the associated recognition of that outlay for tax purposes. This difference will be a key factor in our analysis of the desirability of investments in fixed assets and their impact on the value of the firm.

Here again, the tax rules for depreciation schedules display considerable variation across countries. They also change fairly frequently *within* countries, as legislatures revise and update tax codes. As we shall see, however, the rule for the financial manager is a very simple one: fixed assets should be depreciated for tax purposes *as rapidly* as the existing tax code will allow. This accelerates the timing of the tax savings from the deductions to the maximum extent, and thereby accelerates the timing of the cash flows from an investment. The sooner cash flows are received, of course, the more valuable they are to the firm and its owners.

In most countries, the tax laws permit corporations to average their income over a period of years in determining their tax bills. Thus, if a firm experiences a net loss from operations in a given year, it can "carry back" that loss and combine it with net profits from prior years to obtain a tax refund. Suppose, for example, a company's earnings were as follows:

Year	Income	Taxes Paid, at 40%
1997	$ 750,000	$300,000
1998	500,000	200,000
1999	(800,000)	—

No taxes would, of course, be due for 1999. In addition, the company could combine the 1999 loss of $800,000 with all of 1998 profits and $300,000 of 1997 profits, to claim a tax refund for 1999 of 40% of $800,000, or $320,000. In that manner, total three-year net income would be $750,000 + $500,000 − $800,000 = $450,000 and total taxes would be $300,000 + $200,000 − $320,000 = $180,000 for the firm. This produces an effective three-year tax rate of ($180,000)/($450,000), or exactly 40%, and allows firms to share not only their profits but their losses with the tax authorities.

There are typically some limits on the period over which such averaging is permitted. In the United States, corporations can "carry back" their losses for a maximum of three years. If, however, there are not sufficient profits in those prior three years to offset fully the current year's losses, the firm can also "carry forward" the remaining loss to future years and shelter future profits from taxation as well until a combined net profit is earned. The carry-forward limit in the United States is 15 years. Other countries have similar rules, although the averaging periods vary.

One final feature of the United States tax code should be noted. If a corporation owns shares of stock in another *domestic* corporation, a portion of the dividends it receives on those shares are free from taxation. Under current rules, if a firm owns more than 20% of the common stock of another company, 80% of any dividends received are not subject to tax. If a firm owns less than 20% of another firm's stock, 70% of the dividends are tax-free. For a company in a 40% marginal corporate tax bracket, therefore, the effective tax rates on dividends received from other firms would be:

Percent of Other Firm's Stock Owned	Portion of Dividends Taxed	Effective Tax Rate, at 40%
More than 20%	20%	(0.4)(0.2) = 8%
Less than 20%	30%	(0.4)(0.3) = 12%

The intent of this provision is to prevent what would amount to *triple* taxation of corporate earnings—once on the earnings of the first firm, again on the dividends paid by it to the second firm, and yet again on the dividends paid by the second firm to its shareholders.

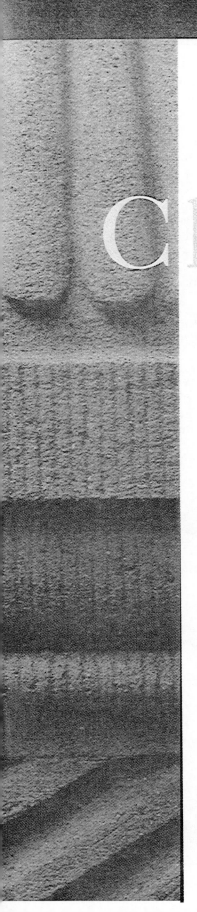

The Accounting Environment: Financial Statements

Accounting is the record-keeping language of corporate finance. Every decision that is made by the financial manager about investing and financing shows up in an immediate change in one or more asset or liability accounts on the firm's balance sheet. The revenues and costs affected by that decision subsequently appear on the firm's income statement. This is how the record of financial decisions is kept, and reported both to shareholders and senior management. Similarly, financial plans for the future are typically developed with reference to their effects on the firm's balance sheet and income statement.

Our purpose in this chapter is to review the nature of the interaction between accounting data and financial decisions. We shall consider first what those data *mean*, and where they come from. We shall then discuss how they can be *interpreted* in order to provide insights into a firm's performance and the future returns it is likely to generate for shareholders. In the process, we shall address the following sorts of issues:

- In the mid-1980s, General Motors Corporation announced a major decision to commit $5 billion to the development of a new car called the Saturn, in completely new manufacturing facilities. How might investors have evaluated that decision's implications for the firm's financial prospects and the firm's risk/return trade-off? What information would they have had available to make their assessment?

- In 1998, the total value of the real estate owned by the 500 largest United States corporations was reported at its original cost of approximately $500 billion on the firms' balance sheets. Yet the real estate could have been sold in that same year for much more than $500 billion. Why did the firms continue to report these assets at their original costs rather than at their significantly higher current market values? How does the difference between market value and original cost affect management decisions?

- In 1996, the Chrysler Corporation and Coca-Cola Corporation each reported total earnings of about $3.5 billion. Financial analysts, however, described Coca-Cola as being more *profitable* than Chrysler. What is the distinction between profits and profitability? Are stockholders and managers more concerned with profits or profitability? What information is available from firms' financial statements to make that distinction?

- Most profitable corporations pay dividends to their shareholders. The usual description of this process is that the dividends are paid *from* profits. Yet, a good case can be made that much of the money to pay dividends for the typical corporation actually comes from borrowed funds. How is this possible? Under what circumstances is it appropriate for a firm to borrow money to pay dividends?

Our goal is to offer some answers to these questions, and to see how the "picture" of the firm, which its financial statements provide, is related to the objective of value maximization.

Figure 2-1 summarizes the role of the accounting environment in the process of financial management. The results to date of the firm's investing and financing decisions are reported publicly in the form of a balance sheet and an income statement. These two statements contain the basic data that are utilized by investors in forming their assessments of the firm's financial health and future prospects. Those assessments in turn are the key to the price at which the company's common stock will trade. As we shall see, the evaluation of the data in the financial statements takes the form of several analytical procedures: (1) the analysis of balance sheet changes; (2) ratio analysis; and (3) cash flow analysis.

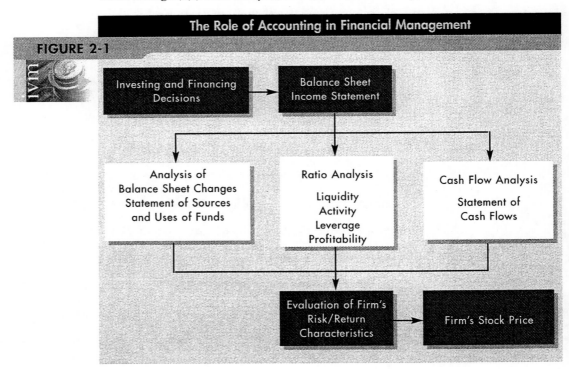

The Role of Accounting in Financial Management

FIGURE 2-1

An *analysis of balance sheet changes* provides information on the nature of the recent investing and financing decisions made by management. *Ratio analysis* highlights resulting financial performance in key aspects of operations. *Cash flow analysis* uses the firm's financial statements to identify the effect of operations on the availability of funds to pay dividends and meet debt obligations. Taken together and in combination with other information that is available about the firm, these three analytical procedures enable investors to appraise the firm's risk/return trade-off, and thereby value its common stock.

THE NATURE OF FINANCIAL STATEMENTS

The income statement and the balance sheet are the basic reports that a firm constructs for use by management and for distribution to stockholders, regulatory bodies, and the general public. They are the primary sources of historical financial information about the firm.

The Balance Sheet

The role of the balance sheet is to summarize a firm's present financial position by listing the types of financing and investing decisions its managers have made to date. Put differently, it summarizes the *sources* of the firm's funds and the *uses* to which those funds have been put. Although all firms follow the same general format in constructing their balance sheets, the particular composition of sources and uses of funds can vary widely even among firms in the same industry. These differences reflect divergent management opinions about the combination of sources and uses that will maximize the returns to be received by the firms' owners.

The amounts shown on the balance sheet are the result of specific management plans to maximize owner wealth. *Investing* decisions alter the amount and composition of *assets*, while *financing* decisions alter the amount and composition of *liabilities and owners' equity*.

The Types of Investing and Financing Decisions. A firm has only two basic sources of funds available to it: debt financing and equity financing. The distinction between these sources reflects two very important differences: the nature of the payment and the length of the financing. Creditors provide *debt financing* in exchange for the firm's promise to repay a *fixed amount at a specific date* in the future. Owners provide *equity financing* for an *indefinite period of time with an uncertain level of payment*. They are entitled only to the residual that remains after all the firm's expenses—including obligations to creditors—have been met. Moreover, the firm is required to repay equity financing only if it goes out of business.

Each of these two major sources of funds is normally broken down into the various components shown on the illustrative balance sheet for Dayton Products, a moderate-sized manufacturer, in Table 2-1. For that firm, total liabilities (debt financing) of $49.9 million represent 58% of its total financing of $87.9 million in 2000. The firm's net worth (equity financing) of $38.0 million represents the remaining 42% of total financing.

From a financial management perspective, there are two distinctions within the liabilities component, which are worth noting. The first is between "spontaneous" and "funded" debt. A **spontaneous liability** is one that arises automatically in the normal course of operating a business, when a firm buys goods and services to produce its products. These liabilities include accounts payable, accruals, and taxes payable. Accounts payable originate from credit purchases of materials,

Spontaneous Liability A source of funds that arises automatically in the course of operating a business, when a firm buys goods and services on credit.

Dayton Products, Inc., Balance Sheets (in Thousands)

TABLE 2-1

	Dec. 31, 1999		Dec. 31, 2000	
Cash		$ 1,800		$ 2,000
Accounts receivable		13,500		15,100
Inventory		26,800		27,500
Other		1,100		900
Current assets		$43,200		$45,500
Plant and equipment	$57,100		$64,500	
Less accumulated depreciation	(23,900)		(26,200)	
Net fixed assets		33,200		38,300
Goodwill		4,500		4,100
Total assets		$80,900		$87,900
Accounts payable		6,800		7,200
Notes payable		5,700		5,600
Accruals		6,300		8,700
Taxes payable		300		400
Current liabilities		$19,100		$21,900
Long-term liabilities		25,000		28,000
Total liabilities		$44,100		$49,900
Common stock				
($2 par; 4 million shares)		8,000		8,000
Retained earnings		28,800		30,000
Net worth or owner's equity		36,800		38,000
Total liabilities and net worth		$80,900		$87,900

fuel, and electricity. Accruals represent temporarily unsettled obligations for such items as employee wages and salaries between payroll dates. Taxes payable consist of income tax liabilities incurred but not due for payment until after the accounting reporting date, or property tax bills due after that date. These sources of funding to support the firm's operations are generally "free," in that the firm is not charged interest on them up to their specified payment date. Nonetheless, they are a form of debt because an explicit obligation to pay a fixed amount is involved.

By contrast, a **funded liability** is one that the firm must take overt action to arrange and on which interest *is* charged. These include loans from banks and other lenders, and debt securities issued to individuals and financial institutions. The notes payable and long-term liabilities listed on Dayton Products' balance sheet fall in this category. Obviously, a firm whose liabilities to creditors consist predominantly of non-interest-bearing obligations is in a different position than a firm that has mostly funded debt, even if the *total* debt of the two firms is the same.

The other important debt distinction is between current and long-term liabilities because it indicates how rapidly the firm must meet its obligations. **Current liabilities** include all those that must be repaid within a year of the balance sheet date. Accounts payable, accruals, and taxes payable are typically due within no more than 90 days. Notes payable may be due within anywhere from a month to a year. **Long-term liabilities** consist of debt financing that need not be repaid until one year or more in the future.

The division of Dayton Products' net worth into common stock and retained earnings provides additional information about the firm's financing strategy. The

Funded Liability A source of funds that a firm must take overt action to arrange and that carries an interest cost.

Current Liability A category of debt that must be repaid within one year.

Long-Term Liability Debt financing that need not be repaid until one year or more in the future.

balance between these two components reveals what portion of equity financing has come from outside the firm (common stock) and what portion has been provided internally (retained earnings). The internal/external equity structure of a firm is a result of its dividend policy. As we shall see later, the ability of financial managers to match their firm's dividend policy with the dividend preferences of its stockholders can be an important determinant of the market value of the firm's stock.

The uses of Dayton Products' total financing of $87.9 million in 2000 are shown in the various asset accounts in Table 2-1, which are subdivided on the balance sheet in terms of their expected life. Current assets are converted into cash within one year. Noncurrent (fixed) assets are not directly converted into cash but are used up over time in the production process. In 2000, Dayton divided its investments almost equally between current and noncurrent assets:

Current Assets	$45,500,000	(52%)
Noncurrent Assets	42,400,000	(48%)
Total Assets	87,900,000	(100%)

The breakdown of assets between current and noncurrent has an important effect on the ability of a firm to meet its obligations. The conversion of current assets into cash is the normal source of the funds necessary to satisfy a firm's current liabilities. Other factors held constant, the larger the level of a firm's current assets, the easier it will be for the firm to make the payments required by current liabilities.

The assets, liabilities, and net worth shown in Dayton Products' balance sheets provide tangible evidence of the specific types of investing and financing decisions that have been made by the firm's financial managers. In order to interpret these data properly, however, it is essential to understand the basis on which they are generated. A crucial element of balance sheet accounting in most countries is the use of *historical costs* rather than current market values.

Historical Cost as a Measure of Value. The balance sheet accounts of Dayton Products in Table 2-1 are based on the **historical cost accounting convention**. The historical cost basis of an asset is the price paid for the asset at the time of its acquisition. The historical cost basis of a liability is the amount received at the time the financing was arranged. Historical cost represents the amount of resources *originally* committed to the acquisition of an asset or obtained from the issuance of a liability. The usefulness of historical cost as a measure of *current value* is limited by the fact that it does not reflect ongoing changes in value over time.

Historical Cost Accounting Convention An accounting technique that values an asset for balance sheet purposes on the basis of the price paid for the asset at the time of its acquisition.

The basic rationale for historical cost is that it is objective and easily verified. Measures of value are much more subjective in nature and difficult to estimate. They also require repeated estimation since they can change over time. Thus, they are not readily verifiable. For instance, the use of the current *replacement cost* of an asset as a measure of its value requires an arbitrary judgment about the appropriate type of new machinery (high technology versus low technology) to select as a replacement for the old machinery. *Reproduction cost* estimates can involve special engineering studies if the old machinery is no longer manufactured. *Resale value* will vary depending on the timing and nature of the sale. Given the practical estimation problems associated with these alternative measures of value, historical cost is generally considered to be the most reliable of a number of imperfect measurement systems.

One aspect of historical cost accounting that deserves special mention is depreciation. Depreciation systematically reduces book value over the life of the asset. For example, the balance sheet for Dayton Products on December 31, 2000, showed the following figures for plant and equipment:

Plant and equipment	$ 64,500,000
Less: Accumulated depreciation	(26,200,000)
Net fixed assets	$ 38,300,000

The purpose of this depreciation procedure is *not* to adjust the historical cost of plant and equipment for declines in value due to deterioration or technological obsolescence. Rather, depreciation is intended simply to recognize each year a portion of the original cost of Dayton's assets as an operating expense. While Dayton originally committed $64.5 million to new plant and equipment, $26.2 million of that historical cost had been included in the firm's income statements as an expense of operations prior to December 31, 2000. Thus, only $38.3 million of the historical cost remained to be recognized as an expense in future income statements. This unrecognized depreciation expense is what Dayton shows on its balance sheet as net fixed assets.

The Income Statement

The role of the income statement is to reveal the *periodic* results of management's investing and financing decisions. It fulfills this role by measuring changes in the

---

■ Valuation

ISSUES

HIDDEN ASSETS

One of the consequences of the use of historical cost as the basis for the construction of a firm's balance sheet is that the resulting figures may be very poor representations of the actual current value of its assets. This is likely to be especially true in connection with the real estate a company owns.

As an example, take the case of a railroad company that might have been established during the late 1800s. At the time of its formation, the firm would have acquired the land on which its tracks were built, the land on which its terminal facilities were constructed, and various parcels of land surrounding both its tracks and terminals. These assets would have been recorded on the firm's balance sheet at their cost at the time they were acquired. Under historical cost accounting, they would still be recorded at that same cost today.

Suppose, however, that what in 1890 was a parcel of land near a terminal in a small town is now a parcel of land in the center of what has grown to be a major metropolitan area. That land might be listed on the firm's balance sheet at an original cost of $100, but could now be worth $100 million instead. Or, suppose that what in 1890 was simply an empty tract of land along the railroad's tracks in the middle of Texas has since turned out to be on top of a major oil field.

Clearly, the firm's balance sheet will be of little use to investors in determining the current value of the firm. Some portion of the actual worth of its assets will be "hidden" in the balance sheet figures presented. One can think of a variety of other illustrations as well: a chain of retail stores that acquired a number of its store locations 25 or 50 years ago, or a company whose headquarters office building was constructed in the middle of Tokyo in 1950.

Investors have become more sensitive to hidden asset values in recent years. One of the services that professional securities analysts provide is to supplement the historical data on companies' balance sheets with estimates of today's asset values. Firms often become the targets of takeover bids by other firms, which are motivated by the intent to realize the target firm's hidden asset values—by selling off undervalued assets following the takeover.

The question of whether accounting systems should attempt to provide more up-to-date estimates of asset values has been debated by the accounting profession and regulators for years. The issue is most acute in countries where inflation rates are high, since inflation is a major influence on changing asset values. As we shall see in subsequent chapters, there are, in fact, a number of countries around the world where adjustments for inflationary effects are a normal part of the preparation of companies' financial statements.

firm's net worth that have resulted from operations during the latest accounting period. The $38.0 million in net worth shown on Dayton Products' Dec. 31, 2000, balance sheet is the share of the firm's total assets to which its stockholders are entitled after deducting the prior claims of the firm's creditors:

Total assets	$87,900,000
Total liabilities	(49,900,000)
Net worth	$38,000,000

The increase in Dayton's net worth from $36.8 million on December 31, 1999, to $38.0 million on December 31, 2000, was the result of operations during 2000, which are presented in detail in Dayton's income statement for the year.

Revenues and Expenses.   The effect of a firm's operations on its net worth is divided into two basic components: revenues and expenses. Revenues increase net worth, while expenses decrease net worth. In the 1999 and 2000 income statements for Dayton Products in Table 2-2, revenues are referred to as sales, while expenses include: cost of goods sold; depreciation; amortization of goodwill; selling, general, and administrative expenses; interest expense; and taxes. Expenses are deducted from revenues to arrive at the *net* effect of operations on net worth during the period: *earnings after taxes*.

The categorization of expenses permits the measurement of the effect on profits of each of the various phases of the firm's operations. The profit attributable to Dayton's manufacturing operations in 2000 is its gross profit of $26.2 million. Cost of goods sold includes specific expenses associated with manufacturing a product: direct labor, raw materials, and overhead. The next stage in the income statement is the subtraction of the remaining operating expenses from gross profit. This will give income from operations (EBIT) of $9.4 million. While they are not directly associated with the product's manufacture, the expenses deducted in this calculation are essential for the product's successful manufacture and sale.

Selling, general, and administrative expenses include nonmanufacturing costs such as the salaries of executives, office workers, and sales representatives. They also include marketing expenses, legal expenses, and research costs. Amortization

Dayton Products, Inc., Income Statements (in Thousands)

TABLE 2-2

	1999	2000
Sales	$105,500	$110,100
Cost of goods sold	(81,800)	(83,900)
Gross profit	23,700	26,200
Depreciation	(2,400)	(2,300)
Amortization of goodwill	(400)	(400)
Selling, general, and administrative expenses	(13,300)	(14,100)
Earnings before interest and taxes (EBIT)	7,600	9,400
Interest expense	(2,500)	(2,800)
Earnings before taxes (EBT)	5,100	6,600
Income taxes	(2,500)	(3,300)
Earnings after taxes (EAT) or net income	$ 2,600	$ 3,300

of goodwill represents the recognition of costs associated with the previous acquisition of another firm. Goodwill represents the excess of the purchase price paid for another firm over the book value of that firm's net assets. This excess is recognized over time as an expense of operations in the form of amortization of goodwill. The last stage of the income statement is the deduction of nonoperating expenses to arrive at the firm's earnings after taxes (EAT) of $3.3 million. Because interest expense on debt financing results from the firm's financing decisions rather than from its investing decisions, it is separated from operating expenses. Interest is tax-deductible, however, so that it must be subtracted to determine the firm's taxable income. Finally, taxes are deducted to arrive at earnings after taxes (EAT), or net income—the residual earnings to which the firm's owners are entitled. As in the case of the balance sheet, proper interpretation of the income statement requires an understanding of the accounting procedures followed in its construction. One of the most important of these procedures is the concept of accrual accounting.

Accrual Accounting versus Cash Accounting. The figures shown in Dayton Products' income statement in Table 2-2 are based on the accounting convention of **accrual accounting**. In an accrual accounting system, cash inflows do not automatically represent revenues for the period, and cash outflows do not automatically represent expenses. For example, assume that all of Dayton Products' sales in 2000 were made on a credit basis under which customers were not required to pay for the goods purchased until 60 days after the purchase date. Under a cash accounting system, no sales revenues would be recorded until the customers paid their bills. Under an accrual accounting system, sales revenues are recognized at the time the sale is *made*, because that is the moment at which the firm is considered to have "earned" the revenues. Thus, it is the customer's *promise to pay rather than the actual payment itself* that determines the recognition of the revenue. Similarly, an accrual accounting system treats the purchase price of a long-lived asset such as a piece of equipment as a fixed asset to be capitalized. The expense arising from the use of the asset is then later recognized in the form of a series of depreciation charges each year over the asset's life. A cash accounting system would merely record the entire purchase price as an immediate expense at the time the equipment was acquired.

Accrual Accounting Convention An accounting system that tries to match the recognition of revenues earned with the expenses incurred in generating those revenues. An accrual accounting system ignores the timing of the cash flows associated with revenues and expenses.

The Relationship Between the Income Statement and the Balance Sheet

The income statement, then, is a record of those elements of a firm's operations over a given accounting period that would cause a change in only *one* item on the firm's balance sheet: its net worth. The final step in reconciling the two statements is to take account of any dividends the firm paid to its shareholders. If Dayton Products' dividend payments during 2000 were $2.1 million, we have the result shown in Table 2-3. The change in the firm's retained earnings in 2000 is equal to earnings after taxes less cash dividends paid.

The roles of the balance sheet and the income statement and their relationship are summarized in Figure 2-2. Each of these financial statements provides its own specific information about the results of a firm's investing and financing decisions. In order to evaluate what those decisions *mean* for the firm's financial condition and performance, however, we need to go further. There are three analytical procedures that can be used for this purpose. The first of these is the analysis of balance sheet changes.

Summary of the Change in Dayton Products' Retained Earnings During 2000

TABLE 2-3

Retained earnings, Dec. 31, 1999	$28,800,000
Earnings after taxes, 2000	3,300,000
	$32,100,000
Less: Cash dividend paid in 2000	(2,100,000)
Equals: Retained earnings, Dec. 31, 2000	$30,000,000

ANALYSIS OF BALANCE SHEET CHANGES

The concept of *sources and uses of funds* is a key element in understanding the decisions of a firm's financial managers. In maximizing value, their task can be described as the selection of the optimal composition of the firm's balance sheet. By its nature, the balance sheet is a *cumulative* record of sources and uses up to the date of the statement. Of equal interest are the periodic *changes* in sources and uses. These reveal the impact of the managers' most recent financing and investing decisions. By comparing two successive balance sheets, such as those shown for Dayton Products in Table 2-1, we can identify what has happened to sources and uses during the interval spanned by the two balance sheets. This analysis is often referred to as a *statement of sources and uses of funds* for the period. A standardized version of such a statement is often included in a corporation's report to shareholders, as a supplement to its balance sheet and income statement.

Construction of a Statement of Sources and Uses of Funds

The following procedure is used to prepare a sources-and-uses-of-funds analysis:

Step 1:   Calculate the change in each balance sheet account over the desired time period and classify each as a source or use of funds.

Step 2:   Decompose the change in retained earnings into two components: a source of funds from net income and a use of funds for cash dividends.

Step 3:   Calculate the source of funds from operations as the sum of net income plus noncash expenses.

Step 4:   Decompose the change in net fixed assets into two components: a use of funds for gross fixed assets and a source of funds from accumulated depreciation.

Step 5:   Group all sources and uses of funds together.

The Relationship Between the Balance Sheet and the Income Statement

SUMMARY FIGURE 2-2

Financial Statement	Purpose	Major Accounting Convention
Balance Sheet	Shows the financial position of the firm at a given moment in time.	Historical Cost
Income Statement	Shows the change in the firm's net worth over the accounting period.	Accrual Accounting

SUMMARY FIGURE 2-3
Rules for Classifying Account Changes as Sources or Uses of Funds

Uses

1. Increase in an asset account
2. Decrease in a liability account
3. Decrease in a net worth account

Sources

1. Decrease in an asset account
2. Increase in a liability account
3. Increase in a net worth account

Classification of Balance Sheet Changes. Figure 2-3 contains the basic rules for this classification. The logic behind these rules should be readily apparent. Increases in liabilities or net worth represent additional financing that has been obtained by the firm. Decreases in assets release funds that had been committed to those assets. Increases in assets tie up additional funds. A reduction in liabilities or net worth is a use of funds since it represents a decrease in the sources of financing available to the firm. Table 2-4 lists the classification of the account changes for Dayton Products during 2000, from the balance sheets shown in Table 2-1.

The focus of our interest is on the two right-hand columns in this tabulation.

Decomposition of Retained Earnings. While Table 2-4 represents a crude but legitimate form of a sources-and-uses-of-funds analysis, the information can be presented in a much more enlightening form. The first modification in the raw data involves providing more detail on the sources of change in the retained earnings account. Table 2-3 reveals that the $1.2 million net change in Dayton Products' retained earnings during 2000 resulted from net income (earnings after taxes) of $3.3 million and cash dividends of $2.1 million. Thus, the *net* source of funds from

TABLE 2-4
Dayton Products, Inc., Balance Sheet Changes from Dec. 31, 1999, to Dec. 31, 2000 (in Thousands)

	12/31/99	12/31/00	Change	Source or Use
Cash	$ 1,800	$ 2,000	$ 200	Use
Accounts receivable	13,500	15,100	1,600	Use
Inventory	26,800	27,500	700	Use
Other current assets	1,100	900	−200	Source
Net fixed assets	33,200	38,300	5,100	Use
Goodwill	4,500	4,100	−400	Source
Accounts payable	6,800	7,200	400	Source
Notes payable	5,700	5,600	−100	Use
Accruals	6,300	8,700	2,400	Source
Taxes payable	300	400	100	Source
Long-term liabilities	25,000	28,000	3,000	Source
Common stock	8,000	8,000	0	—
Retained earnings	28,800	30,000	1,200	Source

the increase in retained earnings can be divided into a *gross* source of funds from net income that is partially offset by a *use* of funds to pay cash dividends to stockholders:

$$\text{Change in Retained Earnings} = \text{Net Income} - \text{Cash Dividends}$$
$$\$1,200,000 = \$3,300,000 - \$2,100,000$$

We therefore replace the "Retained earnings" line in Table 2-4 with the expanded entries:

Net income	3,300	Source
Dividends	2,100	Use

This allows us to identify on the statement both what the firm earned *and* what it paid out during the year. To understand management's decisions, we should be interested in both. Thus, if the $1.2 million increase in retained earnings came from net income of $23.3 million and $22.1 million of dividends, that is obviously a different situation than if, as for Dayton Products, income were $3.3 million and dividends were $2.1 million.

Calculation of Funds from Operations.
The next step is to recognize the effect of the accrual accounting convention on the manner in which net income from operations is calculated. As we noted earlier, the annual charges included on the income statement for depreciation and amortization of goodwill represent allocations to the current period of a portion of expenditures that were made in a previous period. They are not actual cash expenses in the current period. For that reason, the firm's operations, in fact, generated *more* funds during 2000 than the figure listed as "net income" would lead us to believe. The correct figure is instead:

$$\text{Funds from Operations} = \text{Net Income} + \text{Depreciation Expense} +$$
$$\text{Amortization of Goodwill}$$
$$\$6,000,000 = \$3,300,000 + \$2,300,000 + \$400,000$$

The $400,000 reduction in goodwill due to the 2000 amortization of that account already appears on the record of balance sheet changes shown in Table 2-4. Accordingly, we move it down as part of a new combined entry, which becomes:

Funds from operations:		
Net income	3,300	
Depreciation expense	2,300	
Amortization of goodwill	400	
	6,000	Source

Does this imply that depreciation expenses and goodwill amortizations are "sources" of funds? Clearly not; they are merely accounting charges against operating income and represent neither sources nor uses. The point is that *operations* produced more funds for the firm than the net income recorded on the income statement suggests. We add back the noncash expenses that were deducted in computing net income, as *adjustments*, in order to identify how much in the way of funds the firm's operations actually did generate.[1]

Decomposition of Net Fixed Assets.
A corresponding adjustment must also be made to recognize the effect of depreciation expense on the firm's net fixed

---

[1] There is a sense, however, in which depreciation and goodwill amortization can be considered indirectly to be a source of funds. Because both expenses can be deducted for tax as well as accounting purposes, they do reduce a firm's tax bill and thereby improve the firm's net cash flow.

assets. The balance sheet change in that account results from two events: (1) new expenditures on fixed assets; and (2) depreciation charges on those assets. Thus, we can see from Table 2-1 that the following changes took place in 2000 for Dayton Products:

$$\text{Increase in Plant and Equipment} = \$64,500,000 - 57,100,000$$
$$= \$ 7,400,000$$
$$\text{Increase in Accumulated Depreciation} = \$26,200,000 - 23,900,000$$
$$= \$ 2,300,000$$
$$\text{Increase in Net Fixed Assets} = \$ 7,400,000 - 2,300,000$$
$$= \$ 5,100,000$$

The actual *expenditures* on additional fixed assets appear as increases in Plant and Equipment, as they are recorded at their cost. This is the use of funds we are interested in identifying. The amount of the increase in accumulated depreciation arises from depreciation expense for the period. It indicates the portion of expenditures on new plant and equipment that can be financed internally from operations without requiring the firm either to retain some of its earnings or obtain additional funds from creditors. Since we have already taken this source into account by adding back depreciation expense to net income to calculate *funds from operations*, however, we would be double-counting to include it here. The correct use-of-funds figure for plant and equipment therefore is the $7,400,000 shown.

Grouping Sources and Uses of Funds. The final step is to group the calculated sources and uses shown in Table 2-4, as modified, to arrive at the format that is shown in Table 2-5. Magically, it turns out that sources exactly equal uses. This will always be the case. There is, of course, no "magic" involved. The raw materials for the data in Table 2-5 were Dayton Products' 1999 and 2000 balance sheets. Because, by their nature, a firm's balance sheets do "balance," so will a derived state-

TABLE 2-5

**Dayton Products, Inc., Statement of Sources and Uses of Funds
Dec. 31, 1999, to Dec. 31, 2000 (in Thousands)**

Sources of Funds		
Decrease in other current assets		$ 200
Increase in accounts payable		400
Increase in accruals		2,400
Increase in taxes payable		100
Increase in long-term liabilities		3,000
Funds from operations:		
Net income	$3,300	
Depreciation	2,300	
Amortization of goodwill	400	6,000
Total Sources		$12,100

Uses of Funds		
Increase in cash		$ 200
Increase in accounts receivable		1,600
Increase in inventory		700
Increase in plant and equipment		7,400
Decrease in notes payable		100
Dividends paid		2,100
Total Uses		$12,100

ment of sources and uses of funds. Put differently, Dayton Products somehow did acquire the funding for all the new investments it made during 2000 and for the dividends it paid. Thus, there *had* to be sufficient sources for all the uses observed. We have simply categorized them in a comprehensive and systematic fashion.

Utilization of a Statement of Sources and Uses of Funds

The objective of a statement of sources and uses of funds is to reveal the sorts of financing and investing decisions a firm's financial managers have made during the period covered by the statement. While it is difficult to be completely general about how this information can be analyzed, there are some reasonable guidelines we can offer:

1. Concentrate on particularly large sources and uses.
2. Identify sources that would normally be expected to be uses, and vice versa.
3. Compare the current period's statement with those of past periods, and look for major differences.

Although these guidelines will not always permit clear conclusions, they will usually indicate key aspects of operations that deserve attention. For example, Dayton Products' uses of funds in 2000 were dominated by sizable acquisitions of plant and equipment. This fact raises a number of questions. Is this level of spending typical or is the firm engaging in a major capital expansion program? Does the new plant and equipment represent replacements for existing facilities or is it designed to produce new products?

The major sources of financing for these acquisitions were funds from operations and the issuance of long-term liabilities. This also raises questions. Since acquisitions of fixed assets ($7.4 million) exceeded funds from operations ($6.0 million), will the firm be forced to reduce the level of such acquisitions in the future? Can the firm continue to rely on the issuance of long-term debt to provide funds, or will it be forced to sell common stock or reduce future dividends? Other items on the statement that seem to merit investigation include the large increase in accounts receivable and the large increase in accruals.

Both the size and the type of sources and uses are of concern. A growing business will normally show dividends and increases in assets as the major uses of funds, and funds from operations and increases in liabilities as the major sources of funds. While certain of the amounts involved appear to be unusually large, these relationships generally hold true for Dayton Products. If *decreases* in assets are a major source of funds, however, it raises the question of whether the firm is voluntarily reducing its size or has been forced to liquidate assets to finance other uses of funds. Large decreases in liabilities may also be an indication of potential problems since they represent a use of funds to retire debt. Unless this reduction in debt is offset by funds from operations or the sale of stock, the loss of financing may indicate that the firm is having trouble obtaining funds from creditors.

In interpreting a statement of sources and uses of funds, we should stress that it is not appropriate to attempt to "match" particular sources to specific uses of funds. Rather, the correct perspective is that the identified sources *collectively* support the identified uses. The sources come as a package. They are jointly determined and, if one is unusually small, the others together must make up the difference needed to allow the uses to occur.

In that regard, let us return to an issue we raised at the beginning of this chapter. We stated that firms often borrow money to pay dividends. It should now be apparent from Table 2-5 that this is exactly what Dayton Products did in 2000.

Included in the $12.1 million of uses of funds were $2.1 million of dividend payments. Among the $12.1 million of sources were $5.8 million of increases in accounts payable, accruals, and long-term liabilities. In effect, $5.8/$12.1, or 48%, of the funds raised both to make new investments *and* to pay dividends came from new debt. Equivalently, if $2.1 million of dividends had *not* been paid, the firm's requirements for new sources of funds could collectively have been reduced by $2.1 million.

Does it therefore make sense to say that dividends were paid out of the firm's net income? Only in part. A better statement would be that dividends were just *one of many* uses to which the funds raised during the year were put. Some of those funds indeed came from earnings, but not all of them did. A growing firm *will* typically experience increases in its liabilities as its assets grow. In the normal case, only a portion of the funding to support asset growth—or to permit the ongoing payment of dividends—comes internally from operations. That is worrisome only if the rate of increase in the firm's liabilities over time is *greater* than the rate of increase in its equity from retained earnings or new stock issues. In that event, the firm is becoming steadily more dependent on debt to pay dividends and acquire assets. This is the sort of potential problem that our second analytical technique, ratio analysis, is designed to help identify.

■ Valuation ISSUES

TAKING THE BIG HIT

The purpose of preparing and reporting the balance sheet of the firm is to provide investors with information on its financial condition. The net worth figure shown on the balance sheet is a measure of stockholders' investment in the firm and the size of their claim on its assets. Most changes in net worth are the result of the profits retained from the ongoing normal operations of the company.

Occasionally, however, firms engage in "non-normal" actions that affect their balance sheets. Among the more prominent of these in recent years have been decisions to write off, and remove from the balance sheet, assets that have lost their earning power. Often these write-offs are prompted by decisions to discontinue a particular line of business and dispose of the assets that supported that business. In most such instances, the disposal is at a price that is much less than the recorded book value of the assets. The result, of course, shows up as an extraordinary loss on the year's income statement and therefore a "big hit" against both earnings and net worth.

It is not unusual for these events to be followed by an increase in the firm's stock price immediately after the announcement of the write-off. How is it possible that a sizable reduction in net worth can produce a jump in stock price?

There is some logic in that response if we recall the principle that the value of a firm depends upon the *future* returns that investors expect from it. If the discontinued operations were unprofitable, the firm is better off disposing of them than continuing to pursue them. Hence, future total earnings may actually be improved by terminating the activity, even though the immediate *accounting* effect is to reduce reported net worth. It is also likely that investors were aware that the operations were unprofitable and were a drag on corporate earnings. They would then view the write-off as a sign that management is moving aggressively to wipe out past mistakes and set the stage for future earnings growth.

There is a further benefit as well. The accounting loss associated with the big hit can be taken by the firm as a deduction for tax purposes. Thus, the firm may actually *generate* cash from the write-off, which can be used to invest elsewhere in more attractive businesses. This also increases future earning power.

RATIO ANALYSIS

Ratio analysis supplements the balance sheet and the income statement through an analysis of the relationship between two or more accounts on these statements. The usefulness of ratio analysis is derived from the concept that it is the *relative* size of the accounts, not their absolute amount, that determines their significance. For example, suppose the past year's net income of a firm was $100,000. Whether this figure should be evaluated as good or bad depends largely on the size of the firm. If the firm is a small flower shop with total assets of $50,000 and annual sales of $300,000, net income of $100,000 is outstanding performance. If the firm is a large industrial firm with assets of $1 billion and annual sales of $2 billion, however, $100,000 in net income represents extremely poor performance! In order to facilitate the comparison of account balances, a number of ratios have been developed to highlight the most important relationships. These ratios are normally divided into four categories based on the particular aspect of the firm's operations that they are used to evaluate:

1. Liquidity Ratios—measure the firm's ability to meet its short-term payment obligations.
2. Activity Ratios—measure how efficiently the firm is employing its resources.
3. Leverage Ratios—measure the extent of debt financing and the firm's ability to meet its debt payments.
4. Profitability Ratios—measure the effectiveness of management in generating a return on the funds invested in the firm.

Analyses of performance through the use of financial ratios involve two types of comparisons: cross-section analysis and trend analysis. **Cross-section ratio analysis** requires that the analyst *compare the current value of each of the firm's ratios in the above four categories with some benchmark.* The benchmark usually chosen is the average ratio value for all firms in an industry for the time period under study. This type of analysis indicates whether the firm's balance sheet and income statement are out of line with those of its competitors.

  Trend ratio analysis requires the *comparison of the successive values of each ratio for a given firm over a number of years.* This type of analysis signals whether the firm's financial performance is improving or deteriorating over time. It also provides a forecast of what may be expected in the future if a firm continues on its current course. Figure 2-4 summarizes the various aspects of the use of ratio analysis in the evaluation of firm performance.

Liquidity Ratios

A key aspect of a firm's operations is its ability to meet its liabilities as they come due. A firm that cannot generate sufficient cash to pay its debts will quickly be forced out of business regardless of the level of its reported net income. Even a profitable firm could be forced into liquidation by unhappy creditors in a relatively short period of time if it becomes seriously delinquent in its payments. Conversely, a firm can continue in business for a number of years even though it realizes net losses, as long as it meets its maturing obligations. **Liquidity ratios** examine the firm's ability to meet its short-term debt obligations.

Current Ratio. The level of current liabilities indicates the payments the firm must make during the coming year. The level of current assets reveals the available assets that can be expected to be converted into cash over that same period. The relationship between these two items is called the current ratio. Using Table 2-1 data, the 2000 current ratio for Dayton Products is:

http://

Find definitions of ratios, discussion of their uses, and actual ratios for individual companies and industries at http://dodona.lib.sfu.ca/kiosk/efairey/ratioan.htm

Cross-Section Ratio Analysis A method of analysis that compares a current value of the firm's ratios with some chosen industry benchmark. The benchmark usually chosen is the average ratio value for all firms in an industry for the time period under study.

Trend Ratio Analysis The comparison of the successive values of each ratio for a single firm over a number of years.

Liquidity Ratios Ratios that examine the firm's ability to meet its short-term cash outflows in terms of the relationship between current assets and current liabilities.

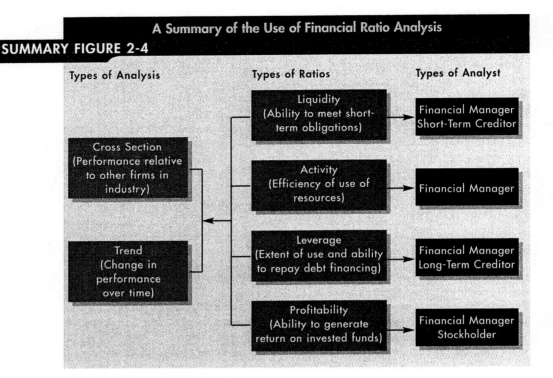

SUMMARY FIGURE 2-4

A Summary of the Use of Financial Ratio Analysis

$$\text{Current ratio} = \frac{\text{Current assets}}{\text{Current liabilities}} = \frac{\$45,500,000}{\$21,900,000} = 2.08$$

For each-dollar of short-term liabilities, Dayton Products had $2.08 in "near-cash" assets (easily converted into cash) to meet those liabilities.

Acid-Test Ratio. This ratio (sometimes called the "Quick" ratio) is calculated by removing the value of inventories from the numerator of the current ratio. The logic behind this modification is that inventories are usually the least liquid of current assets. If they are damaged, out of fashion, or obsolete, they may not be salable at all. Even if they can be sold, they are usually sold on a credit basis. Thus, before they can generate cash, they must be converted into accounts receivable, which then must be collected. The 2000 acid-test ratio for Dayton Products was:

$$\text{Acid-test ratio} = \frac{\text{Current assets} - \text{Inventories}}{\text{Current liabilities}}$$

$$= \frac{\$45,500,000 - 27,500,000}{\$21,900,000} = 0.82$$

Notice that the exclusion of inventories from the liquidity calculation has substantially reduced Dayton's ratio of liquid assets to short-term liabilities from 2.08 to 0.82. If Dayton were not able to convert any of its inventory to cash prior to the maturity of its current liabilities, the firm would not be able to meet all of those obligations from the liquidation of its remaining current assets.

Activity Ratios

As we have seen, financial managers' investing decisions represent the commitment of resources to specific assets. One method of judging the adequacy of the size and composition of a firm's assets is to measure the level of sales generated by those assets. **Activity ratios** measure how effectively a firm's management is utilizing the resources committed to receivables, inventory, and plant and equipment. They consist of calculations that compare the investment in these assets to a measure of overall business activity such as sales.

Activity Ratios Ratios that measure how effectively management is utilizing its resources by relating the magnitude of various assets to revenues or expenses.

Average Collection Period. This ratio measures the efficiency of the firm in managing its investment in accounts receivable. The average collection period (ACP) is also sometimes referred to as days of sales outstanding (DSO) because it represents the average time between a credit sale and the receipt of cash from the credit customer. The 2000 ACP for Dayton Products is calculated as follows:

$$\text{Sales per day} = \frac{\text{Sales}}{360} = \frac{\$110,100,000}{360} = \$305,833$$

$$\text{ACP} = \frac{\text{Accounts receivable}}{\text{Sales per day}} = \frac{\$15,100,000}{305,833} = 49 \text{ days}$$

This ratio indicates that Dayton's year-end accounts receivable balance of $15.1 million represented a total of 49 days' worth of sales. Thus, the firm must be taking 49 days, on average, to collect its credit sales.[2] Whether this figure is high or low depends largely on the terms of sale. For example, if the terms technically require payment within 30 days, an ACP of 49 days may indicate poor collection procedures and/or a large number of uncollectible accounts in the accounts receivable balance.

Inventory Turnover. This ratio is designed to indicate how quickly inventories are sold and replaced by comparing the size of inventories to the total cost of inventories sold during the year. The calculation of the 2000 inventory turnover for Dayton Products is:

$$\text{Inventory Turnover} = \frac{\text{Cost of goods sold}}{\text{Ending inventory}} = \frac{\$83,900,000}{\$27,500,000} = 3.05$$

The calculation reveals that the cost of inventories sold during 2000 was 3.05 times as large as the amount of inventories held as of the end of the year. Consequently, the firm must have sold and replaced its entire inventory about three times during 2000. In general, an increase in inventory turnover indicates that the firm is becoming more efficient in its management of assets because it is supporting more sales with a given amount of inventories. Excessively high turnover, however, could mean that the firm's inventories are too small. This situation increases the likelihood that sales will be lost due to inventory "stockouts."

Average Payment Period. This ratio measures the speed with which the firm makes payments to its suppliers for the materials the firm purchases from them. It is the counterpart of the ACP on the liabilities side of the firm's balance sheet. The Average Payment Period (APP) is also sometimes referred to as the number of days' purchases outstanding (DPO) because it measures the average time between a purchase of materials on credit and the cash payment for that purchase to a vendor

---

[2] The figure for sales per day is computed by assuming a 360-day year (12 months of 30 days each) as a standard convention. Although less frequent, a 365-day year is used by some services that compile industry ratios. Strictly speaking, *credit sales* per day should be used in the ACP calculation. Often, however, firms do not provide a breakdown of total sales into cash sales and credit sales. As a result, the analyst is forced to employ total sales per day in the calculation. Since the vast majority of sales of most firms are credit sales, however, this approximation is normally quite accurate.

or supplier. If it were the case that Dayton Products purchased $59,100,000 of materials from suppliers in 2000, its APP would be calculated to be:

$$\text{Purchases per day} = \frac{\text{Purchases}}{360} = (\$59,100,000/360) = \$164,167$$

$$\text{Average Payment Period} = \text{APP} = \frac{\text{Accounts payable}}{\text{Purchases per day}} = \frac{\$7,200,000}{\$164,167}$$

$$= 44 \text{ days}$$

The implication is that the firm is meeting its payment obligations to suppliers, on average, 44 days after the suppliers ship materials to the firm. As with the ACP calculation, whether this 44-day figure is favorable or unfavorable depends on the terms of sale specified by suppliers. If payments to them are due in 30 days after shipment, the firm is 14 days overdue in its payments, and may run into trouble with suppliers in obtaining materials in the future. If the terms of sale are 45 days after shipment, the firm is paying its bills on time.[3]

Fixed Asset Turnover. The effectiveness of management's investing decisions regarding fixed assets can be analyzed by examining the relationship between sales and fixed assets. Up to a point, the higher the level of sales that is supported by fixed assets, the more efficiently management is using those assets. For example, Dayton Products' 2000 fixed asset turnover was:

$$\text{Fixed asset turnover} = \frac{\text{Sales}}{\text{Net fixed assets}} = \frac{\$110,100,000}{\$38,300,000} = 2.88$$

Every $1 in net fixed assets was used to generate $2.88 in sales in 2000. As was the case with inventory turnover, a low fixed asset turnover suggests that the firm has made an excessive investment in fixed assets or that the assets it has acquired are obsolete or otherwise nonproductive.

Total Asset Turnover. This ratio reveals the *overall* effectiveness of management's investing decisions. The total asset turnover for Dayton Products in 2000 was:

$$\text{Total asset turnover} = \frac{\text{Sales}}{\text{Total assets}} = \frac{\$110,100,000}{\$87,900,000} = 1.25$$

For every $1.00 in total assets, Dayton was able to generate $1.25 in sales during 2000. Often a comparison of this ratio with fixed asset turnover can reveal specific problem areas in the firm.

A firm's financial managers should be concerned with inefficiencies suggested by any of the activity ratios because they have implications for the firm's liquidity and profitability. For example, a long average collection period or a low inventory turnover suggests either that too much investment is tied up in these assets or that inventories may be unsalable and receivables uncollectible. In this latter case, the current ratio and the acid-test ratio both overstate the firm's liquidity because they are inflated by inventories and/or receivables that are not readily convertible into cash. Activity ratios also provide evidence about a firm's profitability. Total asset turnover is a key component of return on assets and return on equity.

---

[3] Often it is not possible to identify a firm's volume of purchased materials during a given accounting period from its financial statements, because they are not separately listed. In that event, a "second best" estimate of the firm's APP can be obtained by dividing the sum of accounts payable and other accruals (both of which arise directly from production activities) by average cost of goods sold per day (a rough estimate of production volume).

Leverage Ratios

Leverage ratios are concerned with measuring the extent and effect of debt financing. Financial leverage (debt financing) can be viewed from two perspectives: its impact on the balance sheet and its effect on the income statement. The ratios concerned with the income statement perspective (the coverage ratios) measure the ability of the firm to make the principal and interest payments required on its debt financing. A firm's failure to make these payments is called **default**. Default carries risk of loss for both a firm's creditors and its owners because the creditors have the legal right to force the firm into bankruptcy proceedings. If the firm is liquidated in these proceedings, the cash proceeds may be insufficient to repay the full amount of either debt or equity financing. The ratio concerned with the balance sheet perspective (the debt ratio) measures the potential loss to creditors and owners in the event of a firm's bankruptcy and liquidation. The size of the loss suffered by these parties will depend on whether the cash proceeds from the sale of the firm's assets are sufficient to meet the creditors' claims.

Debt Ratio. The debt ratio is defined as the ratio of total debt to total assets. The lower this ratio, the smaller is the total claim of creditors relative to the total assets available to *pay* that claim. Creditors prefer a low debt ratio because it indicates less risk of loss to them in the event of liquidation of the firm. The stockholders' viewpoint on leverage is often the opposite of that of the creditors. Stockholders tend to prefer high financial leverage because it can increase the returns on *their* investment in the firm. Any returns that the firm can earn in excess of the required interest on debt financing accrue to the benefit of the stockholders. The debt ratio for Dayton Products in 2000 was:

$$\text{Debt ratio} = \frac{\text{Total debt}}{\text{Total assets}} = \frac{\$21,900,000 + 28,000,000}{\$87,900,000} = 0.57$$

The firm raised 57% of its total financing in the form of debt.

Interest Coverage Ratio. The interest coverage ratio is designed to measure the firm's ability to generate earnings that are sufficient to pay its fixed interest obligations to its creditors. The 2000 ratio for Dayton Products was:

$$\text{Interest coverage} = \frac{\text{EBIT}}{\text{Interest}} = \frac{\$9,400,000}{\$2,800,000} = 3.36$$

For every $1 in interest expense, Dayton had $3.36 in operating earnings available to pay interest. The higher this ratio, the lower is the risk of interest default and bankruptcy. Notice that the interest coverage calculation uses EBIT (earnings before interest and taxes) instead of EAT (earnings after taxes). This is because interest is a tax-deductible expense that can be paid out of pretax income from operations.

Fixed Charge Coverage. In this calculation, the definition of payments is broader than that used in connection with the interest coverage ratio. The reason for this is that a firm is legally obligated to make *all* payments, not just the interest expense, associated with debt financing. For example, some forms of debt require periodic payments of both interest and principal. Failure to make either payment represents default. In a similar manner, failure to make the required payments under a lease agreement also represents default.

Leverage Ratios Ratios concerned with measuring the extent and effect of debt financing.

Default The failure to make the principal and interest payments required on debt financing.

The following calculation shows the 2000 fixed charge coverage for Dayton Products under the assumption of principal payments of $2 million on debt, lease payments of $1 million, and a marginal tax rate of 40%:

$$\text{Fixed charge coverage} = \frac{\text{EBIT} + \text{lease payments}}{\text{Interest} + \text{lease payments} + \text{principal payment} / (1 - T)}$$

$$= \frac{\$9,400,000 + 1,000,000}{\$2,800,000 + 1,000,000 + [2,000,000 / (1 - 0.40)]} = 1.46$$

Since lease payments are part of the firm's selling, general, and administrative expenses, they must be added back to EBIT to determine income available to cover fixed charges. The principal payment is divided by (1 – T) because, unlike interest and lease payments, it is not a tax-deductible expense. Thus, for Dayton Products to be able to make an after-tax principal payment of $2 million, it must earn $3.333 million before taxes. Notice that the addition of lease and principal payments has reduced the coverage ratio considerably from the *interest* coverage ratio of 3.36.

Profitability Ratios

One of the key factors utilized by owners in their evaluation of the firm and its stock is the earnings generated by the firm. From the viewpoint of the stockholders, the earning power of a firm is a basic test of the overall effectiveness of its management and policies. Yet, as we pointed out in our introduction to financial ratios, firm performance cannot validly be measured on an absolute basis. It is not the profits of a firm in isolation that are important but, rather, profits relative to the activity or investment required to generate those profits.

For example, the Chrysler Corporation and Coca-Cola Corporation both recently reported EAT of about $3.5 billion. Chrysler's EAT represented only 6% of its sales, however, while Coca-Cola's EAT represented 19% of its sales. The two firms' performance was similar in terms of *profits* but not profitability. **Profitability ratios** measure a firm's overall performance on a relative basis by relating various measures of profits to either sales or investment.

Profitability Ratios Ratios that measure the firm's overall financial performance on a relative basis by relating various measures of profits to either sales or investment.

Gross Margin. By concentrating on the relationship between gross profit and sales, this ratio indicates the effectiveness of a firm's pricing policy and its production efficiency. Without a sufficient gross margin, a firm's efforts to improve profits by holding down nonproduction expenses is likely to be of little use. For example, a low gross margin might be due to high materials or labor costs associated with manufacturing a firm's products. Reacting to such a problem by reducing the size of a firm's headquarters office staff would reduce total firm expenses but do nothing about the basic manufacturing cost problem.

A high gross margin does not *assure* overall profitability, but a low gross margin can often lead to net losses. Dayton Product's gross margin for 2000 based on the data in Table 2-2 was:

$$\text{Gross margin} = \frac{\text{Gross profit}}{\text{Sales}} = \frac{\$26,200,000}{\$110,100,000} = 23.8\%$$

Equivalently, Dayton's direct production costs (materials, direct labor, and factory overhead) amounted to $0.762 out of every $1 in sales.

Net Margin. This ratio evaluates the relationship between profits after all expenses (including taxes) and sales. It is one of the fundamental measures of overall firm profitability. Dayton's 2000 net margin was:

$$\text{Net margin} = \frac{\text{EAT}}{\text{Sales}} = \frac{\$3,300,000}{\$110,100,000} = 3.00\%$$

Out of every \$1 in sales, Dayton earned only \$0.03 in profits after taxes. Net margin is a very significant measure of profitability because a small change in net margin can result in a large change in total profits and in the return earned by the stockholders on their investment in the firm.

Return on Assets. The first two profitability ratios measured profitability in terms of percentage return on sales. The next two ratios measure profitability in terms of return on some measure of investment. The logic behind these ratios arises because the true indicator of an investment's value to an investor is the returns *per amount invested*.

Return on assets (ROA) relates EBIT to the firm's total assets. The goal of this ratio is to measure the profitability of the firm's investing decisions only. Using EBIT as the profit measure leaves the ratio unaffected by the firm's methods of financing because the calculation of EBIT excludes interest expense on debt. Since financial managers are able to control investing and financing decisions separately, it is useful to be able to measure the firm's profitability both before *and* after its financing decisions. For Dayton Products, the 2000 return on assets was:

$$\text{ROA} = \frac{\text{EBIT}}{\text{Total assets}} = \frac{\$9,400,000}{\$87,900,000} = 10.69\%$$

For every \$1 in assets that Dayton's management had at its disposal, it was able to earn a return of more than \$0.10 before taxes and interest. The relationship between ROA and the cost of debt financing determines the profitability of debt financing. Thus, if a firm earns a 10% rate of return on its investment in assets, and finances part of those assets with debt whose cost is just 8%, the extra 2% goes to the firm's stockholders. This is a key comparison that the ROA calculation permits.

Return on Equity. ROA is an overall indicator of profitability, since it measures the returns from assets that have been financed by both debt and equity funds. Stockholders are primarily interested, however, in the return on the equity funds *they* have provided. The return on equity (ROE) for Dayton Products in 2000 was:

$$\text{ROE} = \frac{\text{EAT}}{\text{Net worth}} = \frac{\$3,300,000}{\$38,000,000} = 8.68\%$$

To refer again to our example of Chrysler and Coca-Cola, Chrysler's ROE was 30.5% and Coca-Cola's was 56.7%, despite the fact that the two firm's *total* earnings for the year were virtually identical.

Earnings per Share. All the profitability measures examined up to this point express profitability on a percentage basis. Another widely used measure expresses profitability on a per-share basis. Earnings per share (EPS) relates total profits to the number of shares of common stock a firm has outstanding. Thus, it is easy to understand and directly comparable to other data of interest to stockholders, such as dividends per share and market price per share. Dayton Products' 2000 EPS was:

$$\text{Earnings per share} = \text{EPS} = \frac{\text{EAT}}{\text{Total shares outstanding}}$$

$$= \frac{\$3,300,000}{4,000,000 \text{ shares}}$$

$$= \$0.83$$

For every share of stock owned in Dayton Products, a stockholder had a claim to $0.83 of the firm's 2000 total EAT of $3.3 million. This EPS figure can be compared to Dayton's EPS in prior years.

Implementation of Ratio Analysis

As we have pointed out, financial ratios for a firm for a single period of time have very little usefulness by themselves. To become helpful to an understanding of the firm's financial performance, they must be compared with similar ratios for other firms or with previous years' ratios for the same firm. When performing *cross-section* analysis, the correct procedure for managers to follow is to compare the ratio they calculate to a benchmark that is as specific as possible to the individual firm. Normally, this benchmark is the average ratio value for the industry in which the firm operates. In many countries, there are a number of sources of information on average financial ratios by industry. In the United States, Dun and Bradstreet, Inc., is perhaps the best known and most widely used source of industry averages. D & B annually calculates 14 key ratios for each of 125 categories of lines of business. Of these, 71 are manufacturing, 30 are wholesalers, and 24 are retailers. In other countries, governmental agencies or industry trade associations typically compile similar data. With *trend analysis*, on the other hand, no external sources of information are required, since the firm's ratios for prior years provide the basis for comparisons with ratios for the current year.

Analysis of Dayton Products' Financial Ratios. Table 2-6 summarizes the previously calculated ratios of Dayton Products for 2000 along with values of these ratios for 1996–2000 and industry data for those years. The data suggest several preliminary conclusions. Dayton's liquidity position seems strong, but its efficiency in the use of assets to generate sales seems somewhat low as indicated by its activity ratios. The leverage ratios reveal that the firm relies more on debt financing than is typical of firms in the industry. Dayton's lower coverage ratios suggest that its above-average use of financial leverage has also increased the firm's risk of default. Finally, the firm's profitability seems slightly low in all areas except ROE in 2000.

This cross-section analysis raises several important questions about Dayton's operations. The combination of high ACP and low inventory turnover with high liquidity ratios suggests that the firm has excessive levels of receivables and inventories. Does Dayton have obsolete, out-of-fashion, or otherwise unsalable inventories? What are the firm's credit terms? Is it providing credit to financially weak customers? Are its collection procedures too lenient or its stated credit period too long?

The firm's leverage and profitability ratios raise additional questions. Why is the firm's reliance on debt financing so heavy? Has it been unable or unwilling to raise equity financing by retaining earnings or selling additional common stock? Does the firm have plans to replace the debt with equity financing in the near future? Why are the firm's profitability measures all below average except for ROE? Is there a problem with cost control or product pricing? Have high interest charges on debt financing adversely affected the firm's profitability?

A trend analysis of Dayton Products' ratios permits the financial managers to extend their analysis to obtain further insight into the firm's strengths and weaknesses. Notice that the firm seems to be attempting to correct the problems it has had with excessive inventories and receivables. The inventory turnover has steadily improved over the five-year period. The same is true of the ACP with the exception of 2000. The firm's fixed asset turnover, on the other hand, has steadily

http://

The differences between countries can make understanding financial information a difficult task. Identify the differences in accounting standards between the United States and Europe at www.louisville.edu/~wcnapi01/

Data for Cross-Section and Trend Ratio Analysis of Dayton Products, Inc.							
						Industry Average	
Ratio	1996	1997	1998	1999	2000	2000	1996–2000
Liquidity:							
Current ratio	3.02	2.75	2.64	2.26	2.08	1.86	2.03
Acid-test ratio	1.23	1.07	0.98	0.86	0.82	0.75	0.85
Activity:							
ACP	55 days	51 days	48 days	46 days	49 days	36 days	33 days
Inventory turnover	2.75	2.83	2.90	3.03	3.09	3.15	3.20
Fixed asset turnover	3.95	3.76	3.54	3.17	2.88	3.00	3.34
Total asset turnover	1.52	1.46	1.37	1.30	1.25	1.35	1.41
Leverage:							
Debt ratio	0.45	0.47	0.50	0.55	0.57	0.50	0.45
Interest coverage	4.40	4.34	3.95	3.40	3.36	3.98	4.10
Fixed charge coverage	1.95	1.89	1.56	1.19	1.39	2.10	2.35
Profitability:							
Gross margin	23.0%	21.7%	20.4%	22.4%	23.8%	24.0%	22.8%
Net margin	3.5%	3.0%	2.7%	2.4%	3.0%	3.3%	3.1%
ROA	9.8%	9.6%	9.2%	9.4%	10.7%	10.9%	10.0%
ROE	7.5%	7.4%	7.2%	7.1%	8.7%	8.2%	7.8%
EPS	$0.75	$0.70	$0.67	$0.65	$0.83	N.A.	N.A.

TABLE 2-6

deteriorated. This suggests that the firm's existing fixed assets are becoming increasingly inefficient, or that Dayton has been acquiring new plant and equipment too rapidly and has excess capacity.

The leverage ratios confirm that Dayton Products has been increasingly relying on the use of debt financing over the five-year period. The steady increase in leverage and the decrease in interest coverage raises the question of how much longer this trend can continue before the firm must take corrective action. The profitability ratios present a mixed picture of the success of Dayton's operations. In the last two years, the firm has largely reversed the downward trend in profitability over 1996–1998. Net margin, however, has still not returned to its 1996 level. Moreover, the firm's ROE and EPS would have declined more rapidly over the first four years except for the magnification effect from the steady increase in financial leverage. The key to further long-term improvement in stockholders' returns most likely lies in continued increases in ROA and net margin rather than in the use of additional debt financing.

Limitations of Ratio Analysis. Successful financial analysis is as much an art as it is a science because its successful application depends upon the *judgment* of financial managers, which must be acquired through experience. While ratios can be extremely valuable tools, they must be used carefully with full knowledge of their limitations:

1. Industries are often difficult to define. Most firms engage in many lines of business. Consequently, an industry classification is somewhat arbitrary.
2. Differences in accounting practices employed by different firms can render comparisons of ratios meaningless. For example, firms may use alternative methods of valuing inventory or depreciating fixed assets, which have different impacts on the balance sheet and income statement.

3. An industry average may not necessarily provide a valid target because it is, in the final analysis, merely a description of the overall performance of the firms in an industry. There is no reason to expect it to be a normative benchmark except for the presumption that the rest of the industry is being operated efficiently.

4. An industry average, which is based on past performance, may not be a valid norm for *future* operations. Changing economic conditions or competitive environments can invalidate the assumption that the past is a proper indicator for the future.

In summary, one should be careful not to expect too much of ratio analysis. It is designed to raise questions and suggest areas requiring further investigation rather than to provide final conclusions. It accomplishes this goal by revealing significant deviations from past performance or industry averages. Conclusions about the causes and significance of these deviations must be drawn cautiously.

CASH FLOW ANALYSIS

We have described how a statement of sources and uses of funds can be used to analyze the sources and uses of funds associated with managers' financing and

■ Valuation ISSUES

INVESTOR INFORMATION AND STOCK PRICES

We posed the question at the beginning of this chapter as to the likely reaction of shareholders to General Motors' announcement that the company intended to invest $5 billion in its new Saturn car line. At the time of the announcement, the company also indicated that the estimated production date for the first car model in the line was five years in the future. Thus, for five years, the facilities investments and associated expenses of tooling up for production would appear on the company's balance sheets and income statements, but there would be no offsetting revenues.

If shareholders relied solely on these published financial reports, one would expect that the Saturn project would depress General Motors' stock price for at least five years. The burden of the investment would show up over that period, but none of the potential profits. Or, in terms of discussion in this chapter, the firm's financial ratios would tend to deteriorate until production of the car line actually began. Other firms undertaking large investments with substantially delayed revenues face similar problems.

Fortunately, current and historical financial statements, while important, are not the only sources of information about corporations which are available to investors. The security analysts who work for brokerage firms provide regular reports to the firms' customers, which examine companies' future prospects as well as their history and current circumstances. There are a variety of investment advisory services available on a subscription basis that provide similar analyses. In many instances, direct discussions with corporate managers are part of the underlying research process for these reports. A company's senior executives, of course, make their own public statements to shareholders and provide information on corporate strategies, which supplements the raw data in the firm's formal financial statements.

There is substantial evidence from empirical studies of the financial markets that investors do take this additional information into account. Stock prices appear generally to reflect investors' reasonably well-informed expectations of firms' future profits, even if those profits are not immediately evident in current financial statements. Thus, it is likely that investors would have responded favorably rather than negatively to General Motors' announcement about the Saturn, despite the project's immediate impact on the firm—as long as they were convinced that the investment would pay off in the longer term.

investing decisions for their firms. In that discussion, we employed the term "**funds**" in its broadest definition to include any form of financing during a given period that would allow assets to be acquired, liabilities to be reduced, or dividends to be paid during the same period. Ultimately, of course, it is necessary for *cash* to be available in order for the firm to meet its operating expenses and to pay for new plant and equipment. Obviously, cash is also required to make principal and interest payments on debt and to pay dividends.

This last point is especially important. We have talked about stockholders having a "claim" on the firm's assets and earnings. That claim, however, has no real *value* unless the stockholders can actually receive some cash payments from it. This is the only way they, in turn, can make consumption expenditures or invest elsewhere in other securities. In subsequent chapters dealing with valuation, we shall concentrate explicitly on cash flows as the fundamental determinant of value. The corresponding perspective is that the firm should be viewed basically as a cash-flow-generating "machine" for stockholders. The job of the financial manager, therefore, is to run the machine in such a way as to make those cash flows have the maximum possible value to the firm's owners.

This perspective motivates our third analytical technique: the **statement of cash flows**. This statement focuses on what the firm's financial statements can tell us about the magnitude and composition of the firm's cash-generating power. The procedure is a variant of a statement of sources and uses of funds, and it uses the same general categories of account changes that we described earlier. The items are rearranged, however, to highlight their impact on cash flows.

Construction of a Statement of Cash Flows

The format for such a statement is presented in Table 2-7, using Dayton Products' 2000 results again as an illustration. The logic behind the classifications contained in the table is to separate out the cash flow consequences of the firm's *operating* and *investing* activities from those of its *financing* decisions. A similar tabulation is often found in many corporate reports to shareholders, although the particular formats used can vary.

The analysis begins with the firm's net income for the year. Suppose all the products the firm sold were paid for by customers immediately in cash. Suppose all operating expenses listed on the firm's income statement represented immediate cash payments by the firm during the year. And suppose the firm had no interest expenses. In that case, the figure listed as net income for the year would also be the firm's net operating cash flow for the year.

As we know, however, certain expenses that are shown as deductions from net income are not current cash expenses. We add back depreciation and amortization of goodwill to recognize this fact. We add back interest expense—which has been deducted in computing net income—in order to separate financing costs from operating costs, and identify cash flow from operations *only*, in the first portion of the statement.

The other additions and deductions from net income represent adjustments for the accrual convention used in determining net income. These are the same items that appear on the statement of sources and uses of funds. Since accruals increased by $2.4 million during the year, some of the expenses recorded on the firm's income statement were not paid for in cash in 2000. Additional credit in the amount of $2.4 million was obtained, and the corresponding cash payments are deferred until 2001. Similarly, because accounts receivable increased, some of the firm's sales were also not collected in cash during 2000. Operating cash flow is less than net income to that extent, and we subtract the increase in receivables. The

Funds Any form of financing that allows assets to be acquired, liabilities to be reduced, or dividends to be paid.

Statement of Cash Flows An analysis of the size and composition of a firm's cash-generating power.

TABLE 2-7

**Dayton Products, Inc., Statement of Cash Flows
December 31, 1999, to December 31, 2000 (in Thousands)**

Cash flows from operating activities:	
Net income	$3,300
Additions:	
Depreciation	2,300
Amortization of goodwill	400
Interest expense	2,800
Decrease in other current assets	200
Increase in accounts payable	400
Increase in accruals	2,400
Increase in taxes payable	100
Deductions:	
Increase in accounts receivable	(1,600)
Increase in inventory	(700)
Net cash flow from operating activities	9,600
Cash flows from investing activities:	
Increase in plant and equipment	(7,400)
Net cash flow from operations and investing	2,200
Cash flows from financing activities:	
Increase in long-term liabilities	3,000
Decrease in notes payable	(100)
Interest expense	(2,800)
Subtotal from debt financing	100
Dividends paid	(2,100)
Net cash from financing activities	(2,000)
Net cash flow for 2000	200
Cash balance, December 31, 1999	1,800
Cash balance, December 31, 2000	2,000

same interpretation applies to the other additions to and subtractions from net income, as shown.

The initial message then is that the firm's manufacturing and selling activities in 2000 produced a $9.6 million positive net cash flow during the year. This is the good news because it indicates that operations were in fact a cash-generator for stockholders. One would hope that this would be the case for most firms in most years. That will not necessarily be true, however. For example, if the firm's net income were small, if large increases in inventory and accounts receivable occurred, and if accounts payable and accruals had decreased rather than increased, it is quite possible that net cash flow from operations could turn out to be negative. Firms *can* show an accounting profit while at the same time be generating no cash from operations. Fortunately, that's not the case for Dayton Products.

The next step is to recognize that part of these operating cash flows were absorbed by investments in additional plant and equipment to support *future* operations. The $7.4 million expenditure listed is directly from the statement of sources and uses of funds in Table 2-5. Net cash flow from operations *and* investing activities therefore was $2.2 million in 2000. This figure is sometimes referred to as a firm's **free cash flow**. It represents the net cash outcome of the firm's *business* activities during the year. It is "free" in the sense that it is available from the business to meet the cash requirements of the firm's *financing* decisions: principal and interest payments on debt, and dividends to shareholders.

On the financing side, several things occurred during 2000. Dayton Products paid $2.8 million of interest on existing debt, repaid a small amount of principal on short-term debt (notes payable), and obtained an additional $3.0 million of new long-term debt. Simultaneously, $2.1 million of dividends were paid to shareholders. Recall our earlier discussion about the fact that firms often borrow money to pay dividends. We see that phenomenon again in the statement of cash flows. Without the $3.0 million of new long-term debt, Dayton Products would not have had sufficient cash flows from its operating and investing activities *alone* to have paid dividends to its common stockholders during 2000, while still meeting its interest obligations.

The result of all this is a net positive total cash flow for 2000 of $200,000. Since the firm started the year with $1,800,000 in cash balances, it ended the year with $2,000,000. That is the change recorded on the firm's balance sheets in Table 2-1.

Interpreting the Cash Flow Statement

The evaluation and interpretation of a statement of cash flows should employ the same guidelines as in the case of a statement of sources and uses of funds: (1) look for unusually large items; (2) look for items that move in an unusual direction; and (3) compare the statement with those from prior periods for the firm. Although we do not have the benefit of earlier years' statements for Dayton Products, there appear to be at least a few issues worth raising, given the information in Table 2-7.

Among these is the large proportionate contribution of increases in accruals to the positive cash flow from operations. Without the increase of $2.4 million shown, operating cash flow would not have covered the firm's needs for expenditures on new plant and equipment, leaving no "free" cash flow from the business to pay lenders and dividends. Because accruals represent a very short-term form of credit, payments on these obligations will be due early in 2001. Unless they are replaced with an equivalent amount of new accruals or taken care of by the rapid collection of accounts receivable, Dayton Products may have a near-term cash flow problem. This could result in an additional and perhaps sizable need for new bank loans (notes payable) in the immediate future.

The expenditures on plant and equipment are themselves worth noting. The $7.4 million spent in 2000 represents approximately a 13% increase during the year from the $57.1 million of (gross) plant and equipment the firm had at the beginning of the year. It is also a 22% increase in *net* plant and equipment from the December 31, 1999, level of $33.2 million (Table 2-1). We commented on this earlier in our evaluation of the firm's sources and uses of funds. The question would be whether these expenditures were *necessary* and whether they indicate the start of a major fixed-asset investment program. If they do, the firm will almost certainly require sizable additional external financing to accommodate such a program.

Finally, we can see that the firm's lenders received more in interest payments during 2000 ($2.8 million) than its shareholders received as dividends ($2.1 million). This may be a further signal that the firm is relying too heavily on debt financing or that its operating profit margins are substandard. Our ratio analysis provided similar signals.

Free Cash Flow The net cash flow from a firm's operating and investing activities during a given period of time.

http://

How much cash can be distributed to shareholders without sacrificing future growth? See how to identify overpriced and underpriced firms in terms of their free cash flow at

www.techstocks.com/ ~wsapi/investor/ Subject-17762

ISSUES

UNETHICAL FINANCIAL REPORTING

The goal of this chapter is to demonstrate how various analytical procedures can be used to evaluate the data contained in a firm's financial statements. Given accurate financial data, these techniques can provide an experi-

enced analyst with considerable insight into the risk/return characteristics of a firm. If the data are inaccurate, on the other hand, even the most skilled analyst can be very easily misled. One of the instances in which this can occur is when a manager intentionally understates a write-off to minimize its impact on reported earnings. Securities and Exchange Commission officials indicate the understatement of write-offs is one of the most common types of fraud investigated by that agency.

It is tempting to conclude that such behavior might typically be limited to managers and firms that pay little attention to ethical values. This conclusion, however, was dramatically contradicted by a recent study of almost 400 business executives and graduate business students. Over 40% of the chief executive officers (CEOs) and controllers and over 70% of the students indicated that they would be willing to hide a write-off if it affected their opportunity for a promotion. Surprisingly, the participants' behavior was not significantly affected by their personal values or the presence of a code of ethics at the hypothetical firm. The authors of the study concluded that such unethical behavior can only be prevented by an all-pervasive ethics program at a firm that involved extensive training, senior executive participation, and rewards for ethical behavior.

INTEGRATED FINANCIAL ANALYSIS

In combination, the information from a statement of sources and uses of funds, an analysis of key operating and financial ratios, and a statement of cash flows can begin to identify major areas of concern and major areas of satisfaction with a firm's performance and prospects. In most instances, further investigation as to *causes* will be required in order to reach definite conclusions. Nonetheless, the three techniques together are powerful tools for assessing the risks and future returns associated with the investing and financing decisions made by a company's financial managers.

The "bottom line" on all this is quite straightforward: the returns must eventually take the form of cash flows to shareholders if an ownership investment in the firm is to have any value. The larger the size, the sooner the receipt, and the lower the risk of those cash flows, the greater will be their value. Our objective has been to demonstrate how one can take the accounting information contained in a firm's standard financial reports and gain some insight into its cash-generating potential. In subsequent chapters, we shall examine the manner in which specific investing and financing decisions can enhance that potential.

SUMMARY

This chapter has provided a brief review of the construction and interpretation of financial statements, and described the basic tools of financial analysis. The starting point was a discussion of the roles and the composition of a firm's balance sheet and income statement. The balance sheet is a cumulative record of the firm's sources of financing (liabilities and net worth) and uses of those funds (assets) over the life of the firm. The income statement is designed to show changes in the firm's financial position over time. Specifically, it reveals changes in the firm's net worth that have resulted from operations during the latest accounting period. Fundamental to the proper interpretation of the information on these two statements is an understanding of their method of preparation. The balance sheet data are based on the accounting convention of historical cost and the income statement data on the convention of accrual accounting.

The information from the balance sheet and income statement can be used to construct a statement of sources and uses of funds. The purpose of this statement is to provide management and investors with additional information on the nature of the firm's investing and financing decisions, by showing changes in the firm's sources and uses of funds during the latest accounting period.

Ratio analysis is designed to assess the success of a firm's operations by putting the balance sheet and income statement data on a relative basis. The major financial ratios are normally grouped into four categories: liquidity, activity, leverage, and profitability. Proper interpretation of these ratios requires norms for comparison. Such norms can take the form of either industry average ratios (cross-section analysis) or a time series of ratio values for a single firm (trend analysis).

The statement of cash flows is an extension of the statement of sources and uses of funds. It rearranges the data to focus directly on the cash flow implications of management's decisions during the accounting period. It provides a breakdown of the origin of those cash flows: from operations, from investing, and from financing activities. The contribution of each segment can then be used to identify potential cash flow problems and to anticipate future cash flow prospects. This statement also performs the calculation of a firm's free cash flow, which is a key element in the valuation model that we develop in the coming chapters.

CONTENT QUESTIONS

1. Explain the purpose of the income statement, the purpose of the balance sheet, and the relationship between the two statements.
2. What are the two major accounting conventions that are used to construct the balance sheet and the income statement?
3. What is the purpose of the depreciation concept in terms of the income statement and the balance sheet?
4. Explain why noncash expenses such as depreciation and goodwill amortization are listed as part of a firm's "sources" of funds.
5. There are three rules of thumb that are useful in classifying balance sheet changes as sources or uses of funds. State them and explain the concepts behind their use.
6. Explain in general terms why ratios are needed to understand financial performance.
7. Explain the general characteristics that are shown by the ratios in each of the four categories.
8. What are the most serious limitations of the use of industry averages in ratio analysis?
9. What is meant by the statement that firms often borrow money to pay dividends?
10. How can a firm be profitable yet not have sufficient cash to meet its obligations to creditors?

SUMMARY OF KEY FINANCIAL RATIOS

	Ratio	Definition
LIQUIDITY	Current ratio	$\dfrac{\text{Current assets}}{\text{Current liabilities}}$
	Acid-test ratio	$\dfrac{\text{Current assets} - \text{inventories}}{\text{Current liabilities}}$
ACTIVITY	Average collection period	$\dfrac{\text{Accounts receivable}}{\text{Sales per day}}$
	Inventory turnover	$\dfrac{\text{Cost of goods sold}}{\text{Ending inventory}}$
	Average payment period	$\dfrac{\text{Accounts payable}}{\text{Purchases per day}}$
	Fixed asset turnover	$\dfrac{\text{Sales}}{\text{Net fixed assets}}$
	Total asset turnover	$\dfrac{\text{Sales}}{\text{Total assets}}$
LEVERAGE	Debt ratio	$\dfrac{\text{Total debt}}{\text{Total assets}}$
	Interest coverage	$\dfrac{\text{EBIT}}{\text{Interest}}$
	Fixed charge coverage	$\dfrac{\text{EBIT} + \text{lease payments}}{\text{Interest} + \text{lease payments} + \text{principal} / (1 - T)}$
PROFITABILITY	Gross margin	$\dfrac{\text{Gross profit}}{\text{Sales}}$
	Net margin	$\dfrac{\text{EAT}}{\text{Sales}}$
	Return on assets	$\dfrac{\text{EBIT}}{\text{Total assets}}$
	Return on equity	$\dfrac{\text{EAT}}{\text{Net worth}}$
	Earnings per share	$\dfrac{\text{EAT}}{\text{Total shares outstanding}}$

CONCEPT QUESTIONS

1. **IVM** Balance sheets and income statements provide historical data on the financial performance of a firm. We have argued, however, that it is *future* performance that determines the value of a firm to its owners. To what extent do you believe a firm's management should include explicit projections of the future, in its formal financial reports to shareholders? What are the potential dangers in such a procedure?

2. The inventory turnover ratio described in this chapter is calculated by dividing end-of-year inventory into cost of goods sold for the year. This is the standard approach. Would it be more logical instead to use *sales* volume for the year rather than cost of goods sold, as the numerator for the calculation? Could

one of these turnover ratios increase from one year to the next, while the other simultaneously decreases?

3. Suppose a firm's average receivables collection period (ACP) was 45 days in 1999 and dropped to 35 days in 2000. Would you interpret this change to be a favorable development, in analyzing the firm's performance? What factors could account for the change?

4. It is often claimed as a rule of thumb that a current ratio of 2.0 is the "correct" ratio for most firms to maintain in their operations, in order to be sufficiently liquid. Would you agree with this recommendation? Why or why not? Is it possible to have *too much* liquidity?

5. It is typical for a growing firm to obtain more funds from creditors as it expands. Sometimes this leads to problems and other times it does not. Identify the factors that are important in defining whether there is likely to be a problem. What financial ratios would be useful in making that evaluation?

PROBLEMS

1. Find the net worth of Bronson Industries if its total assets are $72,550,000 and its total liabilities are $53,680,000.

2. Bronson Industries balance in net fixed assets was equal to $17,370,000 at the end of 1999. During the next year, it spent $5,520,000 on plant and equipment and had depreciation expense of $1,390,000. Find the balance in net fixed assets at the end of 2000.

3. Miami Entertainment has a current ratio of 1.50 and current assets equal to $27,000,000.
   a. What are Miami's current liabilities?
   b. If Miami's quick ratio is 1.0, what is the book value of its inventories?

4. Econo Controls has EBIT of $1.435 billion and interest expense of $265 million. Find Econo's earnings per share on its 35 million shares of common stock if its average tax rate is 40%.

5. Forbes Refinery reported retained earnings of $83,000,000 at the end of 1995, $87,000,000 at the end of 1996, and $83,500,000 at the end of 1997.
   a. Find the net income for 1996 if dividends of $2,000,000 were paid.
   b. In 1997, Forbes reported a net loss of $1,000,000. What was the amount of dividends paid in 1997?
   c. If earnings are expected to be $3,500,000 and dividends $2,750,000 in 1998, estimate the retained earnings for the end of 1998.

The following data apply to problems 6–10:

Easycalc Corporation
Balance Sheets
Dec. 31, 1999 and Dec. 31, 2000
(in Millions)

	1999	2000
Cash	$ 10	$ 15
Other current assets	150	135
Net fixed assets	320	350
Total assets	$480	$500
Current liabilities	$ 70	$ 60
Long-term debt	140	100
Common stock	90	125
Retained earnings	180	215
Total liability and net worth	$480	$500

Easycalc Corporation
Income Statements
1999 and 2000
(in Millions)

	1999	2000
Sales	$700	$800
Cost of goods sold	(435)	(490)
Earnings before interest and taxes	265	310
Interest expense	(15)	(10)
Earnings before taxes	250	300
Taxes	(100)	(120)
Net income	$150	$180

6. What did Easycalc spend to increase plant and equipment in 2000? Depreciation expense in 2000 was $20,000,000.
7. In 2000, what amount of dividend was paid out by Easycalc to its shareholders?
8. Prepare a statement of sources and uses of funds for Easycalc for 2000.
9. Prepare a statement of cash flows for Easycalc for 2000.
10. Calculate the following financial ratios for Easycalc for 1999 and 2000:
    a. Current Ratio   e. Interest Coverage
    b. Fixed Asset Turnover   f. Net Margin
    c. Total Asset Turnover   g. Return on Assets
    d. Debt Ratio   h. Return on Equity

The following data apply to problems 11–14:

**Global Industries
Balance Sheets (in Millions)**

	1998	1999
Cash	$ 210	$ 120
Accounts receivable	230	260
Inventories	310	340
Current assets	750	720
Plant and equipment	1,890	2,200
Accumulated depreciation	(610)	(710)
Net fixed assets	1,280	1,490
TOTAL ASSETS	$2,030	$2,210
Accounts payable	$ 250	$ 340
Notes payable	140	160
Accruals	290	370
Other current liabilities	40	40
Total current liabilities	720	910
Long-term debt	230	290
Common stock	150	150
Retained earnings	930	860
TOTAL LIABILITIES AND NET WORTH	$2,030	$2,210

**Global Industries
Income Statement (in Millions)**

	1998	1999
Sales	$3,320	$2,910
Cost of goods sold	(1,750)	(1,680)
Gross profit	1,570	1,230
Selling and administration	(950)	(1,020)
Interest expense	(40)	(50)
Earnings before taxes	580	160
Taxes	(260)	(70)
Net income	$ 320	$ 90

11. Using the financial statements shown above, what was the amount of dividends paid during 1999 by Global?
12. a. Prepare a statement of sources and uses of funds for 1999 for Global.
    b. What are the major sources and uses of funds and the items that might not be classified as "normal"?
13. Calculate the key financial ratios for Global for 1998 and 1999.
14. a. Prepare a statement of cash flows for Global for 1999.
    b. What are the major positive and negative features of the firm's situation, which are suggested by that cash flow statement?

The following data apply to problems 15–17:

Touraine, Inc.
Income Statements

	2000	2001
Sales	$2,900,000	$3,400,000
Cost of goods sold	(1,800,000)	(2,000,000)
Gross profit	1,100,000	1,400,000
Selling and administration	(400,000)	(400,000)
Depreciation	(100,000)	(200,000)
Earnings before interest and taxes	600,000	800,000
Interest	(100,000)	(100,000)
Earnings before taxes	500,000	700,000
Taxes	(200,000)	(300,000)
Earnings after taxes	$ 300,000	$ 400,000

Statement of Retained Earnings, 2001

Retained earnings, 2000	$ 600,000
Earnings after taxes, 2001	400,000
Less dividend paid	(200,000)
Retained earnings, 2001	$ 800,000

Touraine, Inc.
Balance Sheets

	2000	2001
Cash	$ 200,000	$ 250,000
Accounts receivable	500,000	650,000
Inventories	500,000	700,000
Current assets	1,200,000	1,600,000
Plant and equipment	4,450,000	4,600,000
Less: Accumulated depreciation	(1,600,000)	(1,800,000)
Net fixed assets	2,850,000	2,800,000
Goodwill	150,000	100,000
Total assets	$4,200,000	$4,500,000
Accounts payable	$ 200,000	$ 300,000
Notes payable	400,000	200,000
Other liabilities	500,000	600,000
Current liabilities	1,100,000	1,100,000
Long-term debt	1,000,000	1,000,000
Common stock	1,500,000	1,600,000
Retained earnings	600,000	800,000
Total liabilities and net worth	$4,200,000	$4,500,000

15. a. Prepare a statement of sources and uses of funds for Touraine for 2001.
    b. State the major sources and uses of funds and the items that might not be considered as "normal."
16. a. Calculate the key financial ratios for Touraine for 2001.
    b. What appear to be the company's strengths and weaknesses, given the following industry norms?

Current ratio	1.8
Acid-test ratio	1.1
Average collection period	60 days
Inventory turnover	4.0
Fixed asset turnover	2.0
Total asset turnover	1.2
Debt ratio	0.33
Interest coverage	9.0
Gross margin	0.40
Net margin	0.10
Return on assets	0.25
Return on equity	0.18

17. a. Prepare a statement of cash flows for Touraine for 2001.
    b. What are the major positive and negative features of the firm's situation, which are suggested by that cash flow statement?
18. The president of a small manufacturing firm, Valco Industries, has approached your bank for a $100,000 long-term loan and has presented the income statements and balance sheets given on the next page. As loan officer of the bank, you notice that a statement of retained earnings was not provided by Valco. You realize that information regarding dividends will be important to your analysis. Since you didn't notice that it was missing until the president of Valco left, you decided to go ahead and construct it yourself. Construct the statement summarizing the firm's changes in retained earnings in 1999.

The following data apply to problems 19–22:

Valco Industries Balance Sheets

	Dec. 31, 1998	Dec. 31, 1999
Cash	$ 88,200	$ 87,600
Accounts receivable	105,700	154,300
Inventories	212,300	233,600
Current assets	406,200	475,500
Plant and equipment	495,500	542,800
Less: Accumulated depreciation	(182,200)	(207,200)
Net fixed assets	313,300	335,600
Total assets	$719,500	$811,100
Accounts payable	$154,600	$240,300
Accruals	44,900	68,200
Taxes payable	4,100	3,800
Current liabilities	203,600	312,300
Long-term debt	200,000	170,000
Common stock	250,000	250,000
Retained earnings	65,900	78,800
Total liabilities and net worth	$719,500	$811,100

Valco Industries Income Statements

	1998	1999
Sales	$1,505,300	$1,643,800
Cost of goods sold	(1,053,500)	(1,236,000)
Gross profit	451,800	407,800
Operating expense	(210,900)	(226,700)
Depreciation expense	(24,400)	(25,000)
Operating income (EBIT)	216,500	156,100
Interest expense	(32,200)	(31,600)
Taxes	(91,200)	(58,100)
Earnings after taxes	$ 93,100	$ 66,400

19. As a loan officer, you are interested in learning as much as possible about the financial history of Valco. Thus, you decide that a sources-and-uses-of-funds analysis would be useful.
    a. Construct a statement of sources and uses of funds for Valco Industries.
    b. What were the major sources and uses of funds?
    c. What areas of additional investigation are suggested by the sources-and-uses-of-funds analysis?

20.   a. Prepare a statement of cash flows for Valco for 1999, from its financial statements.
    b. What are the major positive and negative features of the firm's situation, which are suggested by that cash flow statement?

21. You have compiled the industry average financial ratios for Valco's industry and constructed the following table:

	Industry Average	1998	1999
Current ratio	2.10		
Acid-test ratio	1.10		
Average collection period	30 days		
Inventory turnover	6.0		
Fixed asset turnover	4.0		
Total asset turnover	2.0		
Debt ratio	0.45		
Interest coverage	6.0		
Gross margin	0.33		
Net margin	0.06		
Return on assets	0.12		
Return on equity	0.22		

a. Fill in the values of the financial ratios for 1998 and 1999 for Valco.
b. Based on the information provided by your answers to (a), what are the strengths and weaknesses of Valco Industries?

22. a. Should you, as loan officer, approve the loan to Valco? Estimate what some key ratios for 1999 would be if $100,000 of long-term debt were added. Assume a 12% rate of interest and that the loan would be used to reduce current liabilities. Use an average 40% tax rate.
b. If you make the loan, what type of restrictions would you place on the investing and financing decisions of Valco to protect the bank's position?
c. What additional information from Valco would help you make a better decision?

INTERNET EXERCISE

http://

Do you know what is happening in the European economy? You can check out the central banks of Europe at the following Web site and research their current monthly economic report. It has sections on key economic data, interest rates, economic conditions, and many other links. Write a three-page report on the current economic condition in Europe. www.financials.com/cbanks.cfm

SELF-STUDY QUIZ

Roundnumber Corporation
Balance Sheets
Dec. 31, 1999 and Dec. 31, 2000
(in Millions)

	1999	2000
Cash	$ 60	$ 100
Other current assets	540	600
Net fixed assets	1,200	1,400
Total assets	$1,800	$2,100
Current liabilities	$ 500	$ 550
Long-term debt	400	490
Common stock	200	260
Retained earnings	700	800
Total liabilities and net worth	$1,800	$2,100

Roundnumber Corporation
2000 Income Statement
(in Millions)

Earnings before interest and taxes	$570
Interest expense	(70)
Earnings before taxes	500
Taxes	(200)
Net income	$300

1. How large were the dividends paid to the stockholders of Roundnumber Corporation in 2000?
2. If depreciation expense was $75 million in 2000, what was spent by Roundnumber on plant and equipment?
3. Construct the statement of sources and uses of funds for Roundnumber for 2000.
4. Construct the statement of cash flows for Roundnumber for 2000.
5. Calculate the following financial ratios for Roundnumber:
   Current ratio (1999 and 2000)
   Debt ratio (1999 and 2000)
   Interest coverage (2000 only)
   Return on assets (2000 only)
   Return on equity (2000 only)

The External Environment: The Financial System

An economy's financial system—its money and capital markets—defines the primary environment within which the corporate financial manager must seek the funds to support the firm's operations. The basic role of this marketplace, like that of any other market in a private enterprise economy, is to allocate scarce resources to their most productive uses. In the financial system, the resource involved is investment capital, and the allocation scheme employed is the standard one—the price mechanism. Organizations and individuals with funds to invest will select among competing bidders for those funds according to the risk/return trade-off each one offers. The "price" of funds will reflect that trade-off.

In a developed economy, this process requires the assistance of a variety of institutions called financial intermediaries. It also involves a wide variety of financial instruments—securities—which define the specific terms of the bargains which are struck between the users and suppliers of capital. For example:

- In 1998, the business sector in the United States issued approximately $500 billion of liabilities through the domestic financial system. Who provided those funds, and how were they used by the firms that acquired them?

- In 1998, the assets of U.S. financial intermediaries exceeded $22 trillion. Who financed these assets? What services were provided by the intermediaries in exchange for the funds? What types of assets did the intermediaries acquire with those funds?

- More than 2,900 firms' common stock is bought and sold on the New York Stock Exchange (NYSE). The daily volume of shares traded averages between 500 and 700 million shares. Yet, none of the funds transferred between buyers and sellers flows to the firms whose stock is traded. What, then, is the function of the NYSE and why do companies list their shares for trading in that market?
- In January 1999, the interest rate on 3-month Treasury bills was only 4.56%, while the rate on 5-year Treasury securities was 4.72%. On Aaa corporate bonds, a 6.35% rate was observed. What factors account for these interest rate differentials? Why would an investor want to purchase a 3-month Treasury bill rather than a corporate bond?
- In 1981, the interest rate on Aaa corporate bonds reached approximately 16%. By 1999, however, the rate had dropped to under 7%. What could account for this dramatic decline in the cost of funds to corporate borrowers?

In this chapter, we will examine these and related aspects of the financial system that affect the cost and availability of the financing that firms employ. The terms of that financing are important because their features directly affect the valuation of a company's shares. In the following chapter, we shall extend our discussion to the international financial marketplace, which is becoming an increasingly significant provider of capital to firms.

RAISING CAPITAL

In the acquisition of funds, financial managers must make the following choices: (1) debt versus equity financing; (2) short-term debt versus long-term debt; and (3) the retention of earnings versus the payment of dividends. Of these alternatives, only the retention of earnings represents an internal source of funds. The other choices are external sources because they require managers to go outside the firm to the financial markets and to financial intermediaries to obtain the necessary financing. Figure 3-1 outlines how the external environment affects the job of

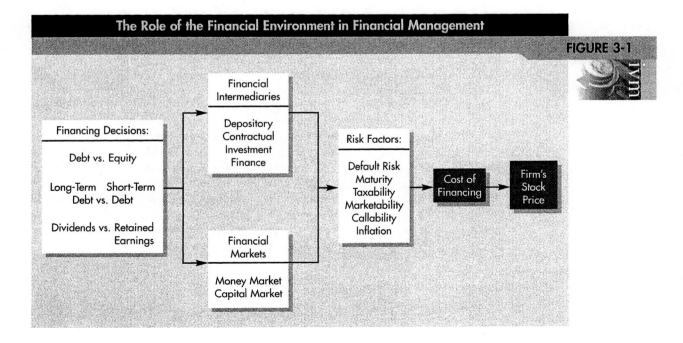

The Role of the Financial Environment in Financial Management

FIGURE 3-1

Financing Decisions:

Debt vs. Equity

Long-Term   Short-Term
Debt vs. Debt

Dividends vs. Retained Earnings

Financial Intermediaries

Depository
Contractual
Investment
Finance

Financial Markets

Money Market
Capital Market

Risk Factors:

Default Risk
Maturity
Taxability
Marketability
Callability
Inflation

Cost of Financing

Firm's Stock Price

financial managers. A firm's financing decisions can be implemented either through private transactions with financial intermediaries or public transactions on financial markets. The significance of these alternatives lies in their impact on the risk accepted by the firm's creditors and investors. This risk, in turn, determines the cost to the firm of its financing decisions. In their attempts to minimize the cost of financing, financial managers are simultaneously striving for the goal of value maximization.

The firm's continuous interaction with the financial system requires that its financial managers be familiar with the system's role and operation. The objectives of this chapter are twofold. First, we describe the institutional setting of financial markets, with particular emphasis on the roles of the money and capital markets. Second, we discuss the major determinants and behavior of interest rates, which are a vital aspect of the operation of financial markets and which strongly influence the cost of both debt and equity capital.

THE NATURE OF THE FINANCIAL SYSTEM

The financial system of an industrialized country consists of a complex of institutions and markets, which serve individuals, corporations, and government by facilitating the exchange of funds from economic units with excess funds to units with deficits. Since this exchange process determines the allocation of productive resources, it has a major impact on the overall productivity and economic welfare of all individuals in the economy.

The Role of Financial Markets

The ultimate purpose of financial markets is to transfer funds from surplus economic units to deficit units. In this context, an economic unit can be an individual household, a partnership, a corporation, a not-for-profit organization, or a government body. A **surplus unit** is one whose portion of income that is saved exceeds its investment spending in a given period of time.[1] A **deficit unit** is one whose investment spending exceeds its saving. Figure 3-2 summarizes the role of financial markets in the transfer of funds.

In Figure 3-2, although the saving of the two units is identical at $150, the deficit unit wishes to acquire $250 in real assets, while the surplus unit only wants to spend $50 on real assets. The financial markets make it possible for both units to be satisfied through a transfer of $100 from the surplus unit to the deficit unit. In the exchange process, the surplus unit receives a financial claim or security (an IOU) from the deficit unit. This security serves as evidence of the transfer and specifies the particular terms of the agreement between the two units.

The T-accounts in the figure indicate the balance sheets of the two units after the transfer of the $100. The surplus unit's net worth of $150 represents its saving for the period, which provided the funds for the acquisition of $50 in real assets and $100 in financial assets. The financial assets of the surplus unit represent the financial claim issued by the deficit unit in exchange for the $100 transferred. This claim is the $100 financial liability shown in the deficit unit's T-account. The deficit unit has financed its investing of $250 in real assets in two ways: the use of its savings of $150 and the issuance of a financial claim for $100.

Surplus Unit An economic unit whose saving exceeds its investment spending for real assets.

Deficit Unit An economic unit whose investment spending on real assets exceeds its saving.

---

[1] At this point in the chapter, we are limiting the term investment spending to the classical economic meaning of the acquisition of *real* assets, such as buildings and machinery.

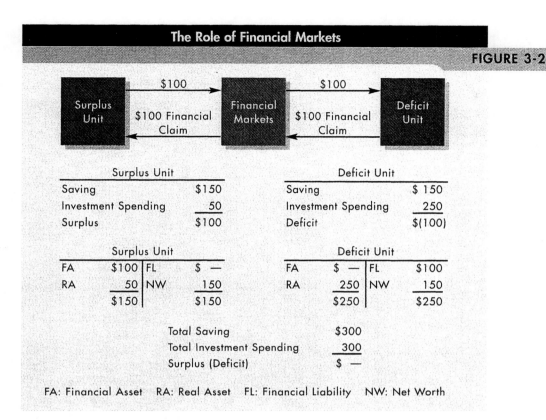

The Role of Financial Markets

FIGURE 3-2

Surplus Unit	
Saving	$150
Investment Spending	50
Surplus	$100

Deficit Unit	
Saving	$ 150
Investment Spending	250
Deficit	$(100)

Surplus Unit			
FA	$100	FL	$ —
RA	50	NW	150
	$150		$150

Deficit Unit			
FA	$ —	FL	$100
RA	250	NW	150
	$250		$250

Total Saving	$300
Total Investment Spending	300
Surplus (Deficit)	$ —

FA: Financial Asset   RA: Real Asset   FL: Financial Liability   NW: Net Worth

Financial Markets and Economic Efficiency

A modern economy resembles our simple example in Figure 3-2. The deficit unit in that figure represents business firms that each year invest in real assets, such as plant and equipment, in amounts generally in excess of their saving. The surplus unit represents households that, as a group, have annual saving considerably greater than their investment in real assets such as homes. Table 3-1 contains estimates of the saving and investing patterns of the household and business sectors in the United States in recent years.

Table 3-1 shows the annual changes in the balance sheets for each sector for a five-year time period. The top half of the table indicates that, in all but one of the five years, the household sector's saving exceeded its investing. This surplus was used to acquire financial assets, which represent transfers of funds to deficit units—including the government. At the same time, the business sector's excess of investing over saving in all of the five years required the issuance of financial liabilities to cover the deficit.

Consider what would happen if financial assets, liabilities, and markets didn't exist. Firms would be constrained to making investments only to the extent they saved. Investments would have to be postponed until sufficient cash had been accumulated. On the other hand, units such as households with excess income would have no convenient outlet for funds that they did not consume or invest in real assets. Without financial assets, their choices for the employment of excess earnings are either unnecessary consumption or the accumulation of idle cash balances. In such an economy, saving cannot be attracted to the most desirable real asset investment opportunities.

	Saving and Investing Patterns in the United States				
TABLE 3-1					

	Annual Flow ($ billions)				
	1994	**1995**	**1996**	**1997**	**1998**
Household Sector:					
Real Assets	$ 865	$ 894	$ 935	$1,000	$1,081
Financial Assets	581	500	575	429	462
Total Uses	1,446	1,394	1,510	1,429	1,543
Financial Liabilities	380	396	430	387	473
Net Worth	1,066	998	1,080	1,042	1,070
Total Sources	1,446	1,394	1,510	1,429	1,543
Saving	1,066	998	1,080	1,042	1,070
Investing	(865)	(894)	(935)	(1,000)	(1,081)
Surplus	201	104	145	42	(11)
Nonfinancial Business Sector:					
Real Assets	$ 641	$ 701	$ 713	$ 826	$ 860
Financial Assets	297	427	418	379	438
Total Uses	938	1,128	1,131	1,205	1,298
Financial Liabilities	298	469	424	469	551
Net Worth	640	659	707	736	747
Total Sources	938	1,128	1,131	1,205	1,298
Saving	640	659	707	736	747
Investing	(641)	(701)	(713)	(826)	(860)
Deficit	(1)	(42)	(6)	(90)	(113)

Source: *Flow of Fund Accounts of the United States*, Board of Governors of the Federal Reserve System

The Development of Financial Systems

There is much more to a modern financial system than the simple existence of financial claims. The financial system encompasses a vast industry within itself, consisting of stock exchanges, brokers, banks, savings institutions, and so on. Their common reason for existence is to support the efficient transfer of financial claims. In addition to this general role, each component of the system serves a specific role, which can best be described by analyzing the evolution of a simple into a more complex financial system.

A Simple Financial System. In the early stages of development, financial claims or securities represent direct agreements between the ultimate supplier of funds (the saver) and the ultimate user of the funds (the investor). This transfer of funds was illustrated in Figure 3-2. The specific financial claim employed can take any one of several forms. In general terms, however, it is called a **direct claim** or security because it is sold *directly to the surplus unit by the ultimate user of the funds, the deficit unit.* How efficient is a financial system that involves only direct claims? In theory, it can work very well, but there are numerous practical problems. The most significant are the time and effort required for surplus and deficit

Direct Claim A financial claim issued by a deficit unit to acquire funds for investment in real assets.

units to locate each other and the potential inability to develop mutually accept-able terms for the direct claim. Clearly, there is some room for improvement in this simple system.

A Complex Financial System. In a free enterprise economy, **brokers** who *specialize in bringing borrowers and lenders together* will come into existence. They may merely serve as a go-between for the two parties or may actually purchase the direct claims from the deficit unit before reselling them to the surplus unit. In either case, brokers help to reduce the problem that savers and investors face in locating each other in a simple financial system. In addition to brokers, **financial intermediaries** will evolve to facilitate the process of transferring of funds. Even if the surplus and deficit units can be brought together, there remains the problem of determining mutually acceptable terms of transfer. Financial inter-mediaries solve this problem by *reaching separate agreements with the borrower and the lender*, as is illustrated in Figure 3-3.

The financial intermediary breaks the transfer process down into two distinct stages or transactions that involve the issuance of two different types of financial claims. When the surplus unit lends $100 to the intermediary in Figure 3-3, it receives a $100 claim on the intermediary itself. The intermediary then relends the $100 to a deficit unit in exchange for a claim on that unit. The claim issued by the deficit unit is the same direct claim as shown in Figure 3-2. The claim issued by the financial intermediary, however, is an **indirect claim** or security because the inter-mediary relends the funds to the deficit unit to enable it to acquire real assets. Thus, the IOU issued by the intermediary represents an indirect claim on the deficit unit that is the ultimate user of the funds.[2] This process, whereby the sur-plus unit channels funds through a financial intermediary before they reach the deficit unit, is called **intermediation**. Although the degree of use of the interme-diation procedure varies over time, it is typically very substantial in developed economies.

Brokers Specialize in bring-ing borrowers and lenders together, and may purchase the direct claims from the deficit unit before reselling them to the surplus unit.

Financial Intermediaries Institutions that produce mutually agreeable terms between borrower and lender by reaching separate agreements with both parties.

Indirect Claim Claim issued by a financial intermediary who relends the funds to the deficit unit to enable it to acquire real assets.

Intermediation The process whereby a surplus unit channels funds through the financial intermediary before they reach a deficit unit.

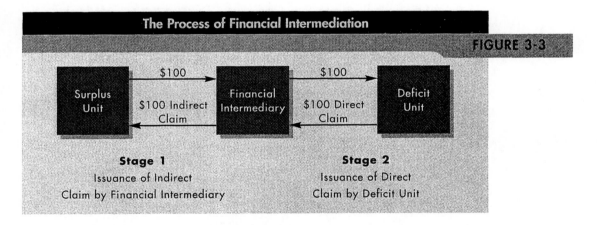

The Process of Financial Intermediation

FIGURE 3-3

$100 → Surplus Unit → $100 → Financial Intermediary → $100 → Deficit Unit

$100 Indirect Claim ← $100 Direct Claim ←

Stage 1
Issuance of Indirect Claim by Financial Intermediary

Stage 2
Issuance of Direct Claim by Deficit Unit

---

[2] The presence of the financial intermediary has doubled the total number of financial claims required to transfer funds from the surplus to the deficit unit. The $100 transfer in Figure 3-3 involves a $100 indirect claim issued by the intermediary and a $100 direct claim issued by the deficit unit. This increase in the number of financial claims is called *financial layering*. In a complex financial system, there may be several intermediaries between the deficit and the surplus unit instead of just the one shown in Figure 3-3. Thus, the degree of financial layering may be considerable.

Primary Market The issuance or original sale of a financial claim by a deficit unit takes place on the primary market.

Secondary Market The resale of an outstanding security by one surplus unit to another takes place on the secondary market.

The final stage in the evolution of a complex financial system involves the creation of secondary markets. The issuance, or original sale, of a financial claim by a deficit unit takes place on the **primary market**. The resale of the claim by one surplus unit to another takes place on the **secondary market**. The purpose of the secondary market is to enable a surplus unit to exchange a financial claim for cash prior to its maturity. In this way, the *secondary market provides both liquidity and flexibility to the surplus unit*. Not only can the unit easily convert the security into cash on the secondary market, but it can also readily shift funds from one type of security to another.

The prime example of a secondary market is a stock exchange such as the New York Stock Exchange (NYSE) or the Paris Bourse. The history of stock exchanges reveals that they had their origins in informal meetings of investors who wished to trade the common stocks of firms. As the knowledge of these meetings spread, other investors requested that the original stock traders carry out trades for them. Over time, the meetings became formalized with a fixed time schedule and meeting place. The original traders became the brokers who facilitated the sale of stock between two other investors.

Figure 3-4 illustrates the operation of the primary market and the secondary market. The transaction that takes place on the primary market results in a $100 inflow of funds to the deficit unit and the creation of a new financial claim. Let us assume that the maturity of the claim is ten years. Without a secondary market, the surplus unit must wait the full ten years before it can receive the $100 back from the deficit unit. If a secondary market exists, however, it can sell the loan to another surplus unit at any time prior to the loan's maturity.

Notice that *secondary market transactions do not result in either the creation of new financial claims or the inflow of funds to deficit units*. These transactions simply involve the resale of outstanding financial claims between surplus units. Why, then, are they so important to the efficient functioning of the financial system? Without a secondary market to make outstanding claims liquid, surplus units would be hesitant to buy long-term claims. Deficit units such as businesses would be forced to rely on the issuance of short-term claims to raise funds. Since most investments in real assets require long-term financing, firms could be reluctant to acquire long-lived assets, and capital formation would suffer. We provide a further description of the secondary securities markets in the Appendix to this chapter.

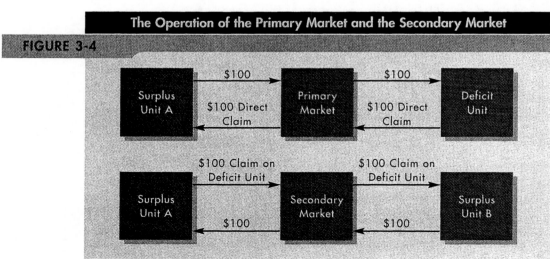

The Operation of the Primary Market and the Secondary Market

FIGURE 3-4

Up to this point, we have discussed the general role of financial instruments and intermediaries in facilitating the funds transfer process. We can now take a closer look at the specific functions performed by financial intermediaries.

The Role of Intermediaries

Financial intermediaries come between the ultimate borrowers and savers by buying direct claims and issuing indirect claims. Through this procedure, they provide a number of benefits:

1. Risk Intermediation
2. Maturity Intermediation
3. Denomination Intermediation
4. Economies of Scale
5. Convenience

Risk Intermediation. A financial intermediary can purchase a large number of direct claims from different economic units in need of funds. There is always the risk that any one of these deficit units might default on its obligation to honor the terms of the agreement that are specified in the claim. By holding a large number of claims, the financial position of the intermediary will not be seriously damaged if one or more of the deficit units fails to repay (defaults) on its claim. Due to their small size, however, *individual* surplus units or savers may be able to own only a small number of direct claims. If the issuer of one of these claims should default, the financial damages suffered by the investor could be severe.

The risk reduction advantage of an intermediary can be passed on to the individual in the form of indirect securities. For example, an individual who deposits $1,000 in a bank savings account is getting an indirect claim on all the direct claims held by the bank. If the bank has 10,000 loans outstanding that amount to $100 million in total, the $1,000 individual deposit represents a partial claim on each of the bank's 10,000 loans. Consequently, a default on one loan will have only a small impact on the bank and on the depositor.

Maturity Intermediation. Financial intermediaries can transform direct securities with any specific maturity into indirect securities with different maturities. Consequently, it is not necessary for the length of time the borrower needs funds to be precisely matched to the needs of the individual saver. For example, a savings and loan association may take in $100,000 in time deposit funds with a maturity of 90 days from many savers and relend the funds to a single home buyer in the form of a mortgage loan with a maturity of 30 years. Due to the very diverse maturity needs of the savers and the borrower, it is unlikely that this transfer of funds could have occurred in the absence of the financial intermediary.

Denomination Intermediation. Financial intermediaries are able to provide small savers with the opportunity to participate in financing large direct claims. An intermediary pools savings to purchase direct claims of various denominations. In addition, it saves the deficit unit the problem of dealing with a large number of small savers. A striking example of denomination intermediation is the operation of "money market" mutual funds. These intermediaries specialize in pooling the savings of small surplus units, such as households, to purchase large-denomination debt securities issued by the government and by banks.

Economies of Scale. Because a financial intermediary handles a large volume of transactions involving direct claims, it can realize economies of scale not available to the individual investor. The operation of a mutual fund or unit trust is a good illustration of these economy of scale benefits. A mutual fund raises capital by selling its own shares of stock (indirect claims) to obtain funds to purchase common stock (direct claims) on secondary markets. On a percentage basis, the brokerage commission paid by the mutual fund on its very large purchases is much smaller than the commission that would be paid by an individual saver.

Convenience.   There are intricate legal and procedural details associated with a direct security both at the time of issuance of the security and throughout its life. In addition, the process of locating a borrower or lender and negotiating the transfer of funds can be quite time-consuming. Especially for the small saver, these inconvenience "costs" can be prohibitive. Financial institutions eliminate the inconvenience by managing all aspects of the acquisition of direct claims for the saver. This convenience benefit is very evident in the operation of a bank or a savings and loan, which takes in funds under simple deposit arrangements and lends them out under intricate corporate loan agreements.

All of the above benefits provided by financial intermediaries arise from the *intermediation* process: the acquisition of direct claims issued by deficit units and the issuance of indirect claims to surplus units. While the general nature of this process is the same for all financial intermediaries, the specific types of direct claims acquired and indirect claims issued vary from one type of intermediary to another.

FINANCIAL INTERMEDIARIES

Financial intermediaries have a number of ways of performing their fundamental function of facilitating the transfer of funds between surplus and deficit units. They are specialized both by the types of indirect claims they issue and by the types of direct claims they purchase. There are four major categories of intermediaries:

1. Depository Types
2. Contractual Types
3. Investment Companies
4. Finance Companies

As an example, the importance of each type of financial intermediary in the United States is shown in Table 3-2.

The size of the assets shown in Table 3-2 indicates the extent to which deficit and surplus units in the U.S. economy make use of the intermediation process shown in Figure 3-3. Roughly 75%–80% of the total annual transfer of funds between surplus and deficit units in the United States is accomplished indirectly through the process of financial intermediation rather than directly between the units themselves.

Depository Intermediaries

Depository Intermediaries
These institutions raise funds by issuing indirect claims in the form of deposits, which can be classified into two basic categories: transaction and time.

As their name suggests, **depository intermediaries** raise funds by issuing indirect claims in the form of deposits, which can be classified into two basic categories: (1) transaction, or demand, deposits; and (2) savings and time deposits. The chief characteristic of transaction deposits is the right of the depositor to withdraw the funds at any time upon demand. Since depositors normally withdraw these funds through the use of a check, transaction deposits are popularly called checking accounts. Savings deposits (such as money market savings and passbook savings) represent financial claims with no specific maturity. In addition, the saver cannot withdraw these funds through the use of a check. Time deposits have

| Financial Assets of U.S. Financial Intermediaries (in Billions) | | | | | TABLE 3-2 |

		1996		1998	
		Assets	%	Assets	%
Depository Types					
Commercial Banks		$ 4,704		$ 5,405	
Savings Institutions		1,032		1,047	
Credit Unions		330		377	
	Subtotal	$6,066	33%	$ 6,829	30%
Contractual Types					
Insurance Companies		$ 3,051		$ 3,582	
Pension and Retirement Funds		4,755		6,267	
	Subtotal	$ 7,806	42%	$ 9,849	43%
Investment Companies					
Mutual Funds		$ 3,233		$ 4,610	
Real Estate Trusts		28		54	
Security Brokers/Dealers		635		824	
	Subtotal	$ 3,896	21%	$ 5,488	24%
Finance Companies		715	4%	796	3%
	Total	$18,483	100%	$22,962	100%

Source: *Flow of Fund Accounts of the United States,* Board of Governors of the Federal Reserve System

specific maturities ranging from one month to several years. Both savings and time deposits can earn interest, as can certain types of transaction deposits. The interest paid on a time deposit tends to vary directly with its maturity: the longer the maturity, the higher the interest.

Depository institutions differ markedly in the types of direct claims they acquire from deficit units. Commercial banks are so named because they stress short-term and intermediate-term loans to businesses. They are also often large purchasers of debt instruments issued by the government. Mutual savings banks and savings and loan associations, on the other hand, use most of their funds to make long-term mortgage loans to consumers and commercial borrowers to finance the purchase of real estate. Finally, credit unions stress short-term consumer loans for a variety of needs of their members, such as the purchase of an automobile or a major appliance. They also make home mortgage loans to their members.

Contractual Intermediaries

The indirect claim issued by a **contractual intermediary** is a contract or an agreement between the financial institution and the individual saver. The contract specifies that the saver will make periodic, fixed payments to the intermediary in exchange for the right to receive payments from the intermediary at some time in the future. The contracts issued by insurance companies promise payments to the insured individual (the saver) in the event of financial losses suffered from some hazard such as premature death, fire, theft, accidents, and sickness. The insured individual promises to make regular premium payments to the insurance compa-

Contractual Intermediary
Issues an indirect claim in the form of a contract that specifies that the individual saver will make periodic, fixed payments to the intermediary in exchange for the right to receive payments from the intermediary in the future.

ny to cover the cost of the protection. Premiums in excess of insurance benefits paid out in a given year are used by the insurance company to make loans to businesses and individuals, and to acquire a variety of securities issued by businesses and government units. The contracts issued by pension funds promise retirement income to the individual saver in exchange for regular contributions to the pension fund during the saver's working years. Excess annual contributions to the pension funds are used to purchase direct claims of deficit units similar to those purchased by insurance companies.

Investment Companies

Investment Companies
Companies that sell their own stock to small surplus units to raise funds for the purchase of direct claims issued by larger deficit units.

The role of **investment companies** is to sell their own stock to small surplus units to raise funds for the purchase of direct claims issued by deficit units. The attraction of investment companies to savers is that they offer the benefits of substantial diversification and professional selection in the acquisition of large portfolios of direct claims. The largest category of investment companies is the open-end investment company, or mutual fund, that specializes in the acquisition of stocks or bonds issued by nonfinancial firms. Since a mutual fund (which, in some countries, is called a "unit trust") normally specializes in a given type of stock or bond, savers can buy the stock of that mutual fund whose investment objective most closely matches their own.

Finance Companies

http://
You can check out the latest news on mutual funds on this Web site.
www.investorguide.com/ MutualFunds.htm

Finance companies raise funds by selling their own debt instruments to surplus units and by borrowing from other financial intermediaries, particularly commercial banks. Personal finance companies make small cash loans to individuals. Sales finance companies make consumer installment loans for the purchase of consumer durables such as automobiles and large appliances. Commercial finance companies specialize in intermediate-term loans to firms to finance the acquisition of machinery and equipment. An important aspect of all three types of finance companies is that they specialize in lending to high-risk deficit units that find it difficult to borrow from commercial banks or other intermediaries. A major category of finance companies is the captive finance company started by a manufacturing firm to finance the sale of its products. General Motors Acceptance Corporation (GMAC) and General Electric Capital are prime examples of captive finance companies.

Finance Companies
Companies that raise funds by selling their own debt instruments to surplus units and by borrowing from other financial intermediaries.

As described earlier, the transfer of funds between economic units involves both direct and indirect financial claims. Let us now take a closer look at the types of *direct* claims issued by deficit units and the markets on which those claims are issued and traded.

TYPES OF FINANCIAL INSTRUMENTS AND MARKETS

The types of securities available on the financial markets are important in two ways. First, the type of claim issued by a firm in a deficit savings position determines the cost and risk impact of the firm's financing decisions. Second, individuals in a surplus savings position and intermediaries must be aware of the differences in the risk/return trade-offs offered by the various direct claims they can purchase. In a similar fashion, a company's financial managers must be aware of the characteristics of the different financial markets that arise from the distinctions in the types of securities that are traded on those markets. We will begin the discussion of financial instruments by considering differences in the nature of their claim on the issuer's *income*.

Nature of the Claim—Contractual Versus Residual

We have used the terms direct or indirect claim to describe the financial instrument involved in the transfer of funds between the surplus and deficit units because the instrument grants the surplus unit a claim on the income of the issuer. A fundamental distinction among financial instruments is the type of claim against the issuer's income that the instrument grants: contractual or residual.

A **contractual claim** specifies an amount that must be paid periodically to the buyer of the security as well as the time at which the principal must be repaid. Securities of this type are also called *debt instruments*. The key element of a debt instrument is that *both the purchaser and the issuer of the security know exactly how much the issuer is obligated to pay for the use of the funds*. In contrast to the contractual claims, **residual claims** do not specify the amount that must be paid periodically or a fixed date for repayment of principal. These securities *have an indefinite maturity and offer payments to the buyer that are contingent on the earnings of the issuer*. This type of claim is also called an *equity instrument*, which refers to the buyer of the security taking an ownership position in the issuing firm. The risk to the buyer of the security is much greater with an equity instrument than with a debt instrument due to the equity instrument's residual claim on income. In addition to differences in terms of the *type* of claim on the issuer's income, financial instruments can also be distinguished in terms of the *maturity* of that claim.

Contractual Claim
Specifies an amount that must be paid periodically to the buyer of a security and the time at which the principal must be repaid.

Residual Claim A claim on a firm's assets and earnings that is associated with equity financing that does not specify the amount that must be paid periodically or a fixed date for repayment of principal.

Maturity of the Claim—Money Market Versus Capital Market

Short-term securities are traded on the **money market**. This market is a *vehicle for economic units to adjust their balance sheets for temporary cash surpluses and deficits*. The term *money market* refers to the ease with which these securities can be bought and sold. From a liquidity perspective, these instruments are "the next best thing to money."

To qualify as a money market instrument, a security must have a maturity of one year or less. Only debt instruments are traded on this market because equity instruments have no maturity date. The debt traded on the money market is typically issued only in very large denominations ($10,000 or greater) by borrowers with the highest credit ratings. Consequently, the money market is actively used by the government and large firms that require short-term financing or wish to earn a return on a temporary surplus of cash. The market is comprised primarily of security dealers and commercial banks. Table 3-3 lists the major U.S. money market instruments and briefly describes each.

Money Market Short-term securities traded on the money market are used by economic units to adjust their balance sheets for temporary cash surpluses and deficits.

United States Money Market Instruments

SUMMARY TABLE 3-3

Instrument	Description
Treasury Bill	Short-term U.S. government borrowing
Banker's Acceptance	Short-term debt issued by a business firm on which a commercial bank has guaranteed payment.
Commercial Paper	Short-term unsecured debt issued by a business firm.
Negotiable Certificate of Deposit	Negotiable securities representing interest-bearing deposits at a commercial bank in denominations of $100,000 or more.

Capital Market Facilitates long-term financial arrangements between savers and users of funds to allocate capital to its most productive uses.

Long-term securities are traded on the **capital market**. This market's role is to *facilitate long-term financial arrangements between savers and users of funds to allocate capital to its most productive uses.* Due to the very temporary nature of the funds transferred in the money market, the issuer of a money market instrument does not usually use the funds to acquire real assets. A capital market instrument, on the other hand, can provide funds to finance the acquisition of plant, equipment, houses, schools, roads, and other long-lived assets. Table 3-4 lists the major U.S. capital market instruments along with a brief description of each.

Although any financial instrument with a maturity in excess of one year qualifies as a capital market instrument, the majority of long-term securities have maturities exceeding 10 years at the time of issuance. In addition, the issuers of these instruments can vary greatly in financial strength and credit rating. Thus, capital market instruments are much less liquid than money market instruments and subject the purchaser to more risk. Capital market instruments are traded both on centralized markets and through networks of brokers and security dealers like those used with money market instruments. Figure 3-5 summarizes the major points of our discussion of financial instruments and markets.

One especially important element of the financial system is the determination and behavior of interest rates. Interest rates establish the cost of debt funds acquired by deficit units and the return on those funds provided by surplus units. They also have a strong indirect influence on the cost of equity capital. In a free enterprise economy, therefore, interest rates are the major factor that determines the nature of the allocation of funds between surplus and deficit units.

THE DETERMINATION OF INTEREST RATES

The general level of interest rates in the economy at any one time is the basic price of capital funds. *Interest rates* are important to the efficient operation of the financial system because they are the *price mechanism by which funds are allocated between surplus and deficit units.* The rationale for a free enterprise economy is that those deficit units that have the most valuable use for available capital will be willing and able to outbid other deficit units to obtain it. If financial managers are to successfully minimize the cost of raising capital, they must understand the determinants of the level of interest rates at any moment and the behavior of rates over time.

United States Capital Market Instruments	
SUMMARY TABLE 3-4	
Instrument	**Description**
Treasury Note and Bond	Long-term U.S. government borrowing. Notes have maturities from 1 to 10 years. Bond maturities run from 10 to 30 years.
Municipal Bond	Long-term debt issued by state and local governments. Interest income is free of federal taxes to purchaser.
Corporate Bond	Long-term debt (out to 50-year maturities) issued by firms.
Mortgage Debt	Long-term debt secured by real estate collateral. Issued by individuals or firms.
Corporate Stock	Residual claim with indefinite maturity issued by firms. Actively traded on secondary markets.

The Major Categories of U.S. Financial Instruments and Markets
SUMMARY FIGURE 3-5

Types of Financial Claims

1. Categorized by Type of Issuer:
   - A. Direct Claim — Issued by deficit unit.
   - B. Indirect Claim — Issued by financial intermediary.

2. Categorized by Claim on Income:
   - A. Contractual (Debt) — Fixed amount and timing of payment. Fixed Maturity.
   - B. Residual (Equity) — Uncertain amount and timing of payment. Indefinite Maturity.

Types of Financial Markets

1. Categorized by Maturity of Claim:
   - A. Money Market — Short-term, high quality, large denomination debt securities. High liquidity. Temporary funds transfer to adjust cash surplus or shortage.
   - B. Capital Market — Long-term debt or equity securities. Less liquidity and more risk than money market. Long-term funds transfer to finance acquisition of real assets.

2. Categorized by Seller of Claim:
   - A. Primary Market — Original issuance of money or capital market security by deficit unit.
   - B. Secondary Market — Trading of previously issued money or capital security by two surplus units.

The Determinants of Interest Rates on Specific Securities

The general level of interest rates on all available securities is determined by the overall supply and demand for loanable funds. Of particular concern to financial managers, however, are the factors that determine the *differences* in the interest rates on different securities at any given point in time. Table 3-5 indicates the structure of interest rates in the United States in January 1999. The differences in the interest rates in that table are known as yield spreads, or differentials. **Yield** is the term used to describe the annual percentage return available to the investors in a security. Notice the size of the differential, or **yield spread**, between corporate Baa bonds and Aaa bonds:

Yield The annual percentage return available to an investor.

Yield Spread The difference in yields between two securities, also known as the yield differential.

Yield Differentials on Various Types of U.S. Securities, in January 1999
TABLE 3-5

Type of Security	Yield (%)
3-Month Treasury Bills	4.56
6-Month Treasury Bills	4.69
5-Year Treasury Notes	4.72
30-Year Treasury Bonds	5.37
Prime Commercial Paper (3-month)	5.15
Prime Banker's Acceptances (3-month)	5.03
Corporate Aaa Bonds	6.35
Corporate Baa Bonds	6.87
Municipal Bonds	4.79

■ Financial

ISSUES

SECURITIZATION

One of the more recent innovations in the financial market is the creation of a new class of financial instruments called "loan securitizations." These instruments benefit borrowers, lenders, and investors by increasing the liquidity and efficiency of the intermediation function.

Financial intermediaries, such as banks and savings and loan associations, obtain funds from depositors in order to make loans to individuals and firms. Traditionally, these loans have been held by the intermediaries as assets on their balance sheets until the loans matured. The drawbacks to this process include the continued assumption of default risk on the loans by the intermediary and the continuous demand on the intermediary's capital to support the assets that the loans represent.

In their attempt to address these problems, intermediaries in recent years have increasingly turned to the technique of securitization. The mechanics are relatively simple. A group of loans with similar terms (interest rate, maturity, borrower type) are grouped together (pooled) by an intermediary. The intermediary then issues to investors a new class of securities, which represent claims to the pooled loans. The original borrowers continue to make loan payments to the intermediary, which then passes these payments, less a servicing fee, to the investors in the new securities. In addition to earning the servicing fee, the intermediary benefits from shifting default risk on the loans to the investors. It also frees up its capital to make additional new loans. The investors, in turn, gain access to generally high-yield investments, which they would not have the expertise to originate or service. Since the new securities can be traded on the secondary market, investors also preserve the liquidity of their investment positions.

The securitization process was originally applied to home mortgage loans. Over time, the concept has been extended to include automobile loans, credit card receivables, commercial real estate loans, and lease obligations. The most recent securitizations have been backed by anticipated revenues on films under production at Hollywood studios. Even the earnings of rock stars have backed securitizations! While first implemented in the United States, the technique has since spread to other countries as well.

Yield Spread = 6.87% – 6.35% = 0.52%

The corresponding spread between 30-year Treasury bonds and 5-year Treasury notes was 5.37% – 4.72% = 0.65%.

Investors must have perceived substantial risk differences in the financial instruments listed in Table 3-5 to have set such diverse required returns. We will now examine the major characteristics of securities that determine their riskiness to investors and thus their yield. These are:

1. Default Risk
2. Maturity
3. Taxability
4. Marketability
5. Callability

Default Risk Uncertainty regarding a borrower's ability to meet the scheduled interest payments and to pay the principal at maturity.

Default Risk. **Default risk** is uncertainty regarding a borrower's ability to meet the scheduled interest payments on a debt instrument and to repay the principal at maturity. Since investors are risk-averse, a positive relationship exists between default risk and the interest rate on a security. While default risk exists on all securities except those issued by the national government and its insured agencies, the *degree* of default risk can vary widely among the deficit units issuing financial claims. Various credit rating agencies evaluate the financial strength of firms and governmental units that issue securities. They summarize their findings in the form of standardized ratings. Table 3-6 on the next page shows the bond rating scale of the two major U.S. credit rating agencies: Moody's Investors Service and Standard and Poor's.[3] The yield on Treasury bonds is the lowest because these securities have no risk of default. While the yields on Aaa corporate bonds exceed those on Treasury securities, they are significantly below the yields on Baa corporate bonds. The default risk premium on the Aaa bonds in Table 3-5 is 0.98% = 6.35% – 5.37% while the default risk premium on the Baa bonds is 1.50% = 6.87% – 5.37%.

Maturity.   The yield on a security is also affected by the length of time remaining until the instrument matures (the term-to-maturity). This characteristic is the factor that accounts for the yield differentials among the first four types of securities shown in Table 3-5. All four types have no default risk because they are U.S. Treasury securities. Even so, investors found 3-month Treasury bills more attractive than 5-year Treasury notes, and still more attractive than 30-year Treasury bonds as indicated by the yield differentials shown. Consequently, investors were willing to accept lower yields for shorter maturity instruments.

The relationship between maturity and yield is called the **term structure of interest rates**. The term structure of interest rates can be expressed graphically in the form of a **yield curve**, which plots the yield of securities on the vertical axis versus the remaining years to maturity on the the horizontal axis. Figure 3-6 shows a number of yield curves for U.S. Treasury securities on different dates. A different yield curve is shown for each date because the yield of securities traded on secondary markets is constantly changing. The yield curves in Figure 3-6 reveal the changing nature of the relationship between yield and maturity. Although the normal or typical relationship is a positive one like that shown in most of the curves, it can become negative as in the case of the curve for July 1981.

Taxability.   Financial instruments are priced on financial markets on the basis of their pretax yields. Given this situation, a security whose payments are nontaxable

Term Structure of Interest Rates Expresses the relationship between the yield and the term-to-maturity of securities that differ only in their term-to-maturity.

Yield Curve The graphical representation of the term structure of interest rates that plots term-to-maturity on one axis against yield-to-maturity on the other axis.

Corporate Bond Ratings		
		TABLE 3-6

Standard & Poor's	Moody's	Degree of Default Risk
AAA	Aaa	Highest quality; little risk of default.
AA	Aa	High grade obligations.
A	A	Upper medium grade.
BBB	Baa	Medium grade; borderline between highly sound and speculative securities.
BB	Ba	Lower medium grade; possess some speculative elements.
B	B	Speculative; lack characteristics of desirable investments.
CCC	Caa	Poor standing; definite danger of default.
CC	Ca	Speculative in a high degree; may be in default.
C	C	Extremely poor prospects of ever paying interest.

Moody's further qualifies its bond ratings by assigning numerical ratings of 1, 2, and 3 within the Aa to B letter scale. Within a given letter category, 1 indicates a high relative ranking, while 3 indicates a low relative ranking. Standard & Poor's qualifies its ratings by adding "+" or "–" to show relative standing within the AA to B scale.

---

[3] Financial markets are definitely sensitive to these credit ratings. For instance, commercial banks and some other financial intermediaries will not, and often cannot, invest in securities rated lower than BBB or Baa. A change of a firm's credit rating can have a dramatic effect on the interest cost of its borrowings.

should carry a lower pretax yield than taxable securities. This is exactly the case in the United States for certain "municipal" securities that are issued by state and local governments. The interest payments on municipal debt instruments are free of federal income taxes and often also free of state income taxes.

The tax-free status of municipal securities makes it possible for an investor to receive a lower *pretax* return on these securities than on taxable instruments and still be better off on an *after-tax* basis. For instance, assume that an investor in a 28% tax bracket has a choice between a municipal security yielding 7% and a cor-

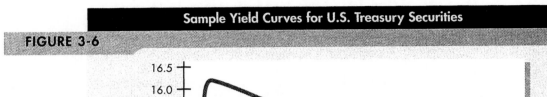

FIGURE 3-6

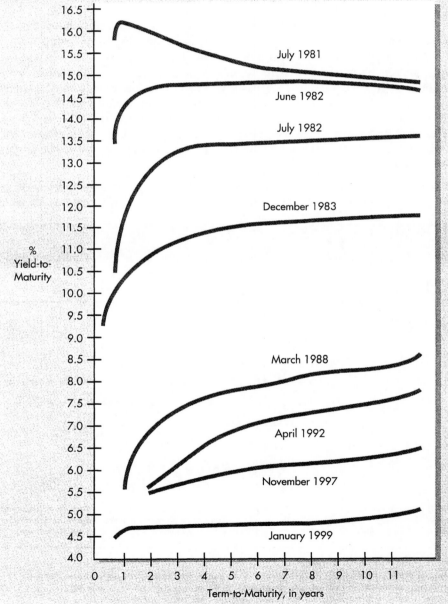

Sample Yield Curves for U.S. Treasury Securities

http://

The current year-end Treasury yield for the last ten years is on this Web site. Check out the latest treasury yield curve and compare it to Figure 3-6.

www.stocktrader.com/yc2. html

porate security yielding 9% before taxes. The following calculations show that the after-tax yield on the municipal security is larger:

Municipal Security:	Pretax Yield	=	7%
	After-Tax Yield	=	7%
Corporate Security:	Pretax Yield	=	9%
	After-Tax Yield	=	(9%)(1 – T) = (9%)(1 – 0.28) = 6.48%

Marketability and Callability.

Marketability refers to the ease and speed with which an investor can resell a security on the secondary market. As we pointed out earlier in this chapter, the ability to sell a security on the secondary market provides the investor with liquidity and flexibility. Thus, a security that is easily marketable is more attractive and carries a lower yield than a security of comparable maturity and default risk which is less marketable.

Treasury Bills and prime (AAA) commercial paper are very comparable in terms of maturity and default risk. If you refer back to Table 3-5, however, you will see that in January 1999 the yield on prime commercial paper exceeded that on 3-month Treasury Bills by 0.59% (5.15% – 4.56%). While some of this differential is due to the slightly higher default risk on the commercial paper, the yield spread may also be due to the lack of marketability of this type of financial claim. Since there is only a thin secondary market for commercial paper, the investor is forced to hold the instrument to maturity.

Callability refers to the right of the issuer of a security to redeem the security prior to maturity by "calling it in" from its owner. This call feature is attractive to issuers because it permits them to replace outstanding high-yield debt instruments with new low-yield securities if interest rates in the financial markets decline. A

Marketability The ease and speed with which an investor can resell a security on the secondary market.

Callability The right of the issuer of a security to redeem the security prior to maturity by "calling it in," or forcing the holder to sell it back.

■ Valuation ISSUES

BOND RATINGS

Because default risk is a key determinant of the yields that investors require from the debt securities they hold, the role of bond rating agencies in affecting corporations' financing costs is a major concern of financial managers.

Investors appear to pay considerable attention to these ratings, since individuals and most smaller financial institutions generally do not have the expertise to investigate thoroughly for themselves the creditworthiness of a company whose bonds they may be thinking of buying. Investors allow the rating agencies to do the analysis for them.

The agencies' decisions about the particular rating a company's bonds deserve are based in part on an analysis of financial ratios like those described in Chapter 2. The agencies have developed their own "norms" for the ranges of those ratios that fit a given bond rating. Not surprisingly, leverage ratios carry an especially heavy weight in the decisions, as do the ratios displayed by other firms in the rated company's industry.

There are subjective elements to the decisions as well. The agencies' staffs will meet with senior executives of the companies being rated, to discuss the firms'

business strategies and future investing and financing plans. They will consider the general economic environment and conditions in the firms' industries. Out of all this will come a specific announced rating. In most instances, the major ratings agencies put very similar ratings on a given company's bonds. Serious disagreements are relatively rare.

Once a company is on the rating list, the agencies then monitor the firm's ongoing financial performance and will regularly review its rating for possible revision. Changes in ratings, either up or down, are typically significant events for firms—and for their financing costs and market value. Although the use of bond ratings was originally restricted to U.S. companies, the bond rating agencies have gone international in recent years. Most major multinational firms, including those with headquarters outside the United States, now have rated debt.

call provision is very often used in this manner to reduce the ongoing interest cost of debt financing. Since a call is performed at the option of the issuer and cannot be refused by an investor, callable securities must offer higher yields in order to compensate the investor for being exposed to a call.

The interest rate on a specific security relative to the interest rates on other securities at any one point in time reflects the *combined* effect of all five factors discussed: default risk, maturity, taxability, marketability, and callability. As the general level of interest rate changes, the yield spreads between different securities can fluctuate over time even though the differences in their default risk, maturity, taxability, marketability, and callability remain constant. Figure 3-6 shows how this can happen for different maturities of U.S. Treasury securities.

The Behavior of Interest Rates Over Time

Financial markets are dynamic. Neither the general level of interest rates nor the relationship between yields on different types of securities is constant over time. Changes in interest rates reflect changes in such broad economic factors as the supply and demand for funds, investor risk aversion, and inflation. The purpose of this section is to examine three aspects of the dynamics of interest rates: (1) the default risk premium; (2) the volatility of short-term interest rates; and (3) the inflation premium.

The Default Risk Premium. While the yield spread between Baa and Aaa corporate bonds is always positive, the size of the yield spread varies from one period to another. The variability in the default risk yield spread is evident from the following calculations:

Default Risk Yield Spread	=	Baa Yield	−	Aaa Yield		
Average 1985 Spread	=	12.71%	−	11.37%	=	1.34%
Average 1987 Spread	=	10.57%	−	9.38%	=	1.19%
Average 1989 Spread	=	10.17%	−	9.26%	=	0.91%
Average 1991 Spread	=	9.80%	−	8.77%	=	1.03%
Average 1993 Spread	=	7.93%	−	7.22%	=	0.71%
Average 1995 Spread	=	8.20%	−	7.59%	=	0.61%
Average 1998 Spread	=	6.87%	−	6.35%	=	0.52%

As can be seen, the spread tends to be greater when the general level of interest rates is relatively high. One possible explanation is that times of high interest rates coincide with periods when investors are especially risk-averse. This phenomenon is illustrated in Figure 3-7, which shows the relationship between default risk and the yield on securities. Since investors prefer certain returns to uncertain returns, they will demand higher yields on securities with high default risk. This is shown in the Yield$_1$ line in Figure 3-7 in which the Baa security carries a higher yield than the Aaa security so that Yield Spread$_1$ is positive, as is the slope of the Yield$_1$ schedule. During periods of recession, severe inflation, or unsettled economic conditions, investors' risk aversion tends to increase. As a result, investors demand a higher yield for accepting a given level of risk. Thus, the schedule pivots upward from position Yield$_1$ to position Yield$_2$. The increase in slope has a larger impact on the yield on the Baa security than on the Aaa security's yield. Thus, the Baa-Aaa default risk premium increases from Yield Spread$_1$ to Yield Spread$_2$.

Interest Rate Volatility. Although changes in the economic environment that affect interest rates will influence the yields on *all* debt securities, the interest rates on short-term instruments are more volatile than the rates on long-term instruments. An indication of this can be seen from the yield curves plotted in

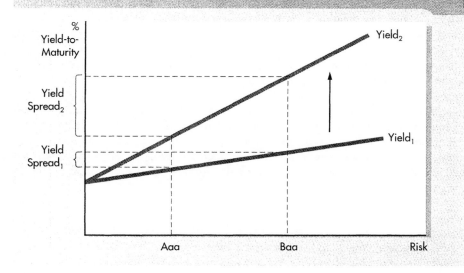

The Response of Yield to a Change in Investor Risk Aversion

FIGURE 3-7

Figure 3-6. Over the period shown, yields on one-year Treasury securities ranged from approximately 4.5% to 16%, while the rates on 10-year securities varied only from 5% to about 15%. Within individual years, the same sorts of differences would be observed.

What explains the greater sensitivity of short-term rates? Those rates are driven primarily by daily fluctuations in the demand for and supply of funds by short-term borrowers and lenders. These are highly sensitive to changes in current economic conditions. Long-term rates, on the other hand, are determined more by the productivity of long-term capital investments made by firms and by long-term savings patterns. Those change much more gradually over time.

There is a "technical" reason for the differences as well, although it is a reflection of the same underlying influences. Specifically, long-term interest rates should be *equal to the average of current and expected future short-term rates*. An investor who is faced with a choice between making a series of five consecutive investments in one-year securities, and one investment in a five-year security, will be indifferent to that choice only if the annual yield on the five-year security is equal to the average of the expected yields on the five one-year securities. If one of those expected one-year yields changes, the corresponding five-year yield will change by a smaller amount because it is mathematically true that an average will change less in value than the change in one of the components that make up the average.

The Inflation Premium. When an individual makes an investment, he or she is making a conscious decision to forego current consumption in favor of future consumption. In order to be willing to wait, the investor must earn a positive return such that the benefit of waiting is the opportunity to consume *more* in the future than would be possible to consume today. Interest rates define the acceptable terms of that trade-off.

In an economy where there was no inflation, interest rates would measure the *extent* to which consumption can be increased by waiting. Thus, if a one-year investment earned interest at 3%, investors could consume 3% more at the end of the year than at the beginning. Suppose, however, inflation began to occur at an annual rate of 10%, raising the prices of all available goods and services at that rate. In order to produce a 3% annual gain in consumption opportunities, investments would now have to provide a return that would compensate investors both for waiting (at 3%) *and* for the price changes in the meantime (at 10%) in the items they wish to buy.

As a consequence, we would expect to find a strong relationship between interest rates and concurrent inflation rates. Interest rates should be relatively high during times of high inflation and relatively low during times of low inflation. This has generally been the case over the years, both in the United States and in other countries. It appears to be one of the major sources of variation in interest rates.

Nominal Interest Rate The total percentage return from investing in debt securities. This return can be observed in financial markets.

The interest rates we *observe* in the financial markets are termed **nominal interest rate**s: the total percentage returns from investing in debt securities. If we adjust those rates for inflation, we obtain what are described as "real" interest rates. An approximate calculation would be:

$$r_R = r - p$$

where r_R is the real interest rate, r is the nominal rate, and p is the prevailing rate of price inflation.[4] The label **real interest rate** refers to the fact that it is a measure of the annual rate of increase in an investor's actual consumption opportunities because the effect of inflation has been taken into account. Equivalently, we can state that

Real Interest Rate A measure of the rate of increase in an investor's consumption opportunities after inflation is deducted from the nominal interest rate. The effective yield on a loan in constant purchasing power terms after adjusting the stated interest rate for inflation.

$$r = r_R + p$$

and p can be thought of as the *inflation premium* which is contained in nominal interest rates. If real interest rates are roughly constant over time, nominal rates will vary directly with inflation rates. Most estimates of the real rate of interest put the figure somewhere in the vicinity of 3% to 4% as a long-run average.

ISSUING SECURITIES IN THE PRIMARY MARKET

Up to this point, we have talked in very general terms about the primary market. We will now examine in some detail the mechanics of security issuance in that market. There are two major alternatives available to a firm for the acquisition of external capital: private placement and public offering. The intent of this section of the chapter is to familiarize you with these two alternatives, with particular emphasis on the roles of the investment (merchant) banker and the Securities and Exchange Commission (SEC), the regulator of the U.S. Securities markets. We will also discuss the nature of flotation costs and the key determinants of those costs.

Private Placement Versus Public Offerings

A private placement of debt or equity securities involves direct negotiation between the issuing firm and the investor. Typically, the investor is an institution such as an insurance company, a pension fund, or the trust department of a commercial bank. While a firm can utilize a private placement to issue either debt or equity securities, debt securities tend to dominate private placements. The key attraction of this financing technique to both the issuer and the investor is that the terms of the security agreement can be tailored to the specific needs of both

http://
You can check out the latest initial public offering IPO's on this Web site. It is a free comprehensive resource for IPO news, information, and insight.
www.investorguide.com/IPOs.htm

---

[4] We shall see in Chapter 24 that this relationship *is* only an approximation—although a very good one in most practical applications.

parties. Furthermore, the transaction is not subject to the extensive regulation that applies to the issuance of securities to the general public.

As the term implies, a public offering involves the issuance of securities by a firm to the general public. The terms of the security agreement are determined by the issuer. Unlike privately placed securities, publicly offered securities are often traded actively on a secondary market subsequent to their issuance. Due to the logistical problems of determining attractive terms, pricing the securities, and locating interested investors, firms normally require the services of an investment banker in a public offering.

The Role of the Investment Banker

Although an **investment banker** may serve in an advisory role in a private place-ment, the primary role is that of a financial intermediary in the exchange of funds between deficit and surplus units. Normally, the investment banking firm will pur-chase the new securities from the issuing firm and then resell them to the gener-al public. In filling this role, it performs a number of important functions, which are summarized in Figure 3-8.

Underwriting.   When an investment banking firm purchases and resells a new security issue, it is said to **underwrite** the issue because it guarantees that the issu-ing firm will obtain the needed capital funds. Once the investment banking firm purchases the securities, it accepts the risk that it will not be able to resell them at a profit. In this sense, the firm is serving as a financial wholesaler who buys at one price and sells (it hopes) at a higher price. The difference between the pur-chase price and the intended selling price is called the underwriting commission.

Distributing.   Due to the large size of most public offerings and the substantial market risk borne by the investment banker, the sale or distribution of publicly offered securities is usually performed by a selling syndicate. The **selling syndi-cate** has two basic purposes: to spread the risk of price declines among a number of investment bankers and to increase the probability of a successful sale of the securities. Risk for any one investment banking firm is reduced because it pur-chases only a portion of the new securities instead of the entire issue. The chances of a successful sale are increased because the number of individuals actively engaged in selling the securities is much greater than would be possible with only one investment banking firm.

The selling syndicate is organized by the managing investment banking firm that initially arranges for the purchase of the securities from the issuing firm. Each

Investment Banker A finan-cial institution that facili-tates the sale of securities by the issuing firm to investors.

http://
You can check out several investment bankers at these Web sites.
www.fbr.com
www.hamquist.com
www.ms.com

Underwriting The process carried out by an invest-ment banker in buying a stock or bond issue and then reselling it. The invest-ment banker takes the risk of price changes during this time.

Selling Syndicate A group of investment bankers that underwrites and issues a firm's securities by buying them from the issuing firm and reselling them to a group of smaller brokerage firms for eventual sale to individual investors.

The Functions of an Investment Banker

SUMMARY FIGURE 3-8

1.	Underwriting	Purchase of securities from issuer and resale to individual investors. Assumption of market risk.
2.	Distributing	Formation of a selling syndicate that is composed of an underwriting syndicate and a selling group. Issuer pays underwriting commission.
3.	Pricing	Underpricing of new securities relative to outstanding securities. Competitive bidding versus negotiated offering.
4.	Advising	Negotiated offering only. Timing, amount, and price of debt or equity securities.

Selling Group Brokerage firms that purchase newly issued securities from investment bankers in relatively large blocks and resell them to individual investors.

Underwriting Commission The fee charged by investment bankers for underwriting a security issue. It is the difference between the purchase price and the intended selling price of the securities.

member of the underwriting syndicate acts as a wholesaler by buying a portion of the issue and reselling it to a network of security dealers and brokerage firms that compose the **selling group**. The members of the selling group, in turn, act as retailers by selling the securities to individual investors. The total number of firms involved in a selling syndicate may number in the hundreds for a large security issue. The members of the syndicate are compensated for their risk-bearing and selling efforts in the form of an **underwriting commission** that is subdivided into an underwriting profit and a selling concession.

To illustrate, take the case of a company coming to market with a $500 million issue of new bonds. Since bonds in the United States typically come in denominations of $1,000 each (their "par" value), the financing will involve a total of 500,000 bonds. The results of the underwriting might be as follows:

	Per Bond	Total
Selling Price to Investors	$1,000.00	$500,000,000
Selling Concession	(3.75)	(1,875,000)
Underwriting Profit	(1.25)	(625,000)
Syndicate Manager's Fee	(1.25)	(625,000)
Net Proceeds to Company	$ 993.75	$496,875,000

In special instances in which the market risk is exceptionally large, an investment banking firm may refuse to underwrite an issue. Instead, it will agree to sell the securities only on a **best efforts basis**. Under this arrangement, the investment banking firm does not buy the securities from the issuer but only agrees to sell them at the best price that can be obtained in the market. Since the market risk remains with the issuer in an offering on a best efforts basis, the participating investment bankers and dealers receive only a selling concession.

Best Efforts Basis An alternative to underwriting a security issue whereby an investment banker agrees only to attempt to sell the securities at the best available price.

During the 30-day period following the initial purchase of securities from the issuing firm, the manager of a selling syndicate will sometimes engage in a practice called *market stabilization* or *price pegging*. Price pegging is designed to reduce the risk of temporary price declines in securities during their resale to the public. The manager will attempt to stabilize the price by placing buy orders at the original offering price. Dealers and underwriters whose securities are repurchased by the manager do not receive any compensation for their sales and are required to purchase the securities if they cannot be resold to the public.

For example, assume that a selling syndicate offers a $200 million bond issue to the public at a price of $1,000 per bond. If the secondary market price of these bonds should fall to $990 before the entire bond issue has been sold, the selling syndicate has a problem. It will be unable to sell the remaining bonds at a price of $1,000 in the primary market because investors can acquire the bonds for $990 in the secondary market. By offering to buy the bonds on the secondary market, the syndicate manager attempts to maintain the secondary market price at a high enough level to enable the syndicate to sell the remaining bonds at a price near $1,000 in the primary market.

Competitive Bidding An auction procedure used to sell a new security issue to the investment banking syndicate that submits the highest bid for the securities.

Pricing. The investment banker can play a major role in the pricing process in two ways. If securities are offered through **competitive bidding**, investment banking firms submit sealed bids for the entire security issue. The issue is then sold to the selling syndicate submitting the highest bid. The price that the winning bidder submits determines both the proceeds to the issuer and the intended resale price to the ultimate investors.

The more typical source of investment banker influence on the price of a new security occurs in the case of a **negotiated offering**. In this case, the issuing firm hires an investment banker to help it design the most attractive terms (including price) for a proposed security issue. In their price recommendations, investment bankers usually suggest that a firm underprice its new issue relative to outstanding securities of similar maturity and risk. The purpose of this **underpricing** is to make the securities sufficiently attractive to new investors to ensure their rapid sale by the investment banker.

Advising.   One reason for the relative unpopularity of competitive bidding is that the issuing firm receives little, if any, advice or assistance from investment banking firms in the design of the security issue. The advice of an investment banker who is in constant contact with the securities markets can be very valuable to the financial managers of a corporation that issues securities only intermittently. In addition to the matter of proper pricing, an investment banker's advising typically covers the question of whether the financing should be in the form of debt or equity, the maturity composition of debt, and the timing of the issuance of securities. Proper advice in these areas can lower a firm's cost of capital by more than enough to offset the investment banker's fees. For this reason, firms often enter into an ongoing relationship with a specific investment banker so that expert advice is always available.

Flotation Costs

The cost of an investment banker's services is one component of the **flotation costs** associated with issuing securities. Since these costs can be significant, a firm's financial managers should be familiar with the factors that determine them. Flotation costs consist of any expenses associated with issuing new securities. For publicly offered issues, the major flotation costs are the underwriting commission, legal fees, printing costs, and the expenses of registration with the Securities and Exchange Commission (SEC). From the financial manager's viewpoint, the key aspect of flotation costs is their level as a percentage of the financing acquired. The major determinants of this percentage are:

1.   The quality (credit rating) of the new securities,
2.   The size of the issue, and
3.   The type of securities issued.

The percentage level of flotation costs tends to be higher as the size and the credit rating of the issuing firm decline. This is due largely to the greater market risk that the selling syndicate must bear with lower quality issues. To compensate for this risk, investment banking firms increase their underwriting commission. Flotation costs are also inversely related to the size of a security issue because many of the costs associated with a public offering are fixed in nature. This is even true of the expenses of the underwriting syndicate. Consequently, flotation costs per dollar obtained decline as the size of the issues increases.

Finally, flotation costs are affected by the type of security that the issuing firm wishes to sell. As the price volatility of the security that is issued increases, the underwriting commission is correspondingly increased. For this reason, the underwriting commission on common stock is much higher than that on bonds. In the United States, the typical flotation cost for a large bond issue would be less than 1% of the total proceeds of the issue. In the case of a common stock issue for a large company whose shares are already actively traded on the secondary market, flotation costs will generally amount to 4% to 5% of total proceeds.

Negotiated Offering A procedure for issuing new securities whereby the issuing firm hires an investment banker to assist in designing the terms of the security issue.

Underpricing Pricing new securities in the primary market below the price of outstanding securities prevailing in the secondary market to ensure the success of the issue.

Flotation Costs The costs incurred by the issuer of securities during the process of issuance.

■ **Ethics**

ISSUES

WHEN A STOCK PURCHASE BECOMES AN ETHICAL PROBLEM

One of the types of underwriting that typically generates substantial interest from investors is the "initial public offering" (IPO) of the stock of a previously privately owned firm. This interest arises from two factors. First, the selling syndicate underprices the shares to increase their appeal. Second, investors have the opportunity to invest "on the ground floor" of a potentially very profitable investment. Of course, if the investor happens to know about major contracts that have been awarded to the firm, the investment may be too attractive to resist.

This is exactly what happened in August 1996 when Tele Tech Holdings, Inc. went public. Approximately thirty managers of United Parcel Service (UPS) bought shares in the IPO because Tele Tech had been awarded a contract to begin operating three dial-in customer service centers for UPS in March of that year. The stock more than doubled in the first seven weeks of trading. At the time of the IPO, Tele Tech's UPS contract was public knowledge, so the UPS managers did not violate any laws that prohibit stock trading based on "inside information." Nevertheless, UPS ordered the managers to sell their shares and give their profits to charity. In addition, the managers were subjected to pay cuts and reassignments.

If the actions in question were legal, why did UPS respond so harshly? A firm spokesperson said that the stock purchases represented a "very, very serious and significant breach of our business ethics. They (the managers) helped write the contracts or they have the appearance of having that relationship. And they should have known better." This incident demonstrates the types of ethical dilemmas faced by managers. Do you think that the response of UPS to its managers' actions was justified? Could UPS stakeholders have been adversely affected by the managers' purchase of Tele Tech stock?

U.S. Regulation of Public Securities Issues

In response to the stock market collapse of 1929, the U.S. Congress passed two landmark pieces of legislation that have had a widespread impact on the securities industry: (1) the Securities Act of 1933, which regulates the issuance of new securities in the primary market; and (2) the Securities Exchange Act of 1934, which regulates the trading of outstanding securities in the secondary market and created the Securities and Exchange Commission (SEC) to enforce both acts. The intent of this legislation and SEC enforcement efforts was to prevent investor losses arising from fraud or misrepresentation. The legislation is not designed to prevent the issuance of speculative securities or investor losses arising from foolish investment decisions. Essentially, *regulation is designed to insure the availability of accurate and detailed financial information* pertaining to new and outstanding securities. The individual investor retains the responsibility to evaluate the information properly.

Only large, public offerings are subject to regulation. Private placements are exempt from SEC jurisdiction, as are security issues that are:

1. Less than $1,500,000 in total amount;
2. Less than 271 days in maturity;
3. Sold only in one state; or
4. Subject to regulation by other federal agencies.

The consequence of this regulation is to increase the delay and cost of issuing securities. Thus, it can influence a firm's financing decisions. For instance, managers can avoid the costs of regulation entirely by selling bonds through a private placement rather than a public offering. The effective maximum maturity of 270 days, which is typical for commercial paper, is based on the desire of firms to avoid the expense associated with regulation. Since the majority of securities are subject to SEC regulation, however, we will conclude this chapter by briefly examining two of its major requirements: the registration statement and the prospectus.

The Registration Statement. Firms planning to issue securities in the United States subject to federal regulation must prepare and file with the SEC a detailed document called a **registration statement**. This document must contain information concerning:

1. The nature and the history of the firm;
2. A description of the proposed security issue;
3. The planned use of the financing;
4. The financial position of the firm; and
5. The security holdings of top management and directors.

There is a minimum waiting period, or cooling-off period, of 20 days during which SEC personnel examine and verify the accuracy of the registration statement. If unsatisfied, the SEC can delay the security issue until the firm corrects or amplifies the statement.

The prospectus. In addition to the registration statement, the issuing firm must also file a **prospectus** with the SEC. A prospectus is a summary of the essential information contained in the registration statement. Copies of the prospectus must be made available to the potential buyers of the securities, so that they can make an informed investment decision.

Figure 3-9 shows the first two pages of a prospectus for an issue of common stock by the Cummins Engine Company. The volume and type of information contained in that document is indicated by the Table of Contents. The appended financial statements referred to in Index F-1 themselves covered 20 pages. The underwriters (Morgan Stanley and First Boston) planned to offer the stock to the public at a price of $57.00 per share. The proceeds to Cummins were to be $55.00 per share. As the small print near the top of the first page noted, the closing market price of the stock was $57.50 in the prior day's trading on the New York Stock Exchange. Thus, the *total* flotation cost of the issue to Cummins, including both the underpricing discount and underwriting commissions, was $2.50 per share. This comes to $2.50/$57.50, or approximately 4.3% of the market value of the shares issued.

Simplified Registration Procedures. The registration statement and prospectus are time-consuming and expensive to construct and file. The time and expense are viewed by the SEC as the price that the issuer of securities must pay in order to provide the data required by potential investors. In the case of large publicly-held firms, however, much of the data in the registration statement and prospectus duplicates data available in other published reports. Thus, in 1978, the SEC instituted a **short-form registration** for large firms. The short-form procedure allows a firm to reduce the size of its prospectus substantially by referencing data available in other reports routinely filed with the SEC. It also permits the firm to sell the new securities 48 hours after filing the registration statement instead of waiting the full 20-day cooling-off period.

In February 1982, the SEC instituted an optional registration procedure that ushered in a new era in the process of issuing securities. The new procedure (Rule 415) allowed large firms to file a **shelf registration** with the SEC. Under the shelf registration, a firm would specify the types and total amount of securities that it

Registration Statement
Must be filed with and verified by the SEC before a firm may issue securities. Contains information concerning the firm and the security issue.

Prospectus A summary of the vital information contained in the registration statement filed with the SEC. Copies of the prospectus must be available to the public.

Short-Form Registration
Allows a firm to reduce the size of its registration statement and prospectus by referencing financial data already on file with the SEC.

Shelf Registration A firm files a general two-year financing plan with the SEC that allows it to sell registered securities at any time during that period without filing additional registration forms or prospectuses.

Example of a Prospectus

FIGURE 3-9

2,000,000 Shares
Cummins Engine Company, Inc.
COMMON STOCK

All the shares of Common Stock offered hereby are being sold by the Company. Of the 2,000,000 shares of Common Stock offered hereby, 1,600,000 shares are being offered initially in the United States and Canada by the U.S. Underwriters and 400,000 shares are being offered initially outside the United States and Canada by the International Underwriters. See "Underwriters." On April 15, 1992, the closing price of the Common Stock as reported on the New York Stock Exchange Composite Tape was $57½ per share.

THESE SECURITIES HAVE NOT BEEN APPROVED OR DISAPPROVED BY THE SECURITIES AND EXCHANGE COMMISSION OR ANY STATE SECURITIES COMMISSION NOR HAS THE COMMISSION OR ANY STATE SECURITIES COMMISSION PASSED UPON THE ACCURACY OR ADEQUACY OF THIS PROSPECTUS. ANY REPRESENTATION TO THE CONTRARY IS A CRIMINAL OFFENSE.

PRICE $57 A SHARE

	Price to Public	Underwriting Discounts and Commissions (1)	Proceeds to Company (2)
Per Share	$57.00	$2.00	$55.00
Total(s)	$114,000,000	$4,000,000	$110,000,000

1. The Company has agreed to indemnify the Underwriters against certain liabilities, including liabilities under the Securities Act of 1933.
2. Before deduction of expenses payable by the Company estimated at $470,000.
3. The Company has granted to the U.S. Underwriters an option, available within 30 days of the date hereof to purchase up to an aggregate of 300,000 additional shares of Common Stock at the price to public less underwriting discounts and commissions for the purpose of issuing over-allotments, if any. If the U.S. Underwriters exercise such option in full, the total price to public, underwriting discounts and commissions and proceeds to Company will be $131,100,000, $4,600,000 and $125,500,000, respectively. See "Underwriters."

No person is authorized in connection with any offering made hereby to give any information or to make any representation not contained in this Prospectus, and, if given or made, such information or representation must not be relied upon as having been authorized by the Company or by any Underwriter. This Prospectus does not constitute an offer to sell or a solicitation of an offer to buy any of the securities offered hereby to any person in any jurisdiction in which it is unlawful to make any such offer or solicitation to such person. Neither the delivery of this Prospectus nor any sale made hereunder shall under any circumstances imply that the information contained herein is correct as of any date subsequent to the date hereof.

No action has or will be taken in any jurisdiction by the Company or by any Underwriter that would permit a public offering of the Common Stock or possession or distribution of this Prospectus in any jurisdiction where action for that purpose is required, other than in the United States. Persons into whose possession this Prospectus comes are required by the Company and the Underwriters to inform themselves about, and to observe any restrictions as to, the offering of the Common Stock and the distribution of this Prospectus.

In this Prospectus, references to "dollar" and "$" are to United States dollars, and the terms "United States" and "U.S." mean the United States of America, its states, its territories, its possessions and all areas subject to its jurisdiction.

TABLE OF CONTENTS

	Page
Available Information	3
Incorporation of Certain Documents by Reference	3
Prospectus Summary	4
Use of Proceeds	5
Price Range of Common Stock and Dividends	5
Selected Financial Data	6
Business	7
Management's Discussion and Analysis of Results of Operations and Financial Condition	9
Description of Capital Stock	14
Certain United States Federal Tax Consequences to Non-U.S. Holders of Common Stock	20
Underwriters	22
Legal Opinions	24
Experts	24
Index to Financial Statements	F-1

IN CONNECTION WITH THIS OFFERING, THE UNDERWRITERS MAY OVER-ALLOT OR EFFECT TRANSACTIONS WHICH STABILIZE OR MAINTAIN THE MARKET PRICE OF THE COMMON STOCK OFFERED HEREBY AT A LEVEL ABOVE THAT WHICH MIGHT OTHERWISE PREVAIL IN THE OPEN MARKET. SUCH TRANSACTIONS MAY BE EFFECTED ON THE NEW YORK STOCK EXCHANGE, IN THE OVER-THE-COUNTER MARKET OR OTHERWISE. SUCH STABILIZING, IF COMMENCED, MAY BE DISCONTINUED AT ANY TIME.

The shares are offered, subject to prior sale, when, as and if accepted by the Underwriters and subject to approval of certain legal matters by Davis Polk & Wardwell, counsel for the Underwriters. It is expected that delivery of the shares will be made on or about April 21, 1992, at the offices of Morgan Stanley & Co. Incorporated, New York, N.Y., against payment therefor in New York funds.

MORGAN STANLEY & CO. Incorporated   **THE FIRST BOSTON CORPORATION**

Reprinted by permission of Cummins Engine Company, Inc.

intended to issue over the next two years. Following SEC approval of the registration, the firm would then be able to sell any part or all of the securities at any time over the two-year period without filing additional prospectuses. In effect, the firm would be able to "take the new securities down from the shelf" and sell them at will.

The logic behind Rule 415 is to facilitate the process of issuing new securities. Shelf registration proved very popular with firms that required long-term financing. By December 1996, the SEC had received almost 5,000 shelf registrations that called for the issuance of approximately $120 billion in securities (over 75% of which were debt instruments). The benefits of the new procedure to the issuing firms included lower flotation costs and greater flexibility in the timing and size of security issues.

The major concern of the SEC with shelf registration was that it might not allow investors and investment bankers adequate time to exercise "due diligence" in analyzing newly announced security issues before committing their funds. This potential problem was most acute in the case of the securities issues of smaller, lesser known firms. Consequently, in November 1983, the SEC permanently extended shelf registration only to firms with at least $150 million in outstanding stock held by outside investors. Thus, the option of shelf registration is at the moment available only to large firms.

▪ International ISSUES

DEREGULATION

Much of the regulatory framework for the financial markets in the United States originated in the Great Depression of the 1930s. Legislation setting forth acceptable rules of behavior, reporting and disclosure requirements, and the jurisdiction of regulatory agencies was established in response to perceived abuses in the markets that may have contributed to the economy's decline. It was not until the late 1970s and early 1980s that moves toward relaxing some of these regulatory restrictions began to be made.

Part of the philosophy for doing so was the belief that the flow of information to investors about the financial condition of the corporations and financial institutions with whom they dealt had improved significantly over the years. Thus, it was thought to be less important for government to attempt to protect investors from being misled. The other driving force was the goal of enhancing competition in the financial marketplace. Institutions that previously had been permitted to engage only in certain well-defined activities were freed to compete with other institutions in a broader range of intermediary functions. In addition, their opportunities to attract investors' funds were expanded.

Savings and loan associations were permitted to offer checking accounts and to make commercial loans to businesses. Ceilings on interest rates payable on time deposits were lifted, both for banks and savings and loans. Interest was allowed to be paid on checking accounts. Banks were made eligible to offer a broader range of securities underwriting services. Perhaps most significantly, restrictions on banks doing business in more than one state were relaxed.

The resultant overlap in the functions of these various intermediaries does appear to have increased competition. Not all of this has a favorable impact, however. Many would argue that deregulation contributed heavily to the serious financial problems of the savings and loan industry during the late 1980s and early 1990s, as these institutions moved into areas in which they had little expertise.

In most other countries, there is a longer history of multiple roles within individual financial institutions. Banks elsewhere have traditionally been able to underwrite securities, sell insurance, manage mutual funds and investment trusts, and act as brokerage firms for securities trading by their customers. The United States is also one of the few countries where, until recently, nationwide banking has been prohibited.

SUMMARY

This chapter examined the crucial role of financial markets in facilitating the transfer of funds between surplus units and deficit units. Without an efficient financial system to allocate funds between savers and investors, capital formation would lag. We also outlined the development of a simple financial system, with just financial assets and liabilities and primary markets, into a complex system with brokers, financial intermediaries, and secondary markets. Financial intermediaries increase the efficiency of the financial system significantly by reaching separate loan agreements with borrowers and lenders. In this process, they offer both parties the benefits of risk intermediation, maturity intermediation, denomination intermediation, economies of scale, and convenience.

The types of direct claims issued by deficit units can be classified on the basis of the type of claim on the issuer's income and the maturity of that claim. While contractual claims specify both the timing and amount of payments to the saver, residual claims offer payments that are contingent on the earning power of the issuer. Money market instruments, which have a maturity of one year or less, are used to adjust liquidity positions. Capital market instruments, on the other hand, are employed in the long-term transfer of funds needed to finance the acquisition of real assets. Numerous factors determine the level of interest rates available on direct and indirect claims at any one point in time, as well as their behavior over time. The yield on a specific security at a given point in time is determined by its default risk, maturity, taxability, marketability, and callability. Variability in a security's yield over time is also a function of its maturity as well as inflationary expectations and investor risk aversion. Yield variability is positively related to inflationary expectations and investor risk aversion, and negatively related to maturity.

The issuance of debt or equity securities by a firm may involve investment banking firms and a regulatory authority. Specific functions of an investment banker include: underwriting the securities (buying them from the issuer); distributing the securities through a selling syndicate (selling them to the general public); pricing the securities; and advising the issuer on various details of a prospective security issue. The role of the regulatory authority is to enforce security laws that are designed to protect individual investors from fraudulent or inaccurate investment information about new securities, and artificial price manipulation of outstanding securities. A standard regulatory requirement for the issuer of publicly-offered securities is the filing of detailed background information and financial data on the company, which must be made available to prospective investors.

CONTENT QUESTIONS

1. What is the ultimate purpose of the financial system?
2. Describe the effect on capital formation of the absence of financial assets, liabilities, and markets.
3. What is the distinction between a primary and a secondary market for financial securities?
4. List and describe the major benefits provided by financial intermediaries.
5. List and describe each of the four major types of financial intermediary.
6. What is the difference between a contractual claim and a residual claim?
7. What is the difference between a money market and a capital market instrument?

8. What are the five determinants of interest rates?
9. Discuss the difference between real and nominal interest rates.
10. What are the principal features of private placements?
11. What are the primary functions of the investment banker?
12. Explain how an investment banker assumes risk by underwriting a security issue.
13. Why is it necessary to *underprice* a common stock issue?
14. Why is the price for most security issues determined through negotiation rather than competitive bidding?
15. Why, for a given size issue, is the flotation cost for common stock greater than for bonds?

CONCEPT QUESTIONS

1. In the United States, individuals who have deposits in a commercial bank or a savings and loan association are insured by the federal government against the loss of those deposits if the bank or savings and loan were to fail. The limit on the insurance is $100,000 per depositor. What effect is this insurance likely to have on the investment behavior of individuals? What effect is it likely to have on the investment decisions of banks? How should it affect the cost and availability of credit to corporations?
2. Would you agree or disagree with the following statement: The purpose of governmental regulation of financial institutions and securities markets is to protect investors from making unwise investment decisions.
3. IVM The prospectus which firms prepare and distribute to investors in connection with the issuance of corporate securities contains information that is restricted by law almost exclusively to historical and current financial data on the issuing firm. Should corporate managers be permitted and encouraged also to include projections of *future* company performance in the prospectus? What would be the advantages and disadvantages of doing so?
4. Ethics What do you see as the major areas of potential conflict of interest between the underwriter of a corporate securities issue and the issuing firm? Between the underwriter and the purchasers of the securities? How should these conflicts be resolved?
5. In the United States, interest rates on the short-term debt instruments issued by government, businesses, and banks fell from approximately 8% in the mid-1980s to 3% in the late 1990s. Who is helped and who is hurt by this decline?

PROBLEMS

1. The following information applies to the household sector of an economy:

Financial Assets	225 billion
Real Assets	653
Total	878
Financial Liabilities	359
Net Worth	519
Total	878

a. How large is the sector's investing?
b. How large is the sector's saving?
c. Does the sector have a savings surplus or deficit?

2. Assume the following information for an economy that consists of two sectors:

	Household Sector	Business Sector
Financial Assets		200
Real Assets	500	___
Total		
Financial Liabilities	100	
Net Worth	___	500
Total		

The Household Sector's saving surplus is 300.
The Business Sector's saving deficit is 300.
   a. How large is the Household Sector's net worth?
   b. How large are the Household Sector's financial assets?
   c. How large are the Business Sector's real assets?
   d. How large are the Business Sector's financial liabilities?

3. Peter Martin just loaned $5,000 to a friend who is opening a small store. The cash is needed to help finance inventory. Once the business is established, the loan will be paid off. Peter's friend signed an agreement to repay $6,000 interest and principal in one year.
   a. Calculate the nominal rate of interest that Peter is charging his friend.
   b. Peter expected the rate of inflation to be 10%. What was the expected *real* rate of interest on the loan?

4. Referring to Problem 3, the year passed and the agreed upon payment of $6,000 was made. However, over the year the actual rate of inflation was not 10% as expected, but was actually 8%. What was the actual *real* rate of interest earned by Peter Martin?

5. Assume that an investor desires to earn a real rate of return of 7% on a loan.
   a. If the expected rate of inflation is 12% per year, what nominal rate of interest should the investor set on the loan?
   b. The investor sets the nominal rate indicated in part (a), but the actual rate of inflation was 10%. What was the actual real rate of interest earned on the loan for one year?

6. John Frank purchased a painting for investment purposes one year ago for $25,000. He has just received an offer from an art dealer. The dealer will pay $30,000 for the painting.
   a. What is the nominal rate of return on this investment if sold to the art dealer?
   b. If the rate of inflation over the year was 5%, what real return on investment could be earned if sold to the art dealer?

7. You are trying to decide where to invest $10,000 for one year. There are two alternatives. One alternative provides tax-exempt interest. The other does not. The rate of interest on the alternative that is not tax-exempt is 15%. What interest rate on the tax-exempt loan would leave you *indifferent* to the two alternatives, assuming that they are similar in every respect except taxability of interest, given the following tax rates:
   a. 20%
   b. 60%

8. Repeat Problem 7 except now assume that the interest rate on the *tax-exempt* loan is 10%. Find the interest rate of the loan with taxable interest that would leave you indifferent to the two alternatives, given the following tax rates:
   a. 20%
   b. 60%

9. On a given day, the following yields were observed in the financial markets:

Security	Yield-to-Maturity
3-Month Treasury Bill	7.55%
20-Year Treasury Bond	8.95%
20-Year Corporate Aaa Bond	9.38%
20-Year Corporate Baa Bond	10.15%

    a. What is the default risk premium on the Aaa corporate bond?

    b. How can you explain the yield spread on the Aaa and Baa corporate bonds?

    c. How can you explain the yield spread on the Aaa corporate bond and the Treasury bill?

10. On a given day, 20-year treasury bonds yield 7.20%, 20-year Aaa corporate bonds yield 8.10%, 20-year Baa corporate bonds yield 9.40% and municipal bonds yield 6.60%. The average term-to-maturity on the municipal bonds is 20 years, and the average investor tax rate is 30%. Estimate the default risk premium on the municipal bonds.

11. Given all the information in Problem 11, if the municipal bonds were to be assigned a bond rating similar to corporate bonds, would they be rated Aaa or Baa?

12. H.T. Technologies issued bonds with a total par value of $100 million in a public offering. The underwriter's commission was composed of $1.50 underwriters profit and $4.00 selling concession. In addition, the syndicate manager's fee was $1.50. Each of the $1,000 par value notes sold for $995.00.

    a. How much cash did H.T. actually receive from this public offering?

    b. What was the flotation cost as a percentage of selling price?

    c. What was the flotation cost as a percentage of par value?

13. Pan American Foods needs $500 million to finance a major expansion. It plans to issue bonds. The sum of the selling concession, underwriter profit, and syndicate manager's fee is expected to be 5% of the bond issue. How large must the bond issue be in order to provide the necessary funds and still cover flotation costs?

14. How large would the bond issue in Problem 13 have to be if the bonds are expected to sell for 98% of par value?

15. On February 20, 1981, the yield-to-maturity on 3-month Treasury bills was 14.70% and on long-term Treasury securities was 9.18%. On February 20, 1993, the yield-to-maturity on 3-month Treasury bills was 3.82% and on long-term Treasury securities was 7.14%.

    a. From this information, describe the general shape of the yield curve on each date.

    b. Considering that, in general, long-term rates can be thought of as an average of expected future short-term rates, how could you explain the difference in the shape of these yield curves?

16. On a given date, the yield-to-maturity on Baa corporate bonds was 10.61%. The yield-to-maturity was 7.94% for 3-month Treasury bills and 9.18% for long-term Treasury securities.

    a. From this information, describe the *general* shape of the yield curve on that date.

    b. What is the default risk premium on the Baa corporate bonds?

17. Graph the yield curve for January 1, 1996, given the following information concerning the yield-to-maturity on that date for Treasury securities:

Yield-to-Maturity	Maturity Date	Yield-to-Maturity	Maturity Date
3.57%	April 1, 1996	4.38%	January 1, 1997
3.31%	February 1, 1996	6.61%	January 1, 2004
3.65%	July 1, 1996	4.95%	March 1, 1998
5.56%	January 1, 2001		

18. On a given date, the yield-to-maturity on municipal bonds was 7.54%, and the yield-to-maturity on comparable risk corporate bonds was 9.65%.
    a. If an investor is in the 20% marginal tax bracket, which of these two investments is preferable?
    b. Investors in which tax bracket will prefer the municipal bonds?

19. Assume that the market's yield schedule for corporate bonds is given by the equation $Y = A + BX$. Y is the yield on a given security; A is the risk-free interest rate; B is the degree of investor risk aversion as measured by the slope of the schedule; and X is the level of default risk connected with a given issuer. Assume that the following scale applies to default risk:

Credit Rating	Value of X
Aaa	0.03
Aa	0.04
A	0.05
Baa	0.06

   If the interest rate on U.S. Treasury bonds is 8% and the slope of the yield schedule is 0.50, what is the yield on bonds in each of the above four credit-rating categories? (Draw a graph of the schedule.)

20. If investor risk aversion in Problem 19 should double, what will happen to the yield spreads between each of the above credit-rating categories? How do you explain this behavior of the yield spreads? (Compare the old and the new yield schedule.)

http://

INTERNET EXERCISE

Go to the Web page listed below and print out the current Treasury yield curve. In a one-page memo to your instructor, explain why the current yield differs from the yield curves in Figure 3-6. www.stocktrader.com/yc2.html

SELF-STUDY QUIZ

Suppose that last Friday the following yields were reported in the financial press:

Type of Security	Yield
3-Month Treasury Bills	5.50%
5-Year Treasury Notes	6.40
20-Year Treasury Bonds	6.80
20-Year Aaa Corporate Bonds	7.60
20-Year Baa Corporate Bonds	8.30
Municipal Bonds	5.70
3-Month Prime Commercial Paper	5.70

1. Sketch the yield curve as it existed on Friday.
2. On Friday, what was the default risk premium on the Aaa corporate bonds? On the Baa corporate bonds?
3. On Friday, what was the yield spread between Aaa and Baa corporate bonds? Explain the reason for the spread.

4. If the average tax rate for investors was 30%, explain why municipal bond yields are so low on Friday.

5. Suppose that one year ago you purchased real estate for $50,000. At the end of the year, you sold the land for $70,000. The rate of inflation for the year was 4%.
   a. What nominal rate of return did you earn?
   b. What real rate of return did you earn?

APPENDIX: SECONDARY SECURITIES MARKETS

Stock Exchanges

Stock exchanges are tangible organizations made up of members who have the right to carry out transactions in the specific issues of common and preferred stocks and bonds that have been listed on the exchange. Members are brokers that handle transactions for individual and institutional investors. There are two U.S. stock exchanges that are national in scope: the New York Stock Exchange (NYSE) and the American Stock Exchange (AMEX). Both exchanges attract issuing companies and investors from across the country. Over the years, the NYSE has accounted for roughly 85% of the value of all common shares traded on exchanges, while the AMEX accounted for about 5% of total volume. Smaller regional stock exchanges in Boston, Chicago, Honolulu, Philadelphia, Salt Lake City, San Francisco, Spokane, and Washington account for the remainder of trading volume.

Listing Requirements. In order to have its stock accepted for trading on an exchange, a company must pass certain requirements regarding its shareholders and financial position. Table 3A-1 gives the requirements for listing on the NYSE. The requirements for listing on the NYSE are stricter than those of other exchanges. This reflects the dominant position of the NYSE and accounts for the fact that only the nation's largest corporations qualify for listing on that exchange.

Benefits of Listing. As a firm grows and prospers, it may eventually qualify for listing first on a regional exchange and then on one or both of the national exchanges. The firm is then faced with the decision whether or not to list. Most people believe that a listed firm will derive a certain amount of prestige and exposure each time its stock is mentioned in any of the various stock market reports and publications of the news media. This may lead to expanded consumer interest in the firm's products. In addition, the investing public may be more interested in investing in a listed company due to the increased liquidity and information about its securities. The increased investor demand may boost the market price of the firm's stock on the secondary market and lower its overall cost of equity financing in the primary market.

Price Quotations

While there are many ways in which stock market trading information is reported,

Listing Requirements for Companies on the NYSE	
	TABLE 3A-1
Current pretax income	$ 2,500,000
Pretax income last 2 years	$ 2,000,000
Net tangible assets	$40,000,000
Shares publicly held	1,100,000
Market value of publicly held shares	$40,000,000
Number of round lot holders (round lot = 100 shares)	2,000

one of the most important is the New York Stock Exchange reporting system, which compiles daily information about stock transactions. Figure 3A-1 is an example of how *The Wall Street Journal* publishes this information. This figure is a small portion of the NYSE transactions section of the *Journal* on Friday, December 4, 1998, which shows the results of trading for Thursday, December 3.

We refer to the Boeing Company (listed as Boeing) to take a closer look at the information provided. The first two columns shown give the highest and lowest prices at which Boeing's common stock traded during the previous 52 weeks. Thus, the stock sold for as much as $56.25 per share and as little as $29.50 per share over that period. (The prices are typically quoted in 1/16 of a dollar increments.) Immediately after the company's name and its listing symbol (BA) is the current per-share annual dividend being paid by the company, which is $0.56 per share. This is followed by the associated cash dividend yield on the shares, 1.8%, which represents the firm's annual dividend divided by the closing market price of its stock. Next is the firm's "price/earnings" ratio, which is the closing stock price divided by the firm's most recent 12 months reported earnings per share. (EPS figures are not listed but are kept track of separately.) According to the stock listing footnotes, the symbol cc indicates that the firm's P/E ratio is 100 or more. This is followed by the volume of trading in the company's shares on December 3, in hundreds of shares. Thus, the figure of 173,523 shown represents volume of 17,352,300 shares on that day. The last four columns provide information on the day's trading prices. Here, Boeing's stock traded during the day at a price of $33.8125 at its highest trade, $31.50 at its lowest trade, and the closing price (the last trade of the day) was $31.875. This closing price represented a change of $1.8125 per share from the closing price of the previous day. The minus sign on the change indicates that the stock closed $1.8125 *lower* than on December 2. (Boeing's stock had fallen some 20% on December 2 and 3 in response to a December 1 announcement that the firm might lay off up to 20,000 employees over the next two years in response to a decline in orders from international airlines following the Asian economic crisis.)

The Over-the-Counter Market

The over-the-counter (OTC) market includes transactions in all stocks not listed on one of the exchanges, or transactions in listed common stocks that do not take place on an exchange. Unlike the organized exchanges, there are no formal memberships or a list of stocks eligible for trading on the OTC. Any stock can be traded on the OTC if a security dealer or broker is willing to accommodate individual investors by "making a market" in the stock. These market makers stand ready to buy from and sell to investors, thereby providing the prerequisite liquidity. Rather than being present together in a single location, dealers are spread throughout the country and communicate through telephones and private lines. They are also tied together by an electronic quotations system called NASDAQ (National Association of Securities Dealers Automatic Quotations).

Based on the number of common stock issues traded, the OTC is larger than both of the national exchanges combined. About 2,900 stocks are traded on the NYSE and 900 issues on the AMEX. Some 10,000 issues, however, are estimated to trade on the OTC. The OTC market is smaller in terms of the volume of shares traded and the value of those securities. In addition to outstanding common and preferred stock, corporate bonds and municipal bonds are traded in the OTC market. The relative importance of organized exchanges and the OTC market for these contractual claims, however, is just the reverse of the case for equity claims. The volume of trading in bonds on the OTC is much larger than that on the organized exchanges.

The Third and Fourth Markets

The **third market** refers to over-the-counter trading of shares listed on an exchange. A dealer who is not a member of an exchange can make a market in a listed stock in the same manner as for an unlisted stock. Most of the trading in the third market is in large amounts by institutional investors as opposed to individual investors. The **fourth market** includes the trading of securities directly between two investors without the aid of a broker or dealer. For a very large transaction such as those often made by institutional investors, brokerage commissions can be substantial. At some size of transaction, the fee is sufficiently high that it becomes economical for institutions to attempt to trade directly with one another. Transactions in both the third and the fourth market are also motivated by the desire to avoid the potential negative price impact of large trades. The growth of these transactions has led to the development of an electronic quotation system called "Instinet" that links major institutional investors.

International Securities Trading

As the world's financial markets have become more integrated, the trading in a company's securities has expanded beyond its own national boundaries. A number of United States companies are listed on the Tokyo and London Stock Exchanges, for example, and a number of European and Pacific Rim companies are listed on the NYSE. We see evidence of this in Figure 3A-1. Among the common shares whose trading is reported are those of British Airways (BritAir), British Petroleum (BritPete), and Broken Hill Proprietary (BrokenHill). The latter is a diversified Australian mining and manufacturing company. In addition, there is a growing "offshore" over-the-counter market where the common stock of both the United States and other countries' multinational corporations are traded by international investors.

Sample of New York Stock Exchange Trading Information, from *The Wall Street Journal* of December 4, 1998

FIGURE 3A-1

52 Weeks Hi	Lo	Stock	Sym	Div	Yld %	PE	Vol 100s	Hi	Lo	Close	Net Chg
38 1/16	22	BlythInd	BTH		...	23	6416	33 5/8	29 11/16	30	–4 3/16
56 1/4	29 1/2	Boeing	BA	.56	1.8	cc	173523	33 13/16	31 1/2	31 7/8	–1 13/16
40 3/8	22 1/4	BoiseCasc	BCC	.60	1.9	dd	2402	31 1/16	30 3/8	30 13/16	+3/8
24 3/4	13 1/16	BorgWarner	BOR		...	9	660	19 1/2	18 1/2	18 1/2	–1/4
12 3/4	6 1/2	BostBeer	SAM		...	22	416	9	8 1/2	8 7/8	+3/8
s40 13/16	20 1/8	BostonSci	BSX		...	dd	18811	27 7/8	26 3/16	26 3/8	–1 3/4
8 3/8	2 1/2	BoydGaming	BYD		...	8	302	3 5/8	3 1/2	3 1/2	–1/16
28 1/2	11 3/8	BoykinLdg	BOY	1.88	13.9	11	432	13 13/16	13 1/4	13 9/16	+3/16
27 3/8	15 3/4	BrndywnRlty	BDN	1.52	8.2	19	885	18 15/16	18 1/4	18 5/8	+5/16
s 23 1/2	9 5/16	BrazilFd	BZF	2.88e	20.8	...	1583	14 7/16	13 7/8	13 7/8	–1 5/16
24 1/4	4 3/4	BreedTech	BDT		...	dd	991	6 7/8	6 7/16	6 7/16	–5/16
11 1/2	5 1/8	BrillAuto	CBA	0.8	1.0	...	6	8	8	8	...
26 5/8	15	BrinkerInt	EAT		...	23	2364	25 11/16	25 1/4	25 1/2	–1/4
^ 129	88 5/16	BrisMyrsSqb	BMY	1.72f	1.4	36	17684	129 1/2	124 5/8	124 7/8	–3 1/2
114 3/4	52 1/8	BritAir	BAB	3.27e	5.1	...	763	66 1/2	64	64 1/16	–2 11/16
97 5/16	73	BritPete	BP	2.91e	3.4	24	17265	86 1/8	85	85 5/16	–3/4
21 1/2	13 1/2	BrokenHill	BHP	.63e	4.3	...	313	15 3/8	14 5/8	14 5/8	–7/8

Money, Time, and Value

Many of the decisions that must be made by the financial managers of firms involve an expenditure of cash in the current year in anticipation of the receipt of a series of cash flows in future years. In the case of a proposal for the construction of a major new plant facility, for example, the sales revenues from the products to be manufactured may be expected to extend ten to fifteen years into the future. Our purpose in this chapter is to establish the basic framework that will permit decisions of that sort, and others of similar character, to be analyzed.

We begin by referring again to the central principle we have stated as the appropriate guide to managerial decisions: take actions that will maximize the value of the firm to its shareholders. It seems obvious that if financial managers are to do this successfully, they first need to know how *investors* measure value. That is the focus of our discussion here. We describe a fundamental valuation process that will enable us to provide answers to such questions as:

- If someone were willing to give you $5,000 today, or $7,000 five years from today, which would you choose? What information would you need in order to be able to make a clear choice?

- You are attempting to decide whether to purchase a new refrigerator for your apartment or to rent that same refrigerator until your lease on the apartment expires. Your lease has two years to run. Given the purchase price of the refrigerator and the monthly payments you would be required to make, should you rent or buy?

- As a parent, you are attempting to accumulate enough money to pay for your child's college expenses. Your child will enter college ten years from now. Counting four years' tuition plus room and board expenses, you expect to need a total of $100,000 by the time your child starts college. How much must you save each year during the next ten years in order to have enough money to pay for four years of college costs?
- You are buying a new house, and you have applied for a mortgage loan from your bank in the amount of $100,000 as part of the purchase price. The bank has offered you two choices: (1) a 15-year loan at a 10% annual interest rate; (2) a 15-year loan at a 9% annual *stated* interest rate, but with 3 points deducted initially from the loan as a financing fee. Which is the more attractive loan?
- You have two Deutschemark investments to choose from. One is a bond that costs DM1,000 and pays interest annually in the amount of DM100 for ten years, at which time the principal of DM1,000 will be repaid to you. The second is a bond that also costs DM1,000 but that pays no annual interest. Instead, at the end of ten years, you will receive a single payment of DM2,840. Which is the better investment?

All these questions deal with the manner in which cash flows of differing amounts that occur at different points in time can be compared on a common basis. That is, we are concerned with what is typically referred to as the "time value of money."

The procedures that individuals use to make the kinds of decisions listed are the *same* procedures they use to place a value on the shares of a company's common stock in the market. If we can identify those procedures, we will then be in a position to make recommendations to a firm's financial managers about the steps they can take to maximize share price.

Our objectives in this chapter are: (1) to examine in detail the concept of the time value of money; and (2) to present the computational techniques needed to give time-value measurement its specific mathematical expression. With that framework established, we may then proceed in subsequent chapters to develop more fully the elements of a comprehensive valuation model that can be applied to financial decision-making in practice. We carry that model through the remainder of the text as a decision-making guide. Importantly, the model has all three attributes that we identified as requirements in Chapter 1. Namely, it is:

- Normative in Character—with value maximization as the specified underlying managerial goal.
- Mathematical in Form—to enable it to provide us with decision rules that are clear, consistent, and repeatable.
- Realistic in Nature—in order that the model can be implemented by practicing financial managers for the decisions they must make for their firms.

Our concentration in this chapter is on the second of these three attributes. Fortunately, while the mathematics of time-value are reasonably powerful, they are also reasonably simple and straightforward. Moreover, they are as useful for individuals' *personal* investing and financing decisions as they are for corporate managers' decisions for their firms—as the questions we posed above would suggest. We shall be able to provide answers to all those questions by the end of the chapter.

VALUATION, CASH FLOWS, AND OPPORTUNITY COSTS

From a financial perspective, valuation is a process that is founded on three basic principles:

http://

Planning for your college tuition can be done on this Web site. It has several links including different planning calculators for costs, savings, goal planning, and loans.

www.americanexpress. com/advisors/cgi-bin/ passer.cgi?step=5

1. Cash flows are what count;
2. Bigger is better than smaller;
3. Sooner is better than later.

Although none of these principles should sound especially controversial, there are some points about them that deserve emphasis.

The focus on *cash flows* as the cornerstone of valuation reflects the fact that an investor cannot realize any tangible economic benefit from an investment unless and until that investment does produce some cash flows. Consumption expenditures and investments elsewhere ultimately require cash as the means of payment. We have made this point before, and it seems self-evident. Similarly, the notion that *larger* cash receipts are more valuable than smaller ones should also not require much elaboration. The principle that *sooner* is better than later where cash flows are concerned, however, is a bit more subtle. The rationale is not merely one of the normal human trait of impatience. The underlying economic argument has to do with the concept of investment "opportunity cost."

Opportunity Cost

To see what this means, consider an investor who is faced with a choice between two alternative investments. Both investments require the same initial outlay, but the expected future cash inflows they are expected to produce differ as follows:

	Expected Cash Inflow From:	
Year	Investment A	Investment B
1	$2,000	$1,000
2	1,000	2,000

A total of $3,000 of cash receipts is expected over two years in both cases. Which of these investments is preferable for the investor and, more importantly, why?

In order to answer that question, let us determine how well off the investor will be *after* two years, depending on the choice made. At the end of the first year, Investment A will generate a $2,000 cash flow, which can then be reinvested elsewhere. Suppose other available investments provide a 10% annual return. Thus, if Investment A were selected, the investor would have a total wealth at the end of two years amounting to:

From Year 1 Cash Flow: ($2,000)(1.10)	=	$2,200
From Year 2 Cash Flow		1,000
Total Wealth, End of Year 2	=	$3,200

The reinvestment of the $2,000 received at the end of the first year grows in value to $2,200 one year later, and is combined with the Year 2 cash receipt of $1,000 from Investment A.

In the case of Investment B, the amount the investor will have at the end of two years, as a result of the same reinvestment process, is instead:

From Year 1 Cash Flow: ($1,000)(1.10)	=	$1,100
From Year 2 Cash Flow		2,000
Total Wealth, End of Year 2	=	$3,100

Investment A therefore is clearly preferable to Investment B even though the *total* cash flows from the two investments are identical over the two years.

The earnings rate of 10%, which is available from other investments, is what produces this result. That earnings rate is the investor's **opportunity cost**. It

Opportunity Cost The rate of return that can be earned from alternative investments. It measures the cost of waiting to receive cash flows.

represents the rate of return that can be earned elsewhere, and it thereby identifies the *cost of waiting* to receive the cash flows from the investments. Investment B requires the investor to wait an additional year to receive the extra $1,000 cash flow, which Investment A provides at the end of the first year. Investment B therefore deprives the investor of the *opportunity* to earn a return on the extra $1,000 in the meantime. That is why sooner is better than later, and why Investment A is superior to Investment B.

Cash Flow Equivalence

We may take the concept of opportunity cost a step further and ask: what would be necessary in order for Investment B to become as *valuable* as Investment A? The answer, of course, is a set of cash flows from Investment B that would cause an investor's wealth at the end of two years to match the $3,200 that Investment A provides. Figure 5-1 shows one of the ways this could occur. If Investment B had an expected cash flow of $2,100 in Year 2, it would then be as attractive as Investment A.

Notice the trade-off involved. Since Investment B produces $1,000 *less* cash flow in Year 1, it must produce $1,100 *more* in Year 2 to be equally valuable. As might be anticipated, the 10% difference in these two amounts is exactly the investor's opportunity cost: the compensation that is required for the extra year's delay. We can generalize this observation. In order for cash flows to have equivalent *values* to investors, *they must become progressively larger the farther in the future they are expected to be received.*

Table 5-1 illustrates the specific nature of that relationship, for an investment opportunity cost of 10% per annum. We see that a cash flow of $1,100 received with a one-year delay is worth the same amount to an investor as $1,000 received immediately. A cash flow of $1,210 received with a two-year delay has the same value, as do cash flows of $1,331, $1,464, and $1,611 received three, four, and five years in the future, respectively. The reason is that $1,000, if it were available immediately, could be invested at a 10% annual earnings rate to *grow* over time to each of the successive amounts listed. From a valuation standpoint, therefore, an investor would be indifferent between having $1,000 now and being promised any *one* of the various other deferred cash flows shown in Table 5-1.

Equivalence of Investment Values at a 10% Annual Opportunity Cost

FIGURE 5-1

Year	Expected Cash Flows: Investment A	Expected Cash Flows: Investment B	Cash Flow Difference, B – A
1	$2,000	$1,000	$(1,000)
2	1,000	2,100	1,100

Investor's Wealth at the End of Two Years, Investment A:
From Year 1 Cash Flow: ($2,000)(1.10)   = $2,200
From Year 2 Cash Flow: 1,000
                                          $3,200

Investor's Wealth at the End of Two Years, Investment B:
From Year 1 Cash Flow: ($1,000)(1.10)   = $1,100
From Year 2 Cash Flow: 2,100
                                          $3,200

TABLE 5-1	Equivalence of Investment Values at a 10% Annual Opportunity Cost	
Expected Time of Receipt, in Years	Effect of Investment Earnings	Cash Flow of Equivalent Value
0	($1,000)	$1,000
1	($1,000)(1.10)	1,100
2	($1,000)(1.10)(1.10)	1,210
3	($1,000)(1.10)(1.10)(1.10)	1,331
4	($1,000)(1.10)(1.10)(1.10)(1.10)	1,464
5	($1,000)(1.10)(1.10)(1.10)(1.10)(1.10)	1,611

Each of those cash flows is, of course, 10% larger than the one for the preceding year. Rather than write out the details of all the calculations, as we have in Table 5-1, we can use a common shorthand notation where

$$
\begin{aligned}
(1.10) &= (1.10)^1 = 1.100 \\
(1.10)(1.10) &= (1.10)^2 = 1.210 \\
(1.10)(1.10)(1.10) &= (1.10)^3 = 1.331 \\
(1.10)(1.10)(1.10)(1.10) &= (1.10)^4 = 1.464 \\
(1.10)(1.10)(1.10)(1.10)(1.10) &= (1.10)^5 = 1.611
\end{aligned}
$$

Thus, the amount of the cash flow that would be necessary to receive five years in the future in order for it to have the same value as $1,000 today is

$$(\$1,000)(1.10)^5 = (\$1,000)(1.611) = \$1,611$$

If instead the investor's opportunity cost were 7% per annum, the Year 5 expected cash flow that would have a value equal to $1,000 today would be only

$$(\$1,000)(1.07)^5 = (\$1,000)(1.403) = \$1,403$$

and this is also a generalizable relationship. The *lower* an investor's opportunity cost, *the smaller is the amount of any future cash flow that will have a value equal to a given immediate cash receipt.*

Table 5-2 provides an illustration of this principle, for opportunity costs of 4%, 7%, and 10% per annum. While it is important to understand the calculations involved, it is more important to understand the economic logic that lies behind them. The key point is that, if an investor has a low opportunity cost, the penalty of having to wait to receive a cash flow is also low, since the investor cannot earn as much from alternative investments in the meantime. As a result, an investor does

TABLE 5-2	The Effect of Opportunity Cost on Cash Flows Having Equivalent Value		
Number of Years Until Cash Flow Is Received	Expected Cash Flow Whose Value Is Equal to $1 Received Immediately, if the Investor's Opportunity Cost Is:		
	4%	7%	10%
0	$1.000	$1.000	$1.000
1	1.040	1.070	1.100
2	1.082	1.145	1.210
3	1.125	1.225	1.331
4	1.170	1.311	1.464
5	1.217	1.403	1.611

not require as large a future cash flow in order to feel that he or she is receiving a payment that is as valuable as a payment received immediately.

We are therefore in a position to answer the first question that we raised at the beginning of this chapter: Would you prefer to have someone give you $5,000 today, or $7,000 five years from today? As should now be apparent, the answer depends on your investment opportunity cost. According to the figures listed in Table 5-2, if you can earn only 4% per year from your other available investments, $5,000 today is worth the equivalent of only ($5,000)(1.217) = $6,085 five years from today. Thus, you would be better off choosing the $7,000 payment in Year 5. The reason is that you could not make $5,000 today grow to an amount *as large as* $7,000 five years from now by investing at 4% in the meantime.

If, on the other hand, you could earn 10% per year from your investments, you could turn $5,000 today into ($5,000)(1.611) = $8,055 five years from now. You would then be better off choosing the immediate payment. At a 7% opportunity cost, $5,000 today would grow to ($5,000)(1.403) = $7,015 in five years. Rounding off, this implies that you would essentially be indifferent to the choice between $5,000 now and $7,000 later. More generally, at any opportunity cost *above* 7%, the immediate cash payment of $5,000 is more valuable. At any opportunity cost *below* 7%, the $7,000 payment five years from now is more valuable. That should sound logical, since a high opportunity cost places an especially large premium on receiving cash flows early because it makes the cost of waiting greater.

The concept of opportunity cost as a determinant of the relative values of cash flows to be received at different points in time is more than merely an abstract computational exercise. It is a very *practical* concept because investors in the real world do in fact have investment alternatives continually available to them that provide positive rates of return. If nothing else, for example, they can put their money into a bank savings account and earn interest annually. Thus, they will necessarily consider timing as an important element in making investment decisions. We have simply formalized that notion here and given it an explicit mathematical content. The mathematics, moreover, are quite straightforward in application. They are also easy to implement, since tabulations like those in Table 5-2 for different opportunity costs covering a wide variety of time periods are readily available. In addition, they are programmed into both handheld calculators and computer spreadsheet software.

COMPOUNDING

The process of determining how rapidly a sum of money will grow over time as it is continually invested to earn a return is called **compounding**. Equivalently, this process identifies how earnings will *accumulate* due to successive reinvestments of prior periods' earnings. To refer again to Table 5-2, we see that $1.000 today will grow to $1.040 in one year and to $1.082 in two years when the earnings rate is 4% annually. If the earnings rate is 10%, a $1.000 investment will accumulate to $1.100 in one year and to $1.210 in two years.

Two things are worth noting about these figures. First, since the *percentage* increases in the cumulative amounts are the same each year at a given earnings rate, the *absolute* increases become progressively larger over time. That is because a return is being earned each year not only on the initial investment but also on all the earnings that have been accumulated during previous years. If this were a bank savings account, we would describe this process as earning "interest on interest" as well as interest on principal each year. We can see the effect in Table 5-3, using a 10% earnings rate as an example, for an initial investment of $1,000.

The second point is that the impact of compounding is greatly magnified

Compounding The process of determining how rapidly a sum of money will grow over time when it is continually invested.

The Effect of Compounding on Increases in Accumulated Investment Amount

TABLE 5-3

Year	Cumulative Investment Amount at a 10% Annual Earnings Rate	Annual Change in Cumulative Amount
0	$1,000	—
1	1,100	$100
2	1,210	110
3	1,331	121
4	1,464	133
5	1,611	147

when the earnings rate increases and is magnified to an increasing extent over time. Table 5-4 shows the relevant comparisons at earnings rates of 4% and 10% annually, again for a $1,000 initial investment. At the end of one year, a 10% annual earnings rate results in an accumulated investment amount that is $60/$1,040, or 5.8%, greater than the amount accumulated at a 4% earnings rate. After five years, however, the difference is $444/$1,217, or 36.5%. This is the power of compounding, and an indication of the progressively more significant payoff from being able to earn higher rates of return.

Figure 5-2 presents these relationships in graphical form. As a reference point, the horizontal line represents the case of a 0% earnings rate. If there is no positive investment return available, the initial sum invested will, of course, never increase. The impact of successively higher earnings rates is evident in the widening distances between the plotted curves over time.

DISCOUNTING

Each of the curves in Figure 5-2 identifies a series of cash flow amounts occurring at different points in time, which all have the same value to an investor as $1.00 available now, for any given earnings rate (opportunity cost). This is because $1.00

The Effect of Compounding on Accumulated Investment Amounts

FIGURE 5-2

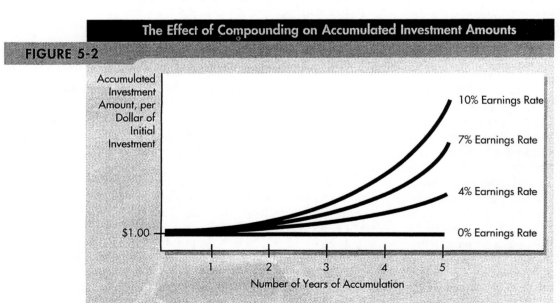

The Effect of Increased Earnings Rates on Accumulated Investment Amount

TABLE 5-4

Year	Accumulated Investment Amounts, at Earnings Rates of: 4%	Accumulated Investment Amounts, at Earnings Rates of: 10%	Difference in Accumulated Amounts
0	$1,000	$1,000	—
1	1,040	1,100	$ 60
2	1,082	1,210	128
3	1,125	1,331	206
4	1,170	1,464	294
5	1,217	1,611	394

invested now would grow with accumulated earnings to *become* each of those future amounts. In the case of a 10% opportunity cost and a four-year deferral period, for example, we saw that

$$(\$1.00)(1.10)^4 = \$1.464$$

and we noted that $1.464 was the future cash flow that was worth the same as $1.00 today.

If we reverse the computational process, we can make an equivalent statement. That is, it is also true that

$$\$1.00 = (\$1.464)/(1.10)^4$$

In this form, we may describe $1.00 as the *present value* of a cash flow of $1.464 that is expected to occur four years in the future, if the investor's opportunity cost is 10% per annum. Obviously, we can make a similar computation to determine the present value of *any* future cash flow for any deferral period. Thus, the present value of a $1.00 cash flow that is expected to occur five years from now, at a 10% opportunity cost, is

$$PV = \$1.00/(1.10)^5 = \$0.621$$

This process is called **discounting**: the computation of the present value of a given future cash flow, recognizing the opportunity that an investor has to earn a return from alternative investments in the meantime.

Discounting is the mirror image of compounding, and it is based on the same concept of equivalent cash flow value. Just as $1.00 available immediately (*at present*) will grow if invested at a 10% annual rate of return to become

$$(\$1.00)(1.10)^5 = \$1.611$$

in five years, so will $0.621 grow to become

$$(\$0.621)(1.10)^5 = \$1.00$$

at the end of five years. Accordingly, $1.00 is the present value of $1.611, and $0.621 is the present value of $1.00, at 10%. In the context of discounting, the opportunity cost or earnings rate used in the calculation is often referred to as the **discount rate**.

In Table 5-5, we show the results of a set of representative present value computations, at the same 4%, 7%, and 10% opportunity costs used previously in Table 5-2. We standardize on $1.00 as the future cash flow whose present value is calculated in each case. We see that the present values decline steadily, as the date of the receipt of the $1.00 cash flow gets progressively farther in the future. This

Discounting The computation of the present value of a future cash flow, recognizing the opportunity to earn a return in the meantime.

Discount Rate The investment opportunity cost used to compute the present value of a future cash flow.

Cash Flow Present Values

TABLE 5-5

Number of Years Until Cash Flow Is Received	Present Value of a $1.00 Future Cash Flow if Opportunity Cost Is:		
	4%	7%	10%
0	$1.000	$1.000	$1.000
1	0.962	0.935	0.909
2	0.925	0.873	0.826
3	0.889	0.816	0.751
4	0.855	0.763	0.683
5	0.822	0.713	0.621

reflects again the established valuation principle that sooner is better than later. We also see that the present values decline more rapidly with time at higher *discount* rates, in the same way that the accumulated investment amounts resulting from compounding increase more rapidly at higher *earnings* rates. We graph these relationships in Figure 5-3.

If an investor's opportunity cost were 7% per annum, therefore, a cash flow of $1,000, which was expected to be received three years from today, would be regarded as being worth the equivalent of ($1,000)(0.816) = $816 today. That is, the investor would be willing to *pay* $816 now for the right to receive $1,000 three years from now. If the $1,000 instead were to be received five years in the future, the investor would be willing to pay only ($1,000)(0.713), or $713, now for the right to receive the later payment. The difference is the (opportunity) cost of waiting an extra two years. If the opportunity cost is zero, waiting involves *no* loss in value, and the present value line in Figure 5-3 is horizontal.

From this perspective, we may return once more to the choice we discussed earlier between receiving $5,000 now or $7,000 five years from now. The present value of $5,000 *now* is, of course, just $5,000. At opportunity costs of 4%, 7%, and 10%, the present values of $7,000 in five years are:

The Present Values of a Single Future Cash Flow of $1

FIGURE 5-3

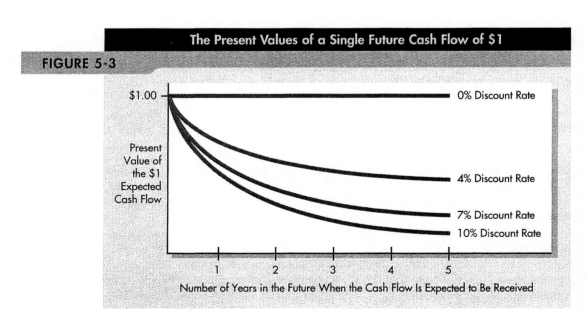

Opportunity Cost (Discount Rate)	Present Value of $7,000 in Year 5
4%	($7,000)(0.822) = $5,754
7%	($7,000)(0.713) = $4,991
10%	($7,000)(0.621) = $4,347

We see again that, at a 7% opportunity cost, the choice is essentially a matter of indifference. At higher opportunity costs, the immediate $5,000 payment is preferred. At lower opportunity costs, the later $7,000 payment is more attractive. This is also consistent with our previous conclusion.

VALUE AND TIMING

Compounding and discounting are the fundamental computational processes that recognize the existence of investor opportunity costs. They determine the value to an investor of any given cash flow, in light of the rate of return available from other investment opportunities. If we are interested in measuring the value of a cash flow as of a point in time *earlier* than the date when the cash flow is expected to be received, we *discount* the cash flow to the earlier date. Its value then is *smaller*. If we are interested in measuring the value of the cash flow as of a point in time *later* than the date of its expected receipt, we *compound* the cash flow forward to the later time. Its value then is *larger*. When we do either of these two things, we are recognizing the basic principle that the value of any cash flow depends not only on its *amount* but also on its *timing*. This is what we mean when we refer to the **time value of money**. The higher an investor's opportunity cost, the greater is the effect of valuing a given cash flow on some date *other* than the date of its expected receipt. Figure 5-4 summarizes the various time-value relationships involved.

Time Value of Money The principle that the value of any cash flow depends both on its amount and its timing.

MULTIPLE CASH FLOWS

What is true of a single cash flow is, by extension, true of a series of cash flows as well. Suppose, for example, that a particular investment promised the following yearly sequence of Swiss Franc cash flows:

A Summary of Compounding and Discounting Procedures

SUMMARY FIGURE 5-4

Compounding: Calculates the value of a cash flow as of a date later than its expected receipt.

Discounting: Calculates the value of a cash flow as of a date prior to its expected receipt.

$$\left.\begin{matrix}\text{Future Value}\\\text{and}\\\text{Present Value}\end{matrix}\right\} \text{Depend on} \left\{\begin{matrix}\text{Cash Flow Amount}\\\text{Date of Receipt}\\\text{Investment Opportunity Cost}\end{matrix}\right.$$

Element	Direction of Relationship
1. Cash Flow Amount	Cash Flow UP, Future Value UP. Cash Flow UP, Present Value UP.
2. Date of Receipt	Cash Flow LATER, Future Value DOWN. Cash Flow LATER, Present Value DOWN.
3. Opportunity Cost	Opportunity Cost UP, Future Value UP. Opportunity Cost UP, Present Value DOWN.

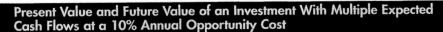

Present Value and Future Value of an Investment With Multiple Expected Cash Flows at a 10% Annual Opportunity Cost

FIGURE 5-5

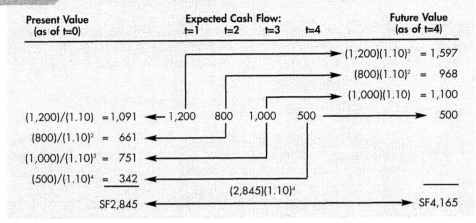

Year	Expected Cash Flow
1	SF1,200
2	800
3	1,000
4	500

At an opportunity cost of 10% per annum, we can compute (a) the present value of these cash flows as of Year 0 and (b) the future value to which they will accumulate as of Year 4. In standard terminology, we shall use "Year 0" or "Time t = 0" to refer to the present. Similarly, the dates of the receipt of the subsequent expected cash flows will be designated as times t = 1 through t = 4, respectively. The relevant calculations are shown in Figure 5-5 for the investment in question. For example, the SF1,000 cash flow at t = 3 is discounted back three years to a present value of 751 and compounded forward one year to a future value of 1,100.

As indicated, the present value of all cash flows is SF2,845, and the time t = 4 future value is SF4,165. The interpretation is that an investor having an annual opportunity cost of 10% would be willing to pay up to SF2,845 now in order to *obtain* the cash flows from the investment. The reason for this maximum purchase price is simple. If the investor did *not* buy this investment but invested the SF2,845 elsewhere at 10%, its future value would be SF4,165 at time t = 4. This is exactly the sum of the future values of the four annual cash flows on the proposed investment. Thus, whether the investor buys this investment or another for SF2,845, the ending wealth position will be the same.

The portrayal in Figure 5-5 of the process of determining future and present values is a useful one conceptually. Keep that picture in mind as we discuss further refinements of the calculations. When you understand it, you will also understand most of what is important to know about analyzing the desirability of corporate investment projects in more realistic settings.

Future Value Notation

In order to make it unnecessary to continue to write out the complete expressions for both future and present values each time we make a computation, we shall introduce some compact notation to represent the various calculations involved.

First, let

K = the investor's opportunity cost
FV = the future value of either a single cash flow or a series of cash flows

Accordingly, if we wish to calculate the future value of a particular cash flow at a point in time N years *after* it is expected to be received, we have

$$FV_N = (Cash\ Flow)(1+K)^N \tag{1}$$

$$FV_N = (Cash\ Flow)(CF_{K,N}) \tag{2}$$

where $CF_{K,N} = (1 + K)^N$ is the *compounding factor* that measures future value N years later at an opportunity cost of K percent per annum. In this form, the future value computations for the cash flows from the investment shown in Figure 5-5 would be:

$$FV = (1,200)(CF_{0.10,3}) + (800)(CF_{0.10,2}) + (1,000)(CF_{0.10,1}) + (500)$$

$$FV = (1,200)(1.331) + (800)(1.210) + (1,000)(1.100) + 500$$

$$FV = 1,597 + 968 + 1,100 + 500 = SF4,165$$

Because these sorts of computations are frequently required in financial decision-making, tabulations of the compounding factors $CF_{K,N}$ for various values of K and N are readily available. We provide such a tabulation in Table I at the end of the text, for opportunity costs ranging from 1% to 20% and for values of N from one year to 50 years. A portion of that table is reproduced in Table 5-6. Most business calculators make the equivalent computations as one of the standard mathematical functions they provide, as do most business software packages for personal computers. We also provide instructions at the end of the text for the use of a financial calculator to solve time value of money problems. Notice again from Table 5-6 how rapidly a sum of money will grow in value over time at high earnings reinvestment rates (high opportunity costs). For example, a dollar invested at 10% will accumulate to approximately $6.73 within 20 years.

Future Value Compounding Factors: $CF_{K,N}$

TABLE 5-6

$$CF_{K,N} = (1 + K)^N$$

Time N	1%	2%	3%	4%	5%	6%	7%	8%	9%	10%	11%	12%
1	1.010	1.020	1.030	1.040	1.050	1.060	1.070	1.080	1.090	1.100	1.110	1.120
2	1.020	1.040	1.061	1.082	1.102	1.124	1.145	1.166	1.188	1.210	1.232	1.254
3	1.030	1.061	1.093	1.125	1.158	1.191	1.225	1.260	1.295	1.331	1.368	1.405
4	1.041	1.082	1.126	1.170	1.216	1.262	1.311	1.360	1.412	1.464	1.518	1.574
5	1.051	1.104	1.159	1.217	1.276	1.338	1.403	1.469	1.539	1.611	1.685	1.762
6	1.062	1.126	1.194	1.265	1.340	1.419	1.501	1.587	1.677	1.772	1.870	1.974
7	1.072	1.149	1.230	1.316	1.407	1.504	1.606	1.714	1.828	1.949	2.076	2.211
8	1.083	1.172	1.267	1.369	1.477	1.594	1.718	1.851	1.993	2.144	2.305	2.476
9	1.094	1.195	1.305	1.423	1.551	1.689	1.838	1.999	2.172	2.358	2.558	2.773
10	1.105	1.219	1.344	1.480	1.629	1.791	1.967	2.159	2.367	2.594	2.839	3.106
15	1.161	1.346	1.558	1.801	2.079	2.397	2.759	3.172	3.643	4.177	4.785	5.474
20	1.220	1.486	1.806	2.191	2.653	3.207	3.870	4.661	5.604	6.728	8.062	9.646

Present Value Notation

We may employ a similar notation for the calculation of the present value (PV) of a cash flow, as of a date N years *prior* to the time of its expected receipt:

$$PV = (\text{Cash Flow})/(1 + K)^N \tag{3}$$

$$PV = (\text{Cash Flow})(DF_{K,N}) \tag{4}$$

where $DF_{K,N} = 1/(1 + K)^N$ is the *discounting factor* for N years at an annual opportunity cost of K. As applied to the investment in Figure 5-5, we have:

$$PV = (1,200)(DF_{0.10,1}) + (800)(DF_{0.10,2}) + (1,000)(DF_{0.10,3}) + (500)(DF_{0.10,4})$$
$$PV = (1,200)(0.909) + (800)(0.826) + (1,000)(0.751) + (500)(0.683)$$
$$PV = 1,091 + 661 + 751 + 342 = SF2,845$$

Tabulations of discounting factors are also widely available. Table III at the end of the text is one that we shall refer to frequently, for subsequent present value computations. A portion of that tabulation is contained in Table 5-7 for our immediate use.

The figures in Table 5-7 demonstrate the heavy influence of an investor's opportunity cost on the present values of future cash flows. A payment of $1 that is expected to be received 10 years from now is worth $0.82 today when the opportunity cost is 2%, but is worth only about $0.32 at an opportunity cost of 12%. As is also apparent, when the date of the receipt is as far as 20 years in the future, cash flows will have very small present values at opportunity costs of 10% and above. Investors with high opportunity costs therefore will strongly prefer investments that have especially large cash flows in the early years.

The Relationship Between Present and Future Values

Due to the mathematics of the discounting and compounding processes, there is a very definite relationship between the measures of value they provide. In particular, it will always be the case for any cash flow that

$$FV_N = (PV)(1+K)^N \tag{5}$$

$$FV_N = (PV)(CF_{K,N}) \tag{6}$$

Present Value Discounting Factors: $DF_{K,N}$

TABLE 5-7

$$DF_{K,N} = 1/(1 + K)^N$$

Time	Opportunity Cost, K											
N	1%	2%	3%	4%	5%	6%	7%	8%	9%	10%	11%	12%
1	0.990	0.980	0.971	0.962	0.952	0.943	0.935	0.926	0.917	0.909	0.901	0.893
2	0.980	0.961	0.943	0.925	0.907	0.890	0.873	0.857	0.842	0.826	0.812	0.797
3	0.971	0.942	0.915	0.889	0.864	0.840	0.816	0.794	0.772	0.751	0.731	0.712
4	0.961	0.924	0.889	0.855	0.823	0.792	0.763	0.735	0.708	0.683	0.659	0.636
5	0.951	0.906	0.863	0.822	0.784	0.747	0.713	0.681	0.650	0.621	0.593	0.567
6	0.941	0.888	0.837	0.790	0.746	0.705	0.666	0.630	0.596	0.565	0.535	0.507
7	0.933	0.871	0.813	0.760	0.711	0.665	0.623	0.583	0.547	0.513	0.482	0.452
8	0.923	0.853	0.789	0.731	0.677	0.627	0.582	0.540	0.502	0.467	0.434	0.404
9	0.914	0.837	0.766	0.703	0.645	0.592	0.544	0.500	0.460	0.424	0.391	0.361
10	0.905	0.820	0.744	0.676	0.614	0.558	0.508	0.463	0.422	0.386	0.352	0.322
15	0.861	0.743	0.642	0.555	0.481	0.417	0.362	0.315	0.275	0.239	0.209	0.183
20	0.820	0.673	0.554	0.456	0.377	0.312	0.258	0.215	0.178	0.149	0.124	0.104

For example, the 1,000 cash flow from the investment in Figure 5-5 that is expected to be received at time $t = 3$ has a present value of $(1,000)/(1.10)^3 = 751$. It also has a time $t = 4$ future value of $(1,000)(1.10) = 1,100$. If we take the ratio of these two values, we have

$$\frac{FV_4}{PV} = \frac{(1,000)(1.10)}{(1,000)/(1.10)^3} = (1.10)^4$$

and, accordingly,

$$FV_4 = (PV)(1.10)^4 = (PV)(CF_{0.10,4})$$
$$1,100 = (751)(1.464)$$

Since the same conclusion holds for each of the investment's individual cash flows, the relationship will hold for the *total* value of the investment as well. That is:

$$FV_4 = (PV)(CF_{0.10,4})$$
$$4,165 = (2,845)(1.464)$$

All this simply reflects the fact that the discounting and compounding processes *are* mirror images of each other. One moves value up to the present, and the other moves value out into the future. For a given opportunity cost, the movements in value are at the same annual rate, and they are connected precisely *by* that rate.

ANNUITIES

There are several special cases of future and present value measurements that arise repeatedly in practice. Because they do, it is convenient to have some additional standard tabulations like those shown in Tables 5-6 and 5-7 in order to simplify the process of making the computations. Among these special cases is that of an annuity.

An **annuity** is the term applied to a series of cash flows for which the amount of the expected receipt or payment is the *same* each period. Certain operating costs of a business might have this character—for example, annual rental payments on a building or a piece of equipment. The same could be true of some portion of revenues if products are being sold under a long-term contract at a fixed price. Importantly, part of the expected cash flows from financial securities like bonds and preferred stock take the form of annuities to the owners of the securities.

Annuity A series of cash flows for which the amount of payment or receipt is the same each period.

Future Value of an Annuity

An illustration of an annuity is provided in Figure 5-6. The specific expectation is for a British pound cash flow of £1,000 at the end of each year for five years. The

http://
Information is available about fixed and variable annuities on the Motley Fool Web site.
www.fool.comFribble/1997/Fribble970404.htm

Future Value of an Annuity of £1,000 for Five Years, at a 7% Annual Investment Opportunity Cost

FIGURE 5-6

Expected Cash Flow:					Compounding Factor, CF	Future Value at t=5
t=1	t=2	t=3	t=4	t=5		
£1,000	£1,000	£1,000	£1,000	£1,000 →	1.000 →	(£1,000)(1.000) = £1,000
					1.070 →	(£1,000)(1.070) = 1,070
					1.145 →	(£1,000)(1.145) = 1,145
					1.225 →	(£1,000)(1.225) = 1,225
					1.311 →	(£1,000)(1.311) = 1,311
					5.751	£5,751

calculations of the future values of those individual cash flows as of the ending date of the annuity are listed, assuming a 7% annual investment opportunity cost. The total future value of the annuity is £5,751 as shown. These are the same sorts of computations we have made before, except that we are now taking advantage of the compounding factors $CF_{K,N}$ contained in Table 5-6 for K = 7% in order to simplify the calculations.

A key point to note is that, since an annuity does consist of a series of cash flows of equal size, all the individual compounding factors are multiplied by the same amount to measure the annuity's future value. We could obviously just as well multiply the *total* of the compounding factors by the annual cash flow as a single computation to obtain the annuity's total future value, that is, (£1,000)(5.751) = £5,751. Equally obviously, if we changed the cash flows in the annuity to £2,000 per year, its future value would simply be (£2,000)(5.751) = £11,502 instead, also as a single computation.

This same convenient feature will characterize an annuity of any specified duration for any given opportunity cost. For that reason, we can greatly simplify the calculations of annuity future values by developing standard tabulations of the totals of the individual years' compounding factors. Table 5-8 provides such a tabulation, for the same time periods and opportunity costs as in Tables 5-6 and 5-7. An expanded version is contained in Table II at the end of the text.[1] We may describe the tabulated figures as *annuity compounding factors* (ACF), where

$$ACF_{K,N} = \text{the future value of a \$1 annuity of N years'}$$
$$\text{duration, at an annual opportunity cost of K percent}$$

Thus, if we were interested in the future value of a 10-year $2,000 annuity when the investor's opportunity cost is 9% per year, we would go to the N = 10 row in

Annuity Future Value Compounding Factors: $ACF_{K,N}$

TABLE 5-8

$ACF_{K,N}$ = the accumulated future value of a $1 annuity of N years' duration, when the annual opportunity cost is K%

Annuity Duration	Opportunity Cost, K											
N	1%	2%	3%	4%	5%	6%	7%	8%	9%	10%	11%	12%
1	1.000	1.000	1.000	1.000	1.000	1.000	1.000	1.000	1.000	1.000	1.000	1.000
2	2.010	2.020	2.030	2.040	2.050	2.060	2.070	2.080	2.090	2.100	2.110	2.120
3	3.030	3.060	3.091	3.122	3.152	3.184	3.214	3.246	3.278	3.310	3.342	3.374
4	4.060	4.122	4.184	4.246	4.310	4.375	4.440	4.506	4.573	4.641	4.710	4.779
5	5.101	5.204	5.309	5.416	5.526	5.637	5.751	5.867	5.985	6.105	6.229	6.353
6	6.152	6.308	6.468	6.633	6.802	6.975	7.153	7.336	7.523	7.716	7.913	8.115
7	7.214	7.434	7.662	7.898	8.142	8.393	8.653	8.923	9.200	9.487	9.784	10.089
8	8.286	8.583	8.892	9.214	9.549	9.897	10.260	10.637	11.028	11.436	11.859	12.300
9	9.368	9.755	10.159	10.583	11.027	11.491	11.978	12.488	13.021	13.579	14.164	14.776
10	10.462	10.950	11.464	12.006	12.578	13.181	13.816	14.487	15.193	15.937	16.722	17.549
15	16.097	17.293	18.599	20.024	21.579	23.276	25.129	27.152	29.361	31.772	34.405	37.280
20	22.019	24.297	26.870	29.778	33.066	36.786	40.995	45.762	51.160	57.275	64.203	72.053

[1] The factors in Table 5-8 can also be calculated using the following equation: $ACF_{K,N} = [(1 + K)^N - 1]/K$. This equation is particularly useful when K is not a round number.

the K = 9% column and determine the future value to be ($2,000)(15.193) = $30,386. More generally, the future value of an annuity can be computed as

$$FV_N = (\text{Annual Cash Flow})(ACF_{K,N}) \tag{7}$$

One of the common uses of annuity future values is to determine how much money would need to be saved each year in order to end up with a desired total sum at the end of the savings period. For example, we asked at the beginning of this chapter about the savings plan that, over 10 years, would allow a parent to accumulate a total of $100,000 to pay for the following four years of a child's college education. In terms of equation (7), the desired future value FV_{10} would be $100,000. If the savings were deposited in a bank savings account that paid 9% interest annually, the annuity compounding factor would be 15.193, and therefore the required annual savings figure is

$$FV_{10} = (\text{Annual Savings})(ACF_{0.09,10})$$
$$\$100,000 = (\text{Annual Savings})(15.193)$$
$$\text{Annual Savings} = (\$100,000)/(15.193) = \$6,582$$

If the parent deposited $6,582 at the end of each year into a savings account, those deposits plus accumulated interest would grow to a sum of $100,000 at the end of 10 years.

It is apparent from Table 5-8 how rapidly the future values can grow over time. The reason is that two things happen each time we add a year to the annuity: (1) an additional $1 cash flow occurs; and (2) earnings continue to accumulate on the earlier cash flows. With time, these effects can add up to a considerable accumulation of funds, and even a relatively modest savings plan can have a very large ultimate payoff. Notice also that all the ACF factors for the future value of a *one-year* annuity are equal to 1.000 regardless of the earnings rate. This is because the first cash flow in the annuity occurs at the *end* of the first year, and no earnings have yet been realized.

Present Value of an Annuity

A similar process can be used to determine the *present value* of an annuity. Figure 5-7 shows the relevant computations for the £1,000 per year annuity that we examined in Figure 5-6. The individual years' discounting factors come from Table 5-7. Once more, the *total* of those discounting factors will always be the same for

Present Value of an Annuity of £1,000 per Year for Five Years, at a 7% Annual Investment Opportunity Cost

FIGURE 5-7

Present Value	Discounting Factor, DF	t=1	Expected Cash Flow: t=2	t=3	t=4	t=5
(£1,000)(0.935) = £935 ← 0.935 ←		£1,000	£1,000	£1,000	£1,000	£1,000
(£1,000)(0.873) = 873 ← 0.873 ←						
(£1,000)(0.816) = 816 ← 0.816 ←						
(£1,000)(0.763) = 763 ← 0.763 ←						
(£1,000)(0.713) = 713 ← 0.713 ←						
£4,100	4.100					

any given combination of annuity duration and opportunity cost. We may therefore define an *annuity discounting factor* (ADF) as

$ADF_{K,N}$ = the present value of a \$1 annuity of N years' duration, at an annual opportunity cost of K percent

and Table 5-9 provides representative values.[2] A more complete version is available in Table IV at the end of the text.

The corresponding generalization is that the present value of an annuity can be calculated conveniently in the form

$$PV = (\text{Annual Cash Flow})(ADF_{K,N}) \quad (8)$$

and we can apply this simplification to help answer one of the other questions that was raised at the beginning of this chapter. The choice offered was between two bonds, both of which would cost DM1,000 to purchase. The first bond provided a DM100 interest payment each year for 10 years and then a DM1,000 principal payment at the end of 10 years. The second paid no annual interest but instead promised a single payment of DM2,840 in year 10. Assume the investor's opportunity cost is 10% per annum.

We can determine the total present value of the cash flows from the first of these alternatives by using the appropriate discounting and annuity discounting factors from Tables 5-7 and 5-9. Thus, the present value is

$$PV = (DM100)(ADF_{0.10,10}) + (DM1{,}000)(DF_{0.10,10})$$
$$PV = (DM100)(6.145) + (DM1{,}000)(0.386)$$
$$PV = DM614.50 + DM386.00 = DM1{,}000.50$$

If the discounting factors had not been rounded off in the tables at the level of the third digit past the decimal point, this present value would calculate out to be

TABLE 5-9

Annuity Present Value Discounting Factors: $ADF_{K,N}$

$ADF_{K,N}$ = the present value of a \$1 annuity of N years' duration, when the annual opportunity cost is K%

Annuity Duration	Opportunity Cost, K											
N	1%	2%	3%	4%	5%	6%	7%	8%	9%	10%	11%	12%
1	0.990	0.980	0.971	0.962	0.952	0.943	0.935	0.926	0.917	0.909	0.901	0.893
2	1.970	1.942	1.913	1.886	1.859	1.833	1.808	1.783	1.759	1.735	1.713	1.690
3	2.941	2.884	2.829	2.775	2.723	2.673	2.624	2.577	2.531	2.487	2.444	2.402
4	3.902	3.808	3.717	3.630	3.546	3.465	3.387	3.312	3.240	3.170	3.102	3.037
5	4.853	4.713	4.580	4.452	4.329	4.212	4.100	3.993	3.890	3.791	3.696	3.605
6	5.795	5.601	5.417	5.242	5.076	4.917	4.767	4.623	4.486	4.355	4.231	4.111
7	6.728	6.472	6.230	6.002	5.786	5.582	5.389	5.206	5.033	4.868	4.712	4.564
8	7.652	7.326	7.020	6.733	6.463	6.210	5.971	5.747	5.535	5.334	5.146	4.968
9	8.566	8.162	7.786	7.435	7.108	6.802	6.515	6.247	5.985	5.759	5.537	5.328
10	9.471	8.983	8.530	8.111	7.722	7.360	7.024	6.710	6.418	6.145	5.889	5.650
15	13.865	12.849	11.938	11.118	10.380	9.712	9.108	8.560	8.061	7.606	7.191	6.811
20	18.046	16.351	14.877	13.590	12.462	11.470	10.594	9.818	9.129	8.514	7.963	7.469

[2] The factors in Table 5-9 can also be calculated using the following equation: $ADF_{K,N} = \left(1 - \frac{1}{(1+K)^N}\right) / K$.

exactly DM1,000.00. That figure should sound right. If you pay DM1,000 for a bond, earn interest at DM100/DM1,000 = 10% each year, and then get your money back when the interest stops, you are realizing a 10% return on your investment. If 10% is also your opportunity cost, the present value of the cash flows you get from an investment that returns you 10% *should* be exactly the amount you invested. We see that this is the case.

For the second alternative, the DM2,840 payment the investor will receive at time t = 10 has a present value equal to

$$PV = (DM2,840)(DF_{0.10,10}) = (DM2,840)(0.386) = DM1,096$$

Accordingly, this investment is superior to the first one, since both cost DM1,000 to acquire.

Installment Loans

Annuity values have a variety of common and useful applications. A major one is in the area of the determination of the terms on installment loans like home mortgages and automobile loans. Suppose, as an illustration, you wanted to borrow $100,000 to finance the purchase of a new house, and the bank you were dealing with planned to charge you a 9% annual interest rate. If the loan was for 20 years, and you were to make a single payment at the end of each year, the size of that annual payment could be determined from equation (8) and Table 5-9.

$$PV = (Annual\ Payment)(ADF_{0.09,20})$$
$$\$100,000 = (Annual\ Payment)(9.129)$$
$$Annual\ Payment = (\$100,000)/(9.129) = \$10,954$$

▪ Financial ISSUES

LOTTERIES COME TO WALL STREET

Although financial markets are sometimes portrayed by the media as a giant casino, Wall Street firms have carefully avoided consciously associating themselves with lotteries—until now. Investment firms have recently begun to make public offerings of securities whose payments are derived from winning lottery tickets. The story behind this financial innovation begins on Main Street where some fortunate individual has purchased a winning ticket in the state lottery. Typically, these winnings are paid out by the state as an annuity over a lengthy period of time. Thus, a $1 million prize actually may take the form of a $50,000 annual payment for the next 20 years.

In the early 1990s, some financial service firms began to offer lottery winners the opportunity to convert their annuities into equivalent present values. In exchange for assigning the prize to the financial service firm, a lottery winner would receive an immediate single lump-sum payment. Initially, these firms would then sell the prize assignment to an institutional investor such as John Hancock or Prudential Insurance.

These investments were particularly attractive because they offered high yields comparable to those on junk bonds. Their risk, on the other hand, was comparable to that on U.S. Treasury securities owned by the state or on annuities purchased by the state from insurance companies. By 1996, annual sales of lottery prizes had reached some $700 million.

In order to expand the market for lottery prize sales, brokerage firms have recently hired Wall Street investment firms to create pools of lottery prizes and issue lottery-backed securities to individual as well as institutional investors. Although the yields offered on these securities are only slightly higher than Treasury bill yields, they are very low risk and can be bought and sold much more easily than the individual lottery prizes. Leave it to Wall Street to convert a lottery ticket into a sure thing.

Thus, you need $100,000 *now* (the PV of the loan). Since a $1 annual payment for 20 years would have a present value of $9.129 at a 9% interest rate, it takes a payment of $10,954 per year to have a present value (to the bank) of $100,000. This is, in fact, the way financial institutions calculate the payments on installment loans.

Take a simpler case, in order to see what's going on behind the numbers. Assume you want a $1,000 loan that you intend to repay in three annual installments. If the interest rate is 12% per annum, your required payment will be

$$\$1,000 = (\text{Annual Payment})(\text{ADF}_{0.12,3})$$
$$\$1,000 = (\text{Annual Payment})(2.402)$$
$$\text{Annual Payment} = \$1,000/2.402 = \$416.35$$

The way this works out is shown in Figure 5-8. You start with $1,000 of credit from the bank and owe interest at 12% per year. At the end of one year, you will owe the bank a total of ($1,000)(1.12) = $1,120 of principal plus accumulated interest. You make your first payment of $416.35 at that time. This reduces the net amount you owe to $1,120.00 − $416.35 = $703.65 as of the end of the first year (and the beginning of the second year). Another year goes by and an additional ($703.65)(0.12) = $84.43 of interest accumulates. The amount you then owe becomes $788.08, and you make a second payment of $416.35 at the end of the year. This reduces your outstanding balance to $371.73. Interest on that balance accumulates during the third year, and it happens that a $416.35 payment at the end of the year exactly takes care of the remaining amount of principal and interest due. *This* is why three annual cash flows of $416.35 each have the same value as $1,000.00 now, at a 12% opportunity cost. The bank has provided you with $1,000.00 initially, and it must receive future cash flows that have an equivalent value.

NON-ANNUAL COMPOUNDING AND DISCOUNTING

The illustrations we have just provided were set up in terms of annual loan payments. In most countries, however, installment loans are payable quarterly or monthly rather than only once a year. In addition, bank savings accounts generally

The Repayment Schedule on a Three-Year Installment Loan of $1,000, at a 12% Annual Interest Rate

FIGURE 5-8

Year	1	2	3
Amount Owed at Beginning of Year	$1,000.00	$703.65	$371.73
PLUS			
Interest Charged at 12% Annually	120.00	84.43	44.62
EQUALS			
Amount Owed at End of Year	$1,120.00	$788.08	$416.35
MINUS			
Amount Paid at End of Year	(416.35)	(416.35)	(416.35)
EQUALS			
Amount Owed at Beginning of Next Year	$ 703.65	$371.73	--

credit interest earnings more often than annually. A number of other investments have similar cash flow characteristics. Thus, we need to adapt the framework we have just outlined to the case of non-annual compounding and discounting periods.

The procedure is basically the same. The only thing to bear in mind is that *the opportunity cost or earnings rate must be defined to fit the time interval in question.* As an example, let us consider how a sum of money will accumulate in value over time if earnings on it are credited more often than just once a year. If the *annual* earnings rate is 12%, the corresponding quarterly and monthly rates will be

$$\text{Quarterly Rate} = 12\%/4 = 3\%$$
$$\text{Monthly Rate} = 12\%/12 = 1\%$$

and, within each year there will be four and twelve times, respectively, when earnings are realized.

Suppose we wanted to identify the future value of $1,000 invested now for a one-year period, with quarterly compounding at a 12% annual earnings rate. We would go to Table 5-6 and look up the compounding factor $CF_{K,N}$ for $K = 3\%$ and a time N that is four periods (four quarters) in the future. We would calculate that future value to be

$$FV_4 = (\$1,000)(CF_{0.03,4})$$
$$FV_4 = (\$1,000)(1.126) = \$1,126$$

If earnings accrued monthly, we would instead need the compounding factor $CF_{0.01,12}$ from Table I at the end of the text, since 12 compounding intervals at 1% per period would be involved. The result is

$$FV_{12} = (\$1,000)(CF_{0.01,12})$$
$$FV_{12} = (\$1,000)(1.127) = \$1,127$$

The effect of increasing the frequency of compounding can be seen by comparing these future values with the value that would be attained if compounding occurred only *once* during the year at a 12% rate. The relationship is shown in Table 5-10.

From our previous discussions, it should be clear why the end-of-year accumulated amount increases as the frequency of compounding increases. When earnings are credited quarterly, earnings are realized each quarter not only on the original investment of $1,000 but also on the *prior* quarters' earnings. When earnings are credited monthly, this bonus occurs twelve times each year. If we went to *daily* compounding, the impact would be even greater.

The result is that the *stated* earnings rate of 12% annually translates into a higher *effective* earnings rate under non-annual compounding, as follows:

The Effect of Non-Annual Compounding on the Future Value of a $1,000 Investment, at a 12% Annual Earnings Rate

TABLE 5-10

Frequency of Compounding	Periodic Earnings Rate	Number of Compounding Periods per Year	Future Value at the End of One Year
Annually	12%	1	$1,120
Quarterly	3%	4	1,126
Monthly	1%	12	1,127

Frequency of Compounding	Effective Earnings Rate
Annually	(1,120 − 1,000)/1,000 = 12.0%
Quarterly	(1,126 − 1,000)/1,000 = 12.6%
Monthly	(1,127 − 1,000)/1,000 = 12.7%

Effective Interest Rate The annual rate at which an investment grows in value when interest is credited more often than once a year.

Thus, monthly compounding produces the same outcome as if earnings were credited only once a year at 12.7%. This is why savings institutions commonly advertise both the stated and the corresponding **effective interest rates** they pay on deposits. We consider the ultimate case of *continuous* compounding in the Appendix to this chapter.

The same impact shows up—in reverse—on investment present values when we allow for non-annual discounting intervals. The present values of a $1,000 cash flow to be received one year from today, at a 12% annual opportunity cost, are shown in Table 5-11. The discounting factors for annual and quarterly discounting come from Table 5-7, and that for monthly discounting from Table III. The present values listed decline as the frequency of discounting increases, for the same reason future values grow: the *effective* discount rate increases.

We can extend the analysis in similar fashion to the cases of the future and present values of annuities as well. One of the questions posed at the beginning of this chapter illustrates the process. The issue was the choice between buying or renting a refrigerator for a two-year period. Let us assume the following facts:

Price of refrigerator	=	£300
Monthly rental fee	=	£12/month
Expected resale value of refrigerator, at the end of two years	=	£50
Opportunity cost	=	12% per annum

If the refrigerator is rented, the present value of the monthly rental fees will be

$$PV = (\text{Monthly Fee})(ADF_{0.01,24}) = (£12)(21.244) = £255$$

where the annuity discounting factor of 21.244 from Table IV reflects a 1% per month opportunity cost, and 24 required monthly payments. If the refrigerator is purchased, an immediate cash outflow of £300 occurs, but 24 months later an inflow of £50 is realized from the resale of the refrigerator. The *net* present value of the cost of purchasing therefore is

$$PV = £300 − (£50)(DF_{0.01,24}) = £300 − (£50)(0.788) = £261$$

On that basis, renting is a better idea because the present value of the cost of doing so is less.

The Effect of Non-Annual Discounting on the Present Value of a $1,000 Cash Flow to Be Received One Year From Today, at a 12% Annual Opportunity Cost

TABLE 5-11

Frequency of Discounting	Periodic Discount Rate	Number of Discounting Periods	Discounting Factor, DF	Present Value: ($1,000)(DF)
Annually	12%	1	$DF_{0.12,1} = 0.893$	$893
Quarterly	3%	4	$DF_{0.03,4} = 0.889$	$889
Monthly	1%	12	$DF_{0.01,12} = 0.887$	$887

Another way to approach the comparison would be to determine *how large* the resale value of the refrigerator would have to be in two years in order to make renting and buying *equally* attractive. Since the present value of the rental costs is £255, the purchase alternative would be acceptable as long as it imposed no greater cost. This would be the situation if

$$
\begin{aligned}
\text{PV of Renting} &= \text{PV of Buying} \\
£255 &= £300 - (\text{Resale Value})(0.788) \\
\text{Resale Value} &= (£300 - £255)/(0.788) \\
\text{Resale Value} &= £57
\end{aligned}
$$

Thus, if the refrigerator could be sold for any more than £57 at the end of two years, the purchase alternative would be preferred. Another common application of the same sort of analysis would be the decision whether to lease or buy an automobile. The answer, as in our case of a refrigerator, will depend on the automobile's initial cost, its projected resale value, and the required monthly lease payments.

As a final observation on non-annual discounting, notice the difference in present values between a series of 24 monthly payments and 2 annual payments. With a 12% annual opportunity cost, 24 monthly payments of £12 each have a present value of £255, as we saw. If instead the same *total* payments were made in two annual installments of $(12)(£12) = £144$ each, the present value of the cost would be

$$
\text{PV} = (£144)(\text{ADF}_{0.12,2}) = (£144)(1.690) = £243
$$

The monthly-payment present value is larger as a result of the net effect of two opposing influences. First, the effective discount rate is greater on a monthly basis, and this tends to reduce present value. Second, however, the average payment is made *sooner* on a monthly schedule than when payments are made only once at the end of each year. This increases their present value. The second influence outweighs the first here, as it will for any opportunity cost.

SPECIAL APPLICATIONS OF DISCOUNTING

Because so many financial decisions involve an immediate expenditure of funds in anticipation of receiving a set of future cash flows in return, the primary valuation technique that is employed in practice is the *discounting* procedure. The associated present value calculations are central to the identification of decisions that will *create* value for a firm's shareholders. We shall see a variety of such applications as we move from the underlying mathematics of time-value in this chapter to the examination of the valuation of corporate investment projects and corporate securities in later chapters. With that in mind, we turn now to some refinements of the basic present-value calculations that will become useful for those subsequent discussions.

Deferred Annuities

Among these refinements is the procedure for measuring the present value of what may be described as a *deferred annuity*. This is a series of equal annual cash flows that are expected to begin only after a few years' delay rather than in the coming year. As an example, consider the annuity that is described in Figure 5-9. The first payment of $1,000 is expected to be received at time t = 3 and then to continue for a total of five years, ending at time t = 7. We assume a 10% annual opportunity cost, and take the listed discounting factors from Table 5-7. If you have any remaining doubts as to where these factors come from, this would be a good time to check back to the table and satisfy yourself that we have the correct numbers.

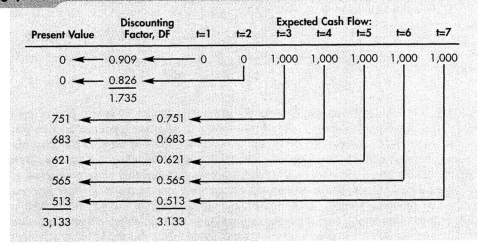

FIGURE 5-9 The Present Value of a Deferred Annuity, at a 10% Annual Opportunity Cost

Present Value	Discounting Factor, DF	t=1	t=2	Expected Cash Flow: t=3	t=4	t=5	t=6	t=7
0	0.909	0	0	1,000	1,000	1,000	1,000	1,000
0	0.826							
	1.735							
751	0.751							
683	0.683							
621	0.621							
565	0.565							
513	0.513							
3,133	3.133							

As the figure shows, the present value of the deferred annuity can be obtained in standard fashion by multiplying each cash flow by the appropriate individual discounting factor. We can take advantage again of the level annual cash flow property of an annuity, however, to simplify the process. Note that the sum of the discounting factors for the "missing" cash flows in the first two years is 1.735. If we add this to the sum of the factors for the five years when the annuity occurs, we get $1.735 + 3.133 = 4.868$ as the total. The latter figure is the annuity discounting factor $ADF_{0.10,7}$ for a *seven*-year annuity. Once more, you may wish to check the ADF tabulation in Table 5-9 to verify that statement.

Consequently, there is an easy way to measure the present value of a deferred annuity. We simply take the annuity discounting factor that applies to an annuity ending on the *last* date of the deferred annuity and subtract the annuity discounting factor for the years *prior* to the beginning of that annuity. In our example here, the calculation would be:

$$PV = (1,000)(ADF_{0.10,7} - ADF_{0.10,2})$$
$$PV = (1,000)(4.868 - 1.735)$$
$$PV = 3,133$$

Put differently, we first compute the value of the annuity *as if* it lasted the full seven years and then adjust for the fact that some early years' cash flows are missing.[3]

---

[3] There is another way to make the calculation as well. We could compute the present value of the annuity as of the beginning of the year it *starts*, and then bring that value back two more years to the present. In this form, we would have

$$PV_2 = (1,000)(ADF_{0.10,5})$$
$$PV_2 = (1,000)(3.791) = 3,791$$

3,791 is the time $t = 2$ present value of a five-year annuity running from $t = 3$ to $t = 7$. We then compute

$$PV_0 = (3,791)(DF_{0.10,2})$$
$$PV_0 = (3,791)(0.826) = 3,131$$

which is its present value at $t = 0$. The difference between this figure and 3,133 is due solely to rounding in the discounting factor tables. You may wish to test your understanding by explaining why this approach is conceptually equivalent.

Present Value of a Perpetuity

A **perpetuity** is the special case of an annuity that is expected to continue *forever*. Although it may be difficult to visualize such a cash flow stream, there are financial securities that provide level perpetual cash flows. Preferred or preference stock is one example. The "consol" bonds, which the British government issued during the Napoleonic Wars, are another. They have no specified maturity date and are not callable. More importantly, the concept of a perpetuity turns out to be fairly useful as a starting point for analyzing a variety of practical valuation problems, as we shall see later in this text. It also provides some additional insight into several of the basic valuation principles we have thus far discussed.

As is true of any set of cash flows, the present value of a perpetuity can be determined by discounting its cash flows back to today. Thus, we can express the present value of a $1 per year perpetuity as

$$PV = (\$1)(DF_{K,1}) + (\$1)(DF_{K,2}) + (\$1)(DF_{K,3}) + \ldots$$

where the DF are our standard individual cash flow discounting factors at the discount rate K. The series of dots at the end of this expression is a notation that

Perpetuity An annuity that is expected to continue forever.

■ Ethics ISSUES

LOTTERY PRIZES AND THE TIME VALUE OF MONEY

The previous *Issues* described the operation of prize brokers that purchase and resell winning lottery tickets. These firms contact lottery winners to remind them of their peculiar dilemma: the prize is paid out as an annuity over a long period of time. The following is an excerpt from a letter written by one of these firms to a lottery winner:

> "Winners like you have been given no choice but to let the lottery invest their prize money at one of the lowest possible yields and then wait for annual payments to be doled out over time like a child's allowance."

While the firms offer a valuable service by converting an annuity into an immediate single lump sum, there is a price paid by the lottery winner. The broker purchases the ticket at a substantial discount from the sum of the total annual payments offered by the lottery. In effect, the purchase of the ticket by the broker represents a loan to the lottery winner. The size of the discount determines the interest rate that the broker charges for this loan.

As an example, take the case of one individual who won over $1.3 million to be paid out in 20 equal annual installments of $65,277 each. After collecting the first eleven payments, the individual was contacted by a prize broker who offered to pay $140,000 for 50% of each of the remaining nine payments. That is, the firm offered $140,000 today in exchange for a total of ($65,277)(0.50)(9) = $293,747 over the next nine years. Equation (8) can be used to determine the opportunity cost involved in this transaction:

$$PV = (\text{Annual Prize Payment})(ADF_{K,N})$$
$$\$140,000 = \$32,639(ADF_{K,9})$$
$$ADF_{K,9} = \$140,000/32,639 = 4.289$$

From Table IV at the end of the text, we can find that $ADF_{0.18,9} = 4.303$. Thus, the purchase price of $140,000 implies that the discount rate is approximately 18%. In effect, the prize broker offered a loan of $140,000 at an annual interest rate of 18%. The federal Truth in Lending Act passed by Congress in 1968 requires lenders to state explicitly in a loan contract the interest rate charged on a consumer loan. That legislation, however, does not apply to prize brokers because the prize purchase is not technically a loan transaction. Given that the broker complained about the low interest rate offered by the lottery on the winner's funds, do you think that it is appropriate to conceal the high interest rate charged by the broker? Should legislation be passed to constrain the behavior of lottery prize brokers?

means that the calculations are to be repeated consecutively into the indefinite future, applying the appropriate discounting factors for subsequent years to each successive $1 annual cash flow.

An initial reaction to this calculation might be that the present value figure obtained would eventually become quite large as we continually keep adding the present value of yet another future cash flow to the total. For reasons that should by now be apparent, however, this is not the case. The farther in the future each successive cash flow becomes, the smaller its present value also becomes. Accordingly, we are continually adding a smaller and smaller number to the total as we move out in time. As we do so, it happens that the total approaches a *limiting* value, which is a quite definite figure for any discount rate K. Specifically, and conveniently, the limit is

$$PV = \$1/K$$

and *this* is the present value of a $1 per year perpetuity.[4] More generally, therefore,

Present Value of a Perpetuity = (Annual Cash Flow)/K   (9)

and we can use the notation $ADF_{K,\infty} = 1/K$ to refer to the *perpetuity discounting factor*.

There should be some intuitive appeal to this result. We have described the present value of any series of cash flows as the amount of money today that an investor would consider to be as valuable as the actual series of cash flows in question. Equivalently, the investor would be indifferent between having a sum of money today equal to that present value, or being promised the future cash flows. Let us look at the present value of a perpetuity from that perspective.

Suppose an investor's opportunity cost is 10% per annum. The present value of a $1 per year perpetuity is

$$PV = (\$1)/(0.10) = \$10$$

and we would conclude that having $10 in hand now is worth as much as being promised $1 a year forever. Why is this? Simply because, if the investor *had* $10 now, he or she could invest the funds to earn 10%, or $1, a year *forever*. The investor could take the $1 earned in the first year and spend or invest it someplace else, and *still* have the original $10 left to reinvest and earn $1 again the next year. This process could be repeated indefinitely (*in perpetuity*). For that reason, $10 available now is equal in value to $1 a year forever because $10 now could be *turned into* $1 a year forever at an earnings rate of 10% per annum. If instead the investor's opportunity cost were 20% per annum, it would only take $5 now to create a cash flow stream of $1 per year forever, and $5 would be the present value of the perpetuity.

We can relate this finding back to the figures listed in the annuity discounting factor (ADF) Table IV at the end of the text. At 10% and 20% opportunity costs, respectively, the present values of annuities of various durations are as follows:

---

[4] More formally, the present value of a $1 per year perpetuity can be represented as $PV = \sum_{t=1}^{\infty} 1/(1+K)^t$

where the "Σ" notation means "the sum of" all the present values $1/(1+K)$, $1/(1+K)^2$, $1/(1+K)^3$ and so on to infinity (forever). Mathematically, it is true that $\sum_{t=1}^{\infty} 1/(1+K)^t = 1/K$ as a standard result.

Annuity Duration	Present Value at Opportunity Cost of: 10%	20%
10 years	6.145	4.193
20 years	8.514	4.870
30 years	9.427	4.979
40 years	9.779	4.997
50 years	9.915	4.999

These values increase as the length of time over which the cash flows are expected to be received increases. Notice, however, that they increase at a diminishing rate, with most of the present value being accounted for by the early years' cash flows. We can see the values approaching the perpetuity values of $10.00 and $5.00 we have identified. At an opportunity cost of 10%, approximately 94% of the total present value of a perpetuity is attained by year 30, and over 99% by year 50. In the instance of a 20% opportunity cost, over 99% is attained by the year 30.

Analyses When the Present Value Is Given

A present value calculation depends on three elements: (1) the size of the expected future cash flows; (2) the length of time over which they are expected to be received; and (3) the discount rate, or opportunity cost, of the investor. Up to this point, we have typically taken these three elements as known inputs and have concentrated on determining the implied present values. There are a range of valuation problems in practice, however, where the present value is given and one of the other three elements is the unknown.

Unknown Annuity. We looked briefly at one such problem when we considered the case of an installment loan. If the required amount of the loan is given, and we know both the proposed duration of the payments and the annual interest rate to be charged, we can determine the *size* of the annual payments that will repay the loan. Because an installment loan is an annuity whose present value is equal to the amount initially borrowed, the relevant equation is:

$$PV = \text{Loan Amount} = (\text{Annual Payment})(\text{ADF}_{K,N})$$

In the instance of an SF100,000 loan payable in twelve equal annual installments at a 9% interest rate, we have:

$$SF100,000 = (\text{Annual Payment})(\text{ADF}_{0.09,12}) = (\text{Annual Payment})(7.161)$$
$$\text{Annual Payment} = SF13,965$$

where the annuity discounting factor $\text{ADF}_{0.09,12}$ is from Table IV. We showed earlier in Figure 5-8 how these annual payments completely take care of the repayment of principal and the interest costs on the loan over its life. In our discussion of non-annual discounting periods, we also showed how similar calculations can be made for the case of *monthly* loan payments.

Unknown Duration. A parallel situation would be one in which a specified amount is to be borrowed at a given rate of interest, but the borrower has a limit on the size of the annual payment he or she is able to make. The same fundamental valuation equation applies, but now the required *duration* of the payments that will repay the loan is the unknown. In the case of an £8,000 loan, an 11% interest rate, and a specified ceiling of £2,000 on the annual payments, the necessary condition is that:

$$PV = £8,000 = (£2,000)(\text{ADF}_{0.11,N})$$
$$\text{ADF}_{0.11,N} = 4.000$$

We therefore need to look down the 11% opportunity cost column in Table IV to find how many years' (N) worth of payments correspond to an $ADF_{0.11,N}$ equal to 4.000. At five years of payments the ADF is 3.696 and at six years the ADF is 4.231. The answer then is somewhere between five and six years.

We can estimate the required period more closely by "interpolating" between the five-year and six-year ADF values. Thus, we need to go from 3.696 at five years to 4.000 to get the needed annuity present value. That is a difference of 4.000 – 3.696 = 0.304. The *total* difference between the five-year and six-year ADF values is 4.231 – 3.696 = 0.535. Accordingly, the correct payment period is approximately

$$0.304/0.535 = 0.57$$

or 57% of the way into the sixth year. This tells us that the £2,000 payment will be required for 5.57 years in order to repay the £8,000 loan originally received.

Among the possible additional applications of this approach would be a situation in which a corporation was making an investment in a piece of labor-saving equipment. The firm's financial managers might wish to determine how *long* a period it would take in order for the present value of the future annual savings to equal the initial cost of the equipment. One could think of this as a kind of break even condition on the investment. We shall have more to say about that sort of analysis in subsequent chapters.

The Rule of 72. A variant on the issue of unknown duration is what is commonly referred to as the "Rule of 72." If you examine the present value discounting factors $DF_{K,N}$ for a single $1 future cash flow in Table III, you will find at least one remarkably consistent pattern. For every combination of K and N for which $K \times N = 72$, the discounting factor is very close to 0.500. For example:

K	N	$DF_{K,N}$
3%	24	0.492
4%	18	0.494
6%	12	0.497
8%	9	0.500
9%	8	0.502
12%	6	0.507

What this implies is that if K is the opportunity cost, a cash flow that is expected to be received N = 72/K years in the future will have a present value equal to half its expected t = N amount. It loses half its value by being deferred until N years from today.

We can turn that observation around and make a corresponding statement about compounding. By definition,

$$DF_{K,N} = 1/(1+K)^N$$
$$CF_{K,N} = (1+K)^N$$

Therefore:

$$CF_{K,N} = 1/(DF_{K,N}) \qquad (10)$$

Consequently, when $DF_{K,N}$ is equal to 0.500, then $CF_{K,N}$ is equal to 2.000. This means that an investment of $1 made today will grow in value with reinvestment of earnings to approximately $2 in the future for all combinations of K and N for which $K \times N = 72$. You could check this conclusion by examining the compounding factors in Table I for the same combinations of K and N listed above that produce a discounting factor that is close to 0.500.

You thereby have an easy rule of thumb for your personal investment planning. You can expect a sum of money that is deposited in a savings account *now* to double in value when the product of the interest rate you are earning and the number of years the money is left on deposit is equal to 72. This turns out to be a very good approximation for interest rates of 12% and below.

Unknown Discount Rate.   At times, the decision problem is one in which there is a specified present value and a given series of expected future cash flows. The unknown to be solved for then is the discount rate that will cause the cash flows to have the requisite present value. A circumstance in which you are requesting a loan and the bank tells you how large your annual payments will be fits this case. What you would be attempting to determine would be the implied *interest rate* on the loan. Alternatively, you are making an investment and you know the future cash flows it is expected to produce. Your objective is to find the implied *earnings rate* on the investment.

We saw an example of the latter situation earlier, although we analyzed it in a different way. Recall the case of a deutschemark bond investment where the bond cost DM1,000 and provided a single DM2,840 payment at the end of ten years. At an opportunity cost of 10% per annum, we found the present value of that payment to be

$$(DM2,840)(DF_{0.10,10}) = (DM2,840)(0.386) = DM1,096$$

and concluded that the bond was a good investment because the present value of the cash flow it promised exceeded the initial cost of acquiring it.

We can also find the "yield," or earnings rate, on the same investment by determining what discount rate K will cause the DM2,840 payment to have a present value equal to the initial outlay of DM1,000. The condition is

$$(DM2,840)(DF_{K,10}) = DM1,000$$
$$(DF_{K,10}) = (DM1,000)/(DM2,840) = 0.352$$

and we seek the discount rate at which the discounting factor for a 10-year future cash flow receipt equals the 0.352 necessary for the indicated condition to hold. From either Table 5-7 or Table III, it turns out that $DF_{0.11,10} = 0.352$ and therefore the implied earnings rate is 11% per annum. Equivalently, an investment now of DM1,000 will grow in value to DM2,840 by the end of ten years at an 11% annual compounding rate. We can refer to the 11% as the *rate of return* on the investment. Not surprisingly, this rate of return exceeds the investor's opportunity cost. Thus, if DM1,096 is the present value of the future cash flow at a 10% discount rate, some *higher* discount rate is needed to reduce the present value to DM1,000.

The same procedure would be followed if there were multiple expected future cash flows. As an illustration, let us examine the one remaining unanswered question we raised at the beginning of the chapter. A borrower was offered a choice between a 15-year $100,000 home mortgage loan at an interest rate of 10% per annum, and one at a stated interest rate of 9% but with three points deducted from the initial amount of the loan as an added financing fee. For the sake of convenience, let us assume that the installment payments on the loan are to be made just once a year, in order that we can use our standard annual present-value tables.

In the case of the 10% loan, the required annual payments over 15 years would be:

$$PV = \$100,000 = (\text{Annual Payment})(ADF_{0.10,15})$$
$$\$100,000 = (\text{Annual Payment})(7.606)$$
$$\text{Annual Payment} = \$13,148$$

For the alternative loan, the corresponding annual payments would be established by using 9% as the interest rate on a *presumed* $100,000 loan, as follows:

$$PV = \$100,000 = (\text{Annual Payment})(ADF_{0.09,15})$$
$$\$100,000 = (\text{Annual Payment})(8.061)$$
$$\text{Annual Payment} = \$12,405$$

However, the actual amount of the loan provided would be only $97,000 because of the deduction of three points initially. (One point equals 1% of the stated loan amount.)

The question therefore is: what interest rate is actually being charged on a $97,000 loan that requires 15 annual payments of $12,405? Obviously, the true rate is higher than 9% per annum. It can be determined from the present-value matching condition that

$$PV = \$97,000 = (\$12,405)(ADF_{K,15})$$
$$ADF_{K,15} = 7.819$$

Since this annuity discounting factor lies between the ADF for a true 9% interest rate (8.061) and that for a true 10% rate (7.606), we know that the actual interest rate being paid is somewhere between 9% and 10%. We therefore know immediately that the loan with the points deducted is the less expensive loan. We could approximate the specific interest rate by interpolating between the ADF values for 9% and 10%. The approximation would be:

$$\frac{ADF_{0.09,1.5} - ADF_{K,15}}{ADF_{0.09,1.5} - ADF_{0.10,15}} = \frac{8.061 - 7.819}{8.061 - 7.606} = 0.53$$

This indicates an interest rate of about 9.5% as the true rate on the loan. As demonstrated at the end of the text, your business calculator or your personal computer could perform all these computations efficiently, without the need for the present-value tables we have been using here. It's important, however, to understand what is going on conceptually with the computations. For that reason, we shall continue to refer to the tables for most subsequent analyses as well.

THE INTERPRETATION OF PRESENT AND FUTURE VALUES

We conclude our discussion of the mathematics of the time value of money with a final illustration to emphasize the interpretation of present and future values. Consider an investment that provides the series of expected cash flows shown in Figure 5-10. They are evaluated at an 8% annual opportunity cost. Given the values shown, we can describe this investment in either of three *economically equivalent ways*:

1. It is expected to produce three consecutive annual cash flows of $1,000, $3,000, and $2,000.
2. It has a future value at t = 3 of $6,406, at an 8% annual earnings rate.
3. It has a present value of $5,085, at an 8% annual discount rate.

The reason (1) and (2) are equivalent is because the three cash flows, when received, can be invested at an 8% annual earnings rate to accumulate in value to $6,406 by the end of three years. The reason (1) and (3) are equivalent is because an investor who had $5,085 in hand now could invest that sum at an 8% annual earnings rate and *reproduce* the three future cash flows.[5] The reason (2) and (3) are equivalent is because an investor who had $5,085 in hand now could invest that sum at an 8% annual earnings rate and have it accumulate to $6,406 at the end of three years.

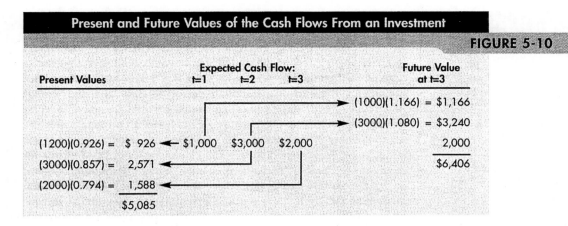

Present and Future Values of the Cash Flows From an Investment

FIGURE 5-10

The investor, therefore, would be *indifferent* between: (1) being promised the indicated three cash flows; (2) being given $5,085 immediately; or (3) being given $6,406 in three years. That's what the computations mean, and that's what the time value of money is all about.

KEY SYMBOLS USED IN COMPOUNDING AND DISCOUNTING

To review our standard notation, we established the following terminology:

FV_N	Future value of a single cash flow or an annuity as of time $t = N$.	$ACF_{K,N}$	Compounding factor for an annuity of N periods duration at an earnings rate of K.
K	The investor's opportunity cost expressed as a percent per period. K is commonly referred to as the discount rate when discounting and the earnings rate when compounding.	PV	Present value of a single cash flow or an annuity.
		$DF_{K,N}$	Discounting factor for a single cash flow that is expected to be received N periods in the future, at the discount rate K.
$CF_{K,N}$	Compounding factor for a single cash flow invested at an earnings rate of K for N periods.	$ADF_{K,N}$	Discounting factor for an annuity of N years duration, at the discount rate K.

SUMMARY

This chapter introduced the concept of the time value of money as the fundamental basis for developing decision rules that will allow financial managers to create value for their firms' shareholders. In order to be able to make value-maximizing decisions, managers must first understand how investors perceive and measure value. The value of any investment depends upon the size and the timing of the cash flows it is expected to generate. Timing is important because investors have alternative investment opportunities on which they can earn a return. Thus, the time value of money depends on investors' opportunity costs. Differences in the amount and the timing of cash flows require compounding or discounting calculations in order to make the value of those cash flows comparable. The two

---

[5] Thus, if the investor started out with $5,085 now, an 8% earnings rate would cause this sum to grow to ($5,085)(1.08) = $5,492 by the end of one year. The investor could withdraw $1,000 from that accumulated fund, leaving $4,492 to invest the second year. At time t = 2, this would have accumulated to ($4,492)(1.08) = $4,851. A withdrawal of $3,000 would leave $1,851 to invest during the third year. At an 8% earnings rate, the amount available at the end of the third year would in fact be $2,000. The investor's funds would therefore be exhausted by withdrawing the last $2,000 to match the full series of cash flows from the investment.

chapter equations

1. $FV_N = (\text{Cash Flow})(1 + K)^N$

2. $FV_N = (\text{Cash Flow})(CF_{K,N})$

3. $PV = (\text{Cash Flow})/(1 + K)^N$

4. $PV = (\text{Cash Flow})(DF_{K,N})$

5. $FV_N = (PV)(1 + K)^N$

6. $FV_N = (PV)(CF_{K,N})$

7. $FV_N = (\text{Annual Cash Flow})(ACF_{K,N})$

8. $PV = (\text{Annual Cash Flow})(ADF_{K,N})$

9. PV of a Perpetuity = $(\text{Annual Cash Flow})/K$

10. $CF_{K,N} = 1/(DF_{K,N})$

procedures move cash flows through time while maintaining their equivalence.

The compounding procedure moves cash flows forward in time to arrive at their future values. The future value of an investment represents the amount to which its cash flows will accumulate with earnings at the end of a specified period of time. The discounting procedure moves cash flows backward in time to arrive at their present value. The present value of an investment represents the amount of money today that is as valuable as the cash flows from the investment. Present and future values can be calculated either for single cash flows or for streams of cash flows. Streams that consist of equal cash flows each period are called annuities. An annuity that is expected to last forever is called a perpetuity. Although the normal time period used in discounting and compounding is a year, present and future values can also be calculated for non-annual discounting and compounding periods, by adjusting the cash flows and the discount or earnings rate to fit the period in question.

The usefulness of the discounting procedure to financial managers arises from two sources. First, the procedure allows managers to use the opportunity cost of the firm's owners to evaluate the impact of both the timing and the amount of the cash flows from any investment proposal. Second, the computation enables managers to represent the value of the expected future cash flows from any investment by a single number—their present value. This number can then be compared to the present values of other investments for decision-making purposes.

CONTENT QUESTIONS

1. Explain what is meant by the time value of money.
2. Why is it important to possess an analytical technique that allows us to adjust the value of cash flows for differences in timing?
3. Differentiate between compounding and discounting.
4. Explain how the compounding factor and discounting factor are affected by changes in the opportunity cost and the number of periods.
5. Define an annuity and a perpetuity.
6. How are the elements of Table III and Table IV in the back of the text related? (Give an example.)
7. Explain the adjustments required to solve problems in which the frequency of compounding is other than yearly.
8. Explain the similarities and differences among the following:
   - a. time value of money
   - b. opportunity cost of funds
   - c. interest rate
   - d. discount rate
   - e. earnings rate
9. Describe the effect of an increase in the discount rate on the discounting factor for a single sum and for an annuity.
10. Describe the effect of an increase in the number of time periods on the discounting factor for a single sum and for an annuity.

CONCEPT QUESTIONS

1. The question as to whether to lease or buy an asset is a common business and personal decision problem. Under what set of circumstances would you

expect to find leasing to be less expensive than buying? Think about the situation of both the lessee and lessor in answering that question.

2. Suppose you are accumulating funds in a savings account for your retirement. To date, the economy of your country has been characterized by relatively low inflation rates. Inflation, however, now begins to increase substantially. Should this make it easier or more difficult to save enough to retire comfortably?

3. We described the Rule of 72 in our discussion in this chapter. From the compounding factor (CF) and discounting factor (DF) Tables I and III at the end of the text, can you suggest any other similar generalizable rules that seem to hold?

4. Draw a graph, similar to that in Figure 5-3, of the relationship between the present value of a $1 per year annuity and the duration of that annuity, for a given discount rate. Graph the same relationship for any higher discount rate. Why do the curves appear as they do?

5. We discussed how to determine the true interest rate on a loan for which the lender deducted points initially as a financing fee. The objective was to compare the interest cost with that of another loan with no points. What would be an alternative way to decide which loan was preferable?

PROBLEMS

1. What amount received at the end of 10 years is equivalent to $1,000 today?
   a. given an opportunity cost of 2%   b. given an opportunity cost of 10%

2. What amount received at the end of 10 years is equivalent to $1,000 received at the end of each year for 10 years?
   a. given an opportunity cost of 2%   b. given an opportunity cost of 10%

3. What present amount is equivalent to $1,000 to be received at the end of 10 years?
   a. given an opportunity cost of 2%   b. given an opportunity cost of 10%

4. What present amount is equivalent to $1,000 to be received at the end of each year for 10 years?
   a. given an opportunity cost of 2%   b. given an opportunity cost of 10%

5. What amount is equivalent to $1,000 today given an opportunity cost of 10%
   a. if received at the end of 1 year?   b. if received at the end of 10 years?

6. Given an opportunity cost of 10%, what is the future value of a $1,000 annuity
   a. for 1 year?   b. for 10 years?

7. Given an opportunity cost of 10%, what present amount is equivalent to $1,000 to be received at the end of:
   a. 1 year?   b. 10 years?

8. Given an opportunity cost of 10%, what is the present value of a $1,000 annuity:
   a. for 1 year?   b. for 10 years?

9. What is the present value of $1,000 to be received at the end of each year forever:
   a. given an opportunity cost of 2%?   b. given an opportunity cost of 10%?

10. Credit Corp. charges interest of 2% per month on its consumer loans. What is the APR of its loans? What is the effective annual interest rate?

11. What is the future value in two years of $1,000 deposited in a savings account paying an annual rate of 12% compounded monthly?

12. Find the present value of $1,000:
    a. to be received at the end of 2 years at 12% compounded quarterly.
    b. to be received at the end of 4 years at 12% compounded semiannually.

13. Francel Motors knows that it will need FF500,000 at the end of 10 years to repay a loan. Starting at the end of the first year, how much will Francel have

to deposit each year into an account that pays 8% interest to accumulate that amount?

14. Given a 15% opportunity cost, which is worth more:
    a. $1.00 now or $2.00 six years from now?
    b. $1.00 three years from now or $2.00 nine years from now?

15. Given an opportunity cost (or discount rate) of 12%, which is more valuable: an annuity of DM1,000 per year for 10 years or a lump sum of DM16,000 received at the end of 10 years?

16. Given a 10% discount rate, find the present value of a cash flow stream of $100 at the end of the first year, $200 at the end of the second, $300 at the end of the third, and $400 at the end of the fourth.

17. Given the cash flow stream and discount rate of Problem 16, calculate the single amount that is equivalent in value to that stream:
    a. if received one year from today?   b. if received three years from today?

18. What is the present value of a 10-year annuity of $3,000 per year if the cash flows begin at the end of the third year? Use a discount rate of 10%.

19. Find the present value of a cash flow stream that promises $2,000 per year for the first 10 years and $3,000 per year for the following 10 years, given a discount rate of 12%.

20. Given a 14% discount rate, find the present value of the following cash flow stream:

Year	Amount
1	SF150
2–10	300
11	–200
12	0
13–19	300
20	1,000

21. What equal annual payment is needed to repay a £50,000 loan at 12% interest over 20 years?

22. You loaned your brother $100, and two years later he repaid $121.00.
    a. What rate of interest did you charge?
    b. What rate of return did you earn on the $100 you invested in your brother?

23. A bank has loaned a company FF1,000,000. The company has promised to repay the bank by making 15 annual installments of FF124,054 each. To what rate of interest did the company agree?

24. Approximately how long does it take for a sum to double in value at an interest rate of 15%?

25. Prepare the repayment schedule for a $10,000 loan at 10% interest. The loan is repaid in equal installments at the end of each year over 5 years (Don't worry if your table is not exactly correct because the discount factors, by necessity, have been rounded off).

26. Frank Tepper will retire in 10 years and wishes to set up a personal savings plan to supplement his employer's pension plan. Frank will deposit £2,000 at the end of each of those 10 years into an account earning 8%.
    a. How much would he have in the account after the last payment is made?
    b. What is the most that he could withdraw in equal amounts over 10 years, starting 1 year after the last payment has been made into the account?

27. Lane Manufacturing can purchase a new machine for $240,000 that is expected to generate cash savings of $60,000 per year for the next five years due to

lower direct labor costs. Assuming an opportunity cost of 10%, should Lane purchase the machine or continue to bear the higher labor expense?

28. You have just inherited SF100,000. You have two investment alternatives. Which alternative is best (assuming they are of equal risk)?

    Alternative 1. Invest SF100,000 in real estate. You estimate that in 10 years you will be able to sell out for SF440,500.

    Alternative 2. Lend SF100,000 to a business associate and be repaid in 10 equal annual installments of SF19,170 each.

29. You have budgeted $300 per month to purchase an automobile. You can obtain a 4-year new car loan for an effective interest rate of 12%. Assuming that you must finance all of the purchase price, what is the most that you can spend on a new car and stay within budget?

30. To celebrate 75 years in business, Riverside Furniture is offering 0% financing on any purchase. Alternatively, you can obtain a 6% discount if purchasing with cash. Is this really a 0% loan? If not, what is the effective interest rate?

31. You have just won the $28,000,000 superbowl lotto. The winnings are paid in 20 equal annual installments. The first payment is tomorrow. You have been contacted by a financial service company that is willing to trade an immediate single lump sum for your 20 payments. What lump sum would be acceptable to you if you had an 8% opportunity rate?

32. You have the choice between leasing a new car for $600 per month for 2 years or purchasing it for $40,000. The estimated value of the car at the end of the 2 years is $30,000. If your opportunity cost is 12%, should the car be leased or purchased?

33. Returning to problem 32, you realize that determining the value of a car 3 years from now is a difficult task. You also realize that resale price is critical to a lease versus buy decision. Consequently, you would like to know the resale price that would make you indifferent between leasing or purchasing. What is that price?

34. Lefty McNuckle, a relief pitcher, just signed a multiyear contract designed to provide lifetime security. The newspaper headlines said it was worth $60 million. On signing, Lefty received a $15,000,000 signing bonus. In the next 5 years, he gets $4,000,000 per year. For 5 years after that he will get $3,000,000 per year. For another 20 years, he will get $500,000 per year. What is the contract's present value if Lefty has an annual opportunity cost of 14%?

35. You have just deposited $100,000 in a bank account paying 7% interest per year. Approximately how long will you have to wait for your money to double? Use the Rule of 72.

36. You just turned 25 years old and are planning for retirement on your sixty-fifth birthday. Starting on your sixty-sixth birthday, you would like to be able to withdraw $50,000 per year indefinitely from a savings account paying 8% interest that you just opened.

    a. What lump sum would you have to place in the account *today* in order to be able to fulfill your retirement plans?

    b. What amount would you need to deposit in the account *each* year through age 65, starting one year from today, in order to fulfill your retirement plans?

    c. You own a $100,000 Treasury note that matures in 10 years. You will deposit the proceeds from the note into the account in addition to your annual savings. What additional amount of savings would you need to deposit into the account each year, starting one year from today, in order to fulfill your plans?

http://

INTERNET EXERCISE

Test your time value of money knowledge on the quiz at this Web site. Print out the results, and submit to your instructor. http://fpc.net66.com/tvmtest.html

SELF-STUDY QUIZ

1. You have just deposited $5,000 into a savings account that pays 12%. What will be the balance in the account after two years:
   a. if interest is compounded annually?
   b. if interest is compounded monthly?
2. What is the effective interest rate for the accounts in Problems 1a and 1b?
3. You are the beneficiary of a trust fund that will pay you $400,000 eight years from today. What is the present value of that fund:
   a. if your opportunity cost is 12% per annum?
   b. if your opportunity cost is 10.75% per annum?
4. Find the present value of an annuity that pays $2,000 per year for nine years:
   a. if your opportunity cost is 12% per annum.
   b. if your opportunity cost is 10.75% per annum.
5. You have borrowed $75,000 from a bank. You will repay the loan in equal monthly payments over the next two years. What is the monthly payment:
   a. if the effective interest rate is 12% per annum?
   b. if the effective interest rate is 18% per annum?

APPENDIX: CONTINUOUS COMPOUNDING AND DISCOUNTING

As mentioned in this chapter, the definition of the time period for compounding and discounting calculations is completely general. It can vary from a year to, *in the limit*, zero! By "in the limit" we mean that the time period approaches zero, while never quite getting there. When the time period approaches zero, the frequency of compounding increases toward infinity. This condition is called continuous compounding.

Continuous compounding is used in practice by savings institutions and is often required in theoretical work in finance. Consequently, it is useful to understand how to discount and compound cash flows under the assumption that the frequency of compounding approaches infinity. If we let K denote an *annually* compounded rate of interest, the standard equations in this chapter can be rewritten to accommodate different frequencies of compounding:

$$FV_N = (\text{Cash Flow})\left(1 + \frac{K}{M}\right)^{NM} \qquad (5A\text{-}1)$$

$$FV_N = (\text{Cash Flow})CF_{K/M,NM} \qquad (5A\text{-}2)$$

where M is the frequency of compounding (the number of times per year that interest is compounded). Equations (5A-1) and (5A-2) contain the adjustments that we described in the chapter. That is, the annual interest rate is *divided* by the frequency of compounding (K/M), and the number of periods is *multiplied* by the frequency of compounding (NM).

A glance at equation (5A-1) does not reveal what happens as M becomes extremely large. While the term K/M decreases toward zero, the exponent NM increases toward infinity. Mathematically, these two opposing effects balance out, and equation (5A-1) converges to another equation as M approaches infinity:

$$FV_N = (\text{Cash Flow})\left[\lim_{M \to \infty}\left(1 + \frac{K}{M}\right)^{NM}\right] = (\text{Cash Flow})e^{KN} \qquad (5A\text{-}3)$$

The term "e" is a constant whose value is approximately 2.71828. This constant is of considerable importance to mathematics, engineering, economics, and finance as a result of its unique properties and its variety of applications. Table 5A-1 shows the limit that an annual interest rate of 12% approaches as the frequency of compounding approaches infinity. The first four future values shown were calculated with equation (5A-1). The effective interest rate represents the earnings rate that is realized over the course of a year with more frequent compounding Since tables and calculators exist that provide values of e raised to any power, the future value in one year of $1.00 compounded continuously at 12% per year can be calculated with equation (5A-3) as follows:

$$FV_1 = (\$1.00)(e^{0.12}) = (\$1.00)(1.1275) = \$1.1275$$

Conversely, a sum may be *discounted* continuously. Equation (5A-3) can be easily transformed to calculate the present value of future amounts:

$$PV = (\text{Cash Flow})\frac{1}{e^{KN}} = (\text{Cash Flow})\,e^{-KN} \qquad (5A\text{-}4)$$

As an illustration, the present value of $1,000 to be received two years from today at 12% compounded continuously is

$$PV = (\$1,000)(e^{-0.12 \times 2}) = (\$1,000)(e^{-0.24}) = (\$1,000)(0.787) = \$787$$

For comparison, the present value of $1,000 to be received in two years at 12% interest compounded annually is

$$PV = (\$1,000)(0.797) = \$797$$

The difference between these two present values is fairly small due to the short time interval of two years. As the time interval lengthens, the effect of continuous compounding on the present value of a future cash flow becomes increasingly significant.

The Limit on the Effective Interest Rate as the Frequency of Compounding Approaches Infinity

TABLE 5A-1

Compounding Interval	Compounding Frequency (Times per Year)	Future Value			Effective Interest Rate
Annual	1	$(\$1.00)\left(1 + \frac{0.12}{1}\right)^{1}$	$= (1.00)(1.12)$	$= \$1.120$	12.00%
Semiannual	2	$(1.00)\left(1 + \frac{0.12}{2}\right)^{2}$	$= (1.00)(1.124)$	$= 1.124$	12.40%
Quarterly	4	$(1.00)\left(1 + \frac{0.12}{4}\right)^{4}$	$= (1.00)(1.126)$	$= 1.126$	12.60%
Monthly	12	$(1.00)\left(1 + \frac{0.12}{12}\right)^{12}$	$= (1.00)(1.127)$	$= 1.127$	12.70%
Continuously	—	$(1.00)(e^{0.12})$	$= (1.00)(1.1275)$	$= 1.1275$	12.75%

Investment Value and Required Rates of Return

When financial managers acquire funds from the capital market and commit those funds to corporate investments, they are acting as agents for their firms' common shareholders. The managers' responsibility is to make investments that will increase the value of the firm *to* the shareholders. We saw in the last chapter that the key determinants of value are cash flows and investors' opportunity costs. If a firm's managers are to make appropriate investment decisions, therefore, they must be able to identify and quantify both of these determinants.

Our purpose in this chapter is to provide the conceptual framework for that identification process, with particular emphasis on opportunity costs. As you shall see, differences among investments in the *risks* they cause investors to bear define the opportunity costs that are relevant to an appraisal of investment values. A "good" investment is one whose potential returns are large enough to compensate for the associated risks. In order to translate that notion into a workable guide to managerial decision-making, we require answers to the following sorts of questions:

- How should risk be measured, and does it depend on who is doing the measuring?

- Are there factors other than an investment's *own* characteristics that determine how much risk it causes investors to bear? If so, what are these factors?

- To what extent are an investment's risks specific to the firm that is considering the investment?

- What role does diversification play in affecting investment risk?

• As a long-run average, investors in the United States have earned a return of over 14% annually from investments in common stocks and about 6% annually from investments in government securities. Why then would investors continue to buy government securities?

As a basis for answering these questions, we introduce in this chapter an Investment Valuation Model (IVM), which can be applied to virtually all of a firm's financing and investing decisions. The model is designed to address the goal of value maximization, which was established in Chapter 1, and to capture the fundamental risk/return decision trade-off discussed in that chapter. It relies on the mathematics of the time value of money described in Chapter 5 and concentrates specifically on measuring the *present value* of a proposed investment.

The IVM can be thought of as a "cost/benefit" model. Consistent with our earlier discussions, it recognizes that the size and the timing of cash flows from an investment are critical to the investment's value. Those cash flows are the benefit component of the model.

The cost component is represented by investors' opportunity costs. We expand here on the definition of that cost to include *risk* as a key element in its determination. The complete description of the opportunity cost K which is applicable in appraising a given investment's value is: The return which is available from alternative investments of *comparable risk*. This is the *required rate of return* (RRR) on the investment. That required return will depend upon several underlying factors: the rate of return available from risk-free investments; the degree of uncertainty associated with the investment's expected future cash flows; and the extent of investors' aversion to risk. As this implies, it is how *investors* perceive and measure value, given their investment alternatives, which is central to the firm's decisions on their behalf.

We summarize the content and scope of the Investment Valuation Model in Figure 6-1. The notation Value = f(Returns, Risk) means that value is a *function of* (value depends upon) both returns and risk. The figure provides an overview of the topics we shall be addressing in this chapter. We begin our discussion with an examination of the characteristics of an investment.

DEFINITION OF AN INVESTMENT

Not all expenditures of funds qualify as investments. Individuals have two choices regarding the use of their money: consumption in the satisfaction of *current* needs or saving in order to satisfy *future* needs. An individual's willingness to sacrifice current consumption should be directly related to the promise of higher future consumption. A return that is large enough to induce an investor to give up current consumption must provide compensation for two things:

• The sacrifice involved in deferring consumption
• The uncertainty the investor sees in the anticipated return.

This relationship between the act of saving and promised returns provides the basis for the formal definition of an investment. An **investment** is the commitment of a known amount today for a specific period of time in return for anticipated future benefits. The benefits must exceed the initial commitment by enough to compensate the investor for the time the funds are committed and for the uncertainty regarding the realization of the future benefits. This definition is purposely general in order that the concept of an investment encompasses a wide range of activities.

Investment The commitment of a known amount today for a specific period of time in return for anticipated future benefits.

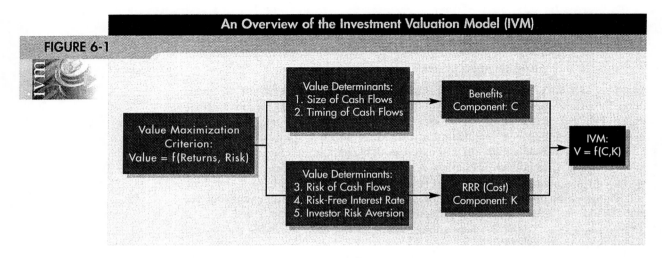

FIGURE 6-1

An Overview of the Investment Valuation Model (IVM)

DETERMINANTS OF INVESTMENT VALUE

The definition also reflects a number of fundamental factors that determine the value of an investment:

1. The size of the anticipated future benefits;
2. The timing of the benefits;
3. The riskiness of the benefits;
4. The risk-free interest rate;
5. Investor risk aversion.

As shown in Figure 6-2, the first three factors are attributes of the *investment* being evaluated, while the last two are characteristics of *investors*. Since each of these determinants plays a key role in the valuation process, we will examine them in more detail.

Size of Anticipated Benefits

The cause-and-effect relationship between the value of an investment and the magnitude of its anticipated returns is straightforward. An investor is giving up current consumption for the expectation of higher consumption at some later date. Clearly, the larger the future returns that are expected to be received, the greater the future consumption possibilities. When the other determinants of value are held constant, therefore, *an increase in the anticipated benefits will increase the value of the investment.*

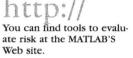

You can find tools to evaluate risk at the MATLAB'S Web site.

http://finprod.mathworks.com

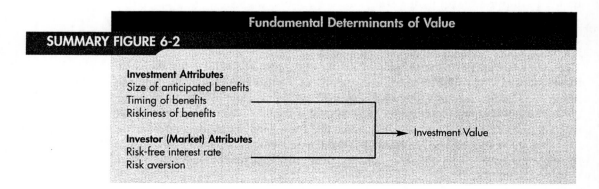

SUMMARY FIGURE 6-2

Fundamental Determinants of Value

Investment Attributes
Size of anticipated benefits
Timing of benefits
Riskiness of benefits

Investor (Market) Attributes
Risk-free interest rate
Risk aversion

→ Investment Value

Timing of Benefits

The sacrifice of current consumption in favor of the opportunity for greater future consumption becomes less attractive to a rational individual the longer the time until the future consumption can take place. Not only do investors give up consumption opportunities while they are waiting for the expected cash benefits, but they also give up the chance of committing their wealth to other investment opportunities in the meantime. Holding all other determinants constant, *the longer the wait for the anticipated benefits, the less valuable is an investment.*

Riskiness of Benefits

Given the ever-changing nature of human affairs, *any* forecast of the future must be viewed as being uncertain. Moreover, proposed investments can vary considerably with respect to the relative confidence investors have that the anticipated future benefits will actually materialize. The promise of a return from an insured deposit in a bank savings account, for example, is much more certain than the promise of a return from exploring for new petroleum deposits.

It is this uncertainty about the realization of future benefits from an investment that is defined as **investment risk**. The greater the uncertainty, the riskier the investment. In general, investors prefer certainty of benefits to uncertainty. An investor who must choose between two investments that promise equally large benefits will pay more for the alternative with the more certain benefits. When the other determinants of value are held constant, *the value of an investment decreases as its uncertainty of benefits (riskiness) increases.*

Investment Risk The uncertainty about the future benefits to be realized from an investment.

The Risk-Free Interest Rate

Even if an investor is certain that the committed funds will be returned at some future date, the investor will demand compensation for sacrificing current consumption. The form that this compensation takes is the interest rate available on a relatively riskless investment such as a security issued by the national government. Since there is no realistic chance of default on such a security, the return it promises compensates the investor only for the temporary sacrifice of consumption associated with owning it. Consequently, the basic return required for foregoing current consumption is called the **risk-free interest rate**. As you shall soon see, there is a negative relationship between the risk-free rate and value. *The higher the risk-free interest rate, the lower the value of an investment.*

Risk-Free Interest Rate The return to an investor in a risk-free security. The risk-free interest rate compensates the investor for the temporary sacrifice of consumption.

Risk Aversion

Most investors prefer certain benefits to uncertain benefits. In some cases, they will select the more certain of two investments even though its anticipated benefits are smaller than those on a more risky investment. For example, a risk-averse investor might invest in a government bond that carries only a 9% annual interest rate, rather than a corporate bond that carries a 12% annual interest rate. The investor views the higher anticipated return on the corporate bond as less attractive than the greater certainty about the return on the government bond. This desire for certainty, or dislike of risk, is termed **risk aversion**.

While investors as a group are generally risk-averse, the degree to which each investor is averse to risk varies both from individual to individual and over time for the same individual. Some people are simply more cautious than others and are unwilling to accept greater uncertainty. Although the degree of risk aversion differs among investors and over time, the basic relationship between risk aversion and value is always a negative one. We will demonstrate later in the chapter that *as the degree of risk aversion increases, the value of an investment decreases.*

http://

The publishers of *Risk Management Report* have a list of current major risk management issues on this Web site.

www.riskinfo.com/rmr.htm

Risk Aversion The preference of investors for certain investment benefits over uncertain benefits of equal expected size.

INVESTMENT VALUATION

Although the previous discussion indicates the direction of a determinant's effect on value, it says nothing about the magnitude of the effect of any one determinant or of all determinants in combination. What is required for investment valuation is a model that will combine *quantitatively* the qualitative effects on value we have described. In this section of the chapter, we will introduce such a valuation model, based on the discounted cash flow procedure.

Investment Valuation Model

Investment Valuation Model (IVM) The basic technique that calculates the value of an investment as the present value of all future cash flows expected to be generated by the investment.

In Chapter 5, we presented a mathematical technique for discounting future cash flows back to their present value. This technique provides the foundation for the **Investment Valuation Model (IVM)** that enables financial managers to apply the value maximization criterion to their proposed investing and financing decisions. The Investment Valuation Model views an investment as a stream of future cash flows. The value of those cash flows depends on their amount, timing, and riskiness. In particular, value can be calculated using the discounting procedure shown in Figure 6-3. The IVM is the fundamental decision-making model in corporate finance.

The mechanics of the discounting procedure of the IVM are identical to those described in Chapter 5. The model utilizes the present value equations from that chapter, both for uneven streams of cash flows and for annuities. For example, suppose a firm's financial managers want to evaluate the following investments at an annual opportunity cost of 10%:

	Investment A			Investment B	
Year	Cash Flow (C)		Year	Cash Flow (C)	
1	$ 100		1	$ 300	
2	200		2	300	
3	300		3	300	
4	400		4	300	
5	500		5	300	
	$1,500			$1,500	

FIGURE 6-3

The Investment Valuation Model (IVM)

Verbal Definition:
- The value of an investment is the present value of all future benefits expected to be generated by the investment.
- The benefits are measured by the cash flows associated with the investment.
- The discount rate applied to the cash flows is the investor's required rate of return (RRR).

Mathematical Definition:

$$V = \frac{C_1}{(1 + K)^1} + \frac{C_2}{(1 + K)^2} + \cdots + \frac{C_N}{(1 + K)^N}$$

$$V = \sum_{t=1}^{N} \frac{C_t}{(1 + K)^t} \tag{1}$$

V = The value of an investment   K = The investor's RRR
C_t = Anticipated cash flow in time period t   N = The horizon of the investment

Although both investments offer the same *total* cash flows, the IVM indicates that Investment B has a higher value due to the earlier receipt of its cash flows:

$$PV_A = (C_1)(DF_{0.10,1}) + (C_2)(DF_{0.10,2}) + (C_3)(DF_{0.10,3}) + (C_4)(DF_{0.10,4}) + (C_5)(DF_{0.10,5})$$
$$= (\$100)(0.909) + (\$200)(0.826) + (\$300)(0.751) + (\$400)(0.683) + (\$500)(0.621)$$
$$= \$90.90 + \$165.20 + \$225.30 + \$273.20 + \$310.50 = \$1,065.10$$

$$PV_B = (C)(ADF_{0.10,5}) = (\$300)(3.791) = \$1,137.30$$

Because accurate estimation of both the cash flows and the discount rate is essential to the valuation process, the IVM must incorporate all five determinants of value in that process. We will now take a closer look at the IVM to see how it integrates all five value determinants and how the discount rate is influenced by the final three.

The Effect of the Fundamental Determinants of Value in the IVM

The present value of an investment depends on two factors: the estimated future cash flows and the discount rate. In terms of equation (1) in Figure 6-3, the first factor is reflected in the numerator (C_t), while the second factor is reflected in the denominator $(1 + K)^t$. As a result, the IVM can be divided into two components. The *benefits component* is the future cash flows. The cost or *required rate of return (RRR) component* is the discount rate. As shown in Figure 6-4, the benefits component measures the effect of the first two determinants of investment value, and the RRR component measures the effect of the final three determinants.

Benefits Component. Reference to equation (1) in Figure 6-3 reveals a positive relationship between the size of anticipated benefits and investment value. Since benefits constitute the numerator (C_t) in that equation, an increase in the size of expected cash flows will increase value. The relationship between the *length of the deferral* of benefits and investment value is negative. That is, the slower the receipt of the cash flows, the smaller an investment's value. Consider the following anticipated benefits from an investment:

Time Period	Expected Cash Flow
1	$100
2	200
3	300

If we assume a required rate of return of 12%, the value of the investment is:

$$V = (\$100)(DF_{0.12,1}) + (\$200)(DF_{0.12,2}) + (\$300)(DF_{0.12,3})$$
$$= (\$100)(0.893) + (\$200)(0.797) + (\$300)(0.712) = \$462.30$$

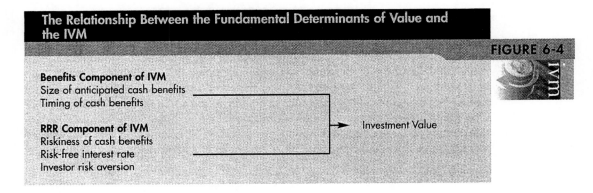

The Relationship Between the Fundamental Determinants of Value and the IVM

FIGURE 6-4

Benefits Component of IVM
Size of anticipated cash benefits
Timing of cash benefits

RRR Component of IVM
Riskiness of cash benefits
Risk-free interest rate
Investor risk aversion

→ Investment Value

Suppose instead that all the cash benefits are expected to be delayed by one year:

Time Period	Expected Cash Flow
1	$ 0
2	100
3	200
4	300

The value of the investment falls to:

$$V = (\$0)(DF_{0.12,1}) + (\$100)(DF_{0.12,2}) + (\$200)(DF_{0.12,3}) + (\$300)(DF_{0.12,4})$$

$$= \quad \$0 \quad + (\$100)(0.797) \quad + (\$200)(0.712) \quad + (\$300)(0.636)$$

$$= \$412.90$$

Even though the amounts of the benefits remain the same, the delay in their receipt decreases the investment's value.

RRR Component. The discount rate K in equation (1) is determined by: the risk-free interest rate, the riskiness of an investment's benefits, and the risk aversion of investors. K is called the **required rate of return (RRR)**. *It is the minimum rate of return that will induce investors to select a particular investment.*

Required Rate of Return (RRR) The minimum annual percentage rate of return required by investors to induce them to select a particular investment.

In Chapter 5, we referred to K as the investor's opportunity cost. The minimum acceptable rate of return on any investment is in fact defined by the returns available on alternative investments of comparable risk. Thus, the terms *opportunity cost of funds* and RRR are synonymous.

The relationship between K and the risk-free interest rate is positive. Recall that the risk-free interest rate compensates an investor for deferring consumption in order to invest in a riskless investment such as a government security. As the returns required to compensate for this deferred consumption increase, the minimum return necessary on a specific *risky* investment also increases. K is also positively related to both the riskiness of an investment and the degree of risk aversion of investors. As the uncertainty of actually realizing the benefits anticipated from an investment increases, investors will require a higher return in order to compensate for the greater risk. In addition, if investors' dislike of uncertainty increases, the RRR they demand on a risky investment rises.

As an example of these relationships, consider the yields available from investments in U.S. Treasury securities and U.S. Aaa corporate bonds in January 1999:

Type of Security	Yield
Corporate bonds	6.35%
Long-term Treasury bonds	5.37
Difference (spread)	0.98%

The 5.37% yield on Treasury securities compensated investors only for deferred consumption. The 6.35% yield on corporate bonds, on the other hand, compensated investors for *both* deferred consumption and the risk of default. If the Treasury securities' yield should rise, the yield on corporate bonds should also rise to reflect the increased need for compensation for deferred consumption. In addition, if investors should become more risk-averse due to concerns about the health of the U.S. economy, the yield on corporate bonds should rise above 6.35% even if Treasury securities continued to offer a 5.37% annual rate of return. Thus, an increase in the "spread" should occur if investors become more sensitive to default risk.

Since K occurs in the denominator of equation (1), the relationship in the IVM between value and the risk-free rate, risk, and risk aversion is negative. *Whenever any of these three determinants increases, it causes an increase in K, which results in a decrease in investment value.* We can illustrate this point by returning to our previous example, where the expected benefits from the investment were:

Time Period	Expected Cash Flow
1	$ 0
2	100
3	200
4	300

At a 12% RRR, the present value of the benefits was $412.90, as computed earlier. Suppose that, due to an increase either in the risk-free interest rate, the riskiness of an investment, or the risk aversion of investors, the RRR rises from 12% to 14%. With this increase, the value of the investment becomes:

$$V = (\$0)(DF_{0.14,1}) + (\$100)(DF_{0.14,2}) + (\$200)(DF_{0.14,3}) + (\$300)(DF_{0.14,4})$$

$$= \quad \$0 \quad + (\$100)(0.769) \quad + (\$200)(0.675) \quad + (\$300)(0.592)$$

$$= \$389.50$$

The increase in the RRR from 12% to 14% causes a decline in the investment's present value from $412.90 to $389.50.

Now that we have seen that the IVM is a valid approach to investment valuation because it correctly incorporates all five determinants of investment value, we will turn our attention to the use of the model in practice. Specifically, we will discuss how to measure the two major elements of the model: the benefits component and the RRR component.

ESTIMATING THE ANTICIPATED BENEFITS

The first step in valuation is the estimation of the anticipated benefits attributable to the investment. The *anticipated benefits* from an investment are the *future cash flows that the investor expects to receive* from the investment.

The emphasis placed on a firm's *profits* by managers and stockholders often leads to confusion about the appropriate measure of anticipated benefits. The value of an investment depends ultimately on the future consumption that it promises. Thus, it is the prospect of receiving cash, and not accounting profits, that gives worth to an investment. Consequently, the investor's main task is to estimate the amount and timing of the cash flows. The cash flows associated with an investment can be categorized as either contractual or non-contractual, depending on the process by which they are generated. This categorization, in turn, determines the procedure that an investor should follow in estimating the size and timing of the cash flows.

Contractual Cash Flows

While it is true that the economic future is inherently uncertain, the returns offered by some investment opportunities are relatively predictable. Their future cash flows can be forecast with considerable accuracy because these cash flows are prescribed by a legal agreement that is enforceable in a court of law. A corporate bond is a good example of this type of investment. The annual interest rate on the bond is fixed for the bond's entire life, and the maturity date is specified in the bond contract. Thus, the expected benefits (annual interest and

■ Ethics

ISSUES

THE DETERMINANTS OF CORPORATE VALUES

In this chapter, we examine the impact of risk on the value of a corporation to its shareholders. Recently, in response to a federal government crackdown on corporate wrongdoing, firms have begun to examine the impact of their corporate values on the risk borne by stockholders. This new emphasis on corporate values and ethics is, at least partially, a response to the 1991 federal sentencing guidelines of the U.S. Sentencing Commission. According to these guidelines, firms that are found guilty of violating federal law will avoid huge fines if they have a serious ethics training program in place. By encouraging such programs, the federal government is hoping to minimize the likelihood of illegal acts by corporate employees.

In response to the sentencing guidelines, firms began to request that the large public accounting firms certify that their ethics training programs would satisfy the requirements of the U.S. Sentencing Commission. The CPA firms, in turn, responded to these requests by setting up units to establish and monitor ethics training programs at their clients. For instance, KPMG Peat Marwick announced in 1996 that it would set up a unit within the firm designed to help clients "create the moral organization." The unit's basic philosophy is that the ethics climate at a firm can be sampled, tested, and measured. Thus, corporate ethics can be audited in the same way that a firm's financial statements can be verified and certified.

KPMG surveyed its clients to determine the major ethical issues and concerns at those firms. The responses identified that the following six risks were viewed as the biggest threats by the firm's legal departments:

1. sexual harassment
2. environmental contamination
3. antitrust violations
4. foreign payments
5. fraudulent financing reporting
6. race issues

Through regular employee surveys concerning the ethics climate, KPMG offers the firms an ongoing "ethics vulnerability risk assessment." This assessment is intended to identify and address potential problem areas before they lead to public relations or legal problems.

repayment of principal at maturity) are defined in a legally binding agreement. For example, a $1,000 corporate bond issued in December 1999 with a 9% interest rate and a five-year maturity would offer the following annual cash flows:

Date	Cash Benefits		
December 2000		$(0.09)(\$1,000) =$	$ 90
December 2001		$(0.09)(\$1,000) =$	90
December 2002		$(0.09)(\$1,000) =$	90
December 2003		$(0.09)(\$1,000) =$	90
December 2004	$\$1,000 +$	$(0.09)(\$1,000) =$	1,090

As long as the bonds carry a high credit rating, an investor can count on receiving $90 each December for four years and $1,090 in December of the last year. While extreme financial distress or bankruptcy could change this, a high credit rating indicates that the payments are virtually certain to be received.

Non-Contractual Cash Flows

The bulk of the investments evaluated by firms do not promise returns that are contractual. The anticipated cash flows are not specified in a legal agreement but are dependent upon the firm's success at utilizing its operating assets in its business. The cash flows actually realized from these assets, moreover, depend on a number of economic factors that are difficult to forecast. This situation greatly complicates the estimate of the benefits component of the IVM.

For example, consider the situation faced by a firm that is evaluating a new product whose sales depend heavily on the general state of the national economy. The basic problem is that the firm's managers are unable to forecast the state of the economy with certainty. Instead, the best they can hope for is to be able to estimate the likelihood of some major possibilities. Suppose they feel that the most likely event is mild economic growth. After estimating the sales based on this assumption, the managers calculate that the investment in the new product could generate cash flows of $500 per year. This is the *most likely* estimate. Without further information, $500 would be accepted as the best available estimate of the investment's annual benefits and would be discounted to a present value by the IVM.

Since the $500 cash flow is not certain, however, there are other possible outcomes for the investment. Each of these outcomes involves different anticipated cash flows and a different probability of occurrence. As an illustration, assume the following estimates are made by the firm:

National Economy	Probability	Cash Flow from the Investment (C)
Recession	0.10	$400
Mild Growth	0.70	500
Rapid Expansion	0.20	800

Which of these three estimates should be used in the IVM? The most likely outcome is $500, but if the firm uses that figure, it is ignoring information about the other possibilities. One approach is to calculate an **expected value**, which is the weighted average of the possible cash flows with the weights equal to the probabilities. For this example, the calculation would be:

$$C = (\$400)(0.10) + (\$500)(0.70) + (\$800)(0.20)$$
$$= \quad \$40 \quad + \quad \$350 \quad + \quad \$160$$
$$= \$550$$

Expected Value The weighted average of the possible cash flows associated with an investment. The weights are equal to the probability of each potential cash flow.

The expected value of $550 now becomes the estimate for the expected cash flow. Notice that it differs from the *most likely* (highest probability) cash flow of $500. As an estimate of anticipated benefits, the expected value of $550 is superior since it takes into account *all* possible outcomes, and not just the most likely one.[1]

By expanding the analysis to recognize a number of possible outcomes, the managers specify a "distribution," which describes the complete set of probabilities for those outcomes. There are two types of **probability distributions**: continuous and discrete. A *continuous distribution* has an infinite number of outcomes and probabilities for ranges of outcomes rather than for individual outcomes. A *discrete distribution*, on the other hand, has a specific number of possible outcomes, each of which has a separate probability. Since there are only three possible outcomes in our example, it is a discrete probability distribution, as shown in Figure 6-5.

Probability Distribution A portrayal that specifies all the possible outcomes associated with an action and assigns probabilities to each outcome.

We calculated the expected value of this distribution to be $550. The expected value of any discrete probability distribution can be found by using the following general formula:

---

[1] The logic behind the expected value as the most useful estimate of an investment's cash flow is based on the results that would be realized from a large number of investments identical to the one under consideration. For any one investment, the cash flow that is realized will be either $400, $500, or $800. If the probabilities are accurate, the $400 flow will occur for 10% of the investments, the $500 flow for 70% of the investments, and the $800 flow for 20% of the investments. Thus, the average realized cash flow for all the investments will be the weighted average of the actual cash flows. This weighted average is the expected value of the possible cash flows, $550.

$$\bar{X} = \sum_{i=1}^{N} X_i p_i \qquad (2)$$

where $\bar{X}$ is the expected value, X_i is the ith possible outcome, and p_i is the probability of the ith outcome. The symbol X is used in order to keep equation (2) as general as possible. In our example, X_i represents the estimated cash flow for each state of the economy where there are $N = 3$ different states:

$$\bar{X} = \sum_{i=1}^{3} X_i p_i \quad \begin{aligned} &= (\$400)(0.10) + (\$500)(0.70) + (\$800)(0.20) \\ &= \quad \$40 \quad + \quad \$350 \quad + \quad \$160 \\ &= \$550 \end{aligned}$$

We have assumed only three states of the national economy. In reality, there are a wide range of possibilities ranging from depression to boom. Thus, a more realistic distribution of cash flows would be continuous, as shown in Figure 6-6. The continuous distribution indicates that there are an unlimited number of possible outcomes associated with the investment in our example, ranging from a low of $0 to a high of $1,000. The expected value of the distribution is $550. The actual value of the outcome within the range $0–1,000 depends on the state of the national economy in the coming years. The likelihood of each possible outcome is indicated by the proportion of the total area under the curve at that outcome. Thus, the likelihood of an outcome between $300 and $800 is greater than the likelihood of an outcome above or below that range.

The uncertainty associated with forecasting non-contractual cash flows is typically much higher than with contractual cash flows. A key question in the evaluation of a proposed investment is whether the forecasted cash flows are sufficiently large to compensate for their uncertainty. The RRR component of the IVM plays a crucial role in answering this question.

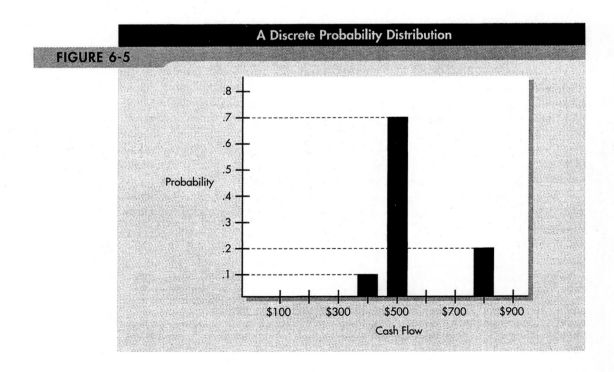

A Discrete Probability Distribution

FIGURE 6-5

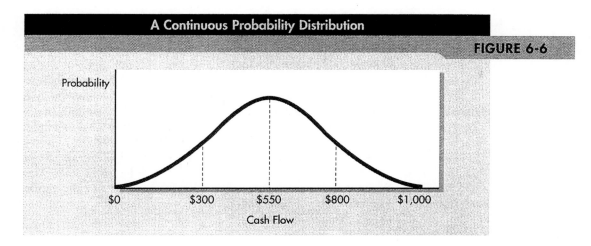

A Continuous Probability Distribution

FIGURE 6-6

ESTIMATING THE REQUIRED RATE OF RETURN

The RRR consists of two elements: the risk-free interest rate and the risk premium. The relative importance of the risk-free interest rate and the risk premium to the estimation of the RRR will vary from one investment to another and from one investor to another. In addition, their relative importance can vary over time for a specific investment or investor. Thus, it is important to know which factors affect the risk-free interest rate and the risk premium. The relationship of the RRR to these elements is shown in equation (3) in Figure 6-7.

Risk-Free Interest Rate

The risk-free interest rate reflects the overall supply of and demand for funds in the financial markets. The supply of and demand for funds is largely determined by monetary policy actions of the Central Bank and fiscal policy actions of the national government. When the Central Bank makes funds more readily available to commercial banks for lending to their customers, the increase in the supply of credit pushes its price down. Conversely, Central Bank actions that decrease the supply of credit at banks will increase the cost of credit. In a similar manner, when the national Treasury has to borrow funds in the financial markets to cover budget

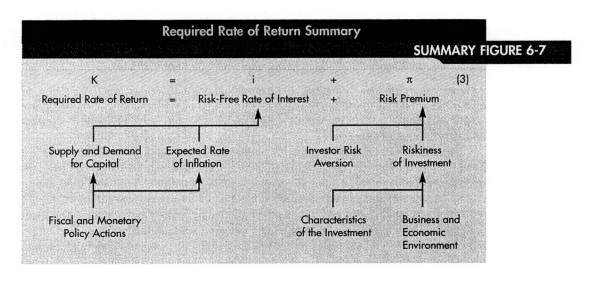

Required Rate of Return Summary

SUMMARY FIGURE 6-7

deficits, the increase in the overall demand for funds increases the cost of credit. Reductions in deficits and Treasury borrowing, on the other hand, should reduce the risk-free interest rate.

In addition to these supply and demand factors, the risk-free interest rate is influenced by investors' expectations about future rates of inflation. As we pointed out in Chapter 3, when inflationary expectations increase, investors will demand a higher return even on riskless investments in order to protect themselves from declines in the purchasing power of their invested funds. For example, assume that investors are willing to accept an annual return of 5% on Treasury securities during a period of no inflation. If instead they forecast an annual rate of inflation of 4%, they will demand a risk-free return of 9% from Treasury securities to compensate for the expected decline in the purchasing power of the future cash flows they receive.

Risk Premium

Risk Premium The portion of an investment's RRR that is a combination of the effects of investment risk and investor risk aversion. Mathematically, the risk premium equals the excess of an investment's RRR over the risk-free interest rate.

The **risk premium** element of the RRR is a combination of the effects of investment risk and investor risk aversion. The risk of an investment is the result of the interaction between the physical characteristics of the investment and the many uncertain aspects of the business environment that affect the investment's cash flows. For example, a $500 million payment to the U.S. government by large U.S. oil companies for the right to explore for oil off the Alaskan shore is a risky investment by its very nature. The ability of the oil companies' geological teams to predict the location of oil without test drilling is relatively limited. Thus, cash flow forecasts based on these predictions are subject to considerable uncertainty.

As mentioned earlier, investor risk aversion is a function of the mental attitude of investors. It is determined by both economic and noneconomic variables and can be subject to great variability over time. The degree of investor optimism and pessimism is affected by national events such as elections, changes in the regulatory environment, and strikes. It is also altered by international events such as wars, oil crises, trade disputes, import and export restrictions, and international lending problems. The effect of changes in risk aversion, as well as in the risk-free interest rate and investment risk, can be evaluated in terms of a *market-determined* RRR schedule.

The Market-Determined RRR Schedule

As agents of a firm's stockholders, managers should evaluate investments in the same way stockholders would. *Thus, managers should use the RRR that shareholders would use if they were evaluating the alternatives themselves.* A large corporation may have thousands of different shareholders, each of whom could differ in terms of his or her degree of risk aversion. How can each investor's attitude toward risk be incorporated into the decision process? The existence of organized financial markets provides a solution to this problem by establishing a *single market-determined required rate of return for each possible degree of risk*, as shown in Figure 6-8.

The line for the required return K begins at the risk-free rate, i, and rises as the level of investment risk increases. The value of i is normally measured as the current interest rate on a national government debt instrument with the same maturity as the investment under consideration. The size of the risk premium (π) that is added to i to specify the RRR on an investment depends on two factors: the location of the investment on the investment risk spectrum, and the slope of the market RRR schedule (which reflects investors' risk aversion). An increase in either factor will increase both π and K.

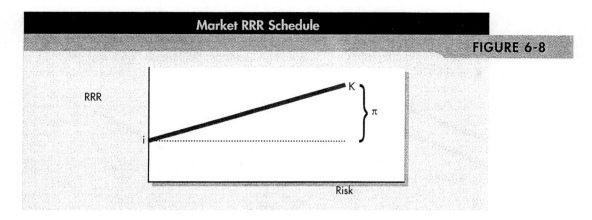

Market RRR Schedule

FIGURE 6-8

The key feature of market-determined RRRs is that they are based on investment alternatives available to everyone. Recall that the RRR for an investment is the opportunity cost of funds for investors as measured by the returns available on alternative, comparable-risk investments. Since all investors face the *same* set of opportunities, there is only one RRR (opportunity cost) for each level of risk. With the existence of organized financial markets, there is no longer a need to worry about different shareholders. *The K established by the market at each level of risk is the RRR for all investments that are characterized by that amount of risk.* Although the **market RRR schedule** will change over time, it is fixed at any one moment in time. The task of financial managers is to determine the current position of that schedule.

Changes in an Investment's RRR

The required return on an investment can change over time in response to changes in the factors that determine it. Specifically, K will fluctuate as the risk-free interest rate, the degree of investment risk, or investor risk aversion changes. These changes in the determinants of K are, in turn, caused by changes in one or more of the factors shown earlier in Figure 6-7.

Changes in the Risk-Free Interest Rate. Let us take the example of an investment whose RRR is 14% as determined by equation (3): $K = i + \pi = 8\% + 6\% = 14\%$. The market RRR schedule and the investment's position on it are shown in Figure 6-9. If an increase in government borrowing or in inflation expectations should cause an increase of 2% in the risk-free rate from 8% to 10%, the market RRR schedule would shift upward to K'. The investment's K would rise from 14% to 16%: $K' = 10\% + 6\% = 16\%$. *An increase in the risk-free interest rate has exactly the same impact on all investments.* An increase in the opportunity cost of deferred consumption by 2% will cause the RRR of all investments to rise by 2% so that the new RRR schedule, K', is parallel to the old schedule, K. Notice also that the *risk premium*, $\pi = K - i = 6\%$, is the same for both schedules. The risk premium is unaffected by a change in the risk-free interest rate.

Changes in the Risk Estimate. Suppose that instead of an increase in the risk-free interest rate, a change in the financial managers' risk estimate occurs. After additional evaluation, the managers increase their estimate of the investment's risk from *Risk* to *Risk'*, as shown in Figure 6-10. The result is an increase in the investment's RRR to 18%: $K' = 8\% + 10\%$. The higher risk estimate has caused the risk premium to rise by 4%: $\pi = 14\% - 8\% = 6\%$; $\pi' = 18\% - 8\% = 10\%$. This *increase in the risk estimate has not altered the market RRR schedule* but merely changed the

**The Effect of a Change in the
Risk-Free Interest Rate**

FIGURE 6-9

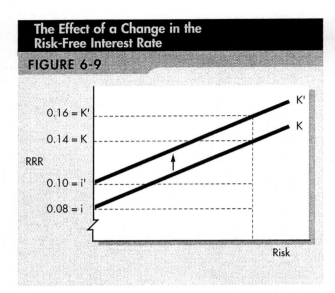

**The Effect of a Change
in Investment Risk**

FIGURE 6-10

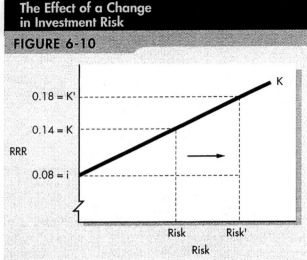

position of the investment *on* the schedule. Thus, the RRR's for other investments are not affected by a change in the risk estimate for one particular investment.

Changes in Investor Risk Aversion. The last source of change in an investment's RRR is an increase or decrease in investor risk aversion. Investors' attitudes toward risk affect the risk premium by determining the *slope* of the market RRR schedule. Suppose unfavorable economic news makes investors more risk-averse in such a way that the market RRR schedule changes from K to K′ in Figure 6-11.

Once again, the investment's RRR has increased due to a rise in the risk premium. The RRR has increased from K = 14% to K′ = 17% because the risk premium has increased from π = 14% - 8% = 6% to π = 17% - 8% = 9%. The impact of this change in risk aversion on the risk premium will vary from one investment to another. The increase in the slope will cause a greater increase in π and K as we

The Effect of a Change in Investor Risk Aversion

FIGURE 6-11

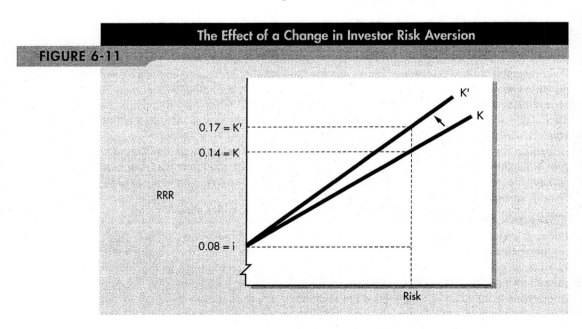

move rightward along the risk axis of Figure 6-11. That is, *an increase in investors' dislike of risk penalizes high-risk investments more than low-risk ones.*

To summarize this section of the chapter, an investment's RRR reflects three of the fundamental determinants of investment value: the risk-free interest rate, investment risk, and investor risk aversion. The risk-free interest rate represents compensation for the deferral of consumption. Investment risk represents investors' uncertainty about their forecasts of the cash flows associated with particular investments. Investor risk aversion is the reaction of investors to uncertain cash flows for all investments.

ALTERNATIVE MEASURES OF RISK

Estimation of the risk premium component of K requires the ability to measure an investment's risk. Due to controversy over the exact nature of investment risk, there is no universally accepted risk measure. We will describe in this section three measures that are commonly used: the standard deviation, the coefficient of variation, and beta. The first two measures estimate the dispersion of the cash flows in a probability distribution specific to a given investment. The third measure estimates the variability of an investment's returns relative to an average of the returns available on all other investments taken collectively.

The Standard Deviation

The **standard deviation** is a measure of the spread of a probability distribution. The greater the variation of an investment's potential cash flows around their expected value, the larger is the standard deviation. To illustrate the calculation and interpretation of standard deviation, let us return to our earlier example of an investment whose annual cash flows are sensitive to changes in the national economy. The cash flows from this investment are shown in the "A" column below. Assume that there is a second investment opportunity whose annual cash flows are shown in the "B" column.

Standard Deviation A measure of investment risk that examines the dispersion of the potential cash flows around their expected value.

National Economy	Probability	Cash Flow from Investment: A	B
Recession	0.10	$400	$ 0
Mild Growth	0.70	500	500
Rapid Expansion	0.20	800	1,000

We previously calculated the expected value of investment A's cash flows to be $550. The expected value of investment B's cash flows is also $550:

$$\overline{X} = \sum_{i=1}^{3} X_i p_i$$

$$= (\$0)(0.10) + (\$500)(0.70) + (\$1,000)(0.20) = \$550$$

Which of these two investments' cash flows is less certain and, therefore, more risky? In order to answer this question, consider the probability distribution of each in Figure 6-12. Clearly, the possible cash flows for investment B are more spread out than those for investment A. Investment B's cash flows can be as small as $0 or as large as $1,000, while A's lower and upper values are only $400 and $800. As a result, an investor would be less certain of the actual outcome of B's cash flows due to the greater *range* of the possible flows around their expected value.

The degree of spread of possible outcomes around their expected value is called the *dispersion* of a probability distribution. The measure of dispersion is the

Comparing Two Probability Distributions

FIGURE 6-12

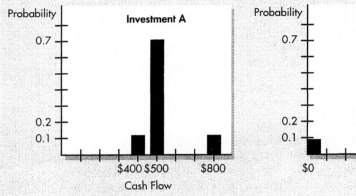
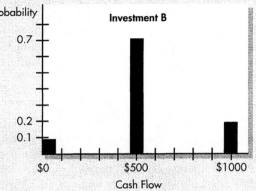

standard deviation. The equation for the standard deviation is:

$$\sigma = \sqrt{\sum_{i=1}^{N}\left(X_i - \overline{X}\right)^2 (p_i)} \qquad (4)$$

where σ (the Greek letter sigma) stands for the standard deviation. The standard deviations for investments A and B are calculated in Table 6-1. Since investment B's standard deviation, \$269.26, is more than twice that of investment A (\$128.45), investment B is the riskier alternative.

Calculation of the Standard Deviation

TABLE 6-1

	Investment A	
$X_i - \overline{X}$	$\left(X_i - \overline{X}\right)^2$	$\left(X_i - \overline{X}\right)^2 (p_i)$
\$400 − 550 = −150	\$22,500	(\$22,500)(0.10) = \$ 2,250
500 − 550 = −50	2,500	(2,500)(0.70) = 1,750
800 − 550 = 250	62,500	(62,500)(0.20) = 12,500
		Total \$16,500

$$\sigma_A = \sqrt{\sum_{i=1}^{3}\left(X_i - \overline{X}\right)^2 p_i} = \sqrt{\$16,500} = \$128.45$$

	Investment B	
$X_i - \overline{X}$	$\left(X_i - \overline{X}\right)^2$	$\left(X_i - \overline{X}\right)^2 (p_i)$
\$ 0 − 550 = −550	\$302,500	(\$302,500)(0.10) = \$30,250
500 − 550 = −50	2,500	(2,500)(0.70) = 1,750
1,000 − 550 = 450	202,500	(202,500)(0.20) = 40,500
		Total \$72,500

$$\sigma_B = \sqrt{\sum_{i=1}^{3}\left(X_i - \overline{X}\right)^2 p_i} = \sqrt{\$72,500} = \$269.26$$

Coefficient of Variation

In cases such as the example just described, the standard deviation was an adequate risk measure because the expected value of each investment's cash flows was identical. When the expected values of two probability distributions are unequal, however, a better measure of risk is needed. To demonstrate this point, let us compare investment A with a third investment, C. The forecasted cash flows of each are:

National Economy	Probability	Cash Flow from Investment: A	C
Recession	0.10	$400	$100
Mild Growth	0.70	500	200
Rapid Expansion	0.20	800	500

The use of equation (2) reveals that the expected value of investment C's cash flows is $250, while equation (4) shows that its standard deviation is identical to that of investment A, $128.45. The expected value is $300 less than that of A. The standard deviations are the same, however, because the difference between each outcome and the expected value is the same in each distribution.

Investments A and C have the same standard deviation, but are they equally risky? The answer is no. An investment from which we expect a cash flow of $250 with a standard deviation of $128.45 is riskier than an investment from which we expect $550 with a standard deviation of $128.45. While the *range* of cash flows associated with a given probability of occurrence is identical for investments A and C, the *percentage* variation of that range around the expected value is much larger for investment C. What is needed is a measure of risk relative to the expected value. The **coefficient of variation (CV)** provides us with such a measure. It is defined as:

Coefficient of Variation A measure of investment risk that defines risk as the standard deviation per unit of expected return.

$$CV = \sigma / \bar{X} \tag{5}$$

where CV is the coefficient of variation. Table 6-2 shows the calculation of the coefficient of variation for investments A, B, and C. The coefficients of variation shown in the table indicate that investment C is riskier than either A or B on a relative basis.

The advantage of using the coefficient of variation as a measure of risk is that it *takes into account differences in expected value by defining risk as standard deviation per unit of expected return*. It is a better measure of risk because the standard deviation can give misleading risk comparisons when investments are of different size. Consequently, the coefficient of variation is useful in more situations and is a more general risk measure than the standard deviation.

Calculation of the Coefficient of Variation
TABLE 6-2

Investment	Expected Value	Standard Deviation	Coefficient of Variation
A	$550	$128.45	$\frac{\$128.45}{\$550} = 0.234$
B	550	269.26	$\frac{\$269.26}{\$550} = 0.490$
C	250	128.45	$\frac{\$128.45}{\$250} = 0.514$

Limitations of the Standard Deviation and the Coefficient of Variation

The standard deviation and coefficient of variation can often be inadequate risk measures because they view the risk of an investment in isolation from that of other investments. This can be an unrealistic view of risk because the typical firm or investor simultaneously owns numerous investments. A strategy of spreading available funds across a number of investments is called **diversification**. Diversification has important ramifications for risk measurements because the resulting group of investments may have less risk in combination than the individual investments themselves.

Diversification A strategy of spreading available funds across a number of different investments.

As an illustration of the effect of diversification on risk, consider the case of a firm that manufactures lawn mowers and snow shovels. The returns realized from its investment in these two product lines depends on the average annual temperature throughout the year. When the average annual temperature is above normal, the sales of lawn mowers are excellent but the sales of snow shovels are poor. The relative returns from the two product lines are reversed when the average annual temperature is below normal. The potential cash flows and the risk/return trade-off for each product line might be as follows:

Average Annual Temperature	Probability	Lawn Mower Division	Snow Shovel Division	Combined Divisions
Below Normal	0.10	$300	$1,000	$1,300
Normal	0.70	500	500	1,000
Above Normal	0.20	800	100	900

	$\overline{X}$	σ	CV
Lawn Mower Division	$ 540	$142.83	0.265
Snow Shovel Division	470	236.85	0.504
Combined Divisions	1,010	104.40	0.103

Both the standard deviation and the coefficient of variation indicate that each of the two divisions is riskier individually than the *combination* of the two. This is due to the negative relationship between the cash flows of the two divisions. High cash flows for the lawn mower division are associated with low cash flows for the snow shovel division, and vice versa. The negative relationship of the cash flows from the individual investments reduces the variability of their combined cash flows.

The implications of this result for the usefulness of the standard deviation or the coefficient of variation in assessing the risk of an individual investment are striking. Both measures can be inadequate because they ignore the risk reduction benefits available from diversification. Since individual investors and firms *can* reduce risk through diversification, the risk premium component of the RRR should be based on the uncertainty of an investment's cash flows that cannot be *eliminated* through diversification. This is the role of beta.

Beta

Although the variability of a firm's total returns can be reduced through diversification, *some* variability is unavoidable. This unavoidable component is due to general economic factors that affect all investments in a similar fashion. For instance, in our previous example, the cash flows from the snow shovel division and the lawn mower division would also both be positively related to the state of the economy. When economic conditions are good, more snow shovels *and* lawn mowers will be sold—regardless of the weather—than when economic conditions are bad. This effect of the economy on the variability of the firm's total cash flows cannot be eliminated by diversification. **Beta** is a risk measure that is proportional to the undiversifiable risk.

Beta (or β, which is the symbol customarily used to denote it) is similar in spirit to standard deviation and coefficient of variation, in that it is a measure of the variability of investment returns. Unlike the other two risk measures, however, beta does not attempt to measure the *total* variability of an investment's returns. Instead, it measures only the portion that is relevant to a *diversified investor*. This is the portion that influences the risk premium component of an investment's RRR because the diversifiable portion can be eliminated by investors in their personal investment portfolios.

Beta A measure of investment risk that assesses only the undiversifiable risk associated with an investment.

Systematic and Unsystematic Risk.

The total risk of the returns on a firm's common stock, which result from the investments the firm makes, can be divided into two parts: systematic risk and unsystematic risk. **Systematic risk** is the *variability in the returns on a stock that is determined by general market factors*, which cause the returns on all securities to rise and fall together. Examples of these market factors include changes in the level of interest rates, fluctuations in the general level of economic activity, and national and international political developments. **Unsystematic risk** is the *variability in returns that is caused by factors specific to a particular firm*. These factors would include labor disputes, management changes, new product developments, major capital expenditures, new securities issues, acquisitions of other firms, and research breakthroughs. While events of this sort will affect a firm's stock price and its dividend-paying potential, they differ from firm to firm and are independent of general market conditions.

Systematic Risk The variability in the returns from an investment that is determined by general market factors.

Unsystematic Risk The variability in the returns from an investment that is caused by factors specific to the investment.

Beta is a measure of an investment's systematic risk. When investors purchase common stocks, they understand that they can eliminate the unsystematic component of risk through diversification. As an illustration, suppose an investor is considering the common shares of 20 different companies as possible investments. The companies are in a low-risk industry whose operations are affected only slightly by changes in the overall economy. Each of those firms, however, has some unique individual characteristics that cause its profitability to be relatively better or poorer than the rest of the industry, regardless of the state of the economy. Because these characteristics can change over time in unpredictable ways, any given company may do better than the industry in some years and worse in others.

In particular, let us assume that the relationship between the state of the economy and the rate of return that an investment in any one of the 20 stocks will provide to an investor is as shown in Table 6-3. If the investor puts all of her funds into the stock of just *one* of the companies, she will realize a return of either 7% or 9% when the economy is in recession. In a situation of mild economic growth, a return of either 9% or 11% will be earned. When the economy is expanding rapidly, a return of either 11% or 13% will be realized. This set of outcomes defines the investor's exposure to risk when the investor's portfolio is *concentrated* in the shares of a single company.

Suppose instead the investor *diversified* her portfolio by dividing the total investment equally among all 20 common stocks. Under that strategy, the investor can expect half the stocks to provide a 7% return in a recession and the other half a 9% return, just by the laws of chance. As a result, the investor can expect the actual realized return to come out to be very close to 8% in a recession, even though she cannot predict *which* of the individual companies will be the good and poor

TABLE 6-3

The Relationship Between the Stock Returns of Companies in a Low-Risk Industry and the State of the Overall Economy

State of the Economy	Possible Rate of Return on a Common Stock Investment	Probability of the Rate of Return
Recession	7%	0.50
	9	0.50
Mild Growth	9	0.50
	11	0.50
Rapid Expansion	11	0.50
	13	0.50

performers in that recession. The same effect will be produced in situations of mild and rapid economic growth. Returns very close to 10% and 12%, respectively, will consistently be earned, despite the peculiarities of the performance of the individual stocks in the portfolio.

Through diversification, the investor has removed the unsystematic or company-specific variability in returns. This reduces total risk only to the exposure to 8%, 10%, and 12% returns on the portfolio. Because those outcomes are determined by general economic conditions, there is no further reduction in risk that is possible from the set of securities described in Table 6-3. Thus, an investor *must* bear the (systematic) risks that are associated with what happens in the overall economy since he or she is part of that economy. The investor, however, does not have to bear the *extra* (unsystematic) risks that are peculiar to the portion of individual securities' returns, which are independent of the general state of the economy. Diversification eliminates this component.

For that reason, only securities' systematic risks are relevant to the rates of return investors will require from those securities. Investors will not have to be compensated for unsystematic risk because they can avoid bearing it. Consequently, the appropriate measure of risk on the horizontal axes of Figures 6-8 through 6-11 *is* systematic risk, in an environment where investors can diversify. The larger this risk for a given investment, the greater will be the required rate of return K which investors will demand in order to undertake the investment. The larger this risk for the investments a *firm* makes, the greater must be the rate of return earned on those investments in order to meet its *shareholders'* return requirements.

Market Risk.   Not all investments, of course, have the same level of systematic risk. Consider the common stocks of companies in a high-risk industry, like those shown in Table 6-4. In contrast to the low-risk stocks in Table 6-3, returns on the high-risk stocks are much more sensitive to changes in economic conditions. The possible returns range from 3% in a recession to 25% in a rapid economic expansion. These stocks therefore have more systematic risk—and the *average* return that they provide must also be higher. For example, if each of the three states of the economy were equally likely to occur, the average (expected) return on a portfolio of the high-risk stocks would be 14%, as compared with just 10% on a portfolio of the low-risk stocks.

We can think of systematic risk as being a form of investment "market risk." In a recession, the rates of return on the stocks of most companies will be low (or even negative) as a reflection of the difficult earnings circumstances of the com-

The Relationship Between the Stock Returns of Companies in a High-Risk Industry and the State of the Overall Economy

TABLE 6-4

State of the Economy	Possible Rate of Return on a Common Stock Investment	Probability of the Rate of Return
Recession	3%	0.50
	5	0.50
Mild Growth	13	0.50
	15	0.50
Rapid Expansion	23	0.50
	25	0.50

panies. The converse should be true in a time of vigorous economic growth. Thus, we could replace the "State of the Economy" headings in Tables 6-3 and 6-4 with the headings "State of the Stock Market," and call the three circumstances:

- Poor Return on the Overall Market
- Normal Return on the Overall Market
- Good Return on the Overall Market

An investment with a high degree of systematic risk is an investment with a high degree of **market risk**. Its outcomes are very sensitive to movements in the general level of securities prices. If we can measure the *extent* of that sensitivity, relative to the securities market as a whole, we can identify the risk premium π that applies to the investment. In turn, we can identify the investment's *required* rate of return in our Investment Valuation Model. That is what beta is designed to accomplish.

Market Risk The extent to which an investment's outcomes are sensitive to movements in the general level of securities prices. It is another name for systematic risk.

The Market Portfolio. The rate of return that is available from a riskless investment in a government security (the risk-free interest rate) defines the *minimum* return requirement for any investment. As we saw, this return provides compensation to investors only for waiting to receive future cash flows and deferring consumption. If risky investments are to be undertaken, they must provide an *expected* return that exceeds the risk-free rate. The additional return requirement is an investment's risk premium. If the investment is of average risk, its risk premium will also be average.

We may use an investment of average (systematic) risk as a standard of comparison for determining other risk premiums. The "average" risky investment is just what the name would imply. It consists of a combination or portfolio of *all* available risky investments. In principle, this portfolio would literally include everything an investor would have available as an investment choice: stocks, bonds, real estate, precious metals, and collectibles such as paintings and sculpture. In practice, however, the returns on most major categories of investments tend to be fairly highly correlated because they are affected by the same set of underlying factors that determine the general condition of the economy. Consequently, we can validly employ a smaller subset of the universe of available investments to represent the average of that universe.

The most frequently-used subset for analyzing investment return requirements in the United States is the diversified portfolio of common stocks contained in the Standard and Poor's 500 Index. The stocks contained in the S&P 500 portfolio

http://
You can find the current, last year, last five years, last ten years, and last twenty-five years of the S&P 500 Index at this Web site.
www.secapl.com/secapl/quoteserver/sp500.html

account for approximately 75% of the market value of all publicly traded common stocks in the United States. The returns on that portfolio are widely followed as an indicator of the general level of stock prices and returns in the U.S. economy. Information about the performance of the S&P 500 is available to investors on a daily basis from a number of business publications. The portfolio is, for obvious reasons, especially well-suited to measuring returns on investments in common stocks. These are our main concern here, given our established focus on share-holder wealth maximization as a guide to managerial decisions. We shall take the S&P 500 to be a reasonable representation of the returns on the stock market as a whole, and will refer to that index as the **market portfolio** for purposes of meas-uring the returns on an "average" securities investment. Accordingly, the *risk* associated with an investment in the S&P 500 also defines the average risk for the universe of common stocks.

Market Portfolio A diversi-fied portfolio used to meas-ure the returns realized on an investment of average risk. In practice, the S&P 500 is the most widely used version of the market portfolio.

The Definition and Interpretation of Beta.

With a specification of the market portfolio, we can then identify the systematic risk measure beta, which applies to individual securities or portfolios of securities that are not of average risk. Table 6-5 provides an illustration. The low-risk and high-risk stock returns listed come from Tables 6-3 and 6-4.

We see that the return on the market portfolio is 12% under normal market conditions, and varies both upward and downward by 6% from that level in good and poor years. Low-risk stocks have an expected return in normal years of 10%, with a variation of 2% around this return as market conditions fluctuate from poor to good. Those movements coincide with changes in the return on the market portfolio. Thus, the movements are *systematic* and linked to general market con-ditions. The beta for the low-risk stocks is:

$$\beta_L = \frac{\% \text{ Change in Low-Risk Stock Returns}}{\% \text{ Change in Market Portfolio Returns}} = 2\%/6\% = 0.33$$

This calculation indicates that beta is a measure of the *relative volatility* in invest-ment returns. Beta will have a value smaller than 1.00 for securities whose returns are less volatile around their *average* return than the market as a whole. This is the case for our low-risk stock category in Table 6-5. The beta of 0.33 for that category tells us that the variation over time in the returns on such securities will be only one-third as great as the variation in the returns on the overall market. Importantly, the same beta also tells us that the returns vary *with* changes in market returns, rather than merely randomly.

From Table 6-5, we can see that the high-risk stock returns vary *more* widely than do the returns on the market as a whole, changing by 10% up and down from their normal level when the market changes by 6%. The corresponding beta is:

$$\beta_H = 10\%/6\% = 1.67$$

which indicates that these securities have substantial systematic risk. The beta of the market portfolio must be 1.00, since it is the standard by which the risks and returns of other securities are judged.

With regard to this last point, consider what an investor could accomplish by dividing his investment portfolio *evenly* between the low-risk and high-risk stocks shown in Table 6-5. The average beta of such a portfolio would be the weighted average beta of its components, with the weights being 50% for each of the two stock categories:

$$\beta_P = (0.50)(\beta_L) + (0.50)(\beta_H) = (0.50)(0.33) + (0.50)(1.67) = 1.00$$

Investment Returns and the Market Portfolio

TABLE 6-5

State of the Securities Market	Return on a Portfolio of Low-Risk Stocks	Return on the Market Portfolio	Return on a Portfolio of High-RiskStocks
Poor	8%	6%	4%
Normal	10	12	14
Good	12	18	24

In similar fashion, the overall returns on the portfolio in each of the three possible states of the securities market would be a weighted average of the returns on the two components:

State of the Market	Portfolio Return
Poor	(0.50)(8%) + (0.50)(4%) = 6%
Normal	(0.50)(10%) + (0.50)(14%) = 12%
Good	(0.50)(12%) + (0.50)(24%) = 18%

Accordingly, both the returns and the systematic risk of the portfolio will exactly match those of the market portfolio.

Clearly, a large number of other such portfolio combinations are possible. The investor can choose to be anywhere he or she wishes on the market risk/return spectrum, by varying the proportions. The resulting relationship between return and risk, however, will be a very specific one. This is the trade-off we described in Chapter 1, and all investors will face the same trade-off. Increasing levels of systematic risk will be accompanied by increasing levels of expected—and *required*—return, whereas unsystematic risk does *not* require any additional return as compensation. Figure 6-13 summarizes these conclusions. We shall provide some empirical evidence on the nature of the relationship between beta and required return later in this chapter.

Investment Risk and Investment Return Requirements

SUMMARY FIGURE 6-13

Total Security Risk	=	Variability in Returns	=	Systematic Risk	+	Unsystematic Risk

Systematic Risk: Is a function of general market factors.
Cannot be eliminated by diversification.
Determines the size of a security's risk premium (π).
Determines a security's beta (β).

Unsystematic Risk: Is a function of security-specific factors.
Can be eliminated by diversification.
Does not affect a security's risk premium.
Has no effect on a security's beta.

Examples of Betas. The common stocks of firms in industries subject to high levels of systematic risk will have betas greater than 1.00, while betas will be less than 1.00 for companies in industries with low systematic risk. We provide some examples of this pattern in Table 6-6. The data come from the *Value Line Investment Survey*, which is an investment advisory service that follows the performance of nearly 2,000 corporations on an ongoing basis.

The observed profile seems reasonable. Industries such as home building, air transportation, computers, and steel are notoriously sensitive to general economic conditions and have high betas. The same is true of securities trading, since the stock market and the economy tend also to rise and fall together. Firms like Mead, Wal-Mart, and Herman Miller have profit cycles that move *with* the economy, but not by *more* than the economy. They are very similar to the market portfolio in their characteristics. Utility companies and food companies are less cyclical than the overall economy because there is a more stable underlying demand for their products and services even in bad times.

Petroleum companies are a fairly volatile business, but their profitability is affected strongly by factors that are not entirely correlated with general economic conditions—in particular, the price of oil on the world market. Thus, they do have considerable risk, but the risk has a substantial *unsystematic* component. The resulting betas therefore are below average. The lowest beta is that of the gold-mining company. This also seems reasonable. When economic conditions are poor and investors are pessimistic, the price of gold often rises because it is thought of as a safe haven in times of distress. Again, gold mining is clearly a volatile business, but it has a low systematic risk element. To some extent, in fact, the business has an *anti*-systematic character.

TABLE 6-6

Value Line Common Stock Betas, February 1999

Company	Industry	Beta
Merrill Lynch	Securities trading	1.95
Kaufman & Broad	Home building	1.55
Compaq Computer	Computer manufacturing	1.45
Owens-Corning Fiberglas	Building materials	1.35
American Airlines	Air transportation	1.30
Bethlehem Steel	Steel products	1.20
General Motors	Automobiles	1.10
Mead	Paper	1.00
Wal-Mart Stores	Discount retailer	1.00
Herman Miller	Furniture	1.00
Bristol-Myers Squibb	Pharmaceuticals	1.00
British Airways	Air transportation	0.90
Kroger	Grocery stores	0.75
Anheuser-Busch	Alcoholic beverages	0.70
McDonald's	Restaurants	0.80
Mobil	Petroleum products	0.75
Honda Motors	Automobiles	0.65
Illinova	Electric utility	0.60
Homestake Mining	Gold mining	0.55

Reprinted by permission of Value Line.

Similar logic applies to a comparison of the relative betas of U.S. and non-U.S. companies within individual industries. The *Value Line* betas listed were computed using the S&P 500 Index to represent the market portfolio, and that Index is comprised primarily of U.S. companies. There is a strong correlation between movements in U.S. stock prices and movements in stock prices in other countries, but the correlation is not perfect because economic conditions in the United States and other countries are not entirely synchronous. Thus, the U.S.-linked beta of British Airways is below that of American Airlines, and the beta of Honda is less than General Motors beta. Although not listed, the beta of a risk-free investment in a government security is equal to zero. If the investment's payoff is both fixed and certain, that payoff has no systematic risk because nothing that happens to the returns on other investments has any impact on it.

BETA AND THE MARKET MODEL

The central role of systematic risk in determining an investment's required rate of return is one of the implications of what is often referred to as **modern portfolio theory**. The insight the theory provides into the risk/return trade-off is that an investment cannot be valued in isolation. Rather, it must be analyzed in the context of the set of other investments that are available concurrently. The risk it causes investors to bear must therefore be judged according to how it affects the risk of an investor's *total* portfolio. This is the systematic component we have described, which cannot be eliminated by diversification.

Modern Portfolio Theory
A framework for investment valuation, which recognizes that investment risk must be viewed according to how an investment affects the risk of an investor's total portfolio.

The Characteristic Line

In order to provide an understanding of how all this works in practice, let us examine how beta would be calculated for the common stock of an illustrative firm, Hesston Mining. Table 6-7 lists the history of the annual rates of return that investments in Hesston Mining's shares and in the market portfolio (the S&P 500) have produced. Those rates of return, R, are measured as the annual dividends received plus annual price changes, expressed as a percentage of each year's beginning price:

$$R = \frac{D + P_E - P_B}{P_B}$$

where D is the annual cash dividend, P_B is the price of the stock at the beginning of the year, and P_E is the price at the end of the year. The difference $P_E - P_B$ is the capital gain or loss on the stock during the year. In the case of the market portfolio, the beginning and end of year prices are the values of S&P 500 Index on those

History of Realized Rates of Return on Hesston Mining Common Stock and on the Market Portfolio

TABLE 6-7

Year	Realized Rates of Return: Hesston Mining	Market Portfolio
1994	– 8%	– 6%
1995	10	8
1996	13	11
1997	10	6
1998	16	14

■ Valuation ISSUES

COMMON STOCK BETAS

In Table 6-6, we presented examples of the betas of individual firms that ranged from a low of 0.45 to a high of 1.80. In practice, the U.S. market betas for the vast majority of companies fall in the range of 0.50 to 1.60, as can be seen from the following distribution reported by *Value Line* in 1999:

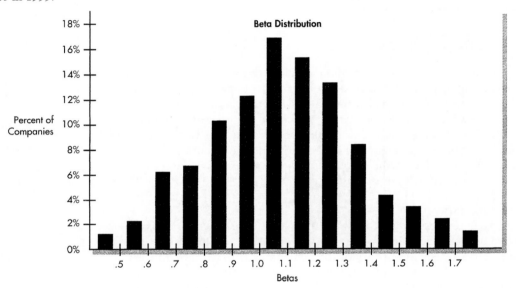

Consistent with the concept of the market portfolio being an average risk investment, the average beta in this distribution is approximately 1.00. Over 96% of the betas are between 0.50 and 1.60, and roughly two-thirds are between 0.80 and 1.30. This is an indication of the strong influence of general market and economic conditions on the stock market performance of individual companies.

Like any other feature of the economic environment, the betas of firms change, albeit gradually, over time, as their operating circumstances and underlying profit performance change. It is important, therefore, to keep estimates of beta continually updated in order to assess investment risk accurately. We shall see in subsequent chapters the kinds of influences that a company's financial and operating characteristics have on its beta.

Characteristic Line A line that represents the rate at which changes in the return on the market portfolio are accompanied by changes in the return on a specific firm's common stock. The slope of this line is the beta of the firm's common stock.

dates, and D represents the total dividends paid during the year on the S&P stocks.[2] The data in Table 6-7 are plotted in Figure 6-14. Each point on the graph represents the realized return on the market portfolio and the associated return on Hesston's stock in a given year. The line through those points describes the average relationship between the two rates of return over the five-year time period in question.

Hesston's beta is the slope of this line. It measures *the extent to which changes in the return on the market portfolio were accompanied by changes in the return on Hesston's common stock.* This line is called the **characteristic line (CL)**

---

[2] It is possible for an investor to "buy" all the stocks in the S&P 500 inexpensively by investing in an "Index" mutual fund, which collects the savings of many small investors and in turn invests those funds in the S&P 500 portfolio. A number of such funds are available.

because it describes the most important characteristic of investments in Hesston stock: how large an impact changes in the general market will have on Hesston's rate of return. That is how risky Hesston's stock is, relative to an average-risk investment.

The characteristic line can be arrived at either graphically or mathematically. The graphical approach involves simply drawing a straight line through the five data points in such a way as to attempt to get all five points as close to the line as possible. The value of beta (the slope of the line) is then found by dividing the change on the vertical axis by the change on the horizontal axis, along the line. The mathematical approach would use linear regression analysis to "fit" the line formally to the data. This is the preferred approach, and the one that is employed by investment services such as *Value Line* that provide betas to investors. Typically, of course, more than just five data points would be available because either monthly or weekly, rather than annual rates of returns, would be used as observations. The fitted regression line would be described by the following equation, in the general case:

$$R_j = \alpha_j + \beta_j R_M \qquad (6)$$

where R_j is the realized return from the jth investment, R_M is the realized return on the market portfolio, and α_j and β_j are the regression intercept and slope, respectively, for the jth investment. The characteristic line for the common stock of Hesston Mining is

$$R_H = 0.22 + 1.21 R_M$$

This equation describes the average relationship between the rate of return on Hesston's stock and the market portfolio over the last few years. It also indicates the risk associated with an investment in Hesston's stock. If the same relationship

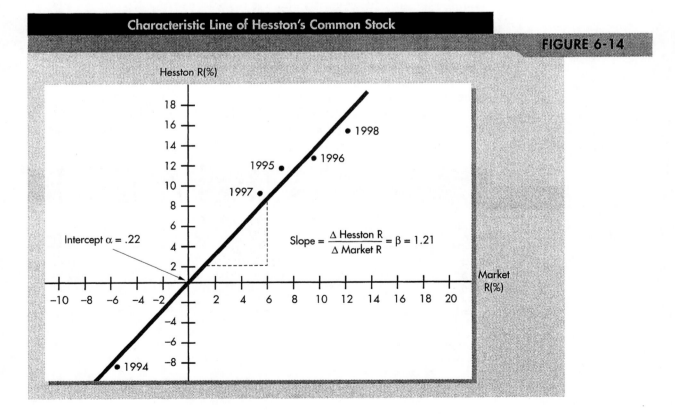

Characteristic Line of Hesston's Common Stock

FIGURE 6-14

holds true in the future, each 1.0% change in the market return will be expected to cause a corresponding 1.21% change in the return on Hesston's common stock. Since the return on Hesston's stock is 1.21 times more variable than the return on the market portfolio, its stock is 21% riskier than "average."

Systematic and Unsystematic Risk in Terms of the Characteristic Line

Notice that while the characteristic line in Figure 6-14 lies *near* the data points, it does not pass directly through them. For instance, in 1997, the realized return on the market portfolio was 6%, while the corresponding return on Hesston's common stock was 10%. The equation for Hesston's characteristic line indicates that the realized return on its common stock *should* have been:

$$R_H = \alpha_H + \beta_H R_M = 0.22\% + (1.21)(6\%) = 7.48\%$$

How should financial managers interpret the difference between Hesston's actual realized return of 10% and its predicted return of 7.48%? Recall that the characteristic line describes the *average* relationship between the historic returns on the market portfolio and those on Hesston's stock. It indicates the influence of the *entire* stock market on the firm's common stock. Thus, 7.48% is that part of Hesston's return that was determined by *general* market factors, which cause the returns on all securities to rise and fall together. The 2.52% difference between the realized return (10%) and the predicted return (7.48%) is that part of Hesston's return that was due to factors *unique* to Hesston. Table 6-8 summarizes the distinction between Hesston's realized return and its predicted return for all five years.

The numbers in column (3) represent the deviation of the actual data points around the characteristic line shown in Figure 6-14. The larger the entries in column (3) for any given security, the less accurate is the characteristic line as a description of the average relationship between the returns on the market and the returns on the security.[3] In other words, *the farther the actual returns vary above and below the characteristic line, the more important are unique firm factors in explaining the returns on a particular security.*

For example, in Figure 6-15, firm factors are more important in explaining the behavior of the returns on Security B than on Security A. Both securities have identical characteristic lines, but Security B's actual returns deviate farther from that line than do Security A's returns. Since Security B's greater unsystematic risk can

TABLE 6-8	Hesston's Realized Return vs. Its Predicted Return		
Year	(1) Realized Return, R	(2) Predicted Return*, $\hat{R} = \alpha + \beta R_M$	(3) Difference $(R - \hat{R})$
1994	–8%	0.22 + (1.21)(–6) = –7.05%	–0.95%
1995	10	0.22 + (1.21)(8) = 9.90	0.10
1996	13	0.22 + (1.21)(11) = 13.53	–0.53
1997	10	0.22 + (1.21)(6) = 7.48	2.52
1998	16	0.22 + (1.21)(14) = 17.15	–1.15
			0.00

*The symbol $\hat{R}$ indicates that the value of the firm's return is a predicted value rather than a realized one.

[3] In statistical terms, the greater the dispersion of data points around the characteristic line, the lower is the correlation between a security's return and the return on the market.

The Influence of General Market Factors and Unique Firm Factors on Security Returns

FIGURE 6-15

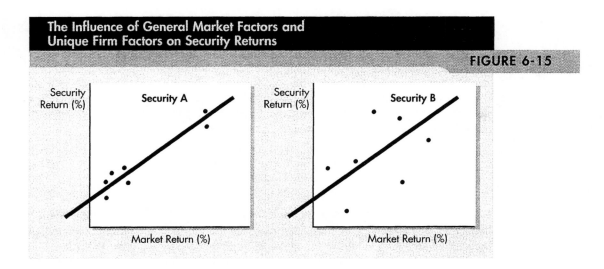

be eliminated through diversification, however, its beta and its risk premium will be identical to those of Security A.

The Security Market Line

Defining risk as market risk establishes a specific relationship between an investment's risk and its RRR. This relationship is known as the **security market line (SML)**, whose equation is

$$K_j = i + (K_M - i)(\beta_j) \qquad (7)$$

where K_j is the RRR on the jth investment and K_M represents an estimate of the future required return on the market portfolio. This equation is an extended version of equation (3), where we can now state that the risk premium (π) is equal to $(K_M - i)(\beta_j)$. A graph of equation (7) is shown in Figure 6-16. The SML in that figure is identical to the market RRR schedule shown in Figure 6-8, given that the appro-

Security Market Line (SML)
The line that establishes a specific relationship between an investment's RRR and its systematic risk as measured by its beta.

The Security Market Line

FIGURE 6-16

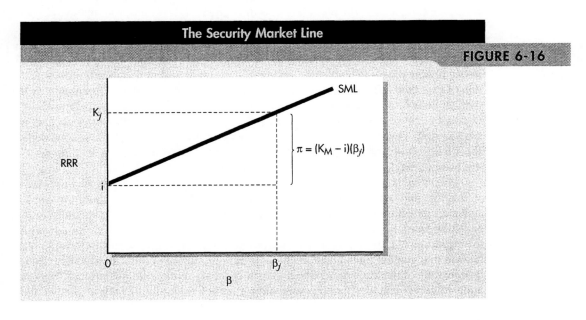

Capital Asset Pricing Model (CAPM) The theoretical model that quantifies the risk/return trade-off associated with an investment in terms of the Security Market Line. The CAPM enables an individual to specify an investment's RRR once one estimates its beta.

priate measure of investment risk is beta. The theoretical model from which the SML is derived is called the **Capital Asset Pricing Model (CAPM)**.

The significance of the SML to a firm's financial managers is that it enables them to calculate an investment's RRR once they estimate its beta. For example, the characteristic line for Hesston Mining common stock indicated that its beta is 1.21. Assume that the risk-free interest rate is 7% and that the estimated average return on the market portfolio in the coming year is 13%. According to the SML, the estimated RRR for Hesston's stock would be:

$$K_H = i + (K_M - i)(\beta_H)$$
$$= 0.07 + (0.13 - 0.07)(1.21)$$
$$= 0.07 + 0.0726$$
$$= 0.1426 = 14.26\%$$

Hesston's RRR of 14.26% exceeds the market return of 13% due to the company's higher-than-average risk. The risk premium for the market portfolio is $(K_M - i)(\beta_M) = (0.13 - 0.07)(1.0) = 0.06$ or 6% because its beta is equal to 1.0 by definition. The beta of 1.21 for Hesston, however, boosts its risk premium to $(K_M - i)(\beta_H) = (0.13 - 0.07)(1.21)$ or 7.26%. Not only is 14.26% the RRR on Hesston's common stock, but it is also the market-determined RRR that applies to *any* investment that has a beta of 1.21. Among such investments, for example, would be ones made by Hesston's management in additional plant facilities for Hesston's existing lines of business. These investments should have the same degree of systematic risk as was measured for Hesston's common stock because the common stock risk is simply a reflection of the nature of the underlying risk of the firm's operations. It is this aspect of beta and the SML that makes the concepts so relevant to financial managers. The appendix to this chapter provides some further elaboration on the Capital Asset Pricing Model and the Security Market Line.

HISTORICAL DATA ON REQUIRED RATES OF RETURN

The SML and the betas that should be used in determining an investment's RRR should in principle be forward-looking in nature, since it is *future* cash flows and opportunity costs that are relevant to an investment's present value. In practice, however, estimates of the SML and betas must necessarily come from historical data.

Typically, betas will be estimated using monthly observations on security returns and market portfolio returns over the most recent two to five years for a given security. If there are reasons to believe a firm's systematic risk has changed in the recent past—for example, because it has made a major investment in a new line of business—its beta might be estimated using weekly rate of return data over the last year or six months. In concept, the interval used to measure these rates of return can be of any length. If systematic risk is present, it should show up just as well in daily or weekly returns as in monthly or annual ones, and the same betas should be observed. Nonetheless, some reasoned judgment must be used in deciding how far back in time to go to collect the data.

The same is true in estimating the profile of the SML. The objective is to arrive at the "normal" relationship between returns on the universe of common stocks and returns on risk-free investments (governmental securities). The specific focus is on the market portfolio's risk premium component $K_M - i$, as the critical input for equation (7). To estimate this component, the historical period chosen should be one that can be considered likely to be representative of the future, in the major dimensions of the economic environment that can be expected to prevail. The balance to be struck is between examining a sufficiently long historical period that

Realized Rates of Return on United States Securities Investments, 1950–1998

TABLE 6-9

Investment	Average Annual Rate of Return
S&P 500 Stocks	14.7%
Long-Term Government Bonds	6.5%
Short-Term Treasury Bills	5.2%

Source: Used with permission. © 1999 Ibbotson Associates, Inc. All rights reserved. [Certain portions of this work were derived from copyrighted works of Roger G. Ibbotson and Rex Sinquefield.]

the estimate is free from merely transitory effects on investment results, while at the same time not going back so far as to render the evidence out-of-date for the current environment.

In the United States, a reasonable choice would be the time period from 1950 to the present. That interval spans a rich variety of investment circumstances and market conditions, to permit one to observe the relationship between stock returns and risk-free interest rates in a wide range of economic settings. To go back further, however, would result in the inclusion of data that come from an environment in which the structure of the economy—including the transition to a peacetime economy after World War II—was substantially different from that of today. Table 6-9 lists the average annual rates of return that have been realized from investments in the S&P 500 stocks and from investments in U.S. government debt securities since 1950.

As the tabulation shows, common stocks have outperformed risk-free securities, on average, over this interval. The higher return is compensation for the extra risk of common stock investments. That risk is evident in Figure 6-17, which plots the series of annual returns on the S&P 500 since 1950. There have been substantial year-to-year fluctuations, ranging from a return of +53% in 1954 to a return of –26% in 1974. The negative returns, of course, are attributable to declines in the prices of the S&P 500 stocks during the years in question. Those fluctuations explain why investors still buy government securities, even though a sacrifice of *average* returns is involved.

A logical estimate of the normal risk premium ($K_M - i$) on the market portfolio would be the difference between the average S&P 500 return and either the average return on long-term or on short-term government securities:

$$\text{Long-Term Risk Premium, } K_M - i = 14.7\% - 6.5\% = 8.2\%$$
$$\text{Short-Term Risk Premium, } K_M - i = 14.7\% - 5.2\% = 9.5\%$$

The choice would depend basically on the horizon for the investment decision in question. Since in practice most corporate investment decisions deal with cash flows that are expected to occur over a series of years, the long-term risk premium of approximately 8.0% would normally be the appropriate measure to employ. Accordingly, our equation for the SML becomes:

$$K_j = i + (8\%)(\beta_j)$$

If the prevailing interest rate on long-term Treasury bonds is 6%, and a particular security has a beta of 1.10, the RRR on the security therefore is:

$$K_j = 6\% + (8\%)(1.10) = 14.8\%$$

If the firm's management were considering investments in additional productive facilities, a rate of return of 14.8% per annum would be required from those invest-

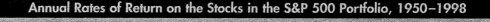

FIGURE 6-17   Annual Rates of Return on the Stocks in the S&P 500 Portfolio, 1950–1998

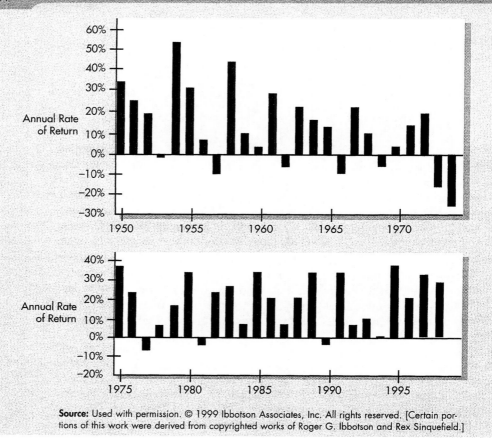

ments.[4] If the present value of the expected cash flows from the investments at that discount rate exceeded their cost, the investments would by definition be desirable. They would be more valuable than the cash outlay required to obtain them. That is the motivation for attempting to identify required rates of return.

SUMMARY

An investment is defined as an outlay of a known amount today in exchange for future cash receipts. The value of an investment is determined by five fundamental factors: the size, the timing, and the riskiness of the future stream of receipts; the risk-free interest rate; and the risk aversion of investors. Value is increased by an *increase* in the size of the anticipated receipts, and by a *decrease* in the riskiness of the receipts, the length of time until their receipt, the risk-free interest rate, and the degree of investor risk aversion.

---

[4] To be more precise, a rate of return of 14.8% would be required on the *portion* of the new investments that were financed by *common equity capital*. We shall amplify this distinction in subsequent chapters.

Each of the five determinants of investment value is incorporated in the Investment Valuation Model (IVM). The IVM calculates the value of an investment as the sum of the anticipated cash receipts discounted to their present value by means of an appropriate discount rate called the required rate of return (RRR). Since the anticipated receipts are typically uncertain, the expected value of the possible receipts is used as the single best estimate of an investment's benefits in the IVM.

The RRR of an investment is a market-determined rate that compensates the investor for three factors: the time value of money, the riskiness of the investment, and investor risk aversion. The task of financial managers is to locate the position of an investment on the market RRR schedule. There are three measures of risk that can be used to measure the uncertainty of an investment's anticipated benefits. The standard deviation and the coefficient of variation measure risk in terms of the variability of possible benefits around their expected value. They are most useful when evaluating the risk of a *single* investment in a situation where investors do not diversify their portfolios.

Beta measures risk in terms of the variability of an investment's returns relative to the variability of returns on the market portfolio. It is a measure of systematic risk, and it applies to a capital market environment where diversification is a feature of investors' portfolios. When risk is measured as beta, the relationship between an investment's risk and its RRR can be specified by the Security Market Line (SML).

chapter equations

$$1.\ V = \sum_{t=1}^{N} \frac{C_t}{(1+K)^t}$$

$$2.\ \overline{X} = \sum_{i=1}^{N} X_i P_i$$

$$3.\ K = i + \pi$$

$$4.\ \sigma = \sqrt{\sum_{i=1}^{N} (X_i - \overline{X})^2 P_i}$$

$$5.\ CV = \sigma / \overline{X}$$

$$6.\ R_j = \alpha_j + \beta_j R_M$$

$$7.\ K_j = i + (K_M - i)(\beta_j)$$

CONTENT QUESTIONS

1. In order to induce an investor to defer current consumption, an investment's return must be large enough to compensate for two things. What are they?
2. Define an investment.
3. List and explain the five fundamental determinants of value.
4. Describe how changes in each of the five fundamental determinants affect the value of an investment.
5. State the Investment Valuation Model mathematically and verbally.
6. Which of the five fundamental determinants of value are measured by the RRR component of the IVM?
7. Explain how changes in the expected rate of inflation will affect the Risk-Return Schedule.
8. In making decisions for their firms, financial managers should use the required rates of return that they would have used if they were making the decisions for their *own* portfolios. True or false? Why?
9. From the point of view of investment decision-making, what is the role of organized financial markets, and what important problems do they solve?
10. Distinguish between certain and uncertain cash benefits.
11. What is the difference between the *expected value* of uncertain cash flows and the *most likely* cash flow?
12. What is the essential difference between a discrete probability distribution and a continuous probability distribution?
13. In the financial markets, what factors determine the risk premium of a specific investment?
14. In your own words, explain what the standard deviation measures.

15. Under what circumstances is the coefficient of variation superior to standard deviation as a measure of risk?
16. What is the difference between systematic and unsystematic risk?
17. Define the term *beta* as a risk measure.
18. Distinguish between the Characteristic Line of a security and the Security Market Line.

CONCEPT QUESTIONS

1. IVM The Security Market Line identifies the relationship between the beta of an investment and its required rate of return (RRR). If that relationship holds, is it possible that the RRR for an investment could be *negative*? Under what set of circumstances, if any, could this occur? Provide an example if you can.
2. IVM Consider the following profile of securities returns and market portfolio returns:

State of the Market	Return on Security A	Return on the Market	Return on Security B
Poor	8%	6%	4%
Normal	11	12	14
Good	14	18	24

   Could a set of returns such as this exist in equilibrium in the market? Explain why or why not.
3. International If the beta for a domestic U.S. company's common stock were recalculated using a "market portfolio," composed of the common stocks of both U.S. *and* non-U.S. companies, would you expect the beta to be larger or smaller than when calculated using only the S&P 500 as the market portfolio? Explain your reasoning.
4. IVM Suppose a firm is evaluating an investment in a line of business that is different from the firm's current line of business. Should the beta that is used to determine the RRR on the investment be the firm's existing beta or the beta that applies to the new line of business? Explain your reasoning.
5. IVM It is generally accepted that the risk-free interest rate tends to rise and fall as expected inflation rates rise and fall. Most empirical evidence would support that notion. If this is the case, how would you modify the procedure for determining a security's characteristic line, which was described in Figure 6-14?

PROBLEMS

1. Jean LeClerc has estimated that an investment will return FF100 per year for 10 years and that, because of uncertainty, the investment must promise a return equal to 10%. What is the value of *this investment to this investor*?
2. Jean LeClerc is also considering another investment that will return FF100 per year for 10 years, but the first FF100 return will not occur until the end of the second year. If the required rate of return is 10%, what is the value of this investment? Compare your answers from Problem 1 and Problem 2.
3. Suppose that Jean LeClerc revises his estimate of the rate of inflation upward by 2 percentage points:
   a. What return would he now require of the investments in Problems 1 and 2?
   b. Now, what are the values of the investments in Problems 1 and 2?
4. What is an investment worth that promises to return FF90 per year for the next 5 years and an additional FF1,000 in the fifth year:

     a. if the required rate of return is 7%?

     b. if the required rate of return is 9%?

     c. if the required rate of return is 11%?

5. What is an investment worth that promises to return FF10,000 per year, given a required rate of return of 15%:

     a. if the benefits are expected for 5 years?

     b. if the benefits are expected for 10 years?

     c. if the benefits are expected for 20 years?

     d. if the benefits are expected indefinitely into the future?

6. You have the opportunity to purchase a contract that promises to pay the owner of the contract $10,000 per year forever.

     a. If your required rate of return is 16%, would you purchase this contract if the offering price were $70,000?

     b. If your required rate of return is 16%, what would be the most you would be willing to pay for this contract?

7. After negotiating with the seller of the contract in Problem 6, you were able to buy it for $66,666.00. What rate of return do you expect to earn now that you own the contract?

8. A company is evaluating an investment that is sensitive to changes in the national economy. If the economy is expanding rapidly, the investment will generate cash flows of $750,000 per year; if mild growth, $500,000; if recession, $250,000. The company's staff economists estimate that there is a two in ten chance that there will be rapid expansion, a six in ten chance of mild growth, and a two in ten chance of recession. What is the expected value of the cash flows from this investment?

9. Given the information in Problem 8, calculate the standard deviation and coefficient of variation of the cash flows from the investment the company is considering.

10. Which of the following investment opportunities is riskier? Explain without calculations.

Opportunity X		Opportunity Y	
Return	Probability	Return	Probability
2,000	0.30	1,200	0.30
1,000	0.40	1,000	0.40
0	0.30	800	0.30

11. Calculate the standard deviation and the coefficient of variation for each of the investment opportunities in Problem 10.

12. Which of the following investment opportunities is riskier? Explain without calculations.

Opportunity Y		Opportunity Z	
Return	Probability	Return	Probability
1,200	0.30	1,200	0.20
1,000	0.40	1,000	0.60
800	0.30	800	0.20

13. Calculate the standard deviation and the coefficient of variation for each of the investment opportunities in Problem 12.

14. Macedonia Oil is drilling an offshore oil well. The following table lists the expected cash flow from each possible outcome and, based on geological studies, the probability of each.

Outcome	Cash Flow	Probability
Dry Well	$-1,000,000	0.30
Natural Gas	1,000,000	0.30
Gas and Oil	2,000,000	0.20
Oil	1,000,000	0.20

Each cash flow will occur one year from today and will fully deplete the well. There is a cash outflow for a dry well due to shutdown expenses.

    a. Calculate the expected value of the cash flows from the well.

    b. Calculate the standard deviation and coefficient of variation of the cash flows.

15. Scandia Petroleum has offered Macedonia Oil $900,000 for the oil well in Problem 14. If Macedonia has a required rate of return of 15%, should it sell the well to Scandia or continue to drill?

16. Admiral Motors has two divisions: its small car division and its large car division. The cash flows from each division in any year are highly sensitive to gasoline prices as shown in the table below.

Price of Gasoline	Probability	Cash Flows (in Millions)	
		Small Car Division	Large Car Division
High	0.3	$50	$ 0
Moderate	0.4	30	20
Low	0.3	10	40

    a. What is the expected cash flow and standard deviation of the cash flows of each division?

    b. What is the expected value and standard deviation of the total cash flows of Admiral Motors?

17. Find the β of a portfolio of three stocks. One-third of the portfolio is invested in each of the stocks. The stocks and their betas are given below:

Stock	Beta
Mallmart	1.10
Peak Power Co.	0.85
Micro Ease	1.40

18. You have two assets in your investment portfolio: a stock mutual fund with a beta of 1.20 and U.S. Treasury securities (assume that they are risk-free). What is the beta of your portfolio if 40% of your funds are invested in the Treasury securities?

19. Over the past six years, the common stock of GF Industries and the "Market" have experienced the following returns:

	Realized Rates of Return	
Year	GF Industries	"The Market"
1	17%	10%
2	5	0
3	12	6
4	-4	-3
5	11	8
6	14	9

    a. Graph these data as in Figure 6-14.

    b. Graphically estimate beta for GF Industries common stock.

    c. Explain the meaning of the value of beta you found.

20. Given that the required return on the market portfolio is 18.8% and the current risk-free rate of return is 8.3%:

    a. Calculate the required rates of return on the common stock of three corporations with the following betas:

        Firm A = 0.10   Firm B = 0.60   Firm C = 1.20

    b. Graph the security market line and show the location of each of these stocks.

21.   a. Find the required rate of return on the stock of Echlin Oil if its beta is 1.3, given that the risk-free rate of interest is 7% and the required return on the market is 14%. Graph the security market line and note the location of Echlin Oil.

    b. Suppose we reevaluate the risk of Echlin Oil and change our estimate of beta to 1.6. Find the "new" required rate of return and note the location on the graph you prepared in part (a).

    c. Suppose that, in addition to the changes in part (b), a government announcement caused us to increase our estimate of the rate of inflation by 3%. Now what is the required rate of return for Echlin Oil? Prepare a graph that shows the effect of this change on the security market line and note the location of Echlin Oil.

    d. Now another government economic report is issued that makes the market pessimistic about the economic future such that investors are less inclined to take risks. The result is that the required return on the "market" increases by 2%. Find the required rate of return for Echlin Oil. Prepare a graph that shows the effect of this change on the Security Market Line and note the location of Echlin Oil (including the changes in parts b and c).

22. The required rate of return on the market is 15%, and the risk-free rate of interest is 7%. You are considering investing in one of two investments. Investment A has a β of 1.5, and you estimate that it will return 18%. Investment B has a β of 0.50, and you estimate that it will only return 12%. Should you invest in A, B, neither, or both if you have enough money?

23. The RRR on Standard Homes common stock is 19.5%, and its beta is 1.25. The risk-free rate is 6%. What is the market risk premium?

24. Ezzon Corporation's RRR is 14.6%, and its beta is 1.2. At the same time, Ortega Airline's RRR is 16.2%, and its beta is 1.4. What is the equation for the security market line?

25. Groton Shipping's common stock has an RRR of 20.6%. If the market risk premium is 8.5% and the risk-free rate is 7%, what is Groton's beta?

26. Financial analysts with Smith Brothers, investment bankers, are in the process of valuing the common stock of a company that its client, Hawk Investments, is trying to acquire. In order to value the stock, Smith Brothers must first estimate the stock's RRR. Smith will use the following average historical returns in its analysis:

Investment	Average Rate of Return
S&P 500	16.0%
Short-Term Treasury Bills	6.0
Long-Term Treasury Bonds	7.0

    a. Estimate the SML that Smith could use to calculate the RRR on any company's common stock.

    b. If the acquisition target's beta is 0.95, what RRR would the analysts use to value the target's common stock?

http://

INTERNET EXERCISE

Try your skill at anticipating the risk/return relationship in the stock market. Develop a portfolio of stocks and try to beat the market measured by the S&P 500 Index for the rest of the semester. Use the Quicken Web page to set up your stock portfolio. Print out a list of the stocks in your portfolio now, and hand it in to your instructor. Bring the results of your selection to class for discussion towards the end of the semester. www.quicken.com/investments/stocks/search

SELF-STUDY QUIZ

1. Find the value of an investment that will return $10,000 per year for 15 years:
    a. if the required rate of return is 8%.
    b. if the required rate of return is 12%.
2. Find the expected value, standard deviation, and coefficient of variation of the cash flow described below:

Probability	Cash Flow
0.4	$\$-20$
0.3	30
0.3	50

3. Using Table 6-6 in the body of this chapter, find the beta of a portfolio composed of equal proportions of Merrill Lynch, General Motors, McDonald's, and Homestake Mining common stock.
4. The risk-free rate of return is 5%, and the estimated required rate of return on the market is 12%.
    a. What is the market risk premium?
    b. What is the equation for the security market line?
    c. The slope of Samson Food's characteristic line is 1.15. What is Samson's beta and RRR?
    d. Suppose the market's expectation of inflation increases by 2%. What is the new SML?

APPENDIX: THE SECURITY MARKET LINE

We stated in the body of the chapter that the Capital Asset Pricing Model specifies that there will be a single overall risk/return trade-off in the financial market, which all investors will confront. That trade-off is captured by the relationship between risk and return called the Security Market Line (SML). The objective of this Appendix is to elaborate on that notion and to provide some intuition.

The market portfolio consists of a fully diversified collection of all risky investments available in the marketplace. The S&P 500 is a good approximation of that portfolio. Any investor can invest in the S&P 500 by purchasing shares in an S&P Index mutual fund. Large institutional investors, such as pension and trust funds, can do this directly by acquiring the S&P 500 stocks. Hence, an investment that duplicates the returns on the market portfolio is readily accessible.

There is another key investment that is readily accessible to all investors: a risk-free investment in government securities or government-guaranteed securities. An insured savings deposit in a bank is an example of the latter. Individual investors can also buy shares in money market mutual funds that invest in government securities. Institutional investors can hold those securities directly.

Consider what this means for investors' risk and return opportunities. They can put together a portfolio in which the proportion z is invested in the market portfolio to earn the expected rate of return K_M and the proportion $(1 - z)$ is invested in government securities to earn the risk-free interest rate i. The overall expected rate of return on such a portfolio will simply be the weighted average of the expected returns on its two component investments:

$$R_P = (1 - z)(i) + (z)(K_M) \qquad\qquad (6A\text{-}1)$$

Thus, suppose the risk-free interest rate is 6% and K_M is 14%. A portfolio in which one-fourth of the investment is in the market portfolio $(z = 0.25)$ and the other three-fourths is in government securities $(1 - z = 0.75)$ will have an expected rate of return equal to

$$R_P = (0.75)(6\%) + (0.25)(14\%) = 8\%$$

Importantly, the *systematic risk* of that portfolio will also be a weighted average of its components' systematic risks. Since the beta of the market portfolio is 1.00, and the beta of the risk-free investment is zero, the overall portfolio beta will be:

$$\beta_P = (1 - z)(\beta_i) + (z)(\beta_M) \qquad\qquad (6A\text{-}2)$$
$$\beta_P = (0.75)(0) + (0.25)(1.00) = 0.25$$

If we alter the investment proportions to one-half in the market portfolio and one-half in government securities, the corresponding R_P and β_P become 10% and 0.50, respectively. Notice that there is an exact match between the values of z and beta.

Clearly, there are an infinite number of possible such allocations. When $z = 0$, the entire portfolio is in government securities, i is the expected rate of return, and $\beta_P = 0$. When $z = 1.00$, the entire portfolio is in the market portfolio, K_M is the expected return, and $\beta_P = 1.00$. If we graphed the results of all the possible allocations between $z = 0$ and $z = 1.00$, we would have the picture shown in Figure 6A-1. The relationship between R_P and β_P is a straight line.

The question then would be: can z ever be *greater* than 1.00? The answer is yes if investors are able to borrow as well as lend. Buying a debt security is called *lending*. The issuer of the security (e.g., the government) borrows, and the investor in the security lends. As an investor, you can also borrow, by "issuing" your *own* debt securities (promises to pay interest). This is what you do when you obtain a home mortgage loan; you issue a promise to pay. You can do the same thing if you want to invest in common stocks.

For example, if you have $10,000 to invest but would like to own a $15,000 stock portfolio, you can borrow the extra $5,000 from your bank or your stockbroker. You thereby owe interest to the lender rather than receive interest from debt securities. The associated values for z and $1 - z$ for your total portfolio are $z = 1.50$ and $1 - z = -0.50$. If your stock investment is in the market portfolio with $K_M = 14\%$ and you pay 6% interest on your loan, your expected overall portfolio return is

$$R_P = (-0.50)(6\%) + (1.50)(14\%) = 18\%$$

because you expect a return of 14% on your $15,000 common stock investment ($2,100 per year) and pay interest at 6% on a $5,000 loan ($300 per year). The expected net return on the $10,000 you started with is then $1,800 per year, or an 18% annual expected return. The associated beta of your portfolio is

$$\beta_P = (-0.50)(0) + (1.50)(1.00) = 1.50$$

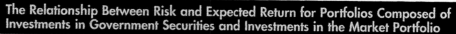

The Relationship Between Risk and Expected Return for Portfolios Composed of Investments in Government Securities and Investments in the Market Portfolio

FIGURE 6-A1

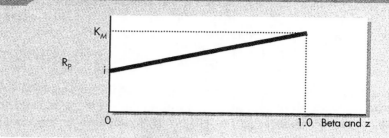

The relationships identified in equations (6A-1) and (6A-2) hold for *any* positive value for z, and we can extend the straight line in Figure 6A-1 beyond the point where z and beta are equal to one.

In that form, the resulting diagram should look familiar. Since R_p is the expected rate of return that is available to an investor from any combination of owning (or issuing) debt securities and investing the remainder of his or her funds in the market portfolio, the investor will not accept a *lower* expected return from any other investment that has the same degree of systematic risk. Accordingly, R_p in Figure 6A-1 also represents the investor's *required* rate of return (RRR) at each level of systematic risk. When extended over the full range of possible values for beta, therefore, the relationship shown in Figure 6A-1 is simply the Security Market Line of Figure 6-16 in the chapter. This is the equilibrium risk/return relationship that will prevail in an investment market where rational investors can—and will— diversify their portfolios to eliminate unsystematic risk.

The Valuation of Securities

The trading of investment securities on the secondary financial markets is a feature of all developed market economies. Changes in stock and bond prices are widely followed, both by the investors in those securities and by the companies and governments that issue the securities. Not only do such changes directly affect investors' personal wealth, but they also provide important information to financial managers about investors' opportunity costs, that is, about the rates of return that investors require. For example:

- On January 4, 1999, 30-year maturity U.S. Treasury bonds were selling at a market price of $1,024.26 for each $1,000 of face value. Why were investors willing to pay more than face value for these bonds? What yield to the investor is implied by this price? What will happen to the price as the bonds' maturity date approaches?

- On January 4, 1999, 10-year U.S. Treasury notes were selling at a price of $982.50 per $1,000 of face value. What accounts for the price difference between the 10-year and the 30-year instruments? Which of the two instruments will have greater price variability over time? What will happen to the price of the 10-year note as its maturity approaches?

- On January 4, 1999, the "yield-to-maturity" of the 30-year bond was 5.09%. This calculation assumes that an investor *holds* the bond until it matures in 30 years. What yield will the investor realize if he or she sells the bond prior to its maturity?

- On January 4, 1999, IBM's common stock was selling at a price of $184 per share on the New York Stock Exchange. How did investors determine this price? How do investor expectations about the future growth in IBM earnings and dividends affect its stock price? What yield to the investor was implied by this $184 stock price?
- How could an investor determine whether $184 was the appropriate stock price for IBM on January 4, 1999? Could the *value* of IBM's stock on that date be greater or smaller than its price on the New York Stock Exchange?
- On October 19, 1987, the Dow Jones Industrial Average of common stock prices fell 23% in a single day. On October 27, 1997, the Dow fell over 7%. What do these collapses indicate about the market's ability to determine stock prices accurately?

Chapter 5 introduced the mathematics of the time value of money, which served as the conceptual basis for the Investment Valuation Model (IVM) developed in Chapter 6. In the current chapter, the IVM is applied to the valuation of financial investments. Specifically, we will discuss three types of financial instruments (securities): bonds; preferred or preference stocks; and common stocks. Our emphasis will be on two aspects of security valuation: (1) calculating the value of a security given its stream of cash flows and the investor's RRR; (2) calculating the RRR, given an investment's cash flows and its value. We will also examine the sensitivity of value to changes in the RRR and in the maturity of a financial instrument.

Figure 7-1 outlines the context of the application of the IVM to security valuation. The IVM states that the value of a security equals the present value of its future cash flows. An investor should decide to buy a security only if its price is no greater than its value, or the security's RRR is no greater than its expected yield. The simultaneous use of the IVM by all investors to value securities leads to an "efficient" market in which value equals price and RRR equals yield. In an efficient security market, the benefits component of the IVM consists of interest and principal payments on bonds and dividends on stocks. The RRR component is the yield on a security. For bonds and preferred stock, the RRR is called the yield-to-maturity and the dividend yield, respectively. For common stock, the RRR consists of a dividend yield and a capital gains yield.

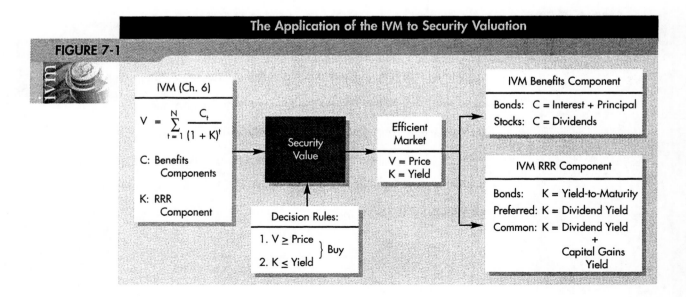

The Application of the IVM to Security Valuation

FIGURE 7-1

IVM (Ch. 6)

$$V = \sum_{t=1}^{N} \frac{C_t}{(1 + K)^t}$$

C: Benefits Components

K: RRR Component

Security Value

Decision Rules:

1. V ≥ Price
2. K ≤ Yield
} Buy

Efficient Market

V = Price
K = Yield

IVM Benefits Component

Bonds: C = Interest + Principal
Stocks: C = Dividends

IVM RRR Component

Bonds: K = Yield-to-Maturity
Preferred: K = Dividend Yield
Common: K = Dividend Yield
+
Capital Gains Yield

It is clearly essential for an *investor* to understand the principles of security valuation. Why do we include such an analysis, however, in a text dealing with *business finance*? The answer is twofold. First, the decision criterion for a firm's financial managers should be the maximization of the value of the firm's stock. Thus, they must understand how investors value securities if they are to apply this criterion successfully. Second, the use of the IVM to analyze investments in *real assets* such as plant and equipment requires that managers first determine an appropriate discount rate (required rate of return). This in turn requires an understanding of security valuation, and the rates of return that investors demand from those securities.

THE VALUATION OF BONDS

A **bond** is a long-term promissory note that is issued by a corporation or government. It represents a loan agreement in which the issuer (the borrower) is contractually obligated to make specific cash payments to the bond's owner (the lender) over a fixed period of time. The cash flows on a bond take the form of periodic interest payments and repayment of principal (usually in one lump sum at maturity). The initial sale or issuance of a bond involves a transfer of funds from the lender to the borrower. After issuance, however, the bond may be resold by the lender to another investor in the financial market. The bond's issuer is unaffected by subsequent resale of a bond except that it must make the contractual interest and principal payments to the new owner of the bond.

Bond A promissory note that is issued by a corporation or government. It is a loan agreement in which the issuer is contractually obligated to make specific cash payments to the bond's owner over a fixed period.

Features of Bonds

There are four terms that are important to understand for bond valuation. These terms are defined in Figure 7-2.

1. Par Value. **Par Value** is also called face value and, in the United States, is normally equal to $1,000. Although par value legally represents the amount of the loan, it is not necessarily either the amount received by the issuer at the time of issuance nor the price received for the bond by the investor if it is resold on the financial markets. Depending on the state of these markets, a $1,000 bond may sell at a price above par (a premium) or a price below par (a discount). Regardless of the original selling price and subsequent market value, however, the issuer is obligated to repay par value to the bond's owner at its maturity.

Par Value The face value of a financial instrument. The par value of a bond represents the size of the loan that the bond's issuer must repay at maturity.

2. Coupon. A bond obligates the issuer to make a specific number of interest payments of a fixed dollar amount. The interest payment is called the bond's **coupon**. The coupon can be expressed either as an absolute amount or as a percentage of par value. For instance, an annual coupon payment of $120 on a $1,000 par value bond represents a coupon interest rate of 12%. Although bond interest may be paid on the basis of any time period, it is most often paid on a semiannual basis. When interest is paid semiannually, one-half the annual coupon is paid every six months.

Coupon The nominal annual rate of interest that the bond issuer is obligated to pay on its bonds. The coupon is normally fixed over the life of the bond.

3. Maturity Date. The bond's issuer is obligated to pay the bond's owner an amount equal to the bond's par value on the **maturity date**. The bond then ceases to exist.

Maturity Date The date on which a bond's issuer is obligated to pay to the bond's owner an amount equal to the bond's par value.

4. Term-to-Maturity. A bond's **term-to-maturity** is the number of periods (years) until its maturity date. Since the maturity date is fixed, the term-to-maturity steadily decreases after the bond is issued. For example, the term-to-maturity on January 1, 1999, of a bond with a maturity date of January 1, 2009, is ten years. The term-to-maturity is an important determinant of a bond's value when market interest rates can fluctuate.

Term-to-Maturity The number of periods remaining until the maturity of a debt instrument.

SUMMARY FIGURE 7-2

Basic Features of a Bond

Term	Definition
1. Par Value	The fixed principal amount that the bond's issuer promises to repay at maturity.
2. Coupon	The fixed dollar or percentage interest payment that the bond's issuer promises to pay each period.
3. Maturity Date	The date on which the issuer repays the bond's par value.
4. Term-to-Maturity	The number of periods remaining until the bond's maturity date.

Calculating the Value of a Bond

Let's illustrate how the IVM can be used to determine the value of a hypothetical bond. In order to finance the acquisition of pollution control equipment, Wabash Power issued $25 million in 20-year bonds at par value on January 15, 1989. The bonds have a par value of $1,000 each and a 9% coupon that is paid annually. If the current date is January 15, 1999, the bonds have a term-to-maturity of ten years.

The IVM calculates value as the present value of future cash flows. Thus, the first step in the valuation procedure is to calculate the anticipated cash flows on the bonds over their remaining life. The annual interest payments are $1,000 \times 0.09 = \$90$ for the next ten years. At the end of that time, the bond will also generate a $1,000 repayment of the principal or par value. Before we can determine the present value of these cash flows, however, the appropriate discount rate (RRR) must be selected. *In order to find the RRR, we must observe the yield (percentage return) offered by bonds of comparable risk and maturity that have been issued by other firms.* This yield represents the market-determined RRR for Wabash Power's bonds.

Let us assume that the market yield on similar maturity and risk bonds of other power companies is currently 12%. We now have all the information needed to calculate the value of each bond. Notice that the cash flows on the bond can be divided into two components: an annuity consisting of the annual interest payments, and a single sum consisting of the repayment of par value. This characteristic of bonds permits us to express the general IVM equation in the following form:

Bond Value = PV of Interest + PV of Par Value

$$V_B = (Int) \sum_{t=1}^{N} \frac{1}{(1+r)^t} + \frac{Par}{(1+r)^N} = (Int)(ADF_{r,N}) + (Par)(DF_{r,N}) \qquad (1)$$

where

V_B = the value of the bond;
r = the required rate of return on the bond;
Int = the annual interest payment;

Par = the par value of the bond;
N = the term-to-maturity, in years.

Figure 7-3 shows the calculations for the valuation of the Wabash bonds. The figure indicates that the bonds have a market value on January 15, 1999 ($830.50), which is considerably less than their par value of $1,000. What is the cause of the discount of $169.50?

Yields on securities have increased since Wabash issued the bonds ten years ago. The firm was able to issue the bonds at par with a coupon of only 9% in 1989

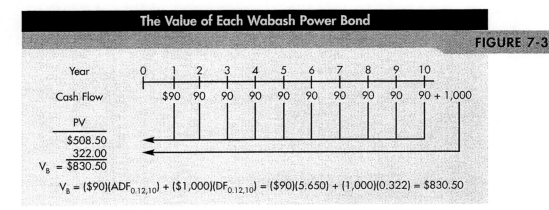

The Value of Each Wabash Power Bond

FIGURE 7-3

$$V_B = (\$90)(ADF_{0.12,10}) + (\$1,000)(DF_{0.12,10}) = (\$90)(5.650) + (1,000)(0.322) = \$830.50$$

because that was the market RRR at the time. Since then, the market RRR has increased from 9% to 12%. If the original investors in the bonds wish to resell them on the financial markets in 1999, they must also offer a yield of 12%. Since the coupon is fixed at 9%, the only way the bond's yield can be increased to 12% is to sell it at a discount. That is, a bond with a par value of $1,000 sells at a market price of $830.50. The discount will provide the new investor with a capital gain of $169.50 at the bond's maturity on January 15, 2009, because Wabash Power will repay the full par value of $1,000 on that date. The combination of the interest income over the 1999–2009 period plus the capital gain at maturity is just sufficient to provide a new investor with the RRR of 12%.

If the market-determined RRR on January 15, 1999, were only 8%, the bonds would sell in the financial markets at a premium (their market price would be greater than par value):

$$V_B = (\$90)(ADF_{0.08,10}) + (\$1,000)(DF_{0.08,10})$$
$$= (\$90)(6.710) + (\$1,000)(0.463)$$
$$= \$603.90 + \$463.00$$
$$= \$1,066.90$$

In this case, the present value of the bond's cash flows exceeds the par value because the RRR of 8% is less than the coupon rate of 9%. This high coupon rate motivates new investors to pay more than par value for the bonds. The coupon of 9% over the life of the bonds will be offset by a capital loss of $66.90 = $1,000 – 1,066.90 at maturity, causing the average annual rate of return on the bond to be just 8%. If the market's RRR in 1999 were 9%, the bonds would sell for par value:

$$V_B = (\$90)(ADF_{0.09,10}) + (\$1,000)(DF_{0.09,10})$$
$$= (\$90)(6.418) + (\$1,000)(0.422)$$
$$= \$577.62 + \$422.00$$
$$= \$999.62 \approx \$1,000$$

The $0.38 discrepancy between V_B and par value is due to rounding in the discounting factor tables. These three examples of the valuation of Wabash Power's bonds demonstrate the three significant relationships shown in Figure 7-4.

Semiannual Interest Payments

In the previous examples, an *annual payment* of interest on the bond was assumed in order to simplify the calculations. In reality, most bonds pay interest on a semiannual basis. Since semiannual interest reduces the size of each period's pay-

SUMMARY FIGURE 7-4

The Relationship Between a Bond's Value and Its RRR

RRR	Bond Value
1. RRR > Coupon Rate	V_B < Par Value
2. RRR = Coupon Rate	V_B = Par Value
3. RRR < Coupon Rate	V_B > Par Value

ment by half and doubles the number of payments, the bond valuation equation can be rewritten as follows:

$$V_B = \left(\frac{Int}{2}\right) \sum_{t=1}^{2N} \left[\frac{1}{\left(1+\frac{r}{2}\right)^t}\right] + \frac{Par}{\left(1+\frac{r}{2}\right)^{2N}} = \left(\frac{Int}{2}\right)\left(ADF_{\frac{r}{2},2N}\right) + (Par)\left(ADF_{\frac{r}{2},2N}\right) \quad (2)$$

The use of equation (2) can be demonstrated by recalculating the present value of the Wabash bonds under the assumption of semiannual payment of interest. We will also assume that the RRR is 12% and the term-to-maturity is 10 years. Thus, the adjusted discount rate is 0.12/2 = 0.06, and the number of time periods is 10 years × 2 = 20. The semiannual interest payment is $90/2 = $45. The bond's value under these assumptions is:

$$
\begin{aligned}
V_B &= (\$45)(ADF_{0.06,20}) + (\$1,000)(DF_{0.06,20}) \\
&= (\$45)(11.470) + (\$1,000)(0.312) \\
&= \$516.15 + \$312.00 \\
&= \$828.15
\end{aligned}
$$

It is important to note that both the interest payments *and* the repayment of par value are discounted at a rate of 6% per period for 20 periods. The standard assumption in the case of a bond that pays semiannual interest is semiannual compounding of interest. Although the par value is a single sum received at the end of the tenth year, the investor has the opportunity to earn interest semiannually on alternative investments. As a result, the par value has a lower present value than if the opportunity cost of funds were stated on an annual basis.

Calculating a Bond's Yield-to-Maturity

http://
This Web page will calculate yield-to-maturity.

www.pathfinder.com/money/smartcalc/pages/bon1.html

Until now, the illustrations of bond valuation have dealt with finding the present value of a bond, given the RRR. Frequently, however, an investor wishes to find the *yield* on a bond that is implicit in its market price. Suppose that you are considering investing in a $1,000 Simcor Industries bond. The bond in which you are interested has a market price of $1,081.10, a term-to-maturity of 15 years, a par value of $1,000, and a coupon rate of 10%. You wish to know what annual rate of return you will earn if you invest in the bond. To find this rate of return, use equation (1) by setting V_B equal to the bond's market price and solving for r. If interest is paid annually, the calculation would be:

$$V_B = (\$100)(ADF_{r,15}) + (\$1,000)(DF_{r,15}) = \$1,081.10$$

The cash flow stream on the bond is not an annuity due to the lump sum repayment of par value at maturity. Consequently, the equation cannot be directly solved for the unknown discount factor, but must be determined by trial and error. First, a guess about r must be made. The corresponding discounting factors from Tables III and IV at the end of the text are then substituted into the equation until the present value at some r is equal to $1,081.10. In order to make a reasonable first guess about r, notice that the market price exceeds the par value. Thus, the correct discount rate must be *less* than the coupon rate of 10%. In addition, the difference between the market price and par value is only $81.10 = $1,081.10 − $1,000. The correct discount rate, then, should not be much below 10%.[1] At a discount rate of 9%, the present value is

$$V_B = (\$100)(8.061) + (\$1,000)(0.275) = \$1,081.10$$

Because this present value equals the market price, the anticipated annual yield on the Simcor bond *is* 9%. This anticipated rate is the RRR on the bond. It is also called the bond's **yield-to-maturity (YTM)** because it is the *interest rate that equates the present value of all future cash flows over the bond's remaining life to its current market price.* If you buy the bond for $1,081.10 today and hold the bond until it matures in 15 years, you will realize a compound annual return of 9%.

If the 10% coupon on the Simcor bonds were paid semiannually rather than annually, adjustments must be made to the discount rate, the number of time periods, and the size of the interest payment per period, as shown in equation (2). Thus, an initial estimate for r of 8% results in the following present value:

$$V_B = \left(\frac{\$100}{2}\right)\left(ADF_{\frac{0.08}{2},(2)(15)}\right) + (\$1,000)\left(DF_{\frac{0.08}{2},(2)(15)}\right)$$

$$= (\$50)\left(ADF_{0.04,30}\right) + (\$1,000)\left(DF_{0.04,30}\right)$$

$$= (\$50)(17.292) + (\$1,000)(0.308)$$

$$= \$1,172.60$$

Since this present value is greater than the market price of $1,081.10, the correct r is larger than 8%.

We would like to recalculate the present value at a discount rate of 9%, but Tables III and IV do not contain discounting factors for a semiannual discount rate of 0.045 (0.09/2). The tables can be used, however, to approximate those discounting factors. Recall that the present value equals the par value of $1,000 when the discount rate equals the coupon rate of 10%. Thus, we know that:

Yield-to-Maturity (YTM) The interest rate that equates the present value of all future cash flows over a bond's remaining life to its current market price. The YTM represents both the RRR and the anticipated annual rate of return on a bond.

---

[1] A useful technique for making a first guess about the value of r is to calculate the average annual return on the bond over its term-to-maturity:

$$\text{Average Annual Return} = \frac{\text{Average Annual Income}}{\text{Average Price}}$$

$$= \frac{\text{Annual Interest Payment} + (\text{Capital Gain (Loss) at Maturity} / \text{Term-to-Maturity})}{(\text{Market Price} + \text{Par Value}) / 2}$$

For the Simcor bond, the average annual return is

$$\text{Average Annual Return} = \frac{\$100 + (-\$81.10 / 15)}{(\$1,081.10 + \$1,000) / 2} = \$94.60 / \$1,040.55 = 9.09\%$$

This technique treats the capital gain or loss as though it were partially realized each year over the bond's remaining life instead of in one lump sum at maturity. Although the average annual return usually provides a close approximation of r, it is not the true annual yield on a bond because it ignores the timing of the capital gain or loss.

r	PV	Market Price	Difference
8%	$1,172.60	$1,081.10	+$91.50
10%	1,000.00	1,081.10	– 81.10

The correct r or YTM therefore must lie between 8% and 10%. Furthermore, the YTM must be approximately 9% because the 8% present value is larger than the market price by about the same dollar amount that the 10% present value is smaller than the market price. If the YTM provided by this procedure is too imprecise, an investor can resort to bond tables, electronic calculators, or computer software packages that provide more precise estimates of the YTM. At the end of the text, we provide instructions for the use of a business calculator to solve for a bond's YTM.

The Components of a Bond's RRR

When the YTM is not equal to the coupon rate, a capital gain or loss is required to obtain the necessary RRR. The return of a bond whose market price is not equal to par value consists of both interest over the life of the bond and a capital gain or loss at maturity. Thus, the RRR on a bond can be divided into two components:

$$r = \text{Current Yield} + \text{Capital Gains Yield}$$

$$\text{Capital Gains Yield} = r - \text{Current Yield}$$

$$\text{Current Yield} = \frac{\text{Annual Interest Payment}}{V_B}$$

The Wabash Power example referred to earlier can be used to demonstrate the application of these relationships. On January 15, 1989, the bonds were issued at par value because the 9% coupon was equal to the market RRR on that date. Let us assume that ten years later on January 15, 1999, the market RRR has changed. If it rises to 12%, the price of the bonds would fall to $830.50. If it falls to 8%, the price of the bonds would rise to $1,066.90. Figure 7-5 shows how these three RRRs on the Wabash bonds can be divided into their current income and capital gains components.

An investor in the Wabash bonds on January 15, 1989, expected to receive a return solely in the form of interest income because the coupon rate was equal to the market RRR. If the market RRR increases to 12% by January 15, 1999, the $169.50 discount ($1,000 – 830.50) increases the current yield to 10.84%. The remaining portion of the 12% RRR comes in the form of a capital gains yield of 1.16%. Alternately, if the market RRR falls to 8% on January 15, 1999, the current

The Current Yield and the Capital Gains Yield on the Wabash Power Bonds

FIGURE 7-5

	January 15, 1989	January 15, 1999 If Interest Rates Rise	January 15, 1999 If Interest Rates Fall
RRR	9.00%	12.00%	8.00%
Annual Interest	$0.09 \times \$1,000 = \$90$	$0.09 \times \$1,000 = \$90$	$0.09 \times \$1,000 = \$90$
V_B	$1,000.00	$830.50	$1,066.90
Current Yield $= \dfrac{\text{Annual Interest Payment}}{V_B}$	$\dfrac{\$90}{\$1,000} = 9.00\%$	$\dfrac{\$90}{\$830.50} = 10.84\%$	$\dfrac{\$90}{\$1,066.90} = 8.44\%$
Capital Gains Yield = RRR – Current Yield	9.00 – 9.00% = 0%	12.00% – 10.84% = 1.16%	8.00% – 8.44% = –0.44%

yield falls to 8.44% because the bond's value rises from $1,000 to $1,066.90. Since the bond's current yield of 8.44% exceeds the RRR of 8.00%, the bond must offer a negative capital gains yield of –0.44%. The capital loss of $66.90 = $1,000 – 1,066.90 at maturity is just sufficient to reduce the overall yield to the RRR of 8%.

Interest Rate Risk: YTM Versus Holding Period Yield

The discussion in the preceding sections concentrated on the case in which an investor holds a bond until it matures. Under this assumption, the YTM at the time of the bond's purchase is the annual rate of return realized by the investor until the bond's maturity. In that case, the investor's holding period is the bond's term-to-maturity at the time of purchase. What if the investor's holding period is less than the bond's term-to-maturity? Is the realized annual rate of return still equal to the YTM at the time of purchase? The answer to these questions depends on the behavior of the bond's YTM over the holding period.

Suppose an investor purchases two bonds with a 10% coupon rate payable annually and a $1,000 par value. The term-to-maturity of one bond is 1 year, while the term-to-maturity on the other is 20 years. If both bonds have a YTM of 8%, their prices can be found in Table 7-1. The short-term bond has a market price of $1,018.60. The long-term bond has a market price of $1,196.80. Assume that interest rates rise over the next year so that after one year the YTM is 9%. The short-term bond matures at the end of the year, and the investor receives the $1,000 par value from the bond's issuer. The investor also liquidates the investment in the long-term bond by selling it on the bond market. At its new term-to-maturity of 19 years and new YTM of 9%, the bond's new market price is:

$$V_B = (\$100)(ADF_{0.09,19}) + (\$1,000)(DF_{0.09,19})$$
$$= (\$100)(8.950) + (\$1,000)(0.195) = \$1,090.00$$

At the time of purchase, the YTM of 8% was the investor's *anticipated annual rate of return* on each bond. The rate of return *actually realized* on a bond, on the other hand, is called the **holding period yield (HPY)**. The formula for the *realized rate of return* or HPY for a holding period of one year is

Holding Period Yield (HPY) The annual rate of return actually realized on an investment in a bond.

$$HPY = \frac{\text{Current Income} + \text{Selling Price} - \text{Purchase Price}}{\text{Purchase Price}} \tag{3}$$

For the short-term bond, the investor's realized annual rate of return was

$$HPY = \frac{\$100 + \$1,000 - \$1,018.60}{\$1,018.60} = \frac{\$81.40}{\$1,018.60} = 8.00\%$$

The Effect of YTM and Term-to-Maturity on the Price of a 10% Coupon, $1,000 Par Value Bond

TABLE 7-1

Term-to-Maturity (N)	Price (V_B) if YTM is:		
	8%	10%	12%
1 year	$1,018.60	$1,000.00	$982.30
10 years	1,134.00	1,000.00	887.00
20 years	1,196.80	1,000.00	850.90

$$V_B = (\$100)(ADF_{r,N}) + (\$1,000)(DF_{r,N})$$

The anticipated return (YTM) and the realized return (HPY) are identical for the short-term bond because its holding period equaled its term-to-maturity at the time of purchase. For the long-term bond, the realized annual rate of return was

$$HPY = \frac{\$100 + \$1,090 - \$1,196.80}{\$1,196.80} = \frac{-\$6.80}{\$1,196.80} = -0.57\%$$

The large difference between the YTM of 8% and the HPY of –0.57% is due to two factors:

1. The fluctuation in the bond's YTM over its holding period.
2. A holding period (1 year) shorter than the bond's term-to-maturity at the time of purchase (20 years).

This example illustrates the significance of a bond's holding period to the risk faced by investors. *If the holding period equals the term-to-maturity*, investors know that they can redeem the bond at maturity for its par value. In effect, the selling price is certain. Thus, *the annual HPY is also certain. When the term-to-maturity exceeds the holding period*, however, the selling price of the bond is uncertain because it depends on the behavior of the YTM after the time of purchase. Consequently, *the HPY is uncertain.*

Interest Rate Risk The uncertainty in the holding period yield on a bond when its holding period is shorter than its term-to-maturity and its yield-to-maturity fluctuates over time.

The uncertainty in the HPY on a bond when its holding period is shorter than its term-to-maturity is called **interest rate risk**. The cause of interest rate risk is the fluctuation in a bond's price that results from changes in its YTM after its purchase. Table 7-1 demonstrates the inverse relationship between YTM and price. Regardless of term-to-maturity, an increase in YTM is accompanied by a decrease in price and a decrease in YTM is accompanied by an increase in price. The table also shows the *positive relationship between the size of the change in YTM and the size of the change in price.* The larger the increase (decrease) in a bond's YTM, the larger the decrease (increase) in its price. For example, if the term-to-maturity is 10 years, an increase in YTM from 8% to 10% results in a price change of only $1,000.00 – $1,134.00 = –$134.00. A change in YTM from 8% to 12%, on the other hand, results in a price change of $887.00 – $1,134.00 = –$247.00.

Figure 7-6 shows the sensitivity of market price to changes in YTM for the three bonds shown in Table 7-1. Since interest rate risk means an exposure to price fluctuations, the figure reveals something about the relationship between interest rate risk and term-to-maturity. Because price sensitivity increases with term-to-maturity, *interest rate risk is always greater for long-term bonds than for short-term bonds.* In Appendix A to this chapter, we examine interest rate risk in more detail.

Up to this point, the theory of bond valuation has been discussed from the viewpoint of the IVM. We have demonstrated how an investor's estimate of a bond's cash flows and its RRR determine its value to that investor. We can now address the issue of whether the prices of bonds traded on financial markets actually reflect the valuation process of the IVM.

PRICE VERSUS VALUE: THE CONCEPT OF MARKET EFFICIENCY

In competitive financial markets, YTM and RRR are such close approximations of each other that these terms can be used interchangeably. The reason for this convergence is that all investors use the market yields (YTMs) available on other bonds of comparable risk as their estimate of the appropriate RRR for a given bond. In essence, when a bond's YTM is taken as the best estimate of the correct RRR, each individual investor accepts the consensus opinion of all investors in the bond market. As long as the market is usually correct in the bond prices it estab-

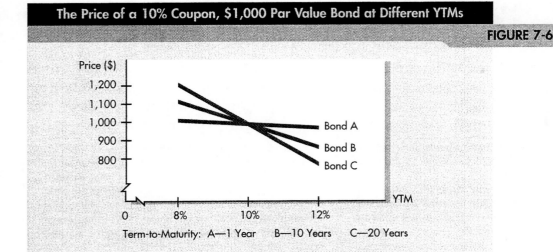

The Price of a 10% Coupon, $1,000 Par Value Bond at Different YTMs

FIGURE 7-6

Term-to-Maturity: A—1 Year   B—10 Years   C—20 Years

lishes, the individual would be making an error *not* to use this approach in determining the RRR.

This does not imply that investors do not change their opinions about the appropriate RRR and value for a bond over its life. In fact, the regular fluctuations in the market price of a bond are due largely to variations in investors' attitudes about the correct RRR. These variations, in turn, are the result of changes in the financial position of the bond's issuer or in the general economic environment. Investors sell bonds whose market prices exceed the revised estimates of their values, and buy bonds whose market prices are less than their values. This process continues until market price equals value for all bonds. The price adjustment process takes place so rapidly, moreover, that the current market price cannot deviate significantly from investors' revised estimate of value except for a very brief period.

It is this speed of adjustment of a bond's price to new economic information that leads to the concept of market efficiency. An **efficient market** is one in which the *current market price of an asset is the best estimate of its value.* Market efficiency is generally characteristic not only of the bond market but also of the markets for other financial instruments. Our discussion of the valuation of bonds and stocks in this chapter is based on the concept of efficient market pricing of these securities. Consequently, in the remainder of this chapter, the terms *price* and *value* will be used interchangeably.[2] Appendix B to the chapter contains a further discussion of the concept of an efficient financial market.

Efficient Market A market in which the current market price of an asset is the best estimate of its value.

THE VALUATION OF PREFERRED STOCK

Preferred stock (sometimes called preference stock) represents a source of equity financing for which the issuing firm promises to pay a specific periodic dividend. Unlike bonds, preferred stock typically has no maturity date nor is the issuer legally obligated to make the payment of dividends. The promised dividends can be stated either as a fixed dollar amount per period or as a percentage of par value. Since

Preferred Stock A source of equity financing on which the issuing firm promises to pay a specific periodic dividend.

---

[2] While the investor's acceptance of market price as a close approximation of value is the correct technique for the selection of financial assets, it is not appropriate for the selection of real assets for which competitive markets are lacking. The lack of efficiency in pricing in the markets for real assets can lead to significant differences between the value of a real asset to the firm and the cost of obtaining that asset. We discuss the correct techniques for valuing real assets in Chapter 9.

■ Financial ISSUES

BOND CALLS

As the general level of interest rates fluctuates in response to changes in the economic environment, the yields that both new and previously issued bonds must provide will also fluctuate. In the case of previously issued, or "seasoned," bonds these fluctuations will affect the secondary-market trading prices of the bonds, as Table 7-1 and Figure 7-6 show.

The calculations that underlie those illustrations do, however, contain an important assumption: that the bonds in question are expected by investors actually to remain outstanding until their *scheduled* maturity date. As we noted in Chapter 3, many corporate bonds contain "call" provisions, which permit the issuing firm to redeem the bonds (call them in from their holders) prior to maturity at a specified premium over par value if the firm wishes to do so. A typical call price might be $1,050 per $1,000 par value of the bonds, for example.

Suppose such a provision existed for the 20-year term-to-maturity bond having a 10% coupon rate, which is shown in Table 7-1. The $1,196.80 price at which the bond is predicted to sell when interest rates (YTMs) drop to 8% neglects the possibility that the issuing firm might decide to call the bond when interest rates drop to that level, rather than continue to pay the 10% coupon rate that was originally set. Since investors will understand that this could happen, the market price of the bond should never rise much above $1,050 even though the present value of the scheduled remaining interest and principal payments *is* $1,196.80.

This is more than merely a theoretical observation. Investors in the United States who purchased bonds in the early 1980s, which had coupon rates of 12% to 16% when they were issued, hoped to be able to hold those bonds until they matured. When interest rates dropped into the range of 8% to 10% in the late 1980s and early 1990s, however, a substantial number of the bonds issued five to ten years earlier were called. Even though the call prices provided the investors with a modest capital gain over the initial par value of the bonds, this gain was not enough to offset the fact that the investors were forced to reinvest the proceeds of the calls at significantly lower earnings rates.

If the reverse had occurred—interest rates had generally risen instead—the issuing firms would not, of course, have called their seasoned bonds. It would have been irrational for a firm to pay $1,050 for a bond that was trading only at $850 in the market, and then have to refinance the bonds at a higher interest rate than the original coupon rate. The existence of call provisions means that the interest rate "bet" that investors make is weighted against them. If interest rates subsequently increase, investors lose the bet because bond prices fall. If interest rates decline, investors also lose the bet because their old bonds are called in at a pre-determined call price and never attain the full price they could have reached if there were no call provision in the bond agreement.

---

there is no repayment of par value at maturity, the major significance of par value is that it serves as a basis for the calculation of dividends.[3] As with bonds, preferred stock can be traded after its issuance among investors on financial markets.

Calculating the Value of Preferred Stock

Because the only cash flow associated with a share of preferred stock is a perpetual stream of dividends, the IVM for preferred stock can be written as:

$$V_P = \sum_{t=1}^{\infty} \frac{D_P}{(1+r_P)^t} \qquad (4)$$

where

V_P = the value of the share of preferred stock;

r_P = the investor's RRR; and D_P = the preferred dividend payment per year.

---

[3] As we shall see in Chapter 13, the stated par value of preferred stock does have one other significance: it determines the claim that preferred stockholders have on a firm's assets in the event the firm is liquidated.

■ Valuation

ISSUes

THE INSTITUTIONALIZATION OF STOCK TRADING AND OWNERSHIP

Among the questions that arise in discussions as to whether the securities markets are "efficient" is that of the nature of the participants in those markets. The United States stock market, unlike similar markets in many other countries, has traditionally enjoyed a broad level of participation by individual investors. As late as the mid-1960s, for example, approximately 85% of all U.S. common stocks were owned directly by individuals in their personal investment portfolios, and roughly 60% of the daily volume of trading on the organized exchanges and over-the-counter markets was accounted for by individuals.

By the early 1990s, however, individuals' direct ownership of common stocks had fallen to just over 50% of the total, and their contribution to daily trading volume had dropped to approximately 20%. The remainder was accounted for by institutional investors such as pension funds, mutual funds, brokerage houses, and insurance companies. In the process, the size of the average trade increased substantially, since institutional investors commonly trade in blocks of 10,000 shares or more rather than the 100-share to 1,000-share blocks that are characteristic of individuals.

Whether these trends have improved market efficiency—that is, whether stock prices now are more likely to reflect the actual underlying *values* of the securities involved—is a subject of considerable debate. On the one hand, it has been argued that institutional investors are able to spend more time and money on careful research into the companies whose shares they might buy, than would be the case for individuals. Thus, the trading decisions of institutions should be better informed and better able to move stock prices closer to true values.

The counterargument is that the large transactions that institutions engage in may tend to drive stock prices away from true values, as the stock exchanges attempt to execute those transactions. In addition, institutions collectively tend to trade in similar directions in response to developing news events. This may lead to increased stock price volatility as large demands for and supplies of stocks arrive on the market together. There is in fact some evidence that daily stock price movements have been more volatile in recent years than was true in earlier times.

Recall from Chapter 5 that an infinite stream of level cash flows represents a perpetuity whose present value is equal to the cash flow per period divided by the discount rate:

$$PV = (C)(ADF_{K,\infty}) \quad ADF_{K,\infty} = 1/K$$
$$PV = C/K$$

Thus, equation (4) can be simplified to:

$$V_p = D_p/r_p \tag{5}$$

For example, if an investor's RRR is 12%, the value of a 9% preferred stock with a par value of $100 is

$$V_p = \frac{\$9.00}{0.12} = \$75.00$$

Calculating a Preferred Stock's Yield

The calculation of the yield or RRR on a preferred stock simply involves rearranging equation (5) to solve for an unknown r_p. Under the assumption of efficient markets for financial assets, the market price of a preferred stock is equal to its value. As a result, the RRR can be found with the following equation:

$$r_p = D_p/P_0 \tag{6}$$

where P_0 is the current price of the preferred stock (the market price at time zero). As an illustration of equation (6), suppose the price of the preferred stock in our previous example rises from $75.00 to $81.00. At the new price, its yield is

$$r_P = \frac{\$9.00}{\$81.00} = 11.1\%$$

Since the issuer is not obligated to repay par value, there is no expected capital gains component of the anticipated yield on preferred stock. Its RRR (anticipated return) therefore consists solely of current income regardless of the level of the RRR. Any fluctuation in the market's RRR for a preferred stock results in a price adjustment that is just sufficient to equate the yield with the RRR. For this reason, r_P in equation (6) is called the preferred stock's dividend yield rather than its YTM, as was the case with a bond.[4]

THE VALUATION OF COMMON STOCK

Common Stock A financial instrument that represents equity financing of a firm and grants a residual claim on the firm's earnings and assets.

The mathematics of the IVM for a **common stock** are identical to those for a bond or a preferred stock. The application of the IVM is considerably more difficult, however, due to the difference in the nature of the cash flow stream. The cash flows on a bond or a preferred stock are fixed in amount. Any investor uncertainty regarding the cash flow streams on these two types of securities stems only from potential financial difficulties that may make it impossible for the issuer to meet the scheduled payments. The dividends on common stock, on the other hand, are residual rather than contractual in nature. Thus, the amount and timing of the dividends is subject to both the firm's *ability* and its *willingness* to make dividend payments.

Calculating the Value of Common Stock

The following form of the IVM can be used to value a common stock:

$$V_E = \sum_{t=1}^{\infty} \frac{D_t}{(1 + K_E)^t} \tag{7}$$

where

V_E = the value of the share of common stock (equity);
K_E = the investor's RRR on the share of common stock; and D_t = the dividend expected in year t.

Although equation (7) appears straightforward, its simplicity is misleading. Unlike the case of a preferred stock, the pattern of the dividend stream is unknown. Future dividends may remain constant, fall, or rise, depending on the firm's financial performance and the dividend decisions of its Board of Directors. Estimating the components of such an infinite stream of unknown dividends is a difficult task. The standard solution to this problem is to project some systematic time pattern of future dividends that enables one to deal with both the perpetual and variable aspects of the cash flow stream.

No-Growth Model. Perhaps the most convenient assumption concerning dividends is that they will continue indefinitely at the level, D_0, paid in the most recent year. In that event, all the expected future D_t in equation (7) are equal to D_0, and the IVM reduces to the perpetuity form used to value a preferred stock;

---

[4] Because a preferred stock's market price *can* fluctuate in response to changes in its RRR, there may be an *unexpected* capital gain or loss realized by the investor in the security.

$$V_E = D_0/K_E \tag{8}$$

Although this equation is mathematically identical to equation (5), there are some important practical differences. First, the value of D_p in equation (5) is fixed while the value of D_0 above is merely the investor's *estimate* of the future annual dividend. Second, the two RRRs, r_p and K_E, are not equal. K_E will exceed r_p due to the higher risk associated with the residual nature of the dividends on common stock. Both the contractual interest on debt and the fixed dividends on preferred stock take precedence over the residual dividends on common stock.

As an example of the use of the no-growth model, suppose an investor wishes to value the common stock of Forest Products Company. The investor estimates that this year's earnings per share (EPS) for the firm will be $6.00 and will remain at that level indefinitely. Furthermore, the firm is expected also to continue indefinitely to pay dividends equal to 50% of earnings. If the investor determines the RRR on the stock to be 15%, its value is:

$$V_E = \$3.00/0.15 = \$20.00$$

and it should trade at that price in the market.

Steady Growth Model.   For many firms, a more plausible assumption about dividends is that they will increase over the long term at some characteristic average annual growth rate, g. If that is the case, the mathematics of compounding can be used to calculate the expected dividend in each future year:

$$D_t = D_0 (1+g)^t \tag{9}$$

where D_0 is the firm's dividend, which was paid in the most recent year (last year). For example, if last year's dividend was $1.50 per share and dividends are expected to grow at an annual rate of 10%, the dividends expected over the next three years will be:

$$D_1 = (\$1.50)(1.10) = \$1.65 \quad D_2 = (\$1.50)(1.10)^2 = \$1.82 \quad D_3 = (\$1.50)(1.10)^3 = \$2.00$$

The relationship in equation (9) therefore can also be expressed in the form

$$D_t = (D_1)(1 + g)^{t-1} \tag{10}$$

When this relationship is substituted into the generalized IVM present value expression of equation (7), the result is the steady growth form of the IVM for a share of common stock:

$$V_E = \sum_{t=1}^{\infty} \frac{(D_1)(1+g)^{t-1}}{(1+K_E)^t} = (D_1) \sum_{t=1}^{\infty} \frac{(1+g)^{t-1}}{(1+K_E)^t} \tag{11}$$

Although this equation looks more complex than the basic IVM in equation (7), it reduces to a much simpler expression.

The forecast in equation (10) is that dividends per share are expected to increase each year at a specific percentage rate, g. Simultaneously, the discount factor applied to them to measure their present value is $1 + K_E$ greater each year than in the preceding year. As a result, each successive year's present value in equation (11) is a fixed percentage of that for the preceding year. A series of numbers of this sort is called a "geometric progression" in mathematics. Conveniently, there is a definite value that any geometric progression reaches when the series of numbers comprising it are added consecutively over an indefinite period of time, as in equation (11), provided that g is less than K_E. When the numerator of the series increases at the rate $1 + g$ each period and the denominator increases at the rate $1 + K_E$, this value is

$$\sum_{t=1}^{\infty} \frac{(1+g)^{t-1}}{(1+K_E)^t} = \frac{1}{K_E - g} \tag{12}$$

Accordingly, equation (11) can be rewritten in a much more compact and usable form as

$$V_E = \frac{D_1}{K_E - g} \tag{13}$$

where D_1 is the dividend per share the firm is expected to pay in the coming year (at time $t = 1$), g is the expected long-term growth rate in dividends per share, and K_E is the RRR for an investment in the firm's common stock. With D_0 being *last* year's dividend, the equivalent expression is

$$V_E = \frac{(D_0)(1+g)}{K_E - g} \tag{14}$$

In order for V_E to be a positive number and therefore result in a meaningful stock price, the requirement is that g must be less than K_E.

Equations (13) and (14) should have some intuitive appeal. If a firm's dividends on its common stock are never expected to increase from their current annual amount, the dividend stream is a level perpetuity. As we saw above, the associated value of the firm's common shares can be obtained by multiplying the expected annual dividend by the level-perpetuity discount factor $1/K_E$, for that case. What equations (13) and (14) indicate is that the present value of a perpetuity that is expected to grow over time at the annual rate g can be obtained by multiplying the *initial* dividend D_1 by the "growing-perpetuity" discount factor $1/(K_E - g)$ instead. The subtraction of g from the discount rate K_E in the denominator of that factor allows for the expectation that dividends will increase from the current annual rate.

Obviously, the present value derived when D_1 is multiplied by $1/(K_E - g)$ is greater than that derived when D_1 is multiplied by $1/K_E$. That is, for a given *initial* dividend, a share of stock whose dividends are expected to grow is worth more than a share of stock for which dividends are *not* expected to grow. Equally obviously, if we substitute $g = 0$ into either equation (13) or (14), we obtain again the no-growth model of equation (8) as a special case.

We may use Forest Products Company once more to illustrate the application of these equations. Suppose the firm's earnings and dividends per share are expected to grow at an annual rate of 10% indefinitely. If last year's dividend was $3.00 per share and the RRR is 15%, the value of the firm's common stock is:

$$V_E = \frac{D_1}{K_E - g} = \frac{(\$3.00)(1.10)}{0.15 - 0.10} = \$66.00$$

The value of Forest Products' common stock increased sharply from $20 per share under the no-growth assumption to $66 per share with an assumed growth rate of 10% per year. A decrease in the assumed value of g will have a similar effect on V_E. Thus, *the estimate of the value of a share of common stock is very sensitive to the assumed rate of growth of dividends.*

Equation (13) can be used with any assumed value of g as long as $g < K_E$. For instance, if Forest Products' earnings and dividends are expected to *decline* at an annual rate of 10%, the value of the stock will be:

$$V_E = \frac{(\$3.00)(.90)}{0.15 - (-0.10)} = \$10.80$$

Not surprisingly, the value of the firm's stock under the assumption of declining dividends is less than its value under the assumption of either constant or growing dividends.

Calculating a Common Stock's Yield

The RRR on a common stock can be estimated with the IVM by rearranging the valuation equations to solve for an unknown K_E. As was true in our calculation of the RRR on a bond or a preferred stock, we use the current market price of a common stock as our estimate of its value.

No-Growth Model. When P_0 (the price at time zero) is substituted for V_E in the no-growth model, the equation can be solved for the RRR:

$$K_E = D_0/P_0 = D_1/P_0$$

Thus, if the current market price of Forest Products' common stock is $20.00 per share and its annual dividends are expected to remain constant at $3.00 per share, the RRR of investors in the stock is

$$K_E = \frac{\$3.00}{\$20.00} = 0.15 = 15\%$$

Steady Growth Model. When P_0 is substituted for V_E in equation (13), that equation can also be solved for the implied RRR:

$$K_E = \frac{D_1}{P_0} + g \qquad (15)$$

For instance, let us return to the earlier steady growth example for Forest Products. Dividends are expected to grow indefinitely at 10% per year, and the current stock price is $66.00 per share. The RRR on the stock must be

$$D_1 = (\$3.00)(1 + 0.10) = \$3.30$$

$$K_E = \frac{\$3.30}{\$66.00} + 0.10 = 0.05 + 0.10 = 0.15 = 15\%$$

In the example in which the annual dividends are expected to decline at 10% per year and the current stock price is $10.80, the RRR is

$$D_1 = (\$3.00)(1 - 0.10) = \$2.70$$

$$K_E = \frac{\$2.70}{\$10.80} + (-0.10) = 0.25 - 0.10 = 0.15 = 15\%$$

This 15% RRR is the same figure used to derive the firm's stock price originally, under each of the various dividend growth expectations.

The Components of a Common Stock's RRR

Individuals who are unfamiliar with the IVM may have difficulty accepting the notion that a model of stock value can be based on expected dividends alone, which is what equation (7) states. They contend that, contrary to the IVM's assumption, investors do not hold a given common stock in their portfolios indefinitely. Rather, investors sell the stock at a capital gain or loss after some limited holding period. Thus, they actually realize both dividend *and* capital gains income. In that situation, the realized return on a common stock can be measured in the same manner as the holding period yield on a bond:

$$HPY = \frac{\text{Current Income} + \text{Selling Price} - \text{Purchase Price}}{\text{Purchase Price}}$$

If investors buy a common stock in anticipation of dividend income and capital gain income, the RRR can again be divided into two components:

$$RRR = \text{Dividend Yield} + \text{Capital Gains Yield}$$

If the planned holding period is one year, the RRR can be measured as:

$$RRR = \frac{D_1}{P_0} + \frac{P_1 - P_0}{P_0} \tag{16}$$

where D_1 = the dividend expected to be received during the year;
 P_0 = the stock's price at the start of the year (its purchase price); and
 P_1 = the stock's expected price at the end of the year (its expected selling price).

Notice that this model *appears* to be different from the form of the IVM in equation (15)

$$K_E = \frac{D_1}{P_0} + g = \text{Dividend Yield} + \text{Annual Growth in Dividends}$$

However, the two models are not contradictory. The only difference in the equations lies in the second component of the RRR and K_E. The IVM includes the annual percentage growth in dividends, while the other model incorporates the percentage capital gain. For equations (15) and (16) to be identical, it must be shown that $g = (P_1 - P_0)/P_0$.

According to equation (13), the price of the common stock at the start of the year is

$$P_0 = V_E = \frac{D_1}{K_E - g}$$

By extension, the price of the stock at the end of the year (at the beginning of the *next* year) is expected to be

$$P_1 = \frac{D_2}{K_E - g} = \frac{D_1(1+g)}{K_E - g} = P_0(1+g)$$

Substitution of this expression for P_1 into the capital gains component of the investors' model in equation (16) results in:

$$\frac{P_1 - P_0}{P_0} = \frac{P_0(1+g) - P_0}{P_0} = g$$

Thus, the expected percentage annual growth in dividends is identical to the expected annual percentage capital gain.

Table 7-2 divides the RRR on the Forest Products common stock of the previous examples into its dividend yield and capital gains yield components. In the no-growth case (g = 0%), the anticipated return must come solely in the form of dividend yield because the constant annual dividend of $3.00 per share implies that the stock price is also expected to remain constant over time. In the steady positive growth case (g = 10%), the anticipated return comes largely in the form of capital gains, which are attributable to the growing dividend. Finally, the dividend yield in the steady negative growth case (g = -10%) must be extremely large (25%) to offset the expected annual decline in the stock price. Despite the differ-

The Effect of Expected Divided Growth on the Price and the Anticipated Return on a Common Stock

TABLE 7-2

g	$P_0 = \dfrac{D_1}{K_E - g}$		K_E Anticipated Return	$=$	D_1/P_0 Dividend Yield	$+$	g Capital Gains Yield
–10%	$P_0 =$	$\dfrac{\$2.70}{0.15 - (-0.10)}$	0.15	$=$	$\dfrac{\$2.70}{\$10.80}$	$+$	(–0.10)
	$P_0 =$	$\$10.80$	0.15	$=$	0.25	$+$	(–0.10)
0%	$P_0 =$	$\dfrac{\$3.00}{0.15 - 0.00}$	0.15	$=$	$\dfrac{\$3.00}{\$20.00}$	$+$	0.00
	$P_0 =$	$\$20.00$	0.15	$=$	0.15	$+$	0.00
+10%	$P_0 =$	$\dfrac{\$3.30}{0.15 - 0.10}$	0.15	$=$	$\dfrac{\$3.30}{\$66.00}$	$+$	0.10
	$P_0 =$	$\$66.00$	0.15	$=$	0.05	$+$	0.10

ences in the three expected growth rates, the anticipated return is the *same* in all three cases because the financial markets will adjust the market price until the anticipated return *does* equal investors' RRR.[5]

A model like the IVM, which states that common stock prices represent the present value of future dividends per share, therefore is consistent with an investment environment in which investors do not hold the shares they purchase forever. It is also consistent with the fact that many investors consciously buy shares of common stock in the expectation of realizing capital gains. The point is that any such capital gains will depend upon expectations of future increases in dividends per share over time, which will lead subsequent purchasers of a stock to pay higher prices than the current price P_0. Ultimately, dividends are the determinant of both current and future stock prices because they represent the *cash flows* that firms distribute to their stockholders.

P/E Ratios and the IVM

In making their decisions about which common stocks to buy, investors in practice will often use a firm's Price/Earnings (P/E) ratio as a guide to the valuation of those stocks. As the name suggests, the **P/E ratio** measures the ratio of the price per share of a stock to the firm's earnings per share. P/E ratios are widely reported in financial publications. The P/E ratio at which a particular common stock should sell can be derived directly from the IVM.

According to the IVM, the value and current price of a share of stock can be expressed as

$$V_E = P_0 = \frac{D_1}{K_E - g}$$

P/E Ratio The ratio of the market price of a share of stock to the firm's earnings per share.

---

[5] In an efficient financial market, even the stocks of firms with poor prospects for their earnings and dividends can be attractive investments. The negative growth case in Table 7-2 will be just as profitable an investment as the positive growth case. Both investments will provide a 15% annual rate of return. The only difference between the two investments is the *form* in which the annual return is earned. The negative growth case offers a very high dividend yield that is partially offset by capital losses. The positive growth case offers a combination of a lower dividend yield supplemented by capital gains. An investor who cares only about the size, but not the form, of returns would find both investments to be equally attractive.

The coming year's dividend per share D_1 can, in turn, be expressed as a percentage of the firm's expected earnings per share E_1:

$$D_1 = (d)(E_1)$$

Dividend Payout Ratio The percentage of a firm's earnings that are paid out to shareholders as dividends.

where d is the firm's **dividend payout ratio**—dividends as a percent of earnings. We can thereby rewrite the IVM valuation equation in the form

$$P_0 = \frac{(d)(E_1)}{K_E - g}$$

If we divide both sides by E_1, this expression becomes

$$\frac{P_0}{E_1} = \frac{d}{K_E - g} \qquad (17)$$

The P/E ratio and dividend payout for the S&P 500 can be found at this Web site.

http://cpcug.org/user/invest/pepayout.html

and P_0/E_1 is the stock's price/earnings ratio. This figure represents the "multiple" of earnings at which the stock should sell in the market, given the dividend payout ratio of the firm in question, the expected annual growth rate in dividends per share for the firm, and investors' RRR from owning the stock. It is the only ratio that is consistent with the underlying valuation framework of the IVM.

As is evident from equation (17), P/E ratios will be higher—with everything else held constant—for stocks with higher dividend payout ratios, higher growth rates, and lower required rates of return. We can illustrate the impact of different growth rates by referring again to the case of Forest Products Company. As previously stipulated, the firm had earnings per share of $6.00 in the most recent year and paid out 50% of those earnings as dividends. The firm's expected earnings per share (E_1), dividends per share (D_1), current stock price (P_0), and the corresponding P/E multiples are shown in Table 7-3 for each of the three projected growth rates of –10%, 0%, and +10% assumed in our previous examples. As the table indicates, the firm's P/E ratio will range from a low of 2.0 to a high of 10.0, depending on investors' expectations about Forest Products' growth prospects.

Can you evaluate risk with P/E ratios? The Value Point Analysis Model gives possible insights into a stock's risk.

www.eduvest.com/vparisk.html

One can think of a firm's P/E ratio as a kind of "quality" statistic for the firm. That is, the price investors are willing to pay *per dollar* of earnings (or per unit of whatever currency the firm's earnings are denominated in) is a measure of how

TABLE 7-3 — The Effect of Expected Growth on the P/E Ratios Implied by the Use of the IVM

g	$P_0 = \dfrac{D_1}{K_E - g}$	E_1	$P/E = P_0/E_1$	$P/E = \dfrac{d}{K_E - g}$
–10%	$P_0 = \dfrac{\$2.70}{0.15 - (-0.10)}$	$5.40	P/E = $10.80/$5.40	P/E = 0.50/(0.15 - (-0.10))
	$P_0 = \$10.80$		P/E = 2.0	P/E = 2.0
0%	$P_0 = \dfrac{\$3.00}{0.15 - 0.00}$	$6.00	P/E = $20.00/$6.00	P/E = 0.50/(0.15 - 0.00)
	$P_0 = \$20.00$		P/E = 3.3	P/E = 3.3
+10%	$P_0 = \dfrac{\$3.30}{0.15 - 0.10}$	$6.60	P/E = $66.00/$6.60	P/E = 0.50/(0.15 - 0.10)
	$P_0 = \$66.00$		P/E = 10.0	P/E = 10.0

▪ Valuation

ISSUES

THE STOCK MARKET COLLAPSE OF 1987

On Monday, October 19, 1987, the New York Stock Exchange suffered its most substantial decline since the fabled market crash of 1929. On that date, the Dow Jones Industrial Average (the most widely quoted market indicator) fell over 500 points, which represented a 23% drop in average stock prices in just a single day. This collapse culminated a decline that began the preceding Wednesday and totaled over 750 points, amounting to a 30% overall reduction in prices. The associated losses to investors in U.S. securities were estimated at more than $500 billion during the five-day period. Simultaneously, similar declines were registered on most stock markets around the world.

This catastrophe resulted in numerous studies of the U.S. financial markets and calls for greater regulation of securities trading. It also reignited the debate over the concept of market efficiency. How could an efficient market in which securities prices are supposed to remain very close to their true values plummet so dramatically in such a short period of time? Is it realistic to assume that the markets were reacting normally and rationally to the arrival of new information, or did both individual and institutional investors merely panic for no good reason?

The case against market efficiency is built on the lack of significant news developments on Monday, October 19, or over the previous weekend. Furthermore, post-crash studies found that pension funds and mutual funds swamped the market with sell orders, driving prices downward. Such concentrated power to move prices is inconsistent with the hypothesis of market efficiency. In a subsequent survey, investors reported that their October 19 selling was a response to worry over market declines on October 14 and 15. Thus, market psychology, rather than a revision in firms' earnings and dividend prospects, seemed to motivate the selling.

Supporters of the notion of market efficiency countered that important new economic and political information did become available during the market decline. Increases in the U.S. trade deficit, and decreases in the dollar's international exchange value would naturally have led to concerns about higher future interest rates and inflation. Corporate earnings and dividends would be harmed in such an environment. Investor uncertainty was intensified by an attack on a U.S. oil tanker in the Persian Gulf, which occurred during this time. Thus, both components of the IVM explanation for stock prices—future dividends and investors' RRR—were adversely affected. In addition, once the selling started, it quickly overwhelmed the capacity of the stock exchanges to maintain an orderly market. The stock price plunge therefore may have been partly attributable to deficiencies in the trading mechanism rather than to underlying irrationality on the part of investors.

valuable investors perceive each dollar's worth of current earnings to be (the *quality* of earnings). Equation (17) says that this value is determined by three factors: (1) the extent to which earnings are distributed to stockholders in the form of dividends because it is ultimately dividends that determine value; (2) how rapidly today's earnings—and therefore dividends—are expected to grow in the future; and (3) the riskiness of the future earnings and dividend stream, as captured in the RRR for the stock in question. Thus, the more earnings can be translated into dividends, the more rapidly both will grow, and the more certain are the receipts, the more investors will pay for *today's* earnings.

A word of caution is in order in interpreting the P/E ratios that are reported in financial publications. In almost all instances, those ratios are computed from a company's current stock price and its reported earnings per share for the *previous* year. Typically, estimates of earnings for the coming year are not made. In Table 7-3, we have used an estimate of next year's earnings (E_1), because it is future, not past, returns that are relevant to valuing securities. If instead the most recent year's EPS of $6.00 were used to calculate P/E multiples for Forest Products, the ratios that would be reported are shown in Table 7-4. Often these are referred to as "trailing" P/E multiples since they are based on earnings (E_0) that *precede* the

	Trailing P/E Ratios for Forest Products Company			
TABLE 7-4				

g	P_0	E_0	$P/E = P_0/E_0$	
−10%	$10.80	$6.00	$10.80/$6.00 =	1.8
0	20.00	6.00	20.00/6.00 =	3.3
+10	66.00	6.00	66.00/6.00 =	11.0

price P_0 that is used in the calculation. While the P/E ratios in Table 7-4 are different from those in Table 7-3, they should in almost all cases follow the same overall pattern. For high-growth stocks, P/E multiples will also be high, even if they are trailing multiples.

From an investor's standpoint, P/E ratios can be useful and compact guidelines as rules of thumb in deciding whether particular common stocks are attractive investments. Thus, if a stock is currently selling in the market at a P/E multiple that is higher than that of other stocks having similar dividend payouts, growth prospects, and risk, the stock may well be overpriced and is likely to come under selling pressure that will reduce its price. The converse would be true of a stock whose multiple is below that of comparable firms.[6] Investment advisory services and brokerage houses often use such guidelines in making recommendations to investors about securities purchases and sales. If the financial markets are efficient, such discrepancies should not persist for very long, and prices should come quickly in line with the underlying values predicted by the IVM.

Common Stock Valuation with Variable Growth Rates

There are some cases in which the assumption of a constant rate of growth in dividends is not justified. For example, as the result of extraordinary technological breakthroughs, a firm may be able to realize very rapid short-term increases in earnings from innovative products, but these increases cannot be sustained indefinitely. More generally, firms tend to go through a life cycle with phases of expansion and maturity that correspond to different rates of change in earnings. Under such circumstances, the steady growth model cannot be used by itself to estimate the value of a firm's common stock. Instead, an alternative procedure is used that combines the basic form of the IVM for common stocks in equation (7) with the steady growth model in equation (13).

The basic procedure is to divide the expected future dividend stream into a number of growth phases. Each phase corresponds to a different expected growth rate. Either equation (7) or (13) is then used to find the present value of the dividends in each phase. Finally, the present values of all the phases are summed to find the value of the common stock. Although this procedure can be used with any number of phases, for the sake of simplicity, the valuation procedure is illustrated here in terms of a common stock with only two growth phases: accelerated (A) and normal (N).

Returning to the example of Forest Products, assume that, due to a recent technological breakthrough, we expect the firm's dividends to grow at an accelerated rate of 26% per year for the next three years and at a normal rate of 10% per year after that. Figure 7-7 compares the behavior of the firm's dividends under this variable growth assumption with the assumption of steady annual growth of 10%.

http://

The Motley Fool examines the importance of combining the P/E ratio with a company's growth rate.

www.fool.com/School/TheGrowthRate.htm

---

[6] In making such comparisons, it is important to identify whether the P/E multiples examined are based on the coming year's expected earnings or are trailing multiples.

■ International ISSUES

MARKET EFFICIENCY REEXAMINED—THE 1997 STOCK MARKET DIVE

On Monday, October 27, 1997, the Dow Jones Industrial Average endured its largest single day point drop in history: 554 points. Ironically, this market jolt occurred almost ten years to the day after the Dow's largest percentage one-day decline since its 1929 crash. Although the 1997 decline was much smaller than the 1987 drop in percentage terms (7% versus 23%), it was large enough to trigger "circuit breakers" that halted trading on the New York Stock Exchange. It also raised new questions about the efficiency of U.S. stock markets.

The efficient market explanation of the market's fall revolves around severe economic and financial market problems in Southeast Asia and their implications for U.S. firms. Real estate speculation, bad corporate loans, and a glut of production capacity were causing severe problems in Indonesia, Malaysia, Philippines, and Thailand. In addition, Japan's economy had been limping along at 1% growth since the early 1990s. Finally, the transfer of control of Hong Kong's economy and markets from the British government to China was a major source of concern. The results of all these negative factors were devastating. From June to September of 1997, the stock markets in some of these countries fell by over 40%. The same was true of the exchange rate of some of their currencies. Hong Kong's stock market alone fell nearly 25% in the four days before October 27. The domestic implication of all this economic turmoil was that U.S. firms would be hurt by competition from low-priced foreign goods both in foreign markets and in the United States. This potential earnings problem was seen by some as the chief cause of the Dow's problems.

The inefficient market explanation for the Dow's dive, on the other hand, emphasizes that U.S. economic performance was remarkably good. Third quarter profits of U.S. firms had exceeded analyst forecasts. The federal budget deficit was the lowest since 1974. Furthermore, inflation remained in check as wages rose less than 1% in the third quarter. Thus, there seemed to be no rational basis for the market's poor performance. This argument is buoyed by the market's response on Tuesday, October 28, when the Dow regained 337 points (4.7%). The erratic valuation of stocks by the stock market is dramatically illustrated by the behavior of the stock of Intel, the leading manufacturer of computer chips. On Monday, October 27, it fell from $85 to $75 per share. The slide continued on Tuesday to $69. By Wednesday, however, the price had rebounded to $85 again. This sort of stock price volatility raises the thought in some observers' minds that significant temporary inefficiencies can arise in otherwise very efficient markets.

The *first step* in the valuation procedure is to calculate the expected dividends in each of the three years of the accelerated growth phase:

$$D_1 = (D_0)(1 + g_A) = (\$3.00)(1.26) = \$3.78$$
$$D_2 = (D_0)(1 + g_A)^2 = (\$3.00)(1.26)^2 = \$4.76$$
$$D_3 = (D_0)(1 + g_A)^3 = (\$3.00)(1.26)^3 = \$6.00$$

The *second step* is to determine the present value of these dividends. Since the dividend stream is not level, we must calculate the present value of each year's dividend separately at the 15% RRR for Forest Products and then sum them:

$$PV = (D_1)(DF_{0.15,1}) = (\$3.78)(0.870) = \qquad \$\ 3.29$$
$$PV = (D_2)(DF_{0.15,2}) = (\$4.76)(0.756) = \qquad \$\ 3.60$$
$$PV = (D_3)(DF_{0.15,3}) = (\$6.00)(0.658) = \qquad \underline{\$\ 3.95}$$

PV of Dividends During Accelerated Growth Phase $\quad \$10.84$

The *third step* requires the calculation of the present value of a stream of dividends growing at an annual rate of 10% from year 4 to ∞. This present value represents the price of the stock at the beginning of the normal growth phase (the end of the accelerated growth phase):

$$\text{Stock Price at the Beginning of Normal Growth Phase} = P_3 = \frac{D_4}{K_E - g} = \frac{(D_3)(1 + g_N)}{K_E - g_N} = \frac{(\$6.00)(1.10)}{0.15 - 0.10} = \$132.00$$

Comparison of Variable and Constant Dividend Growth Rates for Forest Products Company

FIGURE 7-7

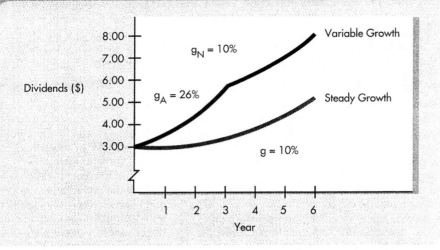

In the *fourth step* , we convert this future stock price into its present value as of today:

$$\text{PV of } P_3 = (P_3)(DF_{0.15,3}) = (\$132.00)(0.658) = \$86.86$$

In the *fifth step*, the current value of Forest Products' common stock is estimated by summing the two present values that were previously calculated:

$$\text{Current Value} = \text{PV of Dividends during Accelerated Growth Phase} + \text{PV of Stock Price at beginning of Normal Growth Phase}$$

$$P_0 = \$10.84 + \$86.86 = \$97.70$$

Thus, Forest Products' common stock should have a current market price of $97.70. At that price, the stock will provide an anticipated annual rate of return

Time Line for the Valuation of Forest Products' Common Stock

FIGURE 7-8

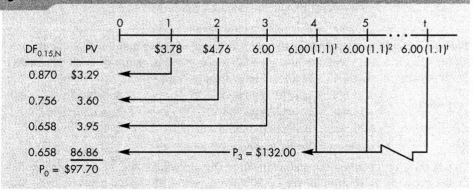

---

[7] Notice how substantially the three years of accelerated dividend growth have boosted the market price. Accelerated growth at 26% for three years increases the price to $97.70 from $66.00. A longer period of accelerated growth would result in an even higher current stock price. Consequently, the stock price is very sensitive to both the length of the accelerated growth period and the accelerated growth rate.

equal to the investors' RRR of 15%.[7] Figure 7-8 contains the time line for the Forest Products example. These relatively simple modifications to the steady dividend growth version of the IVM increase its usefulness. By dividing the future dividend growth pattern into phases, the concept of a firm's life cycle can be incorporated into estimates of the firm's RRR and the value of its common stock.

SUMMARY

In this chapter, the IVM was applied to the valuation of securities. It was also used to calculate the RRR on a security. The market price of a bond is equal to the present value of its expected future interest and principal payments. Since the coupon interest rate on a bond is fixed, the bond will sell at a premium or discount relative to its par value whenever the RRR of investors is smaller or larger than the coupon rate. This premium or discount results in a capital loss or gain at the bond's maturity. Thus, the RRR can be divided into a current yield component (interest income) and a capital gains component. The RRR or yield-to-maturity (YTM) on a bond is calculated by determining the discount rate, which equates the expected cash flows on the bond to its current market price.

The fluctuations in the price of a bond in response to changes in its YTM are positively related to the size of the change in the YTM and the term-to-maturity of the bond. When the market price fluctuates, the YTM at the time of purchase is no longer equal to the holding period yield (HPY) if the bond is sold prior to its maturity date. The possibility that the HPY will be larger or smaller than the YTM is called interest rate risk. The longer the maturity of a bond, the greater is its interest rate risk.

The market price of a preferred stock represents the present value of an infinite stream of level dividend payments. The price is calculated by dividing the expected annual dividend by the investor's RRR. Since there is no maturity date for a preferred stock, there is no expected capital gains component to its RRR. Consequently, the RRR on a preferred stock is called its dividend yield. The dividend yield is calculated by dividing the annual dividend by the current market price.

The valuation of a common stock requires assumptions about the amount and timing of the unknown future dividends. The most common assumption is that dividends will grow indefinitely at a specified annual rate. The steady growth model calculates the price of a common stock as the present value of its infinite future stream of increasing dividends. According to this model, the RRR on a common stock has two components. The dividend yield component consists of dividend income. The capital gains component corresponds to the expected rate of growth in future dividends. In those cases in which the assumption of steady dividend growth is not justified, a variable growth valuation technique is available.

chapter equations

1. $V_B = (Int)(ADF_{r,N}) + (Par)(DF_{r,N})$

2. $V_B = \left(\dfrac{Int}{2}\right)\left(ADF_{\frac{r}{2},2N}\right)$
$+ \left(Par\right)\left(DF_{\frac{r}{2},2N}\right)$

3. $HPY = \dfrac{\text{Current Income + Selling Price} - \text{Purchase Price}}{\text{Purchase Price}}$

4. $V_P = \displaystyle\sum_{t=1}^{\infty} \dfrac{D_P}{(1+r_P)^t}$

5. $V_P = D_P/r_P$

6. $r_P = D_P/P_0$

7. $V_E = \displaystyle\sum_{t=1}^{\infty} \dfrac{D_t}{(1+K_E)^t}$

8. $V_E = D_0/K_E$

9. $D_t = (D_0)(1+g)^t$

10. $D_t = (D_1)(1+g)^{t-1}$

11. $V_E = (D_1) \displaystyle\sum_{t=1}^{\infty} \dfrac{(1+g)^{t-1}}{(1+K_E)^t}$

12. $\displaystyle\sum_{t=1}^{\infty} \dfrac{(1+g)^{t-1}}{(1+K_E)^t} = \dfrac{1}{K_E - g}$

13. $V_E = \dfrac{D_1}{K_E - g}$

14. $V_E = \dfrac{(D_0)(1+g)}{K_E - g}$

15. $K_E = D_1/P_0 + g$

16. $RRR = \dfrac{D_1}{P_0} + \dfrac{P_1 - P_0}{P_0}$

17. $\dfrac{P_0}{E_1} = \dfrac{d}{K_E - g}$

The application of the IVM to the valuation of securities is important to a firm's financial managers in two ways. First, they must understand the process by which stockholders value a firm's stock if they are successfully to apply the value maximization criterion. Second, the evaluation of proposed investing and financing decisions requires estimation of both the cash flows and the RRRs associated with these decisions. By providing estimates of the RRRs on a firm's securities, the IVM enables financial managers to determine the appropriate RRRs for their firm's investing and financing proposals.

CONTENT QUESTIONS

1. Why is the study of financial security valuation important to financial managers?
2. Explain how the amount and timing of the cash flows from a bond are determined.
3. Under what conditions will a bond's market price be: greater than par, equal to par, and less than par?
4. Define a bond's yield-to-maturity.
5. Explain the difference between price and value and the difference between yield and required rate of return.
6. How does an efficient market insure that prices will be reasonable estimates of value?
7. Why do long-term bond prices fluctuate more than short-term bond prices in response to a given change in interest rates?
8. What is interest rate risk?
9. In what basic respects does the valuation of common stock differ from that of bonds and preferred stock?
10. What assumption regarding the time pattern of dividends is necessary to derive the equation that states

$$V_E = \frac{(D_0)(1+g)}{K_E - g}$$

11. Answer a critic of discounted cash flow stock valuation models who says that they are invalid because they are based on dividends only, while everyone knows that investors are primarily interested in capital gains.
12. Explain how the dividend growth rate affects the P/E ratios implied by the IVM.
13. In addition to steady dividend growth, why is it important to understand the valuation of common stock with variable dividend growth rates?
14. What are the two components of a bond's RRR and a common stock's RRR? How are they similar? How do they differ?

CONCEPT QUESTIONS

1. IVM The valuation of common stocks according to the IVM, as discussed in this chapter, is based on the concept that the price today of a share of stock reflects the present value of the future cash dividends expected from the stock. Many firms, however, do not currently pay dividends on their common stock, and many firms have not paid a dividend since the firms were formed. How can you reconcile the fact that the firms' shares still trade at a positive price, with the fact that they do not pay dividends?

2. IVM A company is considering the possibility of issuing bonds to raise funds for a capital expenditure program. Its investment bankers have offered the firm two choices: (1) a 20-year bond with no call provision, and (2) a 20-year bond, which is callable beginning five years after the date it is issued at a call price of $1,050 per bond. Both bonds have a par value of $1,000 and both are intended to be issued at par value. Which of these bonds would you expect to have the higher coupon interest rate? Explain your reasoning.

3. IVM We noted in the chapter that interest rate risk is greater for bonds with long terms-to-maturity than for bonds with short terms-to-maturity. Would you expect interest rate risk to be greater for bonds with high coupon interest rates or bonds with low coupon interest rates if their *terms-to-maturity* are identical? Explain your reasoning.

4. IVM In the case of companies whose common shares are publicly traded, information on their current prices, their current dividends per share, and the projected growth rates in their dividends per share can be used to infer the RRR that investors associate with the firms' stock. This RRR, in turn, would be used by a firm to analyze proposed corporate investment expenditures, in order to be sure those investments provide a rate of return that is consistent with what stockholders could earn for themselves elsewhere. How could a firm whose stock is *not* publicly traded obtain the RRR to use for analyzing its investments?

5. International For an extended period of time, the P/E ratios of Japanese common stocks exceeded the P/E ratios of U.S. common stocks—often by a substantial margin. Many investment analysts pointed to such evidence as an indication that Japanese stocks were overpriced and that the international financial market was inefficient. What would be an alternative interpretation, based on the IVM?

PROBLEMS

1. What is the value of a bond with a DM1,000 par value that has a 6% coupon rate and pays interest annually if the required rate of return is 8% and the term-to-maturity is:
   a. 10 years?   b. 5 years?   c. 1 year?
   d. In terms of your answers to (a), (b), and (c), what is the relationship between value and term-to-maturity?

2. Calculate the current yield and capital gains components of the RRR in parts (a), (b), and (c) of Problem 1. How are they affected by the assumption about the bond's term-to-maturity? Why?

3. What is the value of a $1,000 bond that has an 8% coupon rate and a 5-year term-to-maturity, given a 12% required rate of return:
   a. if interest is paid annually?   b. if interest is paid semiannually?
   c. if interest is paid quarterly?
   d. Explain why the frequency of interest payment affects bond value in terms of your answers to (a), (b), and (c).

4. Atlanta Foods' $1,000 par value, 20-year bonds were issued with a 9% coupon rate paying interest annually.
   a. What was the price of the bonds if they were sold at a YTM of 9%?
   b. Five years after issue, an increase in the general level of interest rates in the economy increased the YTM to 10%. What is the market price at this new YTM?
   c. Ten years after issue, a decrease in the general level of interest rates in

the economy decreased the YTM 8%. What is the market price at this new YTM?

5. Calculate the current yield and capital gains components of the RRR on Atlanta Foods' bonds in parts (a), (b), and (c) of Problem 4.

6. Find the yield-to-maturity of a 10-year, $1,000 par value bond that pays a 12% coupon rate annually:
   a. given a market price of $1,123.40.
   b. given a market price of $895.92.

7. One year ago an investor purchased a newly issued DM1,000 par value bond at par. The bond had a coupon rate of 11%, paid interest annually, and had a term-to-maturity of 15 years. What is the investor's realized return (HPY) on the investment for the year if she sells the bond today:
   a. at a YTM of 10%?   b. at a YTM of 11%?   c. at a YTM of 12%?

8. Calculate the HPY on the investment in Problem 7 (an 11% coupon bond purchased at par value) if the bond is sold after one year at a YTM of 12% and has a term-to-maturity at the time of sale of:
   a. 5 years.   b. 15 years.   c. 30 years.
   d. How do you account for the differences in your answers to parts (a), (b), and (c)?

9. Assume that an investor purchased a $1,000 par value bond with an annual coupon of $50 on January 15, 1965. At the time of purchase, the bond's YTM was 9% and its term-to-maturity was 30 years. If the YTM remained constant until maturity, what was the bond's market price on:
   a. January 15, 1965?   b. January 15, 1975?
   c. January 15, 1985?   d. January 15, 1995?
   e. How do you account for the behavior of the bond's price as the maturity date approached?

10. Baker-Midland Corporation's bonds are selling for $511.65 with a YTM of 13%. If they have a par value of $1,000 and a term-to-maturity of 10 years, what is the coupon rate of Baker's bonds?

11. Find current yield and capital gains yield for Baker-Midland's 10-year bonds described in Problem 10.

12. Osceola Textile's bonds are selling for $1,162.79 with a YTM of 13%. If they have a par value of $1,000 and a 10-year term-to-maturity, what is the coupon rate of Osceola's bonds?

13. Find the current yield and capital gains yield for Osceola Textile's bonds described in Problem 12.

14. In planning an issue of 20-year, $1,000 par value bonds, La Serena Hotel's investment banker recommended a coupon rate of 8.5%. On the day that the offering price was to be set, the yield-to-maturity for similar bonds was 9.0%. What must the offering price be in order to sell the bonds at the market YTM? Express your answer as a percentage of par value.

15. Allied Milling's preferred stock pays $7.00 per year.
   a. What is the value of one share of Allied preferred stock if the required rate of return is 12%?
   b. What is the yield on Allied preferred stock if the market price is $50.00 per share?

16. Hall Technologies is planning to issue preferred stock to raise $10,000,000 for an expansion of its manufacturing plant. It has estimated that investors would require a 15% rate of return.
   a. How many shares would have to be sold if Hall set the preferred dividend at $6.00 per share?

b. How many shares would have to be sold if Hall set the preferred dividend at $9.00 per share?

17. Mid-South Power is planning to raise $200 million for a new power plant. Its investment bank recommends that the firm issue preferred stock with a $7.00 dividend.
    a. If the firm estimated that the market RRR would be 7% at the time of issuance, how many shares should Mid-South plan to offer for sale?
    b. Assume that the issue price of the preferred stock reflected a market RRR of 6.75%. Based on your answer to part (a), what were the actual proceeds of the stock issue?

18. Referring to Problem 16, calculate the total amount of cash dividends that Hall Technologies would have to pay each year after it raises the $10,000,000:
    a. if it set the preferred dividend at $6.00 per share?
    b. if it set the preferred dividend at $9.00 per share?

19. Taft Industries is a mature firm. Most analysts believe that its common stock dividends will remain constant indefinitely at the current level of $4.80 per share.
    a. If the RRR of investors is 15%, what is the market value of a share of Taft common stock?
    b. If the market price is $30.00, what is the market RRR on Taft common stock?

20. Common shareholders of Oxford Brewing just received a £2.75 dividend per share. What is the price of a share of common stock, given a required rate of return of 16%:
    a. if the dividend growth rate is 5%?
    b. if the dividend growth rate is 10%?
    c. if dividends are expected to fall at a rate of 5% per year?

21. Using the information in Problem 20, find the dividend yield and capital gains yield that an investor would receive if he or she purchased Oxford Brewing stock:
    a. assuming the dividend growth rate is 5% per year.
    b. assuming the dividend growth rate is 10% per year.
    c. assuming that dividends are expected to fall at a rate of 5% per year.

22. Continuing with the information in Problem 20, calculate the trailing P/E ratio for Oxford Brewing's common stock if the dividend of £2.75 was 50% of the previous year's earnings per share:
    a. assuming the dividend growth rate is 5%.
    b. assuming the dividend growth rate is 10%.
    c. assuming that dividends are expected to fall at a rate of 5% per year.

23. The current market price for Triton S.A. common stock is SF100.00 per share. Assume that the next annual dividend is expected to be SF4.00 per share and that future dividends are expected to grow at a rate of 12% per year indefinitely.
    a. What required rate of return is implied by the market price?
    b. How is the required rate of return distributed between dividend and capital gains yields?

24. Weis Products just paid a $3.00 per share dividend on its common stock. Given a required rate of return of 20%, what constant rate of growth would be implied by a market price of $33.00 per share?

25. Gulfport Technology, Inc. is experiencing tremendous growth due to a number of successful technological breakthroughs. Due to impending competition

from other firms, however, growth should return to normal in a few years. Analysts believe dividends will grow at a rate of 20% per year for the next five years. After that, they should average about 8% indefinitely. The latest dividend was $1.00 per share. What is the value of a share of common stock if investors require a 14% rate of return?

26. What is the value of a share of common stock that just paid a dividend of FF5.00 per share if dividends are expected to grow each year at the rates shown below? Assume a required rate of return of 12%.

Year	Growth Rate
1	22%
2	22
3	12
4	12
5	10
6	10
7 to ∞	6%

27. Your cousin is trying to sell you an annuity that will pay $1,000 per year for the next 25 years. The first payment will be one year from today. The advertised price of the annuity is $10,675.00. You calculate that you can earn 12% on other investments of similar risk.
    a. What is the value of the annuity to you?
    b. When you decline your cousin's offer, she replies that you are making a serious mistake since she has made numerous sales to other investors at the advertised price. If her reply is true, what does it reveal about the efficiency of the market for these annuities?

28. Compusoft Technologies is experiencing tremendous growth. Because it must finance this growth externally, it will not pay dividends for the next 5 years. After that, dividends will be paid starting in the sixth year with a $2.00 per share dividend, which is expected to grow at 12.5% per year indefinitely. Find the current market price of Compusoft's common stock if the RRR is 16%.

29. Redbrick Corporation, once a solid manufacturing firm, has filed for bankruptcy. The firm has also suspended all dividend payments on its common stock and preferred stock and interest payments on its bonds. You estimate that it will be three years from today before the proceeds from its liquidation will be distributed. You believe that, after all other claims, there will be $75,000,000 left to be distributed to Redbrick's common shareholders. If you have a 15% RRR, what would you be willing to pay today for one of Redbrick's 15,000,000 shares?

30. Hall Management Corporation has a 40% dividend payout ratio. The firm just paid a $3.50 dividend on its shares of common stock. The dividend is expected to grow at 8% per year indefinitely. The market's RRR is 14%.
    a. What is Hall's P/E ratio?   b. What is its "trailing" P/E ratio?

31. Hi-Lite Industries' last dividend was $1.05 per share on its common stock. Due to declining business, its dividend is expected to fall each year by 5%. The market's RRR is 14% and Hi-Lite's payout ratio is 75%.
    a. Find Hi-Lite's P/E ratio.   b. Find Hi-Lite's "trailing" P/E ratio.

INTERNET EXERCISE

Use the bond calculator to calculate the yield-to-maturity of the following bonds.

Price Paid	Face Value	Coupon Rate	Months to Maturity
95	1,000	9%	12
95	1,000	9%	24
95	1,000	9%	36
95	1,000	9%	48

Print out your results, with your observations and comments, and hand in to your instructor. www.pathfinder.com/money/smartcalc/pages/bon1.html

SELF-STUDY QUIZ

1. Find the price of an 8.5% coupon bond with a $1,000 par value and a 15-year term-to-maturity. Interest is paid semiannually. The yield-to-maturity is 10.0%.
2. Find the current yield and capital gains yield of the bond in Problem 1.
3. One year ago you purchased a 9.25% coupon bond for $995.00. Today the market value of the bond is $1,050.00. What was your holding period yield?
4. Calculate the value of a share of common stock that just paid a dividend of $0.75 per share. Dividends are expected to grow at a rate of 11% per year. The RRR is 16%.
5. For the common stock in Problem 5, separate the RRR into its two components.

APPENDIX A: BOND DURATION AND INTEREST RATE RISK

In the body of the chapter, we briefly discussed how a bond's price on the secondary market responds to changes in the RRR on the bond, that is, to changes in its required yield-to-maturity (YTM) after it is issued. These price fluctuations are what is meant by the term "interest rate risk." We saw that bonds with long terms-to-maturity (TTMs) will exhibit greater changes in price due to a given change in YTM than will bonds with short TTMs.

This effect is illustrated in Table 7A-1. There, we calculate the percentage price increase for each of the three 10% coupon rate bonds shown in Table 7-1 in the chapter, in response to a 20% decrease in YTM from 10% to 8%. The percentage increase is 19.7% for the 20-year bond but only 1.9% for the one-year bond. The price *sensitivity* of the three bonds is summarized in the last column of Table 7A-1, by expressing the percentage price change relative to the percentage change in YTM. Thus, the 20% decline in YTM was associated with a 19.7% price increase for the 20-year bond. The price increase therefore was 0.985 times as large as the

The Effect of Term-to-Maturity on the Price Sensitivity of Bonds Having a 10% Coupon					TABLE 7A-1

| Term-to-Maturity | Bond Price (V_B) if r is: | | Percentage Change in: | | Bond Price Elasticity: |
(TTM)	10%	8%	V_B	r	$V_B^E = \dfrac{\% \text{ Change in } V_B}{\% \text{ Change in } r}$
1 Year	$1,000.00	$1,018.60	1.9%	−20%	−0.093
10 Years	1,000.00	1,134.00	13.4%	−20%	−0.670
20 Years	1,000.00	1,196.80	19.7%	−20%	−0.985

Price Elasticity A measure of the sensitivity of a bond's price to changes in its yield-to-maturity. It is calculated by dividing the percentage change in price by the percentage change in YTM.

yield decrease. (The negative sign on that figure in the table signifies that YTM and price move in opposite directions.) This measure of relative price change is known as the bond's **price elasticity** and is indicated by the symbol V_B^E. The higher the value of V_B^E, the more sensitive is a bond's price to a given change in yield to maturity.

Price elasticity is an important concept to an investor because it identifies the extent of the investor's exposure to interest rate risk. While a bond's price elasticity is directly related to its term-to-maturity, it is also affected by another attribute of the bond: the bond's coupon rate. The prices of bonds with low coupon rates are more sensitive to YTM changes than are the prices of high coupon rate bonds of equal terms-to-maturity. That is, price elasticity is inversely related to the size of the coupon rate.

That phenomenon is illustrated in Table 7A-2. We see that the price elasticity (V_B^E) of a 10-year bond having a 10% coupon is –0.670 because the bond's market price rises by 13.4% in response to a 20% decline in YTM. A bond of the same maturity having only a 5% coupon, however, has a price elasticity of –0.760 because its price increases by 15.2% as a result of the 20% decrease in YTM. A bond that pays *no* coupon interest exhibits the greatest price elasticity, by rising 19.9% in value due to a 20% decline in YTM. Consequently, this "zero coupon" bond has a (V_B^E) of –0.995.[1]

Since the price elasticity of a bond is affected both by its term-to-maturity and its coupon rate, a measure of the *combined* impact of both attributes of the bond would be very helpful to investors who are concerned with their overall exposure to interest rate risk. Fortunately, such a measure has been developed. It is referred to as a bond's *duration* and is defined in the following manner:

$$D = \frac{\text{(Sum of the Weighted PVs of Each of the Bond's Cash Flows)}}{\text{(PV of all Cash Flows)}} \qquad (7A\text{-}1)$$

$$D = \frac{[(1)PV(C_1) + (2)PV(C_2) + \ldots (N)PV(C_N)]}{V_B}$$

where N is the bond's term-to-maturity, and V_B (the current price of the bond) is the present value of all the bond's future cash flows. The *weights* applied to each of the individual cash flows are the number of years in the future each cash flow

The Effect of Coupon Rate on the Price Sensitivity of Bonds Having 10-Year Terms-to-Maturity

TABLE 7A-2

Coupon Rate	Bond Price (V_B) if r is:		Percentage Change in:		Price Elasticity: (V_B^E)
	10%	8%	V_B	r	
10%	$1,000.00	$1,134.00	13.4%	–20%	–0.670
5%	693.25	798.50	15.2%	–20%	–0.760
0%	386.00	463.00	19.9%	–20%	–0.995

[1] A zero coupon bond is a special case of bonds known as "original issue discount" bonds, which are issued with coupons substantially below the market-required YTM at the time they are issued. We will examine the valuation of zero coupon bonds further in Chapter 12.

is scheduled to be received. Thus, the present value of the cash flow that is expected to be received one year from now (C_1) is assigned a weight of 1, the present value of the cash flow expected to be received two years from now (C_2) is assigned a weight of 2, and so on throughout the remaining maturity of the bond.

Duration is a more comprehensive measure of the remaining "life" of an investment in a bond than is term-to-maturity. **Duration** identifies how far in the future the *average* cash flow is scheduled to be received, while term-to-maturity identifies how far in the future the *last* cash flow is to be received. Since the price elasticity of a bond is affected by the size and timing of *all* its cash flows—including both coupon interest payments and principal repayments—duration is a more accurate indicator of price elasticity and interest rate risk.

The computations of the durations of the three 10-year term-to-maturity bonds in Table 7A-2 are shown in Table 7A-3. The duration of the 10% coupon bond is only

Duration An alternative to term-to-maturity as a measure of the remaining life of a bond. It identifies how far in the future the average cash flow from the bond is scheduled to be received.

The Durations of Bonds Having 10-Year Terms-to-Maturity, at Yields-to-Maturity of 10%

TABLE 7A-3

Year, t	Cash Flow, C_t	Discount Factor, $DF_{0.10,t}$	Cash Flow Present Value, $PV_t = (C_t)(DF_{0.10,t})$	Time Weight, t	Weighted Present Value, $(t)(PV_t)$
A.	**10% Coupon Rate Bond:**				
1	$ 100	0.909	$ 90.90	1	$ 90.90
2	100	0.826	82.60	2	165.20
3	100	0.751	75.10	3	225.30
4	100	0.683	68.30	4	273.20
5	100	0.621	62.10	5	310.50
6	100	0.564	56.40	6	338.40
7	100	0.513	51.30	7	359.10
8	100	0.467	46.70	8	373.60
9	100	0.424	42.40	9	381.60
10	1,100	0.386	424.20	10	4,242.00
	$2,000		$1,000.00		$6,759.80

Duration = $6,759.80/$1,000 = 6.76 years

Year, t	Cash Flow, C_t	Discount Factor, $DF_{0.10,t}$	Cash Flow Present Value, $PV_t = (C_t)(DF_{0.10,t})$	Time Weight, t	Weighted Present Value, $(t)(PV_t)$
B.	**5% Coupon Rate Bond:**				
1	$ 50	0.909	$ 45.45	1	$ 45.45
2	50	0.826	41.30	2	82.60
3	50	0.751	37.55	3	112.65
4	50	0.683	34.15	4	136.60
5	50	0.621	31.05	5	155.25
6	50	0.564	28.20	6	169.20
7	50	0.513	25.65	7	179.55
8	50	0.467	23.35	8	186.80
9	50	0.424	21.20	9	190.80
10	1,050	0.386	405.35	10	4,053.50
	$1,500		$ 693.25		$5,312.40

Duration = $5,312.40/$693.25 = 7.66 years

Year, t	Cash Flow, C_t	Discount Factor, $DF_{0.10,t}$	Cash Flow Present Value, $PV_t = (C_t)(DF_{0.10,t})$	Time Weight, t	Weighted Present Value, $(t)(PV_t)$
C.	**Zero Coupon Bond:**				
10	$1,000	0.386	$ 386.00	10	$3,860.00

Duration = $3,860.00/$386.00 = 10.0 years

6.76 years, even though its TTM is a full ten years. This is a reflection of the fact that the duration calculation recognizes that the ten coupon interest payments involved occur, on average, five years in the future and that they account for a sizable portion (over half) of the total present value of the bond. The duration of the 5% coupon bond is somewhat longer—7.66 years—because the ten coupon payments on it comprise a smaller fraction of the bond's total cash flows and total present value. Finally, the duration of the zero coupon bond is exactly equal to its term-to-maturity, since the principal payment *at* maturity is the *only* cash flow. If we made similar calculations for bonds with the same coupons but with 20-year TTMs, all the durations would be greater. With the exception of the zero coupon bond, however, all would still be less than the 20-year terms-to-maturity of the bonds.

These are generalizable results. For a given yield-to-maturity, duration increases as term-to-maturity increases, and decreases as a bond's coupon rate increases. The relationships are a direct reflection of the different time weightings of the bond's cash flows in the duration calculation. More importantly, since term-to-maturity and coupon rate determine a bond's price elasticity, duration considers both simultaneously. In particular, the price elasticity of a bond has been shown to be related to its duration in the following manner:

$$V_B^E = -(D)(YTM) \qquad\qquad (7A\text{-}2)$$

Thus, when the current YTM is 10%, the price elasticities of the three bonds in Table 7A-3 are:

$$10\% \text{ Coupon Bond: } V_B^E = -(6.76)(0.10) = -0.676$$
$$5\% \text{ Coupon Bond: } V_B^E = -(7.66)(0.10) = -0.766$$
$$0\% \text{ Coupon Bond: } V_B^E = -(10.0)(0.10) = -1.000$$

The price elasticity of –0.676 for the 10% coupon bond indicates that a 10% increase (decrease) in the bond's required yield-to-maturity will cause a 6.76% decrease (increase) in the bond's market value. As is again evident, price elasticity is inversely related to coupon rate.

The elasticity relationship identified in equation 7A-2 holds strictly only for *small* changes in YTM around the current YTM. In mathematical terms, it would be described as a "point" or "local" elasticity. That is why the elasticities listed in Table 7A-2 for a change in required yield-to-maturity from 10% to 8% are slightly different from those computed from equation 7A-2. A sudden 2% change in YTM would be a relatively large change in the financial marketplace. Nonetheless, the differences are quite small, and the duration of a bond provides a good summary measure of the extent to which fluctuations in interest rates will affect a bond's price and therefore expose an investor to interest rate risk. The larger is duration, the greater is that risk.

APPENDIX B: MARKET EFFICIENCY

In this chapter, we introduced the concept of an efficient financial marketplace in which the prices at which securities are observed to trade on the secondary markets are very close estimates of the true underlying values of those securities. By "true underlying value," we mean the value that would be obtained by discounting the expected future cash flows from the securities at an appropriate required rate of return. That is what the Investment Valuation Model prescribes. Another way to describe an efficient market is to say that all relevant and available *information* about securities' cash-flow-generating potential is reflected in the securities' current prices. Most contemporary finance theory is based on this notion. The question is whether it is a reasonable notion and whether there is empirical evidence to support it.

Requirements for an Efficient Market

Market efficiency requires that information about securities is widely available to most investors at relatively low cost. It also requires that the transactions costs of trading in securities are relatively low, in order that price discrepancies can quickly and effectively be corrected by trading. Furthermore, it requires that the market be comprised of a large number of participants, no one of which can affect a security's price significantly by trading in the security. These requirements are met by many financial markets around the world and are probably most closely met by the U.S. financial markets. A wide range of investment advisory services and brokerage houses provide information to investors for quite modest fees. As the U.S. financial markets have become less regulated and more competitive, the costs of trading have been reduced substantially for investors. The same phenomenon has occurred in a number of other countries as well. As institutional investors have become more important in the markets, their research skills should provide improved information about securities' underlying values and thereby keep prices from getting very far out of line with values. One potential problem with institutional investors is the typically large size of their trades, which can move prices in the short run simply because of supply and demand imbalances. There is also the tendency of many institutions to trade in similar directions at the same time, which can enhance price volatility in the short run.

Implications of an Efficient Market

If the financial markets *are* efficient, investors, whether individual or institutional, should have very limited opportunities to "beat" the market by identifying mispriced securities and acting on that information. Thus, if prices are correct, an investor can only earn the rate of return on a security that is consistent with that security's risk. We saw in Chapter 6 that the relevant risk measure is systematic risk. In an efficient market, then, the returns earned by investing in securities should differ only to the extent that securities' betas differ. Each level of systematic risk assumed by an investor will offer a return that is exactly right for that level of risk—but no more. Rather than attempt to pick out mispriced securities, investors would be just as well off by investing in a broad-based market portfolio like the S&P 500 and simply holding that portfolio over time. Attempts to "time" the market or detect undervalued stocks would in general be wasted efforts.

Another implication is that the past price movements in a security would provide little, if any, indication of future price movements. In particular, if all information that is available *today* about a security is already reflected accurately in its price, the only thing that can change that price is tomorrow's *new* information. Since tomorrow's information is unknown, one cannot predict tomorrow's security price. This is the rationale for the notion that securities' price movements will be random in nature, because new information is also random in nature. Attempts to detect likely future price movements by looking at past price movements and looking for patterns in those prices (what is commonly described as "technical analysis") should be fruitless as well.

Evidence of Market Efficiency

Most empirical studies of securities returns would support that general notion of market efficiency. It appears as though the actual returns that securities have provided historically are about what they *should* have been for the levels of systematic risk involved. It appears as though even large and sophisticated institutional investors, like mutual funds and pension funds, have not been able to "beat" the market. The returns on their portfolios have also been just what they should have been, given the risk levels of the portfolios. Similarly, most studies of the returns from trading on the basis of past price patterns as predictors of future prices show little evidence of any ability to earn abnormal returns from the associated trading rules.

Evidence of Market Inefficiency

Despite the weight of the evidence, however, there are certain phenomena that appear in the data on stock returns that seem to be inconsistent with full efficiency in the markets. A small number of institutional investors have earned returns that are well in excess of what would have been expected for the levels of risk they have assumed—and have done so over extended periods of time. There is some suspicion, therefore, that their analytical skills have been able to detect undervalued securities and profit from that information.

There are also some disturbing anomalies in the historical returns on various subcategories of common stocks, and in the returns from particular investment strategies. For example, it appears as though the rates of return that small-company stocks have been observed to provide are higher than would be expected if investors were being rewarded only for assuming systematic risk. These returns have persisted for a number of years and have generally exceeded the returns from investing in large-company stocks. Additionally, stocks that in one year sell at relatively low P/E multiples tend to outperform stocks that concurrently sell at high P/E multiples, over the next year.

The calendar also seems to have an impact. If one bought U.S. common stocks in December of every year and sold them the following January, one would have outperformed the market during the remainder of the year quite consistently over time. The same would have been true if the trading rule were to buy stocks on Monday of each week and sell them on Friday.

None of these anomalies should persist if the market *is* efficient. Investors should anticipate them and, by attempting to act on them, should eliminate the differential profit opportunities by adjusting stock prices in advance. Nonetheless, the evidence does suggest that for certain investors, for certain types of securities, and for certain trading rules, the concept of market efficiency may not be totally valid. As a generalization for most segments of the market, however, efficiency does seem to be a reasonable characterization, at least in the United States and in many other major industrialized countries having well-developed and broadly based securities markets.

Capital Expenditure Decision Rules

In the preceding chapters, we have applied the fundamental principles of the Investment Valuation Model primarily to the valuation and pricing of corporate securities. The objective was to identify the manner in which *investors* perceive value, in order that a firm's financial managers can develop decision rules that are consistent with value maximization for shareholders. In this chapter, we turn our attention to a major category of financial decisions: the budgeting of funds for expenditures on capital investments. Investments of this sort frequently require very sizable outlays and commit a firm's financial resources for an extended period of time. Thus, they can be critical decisions for the economic health of the firm. They also represent one of the most logical decision areas for the application of the IVM, due to the length of the decision horizons that are typically involved. Among the issues that we shall address are the following:

- Recent surveys of large firms reveal that discounted cash flow (DCF) techniques for capital budgeting decisions are more widely used by financial managers than are non-DCF methodologies. What is the distinction between the two? Do both types of techniques accurately reflect the determinants of investment value that were described in Chapter 6? What accounts for the more widespread use of the DCF methodologies?

- The DCF approaches present certain practical problems in implementation. For example, accurate estimation of a proposed investment's expected future cash flows can often be quite difficult. In other cases, a firm may be unable or unwilling to finance all the investments that are

identified as being acceptable by DCF decision rules. When this occurs, it is necessary to rank investments by their relative attractiveness. How can financial managers deal with these problems?

- DCF decision rules concentrate on cash flows to assess the desirability of proposed capital investments. Most corporations, however, evaluate the performance of their various divisions and business units according to criteria such as ROA, which are based on accounting data. Can this lead to a conflict between the kinds of investments that senior management would *like* to have its operating managers undertake, and the ones those operating managers may *choose* in response to their performance evaluation? If so, how can that conflict be resolved?

This chapter is the first of three in Part 3 that describe the application of the IVM to the decision to invest in real assets. The estimation of both the benefits and the RRR components of the IVM is a much more complex procedure for real assets than for financial assets such as corporate securities. The distinction between the two settings is summarized in Figure 9-1. Recall from Chapter 7 that the existence of efficient markets for securities implies that value equals price, and RRR equals yield, in the case of financial assets. Thus, the search for overpriced or underpriced securities is likely to prove futile for most investors.

The conditions necessary for efficient markets, however, are lacking for real assets. The IVM, therefore, can often be used effectively to identify underpriced or overpriced capital investments. This chapter describes two investment decision

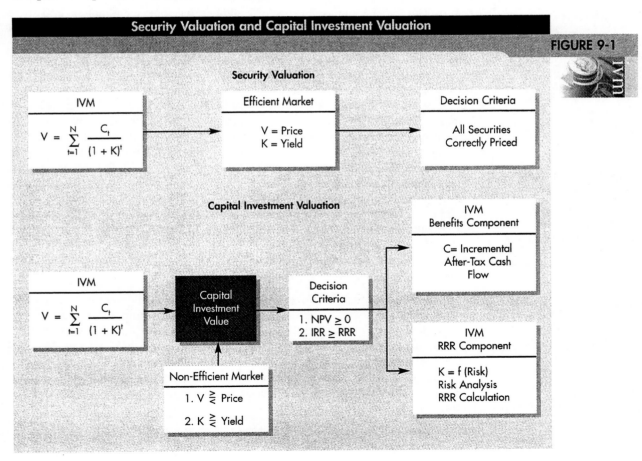

Security Valuation and Capital Investment Valuation

FIGURE 9-1

rules, net present value (NPV) and internal rate of return (IRR), that are derived from the IVM. If an investment's NPV is positive or its IRR exceeds its Required Rate of Return, the investment should be undertaken because it will enhance share-holder wealth. The calculation of NPV and IRR, in turn, requires a careful estimation of both the cash flows and the RRR that are relevant to an investment. Chapter 10 concentrates on the estimation of these cash flows. Chapter 11 discusses how to assess their riskiness, and Chapter 15 utilizes that risk assessment to determine the appropriate RRR for a given investment proposal.

The presentation in this chapter will begin in a general manner by discussing the basic characteristics and importance of investments in capital assets. We then proceed to a detailed analysis of the calculation procedures for the two categories of capital budgeting decision criteria: non-discounted cash flow (non-DCF) and dis-counted cash flow (DCF) methodologies. The conceptual superiority of the major DCF methodologies (net present value and internal rate of return) will be demon-strated in terms of their ability to measure the potential effect of a proposed invest-ment on firm value. The chapter will close with an examination of decisions under capital rationing, and with an analysis of the relationship between DCF decision rules and corporate performance measurements.

THE CAPITAL INVESTMENT DECISION

A **capital investment** is an expenditure of funds made in the hope of realizing future benefits that are expected to occur over a *long period of time*. The expendi-ture can be for tangible assets such as buildings, machinery, equipment, and spare parts. It can also involve intangible items such as an advertising campaign, research and development, employee training, and the exploration for raw materials. The key elements of a capital investment are the *current expenditure* of funds in anticipa-tion of *long-term future cash inflows*. Capital expenditures can be contrasted with operating expenditures such as salaries, office supplies, production materials, and energy, which are made in anticipation of short-term cash inflows. The term **capital budgeting** describes the entire process of analyzing potential capital investments to determine whether they should be selected and how they will be implemented.

The view of financial managers on capital investments is different from that of accountants. Financial managers will often analyze as a capital investment an expenditure that accountants do not capitalize. For example, financial managers may treat the cost of a new advertising campaign or an executive development program as a capital expenditure since long-term benefits are expected from these outlays. Accountants, on the other hand, would usually record the costs as a cur-rent expense of operations.

The effective evaluation and management of capital investments is critically important to a firm and its owners for several reasons:

1. *Long Time-Horizon.* Once a capital investment is implemented, it can affect the profitability and value of a firm over a substantial number of years.
2. *Strategic Nature.* Frequently a capital asset represents a strategic investment that shapes the future of the firm, such as major expansion, a new product, or a new technology.
3. *Magnitude of Resource Commitment.* Many capital investment decisions involve a large expenditure of funds and a significant commitment of mana-gerial time.

Each of these factors justifies careful attention to the capital budgeting process as a key influence on firm value.

---

http://
What is required to formu-late realistic capital expen-ditures and operating cash flows for a capital budget? Examine a capital-intensive new dairy facility at
http://hammock.ifas.ufl. edu/txt/authors/DS138

Capital Investment An expenditure of funds made to realize benefits that are expected to occur in the future.

Capital Budgeting Analyzing potential invest-ing decisions in long-lived assets to determine whether they should be selected and how they will be implemented.

http://
From idea to implementa-tion requires effective man-agement. For a look at a successful launch of a proj-ect, see
www.barcode-system. com/book.htm

CAPITAL BUDGETING CRITERIA: NON-DISCOUNTED CASH FLOW METHODOLOGIES

The importance of capital investments to successful performance has led firms to develop elaborate capital budgeting systems. These systems are designed to assist financial managers in the evaluation, selection, monitoring, and control of capital projects. This chapter concentrates on the evaluation and selection phases of a capital budgeting system. A key aspect of these two phases is the choice of a decision criterion for the evaluation of an investment's desirability. In this chapter, we will describe the most widely used criteria.

Capital investment evaluation criteria can be divided into two broad categories: non-discounted cash flow (non-DCF) methodologies and discounted cash flow (DCF) methodologies. The two major non-DCF techniques, average return on investment (AROI) and payback period, can give financial managers misleading accept/reject signals because those techniques are not based on the value maximization criterion. Nevertheless, we will begin our examination with non-DCF methodologies because they *are* used by some firms to evaluate capital investments. In addition, they serve as a useful starting point for discussing the advantages of the DCF methodologies, which provide the basis for the application of the IVM.

Average Return on Investment

The AROI can be defined in the following manner:

$$AROI = \frac{Average\ Net\ Income}{Investment} \tag{1}$$

As an illustration of this calculation, consider Investments A and B in Table 9-1. The average annual net income over 5 years for Investment A is $6,000 = $30,000/5, and it results in an AROI of:

$$AROI_A = \frac{\$6,000}{\$25,000} = 24\%$$

For Investment B, the average annual net income and the AROI are:

$$Average\ Net\ Income = \frac{\$24,000}{5\ years} = \$4,800$$

$$AROI_B = \frac{\$4,800}{\$20,000} = 24\%$$

Thus, both investments appear to be equally desirable according to their AROI.

Cash Flow and Net Income for Two Investment Proposals

TABLE 9-1

Year	Investment A: Cost = $25,000		Investment B: Cost = $20,000	
	Cash Flow	Net Income	Cash Flow	Net Income
1	$ 4,000	$ 2,000	$12,000	$ 7,000
2	8,000	4,000	8,000	5,000
3	12,000	7,000	6,000	4,000
4	14,000	8,000	6,000	4,000
5	16,000	9,000	6,000	4,000
Total	$54,000	$30,000	$38,000	$24,000

Independent Investments
Investments available to a firm that may be selected individually or in groups because each investment is different in its nature and purpose.

Mutually Exclusive Investments Alternative investments available to a firm that represent different approaches to a single goal or task. A firm can accept only one investment out of a group of mutually exclusive investments.

Hurdle Rate The minimum acceptable annual rate of return for a given investment.

Decision Rules. The AROI decision rule is slightly different for independent investments than for mutually exclusive investments. When a firm is faced with a number of **independent investments**, it *can select any or all of the investments* because they are totally different in their purpose. Conversely, investments are termed **mutually exclusive** if acceptance of one precludes the acceptance of others. Mutually exclusive investments represent different approaches to a single goal or task. As a result, a firm *can select only one out of a group of mutually exclusive investments.* For example, assume that Investments A and B in Table 9-1 are a microprocessor for administrative recordkeeping and a machine for the production line, respectively. In that case, they represent independent investments. The fact that the firm should decide to acquire Investment A in no way precludes it from also acquiring Investment B because the two investments are designed to perform very different tasks. If Investments A and B, however, were both microprocessors made by different manufacturers, they would represent mutually exclusive investments.

The decision rules for the AROI technique are shown in Figure 9-2. Using the AROI technique requires that financial managers calculate a minimum acceptable AROI to serve as a cutoff rate or **hurdle rate**. The estimate of each potential investment's AROI is then compared with the hurdle rate to reach the decisions shown in the figure. For instance, given a hurdle rate of 20% for Investments A and B in Table 9-1, both investments should be accepted if they are independent. If they are mutually exclusive, the firm could accept either investment since they have identical AROIs that exceed the hurdle rate.

Advantages. The principal advantage of the AROI is its familiarity and ease of interpretation. Since it is a standard rate of return calculation like the ROA formula in Chapter 2, it is easily understood by most individuals. In addition, it is mathematically consistent with the ROA and ROE criteria that are commonly used by shareholders and external financial analysts to evaluate the financial performance of a firm. Consequently, when managers use AROI as a decision criterion, they are employing a familiar evaluation system.

Disadvantages. There are three major disadvantages to the AROI as a test of investment desirability:

1. *It Ignores the Timing of Benefits.* Notice that the AROIs for Investments A and B in Table 9-1 are identical even though the time patterns of the net incomes are very different. The averaging process totally ignores these differences.
2. *It Ignores Investment Cash Flows.* An investment's value is determined by its cash flows and not by its accounting income. Cash flows are the correct measure of an investment's benefits because only cash can be used to make expenditures for salaries and wages, dividends, and new investments. AROI, however, measures benefits in terms of accounting net income.
3. *It Requires a Subjective Hurdle Rate.* It is not sufficient that an investment promise a positive AROI. The return must be high enough to meet or exceed

The AROI Decision Rules

SUMMARY FIGURE 9-2

| Independent Investments | Accept *all* investments whose AROI ≥ Minimum Acceptable AROI |
| Mutually Exclusive Investments | Accept the *single* investment with the highest AROI (as long as its AROI ≥ Minimum Acceptable AROI). |

the minimum desired return of the stockholders. Unfortunately, the AROI criterion is not derived from a general economic model that establishes a link between the hurdle rate and returns available to investors in the capital markets. As a result, the financial managers are forced to select subjectively and arbitrarily a hurdle rate with only a vague sense of its accuracy.

On balance, therefore, the AROI cannot be relied upon to provide correct accept/reject signals about investments. The disadvantages are so significant that managers cannot expect the AROI consistently to signal acceptance of investments that will increase firm value.[1]

Payback Period

A second investment evaluation method that does not rely on discounted cash flow analysis is the payback period. It is defined as the number of years required for the expected cash flows on an investment to accumulate to a sum equal to the initial cost of the investment:

$$\text{Payback Period} = \text{Length of Time Needed to Recover the Initial Cost} \qquad (2)$$

For example, the cumulative cash flows of Investments A and B in Table 9-1 are shown in Table 9-2.

The cost of Investment A is more than its cumulative cash flows by year 3 but less than its cumulative cash flows by year 4. Consequently, the payback period is longer than three years but less than four years. More specifically, it is equal to three years plus the proportion of the fourth year required to recover the last portion of the initial cost not recovered by year 3:

$$\text{Payback}_A = 3 \text{ years} + \frac{\$25,000 - 24,000}{\$14,000} = 3.07 \text{ years}$$

Similarly, the payback period for Investment B is exactly two years because the cumulative cash flow in the second year equals the initial cost of $20,000:

$$\text{Payback}_B = 2.0 \text{ years}$$

Decision Rules. The decision rules for the payback period methodology are shown in Figure 9-3. In a manner similar to the AROI technique, the payback period methodology requires financial managers to determine a maximum acceptable

The Cumulative Cash Flows from Investments A and B

TABLE 9-2

	Investment A: Cost = $25,000		Investment B: Cost = $20,000	
Year	Cash Flow	Cumulative Cash Flow	Cash Flow	Cumulative Cash Flow
1	$ 4,000	$ 4,000	$12,000	$12,000
2	8,000	12,000	8,000	20,000
3	12,000	24,000	6,000	26,000
4	14,000	38,000	6,000	32,000
5	16,000	54,000	6,000	38,000

[1] The ROA, however, remains an important *performance* criterion. We will examine the apparent conflict between the usefulness of ROA as a decision criterion and as a performance criterion later in the chapter.

The Payback Period Decision Rules

SUMMARY FIGURE 9-3

Independent Investments	Accept *all* investments whose payback period $\leq$ Maximum Acceptable Payback Period.
Mutually Exclusive Investments	Accept the *single* investment with the shortest payback period (as long as its payback $\leq$ Maximum Acceptable Payback Period).

payback period. This "hurdle" payback criteria is the ultimate determinant of the acceptability of a proposed investment. If the hurdle payback for Investments A and B is 4.0 years and they are independent investments, they would both be judged acceptable. If they are mutually exclusive, only investment B would be accepted.

Advantages. The obvious advantage of the payback technique is its simplicity of calculation and interpretation. Even the smallest firms with relatively untrained managers can evaluate proposed investments in terms of their payback periods. More importantly, unlike the AROI technique, the payback methodology utilizes the anticipated cash flows from a proposed investment. Thus, it evaluates the investment benefits that matter to a firm's stockholders. In addition, the payback period does pay some attention to the time value of money by favoring those investments with more rapid cash inflows.

Disadvantages. In contrast to its limited advantages, the payback methodology suffers from a number of serious shortcomings as an investment decision criterion:

1. *It Improperly Evaluates the Timing of Benefits.* While the payback technique does favor projects with quick returns, it does not properly account for the time value of money. It totally ignores the differences in magnitude and timing of cash flows *within* the payback period. For instance, assume that a financial manager is faced with a choice between Investment B in Table 9-2 and Investment C shown below:

Investment C

Year	Cash Flow	Cumulative Cash Flow	
1	$ 8,000	$ 8,000	
2	12,000	20,000	Cost = $20,000
3	6,000	26,000	
4	6,000	32,000	Payback$_C$ = 2.0 years
5	6,000	38,000	

Clearly, Investment B is preferable to Investment C due to its more rapid inflow of cash in year 1. The payback criterion evaluates both investments as equally attractive, however, since they have the same payback period. The payback methodology simply cannot properly evaluate such a difference in the timing of cash inflows.

2. *It Improperly Evaluates Cash Flows.* While the payback methodology utilizes cash flows instead of net income, it completely ignores cash flows *beyond* the payback period. Consequently, the technique implicitly assumes that the firm is uninterested in the returns generated after the firm has recovered the initial

cost of an investment. For example, assume that a financial manager is comparing Investment B in Table 9-2 with Investment D shown below:

	Investment D		
Year	Cash Flow	Cumulative Cash Flow	
1	$12,000	$12,000	
2	8,000	20,000	Cost = $20,000
3	1,000	21,000	
4	1,000	22,000	$Payback_D$ = 2.0 years
5	1,000	23,000	

The payback methodology indicates that Investments B and D are equally attractive even though Investment B's cumulative cash flows over its five-year life are $15,000 higher.

3. *It Requires a Subjective Hurdle Payback Period.* As was true of the AROI criterion, the payback methodology is not derived from a general economic model. Thus, there is no objective procedure for determining the correct maximum acceptable payback period. Despite its importance to the evaluation procedure, the hurdle payback period must be arbitrarily selected.

Historically, the payback period has been a very common method for evaluating capital investment proposals. Although it is still utilized by many firms, its role should be limited to one of providing supplementary information (for example, about a project's short-term effect on the firm's liquidity) to the DCF evaluation techniques.

CAPITAL BUDGETING CRITERIA: DISCOUNTED CASH FLOW METHODOLOGIES

The goal of financial managers in their role as agents of the firm's stockholders is to make investing and financing decisions that will maximize the value of the firm's stock. In terms of capital budgeting, this goal translates into the search for investments that will maintain or increase the market value of the stock. The two DCF methodologies that will be examined—net present value (NPV) and internal rate of return (IRR)—are designed to facilitate this search. Before we can discuss the mechanics of these two decision criteria, however, we will describe the general manner in which they identify acceptable capital investments.

The Role of NPV and IRR in the Evaluation Process

The price and the value of a security, and its yield and RRR, are equivalent in an efficient market. Whenever price deviates from value, the subsequent buying and selling actions of investors will alter the price so that it is once again identical to investors' estimates of value. A discrepancy between a security's value and its price is described as *disequilibrium* because it induces traders to change the price. Only when price and value are equal will the market be in equilibrium so that the price will be stable.

Figure 9-4 depicts disequilibrium in the market for two common stocks, A and B. Security A's value of $34.12 exceeds its market price of $25.00, with the result that its expected yield of 10.8% exceeds its RRR of 9.25%. For Security B, the situation is reversed. Its market price of $35.00 exceeds its value of $21.42, while its RRR of 11.50% exceeds its expected yield of 10.1%. In an efficient market, these disequilibrium conditions will not continue. Investor demand for Security A will

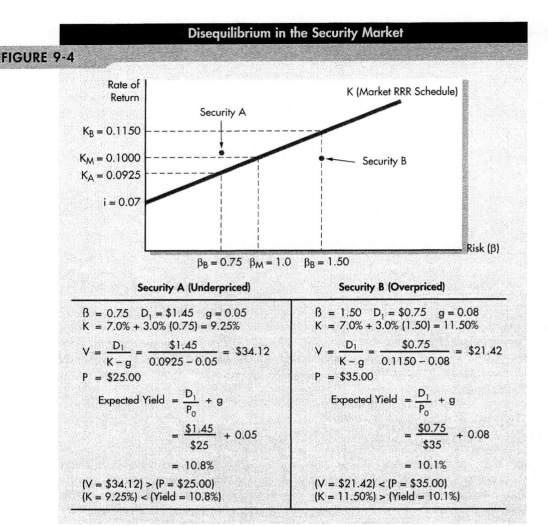

FIGURE 9-4

Disequilibrium in the Security Market

Security A (Underpriced)

$\beta = 0.75 \quad D_1 = \$1.45 \quad g = 0.05$
$K = 7.0\% + 3.0\% (0.75) = 9.25\%$

$$V = \frac{D_1}{K - g} = \frac{\$1.45}{0.0925 - 0.05} = \$34.12$$

$P = \$25.00$

$$\text{Expected Yield} = \frac{D_1}{P_0} + g$$

$$= \frac{\$1.45}{\$25} + 0.05$$

$$= 10.8\%$$

$(V = \$34.12) > (P = \$25.00)$
$(K = 9.25\%) < (\text{Yield} = 10.8\%)$

Security B (Overpriced)

$\beta = 1.50 \quad D_1 = \$0.75 \quad g = 0.08$
$K = 7.0\% + 3.0\% (1.50) = 11.50\%$

$$V = \frac{D_1}{K - g} = \frac{\$0.75}{0.1150 - 0.08} = \$21.42$$

$P = \$35.00$

$$\text{Expected Yield} = \frac{D_1}{P_0} + g$$

$$= \frac{\$0.75}{\$35} + 0.08$$

$$= 10.1\%$$

$(V = \$21.42) < (P = \$35.00)$
$(K = 11.50\%) > (\text{Yield} = 10.1\%)$

push its price up until it reaches $34.12. Conversely, yield will fall until it reaches 9.25%. At this point, equilibrium will exist because price equals value, and yield equals RRR. In the case of Security B, investor selling will drive its price down and yield up to the equilibrium levels of $21.42 and 11.50%, respectively. In terms of Figure 9-4, investors would buy securities such as Security A, whose yield lies above the market RRR schedule, and sell securities like B, whose yield lies below the market schedule.[2]

In light of their role as agents for the firm's owners and their goal of firm value maximization, financial managers should follow the same procedure in evaluating capital investments. The essence of capital budgeting is to identify and select capital investments whose price or initial cost is less than the present value of their anticipated cash flows. Equivalently, financial managers should accept proposed

---

[2] The typical cause of disequilibrium in securities markets is the discovery of new information about the financial outlook for a firm, a specific industry, or the entire economy. Studies have indicated that the market's (all investors) response to disequilibrium conditions is sufficiently rapid that it is very difficult for any individual to consistently buy underpriced securities or sell overpriced securities *before* their price returns to its equilibrium level.

investments whose expected yield exceeds their RRR. The two DCF evaluation methodologies are designed to identify these acceptable investments.

If the markets for operating capital assets such as machinery and buildings were as efficient as the markets for securities, the use of the NPV or the IRR methodology to identify underpriced investments would be largely a waste of time. In an efficient market, the chances of *consistently* locating underpriced assets are very remote. It requires analytical skill, insight, and information that is possessed by few individuals. The markets for operating capital assets, however, are much less efficient than the markets for securities. The reason for this inefficiency is due to the basic nature of these assets.

Securities are very similar in nature (*homogeneous*) and are traded by large numbers of investors on *active financial markets. Operating capital assets*, on the other hand, tend to be *unique* in nature because they are geared to the specific needs of an individual firm. While investors' expectations concerning cash flows on securities may tend to be very similar, estimates of the cash flows that are expected to be generated by a capital asset can vary widely from one firm to another. One firm may possess patents, trade secrets, technological advantages, or gifted employees that make a particular capital investment much more valuable to it than to other firms. In summary, there exists a vast array of potential capital investments available to a firm and relatively little competition in the buying and selling of these investments. Thus, it is quite reasonable to believe that the NPV and IRR techniques can effectively assist financial managers in identifying underpriced operating capital assets.

Net Present Value

The NPV evaluation methodology involves a comparison of the value of a proposed capital investment with its cost. An investment's **net present value** can be expressed in the form of the following equation[3]:

Net Present Value The difference between the present value of an investment's anticipated future cash flows and its initial cost.

$$NPV = \sum_{t=1}^{N} \frac{C_t}{(1+K)^t} - I = \text{Present Value} - \text{Cost of Asset} \qquad (3)$$

where

C_t = the anticipated after-tax cash flow in period t;
K = the risk-adjusted discount rate (the RRR);
I = the cost of the asset (the amount of the initial investment);
N = the number of periods in the useful life of the asset.

The first term on the right-hand side of equation (3) is the mathematical form of the IVM developed in Chapter 6. As stated in that chapter, the value of any investment can be measured as the present value of its anticipated cash flows. The difference between its present value and its cost indicates whether the asset is underpriced or overpriced. *A positive NPV corresponds to an underpriced asset, while a negative NPV corresponds to an overpriced asset.*

Decision Rules. The decision rules for the NPV criterion are shown in Figure 9-5. As was true of the AROI and the payback period methodologies, the NPV criterion involves a benchmark for determining an acceptable investment. With this

---

[3] For now, we will assume that the entire cost of an asset is a lump sum that occurs at time 0. If outlays are required in more than one period, these should be discounted back to time 0 and included in I.

SUMMARY FIGURE 9-5

The NPV Decision Rules

Independent Investments	Accept *all* investments whose NPV $\geq$ 0.
Mutually Exclusive Investments	Accept the *single* investment with the highest NPV (as long as its NPV $\geq$ 0).

evaluation technique, the benchmark is the minimum acceptable NPV, which is an NPV = 0. Whether a given investment proposal can meet or exceed this hurdle NPV depends heavily on the RRR used in determining the present value of the anticipated cash flows. Thus, the RRR plays a major role in the application of the NPV decision criterion.

The RRR will normally vary from one investment proposal to another and for all investment proposals over time. It fluctuates in response to factors such as changes in the risk-free interest rate, investment risk, a firm's marginal tax rate, and a firm's financial structure. The correct technique for determining the RRR for an investment has long been a topic of controversy in the field of finance. This chapter will concentrate on the mechanics and interpretation of the NPV methodology by assuming initially that the financial managers *know* the appropriate RRR. Chapter 11 will examine techniques for measuring a capital investment's risk. We will then use the results of that chapter to demonstrate in Chapter 15 a procedure for calculating a risk-adjusted RRR, which also incorporates the effect of a firm's tax structure and financial structure.

As an illustration of the use of the NPV methodology, let us examine the case of Houston Fabrics, a textile manufacturing firm. Houston's management has under consideration a proposal to expand production by installing an additional finishing line in its Hillgrove, Texas, plant. The firm's financial managers estimate that the line will initially cost $400,000 and generate the incremental cash flows shown below over its useful life. Given a risk-adjusted RRR of 14%, the financial managers calculate the following NPV:

Year	After-Tax Cash Flow	$DF_{0.14,N}$	PV
1	$ 40,000	0.877	$ 35,000
2	200,000	0.769	154,000
3	600,000	0.675	405,000
Total	$840,000		$594,000

$$\text{NPV} = \text{PV} - \text{Cost} = \$594,000 - 400,000 = \$194,000$$

Since the NPV is positive, Houston Fabrics should accept the investment proposal. The NPV calculation indicates that, at an RRR of 14%, the capital investment is underpriced because its value to the firm exceeds its cost by $194,000.

Interpretation of the NPV. While the calculation of an investment's NPV is straightforward and the NPV decision rules are simple to apply, what exactly does the NPV measure? How can this evaluation methodology be used to achieve the goal of stock price maximization? The NPV criterion requires that the financial managers view the value of the firm, not from an accounting viewpoint, but from the viewpoint of the IVM. The value of the firm is the net present value of all cash flows to be generated in the future by the firm's assets. If a firm acquires a new asset with a positive NPV, the value of the firm (the NPV of all its assets) will increase. Thus, the NPV of a proposed investment can be viewed as the *amount by which the value of the firm is predicted to rise if the investment is implemented.*

We can illustrate this interpretation of NPV by returning to the Houston Fabrics example. Assume that the NPV of all of the firm's assets at present is $11 million, including sufficient cash to finance the acquisition of the proposed finishing line. If the firm should implement the finishing line proposal, the firm's NPV will rise to $11,194,000. This increase reflects the effective use by Houston's managers of $400,000 in plant and equipment to generate cash flows with a current value of $594,000. From the viewpoint of the firm's stockholders, the value of the firm to them is equal to the firm's NPV less the value of the liabilities that represent creditors' prior claims on Houston's assets. If the value of the liabilities of the firm remains unchanged after the implementation of the finishing line, the increase in the firm's NPV will also represent an increase in the value of the firm to its owners. This value increase should, in turn, be reflected in an increase in the market price of the firm's stock.

The effect of the finishing line on the value of Houston Fabrics' stock is summarized in Table 9-3. The calculations in the table assume that the firm's liabilities are $3 million and that it has 100,000 shares of common stock outstanding. By accepting the finishing line proposal, Houston Fabrics' management can increase the value of the firm's stock by $1.94 per share. As long as the firm continues to implement capital investment proposals with positive NPVs, it will continue to create economic value that will increase the value of the firm's stock. Thus, there is a direct, quantitative link between NPV and the financial managers' goal of value maximization. *The value of a firm to its owners is maximized by accepting all available investment proposals with NPVs ≥ 0.* If the firm does not possess the cash to finance the proposals, it should raise the cash in the financial markets.[4]

Internal Rate of Return

The IRR evaluation methodology involves a comparison of an investment's anticipated annual yield with its RRR. The anticipated yield is called the **internal rate of return**. The IRR is defined as the discount rate that equates the cost or price of an asset with the present value of its anticipated cash flows. We have already described in a previous chapter the technique for calculating the IRR on a financial instrument. In the case of a bond, the IRR is called its yield-to-maturity (YTM). The computational technique for finding the IRR on a capital investment is identi-

Internal Rate of Return (IRR) The discount rate that equates the cost or price of an asset with the present value of its anticipated cash flows. The IRR on a bond is called its yield-to-maturity.

The Effect of the Finishing Line Proposal on the Value of Houston Fabrics

TABLE 9-3

	Without Proposal	With Proposal	Change
NPV of firm's assets	$11,000,000	$11,194,000	$194,000
Value of liabilities	3,000,000	3,000,000	—
Value of firm to owners	$ 8,000,000	$ 8,194,000	$194,000
Number of shares of common stock outstanding	100,000	100,000	—
Value per share	$80.00	$81.94	$1.94

---

[4] In actual practice, a firm is sometimes unable or unwilling to obtain sufficient funds to finance all acceptable investment proposals. This situation forces the financial managers to ration the available capital among the acceptable projects. We will discuss the selection procedure for capital investments under capital rationing later in this chapter.

cal to the technique that is used to find the YTM on a bond. The IRR can be expressed mathematically as:

$$\text{Cost of Asset} = \text{PV of Anticipated Cash Flows} \qquad (4)$$

$$I = \sum_{t=1}^{N} \frac{C_t}{(1 + \text{IRR})^t}$$

Since the present value of the cash flows is equal to the cost of the asset in equation (4), the NPV must be equal to zero. Thus, the IRR can also be defined as *the discount rate that results in an NPV = 0*. Mathematically,

$$\text{NPV} = \text{PV of Anticipated Cash Flows} - \text{Cost of Asset} = 0 \qquad (5)$$

$$= \sum_{t=1}^{N} \frac{C_t}{(1 + \text{IRR})^t} - I = 0$$

Decision Rules. The decision rules for the IRR criterion are shown in Figure 9-6. The comparison of the IRR and the RRR for a capital investment indicates whether the asset is overpriced or underpriced. *If the anticipated return or yield (IRR) exceeds the minimum required return (RRR), the asset is underpriced.* If the IRR *is less than the RRR, the asset is overpriced.* The decision rules for the IRR methodology involve exactly the same comparison that we previously made in Figure 9-4 between a stock's yield and its RRR. This result leads to another version of the IRR decision rule: *accept a capital investment only if its IRR is located on or above the market-determined RRR schedule.* Notice the pivotal role of the RRR in this evaluation procedure. As was true of the NPV criterion, the RRR determines the acceptability of a capital investment within the context of the IRR criterion.

We can demonstrate the use of the IRR evaluation methodology by returning again to the Houston Fabrics example. The IRR in the case of the proposed finishing line is the discount rate that equates the present value of its cash flows with its initial cost of $400,000. The IRR solves the following equation:

$$\text{NPV} = (\$40,000)(DF_{\text{IRR},1}) + (\$200,000)(DF_{\text{IRR},2}) + (\$600,000)(DF_{\text{IRR},3}) - \$400,000 = 0$$

Since the anticipated cash flows are uneven, the procedure for finding the IRR is equivalent to the trial-and-error process that we used to calculate a bond's YTM.

Table 9-4 shows the calculations for the Houston Fabrics example. In the NPV calculations for this example, we found that, at a 14% discount rate (the investment's RRR), the NPV was $194,000. The IRR must be considerably higher than this RRR because the present value (and the NPV) declines as the discount rate rises. In order to find an NPV of $0, we arbitrarily try 30% as our starting discount rate. As the table shows, even at that discount rate, the NPV is a large positive number. At a discount rate of 35%, however, the NPV is negative. Thus, the discount rate that results in an NPV of $0 must lie between these two discount rates. The project's

The IRR Decision Rules	
SUMMARY FIGURE 9-6	
Independent Investments	Accept *all* investments whose IRR $\geq$ RRR.
Mutually Exclusive Investments	Accept the *single* investment with the highest IRR (as long as its IRR $\geq$ RRR).

Trial-and-Error Calculations to Bracket the IRR

TABLE 9-4

Year	After-Tax Cash Flow	$DF_{0.30,N}$	PV	$DF_{0.35,N}$	PV
1	$ 40,000	0.769	$ 30,760	0.741	$ 29,640
2	200,000	0.592	118,400	0.549	109,800
3	600,000	0.455	273,000	0.406	243,600
	$840,000		$422,160		$383,040

30% Discount Rate: NPV = $422,160 − 400,000 = $22,160 > 0
35% Discount Rate: NPV = $383,040 − 400,000 = −$16,960 < 0

30% < IRR < 35%

IRR can be approximated through interpolation of the results in Table 9-4.[5] Alternatively, the exact IRR can be found through the use of a computer spreadsheet or a business calculator. (We provide instructions for the use of a business calculator to find an investment's IRR at the end of the text.) Since the IRR of 32.8% on the finishing line exceeds the RRR of 14%, Houston Fabrics should implement the capital investment proposal.

Interpretation of the IRR. Since the IRR is stated in terms of an annual yield on a project, it seems very understandable to most individuals. While an NPV of $194,000 may require some explanation, the meaning of an IRR of 32.8% is fairly self-evident. The finishing line is a very attractive investment because it promises an annual yield that far exceeds the minimum acceptable or required return of 14%. In their interpretation of this IRR, Houston's financial managers must be aware of an assumption implicit when relying on the IRR to identify and compare worthwhile projects.

In order to be sure that an investment whose IRR exceeds that of another is a superior choice, it must be assumed that the cash flows generated by each investment can subsequently be reinvested to continue to earn their respective IRRs until the ends of each of their useful lives. In Houston's case, the necessary condition is that the firm will reinvest the $40,000 cash flow received at the end of year 1 and the $200,000 cash flow received at the end of year 2 at a 32.8% annual rate of return until the end of year 3. If the firm cannot actually earn 32.8% through reinvestment of the cash, the future amount to which those cash flows will actually accumulate will be less than the 32.8% calculated yield would imply. Consequently, *the usefulness of the IRR calculation depends, in part, on the realism of the reinvestment assumption.* In the case of unique capital investments that are unusually profitable, that assumption may be overly optimistic.

---

[5] We can solve for the approximate IRR with the following formula:

$$IRR = Lower\ Rate + \left(\frac{Lower\ Rate\ NPV}{Lower\ Rate\ NPV - Higher\ Rate\ NPV}\right)(Higher\ Rate - Lower\ Rate)$$

$$= 0.30 + \left(\frac{\$22,160}{\$22,160 - (-\$16,960)}\right)(0.35 - 0.30)$$

$$= 0.30 + (0.567)(0.05) = 0.30 + 0.028 = 32.8\%$$

[6] The basic assumption of the compounding process is that both the principal and any subsequent earnings accumulate in the future at the annual yield specified.

Advantages of the DCF Evaluation Methodologies

Both the NPV and the IRR techniques represent a substantial improvement over non-DCF methodologies because they address weaknesses in the non-DCF procedures. First, the NPV and IRR criteria measure benefits in terms of cash flows rather than accounting profits. Second, the DCF methodologies evaluate both the magnitude and the timing of an investment's anticipated cash flows. Third, the DCF techniques do not require subjective and arbitrary evaluation benchmarks or hurdles. The RRR for a proposed capital investment is determined by the actions of investors in the financial markets rather than "hunches" of the financial managers.

COMPARISON OF THE NPV AND IRR METHODOLOGIES

The NPV and IRR provide slightly different information about an investment because they evaluate it in a different manner. In this section, we will examine the basic relationship between these two evaluation techniques. We will demonstrate why they can provide conflicting accept/reject signals in the case of mutually exclusive investments even though they will generally give the same signal for independent investments.

The Evaluation of Independent Investments

NPV is a measure of the absolute increase in the firm's value that an investment is expected to produce, while the IRR is an annual rate of return measure. How is an investment's NPV related to its IRR? How can both techniques provide valid accept/reject signals for investment proposals? The answers to these questions can be provided by examining the graph in Figure 9-7. The graph is based on the finishing line proposal under evaluation by Houston Fabrics. The graph is called an **NPV profile** because it shows the investment's NPV at different discount rates or RRRs. For instance, the NPV of $194,000 shown by the curve at a discount rate of 14% is the NPV that we had calculated earlier for the finishing line proposal.

NPV Profile A graph that indicates possible NPVs at different discount rates.

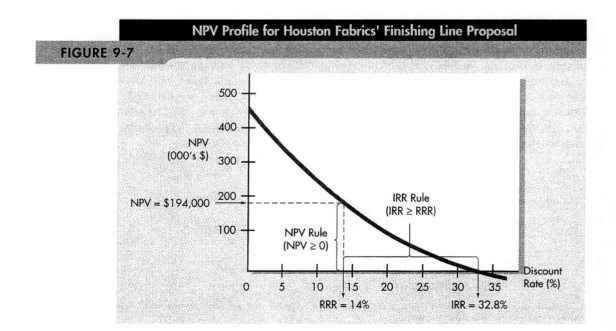

FIGURE 9-7

NPV Profile for Houston Fabrics' Finishing Line Proposal

■ Valuation

ISSUES

CAPITAL BUDGETING TECHNIQUES IN PRACTICE

As described in the body of the chapter, a firm's financial managers can apply either DCF or non-DCF techniques to the evaluation of capital investment proposals. From a theoretical standpoint, the DCF approaches are superior because they are founded on the valuation framework of the IVM, and therefore are consistent with a value maximization objective for shareholders. In practice, however, the use of DCF techniques varies across firms according to the level of sophistication and education of the firms' financial managers.

There have been a series of surveys conducted in the United States that have compiled data on the capital budgeting practices of American companies. While there are differences in the scope and emphasis of those surveys, most have been directed to the Chief Financial Officers (CFOs) of relatively large manufacturing firms such as those on *Fortune* magazine's annual list of the 1,000 largest industrial companies. The history of the responses to questions about the primary technique used by the firms to evaluate the desirability of capital expenditure proposals has been roughly as follows:

Primary Technique Employed	Late 1950s	Survey Dates: Mid-1970s	Early 1990s
Payback Period	34%	9%	2%
AROI	34%	24%	23%
DCF Methodologies	20%	66%	74%
Other	12%	1%	1%

The growing popularity of DCF techniques is evident in these data. Nonetheless, the AROI approach appears still to be employed by a detectable minority of companies, presumably because of its computational simplicity and because it parallels the performance measures that are commonly used by external financial analysts—as we discussed in Chapter 2.

Within the DCF category, the IRR methodology remains the predominant technique. Managers report that this approach, which measures the "yield" on an investment proposal, is easier to explain to senior management and easier to visualize and interpret than the NPV criterion.

The surveys have also found that large firms are more likely to adopt DCF methodologies than are small firms, and that U.S. companies use those methodologies more frequently than do companies in other countries. Finally, a payback period is often calculated as a supplement to a DCF analysis, in order to identify the near-term liquidity consequences of an investment decision.

The graph indicates the negative relationship between the discount rate and NPV. At a discount rate of 0%, the NPV is equal to the total anticipated cash flows on the investment less its cost: NPV = $840,000 – 400,000. At a discount rate of 35%, the NPV is the –$16,960 that was previously calculated in Table 9-4. The graph reveals the IRR as the point of the intersection of the curve with the horizontal axis. At that point (discount rate = 32.8%), the NPV of the proposal equals zero, which is the definition of the IRR. The decision rules for the two DCF criteria are summarized in the figure. The NPV criterion signals acceptance because the proposal has a positive NPV at the RRR of 14%. The IRR criterion signals acceptance because the IRR (32.8%) lies to the right of the RRR (14%).

The investment proposal is, in reality, *characterized by only two points on the NPV profile*: its NPV of $194,000 at the discount rate of 14% and its NPV of $0 at the discount rate of 32.8%. That is, an investment normally has only one NPV and one IRR.[7] Showing the entire profile, however, clearly demonstrates the relation-

---

[7] In some unusual cases, an investment may have more than one IRR. We discuss the cause of this phenomenon and its impact on the usefulness of the IRR decision criterion in the appendix to this chapter.

ship between the investment's NPV and its IRR. Notice that the finishing line proposal's NPV in Figure 9-7 will be positive at any RRR below its IRR of 32.8%. As a result, the NPV decision rule will signal acceptance at all RRRs below the IRR. The IRR decision rule will also signal acceptance at all RRRs below the IRR. For any one investment, the conditions *NPV ≥ 0 and IRR ≥ RRR, or NPV < 0 and IRR < RRR, will almost always hold true simultaneously.* Thus, the NPV criterion and the IRR criterion should generally provide the same accept/reject signal for any given *independent* investment.

The Evaluation of Mutually Exclusive Investments

When financial managers are faced with a choice between two or more *mutually exclusive* investments, they must select the most valuable alternative by ranking the investments. Unfortunately, *the NPV and the IRR methodologies do not always rank mutually exclusive projects in the same order.* When this occurs, the managers must determine which methodology provides the correct ranking.

Suppose Houston Fabrics has a second investment proposal that involves establishing a new weaving center. Since the two capital investments are each designed to fill the same available floor space, they are mutually exclusive. Houston's financial managers anticipate that the weaving center will cost $400,000 and generate annual after-tax cash flows of $239,000 in each of the next three years. That is, the annual cash flows represent a three-year annuity. They estimate the project's RRR to be 14% since it is similar in risk to the finishing line. Based on these forecasts, they calculate the following NPV for the weaving center:

$$NPV = PV - I$$
$$= (C)(ADF_{0.14,3}) - I$$
$$= (\$239,000)(2.322) - \$400,000$$
$$= \$155,000$$

Similarly, the weaving center's IRR can be determined from the following equation:

$$NPV = (C)(ADF_{IRR,3}) - I = 0$$

This equation can be solved for the appropriate discounting factor:

$$ADF_{IRR,3} = I/C = \$400,000/\$239,000 = 1.674$$

In Table IV in the back of the text, the discounting factor closest to 1.674 in the three year row is 1.673, which corresponds to a discount rate of 36%. Thus, the IRR on the weaving center is approximately 36%.

The NPVs and the IRRs for the two competing investments are shown in Table 9-5. Notice that the NPV criterion and the IRR criterion would signal acceptance of both investment proposals if they were independent because NPV > 0 and IRR > RRR for each project. The *conflicting accept/reject signals in Table 9-5 occur as a result of the ranking required by mutually exclusive investments.* Houston's financial managers are now confronted with two important questions. What is the cause of the ranking conflict of the two DCF methodologies? Which methodology gives the correct answer?

The Cause of Conflicting NPV and IRR Rankings.
The anticipated net cash flows (including the initial costs at time t=0) from the two investments are restated on the next page:

Conflicting NPV and IRR Rankings of Houston Fabrics' Investment Proposals

TABLE 9-5

Investment	RRR	NPV	NPV Ranking	IRR	IRR Ranking
Finishing Line	14%	$194,000	#1	32.8%	#2
Weaving Center	14%	$155,000	#2	36.0%	#1

IRR Signal: Accept Weaving Center   NPV Signal: Accept Finishing Line

	After-Tax Cash Flows		
Year	Finishing Line	Weaving Center	Difference
0	−$400,000	−$400,000	—
1	40,000	239,000	−$199,000
2	200,000	239,000	−39,000
3	600,000	239,000	361,000
Total	$440,000	$317,000	$123,000

While the *total* net cash flows from the finishing line greatly exceed those from the weaving center, their timing is much less desirable. Not until the third year do the finishing line's cash flows surpass those of the weaving center. The *present value* obtained from the discounting procedure *reflects both the timing and the size of an investment's cash flows*. Which of these two characteristics is most important in the present value calculation depends on the discount rate selected. *The higher the discount rate, the more important is timing relative to size.*

This point can be demonstrated through a simple example. Suppose that you are offered a choice between two investments. Investment A offers a cash flow of $1,000 at the end of year 1, while Investment B offers a cash flow of $2,000 at the end of year 5. Which of these investments is more valuable to you? Table 9-6 indicates that the answer depends on the discount rate or RRR that is used to value the cash flows.

At low values of the RRR, Investment B is more valuable because the *size* of each investment's cash flows dominates the present value calculation. For instance, the timing difference is totally ignored if the RRR is 0%. As the RRR increases, however, the value of Investment B falls faster than that of Investment A,

The Effect of the RRR on the Relative Importance of the Size and Timing of an Investment's Cash Flows

TABLE 9-6

	Investment A			Investment B			
RRR	$DF_{K,1}$	C_1	PV	$DF_{FK,5}$	C_5	PV	$PV_A - PV_B$
0%	1.000	$1,000	$1,000	1.000	$2,000	$2,000	−$1,000
5	0.952	1,000	952	0.784	2,000	1,568	−616
10	0.909	1,000	909	0.621	2,000	1,242	−333
15	0.870	1,000	870	0.497	2,000	994	−124
20	0.833	1,000	833	0.402	2,000	804	29
25	0.800	1,000	800	0.328	2,000	656	144
30	0.769	1,000	769	0.269	2,000	538	231

$$PV = (C_N)(DF_{K,N})$$

until Investment A becomes more valuable at RRRs of 20%, 25%, and 30%. At these high discount rates, the much more rapid *timing* of Investment A's cash flows more than offsets their smaller size.

This conflict between the effect of timing and size of cash flows on present value is responsible for the ranking conflict for Houston Fabrics' two investment proposals. This fact is readily evident in the NPV profiles for the two investments shown in Figure 9-8. Only at a discount rate of 25% are the NPVs of the two investments identical. At discount rates below 25%, the greater size of the cash flows from the finishing line outweighs the more rapid timing of the cash flows from the weaving center. Thus, the finishing line's NPV is greater at the lower discount rates. At discount rates above 25%, the reverse is true. The more rapid timing of the weaving center's small-size cash flows makes its NPV higher than that of the finishing line.

The discount rate of 25% is critical in the Houston Fabrics example because it is the point at which the two NPV profiles cross over and change relative positions. Above this crossover point, the NPV criterion and the IRR criterion agree. They both rank the weaving center proposal above the finishing line proposal. Only at discount rates below the crossover point does a ranking conflict arise. The cause of the ranking conflict is the fact that the investments' 14% RRR *lies below the crossover discount rate, while the investments' IRRs lie above it.*[8]

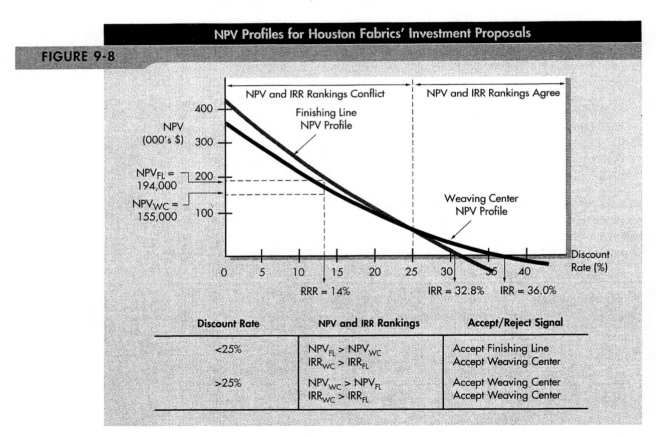

FIGURE 9-8

NPV Profiles for Houston Fabrics' Investment Proposals

Discount Rate	NPV and IRR Rankings	Accept/Reject Signal
<25%	$NPV_{FL} > NPV_{WC}$ $IRR_{WC} > IRR_{FL}$	Accept Finishing Line Accept Weaving Center
>25%	$NPV_{WC} > NPV_{FL}$ $IRR_{WC} > IRR_{FL}$	Accept Weaving Center Accept Weaving Center

---

[8] It is easy to see that an investment's RRR can lie either above or below the NPV profile crossover point. It is also possible, however, for the IRR to be larger or smaller than the crossover discount rate. When the IRR is smaller, the crossover point shown in Figure 9-8 occurs *below* the horizontal axis. That is, one investment's NPV is greater for all discount rates that result in positive NPVs for both investments. When this situation occurs, the NPV and IRR accept/reject signals will be identical at all RRRs.

The Correct Methodology in the Case of a Rankings Conflict. When the NPV and IRR criteria provide conflicting rankings of mutually exclusive investments, the final decision should be based on the *NPV ranking*. The reasoning lies in the manner in which investment opportunity costs are treated in the two methodologies.

As we have noted, the IRR calculation can be relied on only if the cash flows from each investment can be reinvested elsewhere at that investment's specific computed IRR. Consequently, every investment that is being evaluated according to the IRR criterion requires a *different* reinvestment assumption. For example, if a firm were attempting to choose among three investments whose respective IRRs were 15%, 20%, and 25%, the choice would be confounded by the fact that three different assumptions would be made as to the rate of return that could be earned from reinvestment of the cash flows from the three investments. In reality, of course, whatever the reinvestment rate, it should be the *same* for all three investments.[9]

To put the point another way, the IRR approach in effect treats each investment proposal *in isolation*. This is a legitimate approach to a DCF analysis if the investments are independent, so that the decision to undertake one of the investments does not impact the firm's ability to take another investment. An IRR analysis will properly provide a correct accept/reject decision for each investment in that case. When investments are mutually exclusive, however, a ranking is required, and the NPV approach utilizes the measure of investment opportunity cost that is the relevant one to a value maximization objective: the opportunity cost of the firm's *shareholders*, which is the RRR for each project.

The motivation for making an investment should be to enhance shareholder wealth. In order to be sure that this occurs, the investment should be evaluated using the criterion shareholders would use—the rate of return which *they* can earn elsewhere in investments of comparable risk. This is what the NPV technique does, and this is why it provides correct rankings when choices among investments must be made.

There is an additional aspect of the NPV methodology that makes it a superior evaluation technique. The IRR indicates only the direction of the impact of an investment on a firm's value to its owners. The NPV, however, indicates both the *direction* and the *size* of an investment's impact on value. This point is illustrated in Table 9-7, which summarizes the results of the evaluation of Houston Fabrics' two investment proposals. The IRR criterion indicates that, if they were independent investments, both investment proposals would be acceptable because their IRRs exceed their RRRs. As we discussed earlier in the chapter, the condition IRR > RRR reveals that an investment will increase the firm's value because it is underpriced. The IRR technique, however, cannot measure the *amount* of the difference between an investment's cost and its value to the firm. It reveals only that each of Houston Fabrics' investment proposals has *some* value greater than its cost of $400,000.

By comparing an investment's value with its cost, the NPV technique enables Houston's financial managers to estimate both the direction and the magnitude of the impact of each proposal on the value of the firm. Table 9-7 indicates that the finishing line will increase value by $194,000, while the weaving center will increase it by only $155,000. Thus, the NPV evaluation methodology is preferable

---

[9] The significance of the reinvestment assumption to the rankings conflict can readily be seen by determining a new IRR ranking of the Houston Fabrics' proposals under an altered reinvestment assumption. Specifically, if the investments' IRRs are recalculated based upon reinvestment of cash flows at the RRR of 14%, the new IRR ranking will be identical to the original NPV ranking.

	The Impact of Houston Fabrics' Investment Proposals on Firm Value			
TABLE 9-7				

Investment Proposal	Decision Criterion	Cost	Value	Impact on Firm Value
	IRR Technique			
Finishing Line	(IRR = 32.8%) > (RRR = 14%)	$400,000	>$400,000	>$0
Weaving Center	(IRR = 36.0%) > (RRR = 14%)	$400,000	>$400,000	>$0
	NPV Technique			
Finishing Line	NPV = $194,000 > $0	$400,000	$594,000	$194,000
Weaving Center	NPV = $155,000 > $0	$400,000	$555,000	$155,000

to the IRR methodology because it permits managers to rank the competing proposals according to their impact on firm value.

The Rationale for the Use of the IRR Technique

In spite of the NPV methodology's theoretical superiority, surveys of firms reveal that the IRR methodology is widely used by financial managers. What accounts for the practical appeal of the IRR criterion? It is sometimes argued that the IRR criterion is preferable because, unlike the NPV calculation, the IRR calculation does not require the computation of an investment's RRR. While this statement is superficially true, it is also misleading. The *calculation* of an investment's IRR does not require a *prior* calculation of its RRR. But the *application* of the IRR decision rule eventually requires the comparison of an investment's IRR with its RRR. Consequently, the IRR methodology cannot be used as a decision criterion unless both an IRR and an RRR are calculated.

The major reason for the popularity of the IRR methodology seems to be that it measures investment performance in terms of an annual rate of return or yield. Even nonfinancially oriented individuals can readily grasp the significance of an investment's IRR because interest rates and yields are universally used in both business and personal finance. The interpretation of an NPV, on the other hand, requires an understanding of the complexities of the discounting process and the IVM. As a result, the IRR seems to possess a "communications" advantage in the case of individuals whose expertise lies in areas other than financial management.

While the IRR and the NPV techniques give identical accept/reject signals in the case of independent investments, a very real potential problem of ranking conflicts exists in the case of mutually exclusive investments. Despite the IRR's familiarity and communication advantages, financial managers should select projects based on their NPV rankings when such a conflict arises. Use of the IRR rankings risks the possibility of selecting investments that will not maximize the firm's stock price. We turn our attention now to another situation in which the NPV criterion is superior: capital rationing.

Capital Rationing A situation in which a firm is forced to reject investment proposals with positive NPVs due to lack of sufficient financial or personnel resources.

CAPITAL RATIONING

A firm may place limits on the volume of funds available for capital investment in a given time period. Such a situation is termed **capital rationing** because the firm is unable to fund all economically acceptable investment proposals. Because it forces the rejection of projects with positive NPVs, capital rationing is an undesirable situation. *It involves an opportunity cost equal to the lost NPV on the rejected proposals.*

■ Valuation ISSUES

THE USE AND MISUSE OF DISCOUNTED CASH FLOW

Despite their conceptual superiority over non-DCF procedures for evaluating corporate investment proposals, DCF methodologies have often come under criticism by observers of corporate practice. Two major problem areas have been cited: (1) difficulties in estimating future cash flows, and (2) difficulties in estimating required rates of return.

It is clear that the process of *forecasting the future cash flows an investment is expected to generate is not an exact science*. Projections of product prices, market shares, raw materials and labor costs, and the physical productivity of plant facilities often contain considerable uncertainty. It is also easy to overlook the consequences of competitive responses to the firm's investment decisions. For example, if competitors react to an expansion in productive capacity by lowering their own prices, cash flow forecasts that assume the maintenance of current price levels can be seriously overstated.

Similarly, the starting point for many analyses should be the question: what will our cash flows be if we *don't* make the investment? Thus, U.S. automakers delayed getting into the small-car market because the mix of large car models they were producing at the time appeared to be much more profitable. They neglected the longer-term impact of the Japanese automakers capturing the small-car segment of the market, building a reputation for quality and aggressive pricing, and then exploiting that reputation to move into the upper end of the auto market.

Investment hurdle rates also cannot be determined very precisely in many cases. This is particularly true of the RRR on the portion of a firm's capital that common equity provides. Since equity returns are residual rather than contractual in nature, the RRR on equity must be *inferred* from data on dividend yields, expected dividend growth rates, and Beta coefficients. Often those data are "noisy," and judgment is required in arriving at a final figure.

How can financial managers deal with these inevitable ambiguities? There are at least three possibilities. One is to vary the assumptions that underlie cash flow forecasts, and determine whether changes in those assumptions will change the decision to accept or reject an investment project. If a project continues to have a positive NPV even under a reasonable range of alternative scenarios relating to prices, costs, and volume, it seems fair to conclude that the project is acceptable without having to be any more precise. The same sort of sensitivity analysis can be conducted with discount rates. Even if a firm can only estimate a project's RRR to within a range of, say, one percent on either side of the "best" estimate, most investments will be either clearly acceptable or clearly unacceptable within that range. Finally, investments should be evaluated not in isolation but in the context of a long-term strategic plan for the firm. Individual investments that may appear only marginally attractive in themselves may open up opportunities for future growth with subsequent investments and provide an entry into new technologies that can be exploited in the future. In all, since the DCF approach is the correct one in principle, it is better to deal with the ambiguities of the firm's environment in the right conceptual framework of the DCF model rather than by employing non-DCF approaches, which would be deficient even if there were no ambiguities.

Capital rationing may be necessitated by some weakness in a firm's financial position. For instance, a firm with poor recent operating results but numerous investment opportunities may find it excessively expensive or even impossible to acquire external financing. As a result, the firm may temporarily be forced to forego desirable investments. Surveys of large U.S. corporations reveal that capital rationing occurs regularly at over 50% of the firms. Most of these situations are the result of debt limitations imposed either by creditors or by the firm's managers. Capital rationing may also occur in response to shortages of nonfinancial resources. In particular, a limited supply of managers, technicians, or other trained employees may restrain the rate at which a firm can grow through expansion proposals. In this case, capital rationing serves as a technique for avoiding overextension of personnel resources.

http://

For a discussion of capital rationing in the United Kingdom, go to

www.sys.uea.ac.uk/~jwm /Tax.html

Regardless of the cause of capital rationing, the critical question is how best to choose the group of proposals to be implemented. The answer is to use the following procedure to *select those positive NPV proposals that offer the highest NPV as a group*:

1. Determine all combinations of positive NPV projects that can be financed by the available capital budget.
2. Select the single combination that offers the highest NPV.

As an illustration, consider the case of Billings Electric Company, whose management has set a $7 million ceiling on capital expenditures for the coming year. The list of economically acceptable investment proposals available for implementation totals $13 million, as shown in the top half of Table 9-8. The firm's financial managers must determine which of the six projects should be selected.

The first step is to calculate the aggregate NPV of each combination of available projects that fall within the financing constraint of $7,000,000, as shown in the bottom half of the table. For example, the first combination, AB, has an aggregate initial outlay of:

$$\text{Aggregate Outlay} = \text{Initial Outlay (A)} + \text{Initial Outlay (B)}$$
$$= \$4,000,000 + 3,000,000$$
$$= \$7,000,000$$

AB's aggregate NPV is:
$$\text{Aggregate NPV} = \text{NPV (A)} + \text{NPV (B)}$$
$$= \$500,000 + 300,000$$
$$= \$800,000$$

Similar computations would be made for each of the other combinations of projects listed in Table 9-8. As indicated, there are four such possible combinations that can be fit into a $7,000,000 total budget. The next step then is to identify the combination having the largest combined NPV—which is ACD in the case at hand. Thus, Billings Electric should make funds available for the implementation of projects A, C, and D and temporarily reject projects B, E, and F until additional funds become available.

For Billings Electric, capital rationing leads to the rejection of economically desirable investments. This situation is clearly nonoptimal. The NPV foregone due to capital rationing is called a **valuation opportunity cost** because it represents

Valuation Opportunity Cost
The potential increase in firm value associated with investments that are foregone due to capital rationing.

TABLE 9-8 — Capital Investment Proposals Available to Billings Electric

Project	Initial Outlay	Net Present Value
A	$ 4,000,000	$ 500,000
B	3,000,000	300,000
C	1,500,000	180,000
D	1,500,000	200,000
E	2,000,000	220,000
F	1,000,000	70,000
Total	$13,000,000	$1,470,000

Combinations	Aggregate Initial Outlay	Aggregate NPV
AB	$7,000,000	$800,000
ACD	7,000,000	880,000
AEF	7,000,000	790,000
BCDF	7,000,000	750,000

the lost opportunity to increase the value of the firm to its stockholders. This cost can be measured in the following manner:

$$\text{Valuation Opportunity Cost} = NPV_M - NPV_S \tag{6}$$

where NPV_M is the maximum NPV available from taking on all positive NPV projects; and NPV_S is the actual NPV available from the *selected* combination of projects. For Billings Electric, the valuation opportunity cost of capital rationing is:

> Opportunity Cost = NPV From All Good Projects − NPV from Projects A,C,D
> Opportunity Cost = $1,470,000 − 880,000 = $590,000

The NPV of $1,470,000 is the increase in the value of the firm that would be realized if there were no capital rationing. With rationing, however, the value of the accepted projects is only $880,000. The firm's unwillingness or inability to secure sufficient resources to undertake all six projects will cost its stockholders $590,000 in lost value.

Liquidation Proceeds and Capital Rationing

Many investment proposals that arise in the course of a firm's capital budgeting decisions involve expenditures to modify or expand existing operations. Examples would be cost-reduction projects or investments to increase productive capacity. In those instances, it becomes important for the financial managers not only to take into account the new expenditures that are required for the investments, but also to recognize that *liquidation* of the existing operations may make additional funds available for investments in other projects. This perspective is especially relevant in a capital rationing situation.

To illustrate the point, let us suppose that Project C for Billings Electric in Table 9-8 represented a proposal to install new cost-reduction machinery on an existing assembly line in one of the company's factories. Let us further suppose that the present value of the expected future cash flows from the products being manufactured is $2,050,000 under the existing operating cost structure. Finally, let us suppose that the existing machinery and other production equipment could be sold to realize $2,000,000 after taxes if the product line were discontinued. Thus, the product line as it stands is just barely worthwhile to the firm because its expected future cash flows have a value only slightly greater than the amount that could be recovered by liquidating the line. Only if Project C were undertaken would the assembly line provide a significant positive NPV for the firm's stockholders.

Viewed in isolation, Project C costs the firm $1,500,000 and promises future cash flows with a present value of $1,680,000. This results in the $180,000 NPV listed for that project in Table 9-8. Looked at more broadly, however, the true incremental cost of undertaking the project is the $1,500,000 of *new* expenditure required, *plus* the $2,000,000 of liquidation proceeds that could be obtained if Billings Electric instead shut down the assembly line to which Project C would be attached. The foregone liquidation proceeds represent another kind of "opportunity cost" for Project C. Offsetting this $3,500,000 of total cost are expected cash flows whose aggregate present value is $1,680,000 + $2,050,000 or $3,730,000, resulting in a combined NPV equal to $230,000. A more economically meaningful description of the project would be to relabel it Project C' having an initial outlay of $3,500,000 and an NPV of $230,000.

Notice then what this implies for the manner in which Billings Electric should approach its project selection decision under capital rationing. The firm could regard its budget constraint to be the $7,000,000 of new capital that is available; and allocate those funds to what appears to be the optimal combination of projects A, C, and D, as shown in Table 9-8. By doing so, an NPV of $880,000 could be obtained.

Alternatively—and more sensibly—the firm's financial managers should recognize that the budget constraint is really $9,000,000 because an additional $2,000,000 could be made available by liquidating the existing assembly line associated with Project C. In turn, the relabeled Project C' would consume $3,500,000 of that expanded budget if it were undertaken, and the firm's set of projects to select from would be as listed in Table 9-9.

Thus, if Project C' is chosen, there will be only $9,000,000 – $3,500,000 = $5,500,000 left to spend on other projects. This is the same amount that would remain out of a $7,000,000 budget when the liquidation possibility is ignored and the cost of Project C is treated as $1,500,000. If Project C' is *not* chosen, however, the existing production line *can* be liquidated and there will be $9,000,000 of funds available for the remaining projects.

Given the various feasible combinations of projects identified in Table 9-9, the optimal decision is to take Projects A, B, and E and liquidate the production line in question. This will provide $1,020,000 in total NPV to Billings Electric. That NPV exceeds the contribution of all other combinations—including those in which Project C' appears. Notice that the NPV of $50,000, which the existing production line provides even without Project C', is counted as part of the benefit of the project in the list of proposals in Table 9-9. That is what accounts for the benefit of *not* liquidating and is why the NPV of Project C' becomes $230,000 rather than only the $180,000 shown originally in Table 9-8. Even though the existing production line does provide some value to the firm, this value is not sufficient to overcome the greater attractiveness of the other investments Billings currently has available. The firm would be better off by recapturing its investment in that production line and spending the money elsewhere.

If some of the other projects the firm was considering were also "add-on" investments to existing operations, the same sort of recognition of potential liquidating values should be included for them as well. While this will often make the

Investment Proposals for Billings Electric When Potential Liquidation Proceeds Are Taken Into Account

TABLE 9-9

Project	Initial Outlay	Net Present Value
A	$ 4,000,000	$ 500,000
B	3,000,000	300,000
C'	3,500,000	230,000
D	1,500,000	200,000
E	2,000,000	220,000
F	1,000,000	70,000
Total	$15,000,000	$1,520,000

Combinations	Aggregate Initial Outlay	Aggregate NPV
ABE	$9,000,000	$1,020,000
AC'D	9,000,000	930,000
ADEF	8,500,000	990,000
BC'DF	9,000,000	800,000
BC'E	8,500,000	750,000

project selection decision somewhat more complicated than if liquidating values were ignored, it will also result in an improved capital allocation procedure for shareholders. The broader logic is that, if funds are short to make capital investments, each of the firm's existing activities should be tested to determine whether its contribution to shareholder wealth is as great as that from new investments that could be financed by liquidating that activity. Closing down and liquidating an existing operation is seldom an easy decision for a firm's financial managers to make, but it will often be the case that it is in the shareholders' best interest to do so.

The Present Value Index

For Billings Electric, there were only six investment proposals at issue. In practice, however, it is not unusual for companies to have quite a long list of investment projects to choose from in a capital rationing situation. When they do, the process of attempting by trial and error to find the optimal combination to fit into the available capital budget can become fairly cumbersome. There is also no guarantee that the truly optimal combination will actually be identified merely by trial and error when there are a large number of projects under consideration.

Fortunately, there is a simple technique available that will enable a firm's financial managers to come very close to identifying that optimal combination on the first "try." The technique is based on what is commonly referred to as the **present value index (PVI)**. This index is computed for each investment project as follows:

Present Value Index (PVI)
The ratio of the NPV of a project to the initial outlay required for it. An efficiency measure for investment decisions under capital rationing.

$$PVI = \frac{\text{Net Present Value}}{\text{Initial Outlay}} = \frac{NPV}{I} \qquad (7)$$

What the index represents is a type of "efficiency" measure for an investment: the net present value payoff *per dollar* of initial outlay required. As we have seen, when there is a budget constraint, the firm's objective should be to allocate funds in such a way as to realize the greatest *total* NPV payoff with the funds that are available to spend. In turn, the way to accomplish this objective is simply to *rank* projects by their PVIs, and move successively down the list until the budget is exhausted.

We can apply this approach to Billings Electric's capital rationing decision problem. Let us return first to the case in Table 9-8 where Project C is a new investment that would *not* be attached to an existing activity. Thus, the possibility of liquidating the existing operations is not an element in the decision. The PVIs for the six projects the company would be considering are shown in Table 9-10.

If the company allocates its budget first to Project D, then to Project A, and then to Project C, it will consume the entire $7,000,000 of available new capital. Recall that this would be the correct allocation since we noted earlier that the

Present Value Indexes for Billings Electric Projects

TABLE 9-10

Project	Initial Outlay (I)	NPV	PVI=NPV/I	Rank
D	$1,500,000	$200,000	0.133	#1
A	4,000,000	500,000	0.125	#2
C	1,500,000	180,000	0.120	#3
E	2,000,000	220,000	0.110	#4
B	3,000,000	300,000	0.100	#5
F	1,000,000	70,000	0.070	#6

combination ACD *is* the optimal one for a $7,000,000 total budget. No further "trials" of other combinations would be necessary.

This procedure will generally work quite well in practice. If a firm has 50 investment projects to consider but only enough funds to undertake 20 of them, the top 20 as ranked by their present value indexes *will* typically be the optimal set. Under certain circumstances, however, it may not identify the optimal combination of projects. The present value index works least well when the projects under consideration have significantly different initial outlay requirements—and when some of those outlays are fairly large in relation to the total available budget. Notice that both characteristics are present for the investment projects that are listed in Table 9-8 and Table 9-10. The initial outlay needed for Project A is four times as great as that for the smallest Project F. In addition, Project A alone consumes 4⁄7 of the total $7,000,000 budget, and Project B consumes 3⁄7 of that budget. Nonetheless, the PVI rankings did identify correctly the optimal combination to choose.

On the other hand, if the project set were as shown in Table 9-9, with a $9,000,000 budget, the PVI rankings would be:

Project	Initial Outlay	NPV	PVI	Rank
D	$1,500,000	$200,000	0.133	#1
A	4,000,000	500,000	0.125	#2
E	2,000,000	220,000	0.110	#3
B	3,000,000	300,000	0.100	#4
F	1,000,000	70,000	0.070	#5
C′	3,500,000	230,000	0.066	#6

If we start at the top, the initial indication is that projects D, A, and E should be chosen. Collectively, they use up $7,500,000 of the budget and provide $920,000 of net present value. This leaves just $1,500,000 for other investments, and Project F is the only one left that will fit within that constraint. Together, the combination DAEF contributes $990,000 of present value. If we replace D and F with Project B, however, the entire budget is spent, and $1,020,000 of net present value is realized. This is the optimal choice, which we identified in our initial discussion of Table 9-9.

The problem is that the required investment outlays are "lumpy"; they come in large and discrete amounts that do not always fit neatly into the budget constraint. In such a situation, it is quite possible that a single large project like B can be a better choice than several smaller projects, which have PVIs above and below that of B. It is still true, on the other hand, that the highly-ranked projects A and E *were* correctly identified by the rankings as part of the optimal combination.

The appropriate conclusion is that the present value index technique will often work *perfectly* as a decision-making guide under capital rationing. Sometimes, however, it will work only *partially*, so that there will remain some room for trial-and-error analysis on the margin for the last few projects to be included in a constrained capital budget.

PERFORMANCE MEASURES AND DECISION CRITERIA

Most capital investment proposals are originated by the line operating managers of a firm. A potential obstacle to the generation and implementation of sound proposals is a conflict between the manner in which those managers' performance is evaluated by others and the manner in which the managers themselves evaluate proposed investments. It is often the case that an investment that would create

■ Ethics

ISSUES

THE DOWNSIDE OF CORPORATE DIVESTITURES

One of the consequences of the increasing international-ization of the world economy has been a corresponding increase in competition among multinational firms. At the same time, financing costs (RRRs) in many industrialized countries have been relatively high by historical stan-dards in recent years. Thus, operating cash flows have come under increasing pressure, and the hurdle rates used to evaluate investment proposals have been elevated.

As the IVM would indicate, these two influences will tend to make it more difficult for corporations to justi-fy new capital expenditures. The same influences should also make it more difficult to justify the contin-uation of various *existing* operations that were started during a more relaxed competitive environment.

We noted in this chapter that it is logical for firms to compare the value of the expected future cash flows from an existing line of business to the amount of capi-tal that could be freed up for use elsewhere if the busi-ness were liquidated. If continuation of the business line does not provide a positive net present value, it should be terminated. That is, the business should be "divested."

In practice, firms appear to be making that compar-ison much more explicitly and much more regularly than in prior years. Even a quick reading of the finan-cial press will uncover on any given day a series of news items that report corporate divestitures of por-tions of their businesses. In some cases, these are accomplished by selling off the operations to other companies. In other cases, the operations are sold to the current managers and employees, to be run by them as independent businesses. And, in a growing number of cases, the operations are simply terminated and the assets sold in the secondhand market for what-ever prices they may bring. For example, in one week in late 1997, Westinghouse, General Motors, and Eastman Kodak all announced major restructurings and write-offs at their firms. Westinghouse declared its intention to sell its power generation equipment busi-ness for $1.5 billion to a major German competitor, Siemens AG. General Motors stated that it would take a $2-3 billion charge against net income to write down underperforming assets and to cut plant capacity both in the United States and in Brazil. Kodak said it would cut 20,000 jobs and take a restructuring charge of at least $1 billion to eliminate unprofitable investments in digital imaging and to lower costs in its price competi-tion with Fuji Photo Film Company.

The act of terminating a long-standing line of busi-ness, and the dismissal of the managers and other employees who have been associated with the opera-tion, is among the most painful of corporate decisions. Perhaps more than any other decision, it forces finan-cial managers to confront the question as to where a firm's obligations lie. While termination may—and apparently often does—make financial sense for the firm's shareholders, the layoff of the employee group obviously imposes substantial human costs and can have an adverse impact on the economy of the com-munity in which the terminated operation previously was located. In a growing economy, the displaced work-ers will presumably find other employment, but the adverse effect on the local community may persist for years. Thus, these massive restructurings dramatically illustrate the uncertainty associated with global com-petition and raise inevitable questions about the extent of the responsibility of a firm's managers to stakehold-ers who are not owners.

value for shareholders may not be viewed as worthwhile by the managers of one of a firm's business units because the investment may adversely affect the measure by which the managers' performance is judged by senior management.

Measuring Business Unit Performance

As we noted in Chapter 2, the most common measures of the performance of a firm are return on assets (ROA) and return on equity (ROE). These are the criteria typically used by external financial analysts in assessing the firm's profitability per dollar of invested capital. Similar measures are also widely employed internally by firms in evaluating the performance of the firms' component business units. The "business unit" in question might be a division of the firm, a major product line, or an individual plant facility. When calculated for internal use, these criteria are often

TABLE 9-11

Balance Sheet for Houston Fabrics Sport Shirt Division, December 31, 1999 (in Millions)

Cash	$ 1.0	Accounts payable	$ 4.0
Accounts receivable	5.0	Accruals	4.0
Inventories	4.0	Net corporate	
Net fixed assets	8.0	investment	10.0
	$18.0		$18.0

referred to as *return on investment* (ROI) measures, which are commonly used by firms as the basis for the promotion and compensation of managers.

The ROI measures become operational when the firm's internal accounting system produces a balance sheet and an income statement each year for each business unit. These statements are constructed in a manner similar to that in which the firm's overall financial statements are prepared for external reporting purposes. The assets used by the business unit are identified, as well as the current liabilities (accounts payable and accruals), which the unit generates in the normal course of its operations. The difference between these assets and liabilities is a measure of the net investment the parent firm has in the business unit.

For example, the men's sport shirt division of Houston Fabrics Company might have a December 31, 1999, balance sheet like that shown in Table 9-11. The only difference between the format of this balance sheet and the one which is prepared for the company as a whole is that the "Net Corporate Investment" figure of $10 million is not separated into debt and equity components at the business unit level. The reason is that the decision as to the form of financing to employ is made at the central corporate level and is not under the control of the business unit. What is important to the firm is that it must acquire $10 million from *some* combination of sources in order to support the operations of the sport shirt division.

If the division's pretax earnings amount to $4.0 million during the year 2000, and Houston Fabrics' effective corporate tax rate is 40%, the division would be credited with ($4.0)(1 − 0.40) = $2.4 million of after-tax operating profit (ATOP) for the year. This would result in a measured **return on investment (ROI)** for the division equal to

Return on Investment (ROI)
The ratio of the after-tax operating profits of a firm's business unit to the firm's investment in that business unit. A measure of the unit's performance during a specified time period.

$$\text{ROI} = \frac{\text{After-Tax Operating Profit}}{\text{Beginning Net Investment}} = \frac{\$2.4 \text{ million}}{\$10.0 \text{ million}} = 24\% \tag{8}$$

for the year 2000. The calculation is based on the investment in the division as of the *beginning* of 2000 (the end of 1999) because the investment must be in place *before* the year's operations can occur. If Houston Fabrics' required rate of return were 14%, the sport shirt division would be regarded as having performed well during 2000, and its managers would be compensated accordingly. Its ROI exceeds the corporate RRR target. If the division reinvested the depreciation on its fixed assets each year so as to maintain an ATOP level of $2.4 million into the indefinite future, the division would be generating a perpetuity whose NPV would be:

$$\text{NPV} = \frac{C}{\text{RRR}} - I = \frac{\$2.4 \text{ million}}{0.14} - \$10.0 \text{ million} = \$17.14 \text{ million} - \$10.0 \text{ million} = \$7.14 \text{ million}$$

Suppose that late in 1999 the managers of the division had considered a new investment project that would require a $2,000,000 initial outlay and would produce an annual ATOP of $400,000 (given annual reinvestment of depreciation). This project would provide an IRR of $400,000/$2,000,000 or 20% per annum. Since that rate of return exceeds the corporate RRR of 14%, the investment *should* be undertaken by the sport shirt division. If it were, annual divisional cash flows would be $2,400,000 + $400,000 = $2,800,000 and the division would generate an NPV for Houston Fabrics' stockholders amounting to:

$$NPV = \frac{\$2.8 \text{ million}}{0.14} - \$12.0 \text{ million} = \$8.0 \text{ million}$$

after including the cost of the new project. This would be an improvement over the $7.14 million NPV that would be generated if the new investment project were rejected.

The problem for the division's managers is that the same project will also reduce the division's measured ROI to

$$ROI' = \frac{\$2.8 \text{ million}}{\$12.0 \text{ million}} = \$23.3\%$$

Since the division would not appear to senior management to be performing as well as it would in the absence of the new project, the division's managers could be penalized for making an investment that increases stockholder wealth! Thus, it is likely that the division's managers will reject the project despite the fact that it provides a positive NPV for shareholders. A similar conflict will arise for *any* new investment whose IRR is below 24% but above 14%. The investments should be made, but it will not be in the interest of the division's managers to pursue them.

Performance Measures and Cash Flow Timing

A conflict between the NPV decision criterion and the ROI performance criterion can also occur even in the case where a proposed investment has a positive long-term impact on a division's ROI. This conflict can arise when a proposed investment's cash flows begin at relatively low levels and increase sharply over time. The problem is that the investment may be attractive in the long run, but it may unfavorably affect the measured performance of the business unit in the short run.

For example, assume that the previously mentioned investment project for Houston Fabrics' sport shirt division is estimated by managers to produce the following series of annual ROIs:

Year	ROI
1	20%
2	22%
3	24%
4	26%
5 – ∞	28%

The investment would have a positive NPV, and it would also have a positive impact on the division's ROI beginning in year 4. The immediate consequence, however, is that the project's acceptance will *adversely* affect the business unit's overall measured ROI during the first two years of the project's life. Not until the fourth year of its life will the project's inherent value to the firm begin to show up in an improvement in the business unit's ROI as seen by senior management. It is quite possible, therefore, that the unit's managers may reject the project as a result of its short-run impact on their measured performance. This would be especially true if the managers expected to be moving on to *another* business unit within the next three years. Their successors would reap the benefit of the project's

http://
Impressive rates of **ROI** are available from eco-efficiency investments at www.igc.org/eco-ops/nbl/nbl.4.7.html

implementation, while the current managers would bear the costs of low early project ROIs.

The Conflicting Roles of the ROI and NPV Criteria in Capital Budgeting

We have demonstrated in this chapter that the evaluation of a proposed investment's acceptability should be based on the DCF criteria: NPV and IRR. Given the importance of the ROI measures in the evaluation of the performance of a firm and its managers, however, it is unreasonable to expect a division manager to ignore this performance measure in the generation of investment proposals. Unfortunately, conflicts between the NPV and the ROI criterion's conclusions regarding proposal acceptability can easily arise.

There is no easy solution to this problem. Especially if the time horizon of the managers is different from the time horizon of the investments they make, worthwhile projects having relatively large cash flows late in their lives may end up being rejected in favor of less valuable projects with high early cash flows. This is another aspect of the "agency" problem we discussed in Chapter 1. Any performance measurement system that reviews operating results annually may distort managers' decisions. The same potential problem will appear at the senior management level if part of the managers' annual compensation is tied to the level of the current year's ROA or ROE realized by the firm as a whole.

One possible response by a firm's senior management is to notify division managers that they will not be penalized for projects that reduce a division's ROI as long as those projects have positive NPVs and their annual cash flows (ATOP) and ROIs meet the managers' original budget projections. A possible response by a firm's stockholders is to link at least part of managers' compensation directly to the firm's stock price performance. Bonuses, which are payable in the form of shares of the company's common stock and stock option plans, have this characteristic. The goal is to encourage managers to make correct investment decisions because the NPVs of those investments will show up in increased stock prices— and increased managerial wealth. To encourage even lower-level managers to make correct decisions, part of their compensation should also be linked to the firm's stock price. Many firms are moving in that direction over time, in their compensation planning. Nonetheless, a potential discrepancy between what shareholders would *like* managers to do, and what managers *will* do in their own self-interest, remains a substantial agency problem in the large corporation.

SUMMARY

In this chapter, various criteria were described that can be used to evaluate and select capital investment proposals. From the financial managers' viewpoint, a capital investment is any expenditure of funds that is made in anticipation of future benefits that are expected to be realized over a long period of time. According to this definition, capital investments can take the form of expenditures on both tangible and intangible assets. Capital investment decision criteria can be divided into two broad categories: non-discounted cash flow methodologies, and discounted cash flow techniques.

The two major non-DCF techniques are average return on investment (AROI) and payback period. The AROI measures the average annual rate of return on an investment in terms of accounting net income. Although it is a familiar measure of

■ **Financial**

ISSUes

INSERTING RISK IN AN EXECUTIVE COMPENSATION PLAN

One of the most visible and sensitive issues at large corporations today is the topic of executive compensation. In a recent survey, 73% of the general public and 47% of

senior executives at large firms agreed that CEOs are paid too much. On the surface, the data on executive pay seem to support this contention. The total compensation of each of the twenty highest paid CEOs at U.S. firms in 1997 ranged from $20 to $230 million. The average compensation of all CEOs in that year was 220 times that of the average factory worker.

Proponents of CEO pay point out that most of the compensation is tied directly to the performance of a firm's stock in the form of stock options. Thus, executives are paid in proportion to the benefits realized by their firm's stockholders. Critics claim, however, that there is very little downside risk associated with stock options. Even the stocks of firms that underperform their competitors are likely to rise in a bull market. Furthermore, at firms whose stock prices do fall, CEOs frequently renegotiate downward the price at which their stock options can be exercised. This perception of the lack of risk in executive compensation was reflected in the above-mentioned survey, in which 71% of the executives and 79% of the public agreed that top executives were rewarded for positive firm performance but not penalized for negative results. Furthermore, 56% of the executives and 79% of the public stated that top managers at poorly performing firms should take a salary cut.

In response to this type of criticism, the CEO of one large American company recently announced that he would forfeit his base salary ($850,000) if his firm's earnings per share (EPS) did not reach a minimum of $4.00 within two years. He also declared that 16 other senior executives would lose 65% of their salaries if earnings do not reach the target. This compensation plan, which was unique among large U.S. firms, seems directly and dramatically to address a major weakness of executive pay plans. The critics of executive pay, however, were far from satisfied.

Since the firm's EPS was $3.90 at the time, the target EPS of $4.00 in two years seemed to be overly conservative. In addition, the target performance was stated in absolute terms (EPS ≥ $4.00) rather than in terms of superior performance relative to the firm's competitors. Furthermore, EPS can be manipulated by management. Finally, the plan's penalties for poor performance were not symmetric with its reward for good performance. At worst, poor results at the firm will cost the CEO his base salary. If the company's EPS hits $4.75, on the other hand, the CEO will receive incentive compensation of up to eight times his current base salary.

performance, AROI is a poor decision criterion because it measures investment benefits as net income instead of cash flows. In addition, it ignores the timing of the benefits and requires the use of a subjective hurdle AROI as a benchmark. The payback period measures the time required to recover the initial cost of an investment. Although it does measure investment benefits in terms of cash flows, it does not correctly evaluate either the size, the timing, or the duration of those cash flows.

The two DCF methodologies, net present value (NPV) and internal rate of return (IRR), are superior to the non-DCF techniques because they apply the Investment Valuation Model to the evaluation of capital investment proposals. Not only do they properly measure benefits as cash flows, but they also evaluate completely both the size and the timing of the cash flows. In addition, both techniques are founded on a general economic model of asset pricing that provides an objective benchmark for the determination of required rates of return. An investment's NPV measures the effect of an investment on the total value of a firm to its stockholders. Hence, independent investments that have positive net present values should be accepted. An investment's IRR is the discount rate that equates the present value of expected future cash flows to the initial cost of the investment. The

chapter equations

1. $AROI = \dfrac{\text{Average Net Income}}{\text{Investment}}$

2. Payback Period = Length of Time Needed to Recover the Initial Cost

3. NPV = Present Value – Cost of Asset

$$= \sum_{t=1}^{N} \dfrac{C_t}{(1+K)^t} - I$$

4. $I = \displaystyle\sum_{t=1}^{N} \dfrac{C_t}{(1+IRR)^t}$

5. $NPV = \displaystyle\sum_{t=1}^{N} \dfrac{C_t}{(1+IRR)^t} - I = 0$

6. Valuation Opportunity Cost = $NPV_M - NPV_S$

7. $PVI = \dfrac{\text{Net Present Value}}{\text{Initial Outlay}} = \dfrac{NPV}{I}$

8. $ROI = \dfrac{\text{After-Tax Operating Profit}}{\text{Beginning Net Investment}}$

IRR represents the annual compound yield that is provided by the investment. The firm should accept all independent investments for which the IRR exceeds the firm's required rate of return.

The IRR technique is more widely used in practice than the NPV technique because it appears to be easier for nonfinance specialists to understand. The NPV technique's assumption that the rate of return earned on the reinvestment of project cash flows is equal to the RRR, however, is more logical. Thus, in the event of a conflict between the NPV and IRR rankings of mutually exclusive investment proposals, financial managers should base their decisions on the NPV rankings.

There are a number of operational problems often faced by companies in their implementation of effective capital budgeting systems. Many firms have limited financial and other resources that prevent the acceptance of all economically desirable investment projects. This results in the need to ration capital. Under capital rationing, the correct decision rule is to select the combination of projects that will fit into the constrained capital budget and that provides the maximum total NPV within that constraint. In addition, the potential for conflict exists between the measures used to appraise the performance of a firm's business units and the effect of economically desirable investment projects on a firm's value to its stockholders. ROI performance measures are particularly susceptible to creating such a conflict.

CONTENT QUESTIONS

1. Explain the difference between a capital expenditure and an operating expenditure.
2. Why might an accountant and a financial manager differ in their definition of a capital expenditure?
3. Why are the management and evaluation of capital investments extremely important to a firm?
4. What are the advantages and disadvantages of AROI as an investment decision criterion?
5. What are the advantages and disadvantages of payback period as an investment decision criterion?
6. Define and justify the NPV decision criterion, with reference to the price and value of financial securities.
7. Define and justify the IRR decision criterion, with reference to the yield on financial securities.
8. Why might corporate capital investment projects provide an opportunity for enhancing shareholder value, even though financial securities are properly priced in an efficient financial marketplace?
9. Explain how there is a direct quantitative link between NPV and value maximization for shareholders.
10. What is the role of the RRR in the calculation of investment project NPVs and IRRs in order to evaluate the attractiveness of those projects?

11. What properties make NPV a superior decision criterion to IRR when ranking investments in order of desirability?
12. Why should the NPV and IRR methodologies provide the same accept/reject conclusions for an individual independent investment?
13. Explain how there may be a conflict between the NPV and IRR rankings of mutually exclusive investment projects, with reference to the NPV profile.
14. Explain what is meant by the valuation opportunity cost of capital rationing.
15. Why do some firms find themselves in a capital rationing situation?
16. Why is the present value index a useful guide to finding the optimal combination of investment projects to select when capital is rationed?
17. What features of investment projects make the present value index only a partial solution to the selection of the optimal combination of investments under capital rationing?
18. What is the relevance of liquidation values to the selection of investment projects under capital rationing?
19. What is the most common performance measure used in practice to assess the performance of a firm's various business units?
20. What are the potential conflicts between ROI measures of performance and the NPV decision criterion for investments?

CONCEPT QUESTIONS

1. IVM We have discussed in this chapter the economic logic behind using the NPV technique as a guide to the evaluation of capital investment projects. Under what set of circumstances might a firm choose to undertake an investment whose indicated NPV is negative?
2. IVM The NPV profile provides a graphical description of the relative desirability of two mutually exclusive investments at various RRRs. What are the characteristics of investments that will appear more desirable at low RRRs, in contrast to investments that will appear more desirable at high RRRs? Why do these differences arise?
3. Is it possible that an existing operation of a firm could have a negative liquidation value? What factors could cause this to be the case? How would this affect the desirability of continuing with the operation?
4. As a financial analyst, you are examining the financial performance of two companies during the most recent year. Firm A has realized an ROE of 20%, and Firm B has realized an ROE of 15%. What additional information would you need in order to be able to decide which firm has had the better performance during the year?
5. One of the difficulties with an ROI measure of business unit performance is that it is calculated as a ratio. Can you suggest a measure that does not have that shortcoming?

PROBLEMS

1. Calculate the payback period of a $100,000 investment with the following cash flows:

Year	Cash Flow
1	$20,000
2	25,000
3	40,000
4	50,000
5	30,000

2. You are thinking about starting a new business that will require an investment of $250,000. Calculate the AROI of this investment, given the following net income projections for the life of the business:

Year	Net Income
1	$ 50,000
2	100,000
3	150,000
4	200,000
5	200,000
6	100,000

3. A firm is considering two investment alternatives with net income and cash flows as shown. Investment I will cost DM50,000 and Investment II will cost DM40,000.

	Investment I		Investment II	
Year	Net Income	Cash Flow	Net Income	Cash Flow
1	DM 6,000	DM10,000	DM12,000	DM22,000
2	8,000	15,000	12,000	22,000
3	11,000	20,000	6,000	10,000
4	13,000	25,000	3,000	5,000
5	16,000	30,000	3,000	5,000
6	16,000	30,000	3,000	5,000

   a. Calculate the AROI for each investment proposal.
   b. Calculate the payback period for each investment proposal.

4. Find the IRR of the following investments and determine which should be accepted, given an RRR of 10%:
   a. An investment costing $31,140 promising a cash flow of $3,000 per year for 15 years.
   b. An investment costing $46,000 promising a cash flow of $6,000 per year for 20 years.

5. Find the NPV of the investments of Problem 4, given an RRR of 10%. Which of the projects should be accepted?

6.   a. Calculate the NPV of each of the two investments in Problem 3 at an RRR of 12%.
   b. Rank the two investments by each of the three evaluation methodologies: AROI, payback period, and NPV. How do you account for the differences in rankings?

7. A firm is considering an investment with an initial outlay of SF90,000. It is expected to generate after-tax cash flows of SF30,000 the first year; SF60,000 the second year; and SF90,000 the third year.
   a. Find the project's NPV if the RRR is 16%.
   b. Find the project's IRR.

8. Due to construction time, the initial outlay of a project spreads over a 2-year period and amounts to $10,000 per year in year 0 and year 1. After completion, the investment project will produce annual cash flows of $15,000 in year 2 and year 3. The RRR is 14%.
   a. Calculate the NPV.
   b. Calculate the IRR.

9. Louisville Products is considering an investment that requires an initial outlay of $5.5 million. It is expected to generate cash flows that will grow by 10% each year for 5 years. What is the net present value of the investment if the first year's cash flow is $1,500,000? (Louisville will use an RRR of 15%.)

10. Parsa Products is considering an investment in a new product venture. The initial outlay is $30 million. The product will produce no cash flow for the first two years. After two years, it is expected to produce cash flows of $1 million for the next two years. After that, it is expected to generate $4 million per year for the last ten years of the product's life. If Parsa has a 12% RRR, what is the investment's NPV? Should Parsa make this investment?

11. Parsa Products' managers are interested in communicating the decision they reached concerning the new product proposal in Problem 10. They want to communicate the decision in terms of rates of return. Explain Parsa's decision by comparing the investment's IRR with its RRR.

12. A firm has a choice between two mutually exclusive investment alternatives, each requiring an initial outlay of $25,000. Investment A promises cash flows of $2,000 the first year; $2,000 the second year; and $35,000 the third year. Investment B offers $21,000 the first year; $10,000 the second year; and $2,000 the third year. The required rate of return is 8%.
   a. Calculate the NPV of each.
   b. Calculate the IRR of each.
   c. Which of these two mutually exclusive investments should be accepted? Why?

13.   a. At what RRR do the two investments in Problem 12 appear equally attractive to the firm in terms of their NPV ranking?
   b. At what RRRs is Investment A in Problem 12 preferable to Investment B according to the NPV methodology?

14.   a. According to the NPV methodology, what is the impact of Investments A and B on the value of the firm in Problem 12 at the RRR of 8%?
   b. What does the IRR methodology indicate about the impact of the two investments on the firm's value?
   c. Why should the financial managers be more interested in the results of the NPV analysis of the two investments than in the results of the IRR analysis?

15. A firm's financial manager is evaluating the following mutually exclusive investments:

| | Cash Flows | |
Year	Investment A	Investment B
1	$24,000	$16,000
2	22,000	19,000
3	20,000	21,000
4	18,000	23,000
5	16,000	25,000

Each investment has a cost of $65,000 and is equally risky.
   a. Which investment is preferable at a discount rate of 17%?
   b. Which investment is preferable at a discount rate of 0%?
   c. At what discount rate are the two investments equally attractive?

16. Two investments have the following NPVs when their cash flows are discounted at four different discount rates:

Discount Rate	Investment A NPV	Investment B NPV
0%	$35,000	$25,000
7%	15,000	15,000
15%	0	7,000
22%	−12,000	1,000

Each investment has a cost of $20,000.
    a. What is the IRR of each investment?
    b. Calculate the total cash inflows over the life of each investment.
    c. Which of the two investments has the more rapid cash inflows?
    d. Where does the crossover discount rate occur for the NPV profiles for the two investments?

17. A $200,000 investment has expected cash flows over 15 years of $100,000 per year. What is the present value index of the investment given an RRR of 12%?

18. Olympia Manufacturing Company is evaluating its capital budget. Due to the unavailability of funds, capital expenditures are limited to £3,000,000. Olympia has the following projects under consideration:

Project	Initial Outlay	NPV
A	£1,000,000	£200,000
B	800,000	140,000
C	1,200,000	250,000
D	900,000	160,000
E	1,500,000	300,000
F	1,100,000	240,000

    a. Which of these investments should be selected for inclusion in the capital budget?
    b. With your solution to part (a), how much would the value of Olympia be expected to increase?
    c. What is the opportunity cost to Olympia's shareholders of the capital rationing constraint?

19. Assume that projects A and F in Problem 18 are mutually exclusive. That is, the selection of either A or F eliminates the possibility of investing in the other.
    a. What investments should be selected for inclusion in the capital budget?
    b. With your solution to part (a), how much would the value of Olympia be expected to increase?
    c. What is the opportunity cost to Olympia's shareholders of the capital rationing constraint? (Keep in mind that A and F are mutually exclusive *regardless* of the rationing constraint.)

20. Returning to Problem 18, A and F are *not* mutually exclusive as assumed in Problem 19. Olympia has decided to include the possibility of liquidating one of its divisions. Project D is a proposal to spend £900,000 to improve the efficiency of that division. The division is currently generating cash flows with a present value of £1,670,000. The division can be sold for £1,600,000.
    a. If funds were unlimited, should this division be liquidated?
    b. Given the budget constraint in Problem 18, should the division be liquidated and what other investments should be made?
    c. What is the valuation opportunity cost to Olympia's shareholders of the capital budgeting constraint?

http:// INTERNET EXERCISE

Read the article "Capital Budgeting for a New Dairy Facility" and explain why you would or would not make this investment. Base your decision and comments on the material in Chapter 9, such as capital investment decision criteria and **ROI**. Click on Animal Topics, Dairy Science, and Records Management and Economics. http://edis.ifas.ufl.edu.

SELF-STUDY QUIZ

1. A $100,000 investment has expected cash flows for three years of $20,000, $100,000, and $10,000. If the RRR is 10%, should this investment be made according to the NPV rule?
2. Should the investment be made according to the IRR criterion?
3. Find the Present Value Index of an investment of $400,000 that has expected future cash flows of $100,000 per year for the next 10 years, given a required rate of return of 16%.

APPENDIX: THE PROBLEM OF MULTIPLE IRRs

The IRR is the discount rate that equates the present value of an investment's cash flows with its initial cost. When the cash flows of an investment follow the conventional pattern of one outflow at the beginning followed by a series of inflows, there is only one IRR for that investment. This was the case for the finishing line and weaving center proposals for Houston Fabrics in the chapter. In Figure 9-8, notice how each NPV profile slopes continuously downward so that it intercepts the horizontal axis at only one point, which corresponds to the investment's IRR. In the case of these two investments, the IRR methodology provides an unambiguous accept/reject signal for each investment proposal.

Unconventional Cash Flows and a Unique IRR

The IRR computation will also generate a unique IRR for an investment that is characterized by a *series* of cash outflows early in its life followed by a series of inflows over the remainder of its life. For instance, assume that a firm's financial managers wish to evaluate the investment shown in Table 9A-1. In this case, the cash outflows are greater than the $100,000 cost of the investment. The outflows also occur over more than one period. The IRR, however, is still the discount rate that results in NPV = 0. Thus, the IRR can be redefined as *the discount rate that equates the present value of the anticipated inflows with the present value of the projected outflows.*

While we have slightly changed the definition of the IRR from that used in the conventional cash flow pattern case, the result is identical. There is only one discount rate at which the investment's NPV equals zero, 18.53%. This can readily be

The IRR Calculation for an Investment With an Unconventional Cash Flow Pattern

TABLE 9A-1

Year	Cash Flow	$DF_{0.18,N}$	PV	$DF_{0.19,N}$	PV
0	−$100,000	1.000	−$100,000	1.000	−$100,000
1	−50,000	0.848	−42,400	0.840	−42,000
2	−25,000	0.718	−17,950	0.706	−17,650
3	125,000	0.609	76,125	0.593	74,125
4	100,000	0.516	51,600	0.499	49,900
5	80,000	0.437	34,960	0.419	33,520
Total	$130,000		NPV $ 2,335		NPV = −$ 2,105

$$\text{IRR} = 0.18 + \left(\frac{\$2,335}{\$2,335 - (-\$2,105)} \right)(0.19 - 0.18) = 0.18 + (0.526)(0.01) = 18.53\%$$

seen in the investment's NPV profile in Figure 9A-1. The unconventional nature of the cash flow pattern has not altered the basic shape of the NPV profile. As was true of the NPV profiles in Figure 9-8, the profile for the unconventional investment intersects the horizontal axis only once. As shown in Figure 9A-1, the IRR decision rule continues to provide a clear accept/reject signal.

Unconventional Cash Flows and Multiple IRRs

There are unconventional cash flow patterns, however, for which the IRR criterion may *not* provide an unambiguous accept/reject signal. This occurs when cash inflows and outflows are interspersed over an investment's life. The mixture of cash inflows and outflows can result in NPV = 0 at more than one discount rate, so that an investment may have more than one IRR. For example, consider the investment shown in Table 9A-2.

The discounting factors in Table 9A-2 for the 25% discount rate were taken from Table III in the back of the text. The factors for the 100% discount rate were calculated with the basic present value equation:

$$PV = (C_N)(DF_{K,N}) = (C_N)\left(\frac{1}{1+K}\right)^N$$

An NPV = 0 occurs at a discount rate of 25% and at a discount rate of 100%. Thus, the investment has *two* IRRs (25% and 100%), as shown graphically in Figure 9A-2.

Due to the change in the sign of the projected cash flows over the investment's life, the NPV profile has a distinctly different shape than the previous profiles we have examined. Since the curve intersects the horizontal axis at two points, the investment has two IRRs. What is the explanation for this strange NPV profile? In algebraic terms, there are simply two discount rates that result in NPV = 0. Intuitively, the NPV of the projected cash flows can be positive or negative, as the discount rate and the relative importance to the investor of the size and the timing of the cash flows fluctuate.

At a discount rate of 0%, NPV = –$10,000 because the sum of the outflows in years 0 and 2 exceeds the inflow in year 1 by that amount. At this discount rate, the only characteristic of the cash flows that the investor considers is their size. As the discount rate increases, the timing of the flows becomes a factor. The fact that the large outflow of $100,000 is delayed until the end of year 2 while the inflow of $130,000 is received one year earlier influences the investor's evalua-

TABLE 9A-2   The IRR Calculation for an Investment With Multiple IRRs

Year	Cash Flow	$DF_{0.25,N}$	PV	$DF_{1.00,N}$	PV
0	– 40,000	1.000	–$40,000	$\frac{1}{(1+1.00)^0} = 1.000$	–$40,000
1	130,000	0.800	104,000	$\frac{1}{(1+1.00)^1} = 0.500$	65,000
2	–100,000	0.640	–64,000	$\frac{1}{(1+1.00)^2} = 0.250$	–25,000
Total	–$10,000		NPV = $ 0		NPV = $ 0

IRR = 25% and IRR = 100%

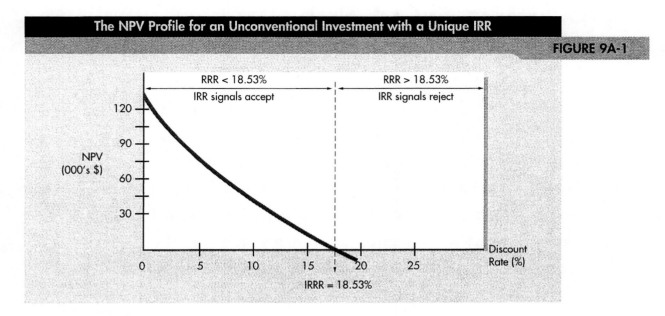

The NPV Profile for an Unconventional Investment with a Unique IRR

FIGURE 9A-1

tion. At discount rates below 25%, the larger size of the two outflows more than offsets the more rapid timing of the inflow. At rates between 25% and 100%, however, the reverse is true. The timing of the inflow makes the investment acceptable to the investor (NPV > 0). Finally, at discount rates above 100%, the importance of timing is so great that the cash flow at time zero dominates the investor's evaluation. Since it is an outflow, the investment is unacceptable (NPV < 0).

In the case of multiple IRRs, the IRR decision rule can give confusing accept/reject signals, as shown in Figure 9A-2. Only if RRR < 25% or RRR > 100% do the two IRRs give the same accept/reject signals. When 25% < RRR < 100%, however, the two IRRs provide conflicting accept/reject signals. What is the solution to this dilemma? The best solution is simply to calculate the investment's NPV. Even an investment with unconventional cash flows and multiple IRRs has only one RRR and one NPV. The NPV technique always provides a clear accept/reject signal regardless of the pattern of an investment's cash flows.

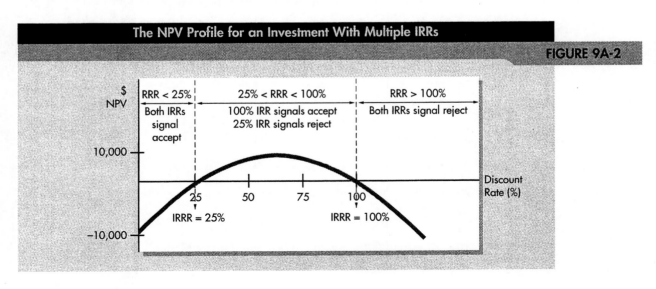

The NPV Profile for an Investment With Multiple IRRs

FIGURE 9A-2

Capital Investment Cash Flows

The previous chapter stressed that only DCF evaluation methodologies can consistently provide theoretically correct accept/reject signals for capital investment proposals. The accuracy of these signals in actual practice, however, depends on the accuracy of the cash flow forecasts and the estimate of the RRR on which the NPV and the IRR evaluations are based. The DCF computational procedures can be relatively easily generalized so that they can be routinely performed on a computer. The estimation of the relevant cash flows and the RRR to be included in the computations, on the other hand, can take considerable time and effort.

Unlike the case of securities with well-defined cash flows, the cash flows on capital investments can be ill-defined and varied in nature. Securities typically have one type of inflow such as dividends or interest payments. Capital investments are characterized by numerous categories of inflows and outflows during each period of the investments' lives. These must be combined into an overall estimate of the net inflow or outflow in each period before a firm's financial managers can calculate an investment's NPV or IRR. The process of cash flow estimation requires that financial managers address a number of important issues:

- Surveys of large multinational firms reveal that the majority of these firms regularly make cash flow forecasts for over 60% of their capital investment proposals. What techniques do the firms use to project investment cash flows? Does the technique vary depending on the type of investment proposal? Are nonoperating cash flows for taxes and interest expense included in the forecast?

- In recent years, institutional investors and takeover specialists have emphasized the analysis of a firm's cash flows instead of its accounting profits. What is the relationship between a firm's earnings and its cash flows? How can the analyst convert an earnings forecast into a cash flow projection? Why are a firm's cash flows so important to analysts?
- Inflation rates in many industrialized countries average less than 3% per year, while in others annual price increases approach 10%. Should a firm's financial managers adjust their forecast of investment cash flows for anticipated inflation over the investment's life? How can such adjustments be made? What are the potential consequences of ignoring inflation's effects on investment cash flows?
- Sometimes financial managers must evaluate investment proposals with unequal lives. Should the managers adjust their cash flow forecasts for this fact or can it be ignored? If adjustments are necessary, how can they be made without biasing the analysis in favor of one of the proposed investments?

In this chapter, we will describe techniques for determining the cash flows that should be included in the evaluation of a capital investment proposal. Figure 10-1 overviews the estimation of the benefits component of the IVM for capital investments which are classified as either expansion proposals or replacement proposals. The significance of this classification is that it affects the calculation of the incremental after-tax cash flows associated with the investment. These cash flows, which should include inflation adjustments but normally exclude the cost of financing the investment, comprise the benefits component of the IVM. In order to simplify their estimation, the cash flows are divided into three categories that differ in terms of their timing. Initial period cash flows occur at the start of the investment's life (C_0). Project life cash flows are generated by the use of the investment each year during its life (C_1 to C_N). Project termination cash flows arise from the liquidation of the investment at the end of its useful life (C_N).

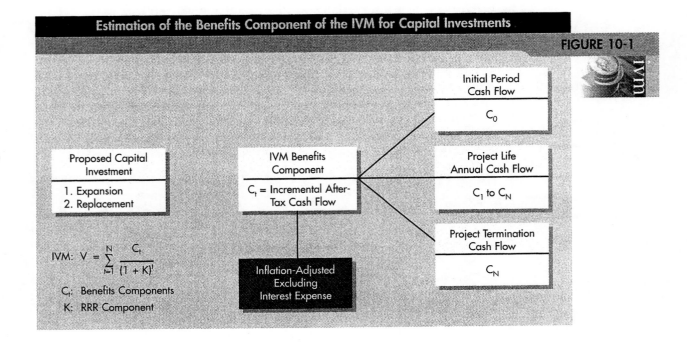

Estimation of the Benefits Component of the IVM for Capital Investments

FIGURE 10-1

RELEVANT CASH FLOWS

The calculation of an investment's relevant cash flows (often referred to as free cash flows) requires an understanding of several key aspects of capital investment. The first of these is the concept of incremental cash flows, which suggests that only the *change* in total firm cash flows attributable to an investment is relevant to its evaluation. Another important concept is that of a sunk cost, which is irrelevant to the evaluation of a proposed investment because it has been incurred in the past.

Additional aspects of capital investment analysis include the role of taxes and the proper treatment of interest expense. Since an investment can affect a firm's cash outlay for taxes, the tax effect of a proposed investment is relevant to its evaluation. On the other hand, the interest expense on debt financing required by an investment is not a relevant cash flow because (as we shall show in Chapter 15) it is included in the investment's RRR. The only exception to this rule is the situation in which the source of financing for a proposed investment is uniquely tied to that specific investment. In this case, the cost advantage or disadvantage of the unique financing arrangement should be reflected in the calculation of the investment's NPV. In this section, we will examine in detail all these determinants of an investment's relevant cash flows.

The Concept of Incremental Cash Flows

The cash flows that are relevant to the calculation of a capital investment's NPV are not always equal to its total cash flows. For the purpose of demonstrating the determination of relevant cash flows, investment proposals can be divided into the two categories shown in Figure 10-2. Expansion proposals increase the size of the firm and boost its sales volume. Replacement proposals are designed to increase the efficiency of the firm at its current sales volume by modernizing its operations. Only if an investment proposal represents an expansion decision should its total anticipated cash flows be included in the NPV calculation. In the case of a replacement proposal, the NPV analysis should include only the difference in cash flows between the new asset and the existing asset that it will replace.

There is a logical explanation for these different treatments of investment cash flows. The impact of a particular investment on the value of a firm's stock depends upon its *net* effect on the firm's cash flows. During their evaluation of investment proposals, financial managers should apply the following rule: *only those cash flows that are **incremental** to a proposed investment are relevant to its evaluation.* In the case of an expansion proposal, the incremental cash flows are equal to the investment's total cash flows. In the case of a replacement proposal, on the other hand, the incremental cash flows are equal only to the difference in cash flows between the new asset and the existing asset that is to be replaced.

Incremental Cash Flows
The net impact of a proposed investment on a firm's cash flows. Only incremental cash flows are relevant to the evaluation of an investment.

SUMMARY FIGURE 10-2

Types of Capital Investment Proposals

Type of Proposal	Nature of Decision	Relevant Cash Flow
Expansion	Add new asset to existing asset structure	Total anticipated cash flows of new asset
Replacement	Substitute new asset for existing asset	Difference in cash flows between new asset and replaced asset

The Effect of Taxes and Sunk Costs

Two additional aspects of cash flow analysis deserve mention. First, the NPV evaluation is accurate only if the cash flows are expressed on an after-tax basis. The only cash flows that are available to the firm for paying dividends or making new investments are after-tax cash flows. Second, the NPV evaluation of an investment proposal is oriented to the future. The calculation of NPV should reflect only cash inflows and outflows that are expected to occur in the future. This time frame of reference is critical to the proper evaluation of an investment proposal that requires the replacement of an existing asset with a new asset.

Taxes.   From the financial managers' viewpoint, the incremental income taxes arising from an investment's revenues are one of many types of cash outflows that reduce the net cash inflows realized from the investment. Consequently, the *cash flows that are relevant* to an investment's evaluation are *incremental, after-tax cash flows*.

Figure 10-3 contains the two rules needed to convert any pretax revenue or expense into its equivalent after-tax cash flow. Revenues increase cash outflows for income taxes while expenses reduce them. The first rule in the figure indicates that a cash revenue must be reduced by the associated corporate income taxes, multiplied by $(1 - T)$, in order to convert it to an after-tax cash flow. For example, a $15,000 increase in sales revenues is equivalent to the following after-tax cash flow for a firm in a 34% tax bracket:

$$\text{After-Tax Cash Flow} = (\$15,000)(1 - 0.34) = \$9,900$$

A cash expense must be reduced by the associated income tax savings. The after-tax outflow associated with the payment of $10,000 in salaries by the firm in our previous example is:

$$\text{After-Tax Cash Flow} = (\$10,000)(1 - 0.34) = \$6,600$$

While the payment of salaries represents a $10,000 cash outflow, it simultaneously reduces the cash outflow for taxes by $3,400 because salaries are a tax-deductible expense.[1]

Figure 10-3 also indicates that noncash revenues and expenses can be converted into after-tax cash flows. How is this possible? A noncash item translates into a cash inflow or outflow whenever it affects a firm's income taxes. Recall from earlier chapters how depreciation expense can be viewed as a source of cash for a firm because it reduces cash outflows for income taxes. Although depreciation is the dominant noncash expense for most firms, the second rule in Figure

http://

Additional tax information is available at

http://www.taxhelponline.com

and

www.irs.ustreas.gov/plain/cover.html

Rules for the Calculation of After-Tax Cash Flows

SUMMARY FIGURE 10-3

Type of Revenue or Expense	After-Tax Cash Flow
Cash Item	After-Tax Cash Flow = Pretax Amount $(1 - T)$
Noncash Item	After-Tax Cash Flow = Pretax Amount $(-T)$ T = Tax Rate

---

[1] The salary expense acts as a tax shield because it reduces the firm's taxable income by $10,000. Our calculation assumes that the firm's revenues are greater than $10,000 so that it can obtain the full benefit of the tax shield. This assumption underlies both of the rules shown in Figure 10-3.

http://

There are several cost issues including sunk costs. Check out the price flexibility index at

http://www.csom.umn.edu/WWWPages/Faculty/ARao/8075_wk2.htm

Sunk Cost A historical cost to the firm that cannot be altered by a firm's future investing decisions. A sunk cost is irrelevant to the evaluation of a capital investment proposal.

http://

The influence of sunk costs on export policy is discussed on the World Bank Web page at

www.worldbank.org/html/dec/Publications/Briefs/db54.html

10-3 applies to any noncash expense that is tax-deductible. The minus sign in front of the T indicates that noncash expenses will generate cash inflows.

Sunk Cost. The evaluation of a capital investment proposal should consider only the future. That is, the NPV of an investment depends only upon the discount rate and the investment's *anticipated* cash flows over its life. As a result, any cost that represents an actual cash flow of the past (a sunk cost) should be ignored. Since a ***sunk cost*** cannot be altered by a firm's future investing decisions, it is *irrelevant to the evaluation of a capital investment proposal*.

The irrelevance of a sunk cost is absolute. It makes no difference how large the cash outflow representing the cost is or how recently it was incurred. A DM1 million sunk cost incurred yesterday is just as irrelevant to the evaluation of a replacement proposal today as a DM1,000 sunk cost incurred ten years earlier. The firm's financial managers should never permit large, recent sunk costs to induce them to ignore subsequent replacement proposals.

Value of Lost Opportunities

While sunk costs are irrelevant because they have occurred in the past, some past events are not irrelevant to the evaluation of a capital investment. Take, for example, the case of a firm that ten years ago purchased 200 acres of prime industrial real estate for $1,200,000. Today the property could be sold for $2,000,000. The firm is evaluating the possibility of building a manufacturing plant on that site. Is the $1,200,000 a sunk cost? The answer is yes. But the event—purchasing the land—is *not* irrelevant. The current market value of the site, $2,000,000, is relevant and should be added to the initial cost of the plant. It is relevant because, once construction begins, the opportunity to sell the site for $2,000,000 is foregone. Based on the principle of measuring the incremental cash flow associated with an investment proposal, the current value of any lost opportunity must be taken into account.

The Treatment of Interest Expense

If a firm plans to use borrowed capital to finance all or part of a capital investment, the after-tax cost of the debt certainly represents an incremental cash outflow connected with the investment. Nevertheless, the interest expense should not be included in the estimated cash flows of the investment proposal. The rationale for this exclusion is that the cost of financing, including its tax consequences, is already taken into account in the discount rate (RRR) used to calculate the NPV. As we shall demonstrate in Chapter 15, the costs of debt and equity financing play a major role in the determination of an investment's RRR. Since financing costs are reflected in the RRR, including them in the cash flows would constitute double counting and lead the manager to underestimate an investment proposal's true NPV. Consequently, financial managers should follow this general rule in evaluating capital investments: *interest expense and any other financing costs should be ignored in calculating an investment's incremental cash flows*.

Special Financing Side Effects

The RRR used to calculate NPV reflects the normal sources of funds that the firm utilizes to finance its investment requirements. In Chapter 15, you will learn that the RRR is calculated based on a target level of debt and equity and on a cost of debt that assumes borrowing at fair market rates. This procedure allows the investment and financing decisions to be separately evaluated. That is, a specific investment alternative is not associated with any particular source of funds. Financing simply provides a pool of cash (some debt, some equity) out of which a project is financed.

From time to time, however, special investment opportunities may arise that offer unique financing arrangements. In such cases, the NPV should be initially calculated as if the unique financing opportunity did not exist. Subsequently, the value that is expected to be created by unique financing can be added to the standard NPV:

NPV = Standard NPV + Value of Financing Side Effect

Consider a situation where a local government offers an incentive to attract a manufacturing plant to its town. The incentive is a below-market rate loan in the form of an industrial revenue bond. The extra value to the firm of such a bond is a function of the difference between the market rate and the lower subsidized rate. The value of this subsidy should be added as a side effect to the standard NPV of the manufacturing plant.

Another unique financing opportunity can take the form of a lease that enables a firm to operate an asset that it does not own. As we will see in Chapter 12, leasing is best thought of as an alternative to borrowing. If the cost of this alternative is low enough, the lease can add value to the firm. In Chapter 12, we will examine how to calculate the incremental value of a lease, which should be added as a side effect to the standard NPV of an asset to arrive at the final NPV of the asset.

Real Option Side Effects

Quite often an investment proposal presents financial managers with a number of operating alternatives that otherwise would not be available. These are termed embedded real options. An option gives management the *chance* but not the *obligation* to take action. The real options provided by investment projects have values that are not captured in the standard NPV calculation. Similar to special financing side effects, the value of real options can be added to the standard NPV:

NPV = Standard NPV + Value of Real Options

Options have value because they can minimize losses, maximize gains, or take advantage of timing flexibility.

The option to abandon a project protects the firm from downside losses in the event that actual cash flows in the early years fall short of forecasts. In that case, the project can be terminated and losses eliminated. Other projects may offer a firm a "foot in the door" to new technology or offer the opportunity to expand if actual results in early years exceed forecasts. In that case, the upside potential gives value to the option. In other cases, there may be options that allow a firm to delay the implementation of a project to collect new information about the project or to take advantage of possible changing conditions in the capital markets.

In theory, the embedded value of real options adds value to a project. Unfortunately, they are currently very difficult to quantify in practice with any reasonable degree of accuracy. This does not mean that their existence should be ignored. Rather, managers should at least subjectively enter real option potential into investment evaluations as an adjunct to their NPVs.

CORPORATE TAXES

In the prior discussion of relevant cash flows, we demonstrated how taxes can alter an investment's cash flows. The payment of taxes is an obligation of every firm; yet the size of the tax payment that satisfies that obligation is not equal for each business enterprise. It is determined by the type or source of income as well as the size of that income. Since the tax burden can vary from one type of investment to another, taxes can be the pivotal factor in some decisions. Our purpose in this section is to survey the relevant tax regulations in order to illustrate how they can influence both the investing and financing decisions of the financial manager.[2]

Income Tax

The corporate income subject to taxes in the United States is determined by subtracting allowable expenses from revenue. Taxable net income earned by a corporation is taxed according to the following graduated tax rate structure:

Taxable Income	Tax Rate
$0 – 50,000	15%
50,001 – 75,000	25%
75,001 – 100,000	34%
100,001 – 335,000	39%
335,001 – 10,000,000	34%
10,000,001 – 15,000,000	35%
15,000,001 – 18,333,333	38%
Over 18,333,333	35%

A corporation that reports taxable income of $200,000 would calculate its corporate income tax as:

$$
\begin{aligned}
0.15 \times \$\ 50,000 &= \$\ 7,500 \\
0.25 \times \quad 25,000 &= \quad 6,250 \\
0.34 \times \quad 25,000 &= \quad 8,500 \\
0.39 \times \quad 100,000 &= \underline{\quad 39,000} \\
&\quad\ \ \$61,250
\end{aligned}
$$

The firm's *average* tax rate can be calculated with the following equation:

$$
\text{Average Tax Rate} = \frac{\text{Total Tax Due}}{\text{Total Taxable Income}} = \frac{61,250}{200,000} = 30.6\% \tag{1}
$$

On average, each dollar of income was taxed at 30.6% even though the first dollar earned was taxed at a rate of only 15%, while the last dollar earned was taxed at a rate of 39%. Thus, the dollar tax burden rises with taxable income for two reasons: (1) taxes due are calculated as a percent of income; (2) the tax rate increases as income rises.

Corporations are required to estimate their annual taxable income for the year at the beginning of the year and pay quarterly installments of the estimated tax on April 15, June 15, September 15, and January 15. At the end of the year, the actual tax liability is compared with the total of the four installments. Differences are settled either by a credit for overpayment or additional charges for underpayment.

Marginal Versus Average Tax Rates

In the context of decision-making, it is important to distinguish between average tax rates and marginal tax rates. An average tax rate represents the tax paid per dollar of total taxable income. The marginal tax rate is the tax that would be paid on the next dollar *added* to that income. For example, a corporation with

---

[2] We will restrict our discussion of taxes here to U.S. federal income tax regulations because they normally impose the largest tax burden on firms doing business in the United States. In addition, the tax regulations at the local and state levels vary so much from one region to another that generalization is not feasible. In those decisions in which state or local taxes are a major factor, managers should apply the same evaluation procedure as that described here for federal income taxes. The tax systems of other countries were discussed in the appendix to Chapter 1.

■ Valuation

ISSUES

INVESTOR USE OF CASH FLOW

Financial managers have historically relied on the NPV and IRR methodologies in the evaluation of the cash flows of proposed investments. Investors, in contrast, have often evaluated firm performance in terms of accounting profit

measures such as EPS, ROA, and ROE. At the start of the chapter, we pointed out that sophisticated investors have begun to place more emphasis on cash flows in their analysis of firm performance. This change has been motivated by two factors: the need to value firms involved in mergers and buyouts, and the increasing difficulty of interpreting reported corporate earnings.

The type of cash flow calculation performed by investors can vary depending on their specific financial interest in the firm under evaluation. An individual or a firm that intends to acquire another company might use the following formula:

$$Cash\ Flow = EBIT + Noncash\ Expenses \\ - Asset\ Expenditures$$

This calculation begins with earnings *before* interest and taxes because the buyer wants the broadest possible measure of cash available to service any debt financing used in the acquisition. This cash flow forecast is fundamental to the buyout negotiations because the final purchase price is often specified as some multiple of this figure.

Other types of investors, institutional investors and security analysts, estimate a firms' cash flow because they have become wary of basing stock purchases or recommendations solely on earnings due to the variety of permissible earnings calculations. For instance, different depreciation techniques can result in large differences in reported earnings at two firms that are otherwise quite similar. These investment professionals adjust for accounting discrepancies by calculating cash flow with an alternative formula:

$$Cash\ Flow = EAT + Noncash\ Expenses \\ - Asset\ Expenditures$$

In this case, the cash flow estimate begins with earnings *after* taxes because only those earnings represent cash available for dividend payments to stockholders. By adding back noncash expenses, such as depreciation, this calculation eliminates the effect of arbitrarily selected depreciation techniques on reported performance. Asset expenditures are deducted in recognition that cash outflows for both fixed assets and current assets are required to support growth in sales.

$200,000 in income would pay an average tax of 30.6% of *all* dollars earned and 39% on the *next* dollar earned.

While the marginal tax rate jumps sharply from one tax bracket to another, the average tax rate increases much more slowly. This fact is important to financial managers because it is the change in income and cash flows arising from a decision that determines the attractiveness of that decision. As a result, it is the *marginal tax rate applicable to a change in income that is relevant to managers when evaluating a proposed investment*.

As an illustration of this concept, assume that a corporation is evaluating the potential effect of a proposed plant expansion on the firm's earnings. The firm's financial managers estimate that expansion will increase taxable income from its current level of $100,000 to a new level of $150,000. The calculation of the expansion's effect on after-tax earnings is:

	Taxable Income	Tax	After-Tax Earnings
Current Plan	$100,000	$22,250*	$ 77,750
Proposed Expansion	50,000	19,500**	30,500
Total	$150,000	$41,750	$108,250

*Tax = ($50,000)(0.15) + (25,000)(0.25) + (25,000)(0.34) = $22,250
**Tax = ($50,000)(0.39) = $19,500

The taxable income of the current plant falls in the first three tax brackets (15%, 25%, and 34%) of the corporate tax rate schedule. As a result, the additional income generated by the proposed expansion falls in the next bracket (39%). The firm's financial managers should evaluate the proposal's acceptability in terms of the increase that it generates in the firm's after-tax earnings. This increase is only $30,500 because the $50,000 increase in taxable income is subject to a marginal tax rate of 39%.

Depreciation

The taxable net income of the firm is determined not only by its revenues but also by its allowable expenses such as depreciation. The cash outflow associated with the acquisition of a long-lived asset usually occurs entirely at the time of the asset's purchase. The recognition of this cash outflow as an expense of operations, on the other hand, occurs over the asset's life as depreciation expense. The *significance of depreciation expense* to financial managers is that the *technique that is used in its calculation can alter the size of a firm's taxable income* and its tax burden for a given year. When a firm makes payments for materials or salaries, the cash outflow corresponds to a tax-deductible expense. When a firm makes an expenditure for a building or a piece of machinery, however, the initial tax-deductible expense is generally less than the cash outflow. The tax-deductible expense arising from the expenditure can only be recognized in periodic increments traditionally called depreciation expense.

In order to calculate the depreciation expense for a capital asset, we need to know: the cost of the asset, the cost recovery period, and the percentage of the cost of the asset that can be depreciated each year. The **cost recovery period** depends on the specific nature of the asset in question. Detailed tax code guidelines, which are beyond the scope of this text, determine the asset class and the recovery period. Most manufacturing assets fall in the 3-, 5-, 7-, or 10-year recovery period classes.[3] It is important to remember that the cost recovery period is not the same as an asset's economic life. Cost recovery periods in the United States are established by Congress, whereas economic life is a characteristic of the specific asset and how it is used. Consequently, an equal cost recovery period and economic life for a given asset would be due solely to coincidence.

Once the recovery period is determined, the annual percentage to be depreciated can be calculated with either of the two methods allowed:

1. Straight-Line
2. Accelerated Cost Recovery (ACR)

The significant difference between these two techniques is the speed with which each permits the firm to recognize the depreciation expense. The straight-line method recognizes the depreciation expense in equal annual amounts over the life of the asset. The ACR method permits larger depreciation expense in the early years of an asset's life.

As an illustration of the tax effect of depreciation, assume that Valley Manufacturing has purchased for one of its plants a new conveyor system with a cost of $100,000 installed. According to tax code guidelines, such an asset has a five-year life, or cost recovery period, for depreciation purposes. Under the straight-line method, the annual depreciation would be calculated as follows:

Cost Recovery Period The number of years to fully depreciate a capital asset. This time period is based on the specific classification of an asset.

---

[3] There are also 15- and 20-year classes for certain specialized assets as well as 21.5- and 31.5-year classes for real property. Only straight-line depreciation is allowed for real property.

$$\text{Straight-Line Depreciation} = \frac{\text{Cost}}{\text{Depreciable Life}} \qquad (2)$$

With this formula, the annual depreciation for the conveyor would be:

$$\text{Depreciation} = \frac{\$100,000}{5} = \$20,000/\text{year}$$

Under current legislation, only one-half of the annual depreciation expense shown above is assigned to the first year of the conveyor's life. The remaining one-half is assigned to a sixth year. This treatment is the "half-year convention" that must be used with straight-line depreciation. This rule requires that a firm depreciate an asset as if it were put in service at midyear regardless of its actual date of acquisition. Consequently, an asset placed in service at the beginning of a year and an asset placed in service at the end of the same year would *both* be entitled to one-half the annual depreciation expense in the first year.

As an alternative to the use of the straight-line method, a firm can determine the annual depreciation expense by multiplying the cost of the asset by the cost recovery percentages reproduced in Table 10-1. In the case of Valley Manufacturing, the depreciation expense for each year of the conveyor's depreciable life is:

Year 1:	$100,000	×	0.20	=	$20,000
Year 2:	100,000	×	0.32	=	32,000
Year 3:	100,000	×	0.192	=	19,200
Year 4:	100,000	×	0.1152	=	11,520
Year 5:	100,000	×	0.1152	=	11,520
Year 6:	100,000	×	0.0576	=	5,760

In Table 10-2 you can see the effect of depreciation over the life of the asset, assuming a 35% marginal corporate tax rate. Notice that the straight-line method tax-deductible expense of $20,000 reduces annual taxable income. Since the depreciation expense reduces taxable income, it is called a **tax shield** whose value reduces income taxes in the following manner:

Tax Shield Any tax-deductible expense of a firm. The expense shields the firm's earnings from taxation by reducing taxable income. The size of the tax shield equals the tax-deductible expense.

$$\text{Reduction in Income Taxes} = (\text{Tax Shield})(\text{Tax Rate}) \qquad (3)$$

For Valley Manufacturing, the impact of the tax shield is:

$$\text{Reduction in Income Taxes} = (\$20,000)(0.35)$$
$$= \$7,000$$

Under straight-line depreciation, the cash expenditure of $100,000 to purchase and install the conveyor results in cumulative tax savings of $35,000 over six years.

The bottom of Table 10-2 shows the tax implication of ACR depreciation. Under either depreciation method, the total depreciation expense ($100,000) and reduction in income taxes ($35,000) is the same. The timing of the depreciation tax shield, however, is significantly different. The ACR method accelerates the recognition of depreciation by providing for a larger expense in the early years of the asset's depreciable life. The attractiveness of the more rapid depreciation is enhanced by the fact that a firm can use different depreciation methods in reporting its earnings to the IRS and to its owners. For instance, Valley Manufacturing could use the ACR method for reporting to the IRS in order to maximize its depreciation tax shelter over the early years of the life of its conveyor system. The firm could simultaneously select the straight-line depreciation method for reporting to

TABLE 10-1

Accelerated Tax Depreciation Schedules by Recovery Period Class

Years	3-year	5-year	7-year	10-year
1	33.33%	20.00%	14.28%	10.00%
2	44.45	32.00	24.49	18.00
3	14.81	19.20	17.49	14.40
4	7.41	11.52	12.49	11.52
5		11.52	8.93	9.22
6		5.76	8.93	7.37
7			8.93	6.55
8			4.46	6.55
9				6.55
10				6.55
11				3.29

Note: These percentages are based on a 200% declining balance switching to straight-line to maximize acceleration. The half-year convention is built into the percentages.

TABLE 10-2

The Effect of Alternative Depreciation Techniques on Valley Manufacturing's Income Taxes

						Straight-Line Method	
Year	Cost	−	Accumulated Depreciation	=	Book Value	Depreciation Expense	Reduction in Taxable Income (Tax Shield)	Reduction in Income Taxes (Tax Rate = 0.35)
1	$100,000	−	10,000	=	$90,000	$ 10,000	$ 10,000	$ 3,500
2	100,000	−	30,000	=	70,000	20,000	20,000	7,000
3	100,000	−	50,000	=	50,000	20,000	20,000	7,000
4	100,000	−	70,000	=	30,000	20,000	20,000	7,000
5	100,000	−	90,000	=	10,000	20,000	20,000	7,000
6	100,000	−	100,000	=	0	10,000	10,000	3,500
					Total	$100,000	$100,000	$35,000

						Accelerated Cost Recovery Method	
Year	Cost	−	Accumulated Depreciation	=	Book Value	Depreciation Expense	Reduction in Taxable Income (Tax Shield)	Reduction in Income Taxes (Tax Rate = 0.35)
1	$100,000	−	20,000	=	$80,000	$ 20,000	$ 20,000	$ 7,000
2	100,000	−	52,000	=	48,000	32,000	32,000	11,200
3	100,000	−	71,200	=	28,800	19,200	19,200	6,720
4	100,000	−	82,720	=	17,280	11,520	11,520	4,032
5	100,000	−	94,240	=	5,760	11,520	11,520	4,032
6	100,000	−	100,000	=	0	5,760	5,760	2,016
					Total	$100,000	$100,000	$35,000

its owners in order to minimize the depreciation expense and maximize earnings over those years.

Our discussion of the benefits of accelerated depreciation raises the question of why a firm's managers would ever select straight-line depreciation. The straight-line method should be selected by a firm's financial managers only if they feel that the firm's earnings will be too low during the early years of an asset's life to benefit from accelerated depreciation.

Investment Tax Credits

In order to stimulate investment in new productive assets, the U.S. Congress has periodically enacted a system of tax incentives called the **Investment Tax Credit (ITC)**. *The ITC represents a direct reduction in a corporation's tax liability as opposed to a tax-deductible expense, which reduces taxable income.* As an illustration of the calculation of the ITC, let us return to the example of Valley Manufacturing's new conveyor system with a cost of $100,000. Assume that it qualifies for an ITC of 10% of its cost:

$$\text{ITC} = (\text{Initial Cost of Asset})(\text{ITC Rate}) \qquad (4)$$
$$= (\$100,000)(0.10) = \$10,000$$

The effective after-tax cost of the new conveyor system to Valley is equal to:

$$\text{Effective After-Tax Cost of an Asset} = \text{Initial Cost} - \text{ITC} \qquad (5)$$
$$= \$100,000 - 10,000 = \$90,000$$

The taxpayer is usually required to deduct all or some portion of the ITC from the depreciable cost (basis) of the asset. While the ITC is not allowed under the current tax code, it is an incentive that has been used frequently in the past whenever Congress desired to boost capital investment. In light of the frequency of tax code revisions, it is possible that the ITC will be reinstated at some time in the future.[4]

Sale of Depreciable Assets

In addition to taxes on ordinary income, a firm is subject to taxes on profits realized from the sale of depreciable fixed assets that are used in the operations of the firm. The gain or loss on the sale of a fixed (operating) asset is calculated on the basis of the selling price relative to the asset's book value. Since gains are added to ordinary taxable income while losses are subtracted from ordinary income, they are subject to the same tax rates as ordinary income. As an example, assume that a firm sells for $25,000 a machine that it has owned for a number of years. While the purchase price of the asset was $110,000, its book value at the time of sale is only $10,000. The tax effect of this gain is:

$$\text{Tax Effect from Sale of an Asset} = (\text{Selling Price} - \text{Book Value})(\text{Tax Rate}) \qquad (6)$$
$$= (\$25,000 - 10,000)(0.35)$$
$$= (\$15,000)(0.35) = \$5,250$$

The net proceeds from the sale of the asset are:

$$\text{Net Proceeds} = \text{Selling Price} - \text{Tax Effect}$$
$$= \$25,000 - 5,250$$
$$= \$19,750$$

If the firm were able to sell the asset for only $6,000, the tax effect of the loss would be:

$$\text{Tax Effect} = (\$6,000 - 10,000)(0.35) = -\$1,400$$

Investment Tax Credit (ITC)
A system of investment tax incentives that serves as a direct reduction in a corporation's tax liability as opposed to a tax-deductible expense, which reduces taxable income.

---

[4] For example, Congress established a 7% ITC in 1962; suspended it in 1966; reinstated it in 1967; eliminated it in 1969; reinstated it in 1971; increased it to 10% in 1975; and eliminated it in 1986.

The net proceeds would be:

$$\text{Net Proceeds} = \$6,000 - (-1,400) = \$7,400$$

The reduction in taxes arising from the loss on the sale represents a cash inflow to the firm, which must be added to the selling price to get the total cash inflow from the sale.

Interest Expense and Dividends

Interest expense and dividend payments represent the cost associated with the financing decisions of the firm. The tax code recognizes the interest paid by a firm on its debt as an expense of operations. Hence, it is deductible for corporate tax purposes. Dividend payments, on the other hand, are not treated as an expense but rather as a distribution of after-tax profits to the stockholders. As a result, they are not tax deductible to the paying firm. Since the U.S. government subsidizes interest expense but not dividends through a tax deduction, firms tend to favor the use of debt financing.

When a corporation receives dividends on stock issued by another unaffiliated corporation, 70% of the intercorporate dividends are exempt from ordinary income taxes.[5] While relatively rare in the past, this situation has become more frequent in recent years as corporations have purchased relatively small amounts of the outstanding shares of other firms prior to an all-out takeover attempt. As is true of an individual stockholder, a corporate stockholder is entitled to the dividends declared on the stock that it owns. For example, if a corporation received $100,000 in dividends, only $30,000 would be taxed as ordinary income. Given a tax rate of 35%, the tax would be

$$\text{Tax} = (\$30,000)(0.35) = \$10,500$$

The effective tax rate on the dividends would be

$$\text{Effective Tax Rate} = \$10,500/\$100,000 = 10.5\%$$

The reason for this tax exemption is that the paying corporation's earnings were subject to income taxes prior to the payment of dividends. If the recipient corporation were to pay taxes on the dividends received, that would represent double taxation. If the recipient corporation were then to pass the dividends along to its stockholders in the form of dividends, the stockholders would pay personal taxes on the dividend income. In order to limit such triple taxation, the tax codes permit the 70% exclusion on intercorporate dividends.

Loss Carry-Back and Carry-Forward

Loss Carry-Back (Forward)
A tax relief that allows operating losses to be used as a tax shield to reduce taxable income in prior and future years. Losses can be carried backward for 3 years and forward up to 15 years under current tax codes.

For some firms, fluctuations in earnings may be so severe that years of negative taxable income are interspersed with years of positive taxable income. In order to provide some tax relief to such firms, the tax code permits *operating losses* to be *used as tax shields to reduce taxable income in other years.* When used to offset taxable income in years prior to the year of the loss, the operating losses are termed **loss carry-backs.** When offset against the taxable income of years subsequent to the loss year, the operating losses are termed **loss carry-forwards.**

Table 10-3 illustrates the calculation of loss carry-backs and carry-forwards for firms in the United States. Other nations have their own ways of providing this

---

[5] If the recipient corporation owns at least 80% of the paying corporation's stock, the tax code permits the firm to treat the dividend as an internal transfer of funds that is not subject to income taxes.

An Illustration of Loss Carry-Backs and Carry-Forwards

TABLE 10-3

	Taxable Income (Loss)	Taxes Paid (35%)	1998 Loss Tax Shield	Post-1998 Taxable Income	Tax Due (35%)	Tax Refund
1995	$ 1,000,000	$ 350,000	$ 1,000,000	$ —	$ N.A.	$ 350,000
1996	1,500,000	525,000	1,500,000	—	N.A.	525,000
1997	500,000	175,000	500,000	—	N.A.	175,000
1998	(10,000,000)					
1999	750,000	N.A.	750,000	—	—	N.A.
2000	1,250,000	N.A.	1,250,000	—	—	N.A.
2001	900,000	N.A.	900,000	—	—	N.A.
2002	1,500,000	N.A.	1,500,000	—	—	N.A.
2003	1,000,000	N.A.	1,000,000	—	—	N.A.
2004	850,000	N.A.	850,000	—	—	N.A.
2005	1,250,000	N.A.	750,000	500,000	175,000	N.A.
1995-1997	$ 3,000,000	$1,050,000	$ 3,000,000	$ —	N.A	$1,050,000
1999-2005	7,500,000	N.A.	7,000,000	500,000	$175,000	N.A.
Total	$10,500,000	$1,050,000	$10,000,000	$500,000	$175,000	$1,050,000

N.A. — not applicable

type of tax relief. The firm in the table had positive taxable income in the period 1995–1997 before it suffered a $10 million loss in 1998. The firm subsequently returned to profitability in the years 1999–2005. The tax code requires that a firm must first use an operating loss to reduce taxable income in the three years prior to the loss, beginning with the most distant year. If the loss exceeds the combined income of those years, it can then be used to reduce taxable income that may be earned up to fifteen years in the future. That portion of the loss that exceeds the combined taxable income of the preceding three years and the following fifteen years is lost.

The firm's 1998 loss of $10 million exceeded total taxable income of $3 million over 1995–97 so that $7 million of the 1998 loss was carried forward as an offset to the taxable income of the years 1999–2005. Since the total taxable income of those years was only $7.5 million, the remaining $7 million loss offset all but $500,000 of the income over that period. The net result of the $10 million loss in 1998 was that the firm received an immediate tax refund of $1,050,000 in that year and did not pay additional income taxes until 2005.

ESTIMATION OF PROJECT CASH FLOWS

Unlike financial securities with well-defined cash flows such as interest or dividends, the cash flows generated by capital investment proposals must be constructed by financial managers from basic economic data. The managers must build their cash flow estimates from data such as forecasts of sales revenue, manufacturing costs for new products, and cost savings arising from the use of more efficient equipment. Figure 10-4 contains a list of the major types of cash flows that are generally encountered in evaluating capital investment proposals. The task confronted by the financial managers is to determine which of these cash flow categories applies to a given investment proposal and to forecast the incremental, after-tax cash flows arising from each.

We will now illustrate the application of the list in Figure 10-4 to a proposal involving an expansion decision and to one involving a replacement decision. We

■ Financial

ISSUES

WHAT THE STOCKHOLDER SEES IS NOT WHAT THE IRS GETS

The income tax payments made by a corporation to the IRS are often less than the taxes due as shown in the annual report to its stockholders. This difference arises from the use of different income calculation techniques on a firm's tax return and on its published income statement. Specifically, a firm can simultaneously use accelerated depreciation to minimize taxable income reported to the IRS and straight-line depreciation to maximize pretax earnings reported to the public. In addition, a firm can utilize any available investment tax credits and loss carry-backs and carry-forwards that cut tax payments without reducing published earnings.

As a result of these tax shelters, the effective tax rate paid on published earnings can be substantially less than the statutory rate. From the 1950s until 1986, the statutory corporate tax rate in the United States remained unchanged at 46%. The average effective tax rate for all corporations, however, was estimated to have declined from 45% to 27%. Some firms did even better in reducing taxes. Despite substantial earnings over the period 1982–1985, General Electric's average effective tax rate was 2.4% while General Dynamics paid no taxes.

In response to such successful use of tax loopholes by corporations, Congress passed the Tax Reform Act of 1986, which eliminated the investment tax credit and reduced the permissible rates of accelerated depreciation. As an offset to these changes, the statutory tax rate dropped to 40% in 1987 and 34% in subsequent years. In 1993, the Omnibus Budget Reconciliation Act raised the highest marginal tax rate to 39%. Despite repeated adjustments to the Tax Code, however, the effective tax rates of many major corporations remain significantly below the highest statutory marginal rate.

should point out that these two examples are not meant to be all-inclusive. Since every investment proposal tends to have unique aspects, our goal is not to present a detailed calculation procedure that can be applied by rote to every proposal. Rather, our objective is to demonstrate the type of reasoning that should be used in determining and measuring the cash flows that are relevant to an investment's evaluation. *Figure 10-4 is intended to be a broad guideline, not a form to be filled in.*

An Expansion Decision

The management of San Paulo Foods is considering expansion of production capacity by building a new processing plant outside Medford, California, on land that will cost $1,000,000. The building and installed equipment will cost $8,000,000 and will qualify for a 10% investment tax credit. It will be depreciated for tax purposes on a straight-line basis over its 20-year life to a zero book value even though the firm's management anticipates a salvage (residual) value of $2

A Chronological List of the Major Types of Cash Flows Arising From a Capital Investment

SUMMARY FIGURE 10-4

A. Initial Time Period
1. Cost of the Investment (including Installment and Set-Up Cost and Foregone Liquidation Value)
2. Sale of Replaced Assets (including Tax Effects)
3. Increase in Net Working Capital
4. Investment Tax Credit (when relevant)

B. Project Life
1. Revenue less Costs on an After-Tax Basis
2. Reduction in Taxes due to Depreciation Tax Shield

C. Project Termination
1. Salvage Value (including Tax Effects)
2. Decrease in Net Working Capital

million.[6] That is, the managers expect that they will be able to sell the building and equipment for $2 million at the end of 20 years. Annual sales revenue is expected to be $10,000,000, while expenses are expected to be $8,000,000 per year. Net working capital has averaged 14% of sales in the past and is expected to remain at that ratio in the future. The marginal corporate tax rate on income is 40%. San Paulo's financial manager estimates that an RRR of 12% is applicable to the investment proposal.

Initial Time Period Cash Flows.   In this example, there are three items to consider in calculating the after-tax incremental cash flows that occur in the initial time period: the cost of the land, building, and equipment; the investment tax credit; and the investment in net working capital. The cash flows associated with these items are shown in Table 10-4.

There is no tax effect from the expenditure for land in the initial time period. There are two tax effects associated with the expenditure on the building and equipment: the investment tax credit and the depreciation tax shield. Since the $8 million expenditure qualifies for a 10% investment tax credit, the investment is accompanied by an $800,000 reduction in San Paulo's income taxes. The effect of depreciation on the firm's cash outlays for taxes is spread throughout the life of the investment and does not affect the cash flows in the initial period.

The remaining item in Table 10-4 that requires explanation is the investment in net working capital. There is a direct and often proportional relationship between net working capital and sales. As a firm's sales expand, an increase in current assets is required to support the higher level of sales. A portion of the increase in current assets is automatically financed by increases in current liabilities. The remainder of the increase in current assets, however, requires a cash outlay by the firm. It is this cash outlay that represents the increase in net working capital associated with a projected increase in sales. The cash outflow required by the net working capital increase arising from San Paulo's expansion proposal has no tax effect because it is not a tax-deductible expense. Rather, it constitutes a portion of the initial investment in assets required by the proposal.

Annual Cash Flows Over the Project's Life.   The incremental cash flows generated by an investment each year (referred to as *operating cash flows*) can be calculated with either of the two methods shown in Table 10-5. The first approach uses an income statement format to calculate the change in the firm's after-tax operating profit (ATOP) that is associated with the investment. Since financing costs are

San Paulo Initial Period Cash Flows

TABLE 10-4

Item	Calculation	Cash Flow
Cost of Land	—	−$1,000,000
Cost of Building and Equipment	—	−8,000,000
Net Working Capital	−(0.14)($10,000,000)	−1,400,000
Investment Tax Credit	+(0.10)($ 8,000,000)	+800,000
Net Investment		−$9,600,000

---

[6] In order to keep the calculations as straightforward as possible, we will use a simplified straight-line depreciation technique that ignores the half-year convention discussed earlier. We will use this simplified technique both for the examples in this chapter and for most of the problems at the end of the chapter.

Annual Operating Cash Flows From San Paulo's Expansion Proposal

TABLE 10-5

	Income Statement Format	Tax Effect	After-Tax Cash Flow
Sales Revenue	$10,000,000	(1 − 0.40)	$6,000,000
Cash Expenses	−8,000,000	(1 − 0.40)	−4,800,000
Depreciation	−400,000	(−0.40)	160,000
Taxable Income	$ 1,600,000		
Taxes (40%)	−640,000		
After-Tax Operating Profit	$ 960,000		
Depreciation	400,000		
Annual Operating Cash Flows	$ 1,360,000		$1,360,000

$$\text{Annual Depreciation} = \frac{\text{Cost}}{N} = \frac{\$8,000,000}{20} = \$400,000$$

ignored in this calculation, taxable income in the table consists of the investment's projected earnings before interest and taxes (EBIT). Since depreciation is a non-cash expense, it is added to the ATOP to arrive at the estimate of the investment's incremental, after-tax cash flows. This income statement approach can also be applied in the form of the following equation:

$$
\begin{aligned}
\text{Annual Operating Cash Flows} &= \Delta\text{ATOP} + \Delta\text{Depreciation} \\
&= (\Delta\text{EBIT} - \text{Taxes}) + \Delta\text{Depreciation} \\
&= \Delta\,(\text{Revenues} - \text{Cash Expenses} - \text{Depreciation}) \\
&\quad (1 - T) + \Delta\text{Depreciation} \\
&= (\$10,000,000 - 8,400,000)(1 - 0.40) \\
&\quad + \$400,000 \\
&= \$1,360,000
\end{aligned}
$$

The symbol Δ stands for the *change* in a revenue or an expense because we are only concerned with the incremental cash flows associated with an investment proposal.

The second computational technique shown in Table 10-5 converts each item of revenue and expense directly into its equivalent after-tax cash flow. It does this by applying the rules shown in Figure 10-3. Each pretax cash revenue or expense is converted into an after-tax cash flow by multiplying by (1 − T). The after-tax cash flows arising from noncash items are found by multiplying by (−T). For San Paulo Foods, the calculations are:

$$
\begin{aligned}
\text{Annual Operating Cash Flows} &= (\Delta\text{Revenues})(1 - T) - (\Delta\text{Cash Expenses})(1 - T) \\
&\quad - (\Delta\text{Depreciation})(-T) \\
&= (\$10,000,000)(1 - 0.40) - (8,000,000)(1 - 0.40) \\
&\quad - (400,000)(-0.40) \\
&= \$1,360,000
\end{aligned}
$$

Both of the approaches in Table 10-5 will produce the same results if they are implemented correctly. The main advantage of the second approach is its analytical flexibility because it calculates the individual contribution of each revenue and expense item to the total after-tax cash flows generated by an investment proposal.

Free Cash Flow.   In general terms, an investment's incremental after-tax cash flows over the project life are equal to annual operating cash flows less any additions to working capital and less any additional capital spending. For example, if

San Paulo expected sales to increase each year rather than stay constant as in the above example, there would be an increase in working capital each year to support those greater sales. Additionally, suppose San Paulo expected to replace a significant amount of machinery in the tenth year of the project's life. The cost of the machinery, along with any increase in working capital, would reduce the amount of cash available to repay creditors and to create value for shareholders.

As we initially pointed out in Chapter 2, the terminology "free cash flow" is often used to describe the excess of operating cash flows over additional investments in current and fixed assets required by a project. The cash flow is "free" in the sense that it is available to pay for the cost of financing the project. If a project's free cash flow is inadequate to pay for the cost of both debt and equity financing, the project will have a negative NPV. We will examine this concept more fully in the appendix to this chapter.

Project Termination Cash Flows.   At the end of the useful life of an investment, there are normally a number of cash flows associated with the termination value of the assets that comprise the investment. Many of the initial period cash outflows will be at least partially converted into cash inflows in the terminal period. The termination cash flows for the San Paulo Foods' expansion proposal are shown in Table 10-6.

San Paulo's financial manager estimates that the land required by the investment proposal can be sold for $1 million at the end of the project's life. Since this sale price is equal to the purchase price (no capital gain or loss), there is no tax effect from the sale. The manager also estimates that the firm will be able to sell the building and equipment at the end of the 20 years for $2 million even though its book value at that time will be zero. At a 40% tax rate, the increase in the firm's taxes associated with this $2 million pretax gain is $800,000.

The last component of the firm's project termination cash flows is the recovery of the cash outflows for the increase in net working capital required by the investment. When the investment is terminated, the incremental sales will cease, as will the need for increased net working capital to finance those sales. As a result, the $1.4 million in incremental funds tied up in net working capital will be released for investment elsewhere. This release of funds can be viewed as a cash inflow at project termination. There is no separate tax effect associated with the recovery of net working capital because taxes are paid on the profits from the operations the working capital supports.

Project Evaluation.   Once the financial manager has calculated the relevant cash flows, she can evaluate the desirability of the expansion proposal with the NPV

San Paulo Project Termination Cash Flows

TABLE 10-6

Item	Calculation	Cash Flow
Sale of Land:		
Selling Price	—	$1,000,000
Tax Effect	—	—
Salvage Value of Building and Equipment:		
Selling Price	—	2,000,000
Tax Effect	(2,000,000)(−0.40)	−800,000
Recovery of Net Working Capital	—	1,400,000
After-Tax Project Termination Cash Flows		$3,600,000

and the IRR evaluation techniques, as shown in Table 10-7. The calculation of the NPV is based on the financial manager's estimate of the proposal's RRR as 12%. The NPV computation in the table is divided into the determination of the present value of each of the three components of the proposal's cash flow stream. The results indicate that the project should increase the value of San Paulo's common stock by $932,200.

The IRR calculation begins at a discount rate of 14% because the proposal has a positive NPV when the discount rate is 12%. Table 10-7 reveals that the NPV is negative at the higher discount rate. The proposal's IRR, then, must lie between 12% and 14%. This estimate of the IRR is sufficiently accurate to enable the financial manager to reach the conclusion that the proposal is acceptable because its IRR exceeds its RRR. For greater accuracy, the equation in footnote #5 from Chapter 9 can be used to interpolate between 12% and 14%, as shown in the table. We also provide instructions at the back of the text for the use of a business calculator to find an investment's NPV and IRR.

A Replacement Decision

A replacement proposal's evaluation differs from an expansion proposal's evaluation in two aspects. First, since the proposal calls for the termination of an existing asset, the cash flows on both the new and the existing asset must be included in the calculation of the proposal's incremental cash flows. Second, replacement proposals do not normally increase the volume of a firm's operations. Hence, these proposals usually do not generate incremental revenues or investment in net work-

TABLE 10-7

The NPV and IRR Evaluation of San Paulo Foods' Expansion Proposal

NPV Evaluation

Type of Cash Flow	Cash Flow	12% Discounting Factor		PV
Initial Period	−$9,600,000	$DF_{0.12,0}$	= 1.000	−$ 9,600,000
Annual	1,360,000	$ADF_{0.12,20}$	= 7.469	10,157,800
Project Termination	3,600,000	$DF_{0.12,20}$	= 0.104	374,400
			NPV = $	932,200

$$NPV = PV \text{ of Inflows} - Cost$$
$$= (\$1,360,000)(7.469) + (3,600,000)(0.104) - 9,600,000$$
$$= \$932,200 \qquad \text{Decision: Since NPV > 0, } accept \text{ proposal.}$$

IRR Evaluation

Cash Flow	12% Discounting Factor	PV	14% Discounting Factor	PV
−$9,600,000	1.000	−$9,600,000	1.000	−$9,600,000
1,360,000	7.469	10,157,800	6.623	9,007,300
3,600,000	0.104	374,400	0.073	262,800
		NPV = $ 932,200		NPV = −$ 329,900

$$12\% < IRR < 14\%$$
$$IRR = 0.12 + \left(\frac{\$932,200}{\$932,200 - (-329,900)} \right)(0.02)$$
$$= 0.12 + (0.74)(0.02)$$
$$= 0.135 = 13.5\%$$
$$RRR = 12.0\% \qquad \text{Decision: Since IRR > RRR, } accept \text{ proposal.}$$

■ Valuation

ISSUES

CASH FLOW ESTIMATION AT LARGE FIRMS

The accuracy of the estimated NPV of a proposed capital investment is dependent on two elements: the cash flow projections and the estimated discount rate. Much attention has been devoted over the years to the development of optimal procedures for estimating the appropriate discount rate (RRR) for investment proposals. The question of cash flow projections procedures, on the other hand, has received less emphasis by researchers even though it is a crucial topic to financial managers. As mentioned at the beginning of the chapter, however, some researchers have surveyed *Fortune 500* companies regarding their cash flow estimation practices.

The responding firms indicated that they regularly estimated future cash flows for the following types of investment proposals:

Type of Proposal	% of Firms*
All Types	59%
New Equipment	25
Replacement	10
Expansion	31

*The sum of the percentages exceeds 100% due to multiple answers by some firms.

Not surprisingly, firms are more likely to require cash flow forecasts for uncertain new equipment and expansion proposals than for the more certain replacement proposals.

When asked about their forecasting methodology, over two-thirds of the firms responded that they use a standard procedure, forecasting model, and/or worksheets for all investments whose cash flows were projected. The firms also identified the key variables for the cash flow estimates:

Financial Variables — tax considerations, project risk, and working capital requirements
Marketing Variables — sales forecast and competitive position
Production Variables — operating and manufacturing expenses and cost of materials

Surprisingly, only about 50% of the firms indicated that they adjusted cash flow forecasts for inflation. This lack of concern about inflation's effects may simply reflect the low rates of inflation in the United States in recent years. In other countries with higher rates of inflation, inflation adjustments are a crucial element in cash flow projections for proposed investments.

ing capital. A major feature of many replacement proposals is the cost savings that arise from the use of more efficient machinery or equipment.

As an example of a replacement proposal, consider the case of Metallwerk AG, a medium-sized metal fabricator operating in Germany. The firm's management is reviewing a proposal to replace an automatic press in its Stuttgart facility with a newer model that is expected to reduce labor and material expenses by DM200,000 per year. The new press will cost DM550,000 plus an additional DM50,000 for installation. It will be depreciated on a straight-line basis over its three-year depreciable life to a book value of zero. At the end of its *economic* life of five years, however, the expected salvage value is DM100,000.[7] The old press can be sold today for DM220,000. It was purchased five years ago for DM350,000 and is being depreciated over its 10-year life to a book value of zero. Management estimates today, however, that the old press will have a cash value of only DM10,000 in five years due to rapid technological improvements in new equipment. Given a marginal tax rate of 40% and an estimated RRR of 12% for the

---

[7] The new machine is assumed to have a 3-year depreciable life to emphasize that an asset's depreciable life and economic life will rarely coincide. Since tax legislation changes frequently, a firm's financial managers must rely on the firm's tax experts to provide current information on the correct depreciation schedule for a specific asset.

proposal, Metallwerk's financial manager must determine whether the firm should purchase the new press.

Initial Period Cash Flows. There are two cash flows to be considered in the initial period of the replacement proposal: the cost of the new press (including installation costs) and the proceeds from the sale of the old press. The difference between these two items is the incremental or net investment associated with the proposal. This difference of $398,000 is shown in the top segment of Table 10-8. One aspect of the initial period cash flows, the tax effect of the sale of the old press, deserves elaboration. Any time an asset is sold at a price that is not equal to its book value, there is generally a tax effect on the sale. In the case of Metallwerk, the old press can be sold for more than its book value. The gain on this sale would result in an increase in taxes that partially offsets the cash inflow from the sale.

As the depreciation calculation at the bottom of Table 10-8 shows, the annual depreciation on the old press is DM35,000. Since the press is currently five years old, its book value at the time of sale would be:

$$\text{Book Value} = \text{Original Cost} - \text{Accumulated Depreciation}$$
$$= 350,000 - (35,000)(5)$$
$$= 175,000$$

From a capital budgeting viewpoint, the sale of the old press would result in a DM220,000 cash inflow from the proceeds of the sale and a noncash taxable gain of DM45,000. According to the second rule in Figure 10-3, the after-tax cash flow associated with this gain is:

$$\text{Tax Effect} = (\text{Gain on Sale})(-\text{Tax Rate})$$
$$= (\text{Selling Price} - \text{Book Value})(-T)$$
$$= (220,000 - 175,000)(-0.40)$$
$$= -18,000$$

Annual Cash Flows Over the Project's Life. There are two sources of annual cash inflows arising from the replacement proposal. The first is the savings in labor and materials cost due to the greater efficiency of the new press. The second is the greater depreciation tax shield provided by the new press. The incremental after-tax annual cash inflows of DM186,000 for years 1–3 and DM106,000 for years 4–5 associated with the investment proposal are summarized in the middle portion of Table 10-8.

The projected decrease in labor and materials cost is equivalent to an annual cash inflow to the firm. The first rule in Figure 10-3 can be used to convert the pre-tax savings into their equivalent after-tax cash flow, shown in Table 10-8. The incremental cash flows arising from the tax shield provided by the new press are smaller than the total cash flows provided by its tax shield. This is due to the replacement nature of the proposal. While Metallwerk acquires a DM200,000 annual tax shield for three years if it purchases the new press, it must simultaneously give up the DM35,000 tax shield available for five years on the old press. The calculations in Table 10-8 show that the total cash inflows arising from the tax shield are DM80,000 on the new press and DM14,000 on the old press. Thus, the *incremental* tax shield cash inflows are only DM66,000 = DM80,000 – DM14,000 in years 1–3, and –DM14,000 = DM0 – DM14,000 in years 4–5.

Project Termination Cash Flows. The termination benefits shown in the bottom portion of Table 10-8 arise from one source: the *incremental* cash flows generated by the salvage value of the new press and the lost salvage value of the old press that is replaced. As was true of the benefits from the depreciation tax shield, the

Incremental DM Cash Flows on Metallwerk's Equipment Replacement Proposal

TABLE 10-8

Item	Calculation	Cash Flow	Years
Initial Period Cash Flows			
Cost of New Press	−(550,000 + 50,000)	−600,000	
Sale of Old Press			
Selling Price	—	220,000	
Tax Effect	(220,000 − 175,000)(−0.40)	− 18,000	
Net Investment		−398,000	0
Project Life Cash Flows			
Labor & Material Savings	(200,000)(1 − 0.40)	120,000	
Depreciation Tax Shield:*			
New Press	(−200,000)(−0.40)	80,000	
Old Press	−(−35,000)(−0.40)	− 14,000	
Annual Operating Cash Flow		186,000	1–3
Labor & Materials Savings	(200,000)(1 − 0.40)	120,000	
Depreciation Tax Shield:			
New Press		0	
Old Press	−(−35,000)(−0.40)	− 14,000	
Annual Operating Cash Flow		106,000	4–5
Project Termination Cash Flows			
Salvage Value of New Press:			
Selling Price	—	100,000	
Tax Effect	(100,000)(−0.40)	−40,000	
Salvage Value of Old Press:			
Selling Price	—	−10,000	
Tax Effect	−(10,000 − 0)(−0.40)	4,000	
Termination Cash Flows		54,000	5

$$*\text{New Press Depreciation} = \frac{600,000}{3} = 200,000 \qquad \text{Old Press Depreciation} = \frac{350,000}{10} = 35,000$$

incremental benefits from the salvaging of the machines are smaller than the total salvage proceeds.

Metallwerk's management estimates the salvage value of the new machine to be DM100,000. The sale of the new machine in five years at this price would have the following tax effect:

$$\text{Tax Effect} = (\text{Selling Price} − \text{Book Value})(−T) = (100,000 − 0)(−0.40) = −40,000$$

As a result, the total after-tax cash flow from the sale is equal to only DM60,000.

Management also estimates that the salvage value of the old press will be DM10,000 in five years even though its book value at that time will be zero.

The DM10,000 gain that would be realized if the old press were scrapped in five years would result in the following cash flow for taxes:

$$\text{Tax Effect} = (\text{Selling Price} − \text{Book Value})(−T) = (10,000 − 0)(−0.40) = −4,000$$

As a result Metallwerk would lose only a DM6,000 net cash inflow generated by the scrapping of the old press in five years if it acquires the new press today. Thus, the net incremental cash inflow at the end of five years is only DM54,000 = DM100,000 − 40,000 − 10,000 − (−4,000).

Project Evaluation. The determination of the NPV and the IRR of Metallwerk's replacement proposal is shown in Table 10-9. The cash flows used in the calculations were taken from Table 10-8. The positive NPV signals that Metallwerk should accept the replacement proposal. The calculations indicate that replacement of the existing machine should increase the value of the firm by DM206,968. Since the NPV at the 12% discount rate is so large, the proposal's IRR must be considerably greater than 12%. The interpolation in Table 10-9 indicates that the IRR is close to 33%. Thus, the IRR evaluation criterion also signals that the replacement proposal should be very valuable to Metallwerk.

Determination of Economic Life

Absolute Physical Life The period after which an asset has deteriorated to such an extent that it can no longer be used.

Economic Life The period over which an asset's NPV is maximized.

When determining the economic life of an investment project, it is important to remember that there is a distinct difference between the absolute physical life of an asset and its economic life. The **absolute physical life** of an asset is defined as the point in time when its condition deteriorates to such an extent that, no matter what we do, the asset can no longer be used. As an example, consider a rusted-out used car. No matter what repairs an individual may be willing to make to the car, it simply cannot be made roadworthy. **Economic life**, on the other hand, is defined as the time period over which an asset's NPV is maximized. In most instances, the economic life of an asset used in calculating NPV is less than its absolute physical life. The major causes of this are technological obsolescence, physical deterioration, and product life cycle. Depending upon the nature of the investment project, any one or any combination of causes may limit economic life.

The NPV and IRR Evaluation of Metallwerk's Replacement Proposal

TABLE 10-9

NPV Evaluation

Type of Cash Flow	Cash Flow	12% Discounting Factor	PV
Initial Period	−398,000	1.000	−398,000
Annual (Yrs. 1, 2 & 3)	186,000	$ADF_{0.12,3} = 2.402$	446,772
Annual (Yrs. 4 & 5)	106,000	$(ADF_{0.12,5} - ADF_{0.12,3}) = (3.605 - 2.402)$	127,518
Project Termination	54,000	$DF_{0.12,5} = 0.567$	30,618
		NPV =	206,908

Decision: Since NPV > 0, *accept* proposal.

IRR Evaluation

Cash Flow	30% Discounting Factor	PV	35% Discounting Factor	PV
−398,000	1.000	−398,000	1.000	−398,000
186,000	1.816	337,776	1.696	315,456
106,000	(2.436 − 1.816)	65,720	(2.220 − 1.696)	55,544
54,000	0.269	14,526	0.223	12,042
	NPV =	20,022	NPV =	−14,958

$$30\% < IRR < 35\%$$

$$IRR = 0.30 + \left(\frac{20,022}{20,022 - (-14,958)}\right)(0.05)$$

$$= 0.30 + (0.57)(0.05) = 32.9\%$$

Decision: Since IRR > RRR, *accept* proposal.

Technological Obsolescence.   A prime example of an asset subject to technological obsolescence is the personal computer. In 1984, the IBM 286 was a state-of-the-art machine. By the late 1990s, it had been replaced by machines with Pentium processors. Most of the replaced computers, however, are still usable. It was a technological advance in computer hardware that made them obsolete, not physical deterioration. Thus, in evaluating the decision to invest in high-tech assets, a manager needs to be careful not to confuse absolute physical life based on physical deterioration with economic life, which is determined by time to technical obsolescence.

Physical Deterioration.   For other types of machinery, there often comes a time before complete physical breakdown when increased maintenance costs and decreased output make it sensible to replace the machine rather than continue its use. An estimate of the time until we expect this to happen is the assets' useful life. This estimate should be used in determining the NPV of such a machine rather than its absolute physical life.

Product Life Cycle.   Another characteristic of an investment project that may determine economic life is product life cycle. For example, suppose we are evaluating construction of a factory to produce a new generation of minicomputer. We estimate the absolute physical life of the building to be fifty years and of the machinery to be fifteen years. Because of anticipated technological obsolescence of the *product* (not the factory), however, we anticipate shutting down production of this particular minicomputer in six years. Consequently, the economic life that we would use when calculating the NPV of the investment would be six years, not fifty or fifteen. Economic life, in this instance, is determined by the life cycle of the product. Since the economic life is much lower than the absolute physical life of the factory, the estimated project termination cash flow should be relatively large since the factory could be sold or put to another profitable use. It is important to remember that the economic life is often determined by the life cycle of products to be produced and that, in such a case, the project termination cash flow captures the remaining value of the physical assets.

Termination Decision.   In all the situations above, it is necessary for the analyst to anticipate the decision to terminate the investment in the future. Since the manager's goal is to maximize the value of the firm to its owners, the economic life of an investment is the life that maximizes the net present value of the investment.

For example, the determining factor for a product life cycle limit to economic life is the relationship between the cash flow contribution margin (the difference between revenue and variable costs) and the fixed cost of production. The economic life of such an investment is determined by an estimate of when future sales will decline to a point where net cash flows become negative because contribution margin is less than fixed costs. A halt in production before that point would eliminate the negative cash flows in the future that would decrease the project's NPV.

INVESTMENT PROPOSALS WITH UNEQUAL LIVES

Up to this point, the discussion of the evaluation of capital budgeting proposals has assumed that competing proposals involve investments with equal useful lives. This assumption was made to simplify the mechanics of the analysis so that we could concentrate on conceptual issues. This assumption, however, is not necessarily realistic in actual practice. Indeed, it seems reasonable to assume that different designs, technology, and quality and quantity of the components of a capital investment will often lead to significantly different useful lives.

The question of the potential impact of unequal useful lives on the evaluation of investment proposals was raised in the chapter introduction. The answer depends on the basic nature of the investment proposal under consideration. If it is an independent proposal, the NPV calculation can validly ignore the issue of unequal project lives. If it is a mutually exclusive proposal, such as the Metallwerk example, specific adjustments must normally be made to the project's cash flows before its NPV can be calculated.

Independent Proposals

When each proposal is independent of other proposals, the fact that proposals under consideration call for projects with unequal useful lives *is irrelevant to their evaluation.* Each proposal with a positive NPV should be accepted regardless of the length of time over which its expected cash flows will be generated. The reason for ignoring the issue of unequal useful lives centers on the type of investment decision required. For example, assume that a firm's managers must evaluate the following independent investment proposals:

Project	NPV	Useful Life
A	FF125,000	5 years
B	50,000	3
C	−15,000	7
D	125,000	10
E	25,000	2

The task is not to select the most valuable project but merely to determine the acceptability of each proposal. Because projects A, B, D, and E have positive NPVs, they should be accepted. Since the NPV methodology automatically adjusts for the time value of money, no other adjustment for a project's life is necessary.

Mutually Exclusive Proposals

If the proposals under evaluation are mutually exclusive, the financial managers may face a much more difficult task. If the life of the product is going to be determined by the life of the investment, the standard NPV criterion can be used. For example, suppose there are two machines that can be used to manufacture a product. One has a life of four years, while the other machine's life is eight years. If the firm is committed to terminate production in either four or eight years, depending on the machine chosen, the financial managers need only compare the NPV of each alternative, one generated over four years and the other eight years. The correct decision is to choose the alternative with the highest NPV.

A firm's production horizon for a good or service often extends beyond the service life of specific investment alternatives. For instance, a firm may plan to produce a given product indefinitely despite the fact that the facilities and machines employed have a finite life. Another firm may estimate a specific fixed production horizon that exceeds the service life of available equipment. In situations such as these, the standard NPV is inaccurate when alternative investment proposals have different economic lives. *An adjustment to the standard NPV criterion may be required if the life of the product to be manufactured is independent of the economic life of either investment.* The specific type of adjustment necessary in the case of mutually exclusive alternatives depends on the firm's production horizon, as summarized in Figure 10-5. If the firm estimates that it will manufacture a product for a limited time period, the financial managers should shorten or extend the useful life of each investment proposal to match the fixed production horizon. If the firm intends to manufacture a product indefinitely into the future, the finan-

The Adjustments Required for Mutually Exclusive Projects With Unequal Lives

SUMMARY FIGURE 10-5

1. Fixed Production Horizon:	Calculate each project's annual cash flows after adjusting its life to equal the estimated life of the good or service to be produced.
2. Indefinite Production Horizon:	Calculate the annualized PV implicit in each project's PV of cash outflows.

cial managers must assume that each investment will be replaced indefinitely into the future, after it physically wears out.

Fixed Production Horizon. As an illustration of the adjustments required in the case of a limited or fixed production horizon, we will examine the case of a firm that is considering an investment in modern equipment that will be used to replace obsolete machinery on the firm's production line. The firm must make a choice between two alternative machines that perform identical functions. The Model 4 is characterized by an initial cost of $60,000, after-tax operating costs (including the associated depreciation tax effects) of $20,000 per year, and a useful life of 4 years. The Model 8 is more expensive ($150,000), has lower annual operating costs ($8,000), and a longer useful life (8 years). At the end of their useful lives, the value of both models will be zero. Regardless of the model selected, the firm intends to terminate production in six years.

It should be evident that it would be incorrect to evaluate either machine in terms of a PV based only on its estimated useful life. The cash flow forecasts for each machine must be adjusted for the firm's production horizon so that the resulting PVs are directly comparable. In order to make the PVs comparable, the machines' cash flows should be adjusted to a common life: the estimated six-year production horizon. The PV of the cash flows should then be calculated for one Model 8 used for only six years and two Model 4s, the second one to be sold after two years' use.[8] Assume that the managers estimate that a two-year-old Model 4 can be sold for after-tax proceeds of $25,000 and a six-year-old Model 8 for $30,000. The relevant cash flows and the PV at an RRR of 10% for each alternative are shown in Figure 10-6.

The numbers for the Model 4 within the box represent cash flows associated with the acquisition of a new machine at the end of year 4 and its operation in years 5 and 6. The –$60,000 is its estimated purchase price, and the $25,000 is its sale price. Likewise, the $30,000 cash inflow in year 6 for the Model 8 is its selling price at the end of the production horizon. The calculations reveal that, over the six-year production horizon, the Model 8 is preferable due to its lower PV of costs.

Indefinite Production Horizon. Frequently, the estimated production horizon associated with a specific product extends indefinitely into the future so that a firm's management knows that it must continually replace technologically or functionally obsolete facilities with new ones. The solution to the problem of comparing mutually exclusive investments with unequal lives under this condition is to think in terms of a continuous series or indefinitely long **replacement chain** of each type of investment. The logic behind the replacement chain concept is that a firm is not actually selecting only one production facility or machine. Rather, it is

Replacement Chain A concept that views a capital investment as an indefinite commitment to a specific type of technology. This concept can be used to allow the comparison of mutually exclusive investments with unequal lives.

---

[8] These two machines can be accurately evaluated without calculating the operating revenues generated by the machines because the revenues are identical for each machine. The investment proposal that will maximize the firm's value is the one that *minimizes* the PV of the costs arising from the acquisition and operation of a new production machine.

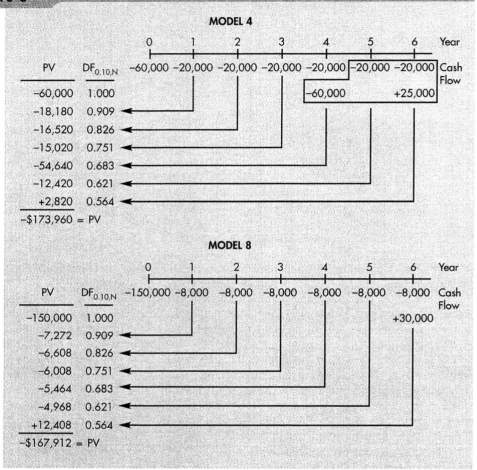

FIGURE 10-6 The PV Calculation for the Model 4 and Model 8 Machines for a Six-Year Horizon

making an indefinite commitment to the technology represented by a given type of capital investment. In order to evaluate mutually exclusive investments in terms of an indefinitely long replacement chain, we should follow a specific procedure:

1. Calculate the PV of the cash outflows of each investment alternative over its estimated useful life.
2. Annualize each investment alternative's PV.
3. Select the investment alternative with the lowest annualized PV.

As an illustration of this evaluation procedure, let's return to our previous example of the Model 4 and Model 8 investment alternatives under the assumption that the firm forecasts an indefinitely long production horizon. Over its useful life of four years, the PV of the Model 4's operating costs is:

$$PV = -\$60,000 - (\$20,000)(ADF_{0.10,4}) = -60,000 - (20,000)(3.170) = -\$123,400$$

For the Model 8, the PV is:

$$PV = -\$150,000 - (\$8,000)(ADF_{0.10,8})$$
$$= -150,000 - (8,000)(5.335) = -\$192,680$$

As we mentioned earlier, these two PVs are not comparable because they are generated over substantially different time periods. One method of converting the PVs into comparable amounts is to annualize them by dividing by the appropriate discounting factor.[9] For the Model 4, the calculation is:

$$\text{Annualized } PV = PV/ADF_{0.10,4} = -\$123,400/3.170 = -\$38,927$$

For the Model 8, the calculation is:

$$\text{Annualized } PV = PV/ADF_{0.10,8} = -\$192,680/5.335 = -\$36,116$$

The **annualized present value** of an investment alternative represents the annual cash flow from an annuity whose life and PV are identical to the life and PV of the proposed investment. An annuity of –$38,927 per year for four years would have the same effect on firm value at an RRR of 10% as the cash flows associated with the Model 4. Likewise, an annuity of –$36,116 for eight years and the cash flows forecast for the Model 8 are equivalent at a discount rate of 10%. *The firm should accept the alternative that offers the lowest annualized PV of costs.* Under this criterion, the Model 8 is a more attractive capital investment for the firm.[10]

Annualized Present Value
The annual cash flow from an annuity with the same life and present value as a specific investment under evaluation.

INFLATION AND CAPITAL BUDGETING

Inflation can dramatically affect the cash inflows and outflows associated with a capital investment. The dilemma that the managers encounter in their attempt to estimate the impact of inflation is that the future rate of inflation is an unknown variable. Forecasts of future inflation are likely to be very inaccurate, particularly in periods of unstable rates of change in the general price level such as occurred in the United States in the 1970s and 1980s. To complicate matters further, inflation's impact may well vary from one type of cash inflow or outflow to another. The rate of inflation is measured in terms of an index that measures the *overall* or average rate of price increase for a number of different types of commodities and services. As a result, the actual rate of change in cash inflows and outflows that is experienced by a firm over the life of an investment can be very different from the rate of change in the general inflation index. Thus, not only must the financial managers *attempt to forecast the general rate of inflation* in the future, but they must also *attempt to estimate inflation's impact on the specific types of cash flows* associated with a given investment.

Given the forecasting difficulties associated with inflation, the best course of action may seem to be simply to ignore inflation's impact altogether! This possible course of action was raised in the chapter introduction. Unfortunately, this is not a

http://
Examine inflation risk and the Consumer Price Index, a measure of inflation, at

www.bankone.com/perbank/investments/securities/straighttalk.shtml
or
http://stats.bls.gov/cpihome.htm

---

[9] Another technique for solving the unequal life problem is to calculate the PV for the machines over the smallest common multiple of their useful lives. In our example, the lowest common multiple is eight years, which represents a comparison of two Model 4s used in sequence versus one Model 8. Although that calculation is simple in this example, it can often become quite cumbersome. For example, the smallest common multiple for a machine with a seven-year life and one with a nine-year life is 63 years. This represents a comparison of nine versions of one machine and seven versions of the other!

[10] An indefinitely long replacement chain of the Model 4 will generate a PV of costs of –$123,400 every four years. This is equivalent to a perpetuity of –$38,927 per year. The PV of this perpetuity is –$389,270 = –$38,927/0.10. The same type of calculations indicate that the Model 8 replacement chain has a PV of –$361,160 = $36,116/0.10. Thus, accepting the investment with the lowest annualized PV of operating costs is equivalent to accepting the investment with the lowest PV of total costs over the production horizon.

■ **Ethics**

ISSUES

THE BODY SHOP HAS TROUBLE MIXING ETHICS AND INTERNATIONAL BUSINESS

One of the factors that can complicate cash flow estimation for investment proposals is a firm's decision to make socially responsible investments. As illustrated by the case

of The Body Shop, the reaction of consumers and investors to such investments can be difficult to predict. Anita and Gordon Roddick started with a single store named "The Body Shop" in Brighton, England in 1976. The business retailed soaps, lotions, and bath accessories with the dual goals of social responsibility and profitability. From its modest beginning, it ballooned to 1,366 stores in 46 countries by 1996. In 1995, profits exceeded $50 million on sales of $349 million.

While this type of growth would be remarkable for any firm, what makes The Body Shop's story so unique is its corporate philosophy of social and environmental responsibility. The Roddicks announced that the firm would use only natural ingredients and would purchase no supplies that had been tested on animals. The company also provided financial support for environmental groups and human rights organizations. It made charitable contributions and bought goods from suppliers located in low-income communities and developing countries.

The Body Shop's philosophy struck a responsive chord among environment-conscious consumers. The firm was cited as the prototype for a new breed of global firm that could stress both profits and social responsibility. Beginning in the 1990s, however, the road to

success turned rocky. Various critics charged the firm with hypocrisy in its social and environmental practices. Management was forced to spend increasing amounts of time publicly defending its record. In 1996, the firm commissioned an outside ethics consulting firm to perform a study that revealed that the firm's business practices failed to live up to its external image. For example, very small percentages of materials were purchased from suppliers in low-income communities and developing countries. Furthermore, a substantial number of its suppliers engaged in animal testing of products not sold to The Body Shop. In addition, charitable contributions were not significantly larger than those made by less activist firms.

All this controversy took its toll on profitability, which fell 26% in the first half of 1996. U.S. operations resulted in operating losses largely due to intense competition from imitators such as the Limited's Bath and Body Works. The stock price in 1996 was down 65% from the high reached four years earlier. In response to stockholder pressures, the Roddicks handed the direction of daily operations over to a professional management team that began to restructure the firm. New control systems and layers of administrative bureaucracy replaced the firm's entrepreneurial spirit and decision-making flexibility.

feasible solution to the problem faced by financial managers. Correct investment evaluation with the NPV or IRR methodology requires accurate estimation of both cash flows and the RRR. As described in Chapter 3, the RRR obtained from financial markets is *automatically* adjusted for inflation. Thus, the financial managers should not ignore inflation's potential impact on an investment's cash flows. Inflation usually has a positive impact on investment cash flows. As a result, failure to include that effect in the estimate of the cash flows will bias the investment's NPV estimate downward.

Nominal Currency The actual amount of a cash flow at some time in the future.

Real Currency The purchasing power in today's currency of future nominal currency to be disbursed or received.

Nominal Versus Real Cash Flows

Another method of saying that a proposal's *estimated cash flows* must be adjusted for inflation is to state that they *should be expressed in nominal currency units* rather than in *real units*. The distinction between nominal and real currency is commonly used by economists to differentiate between the *amount* of currency received and its *value* to the recipient. **Nominal currency** represents the actual amount of a cash flow at some time in the future. **Real currency** represents the purchasing power in today's currency of the future nominal currency amounts.

The calculation of nominal and real currency amounts requires the application of the concept of compounding. The formula for a future nominal currency amount is:

$$C_N = (C_0)(1 + p)^N \qquad (7)$$

where C_N is the cash flow (nominal currency amount) in time period N; C_0 is the cash flow (real currency amount) in time period 0; and p is the annual rate of increase in prices (inflation). Correspondingly, the formula for the conversion of a future nominal amount into its current real currency equivalent is:

$$C_0 = C_N / (1 + p)^N \qquad (8)$$

As an illustration of these calculations, suppose that a U.S. firm is considering an investment in a new machine that will save the firm 500 hours of labor each year for the next three years. Table 10-10 shows the distinction between the nominal and real dollar savings produced by the machine under the assumption of a current wage rate of $8.50/hour and annual rate of inflation of 8%. The table indicates that the real savings associated with the investment remain constant over the three years because the reduction in labor hours is fixed at 500 hours over the investment's life. The nominal savings, on the other hand, increase at an annual compound growth rate of 8%.

The Downward Bias in Real Currency NPV

Since the RRR for a proposal includes an inflation premium, failure to use nominal currency cash flows will bias downward the estimate of an investment proposal's NPV. This bias may, in turn, lead to incorrect rejection of the proposal.

Table 10-11 contains a simple example of how the failure to estimate a project's NPV in nominal currency terms can lead to its incorrect rejection. The top half of the table shows the calculation of the present value of the real after-tax cash flow forecasts associated with an investment over its five-year life.[11] Since the real dollar NPV is negative, the appropriate decision appears to be to reject the investment proposal. The bottom half of the table contains the recalculation of the proposal's NPV under the condition that its nominal cash flows are expected to increase at the forecasted 5% annual rate of inflation.[12]

These calculations assume that the financial markets have automatically included a 5% inflation premium in the proposal's 15% discount rate. The significance of the inflation adjustments is readily apparent in the accept signal provided by the positive nominal dollar NPV.[13] The accuracy of the NPV accept/reject signal depends on the accuracy of the adjustments for inflation's impact on the investment's cash flows.

---

[11] It is important to note that since taxes are a percentage of nominal pretax income, taxes are also nominal.

[12] We should mention at this point that our example assumes, for the sake of simplicity, that the annual rate of increase in the proposal's cash flows is identical to the rate of inflation. Nominal cash flows can increase faster or slower than the rate of inflation or even be totally unaffected. For instance, the cash flows associated with the depreciation tax shield on buildings and equipment are constant regardless of the behavior of inflation because they are based on a depreciation expense that is constant in nominal currency terms.

[13] An accept signal would also be obtained if the real cash flows in the top half of Table 10-11 were discounted at the real RRR = (1.15/1.05) − 1 = 9.52%. The same correct decision will be provided when nominal cash flows are discounted at a nominal RRR and when real cash flows are discounted at a real discount rate. We have stressed the use of nominal data because it is the more convenient of the two procedures in actual practice.

The Distinction Between Real and Nominal Cash Flows

TABLE 10-10

Year	Nominal Wage Rate		Nominal Savings	
1	$8.50(1.08)^1$ = $9.18	500 hours × $9.18 =	$4,590	
2	$8.50(1.08)^2$ = 9.91	500 hours × 9.91 =	4,955	
3	$8.50(1.08)^3$ = 10.70	500 hours × 10.70 =	5,350	

Year	Real Wage Rate		Real Savings	
1	$9.18/(1.08)^1$ = $8.50	500 hours × $8.50 =	$4,250	
2	$9.91/(1.08)^2$ = 8.50	500 hours × 8.50 =	4,250	
3	$10.70/(1.08)^3$ = 8.50	500 hours × 8.50 =	4,250	

An Illustration of Conflicting Accept/Reject Signals Provided by Real Dollar and Nominal Dollar NPVs

TABLE 10-11

	Unadjusted Cash Flows		
Year	Real Cash Flows After Tax	$DF_{0.15,N}$	PV
0	−$55,000	1.000	−$55,000
1	10,000	0.870	8,700
2	15,000	0.756	11,340
3	15,000	0.658	9,870
4	30,000	0.572	17,160
5	10,000	0.497	4,970
	Decision: *Reject* Proposal.		NPV = −$ 2,960

	Adjusted Cash Flows				
Year	Real Cash Flows After Tax	Inflation Factor $(1+p)^{N*}$	Nominal Cash Flows	$DF_{0.15,N}$	PV
0	−$55,000	1.00	−$55,000	1.000	−$55,000
1	10,000	1.05	10,500	0.870	9,135
2	15,000	1.10	16,500	0.756	12,474
3	15,000	1.16	17,400	0.658	11,449
4	30,000	1.22	36,600	0.572	20,935
5	10,000	1.28	12,800	0.497	6,362
	Decision: *Accept* Proposal.			NPV =	$ 5,355

*p = annual rate of inflation = 0.05

SUMMARY

The goal of this chapter is to introduce those factors that determine which of the total cash flows associated with a capital investment proposal are relevant to its NPV or IRR evaluation. An accurate estimation of an investment's relevant cash flows is important because these cash flows determine the acceptability of a proposed investment. The accurate estimation of relevant cash flows relies heavily on the concept of incremental, after-tax cash flows. The impact of an investment on firm value depends on the *changes in future firm cash flows* caused by that investment. These changes in firm cash flows are termed *incremental cash flows*. From a capital budgeting viewpoint, taxes simply represent a specific type of cash outflow connected with an investment. Thus, the incremental cash flows associated with an investment should be measured on an *after-tax* basis.

An expansion proposal's incremental cash flows are equal to its total cash flows. A replacement proposal's incremental cash flows, on the other hand, are normally smaller than its total cash flows. In the case of either type of investment proposal, a firm's financial managers should ignore the financing costs associated with an investment in their determination of its relevant cash flows. They cannot ignore the impact of future inflation on a proposal's incremental cash flows, however, unless they feel that the impact will be insignificant.

The cash flows associated with most capital investment proposals can be divided into three major categories: initial period flows, annual flows, and termination flows. The initial period flows comprise the net investment or cash outflow that occurs immediately at the start of an investment's life. The annual cash flows represent the stream of benefits generated by the investment each year of its useful life. The project termination cash flows consist of the net proceeds realized from the liquidation of the assets no longer required by an investment proposal at the end of the project's life.

There are a number of operational problems faced by a firm in its implementation of a capital budgeting system. The first of these is the downward bias in the NPV estimate for a proposal caused by the failure to adjust for the impact of expected inflation. Accurate project evaluation requires that the cash flow forecasts for a project be stated in terms of nominal currency units. Second, financial managers often cannot validly compare the NPV estimates for mutually exclusive investments unless they have first adjusted for differences in their expected useful lives.

chapter equations

1. Average Tax Rate = $\dfrac{\text{Total Tax Due}}{\text{Total Taxable Income}}$

2. Straight-Line Depreciation = $\dfrac{\text{Cost}}{\text{Depreciable Life}}$

3. Reduction in Income Taxes = (Tax Shield)(Tax Rate)

4. ITC = (Initial Cost of Asset)(ITC Rate)

5. Effective After-Tax Cost of an Asset = Initial Cost − ITC

6. Tax Effect from Sale of an Asset = (Selling Price − Book Value)(Tax Rate)

7. $C_N = C_0(1 + p)^N$

8. $C_0 = C_N/(1 + p)^N$

CONTENT QUESTIONS

1. Distinguish between an expansion proposal and a replacement proposal.
2. What is the relationship between the total cash flows and the incremental cash flows of a replacement proposal?
3. Why are only incremental, after-tax cash flows relevant to the NPV or the IRR evaluation of an investment proposal?
4. Explain the concept of a sunk cost. Why is the cash outflow associated with a sunk cost *not* a relevant cash flow in capital budgeting?
5. Discuss the appropriate treatment of financing costs such as interest expense in the DCF evaluation of an investment proposal.
6. Describe the problems introduced into capital budgeting by inflation.
7. Why should financial managers always attempt to adjust an investment proposal's relevant cash flows for inflation?
8. Explain how and why changes in net working capital required by an investment proposal are incorporated into the evaluation of the proposal.
9. Why is the forecasted salvage value of an existing asset at the end of its useful life included in the DCF evaluation of a replacement proposal?
10. How does a noncash expense affect a firm's after-tax cash flows?
11. Given two investment proposals with unequal lives, when is it necessary to use something other than the standard NPV comparison?

12. In making an accept/reject decision on the basis of annualized NPV, financial managers assume an indefinitely long replacement chain. Why?

CONCEPT QUESTIONS

1. IVM In order to estimate accurately the cash flows associated with a proposed capital investment, a firm's managers must be able to predict the impact of future competitor actions and national business cycles. Given the inherent unpredictability of both these factors, cash flow estimates are necessarily imprecise. Based on this line of reasoning, critics of the NPV and IRR evaluation techniques sometimes argue that the seeming precision of NPV and IRR estimates is very misleading. As a result, such estimates do more harm than good. What is your reaction to this argument?

2. IVM The financial managers of a firm are considering a capital investment proposal that calls for the purchase of expensive machinery that utilizes the latest technological breakthrough. The new machinery would replace equipment that was purchased only one year ago. Although the current equipment was estimated to have a useful life of twenty years, it is now technologically obsolete even though it is functionally in excellent condition. Based on the high cost and recent installation of the current equipment, one of the managers argues that the NPV estimate of the new machinery should reflect the undepreciated cost of the current equipment. Is this argument valid?

3. IVM In this chapter, we stated that only a proposed investment's incremental *cash flows* are relevant to its evaluation. Given this rule, why is depreciation expense included in the calculation of an investment's NPV? Can you think of any circumstances in which the depreciation associated with a proposed investment can be safely ignored?

4. IVM A firm's managers have estimated the cash flows associated with a proposed investment under the assumption of a stable price level. One of the managers then suggests that it is quite likely that inflation will increase the investment's cash flows over its life. In response, another manager argues "that predicting the rate of inflation and its effect on the investment's cash flows is so difficult and uncertain that inflation should be ignored." What is your opinion of this statement? If inflation is ignored, what will be the likely effect on the proposed investment's NPV estimate?

5. IVM Accepted capital investment projects must be financed with some combination of debt and equity financing. In addition, the interest expense on the debt and the dividends on the stock represent cash outflows associated with the projects. Consequently, these cash outflows should be included in the calculation of the projects' NPVs. Is this argument valid? If it is not valid, how are interest expense and dividends accounted for in the estimation of NPV?

PROBLEMS

1. An investment will generate $30,000,000 in sales revenues each year. Annual expenses will equal $10 million for labor, $8 million for materials, and $6 million for other cash expenses. Annual depreciation will equal $2 million. The marginal tax rate is 40%.
    a. Calculate the annual after-tax cash flow of the investment using the income statement approach.
    b. Calculate the annual after-tax cash flow of the investment by converting each item into its after-tax equivalent.

2. What is the after-tax cash flow associated with each of the following pretax cash flow items, given a marginal tax rate of 40% for all cases?
    a. Increase in net working capital of $500,000
    b. Sales revenue of $26,000
    c. Increase in maintenance expense of $50,000
    d. Investment in new equipment for $400,000 that qualifies for a 10% investment tax credit
    e. Sale of machinery for $20,000 that has a book value of $14,000
    f. Sale of machinery for $14,000 that has a book value of $20,000

3. Des Moines Corporation has just purchased a building that it will either lease to another company or use for its own purposes. If it is not leased, Des Moines would be able to move certain operations from a rental building, thereby saving the annual rental expense. Des Moines has collected the following information:
    a. The building cost FF4,350,000.
    b. Depreciation of the building is FF200,000 per year for 20 years.
    c. Estimated salvage value is FF350,000 at the end of the building's 20-year life.
    d. The annual lease payment is FF350,000. (Lessee will assume maintenance.)
    e. Property taxes are FF64,000 per year.
    f. Expected annual maintenance expense is FF75,000.
    g. Rental expense for alternative space is FF375,000 per year.
   Classify each item as either relevant or irrelevant to the question of leasing the building to the company and briefly state why.

4. Determine the marginal and average tax rates for corporations with the following taxable earnings:
    a. $10,000   b. $100,000   c. $1,000,000   d. $10,000,000

5. Oakland Developers reported 2000 taxable income of $12,000,000. What is Oakland's average federal income tax rate? What is Oakland's marginal tax rate? What rate should Oakland use to evaluate investment decisions?

6. Melrose Limited has just purchased a computer that is classified as an asset with a 5-year recovery period, for $100,000. Melrose can use either ACR percentages or straight-line (with the half-year convention). It has an opportunity cost of 10% per year and a tax rate of 40%.
    a. Find the present value of the depreciation tax shield for both depreciation methods.
    b. In the case of this particular computer, explain the impact of accelerated depreciation on the value of Melrose's common stock.

7. Nethers Plastics has purchased a light truck for $30,000. The depreciation method is straight-line for 5 years (with the half-year convention). Given a 40% tax rate, find the after-tax proceeds from the sale of the truck:
    a. if the truck is sold for $10,000 after 3 years.
    b. if the truck is sold for $6,000 after 4 years.

8. Nethers Plastics purchased a light truck for $30,000. The depreciation method is ACR with a 5-year recovery period. Find the after-tax net proceeds from the sale of the truck given a 40% marginal tax rate:
    a. if the truck is sold for $10,000 after 3 years.
    b. if the truck is sold for $6,000 after 4 years.

9. Rohrson Manufacturing incurred a loss in 1995. In other years, it realized taxable income as shown on the next page:

1991	$2,000,000	1996	$1,000,000
1992	1,000,000	1997	2,000,000
1993	3,000,000	1998	5,000,000
1994	1,000,000		

Recompute the taxable income for each year assuming that the 1995 loss was:
a. $1,500,000   b. $4,200,000   c. $5,300,000   d. $6,200,000

10. The Anco Corporation owns 250,000 shares of stock issued by another corporation. The annual dividend on each share is $2.25. Calculate the annual after-tax return realized by Anco on the stock if the firm's marginal tax rate is 40%.

11. Springfield Manufacturing is considering building a new plant that will add significantly to its capacity. After taking into account all tax effects, it has determined that the cash outflow in the initial period will be $4,000,000 and that the annual cash inflow will be $750,000 for the first five years of the project's life and $500,000 for the remaining five years. It also calculates that the after-tax termination cash flow in the tenth year is $800,000. Should Springfield build the new plant if its RRR is 10%?

12. Returning to Springfield Manufacturing's new plant proposal in Problem 11, suppose that the cash inflows will not begin until after a *two-year delay*. That is, the annual cash flow will begin in year 3 rather than year 1, and the project will terminate in year 12 rather than year 10. With these new facts, should Springfield build the new plant?

13. Returning to Problem 11 (ignore the change in Problem 12), suppose that just *after* Springfield paid $4,000,000 to the contractors who built the plant, the local labor union called a strike. Because of the seriousness of the strike issues, Springfield's management estimated that the plant will not be opening for two years. Because of the specialized nature of the plant and the labor unrest, no other company would buy the plant. Should Springfield abandon the plant?

14. Pacific Mills is considering the acquisition of new machinery that will cost $750,000. It will have a 10-year service life and a salvage value of $50,000. It also qualifies for a 10% ITC. The machine is expected to reduce material expense by $125,000 annually for the first 5 years and $75,000 the last 5 years. Assuming an 8% RRR, 40% marginal tax rate, and straight-line depreciation over 5 years (ignore the half-year convention), should the machine be purchased?

15. Now suppose the machine in Problem 14 is intended to replace an older machine. The older machine was purchased 10 years ago for $280,000. At the time of purchase, its projected salvage value at the end of its 20-year life was $40,000. The machine can be sold now for $110,000. Assume the old machine is depreciated on a straight-line basis over 20 years. Reevaluate the investment. Should the new machine be purchased?

16. Bridgewell Industries is evaluating the option of purchasing a fork-lift truck costing $60,000. If purchased, the truck will replace 4 workers, each with an average annual salary of $15,000. However, an experienced fork-lift operator will have to be hired at a salary of $20,000 per year. Fuel and maintenance expense is expected to be $10,000 per year. At the end of its 5-year economic and depreciable life, the truck will have a salvage value of $10,000. Bridgewell uses straight-line depreciation, assigns a 10% RRR for this type of investment, and has a marginal tax rate of 40%. (Ignore the half-year convention for depreciation.)
    a. Should the fork-lift truck be purchased, given the above information?
    b. Should it be purchased if it could only replace 3 workers rather than 4?

17. Case Manufacturing has been purchasing 15,000 units of a component used in the assembly of its main product line at a price of $24.00 per unit. Case is now

considering the alternative of making the component itself rather than buying it. In order to produce the component, Case must purchase $500,000 in additional equipment and invest $75,000 in additional working capital. The equipment has an economic life of 10 years, a depreciable life of 5 years, and a zero salvage value. It would be depreciated on a straight-line basis (ignore the half-year convention) to a zero book value. Variable costs of production are $14.00 per unit. If the firm's marginal tax rate is 40% and the RRR is 14%, should Case continue to buy the component or produce the component itself?

18. In reviewing the make-or-buy decision in Problem 17, the financial vice president notices that the decision is greatly influenced by the number of units of the component needed each year. She feels that this is a difficult number to forecast accurately. Thus, she wishes to know the minimum number of units of the component needed to justify the decision to produce the component. Calculate that number.

19. Oregon Tool Works is considering a proposal to produce a new product. Sales are expected to be $20,000,000 per year and manufacturing and other costs about $16,000,000 per year. Net working capital is estimated to be $2,000,000. The plant site will cost $500,000 and should remain at that value indefinitely. The plant and equipment will cost $10,000,000 and be depreciated on a straight-line basis (ignore the half-year convention) over a 20-year life. The expected salvage value is zero. The marginal tax rate is 40%.
    a. What is the initial period cash flow?
    b. What is the annual cash flow over the project's life?
    c. What is the project termination cash flow?
    d. If the RRR is 12%, what is the investment's NPV?

20. Savannah Mills is considering the acquisition of new machinery at a cost of $1,500,000. The machine will have a 10-year economic life, a 5-year depreciable life, and a salvage value of $100,000. The machinery is expected to reduce material expense by $250,000 per year. It will replace older machinery, which was purchased 10 years ago for $560,000. At the time of purchase, the older machinery was depreciated on a straight-line basis (ignore the half-year convention). It will have a salvage value at the end of its 20-year life of $60,000. It can be sold now for $200,000. Savannah uses straight-line depreciation and has a marginal tax rate of 40%. Considering the low risk, the RRR for this investment is 8%.
    a. What is the initial period cash flow?
    b. What is the annual cash flow over the project's life?
    c. What is the project termination cash flow?
    d. Use the NPV criterion to determine whether the new machinery should be purchased.

21. Oxford International is considering an investment in a new product. The initial period outlay required is £83,000,000. Of this figure, £10,000,000 represents an increase in net working capital and £1,000,000 represents the cost of land for a new plant. The remainder of the outlay represents the cost of new plant and equipment. The product will generate an EAT of £11,000,000 per year over its 20-year life. The plant and equipment will be depreciated on a straight-line basis for 20 years (ignore the half-year convention). The land will have a value of £1,000,000 at the end of the product's life. The plant will have no salvage value. If the RRR is 16%, should Oxford invest in the product? (Hint: You do not need to know the marginal tax rate.)

22. Due to a "bottleneck" in the shipping department caused by an old and inefficient railroad car loading system, Randall Industries has not been able to oper-

ate its plant at capacity and has lost sales as a result. It is considering investing in a completely automated system costing $2,000,000 installed. It would have a 5-year life for straight-line depreciation (ignore the half-year convention). The new system is expected to have a salvage value of $400,000 at the end of its 10-year economic life. The sales increase made possible by the new system will increase pretax cash flows by $300,000 annually and will require an additional $250,000 in working capital. The old system has a zero book value but has a salvage value of $100,000 both now and at the end of the 10 years remaining on its economic life. Randall's marginal tax rate is 40%.

    a. What is the initial period cash flow?

    b. What is the annual cash flow over the project's life?

    c. What is the project termination cash flow?

    d. If the RRR is 12%, should the investment project be accepted?

23. The vice president of Bankers Real Estate Development Corporation is eager to purchase 200 acres of land that should double in value in four years. The land can be purchased for $500,000 and sold after four years for $1,000,000. However, each year the owners must pay $30,000 in property taxes and $5,000 for liability insurance. Because of the risk, the investment is required to return 18%. Given that all the dollar amounts are after-tax:

    a. Should Bankers purchase this land for $500,000?

    b. What is the most that Bankers should offer if the price were open to negotiation?

24. Suppose that a firm usually forecasts cash flows in nominal dollars and uses a market-determined RRR. The manager sponsoring a new investment proposal, however, has provided the following real dollar after-tax cash flow forecasts:

Year	0	1	2	3
Cash Flow	−100	+35	+50	+30

The RRR for this proposal is 15%, and the expected rate of inflation is 10%.

    a. Calculate an NPV by discounting the *real* cash flow estimates by the *nominal* RRR.

    b. Calculate the *nominal* dollar cash flows for the project.

    c. Calculate the NPV by discounting *nominal* cash flow estimates by the *nominal* RRR.

    d. Which NPV calculation is correct? Why?

25. Florida Industries is considering adding equipment to an existing production line in its Tampa plant that will reduce raw materials by 1,000 tons per year. The equipment will cost $8,000,000 and will be depreciated on a straight-line basis (ignore the half-year convention) over its five-year life to a zero salvage value. Although the current cost of the raw materials is $2,000 per ton, expected inflation would increase the cost of raw materials at the rate of 5% per year. The RRR for this investment is 10%, and the marginal tax rate is 40%.

    a. Find the real dollar pretax savings in raw materials costs each year.

    b. Find the nominal pretax savings in raw materials costs each year.

    c. Find the nominal after-tax cash flows of this investment.

    d. Based on its nominal dollar NPV, should this project be accepted?

26. Baxter Foods is evaluating an investment in a new product line. The initial period outlay after taxes is $190,000,000. The net cash flow at termination in 15 years is $25,000,000. The new product line will generate EAT of $20,000,000 the first year. Because of inflation, EAT will increase by 5% each year after that. Annual depreciation is based on the initial cost of the plant and is $10,000,000 per year over the project life. The required rate of return is 15%. Should Baxter make this investment?

27. Now assume for Problem 26 that, in spite of inflation, nominal EAT remains constant (i.e., EAT falls in real terms). Should Baxter make this investment?

28. Brennan Manufacturing is considering the $200,000 purchase of an automated mailing system that will be depreciated on a straight-line basis (ignore the half-year convention) over 5 years. The service life of the system is 10 years, at which time it can be salvaged for $20,000. The pretax operating cost is $30,000 per year. The marginal tax rate is 40%, and the RRR is 8%. Calculate the annualized PV of the automated mailing system.

29. Nashville Products has a choice between two types of machines that will perform the same task in the production of its *major* product. Model X has a life of 3 years with an initial cost of $100,000 and an operating cost per year of $20,000. Model Y has a life of 8 years with an initial cost of $300,000 and an operating cost per year of $15,000. These cash flows are stated on an after-tax basis. If the RRR is 10%, which machine should be accepted?

30. Windy City Printing's financial manager is evaluating two types of printing presses to replace a usable but technologically obsolete press, which has no salvage value. The data on the two presses is shown below:

	Manual Model	Computerized Model
Initial Cost	$60,000	$100,000
Useful Life	8 years	5 years
Annual Pretax Cost Savings	$30,000	$ 50,000

The firm's marginal tax rate is 40%. Either new press would be depreciated over 5 years (cost recovery period) on a straight-line basis with a zero salvage value at the end of its useful life. Which model should the firm accept at an RRR of 12%?

31. Consider two investment projects with a 12% required rate of return and the after-tax cash flows given below:

Year	Investment A	Investment B
0	-$100,000	-$150,000
1	30,000	30,000
2	30,000	30,000
3	30,000	30,000
4	30,000	30,000
5	30,000	30,000
6	—	30,000
7	—	30,000
8	—	30,000
9	—	30,000

a. If the two investments are independent, which should be accepted?
b. If the two investments are mutually exclusive, which should be accepted? Assume a production horizon of five years. At the end of that time, Investment B can be sold for after-tax proceeds of $60,000.
c. If the two investments are mutually exclusive and the production horizon is indefinite, which should be accepted?

INTERNET EXERCISE

http://

You can download the New Media Financial "Lite" software to go with Microsoft's Excel 97 for a 3-day sample. The software will allow you to analyze the article "The Case Against Earnings," which examines cash flow. Take the quiz mentioned at the beginning of the article. Hand in the results of your quiz and analysis of the article.
www.rcmfinancial.com/NewMediaFinancial/NMFhelp/nmflite.asp

SELF-STUDY QUIZ

1. What is the after-tax equivalent of each of the following pretax cash flow items? The marginal tax rate is 40%.
    a. Revenue from sales of $12,000
    b. Increase in net working capital of $200,000
    c. Maintenance expense of $25,000
    d. Sale of equipment for $10,000 whose book value is $6,000
    e. Sale of equipment for $6,000 whose book value is $10,000
    f. $500,000 investment in new equipment that has a 5-year life (Assume straight-line depreciation and ignore the half-year convention.)
    g. The same as (f) under the assumption of ACR percentages for depreciation

2. Evergreen Controls is considering a new machine that costs $750,000. It will be depreciated on a simplified straight-line basis over 10 years and will have a $60,000 salvage value at the end of 10 years. Evergreen has a 40% marginal tax rate and will use an 8% RRR to evaluate this project. If this machine is expected to reduce material expenses by $160,000 per year for the first 5 years of its life and $80,000 per year for the last 5 years, should Evergreen acquire the machine?

3. Suppose that the machine that Evergreen Controls is considering would replace an older machine. The older machine was purchased 5 years ago for $300,000 and is being depreciated on a straight-line basis over 10 years. It has a salvage value at the end of its 15-year service life (10 years from now) of $40,000. It can be sold now for $120,000. Should Evergreen replace this machine?

APPENDIX: INVESTMENT VALUATION AND FREE CASH FLOW

The logic behind the definition of cash flows in the NPV and IRR decision criteria can be seen clearly when we compare the cash flow definitions used in DCF evaluations of investment proposals with the statement of cash flows discussed in Chapter 2. In general, a cash flow statement is merely an historical account of where cash came from and where it went. There are many ways of formatting this information, including the statement of sources and uses of funds and the statement of balance sheet changes, both of which were discussed in Chapter 2. A key prerequisite for the usefulness of any format is that it should highlight the amount of the cash flows which, because they are available to the suppliers of capital (lenders and shareholders), are the source of a firm's value. As we pointed out in the chapter, these cash flows are often described by the term *Free Cash Flow* (FCF). If a project's FCF exceeds the compensation required by a firm's creditors and stockholders, it will have a positive NPV. In this appendix, we will demonstrate how the free cash flow format can be used in the NPV and IRR evaluation of an investment proposal.

Free Cash Flows in the Cash Flow Statement

We will begin our discussion by relating the concept of free cash flow to the statement of cash flows that a firm reports to its stockholders. The left side of Table 10A-1 reproduces the statement of cash flows for Dayton Products that was discussed in Chapter 2. On the far right side is the definition of free cash flow that is used to calculate a project's NPV or IRR. In the middle of the table, the data in the statement of cash flows are rearranged to conform directly to the FCF format. The addition of interest expense to net income yields Dayton's after-tax operating profit (ATOP). Adding depreciation and other noncash expenses to ATOP results in operating cash flow (OCF). Summation of all changes in current assets and current liabilities with the exception of cash equals additions to working capital which, in the FCF calculation, is shown as ΔWC. The change in investment in gross plant and equipment represents capital expenditures (CAPEX). Thus, Dayton Products' FCF in 2000 was:

$$
\begin{aligned}
\text{FCF} &= \text{OCF} - \Delta\text{WC} - \text{CAPEX} \\
&= \$8,800,000 - (-800,000) - 7,400,000 \\
&= \$8,800,000 + 800,000 - 7,400,000 \\
&= \$2,200,000
\end{aligned}
$$

These calculations reveal that $8,800,000 in net cash inflows was generated by operations. A reduction in net working capital contributed another $800,000 to cash inflows. Additional capital investments required $7,400,000 in cash outflows. The remaining $2,200,000 is the net amount of the total cash flows generated by Dayton's assets that is available to support its financing activities.

The bottom portion of the statement of cash flows gives details on the year 2000 distribution of cash flows to the "suppliers of capital." In a long-term sense, this distribution is accounted for in the calculation of Dayton's RRR. Exactly how this is accomplished will be shown in Chapter 15 where we discuss the importance of financial structure to the estimation of a project's RRR.

One item in the statement of cash flows—the net cash flow of $200,000 for 2000—requires further discussion. Strictly speaking, this is a change in a working capital account (cash). A portion of this amount may have been a necessary addition to cash balances to support operations and, therefore, was not available to support financing activities. Thus, it should be deducted from Dayton's FCF of $2,200,000. Based solely on the accounting statement of cash flows, we cannot make this distinction. When estimating the FCF of a proposed capital investment, however, a financial manager should make this distinction and be certain that ΔWC includes any necessary increases in cash balances as well as other working capital requirements.

Complex Project Evaluation in Terms of Free Cash Flows

We will now illustrate how the free cash flow format and computer spreadsheet technology can be utilized to find the NPV and IRR for a project with more complex and realistic cash flows than we assumed in our discussion of capital investment decisions in the body of the chapter. In the example to follow, we will employ accelerated rather than straight-line depreciation and assume increased sales and working capital requirements each year, as well as capital spending after the initial period.

An Expansion Decision. The management of Martin Enterprises is considering a new product with a ten-year life. Martin plans to use an idle factory building that it already owns but which could otherwise be sold for $1,100,000 cash (after taxes) if not used for this project. The equipment necessary to begin production is expected to cost $20,000,000 (including installation) and have a salvage value of $1,000,000. In addition, Martin estimates that another $10,000,000 must be spent to upgrade and expand the production process during the fifth year of production. This upgrade will have a salvage value of $1,500,000. ACR depreciation with a seven-year recovery period will be used for all machinery. Sales and production expenses in the first year are expected to be $15,000,000 and $10,000,000, respectively. Both are forecast to grow at 5% per year. Working capital requirements are expected to equal 10% of sales, and Martin plans to invest this amount at the beginning of the year in which the sales occur. The firm has a marginal tax rate of 40% and will use a 10% RRR to evaluate the cash flows from this project.

TABLE 10A-1

Cash Flow Statement and Free Cash Flow: Dayton Products December 31, 1999, to December 31, 2000 (in Thousands)

Cash flows from operations:			
Net income	$3,300	$ 3,300	EAT
Additions:			
Interest expense	2,800	+ 2,800	+ Interest
		6100	ATOP
Depreciation	2,300	+ 2,300	Depreciation
Amortization of goodwill	400	+ 400	Amortization
		8,800	OCF
Decrease other current assets	200		
Increase accounts payable	400		
Increase accruals	2,400		
Increase taxes payable	100	+ 800	– ΔWC
Deductions:			
Increase accounts receivable	(1,600)		
Increase inventory	(700)		
Net cash flow from operations	9,600	9,600	OCF – ΔWC
Cash flows from investing:			
Increase in plant & equipment	(7,400)	– 7,400	–CAPEX
Net cash flow from operations and investing	**2,200**	**2,200**	**FCF**
Cash flows from financing activities:			
Increase long-term liabilities	3,000		
Decrease notes payable	(100)		
Interest expense	(2,800)		Accounted for over the long term in the calculation of Dayton's RRR
Subtotal from debt financing	100		
Dividends paid	(2,100)		
Net cash flow from financing	(2,000)		
Net cash flow for 2000	**200**		Deduction from FCF shown above, if needed to support operations
Cash balance, December 31, 1999	1,800		
Cash balance, December 31, 2000	2,000		

Initial Period Cash Flows. The initial period cash flows have three components. The first is the initial investment in working capital, which is 10% of the first year sales of $15,000,000:

$$\Delta WC = (\$15,000,000)(0.10) = \$1,500,000$$

The second component is the $20,000,000 cost of the equipment. The third is the value of the lost opportunity to sell the factory building for $1,100,000. Capital expenditures in the initial period are the sum of these last two components:

$$CAPEX = \$20,000,000 + 1,100,000 = \$21,100,000$$

The total cash outflows in the initial period are, therefore, $22,600,000.

Cash Flows Over the Project's Life. As we pointed out in the body of the chapter, the free cash flow in any given year is equal to operating cash flow (OCF) less any additions to working capital and capital spending expected in that year. For the first year, the operating cash flow can be calculated in either of two ways:

OCF = EBIT − Taxes + Depreciation

$\quad$ = (Revenues − Cash Expenses − Depreciation)(1 − T) + Depreciation

$\quad$ = ($15,000,000 − 10,000,000 − 2,856,000)(1 − 0.40) + 2,856,000

$\quad$ = $1,286,000 + 2,856,000 = $4,142,000

$\qquad\qquad$ OR

OCF = (Revenues)(1 − T) − (Cash Expenses)(1 − T) − (Depreciation)(−T)

$\quad$ = ($15,000,000)(1 − 0.40) − (10,000,000)(1 − 0.40) − (2,856,000)(−0.40)

$\quad$ = $9,000,000 − 6,000,000 + 1,142,000 = $4,142,000

The depreciation expense of $2,856,000 was obtained from Table 10A-2, which shows the annual depreciation for both machines, and the associated tax effect. Due to the use of the ACR depreciation rates shown in Table 10-1 in the chapter, the annual depreciation expense will differ for each year. Sales and expenses will also be different each year because they are expected to grow at 5% per year. Consequently, the annual OCFs, which are shown in the spreadsheet in Table 10A-3, are each unique. Notice that all cash flows shown in that table are expressed on an after-tax basis.

Along with the annual OCFs, Table 10A-3 contains the addition to working capital for each year. This addition is necessary to maintain a beginning-of-the-year investment in working capital equal to 10% of the year's sales. For example, at the end of year 1, ΔWC is $75,000, which accounts for the increase in working capital needed to support 5% greater sales in year 2. The same reasoning is used to calculate ΔWC for subsequent years. Lastly, $10,000,000 of additional capital spending in year 5 is included in the FCF calculation in Table 10A-3 for that year.

Project Termination Cash Flows.   The last year in Table 10A-3 contains two items that we previously defined as termination cash flows. These are the recovery of working capital and the after-tax salvage value of the assets. The recovery of working capital of $2,326,000 is the total invested in working capital over the life of the project. It represents the sum of the initial investment in working capital and all the additions that will be made over the project's life.

CAPEX in year 10 is a cash inflow of $2,393,000. This is the sum of after-tax cash flows that are expected from the sale of equipment at project termination.

Net Proceeds = Selling Price − (Selling Price − Book Value)(Tax Rate)

Martin Enterprises Depreciation Schedule

TABLE 10A-2

Depreciation Schedule
ACR Seven-Year Recovery Period
(in Thousands)

	Initial Machinery	Year 5 Machinery	Total Depreciation	Depreciation × 0.40
1	$ 2,856		$2,856	$1,142
2	4,898		4,898	1,959
3	3,498		3,498	1,399
4	2,498		2,498	999
5	1,786		1,786	714
6	1,786	$1,428	3,214	1,286
7	1,786	2,449	4,235	1,694
8	892	1,749	2,641	1,056
9		1,249	1,249	500
10		893	893	357
Total	$20,000	$7,768		

TABLE 10A-3

Free Cash Flow Spreadsheet for Martin Enterprises' Expansion Project (in Thousands)

Year	0	1	2	3	4	5	6	7	8	9	10
(Revenue)(1 − T)		$9,000	$9,450	$ 9,923	$10,419	$10,940	$11,487	$12,060	$12,664	$13,297	$13,962
(−Expense)(1 − T)		−6,000	−6,300	−6,615	−6,946	−7,293	−7,658	−8,041	−8,443	−8,865	−9,308
(−Depreciation)(−T)		1,142	1,959	1,399	999	714	1,286	1,694	1,056	500	357
OCF		4,142	5,109	4,707	4,472	4,361	5,115	5,713	5,277	4,932	5,011
−ΔWC	−$1,500	−75	−79	−83	−87	−91	−96	−100	−105	−110	+2,326
−CAPEX	−21,100					−10,000					+2,393
FCF	−$22,600	$4,067	$5,030	$ 4,624	$ 4,385	−$5,730	$ 5,019	$ 5,613	$ 5,172	$ 4,822	$ 9,730

NPV @10% = $2,088,000   IRR = 12%

The net proceeds from the salvage of the initial equipment expenditure are:

$$\text{Net Proceeds} = \$1,000,000 - (1,000,000 - 0)(0.40) = \$600,000$$

The book value and net proceeds from the salvage of the equipment purchased in year 5 are:

$$\text{Book Value} = \text{Original Cost} - \text{Accumulated Depreciation}$$
$$= \$10,000,000 - (7,768,000)(\text{from Table 10A-2})$$
$$= \$2,232,000$$

$$\text{Net Proceeds} = \$1,500,000 - (1,500,000 - 2,232,000)(0.40)$$
$$= \$1,500,000 - (-732,000)(0.40)$$
$$= \$1,500,000 + 293,000 = \$1,793,000$$

Notice that the salvage of the equipment caused a $732,000 loss relative to the asset's book value of $2,232,000. CAPEX in year 10 is equal to the sum of the net salvage proceeds from both sets of equipment. The FCF of $9,730,000 in the final period is the sum of the OCF and the termination cash flows that take the form of a reduction in working capital and proceeds from liquidation of assets.

Project Evaluation.   At an RRR of 10%, the NPV of the expansion proposal is $2,088,000. That is, implementation of the proposal should increase the value of Martin Enterprises' stock by over $2 million. The project's desirability is also reflected in its IRR of 12%

Abandonment Option.   An interesting element of this example is the presence of an obvious abandonment alternative in the fifth year. Martin's management must decide whether it really makes sense to spend $10,000,000 more on the project in that year. The alternative is to abandon the project and liquidate the associated assets. To make this decision, Martin's managers would compare the liquidation value of the assets in year 5 to the NPV of an expenditure of $10,000,000 that will generate the FCFs shown in Table 10A-3 for years 6 through 10. In this example, we assume that Martin's managers had analyzed the option to abandon and projected that they would not exercise that option when the time came.

Of course, if the actual cash flows in the first few years fall short of the forecasts shown in Table 10A-3, Martin's managers might revise their estimated cash flows for the last five years of the project's life. When the time comes to commit another $10 million, they might well decide to abandon the project as a result of this revision. While they currently do not intend to abandon the project in year 5, they still have the valuable real option to do so.

Financial Leverage

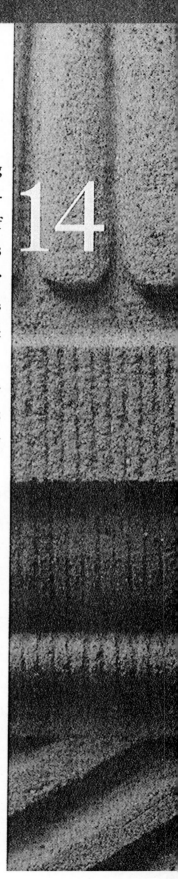

Just as with its investing decisions, a firm's financing decisions can alter its risk/return trade-off. Thus, financial managers must be aware of the potential effects of alternative financing choices on firm value. Perhaps the most important financing decision that a manager can make is the choice between debt financing and equity financing. This chapter evaluates the risk/return implications of the decision to employ debt financing. In this evaluation, we will address the following issues:

- How is the financial leverage associated with fixed interest on debt comparable to the operating leverage associated with fixed operating expenses? Since both types of leverage arise from fixed costs, why should a firm's financial managers analyze them separately?

- The debt/equity decision is important because it can alter a firm's risk/return trade-off. What is the effect of financial leverage on the size and variability of a firm's profits? Does the effect depend on the measure of profits under consideration? Under what conditions will financial leverage be favorable?

- Financial leverage affects a firm's taxes because the interest expense on debt is tax-deductible. How can a firm's managers estimate the value of the tax shelter offered by debt financing?

- The value of a firm's stock is affected by both its beta (β) and its RRR (K_E). What impact does financial leverage have on K_E? Does it have a comparable effect on β?

- Firms utilize debt financing largely because the interest expense is tax-deductible. An offset to this advantage of debt, however, is the increased

risk of financial distress associated with the contractual commitment to make interest and principal payments. Does the tax benefit effect from debt financing always outweigh the financial distress effect? Can the net impact of these two effects on a firm's value to its stockholders be measured? How can financial managers determine the optimal level of debt financing?

The effect of a firm's financial leverage on its value is outlined in Figure 14-1. An increase in debt financing is associated with an increase in both expected stockholder returns and the riskiness of those returns. Whether a firm's value will be increased by simultaneous increases in its expected ROE or EPS and the coefficient of variation (CV) of these returns depends upon the trade-off between the tax effect and the financial distress effect of debt. If the present value of the interest expense tax shelter exceeds the cost of financial distress associated with debt, increased financial leverage will boost firm value. The task of the financial managers of a firm is to determine the *maximum level of leverage* at which this relationship holds. The goal of this chapter is to establish some guidelines that a firm's financial managers can follow in their attempt to select the optimal capital structure.

THE CONCEPT OF LEVERAGE

The way in which the term leverage is used in the everyday language of finance can be confusing. The reason behind the confusion is that there are two types of leverage. We examined the first type of leverage, operating leverage, in Chapter 11, where we pointed out that operating leverage is determined by the financial managers' investing decisions. The second type of leverage, financial leverage, is determined by the managers' financing decisions as we described in Chapter 2. While there are *two different types* of leverage, there is *only one concept* of leverage. **Leverage** refers to the presence of fixed costs in a firm's cost structure. It deals with the relative size of fixed costs whether they are operating costs or financing costs. Before our analysis of the impact of financial leverage on a firm's value, we will examine the exact relationship between operating leverage and financial leverage. We will also investigate the nature of fixed and variable financing costs.

Leverage The presence of fixed costs in a firm's cost structure.

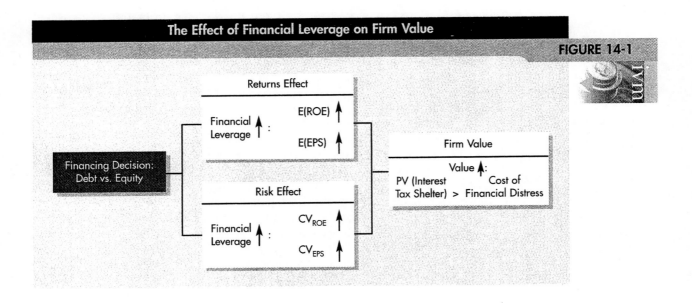

The Effect of Financial Leverage on Firm Value

FIGURE 14-1

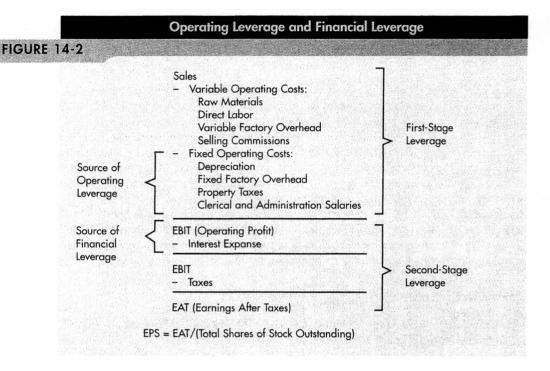

FIGURE 14-2 — Operating Leverage and Financial Leverage

The Relationship Between Operating Leverage and Financial Leverage

The discussion of the nature of the two types of leverage and their impact on a firm's profitability can be summarized in terms of the simplified two-stage income statement shown in Figure 14-2. **Operating leverage** involves the *substitution of fixed for variable operating costs*. The source of this type of leverage is the fixed cost of operating a firm. The higher the level of fixed operating costs, the larger will be the fluctuation in EBIT that is associated with a given change in sales. Thus, a firm's operating leverage is a direct function of the ratio of fixed to variable operating expenses. As this ratio increases, so does the level of operating leverage. For instance, a firm whose ratio of fixed to variable operating expenses is $300,000/$500,000 = 0.60 has higher operating leverage than a firm whose ratio is only $300,000/$1,000,000 = 0.30. Operating leverage can be referred to as first-stage leverage because its impact occurs earlier in the income statement than that of financial leverage. Since the behavior of operating expenses depends on the asset structure of the firm, operating leverage is determined by the investing decisions of a firm's financial managers.

In contrast to operating leverage, **financial leverage** is determined by financing decisions because it involves the *substitution of fixed for variable financing costs*. The source of this type of leverage is the fixed cost of the interest associated with debt financing. The fixed interest expense associated with debt financing alters the relationship between a firm's operating profit and its overall profit. As we will demonstrate shortly, the introduction of fixed interest expense causes EAT and EPS to change at a faster rate than EBIT. A firm's financial leverage is a direct function of the ratio of interest expense to EBIT. As this ratio increases, the level of a firm's financial leverage also increases. A firm with a ratio of interest expense to EBIT of $200,000/$600,000 = 0.33 has a higher level of financial leverage than a firm whose ratio is $200,000/$800,000 = 0.25.

Operating Leverage The presence of fixed operating costs in a firm's cost structure.

Financial Leverage The presence of fixed financing costs in a firm's cost structure.

The effects of the two types of leverage are analyzed individually because they can be controlled separately by financial managers. A firm that has a high level of operating leverage need not have a high level of financial leverage. In fact, a firm with high operating leverage will frequently want to limit its level of financial leverage. The combined effect of fixed operating and fixed financing costs on profits is a firm's total leverage. Total leverage alters the relationship between Sales and EAT or EPS. As fixed costs of any type are introduced into the income statement, the sensitivity of a firm's overall profits to changes in its sales is increased.

Fixed Versus Variable Financing Costs

The use of leverage involves replacing a variable cost with a fixed cost in order to increase profits. In the case of operating leverage, the fixed costs that are substituted for variable costs are shown in Figure 14-2. These costs and the substitution procedure are quite straightforward. The substitution process in the case of financial leverage, however, is rather subtle. The fixed cost that is introduced is the interest expense on debt financing. But what are the variable costs that are reduced? The answer to this question requires that we take a stockholder's viewpoint on firm profitability. What matters most to the individual stockholder is not the firm's overall profits (EAT) but the share of the profits to which each stockholder is entitled for each share of stock owned. Consequently, actions the firm's financial managers can take to improve the firm's EPS will be viewed favorably.

Table 14-1 shows the effect of financial leverage on the level and variability of a firm's EAT and EPS. The two firms in the table are identical except for their level of financial leverage. Firm C has no debt financing, while Firm D has financed 40%

The Effect of Financial Leverage on EAT and EPS — TABLE 14-1

Sales	$90,000	$100,000	$110,000
		Firm C	
EBIT	$20,000	$25,000	$30,000
Interest	—	—	—
EBT	$20,000	$25,000	$30,000
Taxes (50%)	10,000	12,500	15,000
EAT	$10,000	$12,500	$15,000
EPS	$1.00	$1.25	$1.50
		Firm D	
EBIT	$20,000	$25,000	$30,000
Interest	10,000	10,000	10,000
EBT	$10,000	$15,000	$20,000
Taxes (50%)	5,000	7,500	10,000
EAT	$5,000	$7,500	$10,000
EPS	$0.83	$1.25	$1.67

	Firm C	Firm D
Debt	$ —	$100,000
Equity	250,000	150,000
Total Assets	$250,000	$250,000
Total Shares ($25.00 each)	10,000	6,000
Interest (10%)	$ —	$10,000

of its assets with debt and 60% with equity. The information on the financial structures of the two firms is shown at the bottom of the table. Notice that both firms in this table have the same value of EBIT at each of the three sales levels. We have done this to hold constant the effects of operating leverage so that we can concentrate on the impact of financial leverage.

A close examination of Table 14-1 reveals that the impact of financial leverage on EAT and EPS is dissimilar. At all three EBIT levels, Firm D's EAT is smaller than that of Firm C. This seems to indicate that the financial leverage is unfavorable. Yet the effects of leverage on EPS are totally different. Firm D's EPS exceeds that of Firm C when EBIT is $30,000, while the reverse is true when EBIT is $20,000. Moreover, the two firms' EPS are identical if EBIT is $25,000. What is the effect of financial leverage on Firm D's profitability? Is the leverage favorable, unfavorable, or neutral?

Firm D has introduced financial leverage by replacing equity financing with debt financing that has increased the firm's fixed costs by $10,000 in interest expense. It has also reduced the number of shares of stock outstanding from 10,000 to 6,000. This decrease in stock means that there are fewer stockholders to share in the firm's profits. In other words, *the denominator in the EPS equation* (EPS = EAT/[total shares outstanding]) *has fallen. This is the variable "cost" that has been reduced through the leverage procedure.*[1] Both Firm C and Firm D have $250,000 in capital to finance their assets. Some of Firm D's capital suppliers have agreed to exchange their variable claim on the firm (a proportionate share of the firm's EAT for each share of stock) for a fixed claim (the interest payments on the debt). As a result, as the firm's EBIT increases or decreases, the EPS of the remaining stockholders will rise or fall at an even faster rate.

We can now answer the questions we posed above. Since stockholders are more concerned with EPS than EAT, the financial managers should assess the effect of financial leverage in terms of its impact on EPS. *Whether the leverage is favorable or unfavorable will depend on the relative impact on EPS of the increase in fixed cost (the interest expense) and the decrease in variable costs (the number of shares of stock outstanding).* If we assume that Firm D introduces financial leverage when its EBIT is $25,000, the immediate impact of the leverage on the level of EPS is neutral. The reduction in the shares outstanding is exactly offset by the increase in the interest expense so that Firm D's EPS ($1.25) is identical to that of Firm C. At an EBIT of $30,000, however, financial leverage is favorable, while it is unfavorable at an EBIT of $20,000. Since the effect of financial leverage on the size of a firm's EPS is uncertain, the use of leverage increases a firm's risk. We will now utilize a risk measure introduced in Chapter 6 (the coefficient of variation) to quantify the effect of leverage on firm risk.

Operating Risk and Financial Risk

Table 14-1 demonstrates that, if the financial managers are uncertain about the future level of the firm's EBIT, they will also be uncertain about whether financial leverage will be favorable or unfavorable. The effect of financial leverage under conditions of uncertainty can be examined by assuming that the three EBIT levels in that table form the following probability distribution:

---

[1] A reduction in the number of shares of stock outstanding does not qualify as a cost reduction in the conventional accounting sense. To the remaining stockholders, however, the impact of a decrease in shares through the use of financial leverage has an impact on EPS comparable to that of a decrease in variable operating costs through the use of operating leverage. Consequently, the decrease in the shares outstanding can also be analyzed by the financial managers as a type of cost reduction.

EBIT	Probability	EPS-Firm C	EPS-Firm D
$20,000	25%	$1.00	$0.83
25,000	50	1.25	1.25
30,000	25	1.50	1.67
	100%		

Figure 14-3 shows the probability distributions of the two firms' EBIT and EPS as well as their expected value, standard deviation, and coefficient of variation.

The EBIT distributions for the two firms are identical because financial leverage cannot affect either the level or variability of a firm's EBIT. The EPS distributions, on the other hand, are distinctly different. By increasing the sensitivity of Firm D's EPS to changes in EBIT, financial leverage has increased the riskiness of the firm. The dispersion of Firm D's probability distribution, as measured by the standard deviation, is greater than that of Firm C even though the expected value for each EPS distribution is $1.25.

Although we discussed the concept of operating risk in Chapter 11, we can now be more specific about how it can be measured. We can also relate it to the definition of financial risk and to the method that can be used to measure financial risk. **Operating risk** is the *variability of a firm's EBIT*. The amount of operating risk is determined by two factors: the nature of the business and the level of operating leverage. The level of sales and associated expenses is more uncertain for some firms than for others simply due to the industry in which they operate. Certain industries may be more subject to variations in EBIT due to factors such as

Operating Risk The variability in a firm's EBIT.

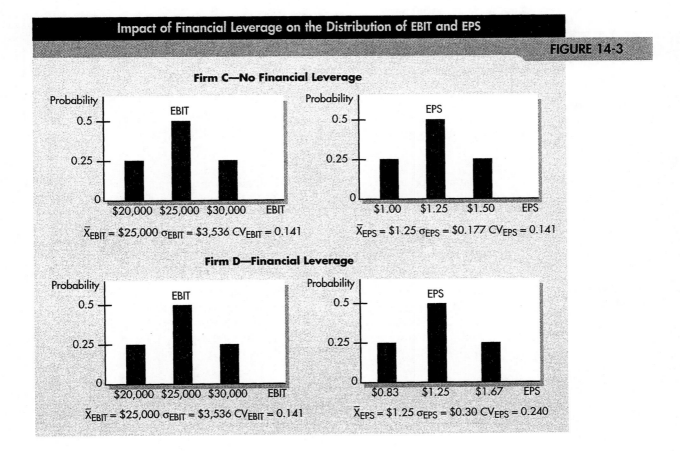

Impact of Financial Leverage on the Distribution of EBIT and EPS

FIGURE 14-3

Firm C—No Financial Leverage

$\bar{X}_{EBIT} = \$25,000 \quad \sigma_{EBIT} = \$3,536 \quad CV_{EBIT} = 0.141$

$\bar{X}_{EPS} = \$1.25 \quad \sigma_{EPS} = \$0.177 \quad CV_{EPS} = 0.141$

Firm D—Financial Leverage

$\bar{X}_{EBIT} = \$25,000 \quad \sigma_{EBIT} = \$3,536 \quad CV_{EBIT} = 0.141$

$\bar{X}_{EPS} = \$1.25 \quad \sigma_{EPS} = \$0.30 \quad CV_{EPS} = 0.240$

■ Valuation
ISSUES

HOW FINANCIAL MANAGERS VIEW THE DEBT VERSUS EQUITY FINANCING DECISION

In this chapter, we have examined the risk/return trade-off involved in the use of financial leverage. The actual financial structure of a firm, of course, will ultimately depend on the managers' perception of that trade-off. The chief financial officers (CFOs) at *Fortune 500* firms were recently surveyed for their view of financial structure decisions. Of the respondents to the survey, the large majority (69%) indicated that they consistently followed a preferred hierarchy of financing sources over time. Furthermore, their answers provide some insight into the reasons behind their preferences.

They were asked to rank the following types of financing in order of preference:

Financing Source	Preference
1. Internal Equity	1st (84%)
2. Straight Debt	2nd (72%)
3. Convertible Debt	3rd or 4th (74%)
4. Preferred Stock	5th or 6th (51%)
5. Convertible Preferred Stock	5th or 6th (66%)
6. Common Stock	6th (40%)

Internal equity (retained earnings) was, by far, the most popular source of financing, while straight debt was a solid second choice. Various sources of external equity were consistently less desirable to the CFOs. Although the managers apparently see advantages to the use of financial leverage, they seem more interested in minimizing the use of external financing, whatever its source.

The managers revealed the reasons for these preferences by indicating various factors that affect the form of financing employed by their firms. The dominant considerations were investment project cash flows and risk, avoidance of restrictive covenants and dilution of common stock EPS, the firm's tax rate, and voting control. Clearly, the managers are concerned about avoiding financial distress as well as protecting the financial interests of stockholders and maintaining flexibility in their own decisions. These concerns were echoed in the managers' ranking of various financial planning principles that might affect financial structure decisions:

Planning Principle	Ranking:	4	5
Financial Flexibility		33%	61%
Long-term Survival		11%	77%
Predictable Source of Funds		39%	36%
Financial Independence		27%	41%
Maximizing Stock Price		34%	38%

(Scale: 5 = most important; 1 = least important)

These responses indicate that avoidance of outside interference and disruptions, as well as maximization of firm value, dominate the financing decisions of these managers.

---

consumer preference changes, technological innovations, labor practices, and weather. The degree of variability in EBIT, however, will be increased if the firm introduces operating leverage into its operations.

Financial risk is determined by the use of financial leverage. As the level of financial leverage increases, the variability of a firm's EPS increases. In Figure 14-3, Firm D's use of financial leverage has increased the variability in its EPS over that of Firm C, which has no debt financing. This *increase in variability in EPS due to financial leverage* is called **financial risk**. The total risk of a firm is the sum of its operating risk and its financial risk. Because variability of a firm's EBIT will also be reflected in the variability of its EPS, total risk can be measured in terms of total variability in EPS. A firm's total risk can be divided into two components:[2]

Financial Risk The variability in the firm's earnings per share not due to operating leverage.

---

[2] We measure risk in terms of the coefficient of variation (CV) in order to adjust for size differences in the EPS and EBIT distributions.

$$\text{Total Risk} = \text{Operating Risk} + \text{Financial Risk}$$
$$= CV_{EBIT} + (CV_{EPS} - CV_{EBIT}) \qquad (1)$$

This division of the total risk of a firm into its components is an important concept for a firm's financial managers. It enables them to determine whether investing decisions or financing decisions have been the major source of variability in firm earnings in the past. For example, when we apply equation (1) to Firm D, we get

$$\text{Total Risk} = CV_{EBIT} + (CV_{EPS} - CV_{EBIT})$$
$$= 0.141 + (0.240 - 0.141) = 0.141 + 0.099 = 0.240$$

This calculation indicates that 60% (0.141/0.240) of the total variability in the firm's EPS is due to operating leverage. The remaining 40% (0.099/0.240) arises from the use of financial leverage.

Figure 14-4 summarizes the discussion of financial and operating leverage. Both types arise from the introduction of fixed costs into the firm's income statement. Fixed operating costs, which occur in the top half of the income statement, alter the sensitivity of EBIT to fluctuations in sales. The risk associated with operating leverage is measured by the variability in EBIT. The fixed interest expense on debt financing, which occurs in the bottom half of a firm's income statement, alters the sensitivity of EPS to fluctuations in EBIT. The risk associated with financial leverage is measured by the variability in EPS that is not caused by operating leverage. We discuss the two types of leverage in further detail in Appendix A to this chapter.

THE EFFECT OF FINANCIAL LEVERAGE ON FIRM PROFITABILITY

In this section, we will initially analyze the factors that determine the effect of financial leverage on the *magnitude* of a firm's profitability. We will then show how the EBIT-EPS breakeven chart can be used to evaluate this effect when EBIT is uncertain. Finally, the effect of leverage on the *variability* of a firm's profitability will be formally measured in terms of the standard deviation and coefficient of variation of various profitability measures.

Magnitude of Return and Financial Leverage

The data in Table 14-2 apply to Merion Controls, whose financial managers wish to examine the impact of each of three different financing plans on various performance measures: No Leverage (0% debt financing), Medium Leverage (40% debt financing), and High Leverage (60% debt financing). The three performance meas-

The Nature of Operating Risk and Financial Risk

SUMMARY FIGURE 14-4

Operating Risk—variability in EBIT
$$= f(\text{Nature of Business, Operating Leverage})$$
$$= CV_{EBIT}$$

Financial Risk—variability in EPS not caused by operating leverage
$$= f(\text{Financial Leverage})$$
$$= CV_{EPS} - CV_{EBIT}$$

ures are ROA (return on assets), ROE (return on equity), and EPS. Since the managers are uncertain about the firm's future sales and EBIT levels, they will examine the effects of the financing plans under each of three possible EBIT levels:

EBIT	Probability
$20,000	25%
35,000	50
50,000	25
	100%

Table 14-3 contains a summary of Merion's performance under each of the proposed financing plans. It reveals that ROA is *unaffected by financial leverage.* At each of the three EBIT levels, ROA is the same for all three financing plans. This result should not be surprising. ROA does not change with the level of debt financing because the level of both operating profits (EBIT) and total assets depends on investing decisions, not financing decisions.

The story changes significantly when the final two return measures, ROE and EPS, are calculated. The magnitude of both measures increases with financial leverage for an EBIT of $35,000 and $50,000 and declines with financial leverage for an EBIT of $20,000. Why does the *behavior of EPS and ROE depend on the level of EBIT*? The answer is that in changing the capital structure, Merion is substituting debt for equity. Whether that change in financing is beneficial to these two measures of returns to stockholders depends on the relationship between what the

The Effect of Financial Leverage on Merion Controls' EAT

TABLE 14-2

	No Leverage (0% Debt)		
EBIT	$ 20,000	$ 35,000	$ 50,000
Interest	—	—	—
EBT	$ 20,000	$ 35,000	$ 50,000
Taxes (50%)	10,000	17,500	25,000
EAT	$ 10,000	$ 17,500	$ 25,000
	Medium Leverage (40% Debt)		
EBIT	$ 20,000	$ 35,000	$ 50,000
Interest	10,000	10,000	10,000
EBT	$ 10,000	$ 25,000	$ 40,000
Taxes (50%)	5,000	12,500	20,000
EAT	$ 5,000	$ 12,500	$ 20,000
	High Leverage (60% Debt)		
EBIT	$ 20,000	$ 35,000	$ 50,000
Interest	15,000	15,000	15,000
EBT	$ 5,000	$ 20,000	$ 35,000
Taxes (50%)	2,500	10,000	17,500
EAT	$ 2,500	$ 10,000	$ 17,500
	No Leverage	**Medium Leverage**	**High Leverage**
Debt	$ —	$100,000	$150,000
Equity	250,000	150,000	100,000
Total Assets	$250,000	$250,000	$250,000
Total Shares ($25.00 each)	10,000	6,000	4,000
Interest (10%)	—	$ 10,000	$ 15,000

The Effect of Financial Leverage on the Magnitude of Merion Controls' Performance Measures

TABLE 14-3

Probability	25%		50%	25%
EBIT	$20,000		$35,000	$50,000
	ROA	**=**	**EBIT/Total Assets**	
No Leverage	8%		14%	20%
Medium Leverage	8		14	20
High Leverage	8		14	20
	ROE	**=**	**EAT/Owners' Equity**	
No Leverage	4.00%		7.00%	10.00%
Medium Leverage	3.30		8.33	13.33
High Leverage	2.50		10.00	17.50
	EPS	**=**	**EAT/# Shares**	
No Leverage	$1.00		$1.75	$2.50
Medium Leverage	0.83		2.08	3.33
High Leverage	0.63		2.50	4.38
Pretax Cost of Debt	10%		10%	10%

company can earn per dollar of funds invested and the cost per dollar of funds borrowed. At an EBIT of $20,000, ROA is 8%, which is less than the cost of debt (10%). At this level of EBIT, as Merion moves from the No Leverage plan to the High Leverage plan, EPS falls from $1.00 to $0.63, while the ROE declines from 4% to 2.50%. The source of this decline is the fact that the firm is financing assets that generate a rate of return of only 8% with debt that has a cost of 10%.[3]

When EBIT is $35,000 or $50,000, however, the ROA of 14% or 20% exceeds the 10% cost of debt. In this instance, both EPS and ROE rise as the proportion of debt financing increases from 0% to 60%. Since the firm has acquired debt with a lower cost than the return on the assets being financed, this difference results in an increase in ROE and EPS. Based on these results, it is possible to generalize about the relationship between financial leverage and EPS and ROE. *Whenever a firm's ROA exceeds the interest rate on debt, EPS and ROE will increase with financial leverage. If the interest rate on debt exceeds ROA, EPS and ROE will decrease. EPS and ROE will be unchanged by leverage when ROA is equal to the interest rate.* We will now examine the importance of the relationship between ROA and the interest rate on debt in terms of the EBIT-EPS breakeven chart.

EBIT-EPS Breakeven Chart

The performance measure that should be of major concern to Merion's financial managers is EPS because it is the share of the firm's EAT that each stockholder is entitled to that is important to any given owner. One convenient technique for analyzing the effect of financial leverage on the size of EPS under uncertain conditions is an EBIT-EPS breakeven chart, such as the one shown in Figure 14-5. The chart is simply a graph showing the values of EPS that will occur, given different values of EBIT.

---

[3] We are comparing the interest rate on debt financing with ROA because both the interest rate and ROA are pretax rates.

FIGURE 14-5

EBIT-EPS Breakeven Chart for Merion Controls

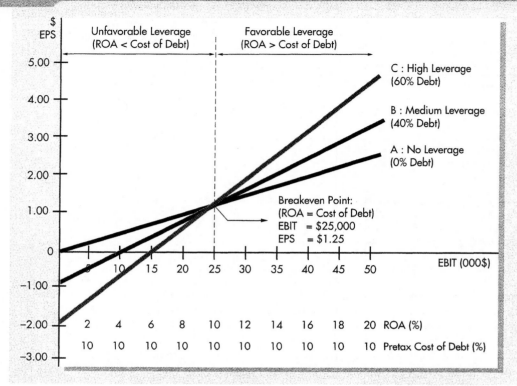

The three lines shown in the figure, which correspond to the three financing plans discussed above in connection with Merion Controls, are based on the EBIT and EPS data presented for Merion in Table 14-3. The heights of the three lines indicate the relative desirability of the alternative financing plans at each level of EBIT. At higher levels of EBIT, the High Leverage plan is most desirable because it maximizes EPS, while at low EBIT the No Leverage plan is most desirable.

The reason for this behavior of the lines becomes apparent in terms of the ROA and interest rate data listed below the graph's *x*-axis, which correspond to the various EBIT levels shown above. At the point of intersection of the three lines, the EBIT of $25,000 corresponds to an ROA of 10%, which is identical to the cost of debt. As stated earlier, under these conditions, EPS is unaffected by financial leverage. At EBIT levels above $25,000, ROA exceeds the cost of debt. Under these conditions, increases in leverage will increase EPS. When ROA is less than the interest rate on debt, increases in leverage will reduce EPS. This occurs at all EBIT levels below $25,000. *The slopes of the lines in a breakeven chart reflect the impact of financial leverage on the sensitivity of EPS to changes in EBIT.* Recall that financial leverage increases the responsiveness of EPS to an increase or decrease in EBIT. The graph demonstrates this point quite vividly. The large slope of the High Leverage plan results in large increases or decreases in EPS as EBIT moves left or right along the *x*-axis.

While the EBIT-EPS chart is a useful tool for analyzing the impact of financial leverage on firm profitability, it does not tell a firm's financial managers which financing plan to select. The basic problem with the breakeven chart is that the most desirable plan depends on an unknown value: the future level of EBIT. For example, Merion's financial managers know that the High Leverage plan will yield the largest EPS if EBIT exceeds $25,000 and the lowest EPS if EBIT is less than $25,000. What they do not know is which EBIT the firm's operations will generate in the future. Moreover, an incorrect guess about EBIT can be a costly mistake, as indicated by the negative EPS that is associated with the Medium and High Leverage plans at EBIT levels below $15,000. What is needed to accurately assess the desirability of financial leverage is a method of determining its impact on the riskiness as well as the magnitude of the firm's returns.

Variability of Return and Financial Leverage

When the financial managers of Merion Controls described three possible EBIT levels and their associated probabilities as shown in Table 14-3, they specified a discrete probability distribution of EBIT. The data from that table can also be used to determine a probability distribution such as Figure 14-3 for each of the three performance measures: ROA, ROE, and EPS. The expected value ($\overline{X}$), standard deviation (σ), and coefficient of variation (CV) of each of these three probability distributions are shown in Table 14-4.

Since operating earnings are not affected by financing decisions, the size and variability of both EBIT and ROA are the same for all three financing plans. However, *increases in financial leverage increase both the mean and the variability of the ROE and the EPS distributions.* Unlike the EBIT-EPS breakeven chart in Figure 14-5, the data on ROE and EPS in Table 14-4 make it readily apparent that the use of financial leverage involves a risk/return trade-off.

Should Merion Controls use debt capital to finance its assets? The firm's financial managers are faced with a dilemma. If they consider *return only*, they would be inclined to say *yes*. The more financial leverage, the higher the expected return to the owners as measured either by ROE or EPS. If they consider *risk only*, they would say *no*. The more debt in the capital structure, the greater the variability of ROE and EPS and, therefore, the greater the risk. Table 14-4 makes it clear that the financial managers must evaluate both risk and return. Their difficult task is to determine whether the increase in return is worth the increase in risk. The general

The Effect of Financial Leverage on the Variability of Merion Controls' Performance Measures

TABLE 14-4

	No Leverage (0% Debt)	Medium Leverage (40% Debt)	High Leverage (60% Debt)
$\overline{X}_{EBIT}$	$35,000	$35,000	$35,000
σ_{EBIT}	$10,605	$10,605	$10,605
CV_{EBIT}	0.303	0.303	0.303
$\overline{X}_{ROA}$	14%	14%	14%
σ_{ROA}	4.24%	4.24%	4.24%
CV_{ROA}	0.303	0.303	0.303
$\overline{X}_{ROE}$	7%	8.33%	10%
σ_{ROE}	2.12%	3.54%	5.30%
CV_{ROE}	0.303	0.425	0.530
$\overline{X}_{EPS}$	$1.75	$2.08	$2.50
σ_{EPS}	$0.53	$0.88	$1.33
CV_{EPS}	0.303	0.425	0.532

SUMMARY FIGURE 14-6

The Effect of Financial Leverage on Firm Profitability

Magnitude of Returns

Performance Measure			Effect
ROA	=	$\dfrac{\text{EBIT}}{\text{Total Assets}}$	No Effect
ROE	=	$\dfrac{\text{EAT}}{\text{Equity}}$	Increase: if ROA > Interest Rate on Debt Decrease: if ROA < Interest Rate on Debt
EPS	=	$\dfrac{\text{EAT}}{\text{Total Shares}}$	Increase: if ROA > Interest Rate on Debt Decrease: if ROA < Interest Rate on Debt

Variability of Returns (CV)

Performance Measure			Effect
ROA	=	$\dfrac{\text{EBIT}}{\text{Total Assets}}$	No Effect
ROE	=	$\dfrac{\text{EAT}}{\text{Equity}}$	Increase
EPS	=	$\dfrac{\text{EAT}}{\text{Total Shares}}$	Increase

effect of financial leverage on the magnitude and variability of a firm's profitability measures is summarized in Figure 14-6.

THE EFFECT OF FINANCIAL LEVERAGE ON FIRM VALUE

The basic rationale behind the Investment Valuation Model is that the proper criterion for any decision made by financial managers is its impact on firm value. This statement applies equally to both investing decisions and financing decisions. Thus, the solutions to the dilemma faced by Merion's financial managers can be found through the application of the IVM to the financial leverage decision. In this section, we will examine the impact of financial leverage on value in two stages. First, we will evaluate the effects of leverage in a tax-free environment. Next, we will introduce corporate taxes into the discussion and compare the effect of financial leverage on firm value under conditions of tax-deductibility and nondeductibility of corporate interest payments. We will then describe a levered firm valuation equation that incorporates the effect of the tax-deductibility of corporate interest payments.

Tax-Free Environment

The stockholders of a firm will favorably evaluate the risk/return trade-off involved in the investing and financing decisions made by financial managers only if they believe that the decisions provide *unique benefits* to them; in other words, if they must believe that they cannot achieve, on their own, the returns generated by the managers' decisions. A strong argument can be made for unique returns from the managers' *investing* decisions due to their expertise in developing and evaluating investment proposals. In fact, it is precisely this managerial investment expertise that induces stockholders to invest in a given firm.

■ Financial

ISSUES

FINANCIAL LEVERAGE HITS NEW HEIGHTS AT PROFESSIONAL SPORTS TEAMS

This chapter discussion of financial leverage stresses the trade-off between the interest tax shield and the costs of financial distress as a firm's level of debt increases. If a firm is to minimize its cost of financing and maximize its value to stockholders, managers must try to identify the level of debt at which the trade-off begins to decrease a firm's value. While the managers and creditors of industrial and service companies seem to be well aware of the limits to financial leverage, professional sports teams and their creditors seem to be unconcerned about the dangers of excessive financial leverage.

In today's market for multimillion-dollar player salaries, team owners have looked to new stadiums as a source of revenue to cover the cost of player contracts. While the additional revenue from skyboxes and advertising appear attractive to owners, the cost of building the stadiums has increasingly fallen on the teams as the public has become reluctant to use tax dollars to finance the new venues. The owners of the St. Louis Blues borrowed $100 million to help cover the $170 million cost of their new hockey arena. The owner of the NBA Washington Wizards and NHL Washington Capitals took on an estimated $225 million in debt to finance the MCI Center, which opened in 1998.

The additional team revenue from these stadiums is approximately $5 to 12 million annually, which can easily disappear in the form of signing bonuses and salary increases. In the meantime, the level of outstanding debt on the teams' balance sheets has skyrocketed. In 1998, the debt at nineteen franchises exceeded 100% of team value. At the San Francisco Giants, outstanding debt represented about 164% of franchise value even before the additional debt required by Pacific Bell Park. The NHL Tampa Bay Lightning's debt of $177 million is more than twice the estimated team value of only $75 million.

The prospects for servicing all this debt are far from assured. The debt service for stadium and arena mortgages, with their 20-to-30-year maturities, is provided mainly by revenues from luxury seating and advertising. Since these contracts must be renewed every three to five years, the risk of default seems very real indeed. This is particularly true in those instances such as Pacific Bell Park, where initial forecasts suggest that stadium cash flows will be barely sufficient to service the debt. In such a situation, poor team performance, accompanied by declining fan interest and attendance, can easily spell financial distress for the team owner.

In a tax-free world, however, the case for unique benefits to stockholders from the managers' *financing* decisions is very weak. Assume that the managers can increase the expected EPS of their firm by 10% through the use of corporate financial leverage. Stockholders can duplicate this increase in returns through the use of *personal* financial leverage. A given stockholder can simply use debt financing to purchase enough additional shares of stock in the firm to boost the share of firm earnings that he or she is entitled to by 10%. Furthermore, the extra risk associated with the increase in expected earnings will be the same for both corporate leverage and personal leverage. Since the risk/return trade-off is identical with both types of financial leverage, *corporate debt and personal debt are said to be perfect substitutes in a tax-free world*.

Effect of Corporate Taxes

In reality, a firm does not operate in a tax-free world. Since taxes are an important part of the firm's environment, their effect on the relationship between financial leverage and firm value should be evaluated. *Ignoring financial distress* for the moment, corporate taxes play the major role in understanding the effect of financial leverage on firm value. In most countries, the tax law favors firms that borrow money because the interest on debt is a tax-deductible expense, while dividend

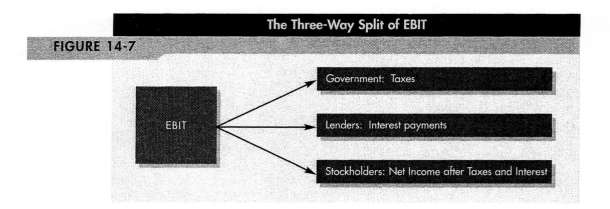

FIGURE 14-7

The Three-Way Split of EBIT

payments on stock are not. The tax-deductibility of interest makes it possible to increase a firm's value through the use of financial leverage.

To understand the role of taxes, it is necessary to consider how the operating earnings of a firm are distributed to the principal claimants. The claimants on a firm's profits are the owners or stockholders, the lenders, and the government. The sum of their claims must equal EBIT because the owners claim the residual that remains after the others have received their payment. This three-way split of EBIT, which is depicted in Figure 14-7, can be expressed in the following form:

$$
\begin{aligned}
\text{EBIT} &= \text{Claims of Government} + \text{Claims of Lenders} + \text{Claims of Owners} \\
&= \text{Taxes} + \text{Interest Payments} + \text{Owners' Net Income} \quad\quad (2)
\end{aligned}
$$

Let's return to Merion Controls, whose total assets are valued at $250,000. Suppose that a group of investors has the opportunity to purchase the company for that amount. After an evaluation of the firm, they feel it is a good investment. Since the investors' available cash is only $150,000, they want to make use of financial leverage by borrowing the remainder of the purchase price. The investors determine that there are *two alternative methods of acquiring the required debt financing*. First, they could borrow money on their own personal account and then pay $250,000 in cash for the company. The financial structure of the firm would then look like the No Leverage case in Table 14-2. While the corporation would have no debt and $250,000 of equity, the owners would have $100,000 *in personal debt* and an investment of $150,000 of their own cash in Merion Controls.

The second financing plan would be to pay the $150,000 of their own money and to promise to pay the remaining $100,000 out of future earnings generated by the firm. Under this plan, the company would borrow the required $100,000. The financial structure of the company would then be that shown for the Medium Leverage case in Table 14-2. There would be $100,000 of corporate debt and $150,000 in equity. Under either financing plan, the investors acquire Merion Controls with an investment of only $150,000 of their own cash.

Interest Not Tax-Deductible. In order to evaluate the effect of taxes on the division of Merion's income, assume initially that interest is not a tax-deductible expense for corporations. If the firm's EBIT is $35,000, the corporate tax rate (T) is 50%, and the interest rate (r) on the debt (D) is 10%, the division of income among the three claimants will be:

	Plan 1 (Personal Debt)	Plan 2 (Corporate Debt)
EBIT	$35,000	$35,000
Corporate Taxes (50%)	17,500	17,500
Earnings Before Interest	17,500	17,500
Corporate Interest = rD	—	10,000
EAT	$17,500	$ 7,500
Personal Interest = rD	10,000	—
Owners' Net Income (Residual)	$ 7,500	$ 7,500

Under either plan, the division of EBIT is identical. Corporate taxes are $17,500; interest expense is $10,000; and residual earnings are $7,500. The only significant difference between the plans is who makes the interest payments to the lenders. Under Plan 1, the owners must make the interest payments on their personal debt out of the firm's EAT. Under Plan 2, the firm pays the interest on its corporate debt. The value of the firm, which is determined by the size of the owners' share of EBIT, will be the same under both plans. Consequently, there is no reason to prefer one plan over the other if interest is not tax-deductible. The division of the firm's EBIT is summarized in Figure 14-8.

These results can be generalized to all investors and the capital markets. *If the assumed conditions of no financial distress and nondeductibility of interest were true,* there would be *no reason for the value of a levered firm to be different from that of an unlevered firm.* As in the case of the tax-free environment, corporate debt and personal debt would be perfect substitutes. Figure 14-9 depicts the relationship between the value of the firm and financial leverage. V_U denotes the value of the unlevered firm (no debt financing), and V_L is the value of the levered firm. Under the assumption of no financial distress and no tax deduction for interest expense, the V_L curve must be flat because financial leverage cannot influence value.

The Three-Way Split of Merion Controls' EBIT When Interest Is Not Tax-Deductible

FIGURE 14-8

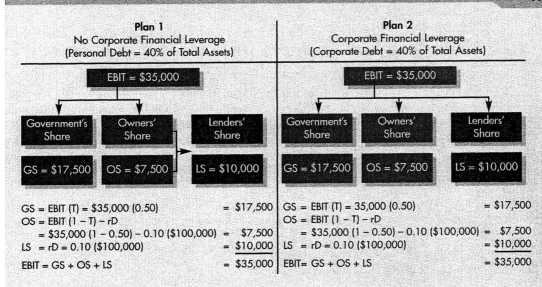

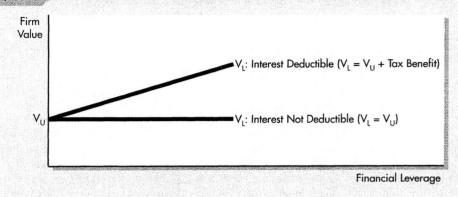

FIGURE 14-9

Firm Value and Financial Leverage Without Financial Distress

Interest Tax-Deductible.   Contrary to the assumption above, interest expense *is* tax-deductible. We will now repeat the analysis of financial leverage under this more realistic tax condition. The effect of the two plans on the three claimants is shown below.

	Plan 1 (Personal Debt)	Plan 2 (Corporate Debt)
EBIT	$35,000	$35,000
Corporate Interest	—	10,000
EBT	35,000	25,000
Taxes (50%)	17,500	12,500
EAT	$17,500	$12,500
Personal Interest	10,000	—
Owners' Net Income (Residual)	$ 7,500	$12,500

Notice how the new assumption about the tax-deductibility of interest has changed the results. The owners' share of EBIT is $5,000 larger under the corporate debt plan. The $5,000 increase in the owners' net income is made possible by a $5,000 decrease in the firm's taxes. Since the firm's tax rate is 50%, the $10,000 corporate interest payment has reduced the firm's taxable income by $10,000 and its taxes by $5,000. In effect, the government is subsidizing the interest by bearing half the cost of debt through reduced taxes. The effect of the new tax assumption on the division of EBIT is summarized in Figure 14-10.

The fact that interest is also a deductible expense to the individual investor does not eliminate the tax advantage of corporate leverage. Including personal taxes into our analysis simply restates the tax advantage on an after-personal-tax basis. For example, if the investors in Merion Controls were in a 30% tax bracket, the marginal effect of their taxes on the dividends that they could receive from Merion each year is:

	Plan 1 Personal Debt	Plan 2 Corporate Debt
Gross Income (Dividends)	$17,500	$12,500
Less: Interest Expense	10,000	0
Taxable Income	$ 7,500	$12,500
Tax (30%)	$ 2,250	$ 3,750

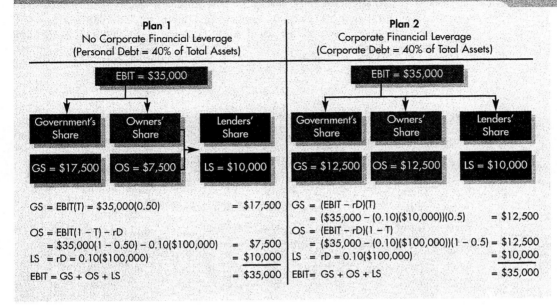

FIGURE 14-10
The Three-Way Split of Merion Controls' EBIT When Interest Is Tax-Deductible

Plan 1	Plan 2
No Corporate Financial Leverage (Personal Debt = 40% of Total Assets)	Corporate Financial Leverage (Corporate Debt = 40% of Total Assets)

Plan 1:

EBIT = $35,000

Government's Share — Owners' Share — Lenders' Share

GS = $17,500   OS = $7,500   LS = $10,000

GS = EBIT(T) = $35,000(0.50) = $17,500

OS = EBIT(1 – T) – rD
= $35,000(1 – 0.50) – 0.10($100,000) = $7,500

LS = rD = 0.10($100,000) = $10,000

EBIT = GS + OS + LS = $35,000

Plan 2:

EBIT = $35,000

Government's Share — Owners' Share — Lenders' Share

GS = $12,500   OS = $12,500   LS = $10,000

GS = (EBIT – rD)(T)
= ($35,000 – (0.10)($10,000))(0.5) = $12,500

OS = (EBIT – rD)(1 – T)
= ($35,000 – (0.10)($100,000))(1 – 0.5) = $12,500

LS = rD = 0.10($100,000) = $10,000

EBIT= GS + OS + LS = $35,000

While it is true that, under Plan 2, more personal taxes are paid, the total government share of EBIT remains smaller:

	Plan 1	Plan 2
Corporate Tax	$17,500	$12,500
Personal Tax	2,250	3,750
Total Taxes	$19,750	$16,250

The difference in the government's share of EBIT is still $3,500 less under Plan 2 than it is under Plan 1. This difference is simply the after-personal-tax proceeds from the extra $5,000 of owners' taxable income under Plan 2: ($5,000)(1 – 0.30). Unless the marginal personal tax rate exceeds 100%, the advantage of corporate leverage remains.[4]

It is possible to extend these results to investors in general and to the capital markets. When *interest is tax-deductible to the corporation*, there is a definite reason for the value of a levered firm to exceed the value of an unlevered firm. *Corporate debt and personal debt are not perfect substitutes.* Stockholders cannot achieve the same cash flow through the use of financial leverage as corporations because tax laws favor the use of corporate debt. Consequently, investors should be willing to pay a premium for shares of a levered firm. *In the absence of financial distress, the value of a firm increases steadily with leverage, as shown in Figure 14-9.*

---

[4] Implicit in our discussion is the assumption that bond income is taxed at the same rate as dividends and capital gains. We have ignored the effect of differential tax rates in our analysis for two reasons. First, it is difficult to generalize about their effect because not all stockholders are in the same tax bracket. Second, the net effect of personal taxes on the relationship between financial leverage and firm value remains an unsettled question among researchers.

The Impact of Leverage on a No-Growth Firm

The reason that the use of corporate debt increases the value of the firm is that the reduction in corporate tax liability cannot be matched through personal borrowing. By looking at the difference between the two tax calculations in Figure 14-10, the difference in corporate tax can be isolated. For the unlevered firm in Plan 1, the tax calculation is:

$$\text{Tax}_U = (\text{EBIT})(T) = (\$35,000)(0.50) = \$17,500$$

For the levered firm in Plan 2, the tax calculation is:

$$\text{Tax}_L = (\text{EBIT} - rD)(T) = [\$35,000 - (0.10)(100,000)](0.50) = \$12,500$$

When Tax_L is subtracted from Tax_U, we get:

$$\begin{aligned}
\text{Tax}_U - \text{Tax}_L &= (\text{EBIT})(T) - (\text{EBIT} - rD)(T) \\
&= (\text{EBIT})(T) - (\text{EBIT})(T) + rTD \\
&= rTD \\
&= (0.10)(\$100,000)(0.50) = \$5,000
\end{aligned}$$

Algebraically, the difference in taxes paid is rTD. This quantity represents the extra Interest Tax Benefit (ITB) available to firms that have debt in their capital structure:

$$\text{ITB} = rTD \qquad (3)$$

It is the tax saving in equation (3) that leads to an increase in the value of a firm as its level of debt rises.

Firm Value. In the case of a firm that is paying out all its earnings as dividends to stockholders, EBIT is not expected to grow over time. Due to the lack of growth, the firm would also plan to have a constant amount of debt in its capital structure. As a result, the Interest Tax Benefit for the firm would be expected to be a level future stream of annual tax savings equal to rTD. From the viewpoint of the IVM, the total valuation benefit from those savings is measured by their present value.

The discount rate to be used in computing that present value should reflect the degree of certainty that the tax benefits will actually materialize, which is essentially the likelihood that the firm will remain in business to claim them. Thus, it is the underlying operating (business) risk of the firm that defines the appropriate discount rate. We can think of this discount rate as the RRR that would apply to value the firm if it were unlevered, and if operating risk were the only risk present for investors.

If we let K_U denote that discount rate, we can express the present value of the anticipated Interest Tax Benefit to a no-growth firm as:

$$\text{Value(ITB)} = \sum_{t=1}^{\infty} \frac{rTD}{(1 + K_U)^t} = \frac{rTD}{K_U}$$

We can simplify this expression by letting the quantity rT/K_U be represented by the Greek letter θ (theta):

$$\theta = rT/K_U \qquad (4)$$

Therefore:

$$\text{Value(ITB)} = \theta D \qquad (5)$$

■ International

ISSUES

EASTERN EUROPE JOINS THE EUROBOND MARKET

Central and eastern European governments and companies historically have found it very difficult to issue debt financing on global financial markets. The political and economic uncertainty in this region has made western

investors very reluctant to become involved with these borrowers. Beginning in the mid-1990s, however, this reluctance was overcome by the desire to earn the high yields available on this segment of the emerging markets. For their part, the private and governmental borrowers have been quick to take advantage of this new interest of institutional investors in the West.

Prior to 1993, external debt financing in central and eastern Europe was a rarity. The major form of outstanding debt was Brady bonds, which were securities that arose from the rescheduling of sovereign debt originally issued by communist governments. Private corporate bonds did not exist. As these centralized governments were replaced by more democratic institutions and as state-owned businesses were privatized, institutional investors in the developed countries began to take notice. By year-end 1996, total debt from the region had reached $5 billion; by 1997, it had quadrupled to $20 billion. Although small by developed country standards, the growth rate in this debt made it the fastest growing segment of emerging markets debt.

The reason for this dramatic growth is straightforward: institutional investors saw a very favorable risk/return trade-off in the debt available from this area of the world. In comparison to debt from other emerging market countries, the debt from eastern Europe offered higher returns for a given level of risk. For example, in June 1997, a three-year Eurobond issued by a Russian bank with a B+ credit rating from Standard & Poor's offered a yield of 420 basis points (4.20%) over three-year U.S. Treasury notes. Comparable risk notes of Brazilian banks, on the other hand, offered a yield spread of only 220 basis points over U.S. Treasuries. Russian debt proved to be particularly popular due to rapid improvements in that country's political and economic stability. Russia initially issued $1 billion in government bonds in 1996. By 1997, that country accounted for some $6 billion in new emerging market debt.

For extremely yield-conscious institutions, the investment grade debt of countries such as Poland, Hungary, and the Czech Republic was too conservative. Furthermore, as investors gained familiarity with Russian debt, the yield spread over the debt of western governments narrowed. As a result, some institutional investors began to seek out higher yield issues from higher risk issuers such as Bulgaria and Ukraine. The highest yields of all were available on debt issued in local currencies. Ruble-denominated Russian government bonds offered yields of 20% to 30% percent in late 1997. The annual yield on ruble bonds of private corporations reached as high as 100%. Ironically, investors realized too late the risk/return trade-off on Russian debt as an economic crisis in 1998 caused massive devaluation of the ruble and default on outstanding debt.

If the value of an unlevered firm is V_U, the value of the same firm levered (V_L) will be greater by the value of the expected Interest Tax Benefit arising from the firm's debt:

$$V_L = V_U + \theta D \qquad (6)$$

The factor θ (a "valuation multiplier" on debt) captures the combined effect of (1) the *riskiness* of the firm's operations, (2) the *interest rate* on its debt, and (3) the corporate *tax rate*. It seems reasonable that all three elements combined would affect the valuation benefit from debt financing in a positive manner. That is, the greater the amount of the firm's debt, the larger is V_L as depicted by the upward sloping line in Figure 14-9.

As an example of the use of equation (6), consider Rathco, Inc., which presently has no long-term debt and has 1,500,000 shares of common stock outstanding selling for $50 per share. All of the firm's EPS of $6.00 is paid out as dividends. The firm is considering borrowing $20 million to change the firm's capital structure by repurchasing common shares. Assume that the corporate tax rate is 40% and that the interest rate on debt is 9%.

With EPS and DPS of $6.00 and a $50 share price, the rate of return that investors require on the common shares of Rathco can be estimated with the no-growth stock valuation equation from Chapter 7:

$$K_U = D_1/P_0 = \$6.00/\$50 = 0.12 = 12\%$$

With no debt, the total market value of the company is ($50)(1,500,000 shares) = $75 million. After taking on debt and repurchasing shares, the new total value of Rathco will be:

$$
\begin{aligned}
V_L &= V_U + \theta D = V_U + (rT/K_U)(D) \\
&= \$75,000,000 + [(0.09)(0.40)/(0.12)](\$20,000,000) \\
&= \$75,000,000 + \$6,000,000 \\
&= \$81,000,000
\end{aligned}
$$

Thus, replacing $20 million of equity with debt will increase the total market value of the company to $81 million from $75 million. Similar calculations can be performed for other levels of debt.

Stock Price. In our example, the increase in the total liabilities of the firm is accompanied by an increase in its value. From the individual stockholder's viewpoint, however, the important question is whether financial leverage increases his or her *personal wealth* as indicated by the firm's stock price.

The new $81 million market value of Rathco, derived from equation (6), represents the total value of both the firm's common shares (V_S) and its debt (D):

$$V_L = V_S + D \tag{7}$$

Substituting the figures from the example into this relationship and solving for the value of V_S gives us:

$$V_S = V_L - D = \$81,000,000 - \$20,000,000 = \$61,000,000$$

The total market value of Rathco's stock should be $61 million after the firm alters its capital structure.

Suppose that Rathco is able to repurchase its common shares in the market at an average price of $53.33 per share.[5] If so, it will be able to repurchase:

$$
\begin{aligned}
\text{Shares Repurchased} &= \frac{\text{Amount of New Debt Issued}}{\text{Average Repurchase Price}} \\
&= \$20,000,000/\$53.33 \\
&= 375,000 \text{ shares}
\end{aligned}
$$

and the market price of the stock after the repurchase will be:

$$
\begin{aligned}
\text{New Stock Price} &= \frac{\text{New Stock Value}}{\text{Original Shares} - \text{Repurchased Shares}} \\
&= \$61,000,000/(1,500,000 - 375,000) \\
&= \$54.22 \text{ per share}
\end{aligned}
$$

---

[5] This is an assumption only. The actual repurchase price in any given situation will depend largely on how the firm goes about the repurchase and on the information that is conveyed to stockholders about the repurchase before it occurs. A price of $53.33 for the repurchase was chosen here simply because it makes some of the other numbers in the illustration come out to round numbers.

To summarize, not only has the use of financial leverage increased the total value of Rathco, but it has also increased the value of the remaining shares of common stock and made every stockholder better off than before. The investors who sold their shares back to the company received an average of $53.33 per share, while the ones who remain have shares worth $54.22 each. In both cases, these values are higher than the $50 per share that prevailed when the firm was unlevered.

Required Rate of Return on Equity. As we noted earlier in this chapter, when a firm adds financial leverage to its operating leverage, the risk borne by common stockholders increases. Consequently, the stockholders will demand some additional compensation in the form of a higher expected (and required) rate of return. Equation (6) allows us to identify exactly how much the RRR on equity will increase.

In the Rathco example, with EPS (and DPS) of $6.00 per share and 1,500,000 shares outstanding when the firm is unlevered, total expected annual earnings after taxes (EAT) are:

$$EAT = (EPS)(Total\ Shares) = (\$6.00)(1,500,000) = \$9,000,000$$

With a corporate tax rate of 40%, the corresponding annual EBIT is:

$$EBIT = (EAT)/(1 - T) = (\$9,000,000)/(1 - 0.40) = \$15,000,000$$

After borrowing $20 million at the assumed interest rate of 9% per annum, Rathco will incur ($20,000,000)(0.09) = $1,800,000 each year in tax-deductible interest costs. Thus, the new level of EAT for the firm will be:

$$EAT = (EBIT - Interest)(1 - T) = (\$15,000,000 - \$1,800,000)(1 - 0.40) = \$7,920,000$$

Since 375,000 common shares are repurchased, 1,125,000 shares will remain outstanding. The new level of EPS and DPS therefore will be:

$$EPS = DPS = EAT/(Total\ Shares) = \$7,920,000/1,125,000 = \$7.04\ per\ share$$

Due to the Interest Tax Benefit from debt, this figure is up by $1.04 per share, or 17.3%, from the $6.00 of EPS and DPS that prevailed before the stock repurchase.

Notice that the stock price rises proportionately less than EPS and DPS. The new price is $54.22 per share, which is an increase of $4.22, or just 8.4% from the original $50 per share when the firm was unlevered. This smaller proportionate increase reflects the additional risk to investors associated with financial leverage in the firm's capital structure. We can directly measure the impact of the extra risk on investors' RRR by calculating the new expected (and required) rate of return on the market value of Rathco's common equity:

$$K_E = DPS/(Stock\ Price) = \$7.04/\$54.22 = 0.130 = 13.0\%$$

which is greater than the RRR on unlevered equity, $K_U = 12.0\%$, that prevailed prior to the share repurchase. Nonetheless, the Interest Tax Benefit outweighs the extra risk, and common stockholders realize an increase in their wealth through an increase in the market price of their shares.

While the indicated effect on the required return on equity depends on the particular numbers chosen for the Rathco example, there is a simple expression for the general relationship between K_U and K_E, which can be derived from equations (6) and (7):

$$K_E = \frac{K_U - rL}{1 - L} \qquad (8)$$

where L represents a firm's "leverage ratio." It is equal to the amount of the firm's debt divided by the total market value of the firm:[6]

$$L = D/V_L \tag{9}$$

Equation (8) is plotted in Figure 14-11. For the unlevered firm, K_E is equal to K_U because $D = 0$. As debt is introduced into the firm's capital structure and L increases, K_E increases in a curvilinear pattern. Using that equation for the Rathco example, K_E for the levered firm is:

$$K_E = \frac{0.120 - (0.09)(\$20,000,000/\$81,000,000)}{1 - (\$20,000,000/\$81,000,000)}$$
$$= (0.120 - 0.022)/(1 - 0.247)$$
$$= 0.130 = 13.0\%$$

which matches our earlier result.

The effect of leverage on K_E can be identified from a slightly different perspective if we focus not on the ratio of debt to *total capitalization* as the measure of the firm's leverage but instead on the ratio of debt to *equity*. An alternative algebraic manipulation of equations (6) and (7) yields the following relationship:

$$K_E = K_U + (K_U - r)\left(\frac{D}{V_S}\right) \tag{10}$$

In this form, the connection between leverage and common stockholders' RRR is perhaps more transparent. Equation (10) indicates that K_E is equal to K_U when the firm has no debt outstanding, but that K_E rises steadily—and linearly—as the ratio of debt to equity increases. Here, we can think of the term $(K_U - r)$ as a kind of "risk premium" factor for financial leverage. It represents the difference between the unlevered RRR on equity for the firm and the interest rate the firm must pay to

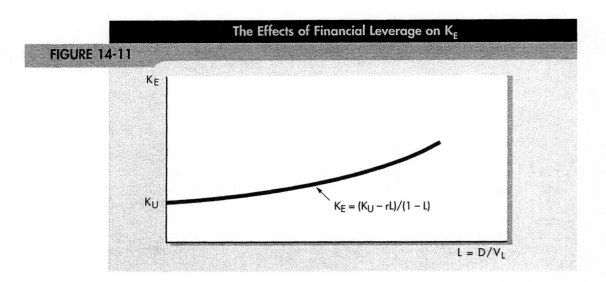

FIGURE 14-11

The Effects of Financial Leverage on K_E

$K_E = (K_U - rL)/(1 - L)$

$L = D/V_L$

---

[6] D should be defined in all these expressions as the market value rather than the book value of the firm's debt. Since we are talking here about newly issued debt, the two will coincide in our case—but that will not necessarily be true for old debt, which may have been issued at interest rates different from today's.

borrow. It is similar in spirit to the risk premium factor $(K_M - i)$ of the Capital Asset Pricing Model that was introduced in Chapter 6. Moreover, just as that factor in the CAPM is multiplied by β to reflect the level of systematic risk of the firm, the factor $(K_U - r)$ is multiplied by the ratio D/V_S in equation (10) to capture the level of the firm's financial risk.

While they have a different look, equations (8) and (10) both express the same underlying relationship, and they will produce the same numerical results. Thus, for our Rathco example, D is equal to $20 million and V_S is the other $61 million of firm value. With K_U equal to 12% and r equal to 9%, equation (10) predicts K_E to be:

$$K_E = 0.12 + (0.12 - 0.09)\left(\frac{\$20,000,000}{\$61,000,000}\right)$$

$$K_E = 0.12 + 0.01 = 0.13 = 13.0\%$$

which is consistent with the answer from equation (8). Equation (10) is plotted in Figure 14-12.

The Impact of Leverage on a Growing Firm

The same relationships we have just outlined apply to a situation in which a firm is retaining some of its earnings to support growth over time. Recall from Chapter 7 that there are two equations that allow us to value a share of common stock:

No Growth in Dividends	Dividends Growing at the Annual Rate g
$P_0 = D_1/K_E$	$P_0 = D_1/(K_E - g)$

The current stock price P_0 represents the present value of the expected future stream of dividends per share. Subtracting g from K_E in the denominator of this present value calculation is what captures the extra value of a growing dividend stream. There is an exact parallel here to the present value of the Interest Tax Benefit for a levered firm.

Firm Value. As a firm grows by retaining earnings, it obviously will build up the equity component of its capital structure over time. If leverage has a positive effect on firm value, the firm's managers should also plan to keep adding debt at the same rate. In fact, this is exactly what the majority of firms do. Their policy about

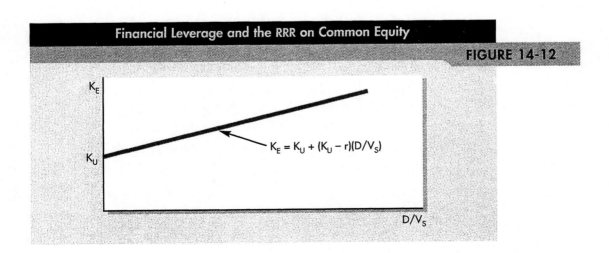

Financial Leverage and the RRR on Common Equity

FIGURE 14-12

$$K_E = K_U + (K_U - r)(D/V_S)$$

borrowing is to choose a target figure for the leverage ratio L and attempt to stay near that ratio as the firm expands. Thus, the magnitude of the firm's debt and its Interest Tax Benefit will be expected to grow at the same rate g at which retained earnings increase.

Under such a policy, the "valuation multiplier" on debt that applies when the associated annual Interest Tax Benefit *begins* at the level rTD becomes:

$$\theta_G = rT/(K_U - g) \tag{11}$$

This new multiplier results in a larger present value for the expected future tax savings than in the case when the firm is not growing ($\theta = rT/K_U$). Accordingly, the equation for the total value of a growing levered company is:

$$V_L = V_U + \theta_G D \tag{12}$$

To see the implications, let us return once more to our Rathco example. With a corporate tax rate of 40%, if the firm is unlevered and expects to earn $15 million of EBIT in the current year, its EAT will be $9 million. Assume the firm decides to retain half those earnings and, as a result, is perceived by investors to be able to grow its earnings and dividends in the future at a 6% annual rate. Taking the value of $K_U = 12\%$, which we had specified as investors' RRR for unlevered Rathco, the total value of both the firm and its common stock will be:

$$V_U = V_S = \text{(Current Year's Total Dividend)}/(K_U - g)$$
$$= (\$4,500,000)/(0.12 - 0.06)$$
$$= \$75,000,000$$

which, by design, is the same figure as for the no-growth case. The present value effect of a smaller initial dividend is just offset by the present value effect of the expected future growth in that dividend. With 1,500,000 common shares outstanding, Rathco's stock price will again be $50 per share as an unlevered company.

Suppose, as before, the firm borrows $20 million at a 9% interest rate in order to engage in a stock repurchase program and is able once more to buy back 375,000 shares at an average price of $53.33 per share, leaving 1,125,000 shares still outstanding. According to equations (11) and (12), the resulting total value of levered Rathco will be:

$$V_L = V_U + [rT/(K_U - g)](D)$$
$$= \$75,000,000 + [(0.09)(0.40)/(0.12 - 0.06)](\$20,000,000)$$
$$= \$75,000,000 + \$12,000,000 = \$87,000,000$$

which is an increase of $12 million rather than only the $6 million figure we calculated when Rathco was not expected to grow. The value of a growing Interest Tax Benefit is greater.

Stock Price. The effect on Rathco's share price is also greater. If the new total value of the firm is $87 million, the new total value of its common stock is:

$$V_S = V_L - D = \$87,000,000 - \$20,000,000 = \$67,000,000$$

and the associated new per-share price, with 1,125,000 shares outstanding, will be:

$$\text{New Stock Price} = \$67,000,000/1,125,000 = \$59.56 \text{ per share}$$

up from the figure of $54.22 per share we calculated in the no-growth case. Since investors will presumably understand that this is likely to happen, it also seems likely that a growing Rathco will have to pay more than just $53.33 per share for the stock it repurchases in its buyback program. Since a higher repurchase price reduces the number of shares repurchased, the result will be a final stock price somewhere between $54.22 and $59.56 per share.

Required Rate of Return on Equity.   We can identify the impact of leverage and the stock repurchase program on the company's required return on equity, K_E, from the growing-firm valuation relationship:

$$V_S = \text{(Current Year's Total Dividend)}/(K_E - g)$$

Since we either already know or can determine all the numbers in this expression except K_E, we can solve for that figure. Thus, after the firm borrows $20 million, the interest costs of $1.8 million will result in EAT in the current year of:

$$
\begin{aligned}
\text{EAT} &= (\text{EBIT} - rD)(1 - T) \\
&= [\$15,000,000 - (0.09)(\$20,000,000)](1 - 0.40) \\
&= (\$13,200,000)(0.60) = \$7,920,000
\end{aligned}
$$

as in the no-growth case.

Because Rathco needed to reinvest $4.5 million of earnings in the current year to support a 6% growth rate when it was unlevered, it will still need $4.5 million of new investments after it is levered. With its debt initially at $20 million and also growing at 6% a year, an extra:

$$(0.06)(\$20,000,000) = \$1,200,000$$

of new debt capacity will become available during the year to provide part of the funding for these investments. Retained earnings must supply the rest of the $4.5 million:

$$\text{Required Retained Earnings} = \$4,500,000 - \$1,200,000 = \$3,300,000$$

which will therefore allow the firm to pay a dividend equal to the difference between total EAT and the needed amount of retentions. That will produce a dividend of:

$$
\begin{aligned}
\text{Current Year's Total Dividend} &= \text{EAT} - \text{Required Retained Earnings} \\
&= \$7,920,000 - \$3,300,000 \\
&= \$4,620,000
\end{aligned}
$$

Notice that this is *larger* than the $4.5 million of dividends that the firm could pay in the current year *before* it became levered. The increase is another aspect of the benefit of debt financing. Since the lenders to the firm are now providing part of the financing for the firm's investments, that leaves more money available to pay dividends.

Given $4,620,000 of total dividends, $67,000,000 of total common stock value, and an expected annual growth rate of 6%, we can calculate the new K_E that applies to Rathco:

$$
\begin{aligned}
V_S &= \text{(Current Year's Total Dividend)}/(K_E - g) \\
\$67,000,000 &= (\$4,620,000)/(K_E - 0.06) \\
K_E &= (\$4,620,000/\$67,000,000) + 0.06 = 0.129 = 12.9\%
\end{aligned}
$$

This figure is slightly less than the $K_E = 13.0\%$ which resulted when Rathco was not expected to grow and borrowed $20 million to repurchase shares. The reason is that the firm's leverage ratio L is now also slightly less. Since $20 million of debt in the current year increases the total value of Rathco to $87 million when the firm is expected to grow, the firm's leverage ratio is:

$$L = D/V_L = \$20,000,000/\$87,000,000 = 0.23$$

Recall that L was equal to $20,000,000/$81,000,000 = 0.25 in the no-growth case, because $20 million of immediate borrowings in that setting only increased total firm value to $81 million. The relationship identified in equation (8) between the levered required return on equity K_E and the unlevered required return K_U still applies when growth is present, however. You can confirm that fact by substituting L = 20/87 in equation (8) and calculating the corresponding K_E. It will match the 12.9% figure for K_E, which we just derived. The same answer results when D/V_S = 20/67 is inserted into equation (10).

An Overview of the Impact of Financial Leverage on the Firm

Given the preceding analyses, we are now in a position to summarize the effects of leverage on the firm and its stockholders, in an environment that includes a corporate income tax. Those effects are shown in Figure 14-13. In Appendix B to the chapter, we also examine the impact of leverage on the β of a firm's common stock.

The underlying assumption for all these statements is that the firm is expected to earn an ROA *that exceeds the before-tax interest rate the firm must pay on its debt*. One could argue that, if this is not the case, the firm not only should avoid debt financing but probably should sell off its assets, distribute the proceeds to stockholders, and go out of business—since its earning power is fundamentally inadequate.

FINANCIAL LEVERAGE AND FINANCIAL DISTRESS

The examination of the effect of the financing decision on firm value to this point suggests that financial managers should maximize the firm's use of debt. Both equation (6) and Figure 14-9 indicate that the value of the firm rises continuously with financial leverage. This analysis is incomplete, however, because it has concentrated on the benefits of leverage while ignoring some potentially major disadvantages.

Financial Distress Inability of a firm to meet its cash flow commitments without seriously disrupting operations.

As a firm increases its financial leverage, it commits itself to a larger fixed interest obligation. The *risk associated with the increased interest expense is that earnings may drop too low in a bad year to allow the firm to pay its contractual obligations without disrupting its operations*. This disruption is termed **financial distress**. During times of distress, the firm finds liquidity falling. In order

SUMMARY FIGURE 14-13	The Impact of Financial Leverage on the Firm and Its Stockholders
	When Leverage Increases:
ROA and K_U	Are unaffected. Only operating risk and operating leverage affect these.
Financial Risk	Increases. The earnings of common stockholders become more volatile.
Corporate Taxes	Decrease. Interest is a tax-deductible expense for the firm.
ROE and EPS	Are expected to increase but will always become more volatile.
Total Value of the Firm	Increases because of the savings in corporate taxes.
Common Stock Price per Share	Increases because firm value increases and the number of common shares is reduced.
K_E	Increases because of the increased risk to common shareholders.

to produce the cash needed for fixed interest obligations, it may have to liquidate certain assets that it would otherwise have kept, or it might forego investments that it would otherwise have made. As a result, its business plans may be altered at the cost of lost opportunities.

If the business conditions causing financial distress deepen or are prolonged, the firm's liquidity problems can also deepen. Suppliers of materials, creditors of all types, and ultimately customers, become nervous about doing business with the firm. They might refuse to continue their relationship with the firm or ask for restrictions on operations in order to protect their positions. Eventually, if conditions become bad enough and the firm cannot pay interest, lenders have the right to force bankruptcy. The result could be liquidation or reorganization, which are discussed in Chapter 23.

The Cost of Financial Distress

On a conceptual level, the effect of financial distress can be summarized by defining a term called the cost of financial distress. This value, C(FD), is an increasing function of financial leverage, as shown in Figure 14-14. For low amounts of debt, the cost and probability of financial distress are small enough to be ignored. As the level of debt increases, however, the cost and probability of financial distress can rise very rapidly. If the expected cost and probability of financial distress could be measured for different amounts of financial leverage for each year into the future, the IVM could be used to estimate the reduction it would cause in the value of the firm in the form:

$$V_L = V_U + \theta D - C(FD) \tag{13}$$

This relationship between total firm value and leverage for a nongrowing firm is shown in Figure 14-15.

As an illustration of the use of equation (13), let us continue with the example of Rathco. Suppose the firm's management estimates that the expected cost of financial distress is $2,000,000 at a level of debt financing of $20,000,000. Given this information, the effect of the increase in financial leverage is:

$V_L = V_U + \theta D - C(FD)$
$= (\$50)(1,500,000 \text{ shares}) + \$6,000,000 - \$2,000,000$
$= \$75,000,000 + \$6,000,000 - \$2,000,000$
$= \$79,000,000$

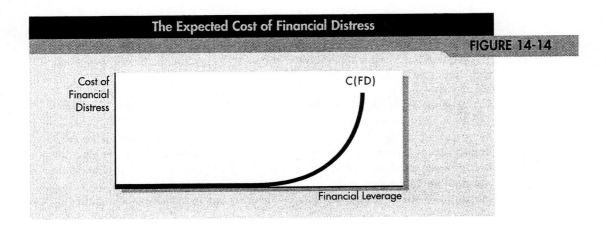

The Expected Cost of Financial Distress

FIGURE 14-14

■ Valuation

ISSUES

THE ALCHEMY OF FINANCIAL DISTRESS: HOW EXCESSIVE DEBT IS TRANSFORMED INTO EQUITY

The chapter discussion of financial leverage points out that once the costs of financial distress outweigh the value of the interest tax shield on debt, a firm should

reduce its financial leverage. The obvious method of making such a change in capital structure is to issue new stock either to finance new assets or repay outstanding debt. This approach, however, is usually viable only for a firm that has not yet encountered severe financial distress. For a company in financial distress, there is usually little interest among investors in purchasing additional shares of stock. Who can such a firm convince to acquire its equity? For Flagstar Companies, the answer to this question lay right on the firm's balance sheet.

Flagstar was a highly leveraged holding company that was the parent of six restaurant chains: 1,500 Denny's, 170 Coco's, 157 Carrow's, 217 El Pollo Loco, 600 Hardee's, and 125 Quincy's Family Steakhouse. Although 1997 sales were close to $3 billion, the firm was in severe financial distress due to $2 billion in outstanding debt incurred in a leveraged buyout (LBO) by management in the early 1990s. In 1992, the famous LBO firm, Kohlberg, Kravis, and Roberts (KKR), acquired 47 percent of Flagstar's equity in exchange for a $300 million infusion of funds. Although the additional equity allowed Flagstar to refinance its high-cost debt at lower interest rates, the firm's subsequent earnings were limited by intense price competition in the restaurant industry. Between 1990 and 1996, Flagstar's cumulative operating losses totaled more than $2 billion.

A new CEO hired in 1995 was unable to turn around the firm's performance despite changing its pricing strategy, selling off non-core assets, and increasing cap-

ital expenditures. In early 1996, he made the controversial decision to use the proceeds from the sale of assets to acquire the Coco's and Carrow's restaurant chains rather than pay off outstanding debt. By 1997, the firm's subordinated debt was rated Caa and its senior debt B3 by Moody's, credit ratings that indicated that default was a real possibility. The company's free cash flow was inadequate to cover annual interest expense of $230 million, much less provide for principal repayment. The market value of the firm's 11.25% coupon bonds fell to 60% of par value, implying a yield-to-maturity of 20%. In the meantime, the value of KKR's equity stake had fallen to $45 million.

Flagstar hired an investment bank to provide advice on changes to its capital structure. The only viable alternative to liquidation of the firm seemed to be the exchange of outstanding debt for new equity. The solution to Flagstar's dilemma took the form of a prepackaged Chapter 11 bankruptcy proceeding. Flagstar emerged from bankruptcy in January 1998 with a new name and a new capital structure. The firm was renamed Advantica Restaurant Group, Inc., and it issued 40 million new shares of stock to former creditors who held senior and junior subordinated debentures and to preferred stockholders. After the capital restructuring, only $500 million of debt remained in the form of senior notes with a 9.75% coupon. KKR, which incurred substantial dilution of its equity position after the debt-equity swap, issued a philosophical public statement: "The leveraged buyout business is not risk-free and not all investments work out as planned."

The $6,000,000 value of the tax shield is partially offset by the $2,000,000 cost of financial distress. Figure 14-15 indicates that the cost of financial distress eventually increases at a faster rate than the value of the tax shield, and V_L actually falls at very high levels of leverage.

Components of the Cost of Financial Distress

The cost of financial distress is depicted in Figures 14-14 and 14-15 as though it has only one component that is initially very small and increases dramatically at high levels of leverage. In reality, however, it is much more likely that this variable is composed of a number of components that can be evaluated separately even if accurate measurement of each is not always feasible. In this section, we will examine three of these components: bankruptcy costs, uncertainty of tax shelter, and agency costs.

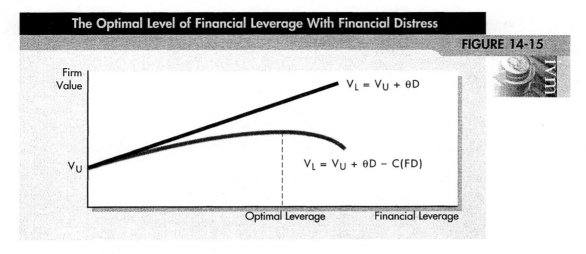

The Optimal Level of Financial Leverage With Financial Distress

FIGURE 14-15

$$V_L = V_U + \theta D$$

$$V_L = V_U + \theta D - C(FD)$$

Bankruptcy Costs. Earlier, we defined financial distress as the inability of a firm to meet its cash flow commitments without seriously disrupting operations. These commitments include a wide range of demands on cash such as payments to suppliers, wages and salaries, product development and marketing expenditures, interest on debt, and dividends on stock. As we will describe in Chapter 23, prolonged financial distress can lead to bankruptcy proceedings under which the firm is protected from creditor demands until the firm is either reorganized for future profitable operations or liquidated to make partial payment to the various claimants. In either case, substantial legal and administrative costs can be incurred during the bankruptcy proceedings. If the firm is reorganized, severe constraints are placed on managers while the firm is directed by a court-appointed trustee. If the firm is liquidated, significant losses may be incurred from the forced sale of assets. All of these explicit and implicit costs of bankruptcy increasingly offset the interest tax benefit of debt as a firm's leverage increases.

Uncertainty of Tax Shelter. The term θD in equation (6) is the present value of a perpetual level stream of tax savings, rTD, which reflects the sheltering of EBIT from taxes by interest expense. We know that actual EBIT will fluctuate around its expected value in response to operating risk. The greater the amount of outstanding debt, the greater the probability that EBIT will be less than interest expense so that the tax saving generated by leverage will be less than rTD. This is depicted in Figure 14-16 where the shaded area shows the probability that the interest tax shield will be less than rTD because EBIT falls below rD. As a firm increases its leverage, rD will move closer to expected EBIT, and the size of the shaded area will increase.

Since the amount of uncertainty in the interest tax shield is directly related to this probability distribution, it is also directly related to the operating risk of the firm's assets. The greater the operating risk, holding rD and expected EBIT constant, the greater will be the spread of the curve and the size of the shaded area in Figure 14-16. The uncertainty of rTD, therefore, is caused by the operating risk of the firm's assets.

Agency Costs. As we will discuss in detail in Chapter 23, a unique set of incentives arise that can cause a serious conflict of interest between stockholders and bondholders when a firm increases the chance of financial distress. For example, consider the position of the bondholders of a firm that has been moderate in its use of debt so that its debt is rated Aaa by Moody's Investors Service.

Uncertain EBIT and Income Shielded by Interest

FIGURE 14-16

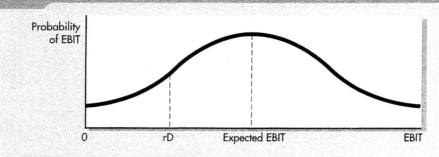

Assume that the firm changes its financial policy and aggressively increases leverage. In response, Moody's drops the rating on the firm's bonds to Baa so that their RRR rises and their market value falls sharply. This type of "event" risk can be devastating to bondholders.

Knowing that such possibilities exist, bondholders will protect themselves by imposing restrictive covenants in the bond indenture. The cost of these covenants is a type of agency cost. The financial managers are the agents whom the bondholders are protecting themselves against. The costs are the restrictions on management flexibility and the need to monitor management decisions. As a general rule, we could expect this type of agency cost to increase with the amount of debt in a firm's capital structure.

In Figure 14-17, we have modified Figure 14-15 to reflect the three separate components of the cost of financial distress. In theory, a variable for each of these components could be inserted into equation (13) to replace C(FD). Measurement problems, however, make such an adjustment practically infeasible. Suffice it to say at this point that θD, by itself, *overstates* the positive effect of financial leverage on a firm's value.

THE OPTIMAL LEVEL OF DEBT

The optimal level of financial leverage for a firm is the amount of debt financing that maximizes V_L in equation (13). Unfortunately, while that equation is conceptually correct, practical difficulties in measuring the cost of financial distress make it infeasible to use directly in practice. Even though equation (13) cannot provide a firm's financial managers with a quantitative answer, it does provide them with qualitative insight into the debt versus equity question.

Why should a firm borrow? It should borrow to take advantage of the interest tax shield provided by the fact that interest is tax-deductible to the corporation. *Why should a firm limit its borrowing* at some point? It should stop borrowing *when increases in the expected cost of financial distress are greater than the increase in value caused by the interest tax benefit.* This is the optimal level of debt where the value of the firm is maximized. In practice, the optimal level of debt is impossible to measure precisely due to the difficulty of estimating the expected cost of financial distress, C(FD). Since the financial managers' ability to quantify C(FD) is limited, they must attempt to measure indirectly its effect on firm value by *estimating stockholder attitudes about the optimal level of debt financing for the firm.* These attitudes determine the effect of the interest tax shield/financial distress trade-off [θD versus C(FD)] on firm value. In order to esti-

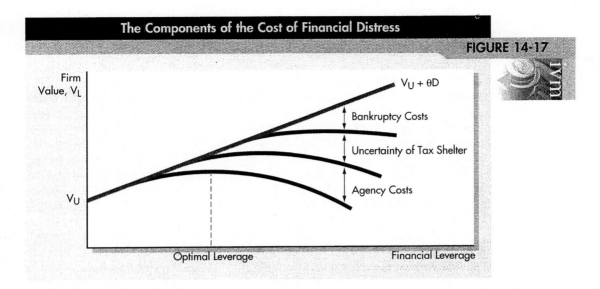

The Components of the Cost of Financial Distress

FIGURE 14-17

mate stockholder attitudes, the managers must *rely on the type of financial indicators that stockholders utilize in forming their opinion about the optimal level of leverage*. In using these indicators, the managers must remember that they are substitutes for the ability to measure C(FD) directly. As a result, they suggest conclusions about leverage that are rough approximations rather than precise targets.

Industry Standards for Financial Leverage

One common approach for estimating stockholder attitudes is simply to *assume that they base their opinions about optimal leverage for a given firm on the financing practices of all firms in its industry*. A firm that attempts to borrow in excess of the average industry leverage may find that investors penalize its stock price due to perceptions of excessive financial risk. In Chapter 2, we defined three different leverage ratios that can be used in this type of cross-section ratio analysis:

$$\text{Debt Ratio} = \frac{\text{Total Debt}}{\text{Total Assets}} \qquad \text{Interest Coverage} = \frac{\text{EBIT}}{\text{Interest}}$$

$$\text{Fixed Charge Coverage} = \frac{\text{EBIT} + \text{Lease Payments}}{\text{Interest} + \text{Lease Payments} + \text{Principal}/(1 - T)}$$

As indicated in that chapter, all three ratios indicate significant aspects of the risk of financial distress. The internal nature of the data needed for the last ratio, however, effectively forces stockholders to rely primarily upon the debt ratio and the interest coverage ratio to make their risk assessments.

Analyst Opinions About Leverage

Due to the difficulty of making accurate risk assessments, *investor opinions are significantly influenced by the evaluations of professional analysts* such as lenders, investment bankers, and credit-rating agencies. Before making their own investment decisions, investors will often seek the advice of these analysts. Consequently, a firm's financial managers can obtain valuable insight into the question of the optimal level of debt financing through discussions with these experts concerning the firm's current and proposed capital structure. Although the professional analysts cannot pinpoint the optimal level of leverage for a firm, they can provide answers to the following questions:

Would additional debt be an attractive investment to creditors?
What impact would additional debt have on the firm's credit rating?
What would be the interest cost of additional debt?

Worst Case Analysis

The opinions of professional analysts about financial leverage are useful in establishing a firm's debt capacity or debt ceiling. A technique available to financial managers for internally verifying these external opinions is the worst case scenario analysis that was introduced in Chapter 11. Recall that this type of analysis indicates the risk of financial distress by projecting a firm's cash flows under the worst possible economic and product demand conditions. Worst case analysis can be used in the context of the financial leverage decision to determine the maximum level of interest and principal payments that a firm will be able to meet even under severely depressed business conditions.

Debt Capacity Versus Optimal Debt Financing

Debt Capacity The level of financial leverage at which adding debt to the financial structure of a firm can cause problems with servicing the debt.

It is unlikely that the market value of a firm's stock will be maximized at a level of debt financing equal to the debt capacity indicated by professional analyst opinion or worst case analysis. **Debt capacity** is the maximum amount of debt that the firm will be able to service (make interest and principal payments) under adverse economic conditions. As we will point out in Chapter 15, the RRR on both debt and equity financing rises rapidly as the level of debt outstanding approaches the firm's debt capacity. The effect of this increase in RRR on firm value is likely to be negative. Consequently, firm value is maximized at some debt level below debt capacity, as shown in Figure 14-18.

SUMMARY

This chapter addressed the question of the appropriate financial structure for a firm because financing decisions can affect the firm's value. The financial leverage provided by financing decisions is analogous to the operating leverage provided by investing decisions. Both types of leverage arise from the substitution of a fixed cost for a variable cost. The two types of leverage differ in the type of fixed cost that is the source of the leverage and in their impact on the income statement.

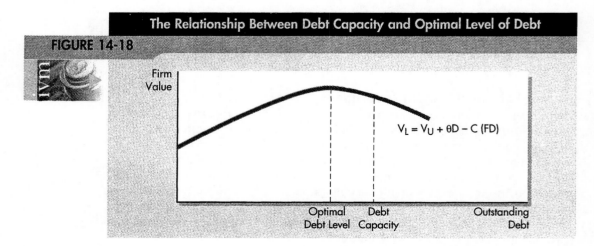

FIGURE 14-18 The Relationship Between Debt Capacity and Optimal Level of Debt

$$V_L = V_U + \theta D - C\,(FD)$$

Operating leverage arises from fixed costs of operations such as depreciation and overhead, while financial leverage arises from the fixed interest expense on debt. Operating leverage alters the responsiveness of EBIT to changes in sales, while financial leverage alters the sensitivity of EAT and EPS to changes in EBIT.

Under conditions of uncertainty about future levels of EBIT, the use of financial leverage involves a risk/return trade-off. Increases in financial leverage are accompanied by increases in both the expected value and the standard deviation of the probability distribution of a firm's EPS. Under the assumptions of no corporate income taxes or no tax deduction for corporate interest payments, the increased risk associated with leverage should exactly offset the increased return, and firm value would not be affected by debt financing. Since corporate interest payments are tax-deductible, however, the value of the interest tax benefit rises steadily with the level of debt financing.

Realistically, the value of the interest tax benefit is offset somewhat by the increase in the probability and cost of financial distress as leverage increases. Financial distress occurs because a firm's EBIT may fall sufficiently in a given year to jeopardize the firm's ability to meet its cash flow commitments, including the interest and principal payments required by debt financing. At high levels of leverage, the expected cost of financial distress outweighs the value of the interest tax benefit. The optimal capital structure for the firm occurs at that amount of debt financing at which an increase in the value of the interest tax benefit is fully offset by an increase in the expected cost of financial distress. Since this optimal capital structure is impossible to identify precisely in actual practice, financial managers must rely on the financial indicators used by investors in forming their opinions about optimal leverage.

chapter equations

1. Total Risk $= CV_{EBIT} + (CV_{EPS} - CV_{EBIT})$

2. EBIT = Taxes + Interest Payments + Owners' Net Income

3. ITB $= rTD$

4. $\theta = rT/K_U$

5. Value(ITB) $= \theta D$

6. $V_L = V_U + \theta D$

7. $V_L = V_S + D$

8. $K_E = \dfrac{K_U - rL}{1 - L}$

9. $L = D/V_L$

10. $K_E = K_U + (K_U - r)\left(\dfrac{D}{V_S}\right)$

11. $\theta_G = rT/(K_U - g)$

12. $V_L = V_U + \theta_G D$

13. $V_L = V_U + \theta D - C(FD)$

CONTENT QUESTIONS

1. Explain how there is one concept of leverage yet two sources of leverage.
2. What does operating leverage have to do with the relationship between the variability of sales and the variability of EBIT?
3. What does financial leverage have to do with the relationship between the variability of EBIT and the variability of EPS?
4. Explain why, as financial leverage increases, the magnitude of ROA remains constant.
5. Why does the behavior of EPS and ROE at different levels of financial leverage depend on the level of EBIT?
6. Assuming that EBIT is large enough to cause EPS to rise with financial leverage, explain how finding the *correct* amount of financial leverage is a question of a trade-off between risk and return.
7. An EBIT-EPS chart can be used to answer the question of the amount of debt a firm should have in the capital structure. True or false? Explain.
8. Name the three primary claimants on the firm's EBIT.
9. Explain why the claim of the stockholders or owners is a residual in the three-way split of EBIT.
10. Assuming that interest is not tax-deductible to the firm, explain how corporate debt and personal debt are perfect substitutes.

11. Explain how, if interest is tax-deductible to the firm, stockholders or owners are better off to the extent that the government is worse off.
12. Explain how the optimal level of debt is determined in theory.
13. Why is it difficult in practice to determine the optimal level of debt?

CONCEPT QUESTIONS

1. We have discussed two forms of leverage in this chapter—operating and financial. What influence do you think the degree of the firm's operating leverage should have on the decision as to how much financial leverage the firm should have?
2. IVM In our examination of the tax consequences of debt financing, we concluded that the personal tax rate paid by investors was not relevant to the tax advantage that debt provided to the firm. Suppose the effective tax rate that investors pay on income received from stockholdings is much less than the rate they pay on income received from owning corporate bonds—and less than the rate at which investors would save taxes on interest they would pay to borrow as individuals. What effect would this have on the desirability of debt financing by firms?
3. IVM At various times in the United States, income that investors earned that was received in the form of capital gains has been taxed at a lower rate than income received in the form of dividends. What effect would you expect this difference to have on the relative required rates of return (K_E) for "growth" stocks and "income" stocks?
4. IVM High levels of debt financing and the associated high levels of interest expenses increase the probability that the firm will encounter financial distress, which has a number of unpleasant consequences for stockholders. Can you think of a *benefit* for stockholders, which a heavy burden of financing costs may produce? Hint: think of the issue of "agency costs" in this regard.
5. We noted that bond ratings might be one of the indicators management should look to in attempting to decide on optimal level of financial leverage for the firm in order to maximize the value of the firm. Is there an optimal bond rating?

PROBLEMS

1. A firm has a capital structure that is half debt and half equity and totals $120,000,000. Sales are $180,000,000 with variable costs equal to 60% of sales and fixed operating costs of $30,000,000. It has 2,500,000 shares of common stock outstanding and interest on debt is 12%. If the corporate tax rate is 40%, find the following:
       a. EBIT   b. EAT   c. ROA   d. ROE   e. EPS
2. Southern Enterprises is analyzing different possible capital structures. It has made the following estimates of EPS.

| | Scenario Analysis | | |
	Pessimistic	Neutral	Optimistic
Low Leverage	$1.00	$2.50	$5.00
High Leverage	0.25	2.90	7.50

Assuming that the probability of each scenario is equal, find the expected value of EPS and the standard deviation of EPS for each amount of leverage.
3. Alpine GmbH is considering financing alternatives as shown on the next page:

	Low Leverage	High Leverage
Debt	SF1,000,000	SF2,000,000
Equity	2,000,000	1,000,000
Total Assets	3,000,000	3,000,000
Shares	100,000	50,000

Alpine has estimated that EBIT will be SF700,000. The interest rate is 10%, and the corporate tax rate is 50%.

    a. Calculate ROA for each alternative.

    b. Calculate ROE for each.

    c. Calculate EPS for each.

4. Alpine (Problem 3) is uncertain about its estimate of EBIT. It feels that EBIT, if the economy is recessionary, may be as low as SF300,000, or could be as high as SF1,100,000 if the economy booms.

    a. Calculate ROE for each EBIT level for both financing plans.

    b. Calculate EPS for each EBIT level for both financing plans.

5. Alpine (Problems 3 and 4) feels that there must be a good way of summarizing the effect of EBIT on EPS.

    a. Using your answers to Problems 3 and 4, construct an EBIT-EPS chart incorporating both financial structures.

    b. Find the EBIT-EPS breakeven point and explain why there is no difference between the EPS of either plan for that EBIT level.

6. Alpine (Problems 3 and 4) did additional economic research and determined that there is an equal probability that EBIT will be SF300,000, SF700,000, or SF1,100,000. For each financing alternative, find the expected value and standard deviation of:

    a. EBIT   b. EPS

7. Winston Products' total assets equal £75,000,000. Its EPS and ROE are unaffected by changes in financial leverage. Given that its cost of debt is 8%, find Winston's EBIT.

8. Viktor GmbH is considering expansion of its assets by DM10 million. The expansion can be financed either through the sale of bonds with an 11% interest rate or through a new issue of common stock at DM25 per share. The firm currently has 300,000 shares of stock outstanding and DM8 million of bonds with a 7% coupon. The tax rate is 46%. Viktor's management estimates that next year's EBIT could be one of four figures: DM2 million, DM4 million, DM6 million, or DM8 million.

    a. Calculate the EPS for each financing alternative at each level of EBIT.

    b. Draw an EBIT-EPS breakeven chart based on your answer to part (a).

9. The management of ACM Corporation is evaluating a change in the capital structure of the firm to benefit from the effects of financial leverage. The firm currently has assets of $10,000,000 financed entirely with 200,000 shares of common stock selling at $50 per share. The firm would alter its capital structure by borrowing funds at an interest rate of 12% and repurchasing shares at $50 per share. Management expects the firm to earn $1,500,000 next year before interest and taxes. The firm's tax rate is 50%.

    a. What is the expected EPS and ROE at next year's expected level of EBIT if the firm remains 100% equity financed?

    b. What is the effect of increased leverage on expected EPS and ROE? Why?

10. The ACM Corporation (Problem 9) is considering two alternative book leverage ratios (debt to total assets): 25% and 50%. Calculate expected EPS and ROE for each of these debt ratios at next year's expected EBIT.

11. ACM's management (Problem 9) wishes to estimate the impact of financial leverage if the firm's EBIT is higher or lower than expected. Management estimates that, in a bad year, EBIT could fall as low as $1,000,000. In a good year, EBIT could rise as high as $2,000,000.
    a. Calculate EPS and ROE at the low and high EBIT levels for book debt ratios of 0%, 25%, and 50%.
    b. Construct an EPS-EBIT breakeven chart and show the breakeven EBIT level.

12. ACM's management (Problems 9, 10, and 11) estimates that there is a 25% chance that EBIT will be as low as $1,000,000, a 25% chance that it will be as high as $2,000,000, and a 50% chance that it will be $1,500,000. Calculate the expected value and standard deviation of EPS for each of the debt ratios mentioned in Problem 10.

13. Lone Star Products is currently financed with 1,000,000 shares of stock with a market price of $20 per share and $10,000,000 of debt with a coupon rate of 8%. It is considering financing a $10,000,000 expansion through either a sale of 10% debentures or a new issue of common stock at $20 per share. Lone Star estimates that there is an equal probability that its post-expansion EBIT will be $2,000,000, $4,000,000, or $6,000,000. The firm's tax rate is 40%.
    a. Calculate the EPS for each financing alternative at each EBIT level.
    b. Prepare an EBIT-EPS breakeven chart.

14. Find the expected value and the standard deviation of EPS for each of Lone Star Product's (Problem 13) financing alternatives.

15. James and JoAnn Robertson are about to start a small corporation. They estimate that they will need about $400,000 for working capital and fixed assets. They have $200,000 in savings that they are willing to put into the business. They can obtain the rest of the funds they need by borrowing at 14% interest. They expect EBIT to be about $500,000 and the corporate tax rate to be 40%. They wonder if it makes any difference whether they borrow money as individuals and put $400,000 into the business as equity or put in $200,000 of equity and the corporation borrows the rest. Assume that interest is *not* deductible for corporate taxes.
    a. Calculate the three-way split in EBIT for each method of financing. That is, find how much of EBIT will be claimed by the government, the lender, and the owners.
    b. Which plan is best, based on your answer to part (a)?

16. Use the same information as Problem 15, except that now assume that interest is deductible for corporate taxes.
    a. Calculate the three-way split in EBIT for each method of financing.
    b. Explain any difference between the financing plans found in (a).
    c. Which plan is best, based on your answers to (a) and (b)?

17. You are about to purchase a small business for $500,000. You only have $300,000, but you can borrow $200,000 from a bank at 10% interest either as a personal loan or as a loan to the new corporation. You estimate that EBIT will be $100,000 per year indefinitely and that the tax rate will be 40%. What is the difference in the amount of EBIT left for you between the corporate borrowing and personal borrowing plans under current tax laws, where interest is deductible to the corporation?

18. Riley Industries currently has no debt in its capital structure. Its 500,000 shares of common stock are selling for $60 per share. The financial manager is considering whether to replace some of his firm's equity with an equal amount of debt through a share repurchase. Riley's EBIT is expected to remain

constant at $5,000,000 per year indefinitely with a tax rate of 40%. The firm pays out all its earnings as dividends. It is considering borrowing $5,000,000, $10,000,000, $15,000,000 or $20,000,000 at an interest rate of 8%.

    a. Find the RRR (K_U) that applies to Riley Industries' unlevered common stock.

    b. Find the value of Riley's common stock for each amount of debt.

    c. Find the RRR on equity (K_E) for each amount of debt.

19. Riley Industries (Problem 18) has decided to recapitalize by borrowing $15,000,000.

    a. Find the price per share of Riley's common stock after the recapitalization, assuming that Riley repurchases shares at each of the following prices: $65 per share, $70 per share and $75 per share.

    b. For each of the prices, explain how the value created by the recapitalization is distributed between those stockholders that sold their shares to Riley and those that held on to their shares.

20. Suppose that Riley Industries was able to estimate the expected cost of financial distress for each level of financial leverage in Problem 18 as given below:

Debt	C(FD)
$ 5,000,000	$ 500,000
10,000,000	1,500,000
15,000,000	3,000,000
20,000,000	6,000,000

    a. Calculate the total value of Riley Industries for each capital structure.

    b. Graph your answer to part (a).

    c. What amount of debt would you recommend and why?

21. Ironwood Products has 10,000,000 shares of common stock selling for $25 per share. It also has $150,000,000 of bonds with a 10% coupon rate. Ironwood's EBIT will remain constant at 70,000,000 per year indefinitely with a tax rate of 40%.

    a. Find the RRR (K_E) that applies to Ironwood's common stock.

    b. What is the total value of Ironwood Products?

    c. Find the RRR (K_U) that applies to Ironwood Products' operating income (or unlevered common stock).

22. Ironwood Products (Problem 21) has decided to sell 6,000,000 additional shares of common stock at $25 per share and use the proceeds of the sale to replace all of its debt.

    a. What will be the total value of Ironwood Products after the debt is replaced with common stock?

    b. What will be the value of Ironwood's common stock after the replacement?

    c. Find the RRR on equity (K_E) after the replacement.

INTERNET EXERCISE

http://

The glossary of risk management terms serves as an index and encyclopedia. Investigate the following terms to find an in-depth article and links to related information. Bring printouts of your investigation to class for discussion.
www.contingencyanalysis.com

Terms

Operations risk	Financial risk	Earnings at risk
Rate of return	Worst-case credit exposure	

SELF-STUDY QUIZ

1. A small business corporation will be purchased for $1,000,000. The new owners plan on investing $600,000 of their own money and borrowing the remaining $400,000 at a 12% interest rate. The money can be borrowed by the individual owners or through the corporation. EBIT is estimated to be $1,500,000 per year. The corporate tax rate is 40%.
   a. Assuming that interest is *not* tax-deductible to the corporation, calculate the three-way split of EBIT for both methods of borrowing.
   b. Assuming that interest *is* tax-deductible to the corporation, calculate the three-way split of EBIT for both methods of borrowing.
   c. Find the value difference between the two methods of borrowing. Evaluate this difference. Assume that K_U is 15% and that EBIT is constant and perpetual.

2. A firm with no debt has 10,000,000 shares of common stock selling for $15 per share. EBIT is estimated to be $25,000,000 for the foreseeable future. The firm is going to borrow $50,000,000 and use that amount to repurchase shares at $16.50 per share. The firm pays out 100% of its earnings as dividends and has a tax rate of 40%. The interest rate is 7.5%.
   a. Find the RRR (K_U) that applies to the common stock of the unlevered firm.
   b. Find the value of common stock after the recapitalization (replacing equity with debt).
   c. Find the RRR on equity (K_E) after the recapitalization.
   d. Find the price per share after the recapitalization.

APPENDIX A: MEASURING THE DEGREE OF FINANCIAL LEVERAGE AND TOTAL LEVERAGE

In the body of the chapter, we pointed out that a firm's degree of financial leverage is directly related to the ratio: Interest Expense/EBIT. As the value of this ratio rises, the level of a firm's financial leverage also rises. While the ratio is a useful indicator of a firm's financial leverage, it is only a general measure. A more precise calculation of the degree of leverage can be performed by looking at the impact of interest expense on the responsiveness of a firm's EAT to fluctuations in its EBIT.

The degree of financial leverage (DFL) is defined as the percentage change in EAT that accompanies a given percentage change in EBIT. The Merion Controls example in this chapter can be used to demonstrate the calculation of DFL. The data in Table 14-2 indicate that, in the medium leverage case, an increase in EBIT from $20,000 to $35,000 results in an increase in EAT from $5,000 to $12,500. Thus, the firm's DFL at an EBIT level of $20,000 must be:

$$DFL = \frac{\text{Percentage Change in EAT}}{\text{Percentage Change in EBIT}} = \frac{\dfrac{\$12,500 - 5,000}{\$5,000} \times 100}{\dfrac{\$35,000 - 20,000}{\$20,000} \times 100} = \frac{150\%}{75\%} = 2.0 \qquad (14A\text{-}1)$$

The DFL of 2.0 indicates that, given a financial structure consisting of 40% debt, any percentage deviation from an EBIT of $20,000 will cause twice that percentage change in EAT.

Notice that equation 14A-1 requires that the financial managers calculate the firm's EAT level at the two different EBIT levels selected. There is an equivalent formula for DFL that eliminates the need to calculate EAT twice:

$$DFL = \frac{EBIT}{EBIT - Interest} \qquad (14A\text{-}2)$$

Use of this equation in the Merion Controls example yields the same result as equation (14A-1):

$$DFL = \frac{\$20,000}{\$20,000 - \$10,000} = \frac{\$20,000}{\$10,000} = 2.0$$

Equation 14A-2 was used to calculate the DFL for Merion Controls at various EBIT levels for each of the three financial structures shown in Table 14-2. The results are shown in Table 14A-1.

Table 14A-1 reveals several important aspects of the DFL calculation:

1. The DFL for a firm with no financial leverage is 1.0.
2. The DFL varies as EBIT fluctuates.
3. The DFL approaches ∞ as EBIT approaches the level of interest expense and approaches 1.0 as EBIT increases beyond the interest expense.
4. A negative DFL occurs at EBITs less than the interest expense.
5. The DFL at any EBIT greater than the interest expense is increased by an increase in interest expense.

As demonstrated in this chapter, both fixed operating costs and fixed financing costs increase the variability of a firm's EAT and EPS. The impact of both types of fixed costs can be combined into an overall measure of their impact on the variability of earnings, called the degree of total leverage (DTL). The following relationship of DTL to DOL and DFL is demonstrated in Figure 14A-1:

$$DTL = \frac{\%\Delta EAT}{\%\Delta Sales} = \frac{\%\Delta EBIT}{\%\Delta Sales} \times \frac{\%\Delta EAT}{\%\Delta EBIT} = DOL \times DFL \qquad (14A\text{-}3)$$

Operating leverage affects the relationship between EBIT and sales, while financial leverage affects the relationship between EAT and EBIT. Consequently, the total effect of both types of leverage alters the relationship between EAT and sales. In equation 14A-3, DTL is defined as the percentage change in EAT that accompanies

The Effect of Financial Structure and EBIT on DFL for Merion Controls

TABLE 14A-1

| | | DFL | |
EBIT	0% Debt (Interest = $0)	40% Debt (Interest = $10,000)	60% Debt (Interest = $15,000)
$ 5,000	1.0	−1.00	−.50
10,000	1.0	∞	−2.00
15,000	1.0	3.00	∞
20,000	1.0	2.00	4.00
25,000	1.0	1.67	2.50
30,000	1.0	1.50	2.00
35,000	1.0	1.40	1.75
40,000	1.0	1.33	1.60
45,000	1.0	1.29	1.50
50,000	1.0	1.25	1.43

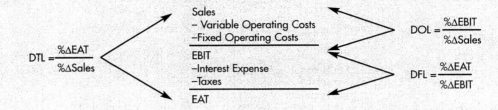

FIGURE 14-A1 — The Relationship Among DOL, DFL, and DTL

a given percentage change in sales. Mathematically, it is simply equal to the product of DOL and DFL. For instance, a firm with a DOL of 4.0 and a DFL of 3.0 would have a DTL of:

$$DTL = DOL \times DFL = 4.0 \times 3.0 = 12.0$$

That is, every 1% increase or decrease in sales will cause a corresponding 12% increase or decrease, respectively, in EAT.

APPENDIX B: LEVERAGE AND BETA

If the required return on equity increases with leverage, the implication is that the beta (β) of the firm's common stock also increases. Recall from our discussion in Chapter 6 that β is a measure of the volatility of a security's returns relative to those of the market as a whole. Since, as we have seen in this chapter, the introduction of leverage into a firm's capital structure raises the variability of its ROE and EPS, we would logically expect the additional variability to be reflected in the firm's β.

We can determine the impact of leverage on β from the definition of β and from the relationship between K_E and K_U in equation (8) of this chapter. We know from Chapter 6 that $K = i + (K_M - i)(\beta)$. Thus,

$$\beta_{KE} = \frac{K_E - i}{K_M - i} \qquad \text{and} \qquad \beta_{KU} = \frac{K_U - i}{K_M - i}$$

Dividing the expression on the left by the one on the right allows us to identify the relationship between the levered and unlevered β's for a firm:

$$\beta_{KE} = (\beta_{KU})\left(\frac{K_E - i}{K_U - i}\right) \tag{14B-1}$$

If we then substitute equation (8) into this equation, we end up with the following rather messy looking (but not especially difficult computationally) expression:

$$\beta_{KE} = (\beta_{KU})\left(\frac{\left[(K_U - rL)\,/\,(1 - L)\right] - i}{K_U - i}\right) \tag{14B-2}$$

To illustrate both the process and the sorts of outcomes that can be expected, consider a situation where the firm's unlevered required return on equity K_U is 14% and its unlevered β_{KU} is 1.00, the going interest rate r on corporate debt is 7%, and the interest rate i on risk-free debt (long-term government bonds) is 6%. Table

14B-1 shows how K_E and the firm's levered β_{KE} increase as the firm's leverage ratio L increases. The effect of the additional leverage on both measures can be noticeable. Given the figures chosen for the illustration, when the firm's leverage ratio goes from zero to 50%, the required ROE increases by 50% and the firm's β by nearly 90%. If we plotted the relationship between β_{KE} and L, it would look almost exactly like the relationship between K_E and L shown in Figure 14-11 in the chapter.

Another—and equivalent—version of the same relationship can be derived from the fact that $K_U = i + (K_M - i)(\beta_{KU})$. If we substitute this expression for K_U into equation (14B-2) and rearrange terms, we can restate the equation as:

$$\beta_{KE} = \frac{\beta_{KU}}{(1-L)} - \left(\frac{r-i}{K_M - i}\right)\left(\frac{L}{1-L}\right) \qquad (14B\text{-}3)$$

The numerical values obtained for β_{KE} from equation (14B-3), as L varies for the firm, will match those from equation (14B-2).

In practice, these computations will most often be done in reverse order, that is, you will know the firm's *levered* β and will be interested in identifying its unlevered counterpart. This is because most firms are already levered and therefore it is their levered β's that are observable. Accordingly, if we solve equation (14B-3) for β_{KU}, we get:

$$\beta_{KU} = (\beta_{KE})(1-L) + \left(\frac{r-i}{K_M - i}\right)(L) \qquad (14B\text{-}4)$$

which makes the estimation of a firm's unlevered β a relatively simple task.

The most common circumstance in which β_{KU} is important to calculate is one in which the firm's financial managers plan to change the firm's leverage ratio (L) from its current value. When leverage changes, the existing β_{KE} no longer applies. In order to estimate the new one, it is first necessary to work backward to infer β_{KU} from equation (14B-4) at the existing leverage ratio. Then, you insert the chosen new value for L in equation (14B-2) to calculate the new β_{KE}, as was done in Table 14B-1.

Finally, notice that the numerical values of the second terms on the right-hand sides of both equations (14B-2) and (14B-3) will tend to be fairly small because the interest rate difference (r - i) for many firms will also be small. Thus, as a practical matter, those terms can frequently be ignored without significant loss of accuracy in translating between levered and unlevered β's for the firm, and the approximations $\beta_{KE} = \beta_{KU}/(1 - L)$ and $\beta_{KU} = (\beta_{KE})(1 - L)$ are used instead.

The Effect of Leverage on a Firm's β

TABLE 14B-1

L	K_E	β_{KE}
0.0	0.140	1.000
0.1	0.148	1.097
0.2	0.158	1.219
0.3	0.170	1.375
0.4	0.187	1.583
0.5	0.210	1.875

The Cost of Capital and the Required Rate of Return

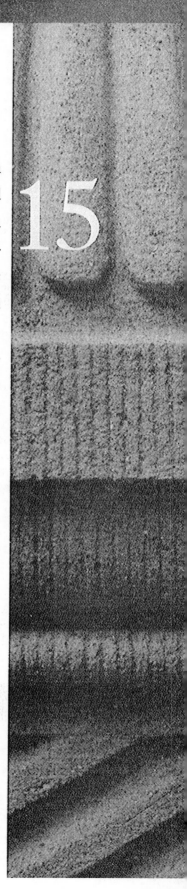

According to the theory of the Investment Valuation Model, the riskiness of a proposed investment should be reflected in the RRR assigned to that investment. In this chapter, we examine the techniques a firm's financial managers can use to determine the appropriate risk-adjusted RRR for a proposed investment. Among the issues we shall consider are the following:

- How is the RRR for a proposed investment related to the cost of the various sources of financing (debt, preferred stock, and common equity) available to a firm? What happens to the RRR as the level of financial leverage rises or falls? How can a financial manager measure the RRRs for the various types of financing?

- Many financial managers argued during the 1980s that the hostile takeovers that occurred at the time were motivated by low stock prices resulting from high RRRs for equity investments. If this were true, what factors might account for a high RRR on a firm's common stock?

- If RRRs are high, how does this affect the relative attractiveness of (a) stocks that pay high current dividends but have only modest growth prospects and (b) stocks that pay low dividends but have high future growth potential?

- While opinions vary about the logic, many firms have followed a strategy of becoming conglomerate enterprises consisting of numerous business units operating in a variety of different industries. Can diversification of this sort reduce the RRRs for a firm's investments?

- In the case of firms that are conglomerates, the individual business units that make up the company may vary quite widely in the degree of risk they face in their respective industries. How should diversified firms measure the RRRs that apply to new investments in each of their businesses?

The RRR is one of the key concepts in business finance because it is the discount rate used to determine the present value of the cash flows from a proposed investment. In the context of the IVM, the RRR compensates investors for the riskiness of the investment. The goal of this chapter is to develop a procedure for calculating the RRR for a capital investment proposal. That required return (commonly called the firm's "cost of capital") depends upon both the *nature of the project* under consideration and also the *mix of financing* the firm plans to employ to fund its capital expenditures. The ability of financial managers to identify positive NPV investments that will increase firm value depends heavily on an accurate estimate of the appropriate RRR for each investment. Figure 15-1 depicts these relationships.

THE CONCEPTUAL FOUNDATION FOR THE REQUIRED RATE OF RETURN

For an investment to be worthwhile for the firm to undertake, it is not sufficient that the investment simply promise a positive rate of return. In order to enhance stockholder wealth, the firm must earn returns on its investments that are *greater than the returns from investments of comparable risk* available to investors elsewhere outside the firm. Those external investment opportunities therefore define the RRRs that apply internally to the firm's projects.

The Market Risk/Return Schedule

In Chapter 6, we discussed the relationship that we believe prevails in the financial marketplace between risk and return for investments in securities. The Capital Asset Pricing Model (CAPM) captures that relationship, in the form:

$$K_j = i + (K_M - i)(\beta_j) \tag{1}$$

where K_j is the required rate of return for investment j, i is the long-term risk-free rate of interest, $(K_M - i)$ is the overall market risk premium for stocks, and β_j is a measure of the systematic risk (relative volatility) of investment j.

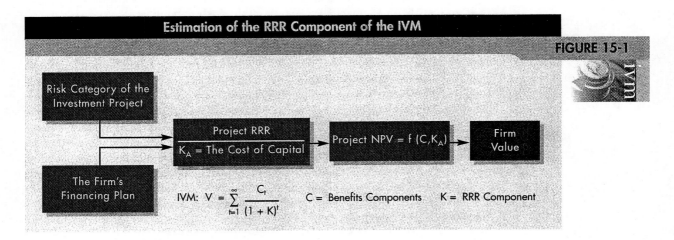

Estimation of the RRR Component of the IVM

FIGURE 15-1

Risk Category of the Investment Project

The Firm's Financing Plan

Project RRR
K_A = The Cost of Capital

Project NPV = $f(C, K_A)$

Firm Value

IVM: $V = \sum_{t=1}^{\infty} \dfrac{C_t}{(1 + K)^t}$

C = Benefits Components

K = RRR Component

While the model was originally developed to explain the profile of returns on securities, it applies equally well in principle to any investment—including the capital expenditures on plant and equipment made by corporations. Thus, if it were possible to do so, the β of each such proposed investment would be measured as we described in Chapter 6, and the RRR for the investment would then be identified from equation (1). The problem, however, is that items of corporate plant and equipment, unlike securities, are not traded in the market on an ongoing basis. Consequently, there is no record of trading prices and periodic returns for real assets to allow direct estimates of their β's to be made.

Estimates of Project Risk

Given that circumstance, it is necessary to use *indirect* measures of the risk of the firm's capital investment projects in order to determine the RRRs that are relevant to calculating the present values of the projects' cash flows. This is typically done by identifying traded securities that are thought to be of similar risk, and using *their* estimated RRRs as the discount rates to measure project NPVs. In some cases, this is a relatively easy task; in others, it can become fairly complex.

Among the easy cases is one in which the firm (a) is predominantly in a single major line of business, (b) is contemplating a new investment that is also in the same line of business, and (c) plans to finance the investment in the same manner as it has financed its past investments. The reason this is the easy case is that the two key underlying determinants of risk that we discussed in Chapter 14 (operating leverage and financial leverage) are essentially identical for the firm as presently constituted and for the new investment being considered. Hence, the RRR for the new investment will logically be the same as that which investors require on the firm's existing securities. Another way to say this is that the firm's *current cost of capital* can be used as the discount rate for the project.

When the new project in question is outside the firm's existing line of business or when the firm is already in multiple lines of business, however, there is not such an equivalence between project risk and overall company risk. Then it is necessary to look elsewhere than at the company itself in order to come up with the RRR that applies for any given project. This is when things become complicated and when it may be necessary to exercise considerable judgment (and perhaps creativity) in attempting to identify comparable risk investments to use as RRR benchmarks. We shall deal with that issue in this chapter and suggest some guidelines to assist in the process. Nonetheless, the level of precision that it is possible to attain in capital expenditure project RRR estimates for multi-business companies is often less than the financial manager might wish to achieve.

Multiple Required Rates of Return

It is important to emphasize that it *is* fundamentally the risk of the investment project in question that establishes the RRR that applies to it. As we shall see, the manner in which a firm finances the project will also have an impact, but the key dimension of the evaluation process is the basic business risk category into which a project falls. If this category is different from that of the investments a firm currently has in place, an RRR that is different from that of those investments is also needed. Thus, a firm will have more than one cost of capital if it is in more than one line of business. An example would be the General Electric Corporation of the United States. The firm manufactures (among other things) jet aircraft engines, railroad locomotives, medical equipment, household appliances, and plastics. The firm also owns a television network and a large financial services company. It seems pretty clear that the risks of these various businesses are not all the same. The appropriate RRRs to use to evaluate new investments in each business therefore will also not be the same.

COMPONENT CAPITAL COSTS

The terms "cost of capital" and "required rate of return" are used interchangeably. They both refer to the discount rate that should be employed to calculate the present value of a proposed investment project's expected cash flows in order to appraise its desirability, given the project's risk and the composition of its financing. That is, the **cost of capital** is the minimum rate of return that a project must earn in order not to diminish stockholder wealth. The reason capital *has* a "cost" is the fact that the investors who provide funds to a firm to support the firm's investments require a return on those funds that at least matches the return they could earn elsewhere. This is true not only of common stockholders, but also of the lenders to the firm and the investors who purchase the firm's preferred stock. Moreover, since lenders and preferred stockholders have priority claims on the firm's earnings and cash flow, any deficiency in returns on the firm's investments will be borne by the firm's common stockholders as the residual claimants. This makes the estimation and effective use of the company's cost of capital a particularly critical matter for them.

Cost of Capital The minimum rate of return an investment project must earn so as not to diminish stockholder wealth.

The cost of capital for each component of the firm's capital structure is the *rate of return investors require in order to be willing to purchase and hold the securities issued by the firm*. Since those return requirements and capital market conditions will change over time, it is important that *current* RRR estimates always be used in defining capital costs. This is consistent with the central concept of marginal (or incremental) analysis we stressed in connection with the proper identification of project cash flows. The investments being made are *new* investments, and they are being supported with *new* financings. The investments must meet current RRR standards rather than historical ones if they are to add *today* to shareholder wealth. The valuation concepts developed in Chapters 6 and 7 can be adapted here to identify these RRRs.

The Cost of Debt

The pretax cost of debt is the *yield the firm would have to offer to investors in order to acquire new debt financing in the current capital market*. We could also describe that yield as the current market interest rate on the firm's debt. If we denote this yield as r, and recognize that interest expense is tax-deductible to the firm, the corresponding after-tax cost of debt is:

$$K_D = (r)(1 - T) \tag{2}$$

where T is the corporate tax rate. As with all forms of capital, we need to measure the cost on an *after-tax* basis, since it is the after-tax cash flows from proposed investments that we discount to obtain their present values.

There are two ways for the firm's financial managers to identify K_D. The first is simply to contact the firm's investment bankers or commercial bankers and ask what interest rate the firm would have to pay to raise new debt capital. These financial institutions will be attuned to current market conditions and have knowledge of the firm's creditworthiness. They should be able to provide a close estimate of the yield r that they and other investors will require. The second procedure would be to calculate the yield-to-maturity on the firm's presently outstanding bonds if the bonds are publicly traded. The logic is that this same yield would apply to new debt as well because it already reflects market conditions and investors' perceptions of the firm's credit standing.

As an illustration of the calculation, assume a firm has bonds with a 10% coupon rate outstanding. These pay interest annually and mature in 15 years. While their par value is $1,000, their current market price is only $864. As shown in Chapter 7, the yield-to-maturity on the bonds is the discount rate that equates the present value of the future debt service obligations to the current market price. The calculation is:

$$(\$100)(ADF_{r,15}) + (\$1,000)(DF_{r,15}) = \$864$$

and an r of 12% satisfies this condition. If the firm's marginal tax rate on corporate income is 40%, the after-tax cost of debt financing is:

$$K_D = (0.12)(1 - 0.40) = 0.072 = 7.2\%$$

in the current market environment.

The Cost of Preferred Stock

The cost of new preferred stock financing is similar to that of debt. It is *the dividend yield the firm would have to offer investors in order to obtain new preferred stock financing.* We shall denote this dividend yield as r_p. Because dividends on preferred stock are not tax-deductible, the after-tax cost of capital for preferred stock is the same as the dividend yield:

$$K_P = r_P \tag{3}$$

Again, the firm's financial managers can get estimates of r_p either from the investment bankers who would issue the new securities or, if the firm already has some outstanding preferred stock, by calculating the current dividend yield on those securities. Since most preferred stock has no specified maturity, the annual dividend stream can be treated as a perpetuity and the yield on the stock determined simply by dividing its annual dividend (D_p) by its current market price (P_0):

$$K_P = \frac{D_P}{P_0}$$

For example, if the annual dividend were $8 and the current market price were $80, the yield would be 10%. This procedure will be a good approximation in most cases even if there *is* a designated maturity, because those maturities tend to be very long ones.

You can see that, if the *pre-tax* costs of debt and preferred stock to the firm are not too far apart (as is generally the case in practice), the after-tax cost of debt will be considerably less than the after-tax cost of preferred stock because of the tax-deductibility of the interest payments on the debt. As we discussed in Chapter 14, this tax feature is the major advantage of debt financing and is its major contribution to enhancing the value of the firm.

The Cost of Common Equity

The cost of common equity is the *rate of return currently required by the holders of the firm's outstanding common stock.* As we saw in Chapter 7, this is the earnings rate they demand in order to be willing to purchase the shares at the current market price from other investors on the secondary market. It is also the earnings rate the firm must provide to stockholders if the firm retains a portion of its earnings rather than distributing them as dividends. In the latter case, since stock-

■ Valuation

ISSUES

AN INNOVATION IN BONDS HELPS FIRMS REDUCE THEIR COST OF CAPITAL

Almost all corporate bonds are issued with a call option that permits the issuing firm to retire its bonds prior to their maturity. This option becomes valuable to the issuer when interest rates drop because it enables the firm to refinance the debt at a lower interest cost. For the bond investor, a symmetric feature is a put option, which allows the investor to sell the bonds back to the issuer prior to their maturity. This option becomes valuable when interest rates rise because it enables the investor to obtain cash (typically par value) from the bond, which can then be reinvested at a higher coupon rate. The motive behind the issuance of a "put bond" is that it reduces the cost of funds to the borrowing firm because it can be issued with a lower coupon than a comparable "plain vanilla" bond. In early 1998, investment banks created a new version of a put bond, which offers even greater interest cost savings than the original form.

One of the drawbacks of a traditional put bond, from the issuer's perspective, is that the institutional investors who dominate the market for corporate bonds are often not willing to give up much coupon interest to obtain the put option. The put option is not very valuable to them because they tend to hold the bonds to their maturity date. Thus, the option to resell the bond at par prior to maturity is not very attractive. Bond underwriters, on the other hand, find such options very valuable because they can use them in their derivatives units either to hedge against or speculate on future interest rate movements. Unfortunately, the traditional put bond does not allow the put option to be detached from the bond so the institutional investor cannot sell the put option to a bond underwriter.

The new form of put bond is known by various commercial names such as REPS (reset put securities) or MOPPRS (mandatory par put remarketed securities). It differs from the traditional instrument in that the call option is detached from the bond and sold to the bond underwriter by the issuing firm. The purchase price of the option helps to offset the interest cost on the bond issue. For example, in 1998, Nabisco, Inc. issued $1 billion in REPS with a 13-year term-to-maturity and both a put option and a call option beginning in the third year. The underwriter paid an estimated $10 to $15 million for the call option. Despite the bonds' 13-year term-to-maturity, the bond investors viewed them as 3-year notes because they will be resold to either Nabisco or the bond underwriter in 2001. If interest rates rise, the bonds will be sold back to Nabisco at par by the investors. If interest rates fall, however, the bonds will be called at par by the underwriter who can then resell them as ten-year maturity bonds at a premium over par value.

All three parties involved in the bond issuance benefit from this new structure. The issuer reduces its cost of financing by selling the option to the underwriter. (Nabisco saved an estimated $10 to $15 million in interest costs by issuing the new bonds.) The underwriter receives an option, which is valuable in its derivatives operations. The investors receive a yield premium of three to five basis points over plain vanilla bonds as an inducement to investing in this unfamiliar security. In the first month of trading, $1.8 billion of these securities were sold. Underwriters were predicting additional volume of $5 billion over the next month and as much as $20 billion over the year.

holders forego the opportunity to invest the retained earnings themselves externally, the firm must compensate them for the returns they could have earned from those other investments.

The challenge in estimating the cost of common equity is that the rate of return investors require is not a contractual one as it is for debt and preferred stock. There is no specified interest payment or stipulated annual dividend that is promised to common stockholders. Instead, stockholders have a claim to the cash flow that is *left* after the firm's obligations to debt and preferred stock have been met. They also have the right to participate in any future growth in the firm's cash flows. The RRR for common equity therefore cannot be observed and objectively calculated as it can for debt and preferred stock. The cost must be *inferred* from other information which is available in the capital marketplace, and there are basically two ways to do this.

Dividend Growth Model. One way to estimate the cost of common equity is to use the model developed in Chapter 7, which expresses the current price of a share of common stock (P_0) as the present value of a growing future stream of cash dividends. The required return on common equity, K_E, is the discount rate:

$$P_0 = \frac{D_1}{K_E - g}$$

where D_1 is the initial annual dividend per share, and g is the expected long-run annual rate of growth in that dividend. In the form that allows us to estimate K_E, the same equation becomes:

$$K_E = \frac{D_1}{P_0} + g \qquad (4)$$

We can find P_0 in the stock tables of any business newspaper. Since firms tend to have a fairly predictable pattern of dividend payments, estimating the coming year's dividend D_1 will generally not be a difficult task. Indeed, many firms' boards of directors announce the coming year's dividend rate on their common stock early in the year. Hence, if we can arrive at a reasonable estimate of g, we will have all we need to estimate K_E with equation (4).

A key consideration in this regard is that it is the dividend growth expectations of *investors* that are relevant because they are the ones who establish the price of the stock by imposing their RRR on the expected dividend stream. If a firm's financial managers want to capture that RRR accurately, they must essentially put themselves in the place of investors and ask: Given the information that is *publicly available* about their company, what might investors expect the long-run growth rate of dividends per share to be? This figure may not match up with management's expectations or hopes. The issue for cost of capital measurement, however, is *investors'* return requirements, and therefore it is *their* perceptions that count.

In forming their expectations of future dividends, it is likely that investors will put considerable emphasis on the firm's historical record of dividend payments. This would be a logical starting point. Since dividends are paid out of earnings, it seems likely that the past record of earnings per share would also be of interest to investors. As an example, take the case of Great Lakes Manufacturing, for whom the DPS and EPS record over the 11-year period 1988–1998 has been:

Year	DPS	EPS
1988	$0.60	$1.20
1989	0.65	1.35
1990	0.75	1.45
1991	0.80	1.60
1992	0.85	1.75
1993	0.90	1.80
1994	1.05	2.15
1995	1.20	2.40
1996	1.25	2.50
1997	1.40	2.85
1998	1.55	3.10

The historical growth rates of dividends and earnings can be found by either (a) averaging the ten year-to-year percentage changes for each variable or (b) calculating the beginning-to-end-of-period compound growth rates of the two. The latter would be done for Great Lakes by solving for g in the following equations:

$$(DPS_{1988})(1 + g)^{10} = DPS_{1998}$$
$$(\$0.60)(1 + g)^{10} = \$1.55$$
$$(1 + g)^{10} = \$1.55/\$0.60 = 2.583$$

$$(EPS_{1988})(1 + g)^{10} = EPS_{1998}$$
$$(\$1.20)(1 + g)^{10} = \$3.10$$
$$(1 + g)^{10} = \$3.10/\$1.20 = 2.583$$

The ten-year growth ratios are the same because dividends have consistently been equal or close to 50% of earnings for Great Lakes. Looking across the 10-year row in Table I at the end of the text (which shows the rate at which a $1 initial amount grows), we see that the ratio 2.583 is very close to the number found in the 10% column. The future value functions of your computer or calculator would identify the same figure. The averages of the ten year-to-year percentage changes in both DPS and EPS are also approximately 10%. To the extent that investors use history to project the future, therefore, 10% per annum would appear to be a reasonable estimate of the market's forecast of Great Lakes' dividend growth prospects.[1]

Investors might also be making use of other sources of information in forming their expectations. Among these sources would be the brokerage houses and investment advisory services who provide analyses of the Great Lakes' prospects and disseminate their opinions to investors. Often, there will be explicit forecasts of the company's growth rate in these published opinions. The *Value Line Investment Survey*, which we cited earlier as one publisher of the betas of common stocks, makes growth forecasts as a regular part of its research recommendations on the stocks it follows. Since we are interested in trying to estimate what investors are expecting, it will often be useful to find out what the people who *tell investors what to expect* are saying.[2] This would be particularly true in situations where the history of a firm's dividends and earnings has not been as steady and stable as it is in our Great Lakes illustration.[3]

Suppose the common stock of Great Lakes has a current market price of $28.25 per share and the company has recently announced its intention to pay a $1.70 per share dividend in the coming year. With an expected dividend growth rate of 10%, the cost of capital for common equity can be estimated to be:

$$K_E = \frac{D_1}{P_0} + g = \frac{\$1.70}{\$28.25} + 0.10 = 0.06 + 0.10 = 0.16 = 16\%$$

This result indicates that investors in Great Lakes' common stock demand an RRR of 16% annually, consisting of a 6% cash dividend yield and a 10% capital gains yield. As with preferred stock, dividends on common stock are not tax-deductible. The 16% cost of equity capital therefore is also *an after-tax RRR*.

---

[1] There is some debate about whether one should give most weight to the past record of dividends or of earnings if the growth rates of the two differ. There is also some debate as to the relative merits of calculating growth rates by averaging the annual changes or using the beginning-to-end compound growth formula. For several reasons, we would place most emphasis on the *dividend* record, and believe an *annual-averaging* approach to the growth rate calculation is most appropriate. Nonetheless, opinions differ, and your instructor may have his or her own views about these two issues.

[2] Another approach to estimating a company's expected growth rate is to determine its "sustainable" growth rate. We discuss the concept of sustainable growth in Chapter 21.

[3] A further question in using the dividend growth model is how *long* a history of dividends and earnings would be relevant to investors in examining a company's past growth record. There is probably no generalizable answer to this question, other than to state that one should go back no further than the point where the major elements of the company's current financial and operating policies were put in place.

http://

Check out the CAPM in an article testing the Fama-French Model of share value at www.maths.tcd.ie/pub/econrev/ser/html/market.html

The CAPM. The alternative approach to estimation of the RRR on common equity would be to use the Capital Asset Pricing Model and calculate that required return directly from the market risk/return relationship specified in equation (1). For example, if the current risk-free rate i is 7%, the historical market risk premium ($K_M - i$) is 8%, and Great Lakes stock has a β of 1.12, the CAPM would estimate the company's cost of common equity to be:

$$K_E = i + (K_M - i)(\beta)$$
$$K_E = 0.07 + (0.08)(1.12) = 0.16 = 16\%$$

Ideally, the dividend growth model and CAPM estimates of this cost will be very close, as in our example. When they are, the financial manager can have some reasonable confidence in the resulting figure. Unfortunately, this may not always be the case in practice.

Each model requires the estimation of one or more key variables (such as g, β, and the market risk premium), which are unobservable because they deal fundamentally with investor expectations. Historical data necessarily must be employed to attempt to capture these expectations, but it's obvious that this is a process in which absolute accuracy is not possible. If the two models give substantially *different* answers, our best advice would be (a) to reexamine the assumptions and data inputs of each more carefully to see if they are reasonable and (b) to make estimates of the cost of common equity for other companies in the industry as benchmarks. Hopefully, these steps will help resolve the discrepancy.

Securities Issuance Costs. As we discussed in Chapter 3, a firm will require the services of an investment banker when it issues new securities to raise funds. Because costs will be incurred by the firm for those services, the firm will receive less money from a securities issue than the full value of the securities that are sold to investors. To make up for the issue costs incurred, the rate of return the firm must earn on the investments that are financed by issuing the securities must be somewhat *greater* than the return that investors require.

For example, suppose a firm issues $100 million of preferred stock that has a 10% dividend rate but receives only $98 million from the issue, net of underwriting costs. The investors who buy the preferred stock require a 10% yield on their investment. The actual cost of the $98 million to the issuing firm is:

$$K_P = \frac{\$10,000,000}{\$98,000,000} = 10.2\%$$

The firm must earn at the 10.2% annual rate on the $98 million of investments it can make in order to cover the $10 million annual dividend on the preferred.

We have not included an allowance for securities issuance costs thus far in our examination of the costs of various forms of capital to the firm. In principle, we should make an upward adjustment in each of the RRRs to recognize those costs. From a practical standpoint, however, it seldom will be necessary to do so. In a well-developed capital market, the issuance costs for a public debt financing of any reasonable size will be quite small in relation to the amount of money raised. The costs will be even smaller for a private placement of debt or for a loan obtained directly from a bank. Hence, the impact on the RRR for debt financing will be minimal and can be ignored. Costs will tend to be somewhat higher for issuing preferred stock, but again not really high enough to make it necessary to take them into account. Essentially, for both debt and preferred stock financing, the extra precision realized in the cost of capital calculation, which will always be an estimated figure in any event, is simply not worth the extra effort.

While there are no issue costs for common equity when earnings are retained, when equity capital is raised by issuing *new shares* of common stock, the associated issuance costs are typically sufficiently large that they do need to be recognized. The costs are comprised of several elements:

(1) *Underwriting Costs.* These consist of the commissions paid to the investment bankers and the out-of-pocket expenses associated with the filings required by legal and regulatory authorities.

(2) *Underpricing Costs.* It is often the case that the new shares being issued will be priced to investors at a slight discount from the current trading price of existing shares, in order to insure a rapid sale of the new securities. This price concession reduces the net funds received by the issuer of the securities in the same manner as does the commission paid to the investment banker.

(3) *Signaling Costs.* When firms announce their intention to sell new shares of common stock, the trading prices of their existing shares typically decline in response to the announcement. There are at least two reasons why this might occur, both of which relate to the "signal" that investors may interpret as being sent by management. One possible message is that the firm intends to reduce the degree of financial leverage in its capital structure by adding to its equity capital. As we saw in Chapter 14, leverage should have a positive effect on the value of the firm and, therefore, less leverage implies less value. A second message could be that common shares are being issued because management believes the shares are currently overvalued in the market and wishes to take advantage of that situation to maximize the proceeds from the sale of new shares. Either of these messages could cause investors to revise downward their assessment of the value of the firm's stock.

Studies have shown that the combination of these costs results in a price decline in the issuing company's stock, which averages about 3% when a new common equity issue is announced. While that figure may not sound like very much, it's important to note that this is a decline of 3% in the *total* value of the firm's stock, not just of the proceeds of the new shares being issued.

Thus, if the typical new stock offering increases the number of the issuing firm's outstanding shares by 20% (which is about average), the resulting 3% price decline for *all* the shares translates into an issuance cost of fully *15% of the value of the new shares issued.* A cost of this magnitude is worth taking into account. The implication is that a firm raising funds by issuing new common shares will have to earn somewhat more than investors' current equity RRR on the additional investments supported by those funds in order to recoup the issue-related costs and valuation losses incurred.

The most direct and convenient way to recognize these costs is to include them as part of the initial outlay in the calculation of investment project present values. For example, suppose the proceeds of new common stock offerings provide 20% of the total funding for a firm's investments over time and that new-equity issue costs are 15% of those proceeds. The issue-cost adjustment factor, λ (lambda), for the firm would be:

$$\lambda = (\%\text{External Equity Funding})(\%\text{Equity Issue Cost}) \qquad (5)$$
$$\lambda = (0.20)(0.15) = 0.03 = 3.0\%$$

and the firm should require that the expected future cash inflows from each investment project have a minimum present value that is equal to $1/(1 - \lambda)$ times the cost of the project. Thus, for an investment necessitating an initial outlay of $1 million, the future cash flows expected from it would need to have a present value equal to:

$$\text{Adjusted Outlay} = \frac{\text{Initial Outlay}}{1 - \lambda} = \frac{\$1,000,000}{1 - 0.03} = \$1,030,928$$

in order for the investment to offset allocated securities issue costs and be just marginally acceptable to stockholders.

THE WEIGHTED AVERAGE COST OF CAPITAL

Having estimated the respective costs of the individual forms of financing available to the firm, the financial manager's next step is to calculate the firm's composite cost of capital. This composite cost will depend upon (a) the identified costs of the individual components of the firm's financing, and (b) the proportions in which those components are combined in the firm's overall financing plan. The resulting weighted average cost of capital is the discount rate that is then used to measure the present value of a proposed investment project. Consequently, the selection and implementation of a financing strategy is central to the determination of project desirability.

Capitalization Targets

Total Market Capitalization The total market value of all the firm's outstanding securities.

Because of its effect on the value of the firm, *the most important element of the financing plan is the degree of leverage the firm chooses to maintain.* As discussed in Chapter 14, the key decision variable in that regard is the leverage ratio L: the ratio of debt to the total market value of the firm (the firm's **total market capitalization**). We saw that the leverage decision involves a trade-off between the tax advantages of debt financing and the expected costs of financial distress, with the optimum leverage ratio being reached when the two effects are in balance. Not all firms will reach the same conclusion as to when that balance has been attained.

In particular, firms in high-operating-risk lines of business will be likely to select relatively low financial leverage ratios. Firms will also differ on the extent to which they may wish to preserve a margin of untapped borrowing power either for emergencies or to take quick advantage of unexpected investment opportunities. Whatever may be the factors considered, the establishment of a **target leverage ratio** is the critical decision for the firm's financial managers. That target ratio becomes the "weight" to be assigned to the cost of debt capital in the calculation of the firm's weighted average cost of capital.

Target Leverage Ratio The ratio of the market value of debt to the total market value of the firm that management seeks to maintain.

A corresponding target ratio (weight) for preferred stock must also be selected, but the effect of that choice on the value of the firm is of minor significance. Because there is no tax advantage to preferred, preferred stock comprises only a very small proportion of corporate financing. What is left over after the target ratios for debt and preferred stock have been established is automatically the target ratio for common equity, since all three ratios must sum to 1.00.

Calculating the Weighted Cost

As an illustration, let us suppose Great Lakes Manufacturing finds that it can obtain new debt financing at a 12% pretax interest rate, new preferred stock at a 10% dividend rate, and retained earnings at an RRR of 16%. Assume Great Lakes to be in a 40% marginal corporate tax bracket and that the firm's future financial plan calls for (a) a target debt ratio of 25% of total capitalization; (b) a target ratio of 5% of capitalization for preferred stock; and (c) the remainder of its financing to come from retained earnings. The **weighted average cost of capital** to the firm (K_A) is:

$$K_A = \text{Weighted Cost of Debt} + \text{Weighted Cost of Preferred Stock} + \text{Weighted Cost of Retained Earnings}$$

$$K_A = (W_D)(K_D) + (W_P)(K_P) + (W_E)(K_E) \tag{6}$$

$$K_A = (0.25)(0.12)(1 - 0.40) + (0.05)(0.10) + (0.70)(0.16)$$

$$K_A = 0.018 + 0.005 + 0.112 = 0.135 = 13.5\%$$

Weighted Average Cost of Capital The discount rate used to calculate the present value of an investment project.

where the W's denote the weights of debt, preferred stock, and retained earnings, respectively. The present values of the cash flows expected from the firm's proposed capital investment projects should be computed by discounting those cash flows at a rate of 13.5% per annum.

This last statement, however, implies somewhat more precision in the calculation than realistically can be obtained. Recall that the component cost of retained earnings is itself only an estimate. For that reason, the resulting weighted average calculation is also subject to estimation error. As a practical matter, therefore, the best one can expect is to be able to come up with a reasonable *approximation* of the weighted cost of capital for a firm, rather than with an absolutely precise figure.

In the case of Great Lakes Manufacturing, for example, a more sensible recommendation might be to advise the firm's financial managers to do a sensitivity analysis and compute the present values of the expected cash flows from the firm's investment projects using a *range* of discount rates centered on 13.5%, such as 13% and 14%. Projects whose net present values are positive at both discount rates can be considered to be acceptable projects. Projects whose net present values are negative at both discount rates are clearly unacceptable. Not only are these easy decisions, but the great majority of project proposals will almost certainly fall in one of the two categories. Conversely, projects whose net present values are positive when 13% is used as the discount rate but negative when 14% is used can be regarded simply as *marginal* projects. To the best of the financial manager's ability to determine, the net present values of those projects are close to zero. The decision whether or not to undertake the projects can then be made on other grounds—they make employees happy, they make managers happy, they make customers happy, or they provide some other hard-to-quantify "strategic" benefit.[4]

The Financial Planning Horizon

Underlying the concept of determining a weighted average cost of capital to use to measure project present values is the principle that the overall target capitalization ratios selected by the firm in its financial plan represent the financing mix *for each individual project* as well. Equivalently, all the investments that comprise the assets of the firm (its *uses* of funds) are supported *equally* by the total set of financings that comprise the claims of securityholders on the firm (its *sources* of funds). The implication is that it is not appropriate to attach a particular component of financing to a particular investment project and use the required rate of return on *that* component as the discount rate to compute the project's present value. This is the case even if the *immediate* financing for the project comes from a single source.

---

[4] Recall also that the *cash flows* from most investment projects are expected rather than known values. Consequently, they are themselves subject to estimation error.

■ Ethics

ISSUES

IS GREEN GOOD FOR BOTH THE ENVIRONMENT AND THE COST OF CAPITAL?

Financial markets in the 1990s have seen a new emphasis by individual and institutional investors on "green" companies that pay serious attention to the environmental impact of their operations. During the 1980s, firms such as The Body Shop in Great Britain and Ben and Jerry's Homemade in the United States were seen as sacrificing profitability to achieve social and environmental goals. In the 1990s, on the other hand, both investors and financial managers were making the argument that environmental awareness is consistent with long-term value maximization. If investors and managers are to act on this belief, however, they must first be able to measure accurately the specific degree of a firm's environmental awareness.

The environmental awareness position argues that good, green behavior increases firm value by improving a company's public image and sales, preempting new environmental regulations, avoiding the costs of environmental lawsuits and cleanups, and boosting employee morale. Most recently, some limited evidence suggests that a green company will also have a lower cost of capital because suppliers of both equity and debt financing view the firm as having less exposure to the risk of environmental accidents. As a result, they will offer better financing terms. While the logic of these arguments is gaining wider acceptance, the inability to measure a firm's exposure and response to environmental risk has seriously hampered their implementation by green investors and managers.

Some early attempts at measuring a company's green performance have occurred in Great Britain. For example, a nonprofit organization called Business in the Environment divides the top one hundred publicly held companies into five levels of achievement that reflect the firms' attempts to manage their impact on the environment. The indicators of environmental management include the assignment of a key board member to environmental issues and the presence of an environmental procurement policy. The ultimate goal of environmental management assessment is to develop quantitative measures that can be used to compare the relative performance of various firms. One step in this direction is a measure of emissions of carbon dioxide that has been developed by London University in partnership with a London insurance company. The role of this measure is to provide investors with an indication of a firm's exposure to penalties for excess emissions of this key greenhouse gas. A British consulting firm, Sum Rating Agency, has constructed an environmental performance rating system that imitates the type of credit ratings provided by Moody's and Standard & Poor's. Perhaps some day these types of quantitative measures of environmental performance will be included in company annual reports, along with the conventional measures of financial performance such as return on assets or return on equity.

The logic behind this principle is that, while firms develop long-term strategies for financing themselves and translate those strategies into a set of target proportions for their capitalizations, it is generally not practical for firms to finance themselves in exactly those same proportions in *every* year. That is because there are economies of scale in the costs of issuing securities. The larger the size of the issue, the smaller are issue costs as a percent of the total proceeds received. Hence, firms tend to raise external capital by issuing securities infrequently in large amounts, rather than frequently in small amounts. In any given year, there may be an unusually heavy reliance on a particular type of financing, just as a matter of efficiency in fund raising. This does not mean, however, that the investments the firm makes in the same year are supported only by that year's financing package.

To see the point, let us return to our Great Lakes Manufacturing illustration. We specified that the firm adopted 25% as its target capitalization ratio for debt. Suppose the company also has a policy of not issuing new debentures in amounts smaller than $50 million. As a consequence, the firm may allow its debt ratio to drift down over several years to perhaps 20% of total capitalization by retaining earnings and adding to stockholder equity, before coming out with a new $50 million debenture offering that takes its leverage ratio immediately up to 30%. Over time, that ratio will drift down again until another large new debenture offering is made. Since the firm's long-run target capitalization ratio for debt is 25%, that percentage of the total value of the firm *will be* debt-financed over the long-term. Nevertheless, there may never be a *single year* in which debt accounts for exactly 25% of the year's financing.

It may be that almost all the funding for the investment projects undertaken in a particular year comes from debt simply because that just happens to be a year in which one of Great Lakes' periodic $50 million debt issues takes place. It would be incorrect, however, to treat those projects as if they were 100% debt-financed and use the cost of debt capital as the discount rate to measure the projects' net present values. While it's true that debt did provide most of the funding for the year's projects, Great Lakes will have to compensate in subsequent years by relying on retained earnings for additional funding until the desired debt/equity balance is restored to its capital structure. In that sense, *all* the firm's investment projects are effectively financed by the long-run set of target capitalization proportions established by the firm, whatever the actual sequence of their funding. Accordingly, *the proper discount rate for all project present value computations is the firm's weighted average cost of capital.*

Book Weights and Market Weights

It is also important to emphasize that the capitalization ratios which are relevant as the weights in the calculation of the weighted average cost of capital are the ratios of the *market values* of debt, preferred stock, and common equity to the total market value of the firm. As we have repeatedly stressed, the objective of the firm's financing and investing decisions should be to enhance the *market value* of its common stock, and the return requirements of both stock and bond investors are based on the market values of the securities involved.

The cost of capital for debt is the current market rate of interest, and the cost of preferred stock is the prevailing market yield on preferred. The RRR on common equity is the discount rate that investors apply to the stream of expected future dividends per share to arrive at the current price they are willing to pay for the stock. Since all these RRRs are market value benchmarks, it is the market weights of the firm's financing that apply in determining its weighted average cost of capital.

This is not to say that the book amounts of debt, preferred, and common equity are unimportant. As we saw in Chapter 2, they are useful in developing internal measures of the financial performance of the firm. Lenders and trade creditors typically define the financial conditions a firm must satisfy in order to qualify for credit in book-value terms. As we shall see in Chapters 16 and 21, the book capitalization of the firm also plays a central role in dividend policy decisions, cash requirements planning, and strategies for funding corporate growth. Nonetheless, for purposes of identifying the desirability of *proposed investment projects*, a market-weighted cost of capital should be used as the discount rate for the present value calculations.

To see how this works, take a simple example where the expected pretax cash flow from an investment proposal is a level perpetuity of $20 million per year. This is the EBIT from the project. Suppose the firm that is considering the proposal plans to borrow $40 million at a 10% interest rate as part of the funding for the project, with the rest of the initial expenditure to be financed with retained earnings. Assume the market-required return on common equity investments in the firm to be 16% and the firm to be in a 40% tax bracket. On that basis, the annual cash flows from the project will be expected to be divided up as follows:

EBIT	$20,000,000	
Interest Income to Lenders	(4,000,000)	(10% on $40 million)
Earnings before Taxes	16,000,000	
Income Taxes	(6,400,000)	(40% of $16 million)
Cash Flow to Stockholders	$ 9,600,000	

The total *value* of the project parallels that of the total value of the firm that we examined in Chapter 14. It is the sum of the market value (D) of the cash flows received by the lenders on the debt financing they have provided, plus the market value (V_S) of the residual cash flows received by stockholders. If 10% is the current market rate of interest, the value of the lenders' portion of the cash flows is, of course, just the $40 million loan they have provided. The value to stockholders is:

$$V_S = \frac{\text{Annual Cash Flow}}{\text{RRR}}$$

$$V_S = \frac{\$9,600,000}{0.16} = \$60,000,000$$

for a total project value of:

$$D + V_S = \$40,000,000 + \$60,000,000 = \$100,000,000$$

This is also the answer you get when you discount the project's after-tax operating cash flows at a market-weighted after-tax cost of capital. Thus, the market weights here are:

$$W_D = \$40,000,000/\$100,000,000 = 0.40$$

$$W_E = \$60,000,000/\$100,000,000 = 0.60$$

and the corresponding weighted average after-tax cost of capital is:

$$K_A = (W_D)(K_D) + (W_E)(K_E)$$

$$K_A = (0.40)(0.10)(1 - 0.40) + (0.60)(0.16)$$

$$K_A = 0.024 + 0.096 = 0.120 = 12.0\%$$

The annual after-tax operating cash flow (OCF) from the project is calculated by ignoring financing costs because these are captured in the cost of capital:

$$\text{Annual Operating Cash Flow} = (\text{EBIT})(1 - T) = (\$20,000,000)(1 - 0.40) = \$12,000,000$$

and the present value of this expected cash flow, calculated using a market-weighted cost of capital of 12.0%, is:

$$PV = \frac{\$12,000,000}{0.12} = \$100,000,000$$

which matches the total of the underlying values to lenders and common stockholders.

Note that the *cost* of the project (which is its book value) does not enter into this calculation. It is only the amount of debt that is raised to *pay* part of the cost that matters. Thus, if the project required an initial outlay of $80 million, lenders would be providing half the funding for it and stockholders the other half. Since the expected future cash flows are worth a total of $100 million, however, stockholders enjoy a $20 million net capital gain from the project. Their contribution to the investment is $40 million, but the residual value of their portion of the project's cash flows is $60 million because the lenders' claims are *fixed* at $40 million. The relationships are as follows:

A. Present Value of Future Cash Flows	$100,000,000
Less: Initial Investment Outlay	(80,000,000)
Equals: Project NPV to Stockholders	$ 20,000,000

B. Present Value of Future Cash Flows	$100,000,000
Less: Value of Lenders' Claim	(40,000,000)
Equals: Value of Stockholders' Claim	$ 60,000,000
Less: Stockholders' Investment	(40,000,000)
Equals: Project NPV to Stockholders	$ 20,000,000

Accordingly, *a project that is calculated to have a positive net present value when the firm's market-weighted average cost of capital is used as the discount rate will be a desirable investment that should create the same amount of value for shareholders.*

Targeting a debt ratio (and thereby implicitly an equity ratio as well) that is fixed in market value terms obviously presents some operational challenges to the financial manager. Taken literally, the task would require either adding to or subtracting from the firm's outstanding debt or equity every day, since stock and bond prices change daily. Clearly, this would be impractical. What firms instead do is adopt the longer-term planning horizon we referred to earlier and aim to achieve their targeted capitalization ratios as *average values* over time. That is a much easier task and simultaneously accommodates the desire to minimize external fundraising costs by having only infrequent issues of securities.

If you recorded and plotted the market capitalization ratios of a typical firm over time, therefore, you would be likely to generate something like the profile shown in Figure 15-2. From time to time, the firm will actually "hit" its targets exactly but generally will have to be content simply with staying within some reasonable range of those targets. Nonetheless, since the targets *will* be attained on average over the long term, they are valid benchmarks for the determination of the firm's weighted average cost of capital.

CHANGES IN THE COST OF CAPITAL

Throughout the discussion in this chapter, we have stressed the need to use estimates of the current cost of capital to calculate a proposed investment's net present value. As we have already pointed out, a firm's current cost of capital can be affected by its investing decisions (which alter the firm's operating risk) and by its financing decisions (which alter its financial risk). In addition, the cost of capital can be altered by changes in the financial market environment even if a firm's investing and financing decisions remain unchanged. In this section of the chapter, we will examine each of these causes of changes in the firm's cost of capital.

Changes in the Leverage Ratio

When undertaking new investment projects in its existing line of business, if the firm adheres to the target capitalization proportions of debt and equity it presently has in place, the current return requirements of investors on both capital components will also carry over to the new projects. We can estimate those RRRs as we have just described and combine them to calculate the firm's weighted average cost of capital. This, as we noted earlier, is the easy case.

If the firm decides to *change* the mix of debt and equity in its capitalization, however, the analysis becomes a bit more complicated. The required return on equity will be affected by that change, due to the associated change in the firm's financial risk. The K_E that would be estimated based on the firm's existing capital-

Characteristic Time Profile of a Corporation's Capitalization Ratios Measured at Market Value

FIGURE 15-2

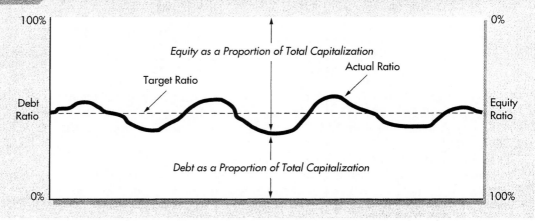

ization therefore will no longer apply. We established the following relationship between leverage and the required return on equity in Chapter 14:

$$K_E = \frac{K_U - rL}{1 - L} \qquad (7)$$

where K_U is the RRR on equity that would be observed if a firm were unlevered, r is the market interest rate on the firm's debt, and L is its leverage ratio. If the leverage ratio planned for the firm in the future is different from the current one, the new K_E that investors will require must be identified from this relationship. The new K_E then is the one that becomes part of the calculation of the firm's new, forward-looking weighted average cost of capital.

We can use Great Lakes Manufacturing again to illustrate the process. We found above that when debt amounted to 25% of the firm's total market capitalization, and the pretax interest rate required on new borrowings was 12%, the required return on common equity for the firm was 16%. From these observations, and equation (7), we can infer the firm's unlevered RRR on equity to be:

$$K_E = \frac{K_U - rL}{1 - L}$$

$$0.16 = \frac{K_U - (0.12)(0.25)}{1 - 0.25}$$

$$K_U = (0.16)(0.75) + (0.12)(0.25)$$

$$K_U = 0.12 + 0.03 = 0.15 = 15.0\%$$

This figure is *less* than the 16% return on common equity required at the firm's existing leverage ratio of 25%. If the leverage ratio is changed to 35%, we can use equation (7) once more to calculate the new K_E which will accompany that change:

$$K_E = \frac{0.15 - (0.12)(0.35)}{1 - 0.35} = \frac{0.15 - 0.042}{0.65} = 0.166 = 16.6\%$$

This return requirement exceeds the current K_E as a result of the increased leverage. The new K_E, along with the new capital structure target for Great Lakes, can then be substituted into equation (6) to determine the firm's new weighted average cost of capital:

$$K_A = (W_D)(K_D) + (W_P)(K_P) + (W_E)(K_E)$$
$$K_A = (0.35)(0.12)(1 - 0.40) + (0.05)(0.10) + (0.60)(0.166)$$
$$K_A = 0.0252 + 0.005 + 0.0996 = 0.1298 = 13.0\%$$

Notice that the firm's average cost of capital has declined from 13.5% in our earlier example because the increase in K_E (from 0.160 to 0.166) has been more than offset by the decrease in W_E (from 0.70 to 0.60). That is, as the firm relies more heavily on less expensive debt financing and less heavily on more expensive equity financing, its weighted average cost of capital falls. The necessary steps in the estimation of the new K_E and average cost of capital are summarized in Figure 15-3.

The reason for having to go through this procedure is that, since the return requirement K_U reflects only the operating risk and operating leverage of the firm, it is *invariant* to changes in financial risk. It is fundamentally a reflection of the firm's line of business, whereas K_E varies upward *from* the underlying K_U as the firm's financial leverage increases.[5]

Among the other effects a change in financial leverage may produce is a change in the interest rate the firm will have to pay to obtain new debt financing. An increase in the leverage ratio L is likely to lead to an increase in that interest rate, because lenders will feel that the risk to them has increased. This effect should also be included in the analysis outlined in Figure 15-3, in the form of a new value for r in Step (3), and the same new r in the weighted average cost of capital calculation in Step (4). Once more, the firm's commercial and investment bankers should be able to provide a good estimate of how r will vary with the firm's leverage.

Steps in the Calculation of the Effect of Changes in the Firm's Leverage Ratio on the Required Return on Common Equity and the Weighted Average Cost of Capital

SUMMARY FIGURE 15-3

(1) Estimate the current required return on common equity (K_E) for the firm at its existing ratio of debt to total capitalization.

(2) Using the current K_E and equation (7), calculate the return of common equity (K_U) that investors would require if the firm were unlevered.

(3) Given K_U and the planned new ratio of debt to total capitalization, insert these values into equation (7) and compute the new K_E that will prevail at the firm's new leverage position.

(4) Use the new K_E as the cost of common equity capital, and the new weights of debt and equity, to determine the firm's new weighted average cost of capital.

[5] The presence of preferred stock in a firm's capital structure also increases the risk to common stockholders because of the fixed and senior claim that preferred has on the firm's income. This senior claim is much like that of bondholders. Hence, it would be logical to include the sum of both debt and preferred stock in defining the leverage ratio L in equation (7), and in identifying the impact of leverage changes on the RRR for common equity, even though we have not done so here in the Great Lakes example. Since the interest rate on debt and the dividend rate on preferred for a given company will generally be quite similar, the debt interest rate can still be used as r in the rL term in equation (7) as a reasonable approximation.

Optimum Leverage Ratio
The leverage ratio that maximizes the value of the firm.

The Optimum Degree of Leverage

While it is often difficult to pin down exactly, there should be an **optimum leverage ratio** for each firm that will maximize the market value of the firm (for a given set of assets) and simultaneously provide the maximum value for the firm's common stockholders. *This will be the same leverage ratio at which the firm's weighted average cost of capital is minimized.* We saw in Chapter 5 that the lower the discount rate which is applied to a given stream of future cash flows, the higher is the resulting present value of those cash flows. Necessarily, then, when value is maximized, the associated discount rate is minimized.[6]

It is primarily the trade-off between the tax advantage of debt and the expected costs of financial distress that determines the optimum leverage ratio. Initially as leverage increases, the value of the firm increases and the per-share price of the firm's stock rises. The increasing proportion of debt in the firm's capitalization also lowers the firm's weighted average cost of capital. At some point, however, the firm's debt obligations become large enough that investors become concerned about the firm's ability to meet those obligations. That concern causes the value of the firm and its common shares to stop rising and begin to turn downward. The effect is the same as if the required return on common equity for the firm started to increase especially rapidly at the same point—in reflection of the risks and possible costs of financial distress. Coupled with an increase in the interest rate the firm will have to pay to obtain new debt financing, the higher RRR for equity causes the firm's weighted average cost of capital to rise as well.

The simultaneous impacts of the firm's leverage ratio on its required return on common equity, its weighted average cost of capital, and the price of the firm's common stock are portrayed in Figure 15-4. While the specific shape of these relationships will vary from firm to firm, they should all have the same general character shown.

Changes in Operations

Another action that can affect the firm's cost of capital is a change in the line of business in which the firm operates. The unlevered required return on common equity, K_U, is the basic determinant of the cost of common equity. It is determined by investors' perceptions of the risks inherent in the firm's operations. Accordingly, if the nature of those operations changes, so also may K_U and K_E.

A good example of a situation of this sort in the United States is the company that used to be known as Westinghouse Electric Corporation. In 1994, just after a new Chief Executive Officer was hired, the firm manufactured railroad locomotives, electrical power generating equipment, electronics for military applications, and industrial refrigeration equipment. By the end of 1997, the new CEO had sold off all these businesses, had bought a television broadcasting network and several hundred radio stations, had moved the company's headquarters from Pittsburgh to New York City, and had even renamed the firm the CBS Corporation. Since the businesses of the company in 1997 were not the same as they were in 1994, it is highly likely that the required returns from those businesses were also not the same.

Changes in the Market Environment

Finally, the weighted average cost of capital can change without any direct action by the firm if changes occur in the securities market which are outside the financial manager's control. Among the key noncontrollables are:

---

[6] Strictly speaking, total firm value and common stockholder wealth (per-share stock price) may not be maximized at exactly the same leverage ratio, but the two peaks will typically closely coincide. Maximum firm value and minimum cost of capital, however, *will* coincide.

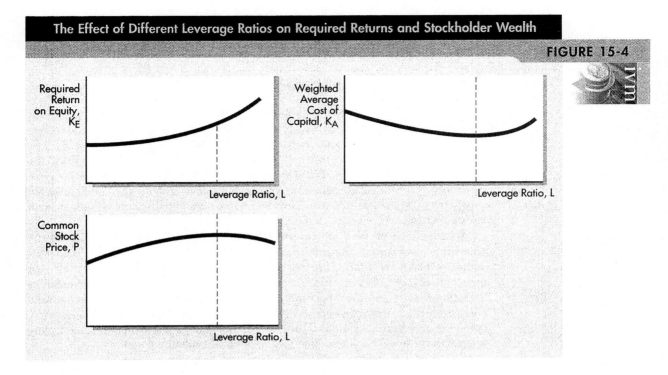

The Effect of Different Leverage Ratios on Required Returns and Stockholder Wealth

FIGURE 15-4

(1) *Changes in the perceptions of investors as to the degree of risk associated with investments in common stocks.*   Thus, the firm's β may not change, but investors may revise their opinions about the risk that is present for the market as a whole. This would show up in the Capital Asset Pricing Model as a change in the required rate of return (K_M) on the market portfolio, and that change would affect all stocks.

(2) *Changes in investors' attitude toward risk.*   Even if there is no change in perceptions about the *level* of investment risk that prevails, it could be that investors simply come to feel differently about *incurring* that risk. This in turn will also alter the RRR for all securities.

(3) *Changes in investors' expectations about future inflation rates.*   We discussed in Chapter 3 the relationship between inflation expectations and the RRR on investments. Specifically, the higher the expected future inflation rate, the higher the rate of return investors will require from their investments, including both stocks and bonds.

Phenomena of this sort have often been cited as having major influences on the prices of securities. In the early 1980s, for example, both short- and long-term interest rates in the United States were in the vicinity of 15% because inflation rates were in excess of 10% and were forecasted to remain high. With such high returns available from bond investments, high returns were required from stocks as well, and the high RRRs resulted in depressed stock prices at the time. Well into the 1980s, the performance of the U.S. stock market appears to have been adversely affected by lingering concerns about inflation and by the perception that the future earnings of American companies were at substantial risk because the firms were not competitive in the international marketplace. Inflation fears largely receded, interest rates declined, and American firms cut costs and improved product quality beginning in the late1980s and early 1990s. The overthrow of the communist governments of central and eastern Europe also may have removed an

http://

The National Institute of Economic and Social Research (NIESR) publishes economic forecasts and related economic articles. For an article based on forecasts published in the NIESR and comments on inflation rates in England, see

www.hm-treasury.gov. uk/pub/html/panel/nov95/ anxa.html

element of perceived risk in the general investment environment. Presumably in response, the U.S. stock market subsequently experienced major and sustained upward movements in prices.

THE IMPLICATIONS OF CHANGES IN THE COST OF CAPITAL

Fluctuations in a firm's cost of capital will affect the RRR and NPV for *proposed* investment projects in its existing line of business. Those same fluctuations, however, will also affect the RRR and NPV for the firm's *current* investments. The amount of the change in value will depend not only on the magnitude of the change in the cost of capital, but also on the size and timing of a firm's cash flows. An example is the differential impact on the prices of "income" and "growth" stocks, even when the RRRs on common equity for the two are identical both before *and* after the change in the broader market.

Take the case of two firms operating in the same industry and therefore in the same business-risk class. Assume that both have the same leverage ratio, that their common shares are both currently trading at a price of $30 per share, and that investors require a 15% annual rate of return (K_E) from investments in the stocks of each company. Suppose that since one company (the *income* stock) pays out a large proportion of its earnings as dividends ($3.00 per share in the current year), it is considered to have only a modest 5% per annum growth potential. In the framework of our basic common stock valuation model:

$$P_{0,I} = \frac{D_1}{K_E - g} = \frac{\$3.00}{0.15 - 0.05} = \$30.00$$

where the added subscript "I" denotes the price of the income stock. The other company (the *growth* stock) retains and reinvests the majority of its earnings and is perceived as having strong future growth prospects. Its current dividend is half that of the income stock (only $1.50 per share), but the dividend is expected to increase in the future at an annual rate of 10%. Accordingly, for the growth company (subscript G):

$$P_{0,G} = \frac{D_1}{K_E - g} = \frac{\$1.50}{0.15 - 0.10} = \$30.00$$

Suppose then that investors' aversion to risk increases for *all* investments and, as a result, the RRR on equity for our two firms increases from 15% to 20%. The new share prices that will be observed are:

$$P_{0,I} = \frac{D_1}{K_E - g} = \frac{\$3.00}{0.20 - 0.05} = \$20.00$$

$$P_{0,G} = \frac{D_1}{K_E - g} = \frac{\$1.50}{0.20 - 0.10} = \$15.00$$

Despite the fact that the two stocks *still* have identical RRRs, the change in required return has caused the price of the growth stock to fall from $30 to just $15 per share, while the price of the income stock declines only from $30 to $20 per share. Similarly, if K_E had decreased rather than increased, the upward impact on the price of the growth company's stock would also be greater.

The reason for the difference is a simple present-value principle that we discussed in Chapter 5: *the farther in the future are the cash flows from an investment, the larger is the effect on their present value of a change in the discount rate applied to them.* Because the cash flows (the dividends) from the income stock start out high, an increase in the RRR on the stock has a relatively moderate

■ Financial ISSUes

THE RESPONSE OF FIRMS TO CHANGES IN THE COST OF CAPITAL IN THE 1990S

The discussion in this chapter points out that a firm's cost of capital reflects not only the financial characteristics of the firm itself but also the market environment in which

the firm operates. The market environment of the late 1990s provides a dramatic example of how market conditions can influence the cost of capital and the investing and financing decisions of firms. Both the level of stock prices and interest rates in the late 1990s seemed to indicate historically low costs of debt and equity capital:

	S&P 500 Index	S&P 500 P/E Ratio	30-Year U.S. Treasury Bond Yield
1981	100	8	15%
1985	200	10	10
1990	370	15	9
1995	600	17	7
1998	1,000	26	6

The yield on U.S. Treasury bonds reached a peak of 15% in 1981 in response to double-digit U.S. inflation rates that resulted in a large inflation premium. By 1998, annual inflation rates of less than 3% for six consecutive years had pushed the long-term Treasury yield to a 40-year low of 6%. The response of firms to this dramatic decline in long-term interest rates was predictable. New debt issues in the capital market reached record levels of some $300 billion annually. The net increase in debt outstanding, however, did not match the gross issuance of new debt because much of the new debt represented a refinancing of outstanding

debt at lower yields. For example, Toro Co. reduced its average cost of debt from 11% to 8% through a series of refinancings during the 1996–97 period. Other firms, such as Disney, J.C. Penney, and IBM, took advantage of the historically low yields by issuing bonds with 100-year terms-to-maturity.

The reliance on debt financing may have been even more pronounced were it not for the impressive rise in stock prices. Not only did the value of the S&P Index rise by 900% from 1981 to 1998, but price/earnings ratios more than tripled. As investors paid even higher multiples of current earnings, the cost of equity financing to firms declined steadily. In response, annual new equity issues also hit record levels of over $100 billion. Interestingly, the net level of equity financing outstanding actually fell since the late 1980s as firms retired equity through mergers and stock repurchase programs. Particularly in the 1990s, company profits were so strong that firms were able to finance the majority of their investments through retained earnings while simultaneously engaging in large stock repurchases. For example, General Motors repurchased $5 billion of its stock in 1997 and announced that it would repurchase another $4 billion in shares in 1998. At the same time, the firm's annual capital expenditures amounted to about $10 billion, and its cash and marketable securities had reached a level of $14 billion.

impact on the value today of its future dividend stream. By contrast, the weight of the growth stock's dividends are much farther in the future because they grow from a low current base. Thus, an increase in the RRR severely penalizes the present value of those dividends. Another way to think of these outcomes is to recognize that the growth stock is an investment that effectively has a longer "duration" than the income stock. The longer the duration, the greater the sensitivity of the value of the investment to changes in the RRR. (See the Appendix to Chapter 7.)

ESTIMATING PROJECT RRRS FOR DIVERSIFIED COMPANIES

Up to this point, we have concentrated our analysis on the estimation of the RRR for a proposed investment in a firm's existing line of business. For this type of investment, the appropriate RRR is the firm's current weighted average cost of capital. When a firm has multiple lines of business or is considering investments in new lines of business, the determination of the appropriate RRR for proposed projects becomes somewhat more of a challenge. For a diversified company, a cost of

capital calculation will lead to a figure that reflects the *composite risk* of the firm's existing businesses but that will not be applicable to any of the *individual* businesses unless they accidentally happen to be of average risk for the firm. Similarly, if the firm is evaluating investment projects outside its current businesses, the RRR for those projects is likely to be different from the RRR for investments in existing operations. In both instances, therefore, measuring the cost of capital for the firm as it stands is not a very useful exercise.

The key to doing something that *is* useful lies in the principle that the fundamental determinant of the RRR for any investment is its level of risk, and the CAPM tells us that *the only risk that is relevant is systematic* risk. Two important conclusions follow from this:

(1) The appropriate RRR for a project is *independent* of the firm that is considering the project.
(2) If we can find an existing investment whose systematic risk is similar to that of the proposed project, we can use the RRR on *that* investment as the discount rate to compute the project's NPV.

A given investment project certainly may affect the unsystematic risk of different companies to different degrees, but *unsystematic risk does not bear on investment return requirements.* Thus, a chemical manufacturer and an electronics company may both be considering a new investment in the furniture business. If so, both should use the same discount rate to evaluate the investment—one that is consistent with the risks of the furniture business.

Value Additivity Principle
The value of a given investment is independent of the firm making the investment.

The concept of relevant risk is related to what has been termed the **value additivity principle**. This principle states that the value that a given investment (that is, one with a given set of expected future cash flows) will add to a firm is the same regardless of the firm making the investment. That is why a chemical manufacturer and an electronics company should both use the same discount rate to calculate the present value of an investment in the furniture business.

The corollary proposition is that a firm cannot create additional value for stockholders merely by diversifying. If investment value is independent of context, combining investments within a firm will simply result in the firm being worth the total of the separate values of those investments. This argument is especially compelling when you consider that diversification also is *something investors can do for themselves* by combining the stocks of different companies in their own portfolios. Thus, there is no reason to expect investors to value a firm more highly than the sum of its parts, because they can sum the parts on their own.[7]

This is not to rule out the possibility that different firms may be able to generate different levels of cash flows from investments in a given business. If that is the case, some firms will be able to create more value than others, and their stockholders will differentially benefit. The extra value created, however, will depend only on the size of the cash flows and not on the firm that generates them. Each investment must still be evaluated using a discount rate (cost of capital) that reflects its particular systematic risk, and *that discount rate will not be dependent on the firm's other investments.*

---

[7] In fact, there is some evidence that conglomerate firms may actually sell at a discount from the total value of their component parts. Two reasons have been suggested: (1) the firm becomes too diverse for management to be able to focus properly on its major core businesses, and (2) the firm is too complex for investment analysts to be able to understand and evaluate its operations effectively.

The Pure Play Approach

The question then is how to estimate the appropriate discount rates when a firm either has more than one business at the moment or is considering investing in something new. The simplest and most direct approach would be to identify other firms that are already in the line of business being considered and estimate *their* costs of capital to use as the discount rate. If there is more than one such firm, the estimated costs of capital for the individual companies would be expected to fall in a fairly narrow range and can be averaged.

This approach will work best if the comparison firms are exclusively in the line of business in question, that is, they are what would be described as **pure plays** in the business. The approach will work respectably well if the other firms are at least *predominantly* in that line of business. In practice, it will often be difficult to find the exact comparison firms one would like, and it may be necessary to exercise some judgment and creativity in selecting the group. For example, suppose a firm is evaluating an investment in the manufacture of luggage and there are no publicly traded luggage companies available as benchmarks. The firm may have to turn to publicly traded hotel and airline companies instead—on the notion that there is some commonality of risks among firms that are basically in the travel business.

Pure Play A firm that operates in a single line of business.

One step that will typically be necessary in using comparison companies to estimate costs of capital is to adjust for differences among them in their leverage ratios. Even if the firms all have the same underlying business risk, they may have different financing strategies. The way to adjust is summarized in Figure 15-3: work back from the various firms' existing leverage ratios, and levered required returns on equity, to identify the *unlevered* required return on equity, K_U, for each.[8] These are the figures that, ideally, should fall in a relatively narrow range and would be averaged. The final step then is to derive the K_E that applies to the equity component of the proposed project's financing, by using the particular leverage ratio the investing firm intends to adopt.

An example of the kinds of numbers one might see in implementing this approach is provided in Figure 15-5. Estimates of K_E for several comparison companies are made, their unlevered returns on equity are inferred, and the average of the latter figures is "levered up" to derive the K_E for the investing firm. Whether the numbers will always come out so neatly in practice is, of course, a question.

The Simulated CAPM Approach

When suitable comparison firms cannot be identified, an alternate strategy is to attempt to develop an *indirect* estimate of the β of the line of business into which a proposed project falls. As we noted in Chapter 6, the standard way to calculate β for a security is to regress observations of the security's historical returns on the simultaneous returns on a market portfolio like the Standard and Poor's (S&P) 500. The coefficient from the regression model is the security's β. If security return data are not available, among the possible substitutes would be historical data on the *operating cash flows* from the line of business at issue. Periodic changes in those cash flows could be used to define a surrogate return series.

Thus, suppose a diversified firm is considering new investments in one of its existing businesses for which there are no publicly traded pure play firms to rely on to estimate investors' RRRs. From internal accounting data, the firm could

---

[8] An alternative would be to work back to find the comparison firms' unlevered β's, using the procedure outlined in the Appendix to Chapter 14.

FIGURE 15-5

Example of the Pure Play Approach to Estimating the Required Return on Common Equity for a Business Unit of a Conglomerate Company

Pure Play Company	Estimated K_E	Leverage Ratio, L	Inferred K_U^*
A	18.2%	0.40	14.9%
B	16.4%	0.20	15.1%
C	20.3%	0.50	15.2%
D	16.8%	0.30	14.8%

For the Conglomerate's Business Unit:

Estimated K_U (average of companies A–D)	15.0%
Selected Leverage Ratio	0.25
Estimated K_E^*	16.7%

*From the relationship $K_E = (K_U - rL)/(1 - L)$ of equation (7)

compile a record of the operating cash flows that had been generated by that business each calendar quarter for perhaps the last five years. The series of percentage changes in those quarterly cash flows could then be used in a regression on the quarterly returns on the S&P 500, to estimate a surrogate unlevered β for the line of business involved. We suggest using quarterly data for this purpose only because it is unlikely that many firms will account internally at the business unit level any more frequently than quarterly. The unlevered β derived from this process can then be adjusted for the firm's planned leverage ratio.

Corporate Debt Capacity and Diversification

When operating risks vary among business lines, it would be logical for the financing plans for the businesses to vary as well. Certainly, there are indications of characteristic differences across industries in the financing strategies employed by the firms in those industries. Since a large diversified company is essentially a collection of smaller single-business firms operating in different industries, the company may not adopt the same long-term financing plan for each of its businesses.

From this perspective, the company's overall capital structure will be the *result* of the financing plans that are selected for the company's individual business units. If the firm directs more of its investments into businesses that inherently have proportionately more debt capacity, the firm's composite leverage ratio will increase as it finances those investments with above-average amounts of borrowings. Conversely, if the firm moves more heavily into low-debt-capacity businesses, its composite leverage ratio will decline due to the below-average amounts of debt being obtained for those businesses. Thus, even though the firm will inevitably end up with a single combined leverage ratio that investors will observe at the *aggregate* firm level, the firm may have a wide variety of *separate* financing strategies being implemented for its various underlying businesses. The RRR used to value a proposed investment project should reflect the financing plan for the specific line of business in question, not the firm's composite capital structure.

There is a side effect to being a diversified firm that can affect its separate line of business financing strategies, once we recognize the possibility and costs of financial distress. Since investors can diversify their own portfolios, they should not, in general, value a diversified firm more highly than the sum of its parts. There *is* one feature of being a diversified firm, however, that investors *cannot* duplicate in their portfolios. By putting together a collection of businesses whose *unsystematic* risks partially balance each other out, the firm can create for itself a combined income stream that is less variable (a smaller coefficient of variation) than that of any of the individual businesses it operates. This less variable income stream, in turn, may allow the firm to have an overall leverage ratio that is *greater* than the average of the "normal" leverage ratios of its business units because lenders perceive the likelihood of the firm experiencing financial distress to be diminished. If leverage adds value to the firm, then, there may be at least one valuation "bonus" from corporate diversification. This is the **unique diversification benefit** a conglomerate firm may be able to provide.

Unique Diversification Benefit The reduction in the likelihood of financial distress for a conglomerate firm, due to its diversified investments.

We illustrate the process in Figure 15-6. The firm in question has two business units, each of whose annual earnings before interest and taxes are either $20 million or $60 million, depending on which one of the two possible states of the economy happens to occur in any given year. The earnings results of the two businesses are asymmetrical, however. When Unit A earns $20 million, Unit B earns $60 million, and vice versa. Assume an equal likelihood of either state of the economy occurring and an interest rate of 10%.

If the two businesses were *independent* companies and each borrowed $200 million at a 10% interest rate, each of their annual interest obligations would be:

$$\text{Annual Interest Obligations} = (\$200,000,000)(0.10) = \$20,000,000$$

Their respective minimum EBITs of $20 million would just cover those obligations, allowing both businesses to avoid financial distress even under their worst-case earnings outcomes. If the businesses were part of a single diversified firm, on the other hand, the combined EBIT of that firm would be an assured $80 million *every* year because of the complementary earnings of its two business units in the two states of the economy. The firm would thereby be able to support up to $80 million of annual interest costs, and it would have an associated $800 million debt capacity.

This is an exaggerated example. In practice, there will be multiple possible outcomes for the annual EBITs of a firm's constituent business units; those outcomes will never be perfectly offsetting; and no firm would commit the full amount of its earnings to lenders. Nonetheless, the example captures the general spirit of how increased debt capacity can be created within a diversified firm.

Coinsurance Effect The process by which the business units of a diversified company pool their earnings to meet the company's debt obligations.

A good way to think about the process is to envision diversification within a firm as giving rise to a **coinsurance effect**. That is, a bad year in some of its business units that would mean default on the debt obligations incurred to finance those units if they stood alone is compensated for by a good year in other business

An Illustration of the Effect of Diversification on Corporate Debt Capacity

FIGURE 15-6

	Business Unit A	Business Unit B	Units Combined in One Firm
State of the Economy #1 (Probability = 0.5):			
EBIT	$20 million	$60 million	$80 million
State of the Economy #2 (Probability = 0.5):			
EBIT	$60 million	$20 million	$80 million
Maximum Annual Interest Obligations to Avoid Financial Distress:			
	$20 million	$20 million	$80 million
Resulting Debt Capacity, at a 10% Interest Rate:			
	$200 million	$200 million	$800 million

units that provide the funds to meet the obligations. Investors *can* combine stocks in their portfolios to smooth out fluctuations in EBITs across companies, but they cannot have the firms in those portfolios provide the coinsurance of each other's debt service payments that automatically occurs in a diversified company. This is the good news about corporate diversification, and it can increase the borrowing power of all a firm's business units.

SUMMARY OF PROJECT RRR ESTIMATION

Figure 15-7 summarizes the procedures that we have described for estimation of a proposed investment project's RRR. If the project represents a new investment in the firm's existing line of business, the appropriate RRR is the firm's current weighted average cost of capital as long as the firm's current capital structure approximates its target structure. A target structure that is significantly different, however, requires reestimation of the firm's cost of capital. The current weighted average cost of capital is also of little use as an RRR for a proposed project that is a substantial departure from the firm's existing line of business. In that case, the RRR can be estimated most accurately through the pure play approach or the simulated CAPM approach. Under either approach, the financial manager must include an adjustment for the target capital structure that is to be associated with the proposed project's line of business.

When multiple costs of capital are employed by a firm as the discount rates to calculate the net present values of proposed investment projects, the resulting NPVs are directly comparable even though they have been arrived at by discounting at different rates. The differences in the risks of the projects are properly recognized by the different discount rates used, and therefore they have a consistent meaning. Each NPV computed represents an estimate of the added value the project will provide to stockholders, *given* the return required by investors for taking on the (systematic) risk level of the project. In fact, the reason the project NPVs *are* comparable is because they *have* been calculated at different discount rates, to reflect risk differences.

Procedures for Estimation of a Project's RRR

SUMMARY FIGURE 15-7

When the Project Is in an Existing Line of Business
 A. If the Financing Target Is the Existing Capital Structure
  Project RRR = Firm's Current Weighted Average Cost of Capital = K_A
  $K_A = (W_D)(K_D) + (W_P)(K_P) + (W_E)(K_E)$
 B. If the Financing Target Is a New Capital Structure
  1. Recalculate Equity RRR: $K_E = \dfrac{K_U - rL}{1 - L}$ 2. Reestimate K_A with new W_D, W_P, W_E, and K_E

When the Project Is in a New Line of Business
 A. Pure Play Approach
  1. Estimate K_U for a firm in same line of business as the proposed project.
  2. Estimate K_E by adjusting K_U based on the project's target financing plan.
  3. Estimate K_A based on the project's target financing plan.
 B. Simulated CAPM Approach
  1. Estimate a surrogate unlevered ß, based on the correlation of market returns with changes in the operating cash flows of a firm in the same line of business as the proposed project.
  2. Adjust the estimated ß for the project's target financing plan, and use it to calculate K_E.
  3. Estimate K_A based on the project's target financing plan.

SUMMARY

This chapter describes the techniques that financial managers can use to estimate the required rate of return for a proposed investment. That RRR is commonly called the firm's cost of capital. It depends on both the business risk characteristics of the project being considered and the mix of financing that will be employed to fund the project. Projects that have positive net present values, when discounted at the costs of capital applicable to their respective risk levels and financing mixes, should increase stockholder wealth by the amount of the calculated NPVs.

The determination of the costs of the various forms of capital available to the firm, which should always be measured as after-tax costs, is a forward-looking process. The focus is on current market conditions and the firm's long-term future financing plans. The identification of the costs is relatively straightforward in the case of debt and preferred stock financing. The returns required by the investors who provide the funds are fixed and are specified as part of the formal terms either of the loan agreement entered into or the securities that are issued. In the case of common equity financing, however, required returns can only be estimated because investors have a residual rather than a contractual claim to the firm's cash flows. Both the capital asset pricing model and the dividend growth model can be used to make these estimates. When common equity capital is raised externally by issuing new shares of common stock, transactions cost can be material and should be taken into account by requiring the present values of projects' expected future cash flows to compensate for those costs.

The firm's weighted average cost of capital is calculated by multiplying the costs of the individual forms of capital in the firm's long-term financing plan by the proportions of the firm's total market capitalization, which those forms represent. The weighted average cost of capital is the proper discount rate to be used to evaluate investment projects.

For a firm operating in a single line of business, the mix of funds in the firm's overall long-term financing plan supports all the firm's investments equally, and the firm has a single cost of capital. When a firm is instead in multiple lines of business, it has multiple costs of capital and may have different financing plans for different businesses as well. The most direct way to estimate the costs of common equity for a diversified firm's various business units is to derive the estimates from other publicly traded companies that are in the same lines of business. If that is not possible, an approximation may be able to be obtained from a variant of the Capital Asset Pricing Model. The proportions of a diversified firm's total capitalization that debt, preferred stock, and common equity will comprise are the result of aggregating the different financing plans of the individual business units. Diversification by a firm has no intrinsic additional value for stockholders because investors can replicate that diversification in their own portfolios. It is possible, however, that a firm's debt capacity can be increased when it is diversified. This could have some positive impact on the firm's value.

chapter equations

1. $K_j = i + (K_M - i)(\beta_j)$

2. $K_D = (r)(1 - T)$

3. $K_P = r_P$

4. $K_E = \dfrac{D_1}{P_0} + g$

5. $\lambda = $ (% External Equity Funding) (% Equity Issue Cost)

6. $K_A = (W_D)(K_D) + (W_P)(K_P) + (W_E)(K_E)$

7. $K_E = \dfrac{K_U - rL}{1 - L}$

CONTENT QUESTIONS

1. Why is the required rate of return a key concept in business finance?
2. Why is the return to a securityholder a cost to the firm?
3. What are the two elements that determine a firm's cost of capital?
4. Should the cost of capital be measured as a pretax or an after-tax figure?
5. Which source of financing has a cost that can only be estimated rather than observed in the securities market?
6. Should market capitalization weights or book capitalization weights be used to calculate the firm's cost of capital?
7. What are the two approaches to estimating the cost of common equity?
8. Why are securities issuance costs relevant to estimates of the cost of capital?
9. How can a firm have more than one weighted average cost of capital?
10. Can a firm have more than one financing plan?
11. Company A and Company B are currently in different industries. Both, however, are considering the same new investment project. Will the RRR for that project differ between the companies?
12. Why is corporate diversification unlikely to provide extra value to stockholders?

CONCEPT QUESTIONS

1. What are the underlying conceptual differences between the dividend growth model and the capital asset pricing model approaches to estimating the cost of common equity capital? Why might they produce different estimates?
2. IVM Why is it that preferred stock is characterized as having little impact on the value of the firm? If it does not, what might account for the fact that some firms still do raise funds by issuing preferred stock?
3. IVM How is it possible that the leverage ratio that maximizes the total value of a firm would not be the same leverage ratio that maximizes the value of the firm's common stock?
4. Describe how you would go about estimating the cost of capital for firms whose common shares are not publicly traded.
5. International The weighted average cost of capital for investments in a firm's home country is 12%. The firm is now considering an investment in a foreign country, in the firm's current line of business. How would you advise the firm to estimate the cost of capital for that investment?

PROBLEMS

1. Standex Products has estimated that its after-tax cost of debt is 6% and its cost of equity is 16%. Standex expects to continue a policy of borrowing 30% of its needed capital. Calculate its weighted average cost of capital.
2. Midland Rubber sold bonds three years ago with a coupon rate of 12%. After discussions with its investment banker, Midland found that now it could sell additional bonds at par with a 9% coupon rate. Calculate the cost of debt, assuming that the marginal corporate tax rate is 40%.
3. Land and Blunt Ltd. have outstanding bonds with a 12% coupon rate that are currently yielding 9.75%. Calculate the cost of debt, assuming the following marginal corporate tax rates.
       a. 40%   b. 30%   c. 15%

4. The market price for Dieppe Chemical's 12% coupon bonds is FF1,l70.70. Interest is paid annually, and there are 20 years until maturity. Find its cost of debt if the marginal tax rate is 40%.

5. Dieppe Chemical's FF8.00 preferred stock is currently selling for FF57.00. Find the cost of preferred stock.

6. Ametek Shipping's last annual dividend was DM2.50 per share. Its common stock is selling for DM36.00 per share. If analysts are projecting 11% growth in earnings and dividends for the foreseeable future, what is Ametek Shipping's cost of equity?

7. NIPSCO Electric has had a stable and consistent growth in earnings and dividends over the past 8 years. In 1990, its earnings per share were Ptas. 400. In 1998, they were Ptas. 640. NIPSCO is expected to pay out 50% of its earnings. Estimate the firm's cost of equity, given a market price per share of Ptas. 5,650.

8. Wedington Industries has a $\beta = 1.20$. What is its cost of equity if the yield on long-term government bonds is 7% and the expected market return is 13%?

9. Howell Technology has compiled the following information:

    Debt: Yield-to-maturity = 10.6%
    Preferred Stock: Current market price = $60.00, dividend per share = $7.00
    Common Stock: Current market price $73.00 per share, expected growth rate = 9%, next expected dividend per share = $4.38

Howell plans to maintain a target capital structure composed of 30% debt, 15% preferred stock, and the remainder in common equity. Calculate Howell's weighted average cost of capital if its marginal tax rate is 40%.

10. Nalin Machine Corp. is considering an investment of $100 million in a new product. It anticipates that 25% of this amount will come from external equity. New equity issue costs have averaged 16% of the proceeds of the issue. What amount should Nalin use as the initial outlay for this investment?

11. Martin Metals is considering a $50,000,000 investment. Without considering flotation costs, the investment has an NPV of $2,000,000. Over time, external equity has provided 25% of investment funding. Flotation costs were 20% of the proceeds. Given these flotation costs, should the investment be made?

12. Peabody Limited has no debt or preferred stock in its capital structure. It has estimated its cost of equity to be 12%. It is considering borrowing at an interest rate of 8% to replace equity. The tax rate is 40%.
    a. What is Peabody's current cost of capital?
    b. What would its cost of capital be if it borrowed up to a leverage ratio (L) of 10%?
    c. What would its cost of capital be if it borrowed up to a leverage ratio of 25%?

13. Guilford Products currently has a leverage ratio (L) of 20%. Its cost of equity is 16%. It is considering increasing its leverage ratio to 50%. It can borrow at 10%, and the tax rate is 40%.
    a. What is Guilford's current cost of capital?
    b. What will Guilford's cost of capital be after the leverage ratio is increased to 50%?

14. Dijon Foods has neither debt nor preferred stock. Its equity beta (β_E) is 1.25. It is planning to recapitalize by borrowing at a 9% interest rate, up to a leverage ratio (L) of 25%. The current risk-free rate is 5%, and the market risk premium is 8%. If the tax rate is 40%, what will be Dijon's cost of capital after the recapitalization?

15. McGraw Chemicals has been using 16% as its cost of capital for a number of years. This number was estimated in 1997. At that time, long-term government

securities yielded 10.5%, and Aaa corporate bonds yielded 13.5%. Currently, long-term government securities yield 6.5%, and Aaa corporate bonds yield 9.5%.

    a. Approximate the current cost of capital for McGraw.

    b. State two of the most important assumptions that are necessary to approximate the cost of capital from the information in the problem.

    c. Assuming the lower interest rates have prevailed for the last two or three years, what effect did the use of the 1997 cost of capital have on the investments evaluated recently by McGraw?

16. Federal Airlines and National Airlines have similar routes and, therefore, are in the same business risk class. The required rate of return (K_E) on each company's common stock is 16%. Federal's next dividend is expected to be $7.00 per share with a growth rate of 6%. National is expected to pay $3.50 per share but grow at 11% per year.

    a. Find current stock price for Federal and National Airlines.

    b. Suppose that, because of recent problems in the airline industry, the RRR of each airline increases to 21%. Find the price of each airline's common stock, given this new information.

17. Returning to Problem 16, suppose the RRR on airline stocks falls from 16% to 14%. Find the new price per share of common stock for each airline.

18. Two independent companies are about to merge. Information about each company is given below:

State of Economy	EBIT: Company 1	EBIT: Company 2
Recession	$50 million	$10 million
Expansion	$10 million	$50 million

Each firm can borrow at 8%, and each state of the economy is equally likely.

    a. Find the debt capacity of each company standing alone.

    b. Find the debt capacity after the merger.

19. Jason Electronics is considering expanding into the software industry. The project is expected to require a $1.4 billion investment over the next 5 years. It has compiled the following information about three pure play software companies:

	Estimated K_E	Leverage Ratio (L)
City Software	13.0%	30%
Nevada Systems	13.4%	40%
Key Computing	12.5%	20%

The borrowing rate of interest for all the firms is 10%, and the tax rate is 40%. If Jason Electronics believes that the debt capacity of its new software division would be a leverage ratio (L) of 25%, what discount rate should it use to evaluate the $1.4 billion investment in the software business?

20. Carlisle Foods, a frozen-food processor, is considering two investment proposals that have the same free cash flow patterns. Both require an initial investment of $18,500,000 and are expected to generate annual after-tax cash inflow of $4,000,000 per year for 10 years. One investment will expand the capacity of its existing frozen-food lines. The other investment will allow Carlisle to break into the beverage field by producing canned fruit juices. The required rate of return (K_E) of Carlisle's common stock is 16%. Its leverage ratio (L) is 30%, the interest rate on its debt is 10%, and the tax rate is 40%. Carlisle has also gathered information concerning the canned juice industry. Based on averaging data concerning three companies, the average required

rate of return on "canned juice" common stocks is 21%, and the average leverage ratio is 20%. Carlisle believes that 20% is a good estimate of the debt capacity of that industry.

    a. Calculate the discount rate that should be used to evaluate the investment to expand capacity of frozen foods.

    b. What is the NPV of the expansion proposal? Should the investment be made?

    c. Calculate the discount rate that should be used to evaluate the investment in the canned juice industry.

    d. What is the NPV of the canned juice proposal? Should the investment be made?

21. Mega Home Products is considering purchasing Old Hickory Furniture, a manufacturer of fine furniture in North Carolina. Mega Home has an equity β of 1.05 and a leverage ratio (L) of 30%. Old Hickory has an equity beta of 2.55 and a leverage ratio (L) of 50%. The interest rate on debt is 10%, and the tax rate is 40%. Mega's managers believe that Old Hickory's leverage is too high and believe that it can only borrow 30% against Old Hickory's assets. The risk-free rate is 6%, and the market risk premium is 8%. What required rate of return should Mega Home Products use to determine Old Hickory's value?

INTERNET EXERCISE

Corporate Financial Spreadsheets is a Web site that offers free downloads of financial spreadsheet templates in the Excel 5.0 format. Download the Optimal Capital Structure file and open in Excel. Use the spreadsheet template to find the optimal capital structure in the Self-Study Quiz number 3. Printout the results and hand in for a class assignment. http://schroeder.wustl.edu/faculty/back/general.htm

SELF-STUDY QUIZ

1. Dressler Brands has a history of steady growth in earnings and dividends for the past nine years. In 1989, earnings per share were $2.25, while in 1998 they were $4.50. Dressler pays out 40% of its earnings as dividends. Estimate Dressler's cost of equity (K_E) immediately after the 1998 dividend was paid. At that time, the market price per share was $21.34.

2. Smyth Resources has a target capital structure of 50% equity, 40% debt, and 10% preferred stock. It has gathered the following data on its securities:

    Common stock: β = 1.75, 5.0% = risk-free rate, and 8.0% = market-risk premium
    Preferred stock = Price per share = $30, Dividend = $4.50
    Debt: Current yield-to-maturity = 12%

If the corporate tax rate is 40%, find Smyth's cost of capital.

3. A firm currently has no debt in its capital structure and a cost of equity (K_E) equal to 13%. It is considering borrowing at a 10% interest rate and using the proceeds to reduce equity. The tax rate is 40%, and there is no preferred stock.

    a. Find the cost of capital of the firm with no debt.

    b. Find the cost of capital of the firm if it borrows up to a leverage ratio (L) of 0.15.

    c. Find the cost of capital of the firm if it borrows up to a leverage ratio (L) of 0.30.

Working Capital Policy

This chapter introduces the issues associated with investing and financing decisions that involve current assets and liabilities. It provides an overview of the risk/return trade-offs of working capital decisions that will be examined in detail in the next three chapters. In those chapters, we will use NPV analysis to apply the IVM to proposed decisions to acquire current assets and to issue current liabilities.

Current assets and liabilities are important because they can affect the firm's risk/return characteristics through their impact on liquidity and profitability. Without sufficient cash, a firm faces the risk of financial distress. Without adequate levels of accounts receivable and inventories, sales and profits will be impaired. Accounts payable and short-term loans represent both a major source of financing for a firm's current assets and a major claim on the firm's short-term cash flows. Given the potential effect of current assets and liabilities on a firm's value to its owners, financial managers should carefully evaluate short-term investing and financing decisions that involve the following issues:

- A recent survey of large U.S. manufacturing firms revealed that financial managers devote as much time to working capital policy as they do to long-term investing and financing decisions. The managers also believe that the skill levels required for effective decision-making are comparable in both areas. What types of decisions are involved in working capital policy? Why are these decisions so important to financial managers? How is a firm's value related to its working capital policy?

- Working capital policy involves operating assets and liabilities that are classified as current assets and liabilities on a firm's financial statements. Yet the dollar amount of these balance sheet accounts may not decline but, instead, grow over time. How can a financial manager reconcile this apparent contradiction between the accounting treatment of these accounts as short term, and the operational reality of their permanence? Is this contradiction relevant to investing and financing decisions? Should it be considered in the establishment of working capital policy?
- One of the important aspects of working capital policy is the maturity of the financing used to acquire assets. How can financing maturity affect a firm's value? What are the risks involved in the use of short-term financing? What are the risks involved in the use of long-term financing?

The *characteristics* of current assets and liabilities are distinctly different from the long-term sources and uses of funds discussed in previous chapters. The financial manager's *objective* in both long-term and short-term decisions, however, is the same: to select that combination of assets and liabilities that will maximize the value of the firm to its owners.

The goal of this chapter is to demonstrate the basic risk/return trade-off that managers must evaluate in their determination of a working capital policy for the firm, which involves investing decisions regarding current assets and financing decisions regarding current liabilities. The discussion begins with a description of the role of working capital in the operation of the firm. After an examination of the risk/return characteristics of working capital policy, the important concepts of temporary and permanent assets and financing will be introduced.

Figure 17-1 outlines the components of working capital policy discussed in this chapter. The investing decisions made by managers concerning the level of current assets have an effect on firm value through their impact on the firm's risk/return trade-off. Specifically, an increase in current assets will tend to boost *expected* operating earnings E(EBIT) while reducing the risk of financial distress. These two positive effects on value are opposed by the negative value effect of the increase in the *uncertainty* of EBIT (σ_{EBIT}) that is associated with an expansion of current assets.

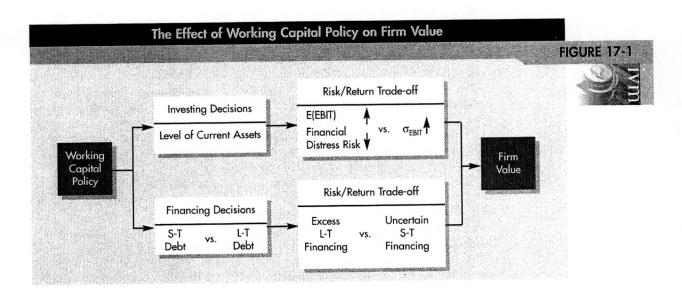

FIGURE 17-1

The Effect of Working Capital Policy on Firm Value

Working capital financing decisions concentrate on the choice between short-term debt and long-term debt to finance current assets. The use of long-term financing reduces profits because it usually results in a temporary surplus of financing. Short-term debt, on the other hand, increases firm risk due to its uncertain availability and cost. Consequently, working capital financing decisions can also alter value through their effect on a firm's risk/return characteristics.

THE NATURE OF WORKING CAPITAL

Working Capital The sum of a firm's current assets.

Net Working Capital The difference between current assets and current liabilities

The term **working capital** refers to the sum of a firm's current assets. The term **net working capital** is defined as the difference between current assets and current liabilities. The major current asset accounts that we will be concerned with here and in the following three chapters are:

1. Cash
2. Marketable Securities
3. Accounts Receivable
4. Inventories

Operating Assets Another term for working capital.

These assets are sometimes referred to as **operating assets** because they arise in the process of generating operating income and are related to the level of sales activity. They normally rise and fall in response to either seasonal or cyclical fluctuations in sales.

The concepts of working capital and net working capital are significant to financial managers because they are indicators of the liquidity of a firm. In general, the higher the level of either measure, the greater is the firm's liquidity and the lower is its risk of financial distress. These measures also serve as indirect indicators of a firm's profitability. A firm must have current assets in order to provide a product or service to its customers and generate profits for its owners. As we shall see shortly, however, excessive levels of current assets can reduce profitability if additional operating income fails to keep pace with the additional investment in current assets.

In order to demonstrate the role of current assets in the operation of a firm, we will refer to the diagram in Figure 17-2. The figure contains a time line that shows the relationship among the various operating assets of a manufacturing firm. The time line enables us to visualize the sequential flow of a given dollar balance through each of the operating assets during the production and sales cycles associated with the firm's product. During the manufacturing phase, the initial expenditure on raw materials is transferred from that inventory account to the work-in-process account and finally to the finished goods account. The credit sale of the product results in a transformation of the inventory balance into an accounts receivable balance, which is ultimately converted into a cash balance upon payment by the buyer. Excess cash balances may temporarily be exchanged for marketable securities as the firm attempts to minimize non-earning assets. Although the dollar balance moves through many accounts, the elapsed time is relatively short—only slightly more than three months.

In interpreting the time line, it is important to keep in mind that the line represents a cash-to-cash cycle. The movement of a given dollar balance out of one account does not reduce the account balance to zero. Rather, the first dollar balance is immediately replaced by a second dollar balance representing another expenditure. In this sense, the time line can be viewed as a pipeline through which dollar account balances flow. As one balance moves through the pipeline from beginning to end, it is preceded and followed by similar dollar balances. As a result,

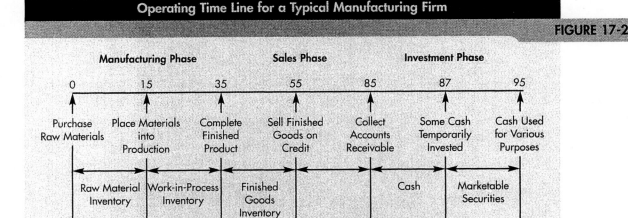

Operating Time Line for a Typical Manufacturing Firm

FIGURE 17-2

the pipeline is never empty for a going concern. Given this background on the role of working capital, we can now examine its effect on the risk/return characteristics of a firm.

THE EFFECT OF WORKING CAPITAL ON FIRM VALUE

The commitment of funds to fixed assets is readily understandable as an investment, due to the strategic nature and long economic life of such assets. Unlike the case of fixed assets, it is easy to overlook the importance of managing the level of investment in working capital. Since working capital consists of current assets, the short life of these assets seems to preclude viewing this use of funds as an investment. Furthermore, current assets seem to arise automatically from operations. As sales rise and fall, the level of inventories needed to support sales and the level of receivables arising from credit sales would seem also to fluctuate independent of management control. This viewpoint is overly simplistic. It is true that the investment in current assets will fluctuate over time in response to changes in sales. Financial managers, however, can alter the level of current assets associated with a given volume of sales at any point in time. Policy decisions regarding inventories, accounts receivable, cash balances, and marketable securities can control the amount invested. In addition, as we shall soon explain, the commitment of funds to current assets can be just as permanent as the commitment of funds to fixed assets.

If a firm's managers are to select the level of current assets that is optimal, they must have a goal to guide their decision-making: maximize the value of the firm to its owners. How can working capital decisions affect firm value? They can alter value through their impact on the size and riskiness of the returns generated by the firm. In order to understand the relationship between the level of working capital and firm value, recall the following equations from Chapter 10:

Operating Cash Flows = EBIT – Taxes + Depreciation

Free Cash Flows = Operating Cash Flows – ΔWorking Capital – ΔFixed Assets

Working capital decisions affect firm value by altering either the size of free cash flows or the RRR at which they are discounted. A change in cash flow size or RRR will, in turn, alter a firm's NPV.

Figure 17-3 indicates the nature of this risk/return trade-off. The left graph shows the general impact of the level of working capital or current assets on firm risk. Additional investment in current assets initially decreases the risk of cash deficiency and financial distress by increasing the firm's liquidity. At some point (point A in the graph), the liquidity provided by current assets effectively eliminates all but the smallest probability of cash deficiency. Accordingly, increasing the investment in current assets beyond this point has little or no impact on a firm's risk and its RRR.

The middle graph depicts the relationship between returns and the investment in current assets. In addition to providing liquidity, working capital is essential to the profitable operation of a firm. Without inventories, a firm would be able to fill customer orders only by producing goods in response to orders previously placed. Without receivables, sales would be limited to cash customers. Inadequate inventories and buyer financing can result in lost sales as potential customers acquire the goods from other suppliers or decide to forego the purchase altogether. Consequently, expansion of a firm's investment in current assets is initially accompanied by sharp increases in EBIT and operating cash flows as the opportunity cost of lost sales falls rapidly. Once the fundamental operating needs have been satisfied, however, further expansion of current assets (beyond point B in the graph) represents excess investment that does not increase operating cash flows and EBIT.[1]

The impact of this risk/return trade-off on firm value is shown in the right graph in Figure 17-3. *The relationship between firm value and working capital reflects the combined impact of the expansion of current assets on firm risk and return.* Below point C, firm value rises sharply as current assets expand due to the positive effects of reduced risk and increased return. Beyond that point, current asset expansion neither increases EBIT nor reduces risk. The only change is that free cash flows will fall due to the cash outflows for increased investment in working capital. The net result is that the NPV associated with the expansion is negative. Thus, the optimal level of working capital for the firm is the level of current assets represented by point C.

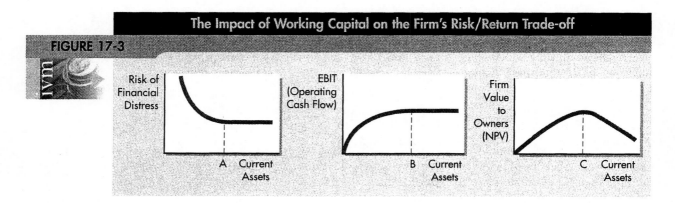

The Impact of Working Capital on the Firm's Risk/Return Trade-off

FIGURE 17-3

---

[1] In fact, the case can be made that overexpansion of inventories and receivables can cause the curve in the middle graph to decline beyond point B. This is due to the decline in EBIT that results from the high costs such as storage expense, damage, bad debts, and collection expense associated with excess inventories and receivables. We will examine these costs in detail in Chapter 20.

■ Financial

ISSUES

THE IMPORTANCE OF WORKING CAPITAL MANAGEMENT AT MAJOR U.S. FIRMS

This chapter stresses the key role of working capital policy in the determination of a firm's risk/return characteristics. It also points out the importance of financial planning for the evaluation of investing and financing decisions. A survey of chief financial officers (CFOs) at *Fortune 1000* firms reveals the significance of working capital management and financial planning to financial managers. The respondents to the survey were initially asked about the relative importance and time allocated to various investing and financing decisions. Their responses are summarized below:

Activity	Greatest Importance	Average Time Allocated
Financial Planning/Budgeting	59%	35%
Working Capital Management	27	32
Capital Expenditure Management	9	19
Raising Long-Term Funds	5	14
	100%	100%

Eighty-six percent of the CFOs indicated that either financial planning or working capital management was their most important activity. Furthermore, these two activities accounted for ⅔ of the total time allocated to all four listed activities.

When questioned about the allocation of their time to the general area of short-term financial management, the CFOs responded as follows:

Activity	Average Time Allocated
Accounts Receivable Management	15%
Cash Management	15
Short-Term Financial Planning	15
Inventory Management	15
Banking Relationships	11
Accounts Payable Management	10
Short-Term Investments Management	10
Short-Term Borrowing	9
	100%

The surveyed managers divided their time fairly evenly among the individual activities, although investing decisions as a group accounted for 55% of manager time as opposed to 30% for financing decisions.

Finally, the executives were asked to assign skill level requirements associated with various financial activities within their firms:

	Average Skill Level Requirement*	Highest Skill Level Requirement**
Financial Planning/Budgeting	2.1	58%
Cash Management	3.1	21
Long-Term Financing	3.5	22
Capital Expenditure Management	4.1	9
Accounts Receivable Management	4.3	9
Pension Fund Management	4.6	8
Short-Term Investments Management	4.7	10
Accounts Payable Management	5.9	3

*Highest Skill Level = 1
 Lowest Skill Level = 8
**Skill Level = 1

On a scale from 1 to 8, financial planning ranked highest in terms of skill required of individuals performing that activity. Moreover, 58% of the CFOs assigned a skill level requirement of 1 to financial planning. While the skill level requirements of the various working capital areas varied considerably, they are comparable to the results for long-term financial activities.

THE MATURITY COMPOSITION OF OPERATING ASSETS AND LIABILITIES

Although working capital consists of current assets, it is not true that working capital policy deals only with short-term assets. In fact, many of the dollar balances in current asset accounts that are classified as short-term within an accounting framework are as long-lived as fixed assets from the financial managers' viewpoint! The same statement can be made about a firm's current liabilities. From the perspective of the financial managers, many current liabilities represent long-term debt financing. Accordingly, before we can discuss working capital policy alternatives, we need to introduce the concept of a permanent current asset and liability.

Permanent Versus Temporary Assets

A firm's investment in operating and fixed assets can fluctuate over time, as shown in Figure 17-4. The graph in the figure typifies the behavior of the assets required by a growing firm with a seasonal or cyclical pattern in its sales. The investment in fixed assets and other long-term investments demonstrates a steady, gradual upward trend in response to long-term growth in sales. Current assets, on the other hand, fluctuate around their upward trend in response to short-term fluctuations in sales.

Permanent Assets Fixed assets (plant and equipment) and permanent current assets.

A firm's permanent assets consist of those assets that are very stable over time. They rise steadily for a growing firm, fall steadily for a declining firm, or remain constant for a mature firm. Since they exhibit this constant behavior pattern, they represent a very long-term investment or use of funds by a firm. ***Permanent assets have two components: fixed assets and permanent current assets.*** In Figure 17-4, the firm's permanent assets are represented by the straight line that touches the total asset curve at each of its two troughs.

Fixed assets qualify as permanent assets due to the long-term commitment of funds involved in their acquisition and their lack of response to short-term variations in sales. A portion of the firm's current assets in the figure also qualify as permanent assets because they exhibit the same behavior as the firm's fixed assets. From the financial managers' point of view, the duration of the firm's commitment of funds to an asset is a more important characteristic than the traditional accounting classification of the asset. Since a firm must have some minimum level of current assets at all times to continue operation, the investment represented by that minimum is every bit as permanent as the investment in fixed assets. Hence, it is called a **permanent current asset**. To return to our earlier metaphor, the pipeline of current assets is never empty for a going concern.

Permanent Current Assets The minimum level of current assets needed by the firm to continue operation.

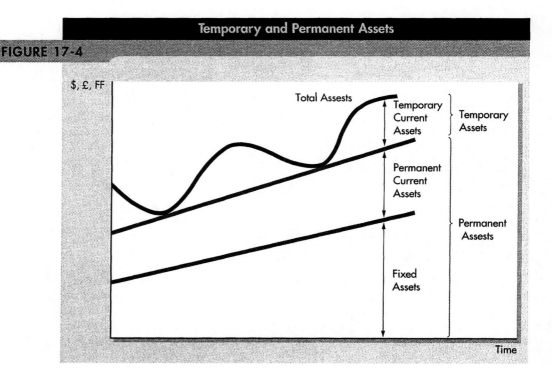

FIGURE 17-4

Temporary and Permanent Assets

As their name suggests, temporary assets have a short life. This is important to financial managers because they require only a short-term commitment of funds. For the firm depicted in Figure 17-4, temporary current assets are equal to the fluctuation of total assets due to seasonal variation in sales. Since only current assets respond to seasonal sales patterns, *temporary assets consist solely of current assets.* Thus, working capital can be subdivided into two components with very different characteristics: temporary current assets and permanent current assets.

Temporary Assets That portion of a firm's current assets that fluctuates in response to seasonal variations in sales.

Permanent Versus Temporary Financing

Figure 17-5 shows the minimum financing requirements that correspond to the investing pattern shown in Figure 17-4. Due to their long life, both fixed assets and permanent current assets require permanent or long-term financing. **Permanent financing** consists of any long-term source of funds. *It has three major components: long-term debt, equity (internal and external), and permanent spontaneous current liabilities.* Long-term debt and equity financing are well-suited to meet the capital requirements posed by a firm's long-term commitment of funds to both fixed assets and permanent current assets. Less obvious is the role of spontaneous current liabilities.

Permanent Financing Any long-term source of funds.

Spontaneous current liabilities are those short-term obligations that automatically increase and decrease in response to changes in financing requirements. The major example of a spontaneous current liability is trade credit. When a firm expands its inventories by buying goods on a credit basis from its suppliers, it is simultaneously making both an investing and a financing decision. The firm is committing financing obtained from the suppliers to the acquisition of goods sold by the suppliers. The net result is essentially the same as if the firm had used the proceeds of a bank loan to purchase goods on a cash basis from its sup-

Spontaneous Current Liabilities Short-term obligations that automatically increase and decrease in response to financing needs.

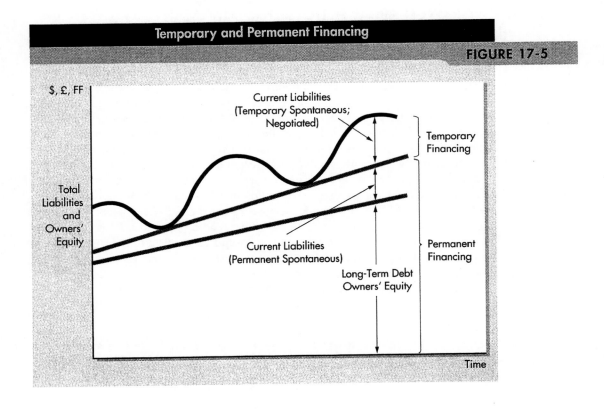

Temporary and Permanent Financing

FIGURE 17-5

pliers. With trade credit, however, the firm's financial managers need not make separate arrangements for financing the inventories because the inventories are automatically financed by the suppliers who sell on a credit basis. The automatic nature of this financing leads to the term "spontaneous current liability."

Although all trade credit is classified as a current or short-term liability in an accounting sense, a portion of this spontaneous liability represents permanent financing. As long as a firm continues to purchase inventories on a credit basis, it will continue automatically to generate financing. Just as a going concern continually replaces each dollar of inventory or receivables over time, it also steadily rolls over each dollar of trade credit or accounts payable. For example, assume that a firm buys goods from its suppliers under trade credit terms that allow it to pay for the goods one month after they are purchased. If the firm purchases $1 million in goods every month, it will acquire $1 million in trade credit for the current month's purchases at the same time that it pays $1 million for the previous month's purchases. As a result, the firm will always show $1 million in accounts payable on its balance sheet even though it makes a payment of that size to its suppliers every month. Thus, for the firm depicted in Figure 17-4, a substantial amount of the financing required for permanent current assets can be obtained through **permanent spontaneous current liabilities**.[2]

Not all spontaneous current liability account balances on a firm's balance sheet at any one moment represent permanent financing. For instance, the fluctuations in current assets shown in Figure 17-4 can be financed though the fluctuations in current liabilities as shown in Figure 17-5. The fluctuations can take the form either of **negotiated current liabilities**, such as a bank loan, or changes in spontaneous current liabilities. These are the two components of **temporary financing**.

Permanent Spontaneous Current Liabilities The minimum level of spontaneous current liabilities that is continuously maintained by a firm.

Negotiated Current Liabilities That part of current liabilities that does not respond automatically to financing needs.

Temporary Financing The sum of negotiated current liabilities and temporary spontaneous current liabilities.

WORKING CAPITAL POLICY ALTERNATIVES

Working capital policy deals with both investing and financing decisions because both types of decisions can affect the value of the firm. The investing decision will be discussed in Chapters 19 and 20 where we will demonstrate how the IVM of Chapter 6 can be used to determine the optimal level of the various types of current assets. In the remainder of this chapter, we examine the financing decision. Specifically, we address the question of whether the maturity composition of a firm's debt can affect the value of a firm to its stockholders. After examining the risk/return implications of the maturity composition of a firm's debt, we will describe the major alternative short-term financing policies available to a firm.

Figure 17-6 summarizes the risk/return effects of two extreme working capital financing policies. An aggressive policy involves the partial use of temporary financing to finance assets, while a conservative policy relies exclusively on permanent financing. The aggressive policy offers high return and risk because it eliminates temporary excesses in financing but exposes the firm to the uncertain cost and availability of short-term debt. Conversely, the conservative policy entails low return and risk because the certainty of permanent financing's cost and availability carries with it the problem of temporary surpluses in financing.

---

[2] Notice that it is normally not possible to finance all of a firm's permanent current assets with spontaneous current liabilities. A firm's financial managers do not have the option of financing current assets such as cash, accounts receivable, or marketable securities with trade credit. If a firm wishes to use debt to finance these assets, it must negotiate this financing with a lender such as a bank, prior to the acquisition of the asset.

■ Ethics

ISSUES

AGENCY ISSUES IN WORKING CAPITAL MANAGEMENT

In this chapter, we state that the goal of the manager in working capital decisions should be the same as in any other decision: to maximize the value of the firm to its owners. As we pointed out in our discussion of agency problems in Chapter 1, however, managers may succumb to the incentive to substitute their own interests for those of the owners. Working capital management decisions have historically been affected by agency problems, which firms have recently begun to address in a formal fashion.

The agency dilemma arises from attempts by vendors to influence the decisions of inventory buyers as potential customers through the use of gifts, entertainment, and other gratuities. While this is a traditional practice among industrial suppliers, its abuse has led to serious ethical and legal problems at some firms. For example, in the mid-1990s, executives at General Motors' Opel unit in Europe were accused of accepting kickbacks from suppliers. An executive in Kmart's real estate division pleaded guilty to taking $750,000 in bribes. Kmart's CEO hired an investigative firm to probe the integrity of its buyers after the firm was forced to liquidate $700 million in unsalable merchandise.

In response to these problems, firms have begun to adopt or revise codes of ethics that set explicit limits on gifts. GM's new policy is outlined in a 12-page document that includes instructional scenarios with examples of unacceptable behavior. GM buyers are no longer permitted to accept stadium box seats, steak dinners, or weekend golf outings. Acceptance of any gift that has more than a minimal value is no longer permitted. Curiously, the policy makes exceptions in the case of non-U.S. employees who may accept gifts if they are consistent with local business practice. The code also permits GM employees to *provide* limited amounts of gifts and meals to customers, such as auto dealers, if they are consistent with the customers' own gift policies.

Kmart's revised ethics code attempts to regulate the behavior of both its own buyers and that of its suppliers. The code states that employees cannot accept "bribes, commissions, kickbacks, payments, loans, gratuities, or other solicitations" from its suppliers. In addition, the code requires suppliers to sign a pledge not to engage in such practices with Kmart employees. Perhaps the strictest but most simple code of ethics for gifts is that of Wal-Mart, which bars acceptance of anything with monetary value. Suppliers must meet with Wal-Mart buyers in glassed-in rooms at company headquarters where wall posters state the firm's policy and warn that: "Any items received will be returned to senders at their expense." Employees who violate this policy are subject to immediate dismissal.

The Issues Involved in the Maturity Composition of Debt Financing

As stated previously, a financing decision is significant only if it can alter the value of the firm. *The potential impact of the maturity composition of a firm's debt on its value arises from its effect on the firm's risk/return trade-off.* The use of short-term debt offers the prospect of

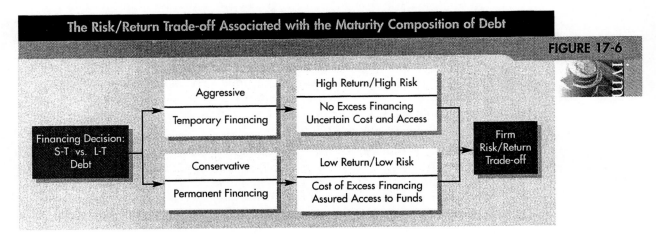

The Risk/Return Trade-off Associated with the Maturity Composition of Debt

FIGURE 17-6

Financing Decision: S-T vs. L-T Debt

Aggressive / Temporary Financing → High Return/High Risk / No Excess Financing Uncertain Cost and Access →

Conservative / Permanent Financing → Low Return/Low Risk / Cost of Excess Financing Assured Access to Funds →

Firm Risk/Return Trade-off

increased returns to the firm. These returns are the result of the reduction in the opportunity cost of excess financing that is associated with long-term debt. Unfortunately, increased returns come at a price: an increase in the risk of financial distress. It is the challenging task of the financial manager to evaluate this risk/return trade-off.

Return Considerations. If a firm has some temporary assets, financing those assets with long-term instead of short-term debt will reduce profitability. During those periods when the temporary asset balances are below their maximum, the use of long-term debt will result in excess financing. Since the firm must pay interest on the long-term debt regardless of whether it is needed, there is an explicit cost of excess financing. The firm can offset part of this cost by temporarily investing the excess funds in short-term marketable securities. *From the stockholders' point of view*, however, there is *an opportunity cost associated with excess financing* even if it is invested in marketable securities. The opportunity cost lies in the fact that the interest rate earned on those securities will almost always be less than the interest rate paid by the firm on its long-term borrowings.

Risk Considerations. The potential for risk reduction implicit in the use of long-term debt is readily evident when you compare the characteristics of short-term and long-term debt. While short-term debt provides a firm with greater financing flexibility, it also carries with it greater uncertainty concerning the cost and availability of future financing. Changes in general credit market conditions and/or a firm's financial position may make the renewal of a short-term loan excessively expensive or even infeasible. The high cost or unavailability of required financing may, in turn, subject the firm to financial distress, resulting in forced sale of assets, elimination of dividends, or failure to meet payrolls and pay bills.

The use of long-term debt enables a firm to avoid these problems because it assures the firm of the availability of financing over a fixed period of time at a fixed cost. The greater certainty associated with *long-term debt can reduce substantially a firm's risk of financial distress*. The degree of risk reduction associated with each additional dollar of long-term debt, however, is not constant. Additional long-term financing for a firm characterized by small amounts of short-term debt provides very small risk reduction benefits.

Balancing the Maturity of Operating Assets and Liabilities

The *risk/return trade-off* involved in the decision regarding the maturity composition of debt is clear-cut. The *financing decision to use long-term debt* has a *positive* impact on value due to the reduction in the risk of financial distress. The *investing decision to periodically acquire marketable securities with the excess financing* that results from the use of long-term debt has a *negative* impact on value. The difficult task is to determine at which point the positive effect of the financing decision ceases to outweigh the negative effect of the investing decision. The optimal financing decision regarding debt maturity depends on previous investing decisions regarding asset maturity. It is the *relationship between a firm's temporary assets and permanent assets that determines the optimal decision about maturity composition of debt.*

Financing Permanent Assets. By definition, permanent assets, whether classified as current assets or fixed assets, require continuous financing. Due to their financing requirements, these assets should be funded with permanent financing (long-term debt, owners' equity, and permanent spontaneous current liabilities). The use of temporary financing (temporary spontaneous or negotiated current liabilities)

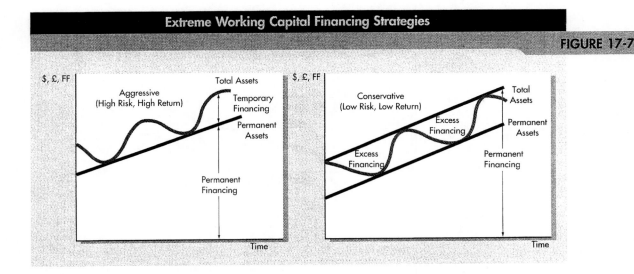

Extreme Working Capital Financing Strategies

FIGURE 17-7

to continuously finance permanent assets is inappropriate for two reasons.[3] First, the financing flexibility provided by temporary financing is not needed with permanent assets because the financing requirement does not exhibit short-term fluctuations. Second, the use of temporary financing subjects the firm to substantial risk of financial distress. The firm's inability to renew maturing short-term debt needed to finance long-lived assets could cause a major financial crisis.

Financing Temporary Assets. The appropriate strategy for financing temporary assets is not as straightforward as the strategy for permanent assets. The most logical approach would seem to be to finance all temporary assets with temporary financing, as shown in the left graph in Figure 17-7. This strategy is labeled aggressive because it calls for increasing the expected returns of the firm by eliminating the opportunity cost of excess financing. At the same time, however, it increases the firm's risk of financial distress due to the heavy reliance on short-term debt. An alternative strategy is shown in the right graph in the figure. It is termed conservative because it seeks to minimize the risk of financial distress by using permanent financing for all assets, both permanent and temporary. The price of this risk reduction is the high opportunity cost of the excess financing.

The strategies shown in Figure 17-7 represent extremes. In reality, it is quite likely that some compromise strategy, such as depicted in Figure 17-8, will be optimal. The compromise strategy involves financing all permanent assets and a portion of temporary assets with permanent financing. The remaining portion of the temporary assets is financed with temporary financing. This strategy represents a compromise because it requires the firm to accept some excess financing in order to moderate the risk of financial distress. It is not possible to establish for all firms a single optimal proportion of temporary assets to be financed with temporary financing. A firm should be able to increase its reliance on short-term debt, however, under the following conditions:

http://

Financing the necessary working capital for a business involves developing strong relationships with banks and other institutions. For a small business, the Small Business Administration (SBA) can be very helpful. See these sites

www.cbsc.org/ontario/bis/2015.html,

www.iep.doc.gov/bisnis/finance/sba.htm, and

www.exim.gov/press/jan2496b.html

---

[3] Due to factors such as temporarily unfavorable market conditions or the need to sell large issues of bonds or stocks, a firm may temporarily finance permanent assets with short-term debt. In such a case, a firm normally recognizes the risk that it is accepting through the use of short-term debt. It will eliminate this risk through the sale of long-term debt or equity as soon as is feasible.

FIGURE 17-8

A Compromise Working Capital Financing Strategy

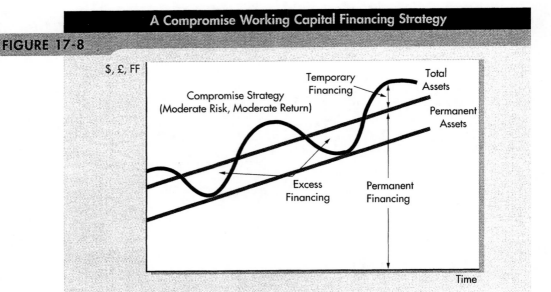

1. the existence of a strong relationship with a bank that provides ready access to short-term financing;
2. the ability to issue commercial paper as an alternative to bank financing; or
3. stable sales and low operating risk, which reduce the risk of financial distress.

An Illustration of Working Capital Policy. The financial managers of Industrie Berne (IB) are constructing a financial plan for the coming year. They estimate that fixed assets will remain constant at SF80 million throughout the year but that current assets will fluctuate in the following pattern:

Month	Current Assets (in Thousands)	Month	Current Assets (in Thousands)
Jan.	SF20,000	July	SF20,000
Feb.	22,000	Aug.	22,000
Mar.	25,000	Sept.	25,000
Apr.	23,000	Oct.	23,000
May	21,000	Nov.	22,000
June	19,000	Dec.	21,000

The managers wish to determine the financing requirements implied by the above asset levels. Equity financing is expected to remain unchanged at SF50 million during the year, and spontaneous current liabilities will average 20% of the firm's required current assets. The firm's working capital financing strategy requires that sufficient permanent financing be acquired to finance all permanent assets and 50% of maximum temporary current assets.

The first step in estimating the firm's financing requirements for the coming year is to determine the projected level of temporary assets and permanent assets:

$$
\begin{aligned}
\text{Permanent Assets} &= \text{Fixed Assets} + \text{Permanent Current Assets} \quad &(1)\\
&= \text{SF80,000,000} + 19,000,000 = \text{SF99,000,000}\\
\text{Maximum Temporary Assets} &= \text{Maximum Total Assets} - \text{Permanent Assets} \quad &(2)\\
&= \text{SF105,000,000} - 99,000,000 = \text{SF6,000,000}
\end{aligned}
$$

Permanent current assets equal SF19 million because that is the minimum projected level of current assets at any time during the coming year. Since the maximum projected level of total assets is SF105 million (SF80 million fixed assets plus

■ Financial ISSUES

HAS THE INTERNET ELIMINATED THE NEED FOR INVENTORIES?

One of the most intriguing and promising aspects of the Internet for financial managers is the development of electronic commerce and its implications for retailer investment in both current assets and fixed assets. Use of Web sites to market and sell products seems, at first glance, to offer the potential to eliminate the need for investment in physical facilities and inventories. Yet the early experience of Internet sellers suggests that electronic commerce has not completely severed the link between sales and assets.

Amazon.com was one of the pioneers of Internet commerce when it set up its electronic bookstore on the Web in 1996 to compete with industry giants such as Borders and Barnes & Noble. Amazon's philosophy and competitive advantage was quite simple. Take orders electronically; obtain the books from book wholesalers and publishers; and then ship the books to the customers. In the process, the firm would eliminate the need for massive investment in elaborate bookstores and extensive inventories sitting on shelves. The concept was an overnight success. In just two years, Amazon's sales had reached an annual level of $110 million. In March 1997, the firm engaged in an initial public offering of its shares. By September of that year, the market value of the firm totaled some $670 million. The demise of the traditional bookstore seemed to be on the near horizon.

Unlike this upstart operation, industry giant Barnes & Noble, with $3 billion in annual sales, not only maintained superstores nationwide but also kept an inventory of 400,000 titles stocked in its central warehouse. In response to the Amazon threat, B&N launched its own Web site in 1997. Due to its extensive inventories of books, however, B&N's Web site has two crucial advantages. First, the firm's volume discounts from publishers enabled it to offer a 30% discount on all hardcover books purchased through its Web site. Second, the availability of so many titles in its central warehouse allowed B&N to fill customer Web site orders much more quickly than Amazon.

Amazon's reaction to this new competition involved a major revision of its "no inventory" philosophy. In order to match B&N's 30% discount and quick delivery, the firm expanded the number of titles that it stocked, from a small list of bestsellers to a much broader collection. Amazon's experience provides a valuable lesson in working capital management. Even in a world of electronic commerce, inventories continue to play a crucial role in the operation of a firm.

SF25 million current assets) in March and September, the firm's maximum temporary assets will be SF6 million in those months.

Given this information, the firm's long-term debt requirements for the next year can be calculated:

$$
\begin{aligned}
\text{Permanent Financing Required} &= \text{Permanent Assets} + \text{Permanent Financing of Maximum Temporary Assets} \quad (3) \\
&= \text{SF99,000,000} + (0.50)(6,000,000) \\
&= \text{SF102,000,000}
\end{aligned}
$$

$$
\begin{aligned}
\text{Long-Term Debt Required} &= \text{Permanent Financing Required} - \text{Owners' Equity} - \text{Permanent Spontaneous Current Liabilities} \quad (4) \\
&= \text{SF102,000,000} - 50,000,000 - (0.20)(19,000,000) \\
&= \text{SF48,200,000}
\end{aligned}
$$

Permanent financing will be needed for both fixed assets and 50% of the firm's maximum temporary assets. Consequently, IB's financial managers must make plans to provide SF102 million in permanent financing next year. Their forecast of owners' equity will provide only SF50 million of the needed funds. Since permanent spontaneous liabilities represent 20% of the firm's permanent current assets, they can provide another SF3.8 million of the needed funds. The remaining SF48.2 million must come from long-term debt. Whether this will require the issuance of additional debt depends on the firm's current level of outstanding long-term debt.

The data on permanent and temporary assets can also be used to calculate the firm's requirements for negotiated current liabilities:

$$
\begin{aligned}
\text{Maximum Temporary Financing Required} &= \text{\% of Temporary Assets Financed with Temporary Financing} \times \text{Maximum Temporary Assets} \quad (5) \\
&= (0.50)(\text{SF6,000,000}) \\
&= \text{SF3,000,000}
\end{aligned}
$$

$$
\begin{aligned}
\text{Maximum Negotiated Current Liabilities Required} &= \text{Maximum Temporary Financing Required} - \text{Maximum Temporary Spontaneous Current Liabilities} \quad (6) \\
&= \text{SF3,000,000} - (0.20)(6,000,000) \\
&= \text{SF1,800,000}
\end{aligned}
$$

The maximum level of temporary financing needed over the coming year is only SF3 million because the firm's working capital policy calls for permanent financing for 50% of temporary current assets. Of that SF3 million, SF1.2 million will be automatically provided in the form of spontaneous credit. The remaining SF1.8 million must then take the form of negotiated current liabilities.

The results of the financial managers' balance sheet projections and the firm's working capital policy are summarized in Figure 17-9. Since IB intends to finance half of its maximum temporary assets with permanent financing, excess financing will occur periodically. For example, permanent financing of SF102 million will exceed June's total financing requirements of SF99 million. The firm's financial managers should plan to invest the excess financing depicted by the graph. Conversely, the managers must make arrangements to acquire temporary financing, such as a bank loan, during those months in which temporary current assets exceed the SF3 million permanent financing available for these assets. For example, the firm's total assets of SF105 million in March and September will exceed its permanent financing of SF102 million. While temporary spontaneous current liabilities will provide SF1.2 million of the SF3 million financing shortfall, the remaining SF1.8 million must come from negotiated current liabilities.

SUMMARY

This chapter demonstrated how a firm's working capital policy can affect the value of the firm. Working capital policy has two dimensions: investing decisions concerning the level and composition of current assets; and financing decisions concerning the maturity composition of a firm's debt. Both types of decisions affect the value of the firm through their effect on the expected level and riskiness of a firm's returns.

As is true of fixed assets, the size of a firm's investment in working capital, or current assets, is controllable by the financial managers. Initially, as current assets expand, they increase the value of the firm for two reasons. First, they increase its liquidity, thereby reducing the risk of financial distress. Second, they increase its profitability by reducing the opportunity cost of lost sales. At some point, both of these positive benefits cease. Further expansion of current assets will reduce the firm's value because the cost of the additional investment is not justified by the benefits generated.

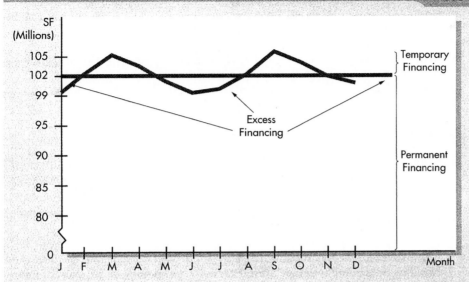

FIGURE 17-9

Industrie Berne's Working Capital Financing Strategy

A firm's assets can be divided into permanent and temporary categories. In the same way, financing consists of temporary and permanent components. From the financial manager's viewpoint, the length of the commitment of funds to an asset or the availability of funds from a given type of financing is not always described accurately by the traditional accounting classification of short-term or long-term. The maturity composition of a firm's debt can affect its risk/return trade-off. Short-term debt increases a firm's profitability by reducing the opportunity cost of periodic excess financing that accompanies the use of long-term debt. Long-term debt, on the other hand, minimizes the risk of financial distress due to the inability to renew maturing short-term debt. Permanent assets should be financed with permanent financing due to their long-term nature. Temporary assets should normally be financed with some combination of temporary and permanent financing. The permanent financing portion maintains the risk of financial distress at an acceptable level. The temporary financing portion moderates the opportunity cost of excess permanent financing. The optimal proportion of temporary financing is directly related to a firm's access to sources of short-term funds and inversely related to its level of operating risk.

CONTENT QUESTIONS

1. What is the basis for classifying certain current assets as operating assets?
2. In what respect are current assets different from fixed assets and in what respects are they similar?
3. Explain why there is some point after which additional investment in current assets ceases to reduce the risk of financial distress.

chapter equations

1. Permanent Assets = Fixed Assets + Permanent Current Assets

2. Maximum Temporary Assets = Maximum Total Assets – Permanent Assets

3. Permanent Financing Required = Permanent Assets + Permanent Financing of Maximum Temporary Assets

4. Long-Term Debt Required = Permanent Financing Required – Owners' Equity – Permanent Spontaneous Current Liabilities

5. Maximum Temporary Financing Required = % of Temporary Assets Financed with Temporary Financing × Maximum Temporary Assets

6. Maximum Negotiated Current Liabilities Required = Maximum Temporary Financing Required – Maximum Temporary Spontaneous Current Liabilities

4. Explain why overexpansion of current assets can decrease a firm's value.
5. Distinguish between a firm's temporary and permanent current assets.
6. What is a spontaneous current liability?
7. Using trade credit as an example, explain how a spontaneous current liability can represent either temporary or permanent financing.
8. What are the components of a firm's permanent financing?
9. Why is a working capital financing strategy that calls for financing all temporary assets with temporary financing considered to be aggressive?
10. What factors determine the optimal proportion of permanent and temporary financing that should be used to finance temporary assets?

CONCEPT QUESTIONS

1. When deciding how to allocate their time, a firm's managers argue that little time should be devoted to working capital management due to the short-term nature of the commitment of funds. Furthermore, the level of working capital required is largely outside the control of financial managers. What is your reaction to these statements?
2. IVM A firm's managers are trying to decide how to finance a buildup in the firm's inventories and receivables associated with an increase in sales. How can they determine whether they should use temporary or permanent financing?
3. A firm's managers are attempting to categorize the firm's financing into temporary and permanent components. Can this be done by examining the firm's balance sheet?
4. Spontaneous financing, such as trade credit, represents a major source of financing for both temporary and permanent current assets. Why can't all of a firm's permanent current assets be financed with permanent spontaneous financing?
5. Assume that a firm that has been growing rapidly for the last three years has financed the associated growth in working capital with short-term negotiated bank credit because the assets are classified as current assets on the balance sheet. Would this financing policy be classified as aggressive or conservative? What are the risks associated with the policy?

PROBLEMS

1. Perry Chemicals is in the process of constructing a financial plan for the coming year. It has estimated that fixed assets will be equal to £200,000,000 for the year and that current asset requirements vary between a minimum of £50,000,000 and a maximum of £80,000,000 during the year.
   a. What is the amount of permanent assets?
   b. What is the maximum amount of temporary assets?
2. Perry Chemicals (Problem 1) estimates that owners' equity for the coming year will equal £160,000,000 and that spontaneous current liabilities will average 25% of the firm's current assets. Its managers want to produce alternative financial plans with different levels of permanent financing of current assets.
   a. Find the required permanent financing and the required long-term debt if Perry would finance *none* of its temporary assets with permanent financing.
   b. Find the required permanent financing and the required long-term debt if Perry would finance *60%* of its temporary assets with permanent financing.

3. Returning to Perry Chemicals (Problems 1 and 2), calculate the maximum temporary financing and the maximum negotiated current liabilities required:
    a. if Perry finances *none* of its temporary assets with permanent financing.
    b. if Perry finances *60%* of its temporary assets with permanent financing.

4. During 1999, Takeo Electronics' fixed assets remained constant at ¥15 billion. Its current assets fluctuated as shown below:

Month	Current Assets (in Millions)	Month	Current Assets (in Millions)
Jan.	¥5,000	July	¥6,000
Feb.	5,000	Aug.	9,000
Mar.	7,000	Sept.	10,000
Apr.	9,000	Oct.	12,000
May	10,000	Nov.	8,000
June	8,000	Dec.	7,000

    a. What was the level of Takeo's permanent assets during 1999? What percentage of permanent assets were permanent current assets?
    b. What was the maximum level of temporary assets in 1999?
    c. What was the level of temporary assets in June?

5. Assume that Takeo Electronics' (Problem 4) spontaneous current liabilities averaged 15% of current assets during 1999. The firm's working capital financing strategy called for financing all of its temporary assets with temporary financing.
    a. What was the level of spontaneous current liabilities in October?
    b. What was the level of temporary and permanent spontaneous current liabilities in October?
    c. What level of negotiated current liabilities in October is implied by your answer to part (b)?

6. Given the information on Takeo Electronics in Problems 4 and 5, calculate the long-term debt required in 1999 if owners' equity in that year remained constant at ¥10 billion.

7. What would happen to your answer in Problem 6 if:
    a. Takeo's working capital policy called for financing 50% maximum temporary assets with permanent financing?
    b. spontaneous current liabilities averaged 25% of current assets (assume the original working capital financing strategy)?

8. After you have taken the Self-Study Quiz, repeat its questions 1 to 4. This time assume that Troy Equipment finances none of its maximum temporary assets with permanent financing.

9. The sales of Falcon Manufacturing follow a seasonal pattern that causes its assets and liabilities to reach a peak in July and a trough in April and October. The firm follows a policy of financing all of its temporary assets with temporary financing. The firm's balance sheet for those months is shown below:

	April (October)	July
Current Assets	$ 6,000,000	$20,000,000
Fixed Assets	25,000,000	25,000,000
Total Assets	$31,000,000	$45,000,000
Current Liabilities	$ 3,000,000	$17,000,000
Long-Term Liabilities	15,000,000	15,000,000
Owners' Equity	13,000,000	13,000,000
Total Liabilities and Equity	$31,000,000	$45,000,000

a. What was the level of the firm's maximum temporary assets and permanent assets?

b. If the firm's spontaneous current liabilities averaged 50% of current assets during the year, what was the level of permanent spontaneous current liabilities?

c. Calculate the firm's permanent financing.

10. In the case of Falcon Manufacturing (Problem 9):

a. Calculate the three components of the firm's current liabilities in April and July: permanent spontaneous, temporary spontaneous, and negotiated.

b. Calculate the firm's temporary financing in April and July.

11. Delta Industries follows the strategy of financing all of its temporary assets with temporary financing. The firm's financial managers forecast that fixed assets will remain constant at $30 million over the next year, while owners' equity will be $15 million. They estimate that current assets will follow the pattern shown below:

Month	Current Assets (in Thousands)	Month	Current Assets (in Thousands)
Jan.	$14,000	July	$16,000
Feb.	15,000	Aug.	14,000
Mar.	13,000	Sept.	13,000
Apr.	10,000	Oct.	11,000
May	12,000	Nov.	10,000
June	13,000	Dec.	12,000

a. Calculate the level of permanent financing required over the year.

b. Calculate the maximum level of temporary financing required during the year.

12. If spontaneous current liabilities for Delta Industries (Problem 11) are expected to average 20% of current assets:

a. calculate the level of long-term debt required.

b. calculate the maximum level of negotiated current liabilities required.

c. construct a balance sheet for July, showing the components of current assets and current liabilities.

13. Assume that Delta Industries (Problem 11) alters its financing strategy to call for financing one-third of its maximum temporary assets with permanent financing.

a. Recalculate the level of permanent financing and maximum temporary financing during the year.

b. If spontaneous current liabilities average 20% of current assets, what will be the maximum level of negotiated current liabilities?

c. If spontaneous current liabilities average 20% of current assets, what is the maximum amount of excess permanent financing? In what month will it occur?

d. Construct a balance sheet for that month, showing the components of current assets and current liabilities.

14. State Enterprises is about to arrange seasonal temporary financing for the year with its bank. The bank wants to know the maximum amount that State would borrow. Find the maximum amount that State would need to borrow given the following information:

1) Long-term debt $1,900,000; 2) Owners' Equity $ 800,000; 3) Maximum Current Assets $1,600,000; 4) Fixed Assets $2,000,000; 5) Spontaneous Current Liabilities will be 25% of Current Assets

15. If the minimum level of current assets for State Enterprises (Problem 14) is $800,000, what is the maximum excess financing?

16. Classic Computers' current assets are expected to reach their highest level of $48,000,000 in June and their lowest level of $28,000,000 in December. Classic's fixed assets will remain constant at $75,000,000 and owners' equity is $46,000,000. Spontaneous liabilities are expected to average 30% of current assets. Classic has established a working capital policy of financing 50% of its maximum temporary assets with permanent financing.

    a. What is the amount of permanent assets and the maximum temporary assets?

    b. What is the amount of permanent financing and the amount of long-term debt?

    c. What is the amount of temporary financing and the amount of negotiated current liabilities in June?

17. Repeat Problem 16 under the assumption that Classic has established a working capital policy of financing none of its maximum temporary assets with permanent financing.

INTERNET EXERCISE

Most people starting a business do not have strong business skills. What's involved in running a successful business? The following Web site investigates the mistakes and outlines the responsibilities of business owners. Make a list of the items that relate to working capital policy and bring it to class for discussion.

www.eweekly.com/news/news36.html

http://

SELF-STUDY QUIZ

During the process of constructing a financial plan for the coming year, Troy Equipment has estimated its current assets requirement, as given below.

Month	Current Assets (in Millions)	Month	Current Assets (in Millions)
Jan.	$50	July	$100
Feb.	40	Aug.	90
Mar.	60	Sept.	80
Apr.	70	Oct.	70
May	80	Nov.	70
June	90	Dec.	60

Fixed assets are forecast to remain constant at $200 million. Troy will finance 40% of its maximum temporary assets with permanent financing.

1. What is Troy's investment in permanent current assets and its maximum temporary assets?

2. Calculate the level of permanent financing for the year.

3. Calculate the maximum level of temporary financing for the year.

4. If spontaneous current liabilities are 25% of current assets and owners' equity is $100 million, find:

    a. the level of long-term debt.

    b. the maximum level of negotiated liabilities.

    c. the maximum level of excess permanent financing.

Management of Accounts Receivable and Inventory

Accounts receivable and inventories are necessitated by competitive conditions in an industry. The level of funds committed to these assets, however, is not *mandated* by competition but is subject to management control. Thus, financial managers must understand the factors that determine the size of receivables and inventories. They also must be able to evaluate the effect of changes in these assets on the value of a firm to its stockholders. In this chapter, we will address the following questions:

- The sale of goods or services on a credit basis gives rise to accounts receivable on a firm's balance sheet. The size of the investment in receivables is directly affected by a firm's credit policy. What are the components of credit policy? How do changes in these components affect credit sales and receivables? Are the components interdependent or can they be controlled independently by financial managers?

- Proposed changes in a firm's credit policy should be evaluated on the basis of their potential effect on firm value. How is a firm's risk/return trade-off altered by changes in credit policy? What effect do changes in the components of credit policy have on a firm's cash flows? How can the impact of these cash flow effects on a firm's value be quantified?

- Along with accounts receivable, inventories represent the largest current asset for many firms. What is the role of inventories in the operation of a business? What effect do changes in inventory policy have on a firm's cash flows? How can financial managers measure the effect of a proposed change in inventory policy on firm value?

The "how and why" of management's control over the level of current assets can sometimes be difficult to understand. The commitment of funds to receivables and inventories is frequently viewed as a by-product of the firm's marketing and production strategies. As a result, it seems a reasonable conclusion that a firm's investment in these assets does not reflect a conscious management policy. Logical though this may seem, on close examination it turns out to be inaccurate. The balance in receivables and inventory is not determined in an arbitrary or a random fashion. Rather, it should be the result of a careful evaluation of the risk/return trade-off associated with these two investments.

The significance of the level of receivables and inventory for a firm's value is highlighted in Figure 20-1. An increase in either or both of these variables is generally associated with increased sales and a corresponding increase in expected returns: E(EBIT). Since the increase in sales and earnings is uncertain, however, the variability (σ_{EBIT}) of earnings will also increase. Thus, the firm faces a risk/return trade-off in expanding receivables and inventory. The firm's financial managers must evaluate this trade-off in their determination of inventory and credit policies. Only those policy changes associated with an NPV ≥ 0 should be accepted.

In the first section of the chapter, the components of a firm's credit policy and their effect on the level of a firm's receivables will be examined. In the second section, we will utilize the IVM to evaluate proposed changes in credit standards, credit terms, and collection procedures. In the third section, a similar examination of inventory policy will be performed. The first task will be to describe the role and characteristics of raw materials, work-in-process, and finished goods inventories. We will then demonstrate how the IVM can be used to estimate the effect of proposed changes in inventory policy on firm value.

THE RELATIONSHIP BETWEEN CREDIT POLICY AND ACCOUNTS RECEIVABLE

The size of the accounts receivable balance is determined by the combination of a number of factors, only a portion of which are controllable by a firm's management. A firm's receivables are equal to the product of two variables: credit sales per day and the average collection period (ACP). Although many factors can have a significant impact on a firm's investment in receivables, the intent in this chapter is to concentrate on the effect of one particular factor, credit policy, which is directly

http://
Explore bootstrap financing that maximizes the cash balance by improving receivable collection and cash distribution for inventory at

www.dtonline.com/finance/bgintfin.htm

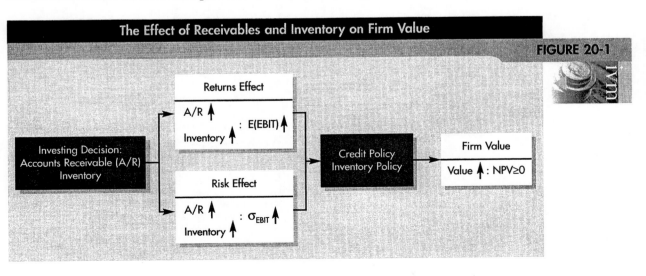

The Effect of Receivables and Inventory on Firm Value

FIGURE 20-1

controllable by a firm's financial managers. In this section, we will examine how the three components of credit policy (credit standards, credit terms, and collection procedures) can affect a firm's receivables through their impact on credit sales and average collection period. The manner in which each of these components affects receivables, which will be discussed below, is summarized in Figure 20-2.

Credit Standards

Credit Standards The guidelines followed in determining whether a credit applicant is credit-worthy.

The most basic decision regarding accounts receivable is to differentiate customers that qualify for credit from those that do not by setting **credit standards**. The problem faced by the financial managers is to determine the optimal amount of risk of nonpayment to accept after considering the returns that are expected from the expansion of credit sales. Let us take a look at the costs and benefits of granting credit. The fundamental source of benefits from offering credit is the recapture of sales that would be foregone if no credit were offered. The major benefit derived from these additional sales is the incremental cash profit realized by the firm. There are a number of costs associated with the extension of credit terms:

1. Investigation expenses
2. Collection expenses
3. Bad debt expenses

Investigation expenses are the costs of looking into the financial and credit history of potential customers. Some of these costs will increase as credit standards are lowered since more applications will be considered in depth and more care taken in assessing each applicant. Collection expenses are the costs of following up on delinquent accounts. These expenses can range from the cost of mailing additional invoices or special warnings about potential loss of credit standing, to the expense of hiring a collection agency. As credit standards are eased, these costs can also be expected to increase.[1]

The Three Components of a Firm's Credit Policy

SUMMARY FIGURE 20-2

Credit Policy Component	Type of Influence on Sales and Receivables	Change in Component That Will Increase Credit Sales and Receivables
1. Credit Standards	*Who* can buy on a credit basis?	*Lower* credit rating required of credit customers.
2. Credit Terms	*How much* is the cost of credit to the customer?	*Decrease* the percentage cash discount.
	How long is the maximum discount period?	*Shorten* the discount period.
	How long is the maximum credit period?	*Lengthen* the net period.
3. Collection Procedures	*What* procedures will the firm use to collect overdue accounts receivable?	*Reduce* the number and expense of collection procedures.

---

[1] The state of the economy influences the level of collection expenses. When the economy enters a recession or credit becomes difficult to obtain in the credit markets, the incidence of credit delinquency increases significantly. When this happens, firms increasingly call on collection agencies to recover overdue payments. The services of these agencies are expensive. Commercial collection agencies typically keep 20%–25% of whatever they collect. Consumer or retail agencies may charge as much as 50% of their collections. A low credit-risk customer in boom times may become a high-risk customer if the economy enters a severe recession.

Bad debt expense is the amount of credit that is uncollectible. At some point, the selling firm will be forced to acknowledge that some of its customers have defaulted on their obligation to pay. A firm should be willing to take a chance on easing credit standards if the percentage of new customers that default is low enough to be offset by the profitability expected from those new customers that do pay. As a result, while the credit managers might strive for zero bad debts, the financial managers should realize that there is some level of bad debt expense that is acceptable.

In setting credit standards, the sum of these three credit expenses are compared with the profits on incremental sales. Figure 20-3 shows how credit standards can alter the value of the firm. The *optimal credit standards* occur when the *incremental profits and expenses connected with a change in standards exactly offset each other*.

Credit Terms

In Chapter 18, it was demonstrated how changing the cash discount, the discount period, or the net period can alter the effective cost of trade credit. Presumably, a credit customer's demand for a firm's products will be influenced by this cost. The higher the cost of obtaining short-term credit from a supplier, the lower is the level of a firm's credit sales and receivables.

For example, assume that a firm's current credit policy calls for credit terms of 2/15; *net 30*. This represents an annual percentage rate (APR) of 49.0% and an effective interest rate (EIR) of 62.4% to customers that do not pay until one month after purchase. The firm is considering replacing the current credit terms with one of the following:

Proposed Credit Policy	New Credit Terms	Change from Current Credit Terms (2/15; net 30)	APR	EIR
A	1/15; net 30	Decreased Cash Discount: 2% – 1% = 1%	24.2%	27.3%
B	2/10; net 30	Shortened Discount Period: 15 – 10 = 5 days	36.7	43.8
C	2/15; net 45	Lengthened Net Period: 45 – 30 = 15 days	24.5	27.4

The changes represented by the three proposed credit policies are those described in the credit terms section of Figure 20-2. Policy A reduces the APR and

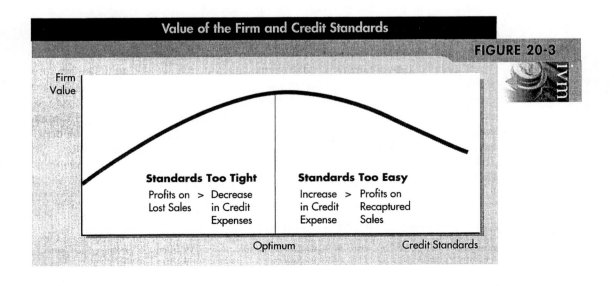

FIGURE 20-3

Value of the Firm and Credit Standards

■ Financial

ISSUES

HOW ONE FIRM HAS CASHED IN ON THE CONSUMER CREDIT CRISIS

Turning receivables over to a credit collection agency is a last-ditch effort on the part of a firm to obtain payment on outstanding accounts receivable. Since the collection agency collects a small percentage of these receivables and charges high fees for its efforts, the net proceeds to the selling firm are minimal. They are preferable, however, to a complete write-off of bad debts. Aggressive issuance of credit cards by U.S. banks in the early 1990s led to historic highs in delinquent credit card receivables and personal bankruptcies later in the decade. While this was bad news for the banks, it created a booming business for collection agencies.

One of the most successful of these firms was Commercial Financial Services (CFS), which specializes in delinquent credit card debts. Between 1990 and 1997, employment at the firm increased from 17 to 2,350. In 1996, the company earned $137 million on revenues of $206 million, an incredible net margin of 67%. The firm is unique not only in its profit margins but also in its operating approach. Unlike most collection agencies that work for a fee stated as a percentage of collections, CFS buys the bad debts outright from the banks. It has an exclusive agreement with 15 of the top 25 bank credit card issuers. The firm pays up to 10% of the face value of the debt and collects some 30% of the total debt purchased, about twice the success rate of the banks themselves. This high success rate is attrib-uted to careful training of employees and extensive use of computers to track down elusive debtors. Ownership of the debts also gives the firm's employees the flexibility to cut deals with the debtors for partial payments.

As of year-end 1997, CFS managed a bad debt portfolio of 2.5 million accounts with a face value of almost $8 billion. As a method of financing these assets, the firm pioneered the adaptation of securitization to bad consumer loans. Since 1995, the firm has sold nine security issues with a market value of $840 million. The firm sells the securities to investors while it continues to collect the payments on the underlying consumer debt. The attraction to investors is the securities' A credit rating from the Standard & Poor's and a yield that is 65 basis points (0.65%) higher than comparable risk and maturity debt instruments. The firm has been so successful collecting from high-risk consumers that it has even set up a separate consumer loan subsidiary. It plans to extend additional credit to those individuals who have faithfully made payments under the credit card payment plan originally negotiated with CFS. If the borrowers default on these new loans, presumably CFS will know how to collect the bad debts.

---

the EIR because the cash discount represents a finance charge to credit customers. Policies B and C both reduce the APR and EIR because they increase the maturity of the financing provided to credit customers. Under the current credit terms, this maturity is 15 days (30–15). Policy B will increase it to 20 days (30–10), while Policy C will increase it to 30 days (45–15). The lower costs of these proposed credit policies should result in an increase in the firm's credit sales.

Credit Terms The conditions under which credit will be extended to a customer. The components of credit terms are: cash discount, credit period, net period.

Typically, a given firm's **credit terms** are dictated by competition because similar terms are offered by all the firms in an industry. The existence of standard credit terms, however, does not mean that they should be overlooked as a potential decision variable. Blindly following industry norms concerning credit standards is no more valid than mimicking other investing decisions of the competition. Since credit terms affect a firm's investment of funds in receivables, an attempt should be made to determine those terms that will maximize the value of the firm to its owners.[2]

---

[2] As a further complication, the payment behavior of customers in response to a given set of credit terms is not constant over time. Unless the selling firm adjusts its credit terms accordingly, a sharp or prolonged increase in interest rates can cause a slowdown in customer payments as trade credit becomes a relative bargain.

A common practice in the computer industry is for manufacturers to wait until the end of a calendar quarter to place orders with their vendors. The vendors, who are under tremendous investor pressure to produce continuous growth in sales and earnings, will frequently grant special credit terms as an inducement to place a sales order before the end of the quarter. Consequently, the captured sales come at the price of reduced margins, which are not necessarily in the best interests of the vendor firm's owners. This problem worsens over time for vendors who gain a reputation for special end-of-the-quarter discounts. Vendors that refuse to offer such special discounts are likely to produce more stable sales and earnings in the long term.

Collection Procedures

The primary concern in establishing collection procedures is to decide when and how rigorously to demand payment. The selling firm must be careful not to lose the goodwill of valuable customers who are basically creditworthy but have failed to pay on time because of an oversight or a temporary liquidity problem. Excessive leniency, on the other hand, not only slows cash inflows but also carries the risk of a permissive reputation and dramatic increases in the average collection period as customers stretch trade credit.

The relative size of the buyer and the seller has a major influence on a firm's collection procedures. Collection efforts by both the seller and collection agencies are much more subtle and diplomatic with regard to trade credit than consumer credit. The apparent reason for this is the larger size of the buyers that make use of trade credit. The loss of future sales due to alienation of a consumer is normally insignificant even to a small seller. The loss of the sales of an alienated firm that buys on credit, on the other hand, can be disastrous. This is particularly true of small-to-medium size suppliers who rely heavily on sales to a few large customers. That is what happened in the early 1990s when Sears informed its suppliers that it was going to pay its bills in 60 days rather than in 30 days, as it had previously done. To refuse these new terms would mean the loss of their major customer for many of the suppliers.

The Role of Credit Information

The purpose of credit investigation is to estimate the potential of a slow payment or a bad debt. While no investigation can ever reveal, with certainty, whether an account will result in a bad debt or slow payment, a thorough analysis can enable a firm to make a reasonably accurate estimate of default. The ultimate decision to grant credit will depend on the relationship among the costs, benefits, and investments associated with the customers in a particular risk category. The type of information that is desirable and available differs greatly between trade credit and consumer credit. The primary sources of information about other businesses are:

1. Credit Rating Agencies
2. Financial Statements
3. Banks
4. Other Firms
5. The Seller's Own Experience

Credit rating agencies compile credit information and make credit evaluations of a large number of companies. In addition to a credit rating, these agencies make available credit reports containing information on principal managers, the nature of the business, financial data, and a credit repayment history of the company. Financial statements are excellent sources of information because they provide

Credit Rating Agencies
Firms that compile information on and establish credit ratings for companies.

detailed and more recent information than that which is available from a credit rating agency.[3]

Banks are most useful as a source of credit information if a firm has specific questions in mind about the credit applicant's financial position. This type of information is best requested through the seller's own bank who will then contact the applicant's bank. Credit information is frequently exchanged among companies selling to the same customer. It can be done on a firm-to-firm basis or through a trade association or credit association, which functions as a clearinghouse of credit information. Finally, the firm's own experience regarding the payment habits of a current customer is perhaps the most important source of information for reassessing creditworthiness.

THE EVALUATION OF ALTERNATIVE CREDIT POLICIES

Each of the components of a firm's credit policy (credit standards, credit terms, and collection procedures) affects the level of receivables through its impact on credit sales or average collection period. A relaxation of credit standards and terms or collection procedures can lengthen the average collection period as well as boost credit sales. Whether the incremental profits associated with such a sales increase are sufficient to compensate for the additional investment must be determined by a firm's financial managers. The IVM is a valuable tool for this purpose.

The impact of a particular credit policy on firm value can be determined by calculating the net present value of the proposed policy:

$$NPV = PV \text{ of Cash Flows} - \text{Incremental Investment} = \sum_{t=1}^{N} \frac{C_t}{\left(1 + K_j\right)^t} - I \qquad (1)$$

where I = the incremental investment required by the policy; C_t = the expected net cash inflow generated by the policy in time period t; N = the number of time periods the policy will be in effect; and K_j = the RRR appropriate to the riskiness of the policy.

If it is assumed that the proposed policy will be in effect indefinitely and that the cash flows generated each period are constant, equation (1) reduces to a simpler perpetuity form:[4]

$$NPV = \frac{C}{K_j} - I \qquad (2)$$

The specific calculations of net cash inflow and incremental investment involved in the evaluation of a proposed credit policy with equation (2) will depend on which of the three components of a firm's current policy is being changed. The general sequence of calculations, however, is outlined in Figure 20-4. We will apply this procedure to the evaluation of changes in each of the three components of credit policy: credit standards, credit terms, and collection procedures.

---

[3] The usefulness of the financial statements provided by an applicant depends on their validity and reliability. In the case of statements that are audited by public accounting firms, this reliability is generally quite good. In the case of unaudited statements, the selling firm's managers must rely on their own judgment and the integrity of the credit applicant.

[4] The major instance in which this formula may lead to an inaccurate assessment of a credit policy's NPV is in the case of significant levels of inflation over the life of the credit policy. In that case, we could either switch to real cash flows and a real discount rate, or employ the constant growth model described in Chapter 7.

A General Procedure for the Evaluation of Proposed Changes in Credit Policy

SUMMARY FIGURE 20-4

1. Identify the proposed credit policy alternatives.

2. Calculate the incremental after-tax cash flow (C) for each policy.

3. Calculate the incremental investment (I) for each policy.

4. Calculate the NPV for each policy. Accept a policy if its NPV is positive.

Credit Standards—The Credit Granting Decision

The setting of credit standards determines which credit applications are accepted and which are rejected. While a *rejection means a lost sales opportunity, an acceptance means increased investment in accounts receivable as well as potential additional bad debts and credit department expense.* All these factors must be reflected in the calculation of the NPV of a proposed policy. Instead of evaluating applicants on an individual basis, a firm's financial managers will often classify applicants into categories or groups with similar risk characteristics. They will use equation (2) to calculate NPV by risk category to determine the optimal policy concerning which categories should be granted credit. The firm's credit managers will then grant credit only to applicants that fall in an acceptable category.

Let's turn to an example of the credit granting decision. Eller Mills classifies its customers into a number of risk classes. The firm's financial managers are considering an extension of credit to three of the more risky groups of applicants (risk categories C, D, and E) in hopes of increasing sales. The firm currently sells on terms of net 30. While these terms would apply to all credit customers, the average collection period is expected to be higher for riskier categories. In addition, the default rate and credit department collection expense are also expected to increase with risk. The first step in the evaluation procedure shown in Figure 20-4 is performed in Table 20-1, which contains special information about each risk category.

Eller Mills' variable costs, which include expenses such as materials, labor, and the variable portion of overhead, are 70% of sales. Since these costs are variable, they only include cash expenses. This variable costs/sales ratio is important because the NPV calculation utilizes only the incremental cash flows associated with a proposed credit policy. Eller's ratio of 70% means that every $1.00 of cash inflows from sales is partially offset by $0.70 in cash outflows for variable costs, resulting in a net cash inflow of only $0.30.

The second step in the NPV analysis of Eller's proposed changes in credit standards is to calculate the incremental after-tax cash flows for each risk category:

Eller Mills' Risk Categories C, D, and E

TABLE 20-1

Category	RRR	ACP	Increase in Sales	Bad Debts	Increase in Collection Expense
C	25%	40	$300,000	10%	$10,000
D	30%	50	250,000	15%	13,000
E	40%	60	150,000	18%	15,000

$$\text{Net Cash Inflow} = [(\text{Incremental Sales})(1 - \text{Variable Cost\%}) - (\text{Incremental Sales})(\text{Bad Debt\%})$$
$$- \text{ Incremental Collection Expense}] \,(1 - \text{Tax Rate})$$
$$C = [(\Delta S)(1 - VC) - (\Delta S)(BD) - \Delta CE](1 - T) \tag{3}$$

Given a corporate tax rate of 40%, the calculations for each of the three risk categories are shown in Table 20-2.

To understand these calculations better, we will review the after-tax cash flows expected from risk class C. The first term, $(\Delta S)(1 - VC)$, represents the net contribution to cash flow of each dollar of new sales. The next term, $(\Delta S)(BD)$, represents the dollar bad debt expense. Since 10% of new sales is not expected to be paid, bad debts reduce the net cash flow contribution of sales by $30,000. Finally, the $10,000 added collection expense in the credit department, ΔCE, associated with granting credit to risk category C is subtracted to arrive at the incremental cash flow of $30,000.

The third step in the analysis is to calculate the incremental investment for each of the three risk classes. The increase in accounts receivable that is attributable to each risk category is the product of new credit sales per day and the expected average collection period (ACP) of the risk category.[5] Only part of this increase is investment. The remainder is merely an *anticipated benefit*. For Eller Mills, each dollar added to accounts receivable is composed of $0.70 of incremental cost and $0.30 of profit. As a result, only 70% of the additional accounts receivable represents incremental investment required of Eller. This investment can be calculated as follows:

$$\text{Incremental Investment} = \text{Average Collection Period} \times \text{Incremental Daily Sales}$$
$$\times \text{Variable Cost \%}$$
$$I = (ACP)(\Delta S/360)(VC) \tag{4}$$

Table 20-3 shows the incremental investment associated with each of Eller's risk categories.

Calculation of Incremental Cash Flows for Eller Mills

TABLE 20-2

$$C = [(\Delta S)(1 - VC) - (\Delta S)(BD) - \Delta CE](1 - T)$$

Risk Category	Net Cash Inflow
C	C = $[(300,000)(1 − 0.70) − (300,000)(0.10) − 10,000](1 − 0.40)$ = $[90,000 − 30,000 − 10,000](0.60)$ = $30,000
D	C = $[(250,000)(1 − 0.70) − (250,000)(0.15) − 13,000](0.60)$ = $[75,000 − 37,500 − 13,000](0.60)$ = $14,700
E	C = $[(150,000)(1 − 0.70) − (150,000)(0.18) − 15,000](0.60)$ = $[45,000 − 27,000 − 15,000](0.60)$ = $1,800

---

[5] We make the simplifying assumption that receivables are the only asset affected by the change in credit policy. In some instances, it is possible that other assets, such as inventories, cash balances, or fixed assets, might be altered. If so, their change should be included in the estimate of incremental investment.

Calculation of Incremental Investment for Eller Mills

TABLE 20-3

$$I = (ACP)(\Delta S/360)(VC)$$

Risk Category	Incremental Investment
C	$I = (40)(\$300,000/360)(0.70) = \$23,333$
D	$I = (50)(\$250,000/360)(0.70) = \$24,306$
E	$I = (60)(\$150,000/360)(0.70) = \$17,500$

Calculation of the NPV for Eller Mills' Proposed Changes in Credit Standards

TABLE 20-4

	Risk Category	NPV
	C	$NPV = \$30,000/0.25 - \$23,333 = \$96,667$
$NPV = \dfrac{C}{K_j} - I$	D	$NPV = \$14,700/0.30 - \$24,306 = \$24,694$
	E	$NPV = \$1,800/0.40 - \$17,500 = -\$13,000$

The final step in the analysis is to calculate the NPV for each risk category, as shown in Table 20-4. The calculations reveal that credit standards should be relaxed to include customers in risk categories C and D.

The Credit Terms Decision

Penn-Ohio Industries is considering changing its credit terms from net 30 to net 60 with the hope of gaining additional sales from firms attracted by the more liberal credit terms. The new customers attracted are likely to be a little less creditworthy than current customers. Accordingly, Penn-Ohio estimates that bad debt expense will be around 2% of the anticipated new sales of $600,000 per year, that collection expense will not change significantly, and that the current ACP of 35 days will lengthen to 65 days after the change in terms. The firm's variable costs are 75% of sales; its corporate tax rate is 40%; and its RRR on the proposal is 20%.

The first step in the evaluation procedure is to identify the policy alternatives, as shown in Table 20-5.

The second step is to calculate the net cash inflows attributable to the policy change with equation (3):

$$
\begin{aligned}
C &= [(\Delta S)(1 - VC) - (\Delta S)(BD) - \Delta CE](1 - T) \\
&= [(\$600,000)(1 - 0.75) - (600,000)(0.02) - 0](1 - 0.40) \\
&= [\$150,000 - 12,000](0.60) \\
&= \$82,800
\end{aligned}
$$

Penn-Ohio Industries' Credit Terms Alternatives

TABLE 20-5

	Current Net 30	Proposed Net 60
Sales	$8,000,000	$8,600,000
ACP	35 days	65 days
Bad Debts		2% of incremental sales

The third step is to calculate the incremental investment attributable to the change in credit terms. Because the proposed credit terms are effective for both *old* and *new* customers, there are *two distinct components to incremental investment.* The first is the *additional investment in accounts receivable due to the acquisition of new customers.* This calculation is equivalent to the one performed above with equation (4) in the example of Eller Mills:

$$I_N = (ACP)(S_N/360)(VC) \qquad (5)$$

where the subscript N indicates that the value of the variable is for new customers only. The incremental investment associated with new customers for Penn-Ohio is:

$$I_N = (65)(\$600,000/360)(0.75) = \$81,250$$

The second component is the *increased investment in accounts receivable due to extending the longer credit period to the firm's existing customers.* The added investment due to the delayed collection of old sales includes both the cost and the profit proportion of sales. The profit on old sales will be realized regardless of which of the two credit periods Penn-Ohio selects. Since the cash inflow from the collection of this profit will be delayed under the net 60 terms, the incremental investment is equal to the full amount of the change in accounts receivable:

$$I_O = (\Delta ACP)(S_O/360) \qquad (6)$$

where the subscript O designates the appropriate value for a firm's old customers. Since Table 20-5 indicates that sales to old credit customers under the current terms of net 30 are $8,000,000, the incremental investment associated with old customers for Penn-Ohio is:[6]

$$I_O = (65 - 35)(\$8,000,000/360) = \$666,667$$

The total incremental investment is the sum of these two components:

$$I = I_N + I_O = \$81,250 + 666,667 = \$747,917$$

The final step in Penn-Ohio's analysis is the calculation of the proposed credit terms' NPV:

$$NPV = C/K_j - I = \$82,800/0.20 - \$747,917 = -\$333,917$$

The very large negative NPV reveals that the benefits from attracting new customers are not even close to justifying the added investment required.

The Credit Collection Decision

In general, as a *firm increases the amount spent on the collection of overdue accounts,* both the *average collection period and the percentage of bad debts decline.* As an illustration, Riley Textiles is unhappy with its current credit collection procedures because its bad debt expense and ACP on annual sales of £50,000,000 are higher than industry averages. It is considering a complete reorganization and expansion of the credit collection department. Table 20-6 compares the current and proposed collection situations.

---

[6] Notice the large size of the incremental investment associated with the firm's existing customers. The proposed credit terms of net 60 will delay the collection of the accounts receivable from credit sales to these customers by 30 days. If Penn-Ohio should implement the new terms of net 60, it would be granting additional interest-free loans to its existing customers equal to $666,667 on an annual basis.

	Current and Proposed Collection Procedures of Riley Textiles	
		TABLE 20-6

	Current	Proposed
Collection Expense	£150,000	£800,000
Bad Debt Expense	2%	1%
ACP	45 days	35 days

The incremental cash flows attributable to the proposed collection procedures are the difference between the reduction in bad debt expense and the additional collection expense. They can be calculated as follows:

$$\text{Net Cash Inflow} = (\text{Decrease in Bad Debts} - \text{Incremental Collection Expense})(1-T)$$
$$C = [(S)(\Delta BD) - \Delta CE](1 - T) \tag{7}$$

The computations for Riley Textiles indicate that the proposed collection procedures will *reduce* the firm's net cash inflows by £90,000:

$$C = [(£50,000,000)(0.02 - 0.01) - (£800,000 - 150,000)](1 - 0.40)$$
$$= (£500,000 - 650,000)(0.60)$$
$$= -£90,000$$

Riley must now determine whether the reduction in investment in accounts receivable caused by decreasing the ACP is sufficiently large to justify an annual net cash outflow of £90,000. The full reduction in accounts receivable represents a decrease in the investment required by the firm because these receivables will become cash inflows more rapidly with the proposed collection procedures. The incremental investment associated with the proposed changes is:

$$I = (\Delta ACP)(S/360) = (35 - 45)(£50,000,000/360) = -£1,388,889 \tag{8}$$

The last step is to find the NPV of the proposed change by using equation (2). In the calculation of the NPV of this proposal, it is essential to remember that both the incremental investment and the cash flows are negative. Since Riley has estimated the RRR to be 20%, the NPV for the proposed reorganization and expansion of the credit collection department is:

$$NPV = C/K_j - I_0 = -£90,000/0.20 - (-£1,388,889) = £938,889$$

The large positive NPV indicates that the immediate reduction of funds committed to accounts receivable outweighs the value of the future annual £90,000 net cash outflow required by the proposed collection procedures.[7]

In this discussion of accounts receivable, we have demonstrated that the level of funds invested is at least partially controllable by a firm's financial managers. Changes in credit standards, credit terms, or collection procedures can alter both the level of a firm's sales and its investment in receivables. Evaluating these changes in the context of the IVM allows managers to estimate the impact of the changes on a firm's value to its owners. Use of the IVM requires that a firm's financial managers

---

[7] Another way of interpreting these results is to view the reduction in accounts receivable as a source of immediately available funds. Just as with a bank loan or the sale of stock, there is a cost associated with this financing. The cost is the £90,000 annual net cash outflow required by the new collection procedures.

estimate both the incremental sales and expenses and the incremental investment in receivables that is associated with proposed changes in credit policy.

MONITORING RECEIVABLES COLLECTION

In the previous sections of this chapter, we developed methods for analyzing decisions concerning credit standards, credit terms, and collection procedures. Estimating Average Collection Period under different alternatives was an important factor in the decision process. Once credit policy is determined, a firm must keep track of the payments made by customers in order to determine whether the policies are working as expected. Consequently, monitoring the performance of its collection effort is an important issue to any firm.

Average Collection Period and Aging Schedule

Take a look at suggestions on reducing accounts receivable aging at http://guide.sbanetweb. com/press/collection.html

Two traditional methods for monitoring receivables collection patterns are to watch for significant changes in ACP and to look for significant changes in an accounts receivable aging schedule. Unexpected increases in ACP or in the age of receivables signal the potential problem that it is taking longer for customers to pay.

An accounts receivable aging schedule takes a closer look at the makeup of the accounts receivables balance than does the ACP. Table 20-7 is an example of an aging schedule for a firm as of the end of March. The schedule tells us that, of the $100,000 balance in accounts receivable, 10% is 60 to 90 days old, 20% is 30 to 60 days old, and 70% is less than 30 days old. This aging schedule would be compared with previous monthly aging schedules to detect whether collections are slowing. If sales are relatively stable, either the ACP or aging schedules produce reliable signals.

An increasing ACP or an increasing percentage of older accounts could signal a problem in collection or the accumulation of bad debts. On the other hand, if sales are seasonal or simply variable, neither technique is a reliable indicator of customer payment patterns.

The Effect of Variability in Sales

If sales are variable, changes in the ACP or accounts receivable aging schedule can be misleading. To understand why this is the case, consider Table 20-8. Essentially, the first two columns and the fourth column of Table 20-8 are the accounts receivable aging schedules for the first three quarters of the year. Notice that the aging schedule in Table 20-7 is the first quarter aging schedule in Table 20-8. In addition, note that the third column in Table 20-8 is the percent of a particular month's sales that remain uncollected at the end of the quarter. For example, 12.5% of January sales is uncollected at the end of March, 25% of February sales is uncollected at the end of March, and 87.5% of March sales is uncollected. The last item in Table 20-8 is the ACP for each quarter. The first quarter ACP is:

ACP = Receivables/Average Sales per day = $100,000/($240,000/90) = 37.50 days

	Accounts Receivable Aging Schedule for March	
TABLE 20-7		

Age of Accounts	Receivables	Percent of Total
60–90 days	$ 10,000	10%
30–60 days	20,000	20
0–30 days	70,000	70
Total	$100,000	100%

■ International

ISSUES

THE WAL-MART WAY TURNS OUT TO BE THE WRONG WAY IN SOUTH AMERICA

In its U.S. operations, Wal-Mart is renowned for its aggressive marketing and sophisticated operations management that vaulted it to the position of Number 1 U.S. retailer with over $100 billion in sales by 1997. Saturation of the U.S. market, however, had the firm's managers setting their sights on duplicating its success in international markets. In Canada and Mexico, this retailing behemoth acquired existing stores from other retailers. In Argentina and Brazil, on the other hand, the firm tried to recreate its U.S. empire from scratch. The problems encountered in this effort provide a valuable lesson in the hazards of international expansion.

By the end of 1997, Wal-Mart had opened 16 stores in Brazil and Argentina, with plans to double that number in 1998. Unlike its U.S. approach of locating in small communities, the South American stores were located in major cities where they were outnumbered by the major competitor by almost four-to-one. As a result, Wal-Mart was in the unfamiliar position of having smaller economies of scale. In addition, it was saddled with higher overhead, since its stores stocked 58,000 items versus only 22,000 items at the competition's stores. Due to lower purchase discounts and higher carrying costs, Wal-Mart suffered from a competitive disadvantage. The firm's inventory problems were compounded by logistical difficulties because it initially did not own its own distribution system in South America. Thus, it was forced to rely on suppliers and local trucking firms to supply its stores. The result was a logistical nightmare, with some stores handling up to 300 deliveries per day as opposed to the typical 7 daily deliveries at U.S. stores. Handling all these deliveries became even more problematic when Wal-Mart discovered that stock-handling equipment imported from the United States did not work with local pallets.

Wal-Mart's inventory problems also extended to its relationship with suppliers both in the United States and in South America. Its aggressive demands for purchase discounts prompted some local suppliers to refuse to sell to the U.S. retailer. In addition, because many local suppliers could not meet Wal-Mart's stringent product specifications, the firm was forced to rely on imported inventories. Many U.S. suppliers, however, balked at providing substantial discounts due to the small scale of Wal-Mart's purchases for its international operation.

Perhaps the biggest problem encountered by Wal-Mart's managers was their unfamiliarity with the local culture and consumer preferences. For example, its Brazilian stores initially refused to accept postdated checks, which were the most common form of consumer credit in that country. Even more troublesome was the firm's choice of inventories. American footballs, tanks of live trout, cordless tools, leaf blowers, and pricey American-style jeans held little appeal to apartment-dwelling South American consumers with limited incomes who preferred soccer and sushi. Much to the disappointment of its managers, Wal-Mart's attempt to extend its U.S. formula for success to South America lost a lot in the translation.

Sales per day is found by dividing quarterly sales by 90. In Chapter 2, when ACP was introduced, sales per day were calculated as annual sales divided by 360. The key to a correct calculation is to match the period of sales to the corresponding number of days.

Table 20-8 shows that at the end of the second quarter, ACP increased to 48.75 days, while the aging schedule has improved—with a smaller percentage of accounts over 30 days old (3.8% + 15.4% = 19.2% versus 10% + 20% = 30% in Quarter 1). Are collections faster or slower by the end of the second quarter? ACP suggests slower; the aging schedule suggests faster. Comparing the second quarter to the third, ACP is lower at 26.25 days but a higher percentage of receivables (21.4% + 28.6% = 50%) is over 30 days old. Are collections faster or slower? ACP suggests faster; the aging schedule suggest slower. Which technique is correct? Actually, neither conclusion is valid. The changes in ACP and aging schedules are due simply to the monthly variation in sales. In fact, there is no change in the speed of collection. In *each* quarter, 12.5% of sales remains uncollected at the end of two months after the sale, 25% remains uncollected at the end of one month after the sale, and

The Effect of Sales Patterns on Average Collection Period and Aging of Receivables

TABLE 20-8

Quarter 1: Constant Monthly Sales (in Thousands)

Month	Sales	Receivables	Receivables as % of Monthly Sales	Receivables as % of Quarterly Receivables	ACP for Quarter
January	$ 80	$ 10	12.5%	10.0%	37.50 days
February	80	20	25.0	20.0	
March	80	70	87.5	70.0	
Quarter Total	$240	$100		100.0%	

Quarter 2: Increasing Monthly Sales

Month	Sales	Receivables	Receivables as % of Monthly Sales	Receivables as % of Quarterly Receivables	ACP for Quarter
April	$ 40	$ 5	12.5%	3.8%	48.75 days
May	80	20	25.0	15.4	
June	120	105	87.5	80.8	
Quarter Total	$240	$130		100.0%	

Quarter 3: Decreasing Monthly Sales

Month	Sales	Receivables	Receivables as % of Monthly Sales	Receivables as % of Quarterly Receivables	ACP for Quarter
July	$120	$ 15	12.5%	21.4%	26.25 days
August	80	20	25.0	28.6	
September	40	35	87.5	50.0	
Quarter Total	$240	$ 70		100.0%	

87.5% at the end of the month of sales. The speed at which any month's sales is collected has not changed at all. Because collections are stable, it is sales variability that is causing changes in ACP and the aging schedule in Quarters 2 and 3.

Uncollected Balance Profile

A better way to monitor accounts receivable is to look directly at receivables as a percent of the sales that gave rise to them, and track how that relationship changes over time. This has been done every three months in Table 20-8. For example, at the end of March, 87.5% of that month's sales remain uncollected, 25% of one month earlier sales is uncollected, and 12.5% of two months' earlier sales is uncollected. Receivables as a percent of sales could be tracked monthly by constructing a table such as Table 20-9.

The collection experiences at the end of the first and second quarters are the highlighted March and June numbers in the table. The other numbers are the percent of sales for the month and two months previous to the month listed at the top of each column. As long as the percentages *across the rows* in the table do not change significantly, there is no change in the speed of collections, even though the ACP and aging schedules may be changing because of sales variability.

Percent of Receivables Outstanding at the End of Month

TABLE 20-9

	January	February	March	April	May	June	July
Month of Sale	88.0%	90.0%	**87.5%**	87.0%	89.0%	**87.5%**	88.0%
1 Month Prior	24.0	25.5	**25.0**	24.5	26.0	**25.5**	26.0
2 Months Prior	12.0	13.0	**12.5**	14.0	12.0	**12.5**	11.5

INVENTORY MANAGEMENT

Inventory management is similar to the management of accounts receivable, to the extent that both types of assets are closely related to sales. Unlike its investment in accounts receivable, however, a firm's commitment of funds to inventory is divided among a number of different types of inventories. In this section of the chapter, we will examine the nature of a firm's investment in inventories. We will also discuss the types of benefits and costs associated with a change in inventory policy and their evaluation within the context of the IVM.

The Components of Inventory

In later analysis of the inventory policy decision, we will talk about the level of inventory investment without reference to the specific type of inventory under discussion. Nevertheless, it is important to have a general understanding of the types of inventory and the motives for investing in inventory. Consequently, before we discuss the NPV evaluation of inventory investment decisions, we will describe the basic nature of the different types of inventories:

1. Raw Materials
2. Work-in-Process
3. Finished Goods

Raw Materials. This inventory category includes items that are purchased from outside the firm to be used directly in the manufacture of the final product. Raw materials may consist of metals, chemicals, and other basic commodities and semi-finished items such as electronic components and motors purchased from other manufacturers. The purpose of holding raw materials is to separate or *uncouple the purchasing function from the manufacturing function* so that, if necessary, each can proceed at a different rate. With a reserve of raw materials, an increase or decrease in the rate of production need not alter the rate of raw material acquisition, and vice versa.[8]

Work-in-Process. Work-in-process inventory consists of all the partially completed products that are being worked on or await further work in the production process. There is investment in work-in-process simply because the production pipeline must be filled if production is to proceed. Additional investment in work-in-process can be made to separate or *uncouple various states within the manufacturing process* so that the stages can operate at different rates. For example, if one of the stages suffers a breakdown, the additional work-in-process inventory allows the other stages to continue operations.

Finished Goods. As products are completed, they are transferred out of work-in-process to finished goods inventory, where they await sale. Finished goods inventory separates or *uncouples the manufacturing function from the sales function* because sales can be made from inventory. Customers do not have to wait until the particular product they desire is placed into production and completed. In addition, an unexpected shutdown of production will not stop sales.

http://

How can you improve the performance of working capital invested in inventory? You can explore reengineering inventory investment to improve availability of inventory while reducing working capital investment. See

www.execulink-invtry.co.uk

---

[8] The importance of a raw materials inventory becomes apparent in light of all the possible disruptions to the steady flow of raw materials to a firm. Strikes at suppliers, political upheavals, war, international politics, real or artificial shortages, and natural catastrophes are just a few of the possible sources of interruption in the supply of raw materials.

■ Valuation

ISSUES

FIRMS GET SERIOUS ABOUT INVENTORY CONTROL

Inventories represent a major commitment of funds by firms operating at all stages of the distribution process: manufacturing, wholesaling, and retailing. As pointed out in this chapter, the decision to invest in inventory requires an evaluation of the trade-off between the opportunity cost of lost sales and carrying costs. In response to high inventory carrying costs, firms have aggressively pursued techniques for reducing inventories while minimizing the opportunity costs of lost sales.

Some of the techniques have involved the use of technology. McKesson Corporation, a distributor of pharmaceuticals, has linked itself through computers to its 15,000 customers and 2,000 suppliers. Other approaches, such as that used at Avery International, base managers' compensation partially on their ability to reduce the ratio of inventory to sales. Perhaps the most widely publicized inventory control technique is that of "just-in-time" inventory ordering and delivery that was pioneered by Japanese industry. The concept behind this technique is simple: maintain only a few days' or hours' supply of inventory instead of a few weeks' supply. Required supplies are ordered almost continuously and arrive from suppliers just-in-time to

be used in the production process. Although it originated in Japan, this technique has been widely adopted by firms elsewhere. A mid-1990s survey indicated that over 70% of U.S. manufacturers utilize just-in-time methods.

The implementation of the technique, on the other hand, can be quite complex because it requires exact timing and close coordination of the buyer and the supplier. For example, General Motors requires one of its suppliers to deliver truck transmissions four times daily to a plant in Pontiac, Michigan. The supplier makes the transmissions in Brazil and ships them to a warehouse/assembly facility in Kalamazoo, Michigan. This facility can assemble the transmissions in different configurations, depending on GM's needs. The results of the just-in-time program have been substantial. GM reduced parts inventories from $10 billion to $8 billion in three years even though production increased over that period.

The Evaluation of Alternative Inventory Policies

Determination of the appropriate level of inventory is an investment decision that should be analyzed with the same technique used to evaluate the decision to invest in any other asset: the IVM. A firm's financial managers must first determine the costs and benefits that can be attributed to a change in the level of investment in inventory. Given these data, the effect of a given inventory policy on the firm's value to its owners can be estimated in terms of NPV.

Inventory Policy Decision Variables. In order to assess properly the impact of a change in inventory policy on firm value, the financial managers must be able to identify the incremental cash flows that are generated by the change. These cash flows can be grouped into the following categories:

1. Carrying Costs
2. Ordering Costs
3. Opportunity Costs of Lost Sales
4. Production Costs

Carrying Costs Costs associated with maintaining an inventory that increase as the level of inventory increases.

Ordering Costs Costs associated with placing orders that are fixed regardless of the size of the order.

Carrying costs represent those expenses that increase as the level of inventory rises. They include the costs associated with both the storage and the servicing of the inventory such as rent, utilities, insurance, property taxes, labor costs, and deterioration. Since these costs vary directly with the level of inventory, they are often expressed as a variable cost per unit of inventory. The **ordering costs** category includes those expenses that are fixed per order regardless of order size, such as the administrative costs of placing an order for goods. Since these costs are the same for each order, they fall as the average level of inventory rises, and the number of inventory orders declines. Fewer orders may also decrease the unit price of the goods ordered because the orders may qualify for quantity discounts due to their larger size.

The cost of a lost sale is an opportunity cost rather than an out-of-pocket expense. When a firm loses a sale due to a stockout, it foregoes the net cash inflow that would have been generated by the sale. Clearly, the firm can reduce this cost by increasing the size of its inventories. The **production costs** category includes those expenses associated with shutting down a production line and then restarting it. They can be reduced by increasing work-in-process and raw materials inventories, which reduce the chance of production delays caused by running out of essential materials.

Production Costs Costs associated with shutting down a production line and then restarting it.

The difficulty in evaluating these four types of inventory costs is apparent from a look at Figure 20-5. While an increase in the average size of inventory reduces ordering costs, production costs, and the opportunity cost of lost sales, it increases carrying costs. As a result, the *optimal inventory level that will minimize the total of these four types of inventory costs* depends on the relative size of each type of cost.

Inventory Policy Analysis. Since the determination of the level of inventory is an investment decision, it can be analyzed by calculating the NPV of a given policy using equation (2) that was presented earlier. The general procedure for the evaluation of alternative inventory policies is similar to that used to evaluate credit policy alternatives. Although we will demonstrate the use of this procedure in terms of finished goods inventory, it is just as applicable to the evaluation of raw materials or work-in-process inventory policy.

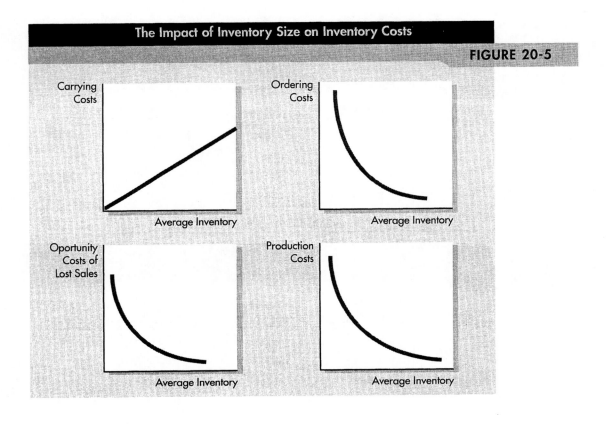

The Impact of Inventory Size on Inventory Costs

FIGURE 20-5

As an illustration of the use of this procedure, we will examine the case of Technidyne S.A. as it analyzes the effect of alternative inventory policies. Technidyne is concerned with the amount of sales that have been lost due to the firm's inability to quickly fill orders out of finished goods inventory. These losses have averaged an estimated SF1,600,000 each year. Since variable costs are 70% of sales, lost sales have resulted in lost profit contribution of SF480,000 each year.

Technidyne has compiled information on four alternative inventory policies, including the current policy (A), which requires an average inventory of SF1,000,000. Data on the four policy alternatives is shown in Table 20-10. The table indicates that the RRR increases with the level of inventory to reflect the increased risk that inventory will lose value due to deterioration, technological obsolescence, and changes in customer preferences. It also reflects the risk that lost sales will not be recovered because the figures in the table are merely management estimates. There is no guarantee that actual sales will increase by the amounts shown if inventory levels are increased.

In order to facilitate the analysis, Table 20-10 is rewritten in incremental form in Table 20-11 by taking the differences between the figures in the same column of Table 20-10 for two successive inventory policies. The data in Table 20-11 are based on successive inventory policies in order to stress the *incremental* effect of moving from one inventory level to another. For example, Policy B's inventory level of SF1,500,000 represents a SF500,000 increase over the inventory level of Policy A. Notice that, unlike the case of accounts receivable, the incremental investment in inventory for each policy is identical to the total increase in inventory required by that policy:

$$\text{Incremental Investment} = \text{Change in Inventory}$$
$$I = \Delta \text{ Inventory} \qquad (9)$$

Technidyne Alternative Finished Goods Inventory Policies

TABLE 20-10

Policy	Inventory Level	Carrying Cost	Annual Lost Sales	RRR
A	SF1,000,000	SF30,000	SF1,600,000	13%
B	1,500,000	50,000	900,000	15
C	2,000,000	60,000	300,000	20
D	2,500,000	65,000	0	25
		Marginal Tax Rate = 40%		

The Incremental Values of Technidyne's Inventory Policy Variables

TABLE 20-11

Policy	Incremental Investment (I)	Incremental Carrying Costs	Decrease in Lost Sales	RRR
B	SF500,000	SF20,000	SF700,000	15%
C	500,000	10,000	600,000	20
D	500,000	5,000	300,000	25

This equation is valid because inventory is valued at cost, not market value.

The next step in the analysis is the calculation of the incremental after-tax cash flows for each inventory level. The cash inflows produced by the expansion of inventories are partially offset by additional carrying costs:

Net Cash Inflow = [(Decrease in Lost Sales)(1 − Variable Cost %)
− Incremental Carrying Costs](1 − T)

$$C = [(\Delta S)(1 - VC) - \Delta CC](1 - T) \tag{10}$$

The calculations for Technidyne's policy alternatives are depicted in Table 20-12.

Given all this information, the NPV of each inventory policy alternative can now be calculated. The NPVs shown in Table 20-13 are based on the RRR for each policy from Table 20-10, the incremental inventory investment from Table 20-11, and the incremental cash flows from Table 20-12. From the NPV calculations, we can see that Technidyne should switch from Policy A to Policy C. Increasing inventory by SF500,000 to SF1.5 million (Policy B) will generate an NPV of SF260,000. A further inventory increase to SF2.0 million (Policy C) will generate an additional NPV of SF10,000. Thus, the NPV associated with switching from Policy A to Policy C is SF270,000. This positive NPV indicates that the additional cash inflows generated by the recovery of lost sales more than compensates for the incremental carrying costs and investment.

As was true of credit policy, a firm's inventory policy affects its level of investment in current assets. In altering inventory policy, a firm's financial managers should evaluate the trade-off between the change in the opportunity cost of lost sales and the change in carrying cost. The IVM enables the managers to compare the incremental revenues and expenses generated by a change in inventory policy with the incremental investment in inventories associated with the policy. Once again, the IVM brings into clear focus the investing nature of the decision to alter inventory policy.

Calculation of Net Cash Inflows for Technidyne's Alternative Inventory Policies

TABLE 20-12

$$C = [(\Delta S)(1 - VC) - \Delta CC](1 - T)$$

Policy	Inventory Level	Net Cash Inflow
B	SF1,500,000	C = [(SF700,000)(1 − 0.70) − 20,000](1 − 0.40) = SF114,000
C	SF2,000,000	C = [(SF600,000)(1 − 0.70) − 10,000](1 − 0.40) = SF102,000
D	SF2,500,000	C = [(SF300,000)(1 − 0.70) − 5,000](1 − 0.40) = SF51,000

Calculation of the NPVs for Technidyne's Alternative Inventory Policies

TABLE 20-13

	Policy	NPV
$NPV = \dfrac{C}{K_j} - 1$	B	NPV = SF114,000/0.15 − 500,000 = SF260,000
	C	NPV = SF102,000/0.20 − 500,000 = SF10,000
	D	NPV = SF51,000/0.25 − 500,000 = −SF296,000

■ Valuation Issues

WHEN INVENTORY CONTROL PROGRAMS ARE COUNTERPRODUCTIVE

Firms that are concerned about inventory carrying costs are constantly searching for techniques that will permit reductions in inventories without resulting in substantial increases in the opportunity cost of lost sales. Indeed, the just-in-time approach to inventory control is a classic example of such a technique. When a firm sells a single product, the trade-off between the opportunity cost of lost sales and inventory carrying cost is a straightforward concept. When multiple product lines are involved, however, the trade-off can be much more complex.

For example, assume that a firm sells two products with very different inventory turnover ratios because one product is an active seller, while the other is very slow moving. If the firm reduces the inventory of both products by 50% in order to reduce carrying costs, the net result would probably be a large drop in sales of the popular product and an inventory dominated by the unpopular product. The opportunity cost of lost sales could easily outweigh the reduction in carrying costs. While the combined inventory falls by 50%, the decrease in the inventory of the popular product will be much larger than that of the unpopular product.

One effective method of handling this inventory problem is to reduce only the slow-moving inventory by selling it at a substantial discount. Although managers are naturally reluctant to incur the loss associated with the discount, they must be aware that failure to sell the product results in steady increases in carrying costs over time. In order to make the proper decision, the managers should compare the estimated discount required to immediately sell the product with the cumulative carrying costs as of the expected sales date if the product is not discounted. For example, assume that the cumulative carrying costs on a non-discounted product represent 35% of its price at the time of sale, while a 25% discount would result in immediate sale. Clearly, the firm will be better off with the latter result. Effective inventory control decisions require that a firm's managers be aware of the sometimes complicated outcomes of attempts at inventory reduction.

Seasonal Sales, Inventories, and Production Planning

Firms whose sales are seasonal are faced with a decision that combines production planning with inventory management. A firm with seasonal sales has two choices. It can match its production plan to its sales forecasts by producing next month's sales this month. As a result, production will be high in peak sales seasons and low in slack sales seasons. Conversely, the firm can forecast total annual sales and plan to produce $\frac{1}{12}$ of that amount each month. In the low sales season, finished goods inventories would increase because production is higher than sales. In peak sales season, inventories would fall because production is less than sales.

Which approach to inventory/production planning is best depends on the trade-off between a decrease in investment in inventory and in carrying costs against the potentially higher cost of producing goods on a seasonal basis. It is clear that seasonal production will minimize investment and carrying costs of inventory. Depending upon the product and production process, however, seasonal production could increase production costs significantly. With seasonal rather than level production, there are the costs of idle capacity, lower employee productivity, layoffs, and possible costly union problems during low seasons. During peak production, there can be overtime pay, training costs for expanded payrolls, overutilization of machinery, and so on.

The trade-off between seasonal and level production can be evaluated the same way all decision alternatives are evaluated. Choose the inventory/production plan that promises the highest net present value. Whether seasonal production is better than level production or vice versa will depend on the details of the production process. For example, the NPV of a product that can be produced with unskilled labor and little capital investment would most likely be higher with seasonal production. The opposite would be true of a product that requires highly skilled employees and a large capital investment. While each situation may be unique, the fundamental approach to decision-making remains constant: select the alternative that maximizes NPV.

SUMMARY

This chapter examined accounts receivable and inventories on both a descriptive and an analytical level. At the descriptive level, there are three components of a firm's credit policy: credit standards, credit terms, and collection procedures. Credit standards determine which customers will be granted credit. Credit terms establish the cost of credit and the maximum length of the credit period. Collection procedures dictate the extent of a firm's efforts to collect past-due accounts. Together, these three components of credit policy help determine the size of a firm's accounts receivable. Easing one or more of the three components will increase accounts receivable, while tightening one or more will decrease the firm's receivables. Once a firm establishes credit standards, it must implement them through a credit analysis of prospective customers. There are numerous sources of the financial information needed for this analysis such as credit rating agencies, customer financial statements, banks, and credit applications.

In general, the role of inventories in the operation of the firm is to serve as a buffer to uncouple the different stages of the production process. Inventories minimize the impact on the production process of fluctuations in the rate of sales or acquisition of raw materials. They also limit the effect of production problems on the acquisition of raw materials and on sales.

At the analytical level, a firm is making an investing decision when it establishes a given credit policy or inventory policy. As a result, these policies should be evaluated in terms of their impact on the value of the firm to its owners. The specific evaluation technique that should be used is the calculation of a policy's net present value (NPV) as measured by the Investment Valuation Model (IVM). The same procedure can be followed in the analysis of credit policy and inventory policy. After the policy alternatives are identified, the incremental cash flows associated with each alternative must be estimated. The managers must then determine the incremental investment that is required by each policy. Finally, they must calculate each policy's NPV by deducting the incremental investment from the present value of the incremental cash flows. Those policies with positive NPVs are acceptable because they will increase the firm's value.

chapter equations

1. $NPV = \sum_{t=1}^{N} \dfrac{C_t}{\left(1 + K_j\right)^t} - I$

2. $NPV = \dfrac{C}{K_j} - I$

3. $C = [(\Delta S)(1 - VC) - (\Delta S)(BD) - \Delta CE](1 - T)$

4. $I = (ACP)(\Delta S/360)(VC)$

5. $I_N = (ACP)(S_N/360)(VC)$

6. $I_O = (\Delta ACP)(S_O/360)$

7. $C = [(S)(\Delta BD) - \Delta CE](1 - T)$

8. $I = (\Delta ACP)(S/360)$

9. $I = \Delta Inventory$

10. $C = [(\Delta S)(1 - VC) - \Delta CC](1 - T)$

CONTENT QUESTIONS

1. Define the three major credit policy decisions.
2. In your own words, what does it mean when a firm has an average collection period of 35 days?

3. Why would a business grant credit to a customer when it is not certain that the customer will pay?
4. Describe five sources of trade credit information.
5. Explain how the three components of credit terms affect the balance in accounts receivable.
6. Why is the incremental investment defined differently for old customers and new customers when credit terms are lengthened?
7. How can a firm's ACP or accounts receivable aging schedule be misleading when sales are variable?
8. Describe the function of each of the three types of inventory.
9. Define the terms "carrying costs" and "ordering costs" and explain how each is affected by the level of investment in inventory.
10. Describe why the incremental investment associated with a change in inventory policy equals the change in inventory.
11. Explain why seasonal production would be preferable to level production for a product that can be produced with unskilled labor and little capital investment.

CONCEPT QUESTIONS

1. IVM In a discussion with a firm's financial manager, the firm's credit manager proposes tightening the firm's credit standards in order to reduce bad debts. The financial manager responds that the proposed change might be undesirable even if it does eliminate bad debts. Under what circumstances will this response be correct?

2. IVM A firm's financial managers are trying to measure the increased investment in receivables associated with lengthening the net period. One manager argues that the change in investment equals the entire increase in the average level of receivables. Another manager responds that the change in investment equals only the variable cost portion of the increase in average receivables. Which manager is correct?

3. IVM A firm has experienced a decrease in sales over the last two years due to increased competition from new competitors. The firm's managers are considering lengthening its net period to offset the decline in sales. What problem will the firm have with its receivables if the increase in credit period does not recapture lost sales?

4. IVM A financial manager has estimated the following NPVs for alternatives to the firm's current inventory level of $2 million:

Policy	Incremental Investment	Incremental NPV
A	$1,000,000	$155,000
B	1,000,000	72,000
C	1,000,000	− 57,000

Based on these data, what is the optimal level of inventory? If inventory can be increased in smaller increments of $1 million, what is the optimal inventory level? What problem would occur if the manager only calculated the NPV for an inventory level of $5 million?

5. IVM A firm has inventory that consists of equal amounts of a rapidly selling product and a poor selling product. The firm's managers are considering a 25% reduction in total inventory to decrease the investment in inventory. What will be the likely negative effects of this reduction in inventory?

PROBLEMS

1. What is the average collection period (ACP) for a firm with annual credit sales of FF60,000,000 and a balance in accounts receivable of FF6,000,000?

2. A firm has annual credit sales of $30,000,000.
    a. Find its ACP if the balance in accounts receivable is $2,600,000.
    b. Find its ACP if the balance in accounts receivable is $3,200,000.

3. Pentec Electric is in the process of forecasting accounts receivable. However, the company is unsure of the amount of credit sales and whether the ACP will be 30 or 40 days.
    a. If annual credit sales are $45 million, find the balance in accounts receivable for an ACP of 30 and an ACP of 40.
    b. If annual credit sales are $60 million, find the balance in accounts receivable for an ACP of 30 and an ACP of 40.

4. Find the annual percentage rate (APR) of trade credit for the following:
    a. 0.5/10; net 60   b. 2/10; net 45   c. net 30

5. Find the effective interest rate (EIR) of trade credit for the following:
    a. 0.5/10; net 60   b. 2/10; net 45   c. net 30

6. Murray Industries is evaluating a proposed credit policy. The estimated value of the incremental investment is $600,000 and of the expected after-tax cash flow is $115,000 per year. The required rate of return is 20%. Calculate the NPV of Murray's proposed credit policy.

7. Majer GmbH is considering extending credit to higher risk customers. The company has estimated variable costs as 75% of sales and the tax rate as 40%. Given the information below, which of the risk categories should be granted credit?

Risk Category	RRR	ACP	Sales
A	15%	35 days	DM500,000
B	20	40 days	DM350,000
C	25	60 days	DM250,000

8. In Problem 7, Majer had forgotten to include critical information that is provided below. Given this added information, which of the risk categories should be granted credit?

Risk Category	Bad Debts	Extra Credit Expense
A	5%	DM 5,000
B	10	DM10,000
C	15	DM15,000

9. York Products is considering the extension of credit to a higher risk category. York estimates that annual sales to these new customers will be $1,000,000 per year, ACP will be 36 days, bad debts will be 10% of sales, and extra collection expenses will be $15,000. Variable costs are 80% of sales, and the company's tax rate is 40%. The RRR is 20%. Should York extend credit to these higher risk customers?

10. Bettner Products has had the policy of extending credit only to customers who were virtually certain to pay their bills on time. It is considering the possibility of extending credit to another group of customers who are thought to be less creditworthy. Sales to these customers are expected to equal $2,500,000 annually. The ACP is expected to be 40 days with bad debts amounting to 2% of sales. Bettner's variable costs are 80% of sales. Bettner expects collection expenses to

increase by $75,000 per year. Should Bettner extend credit to this group of customers, given a tax rate of 40%? The RRR is 20%.

11. In order to attract new customers, Media Technique is considering changing its credit terms to net 60 from the current terms of net 30. Currently, Media's ACP is 40 days and is expected to increase to 70 days if the terms are extended to net 60. The liberal credit period is expected to add FF30,000,000 in new annual sales to the current sales level of FF150,000,000.
   a. What is Media's current balance in accounts receivable?
   b. What will Media's balance in accounts receivable be if the longer credit period is made effective?

12. Media Technique's (Problem 11) variable costs are 60% of sales, and the corporate tax rate is 40%. The RRR is 18%. Given the information in Problem 11:
   a. Calculate the total investment that is required for the extended credit period.
   b. If bad debts are expected to be 1% of new sales, should Media extend its credit period?

13. Bundi Steelwerk is considering a proposal to improve the efficiency of its credit collection department. The proposal promises to reduce bad debts from 3% to 2% on sales of DM20,000,000 and reduce the ACP from 50 days to 30 days. While these results are appealing to Bundi's management, the new credit department's operating budget will be DM375,000 above the old budget. Given that the RRR is 21% and that the corporate tax rate is 46%, should Bundi implement the proposed changes in its credit collection department?

14. Evans Technical Products is considering reducing the size of its credit collection department in order to save $500,000 per year in collection expenses. While it expects bad debts to be unaffected by the reduction, it does believe that the collection period will increase by 5 days due to staff reductions. It has $100,000,000 annual sales and a 40% marginal tax rate. Given a 20% RRR, should Evans go ahead with the plan to reduce the size of its credit collection department?

15. Merrick Engineering is considering lengthening its credit terms from net 30 to net 60. Its current ACP of 25 is expected to increase to 65 days. $12,000,000 will be added to its current annual sales of $36,000,000. Bad debt expense on new sales is expected to be 2%. Variable costs are 70% of sales, and the tax rate is 40%. Should Merrick lengthen its credit period if the RRR is 15%?

16. Crown Metals is considering a proposal to improve the efficiency of its credit collection department. Bad debts will be reduced from 5% to 3% of sales, and the ACP will be reduced from 48 days to 30 days. There will be additional credit collection expenses of $300,000 per year. The tax rate is 40% on annual sales of $10,000,000. Variable costs are 80% of sales. The RRR is 17%. Should Crown accept the proposal?

17. Cooper Products is considering a proposal that promises to cut its bad debts from 4% to 1% and reduce the ACP from 60 days to 35 days. The proposal will add $500,000 to collection expenses. The tax rate is 40% on sales of $10,000,000. If the RRR is 20%, should the proposal be accepted?

18. Gates Chemicals has experienced significant sales losses due to stockouts. It has adhered to its policy of maintaining a finished goods inventory of $2,000,000 but has lost about $4,000,000 in sales annually because of stockouts. Variable costs are 60% of sales, and the carrying costs of inventory are 5% of the value of the inventory. The corporate tax rate is 40%. Given the information below on three alternative levels of finished goods inventory, which level is best for Gates Chemicals?

Inventory Level	Annual Lost Sales	RRR
$3,000,000	$2,000,000	15%
4,000,000	500,000	20
5,000,000	100,000	25
6,000,000	0	30

19. Industrie Pilot's planning committee is evaluating a proposal to restructure its finished goods inventory policy. The proposal calls for a reduction in average inventory from FF8,000,000 to FF5,000,000 by stocking only the most popular model of its products. There is an estimated savings of warehousing and other carrying costs of FF200,000 per year. However, the marketing department is against the plan because they estimate that this policy would result in lost sales of about FF4,000,000 per year. Variable costs are 75% of sales. Is this proposal acceptable to Pilot, given a 20% RRR and a 40% corporate tax rate?

20. Tartan Fabrics is considering increasing its finished goods inventories from its current level of $200,000 to $400,000. Sales lost as a result of stockouts are expected to fall from $1,500,000 to $500,000. Carrying costs are 5% of inventory. Variable costs are 75% of sales, and the tax rate is 40%. The RRR on the proposal is 20%. Should Tartan increase its inventory from $200,000 to $400,000?

INTERNET EXERCISE

The Society for Food Science and Technology offers a lesson on inventory management. Read through the lesson, click on the questions, and answer the questions for Lesson 5. Turn in a printout of the answers to your instructor.

www.ift.org/car/food_ind/mod6.html

SELF-STUDY QUIZ

1. Douglas Tire Company currently extends credit only to low-risk customers. It is considering extending credit to customers that it classifies as moderate and high risk. Douglas's variable costs are 70% of sales, and its tax rate is 40%. Given the following information, should Douglas extend credit terms to either risk category?

Risk	RRR	ACP	Sales	Bad Debts	Extra Credit Expenses
Moderate	20%	45	$2,000,000	5%	$10,000
High	30	80	1,000,000	20	25,000

2. Inland Services is considering changing its credit terms from net 15 to net 30. If this change is made, the ACP will increase from 20 days to 40 days, and $50,000,000 of new sales will be added to current sales of $300,000,000. New customer bad debts are expected to be 2% of sales; variable costs are 75% of sales; the tax rate is 40% and the RRR is 20%. Should Inland extend its credit period to 30 days?

3. Talbert Corporation maintains an inventory of $100,000 and estimates that it loses $400,000 in annual sales due to stockouts. Its variable costs are 70% of sales, and carrying costs are 5% of inventory. Given a 40% tax rate and the information on the next page, which is the best level of inventory for Talbert?

Inventory Level	Annual Lost Sales	RRR
A. $200,000	$200,000	20%
B. 300,000	50,000	25
C. 400,000	0	30

Financial Planning and Corporate Growth

Throughout the text, we have described the financial managers' job as one of making investing and financing decisions. This decision process requires that the managers perform two basic tasks: analyze the past and forecast the future. Chapter 2 described the basic tools for financial analysis that are available for executing the first task. From that point on, we concentrated on the analysis of the potential impact of the cash flows anticipated from investing and financing alternatives, on the value of the firm. For the most part, proposed decisions were analyzed without direct reference to their effect on the firm's future income statements and balance sheets. This chapter will remedy that omission and address issues such as the following:

- Cash budgets are constructed to show the size and timing of a firm's estimated cash inflows and outflows over time. Cash surpluses should be temporarily invested in marketable securities, while cash deficits must be covered by temporary financing such as a bank line of credit. What are the key operating characteristics of the firm that determine whether it will produce positive or negative cash flows during the coming period? How can a firm determine the amount of the line of credit it should arrange with its bank to finance its operations?

- Pro forma balance sheets and income statements reflect the impact of projected operations on a firm's future financial performance. What role does the cash budget play in the construction of pro forma statements? How can historical financial ratios be used to project future performance on pro forma statements? Why does the sales forecast play a critical role in the construction of the pro forma balance sheet as well as the pro forma income statement? How frequently should pro forma statements be constructed?

- Growth in sales is often seen by a firm's managers as the fastest method of maximizing the value of a firm to its owners. Additional sales, however, require additional assets that must be financed with either debt or equity funds. How can a financial manager estimate the relationship between a firm's operating characteristics and its financial policies as its sales grow over time? Which financial policies have the most impact on the firm's ability to achieve its growth objectives? What are the financial implications of excessively rapid growth in sales?

One aspect of financial planning involves integrating the expected results of a firm's many decisions into a cash budget that indicates the detailed timing and amount of cash inflows and outflows. The role of the cash budget is to enable a firm's managers to identify temporary cash deficits that must be covered with borrowing, and cash surpluses that can be temporarily invested. Forecasted balance sheets and income statements are also an important part of financial planning. In these statements, the *anticipated* results of the firm's decisions are expressed in the same format as the *actual* results, which will eventually be reported to the stockholders. The first section of this chapter describes procedures for the construction of cash budgets and forecasted financial statements.

The financial planning process also serves as a final test of feasibility in which the financial implications of all the firm's decisions are carefully examined. At this stage of the decision process, a manager must determine if "all the pieces fit together." The last section of this chapter introduces the concept of sustainable growth as a tool for testing and analyzing the compatibility of the firm's investing and financing decisions. By calculating sustainable growth, managers can tell whether their plans are feasible and which adjustments to those plans may be necessary.

FINANCIAL PLANNING

The fundamental purpose of financial planning is to anticipate the financial implications of a firm's many operating and financial policies. As such, the financial plan represents the final stage of a larger planning process, as shown in Figure 21-1. A complete planning system begins with a *corporate mission*, which is a statement of the basic purpose and goals of the firm. To become operational, the mission statement must be converted into strategic operating plans for each of the major functional areas within the firm. From these operating plans, a strategic financial plan is derived, which usually consists of pro forma balance sheets and income statements that span a 3–5 year time period.

The *first year of the strategic plan* is often *used as the profit plan* or budget, which is a detailed forecast of the firm's performance with regard to specific products and markets. It is sufficiently accurate to be used as the *benchmark against which actual performance is compared throughout the year*. The profit plan is also *used to formulate the immediate financial needs of the firm*. In addition to a pro forma balance sheet and income statement, many firms produce a cash budget as part of their plans. Since cash flows are essential to the survival of the firm, the cash budget is an integral part of the profit plan and a key to successful working capital management.

http://

Explore a five-year forecast explained by the Corporate Financial Group at

http://www.gonnerman.com/plan.html

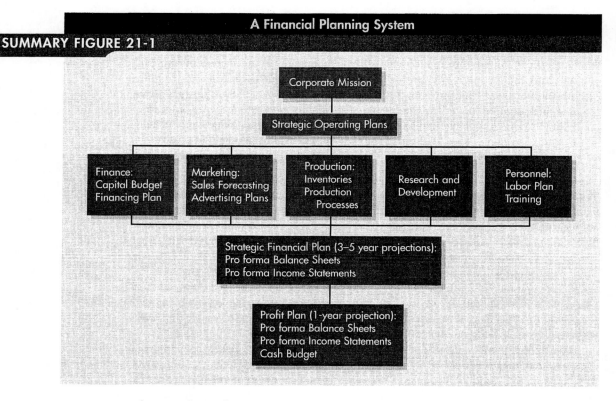

A Financial Planning System

SUMMARY FIGURE 21-1

The Cash Budget

A cash budget is a projection of cash receipts and disbursements of the firm over some time period. The purpose is to determine both *the amount and the timing* of expected inflows and outflows of cash. Within the planning period, *cash inflows and outflows are rarely in synchronization*. As sales increase, outflows tend to exceed inflows. When sales decline, inflows tend to exceed outflows. Consequently, if a firm's sales fluctuate over time, even though a net cash inflow is forecast over the entire accounting period, a cash deficit may occur *within* the period.

Cash Inflows. As long as a firm sells on credit, its sales volume will not be equal to its cash inflows for any period. In order to predict cash inflows, the managers must have knowledge of the *payment* habits of the firm's credit customers. For example, Union Garden Products has annual sales that peak in March as retailers stock up for spring. In order to plan its cash needs, Union's financial managers are preparing a monthly cash budget for the six-month period beginning with January. The following sales information was provided by the marketing department:

	Sales (in Thousands)	Data Source
November	$3,244	Actual
December	3,292	Actual
January	3,400	Forecast
February	4,600	Forecast
March	8,000	Forecast
April	6,000	Forecast
May	5,000	Forecast
June	3,000	Forecast
July	4,000	Forecast

Union Garden Products' Forecast of Sales Receipts (in Thousands)

TABLE 21-1

	Jan.	Feb.	March	April	May	June
Total sales	$3,400	$4,600	$8,000	$6,000	$5,000	$3,000
Collections:						
Cash (25%)	$ 850	$1,150	$2,000	$1,500	$1,250	$ 750
One month (50%)	1,646*	1,700	2,300	4,000	3,000	2,500
Two months (25%)	811***	823**	850	1,150	2,000	1,500
Total collections	$3,307	$3,673	$5,150	$6,650	$6,250	$4,750

*50% of December's actual sales of $3,292
**25% of December's actual sales of $3,292
***25% of November's actual sales of $3,244

Union's credit department has determined that, on average, over the past few years, 25% of the sales are on a cash basis, 50% are collected the month after the sale, and the remaining 25% are collected the second month after the sale. With this information, the managers estimate Union's monthly cash receipts from sales as shown in Table 21-1.

The receipts from any month's sales are spread over three months. Out of January's sales of $3,400,000, $850,000 (25%) are collected in January, $1,700,000 (50%) in February, and $850,000 (25%) in March. The table is filled out by repeating these calculations for the other months' sales and totaling the receipts for each month. In addition to sales receipts, there are other anticipated cash inflows. Union expects to receive $100,000 in May for real estate sold last year and $300,000 in February for an insurance claim filed last year. Total forecasted cash receipts are shown in Table 21-2.

Cash Outflows.

Cash outflows are similarly budgeted to specific months by Union's financial managers, who divide total disbursements into two schedules. The first schedule represents the monthly expenses for operating the business, including all production and administrative expenses. The second schedule includes other expenditures that the firm plans to make, such as outlays for plant and equipment, taxes, and dividends.

The operating portion of the disbursements schedule that is shown in Table 21-3 is dependent upon Union's production schedule. Although some firms smooth production during the year by building inventory toward the peak sales month, Union follows an alternate production policy. Its production department schedules production that is sufficient to cover only the next month's forecasted sales. That is, production in January is based on the forecast of February's sales, and so on. The cost of materials used in the production process averages 35% of sales. The materials are purchased in the month of their use in the production process

Union Garden Products' Forecast of Cash Inflows (in Thousands)

TABLE 21-2

	Jan.	Feb.	March	April	May	June
Sales receipts	$3,307	$3,673	$5,150	$6,650	$6,250	$4,750
Other receipts		300			100	
Total cash inflows	$3,307	$3,973	$5,150	$6,650	$6,350	$4,750

but are paid for one month later in the month of the sale of the finished product. Direct labor at 25% of sales is paid for in the month of production. Factory overhead is estimated at $400,000 each month, while selling and administrative expenses are expected to be $600,000 per month.

Table 21-4 contains the schedule of other anticipated disbursements during the coming six months. Union plans to purchase new machinery at a cost of $125,000 in January and $175,000 in May. In addition, the board of directors is expected to approve quarterly dividend payments of $100,000 to the common stockholders in March and again in June. According to a long-term loan agreement, $225,000 of interest on the loan is to be paid in January. Union plans to pay half the estimated taxes of $2,150,000 for the period on April 15 and half on June 15.

The data in Tables 21-3 and 21-4 have been combined in Table 21-5 to summarize Union's forecast of total cash outflows for the coming six months. Table 21-6 shows Union's cash budget for the next six months. It was constructed by combining the data in Tables 21-2 and 21-5. The cash budget reveals the implications of Union's monthly cash flows for its investment opportunities and financing requirements. Under the assumption of a beginning cash balance of $500,000 in January, the cash budget indicates that Union will run out of cash in February. Moreover, the cash balance will not turn positive until April. Since Union cannot, in reality, have negative cash balances, the firm's financial managers must arrange short-term financing to cover these temporary cash deficits. In addition, if Union desires to maintain a minimum cash balance above zero, the managers will have to

Union Garden Products' Forecast of Cash Outflows for Operating Expenses (in Thousands)

TABLE 21-3

	Jan.	Feb.	March	April	May	June
Sales forecast	$3,400	$4,600	$8,000	$6,000	$5,000	$3,000
Production schedule	$4,600	$8,000	$6,000	$5,000	$3,000	$4,000
Direct materials*	$1,190	$1,610	$2,800	$2,100	$1,750	$1,050
Direct labor**	1,150	2,000	1,500	1,250	750	1,000
Factory overhead	400	400	400	400	400	400
Selling and administration	600	600	600	600	600	600
Total cash outflows for operating expenses	$3,340	$4,610	$5,300	$4,350	$3,500	$3,050

*35% of the current month's sales forecast (Production leads sales by one month but payment is delayed one month.) Jan.: $1,190 = (0.35)($3,400)

**25% of the production schedule (Production and the payment for direct labor both lead sales by one month.) Jan.: $1,150 = (0.25)($4,600)

Union Garden Products' Forecast of Other Expenditures (in Thousands)

TABLE 21-4

	Jan.	Feb.	March	April	May	June
Other Expenditures:						
Capital expenditures	$125	$—	$ —	$ —	$175	$ —
Dividends	—	—	100	—	—	100
Interest payment	225	—	—	—	—	—
Taxes	—	—	—	1,075	—	1,075
Total	$350	$ 0	$100	$1,075	$175	$1,175

Union Garden Products' Forecast of Cash Outflows (in Thousands)

TABLE 21-5

	Jan.	Feb.	March	April	May	June
Operating expenses outflows	$3,340	$4,610	$5,300	$4,350	$3,500	$3,050
Other expenditures	350	0	100	1,075	175	1,175
Total cash outflows	$3,690	$4,610	$5,400	$5,425	$3,675	$4,225

Union Garden Products' Cash Budget (in Thousands)

TABLE 21-6

	Jan.	Feb.	March	April	May	June
Total cash inflows	$3,307	$3,973	$5,150	$6,650	$6,350	$4,750
Less: Total cash outflows	3,690	4,610	5,400	5,425	3,675	4225
Net cash flow	$ -383	$ -637	$ -250	$1,225	$2,675	$ 525
Beginning cash balance	$ 500*	$ 117	$ -520	$ -770	$ 455	$3,130
Net cash flow	-383	-637	-250	1,225	2,675	525
Ending cash balance without external financing	$ 117	$ -520	$ -770	$ 455	$3,130	$3,655

*Given

arrange financing for this requirement also. For example, if the firm's minimum desired cash balance is $500,000, it will have to borrow sufficient funds to cover any projected deficit plus the additional funds needed to increase the ending cash balance to $500,000:

	Jan.	Feb.	March	April	May	June
Ending cash balance —No financing	$ 117	$ -520	$ -770	$ 455	$3,130	$3,655
Less: minimum desired balance	-500	-500	-500	-500	-500	-500
Cash surplus or deficit	$-383	$-1,020	$-1,270	$ -45	$2,630	$3,155
Required loan	$ 383	$ 1,020	$ 1,270	$ 45	$ —	$ —

The primary goal of a cash budget is to uncover such financing needs in advance so that short-term financing can be arranged to avoid a cash crisis. With a cash budget, the financial managers can inform potential lenders of both the amount and the timing of the required financing as well as the firm's ability to repay the loan. A secondary goal of the cash budget is to enable the firm to generate income by temporarily investing excess cash in short-term investments.

Pro Forma Financial Statements

In addition to the effect of future operations on cash flows, financial managers should estimate the effect on the firm's financial position and performance in terms of a pro forma balance sheet and income statement. These statements can be prepared either directly from the firm's operating plans or indirectly from its cash budget. The preparation of the pro forma balance sheet also requires data from the firm's actual balance sheet at the beginning of the forecasting period. As with cash budgeting, the accuracy of the forecasted balance sheet and income statement depends largely on the accuracy of the sales forecast.

■ **Ethics**

ISSUES

HOW MANY McDONALD'S OUTLETS ARE TOO MANY?

McDonald's is the reigning king of the fast-food world with more than $30 billion in sales and over 12,000 U.S. stores. Despite its near saturation of the U.S. market, the firm continues to open additional domestic outlets at the rate of 600 stores per year. The purpose behind this campaign is to lock up choice locations so they are unavailable to competitors such as Burger King that have been increasing their market share at McDonald's expense. Although this strategy protects the corporation's interests, a number of disgruntled franchisees contend that the parent firm has failed to live up to its obligation to them.

The angry franchisees charge that the additional stores have cannibalized sales and profits from existing outlets located nearby. Sales data seem to support this claim. Although overall sales (85% of which are produced by franchise stores) have grown, sales at existing stores decreased in both 1995 and 1996. While McDonald's has a program to compensate franchisees for lost sales, operators say that it pays too little, too late, to prevent their profit margins from falling. One group of franchisees has formed an organization called Consortium Members, Inc., which has publicly called for slower expansion and legislation that would protect franchisees' rights. The group charges that McDonald's has a vested interest in establishing new stores to boost overall volume because that increases the parent's collections from franchisees, which are calculated as a percent of sales. In addition, the firm is able to charge higher rent for new outlets.

McDonald's executives respond that the preponderance of existing franchisees want growth so that they can acquire additional stores to boost their own sales and earnings. They also note that the firm has begun to alter its program that compensates existing franchisees for sales lost to new stores. Finally, they point out that McDonald's outlets are tremendous opportunities for franchisees who average free cash flow of $180,000 per store annually. Burger King outlets average only about $125,000 per year. Nevertheless, a recent headquarters survey of franchisees revealed that, although 70% of the respondents were satisfied with being part of McDonald's, 66% felt they were undercompensated for cannibalization of sales by new outlets. This controversy over outlet expansion indicates how complicated the relationship between a firm and its franchisees can be.

The Pro Forma Income Statement. As an illustration of the planning procedure, we will prepare the pro forma income statement for Union Garden Products for the six-month period covering January through June. The starting point is to estimate total sales over the period. By simply adding the firm's sales forecasts for each month, we have: Estimated sales = $3,400,000 + 4,600,000 + 8,000,000 + 6,000,000 + 5,000,000 + 3,000,000 = $30,000,000. Since Union's accounting system follows the standard accrual method, sales are recognized when goods are sold, not when actually paid for. Thus, all sales forecasted for the six-month period are included in the pro forma income statement shown in Table 21-7.

Direct material and labor are estimated at 35% and 25%, respectively, of sales. *Unlike the case of the cash budget, the financial managers need not determine when these expenses will actually be paid because the pro forma income statement is based on accrual accounting.* Factory overhead is estimated at $400,000 per month, while selling and administrative expenses are forecast to be $600,000 per month. Depreciation was not mentioned in the discussion of cash budgeting since it is a noncash item. It is included in the pro forma income statement, however, because it is an expense for the purpose of determining earnings before tax. For Union, the monthly depreciation expense is $200,000, or a projected total over six months of $1,200,000. The last expense on the pro forma statement is the interest on Union's outstanding long-term debt of $4.5 million. Since the annual rate of interest is 10%, the $225,000 shown on the income statement represents the interest expense for six months. Finally, Union's taxable income is taxed at an

Union Garden Products' Semiannual Pro Forma Income Statement

TABLE 21-7

	Amount (in Thousands)	Basis for Calculation
Sales	$30,000	Sales Forecast
Cost of goods sold:		
Direct material	(10,500)	35% of sales
Direct labor	(7,500)	25% of sales
Factory overhead	(2,400)	6 × $400
Gross profit	9,600	
Selling and administrative expenses	(3,600)	6 × $600
Depreciation	(1,200)	6 × $200
EBIT	4,800	
Interest expense	(225)	0.05 × $4,500
EBT	4,575	
Taxes	(2,150)	0.47 × $4,575
EAT	$ 2,425	

average rate of 47% (which includes local, state, and federal taxes) to arrive at its projected net income of $2,425,000.

The same procedure can be followed to arrive at the monthly pro forma income statements shown in Table 21-8. The summation of any item across all six months equals the value of that item on the six-month statement in Table 21-7. Notice the difference between the monthly direct labor amounts shown in Table 21-8 and those shown in Table 21-3. This difference is due to the *distinction between the cash outflows for direct labor and the accrual accounting recognition of direct labor expense*. For example, Union forecasts in Table 21-3 that it will pay $1,150,000 in January for direct labor arising from the production of goods to be sold in February. This expenditure (cash outflow) for wages is not recognized as an operating expense in Table 21-8, however, until the goods are sold in

Union Garden Products' Monthly Pro Forma Income Statements

TABLE 21-8

	Jan.	Feb.	March	April	May	June	Total
Sales	$3,400	$4,600	$8,000	$6,000	$5,000	$3,000	$30,000
Cost of goods sold:							
Direct material*	(1,190)	(1,610)	(2,800)	(2,100)	(1,750)	(1,050)	(10,500)
Direct labor**	(850)	(1,150)	(2,000)	(1,500)	(1,250)	(750)	(7,500)
Factory overhead	(400)	(400)	(400)	(400)	(400)	(400)	(2,400)
Gross profit	960	1,440	2,800	2,000	1,600	800	9,600
Selling and administrative expenses	(600)	(600)	(600)	(600)	(600)	(600)	(3,600)
Depreciation	(200)	(200)	(200)	(200)	(200)	(200)	(1,200)
EBIT	160	640	2,000	1,200	800	—	4,800
Interest expense	(37)	(38)	(37)	(38)	(37)	(38)	(225)
EBT	123	602	1,963	1,162	763	(38)	4,575
Taxes	(58)	(283)	(923)	(546)	(358)	18	(2,150)
EAT	$ 65	$ 319	$1,040	$ 616	$ 405	$ (20)	$ 2,425

*35% of current month's sales forecast Jan: $1,190 = (0.35)($3,400)
**25% of current month's sales forecast Jan: $850 = (0.25)($3,400)

February. In the same way, the $2,000,000 expenditure for direct labor in February is recognized as an expense of March operations. Whether a firm would go to the expense of preparing monthly as opposed to longer-term pro forma income statements will depend on their purpose. For reporting expected performance to individuals external to the firm, such as lenders, longer time spans are usually sufficient. On the other hand, pro forma income statements used as benchmarks for judging managerial performance are usually prepared monthly to provide timely warning of deviations from goals.

The Pro Forma Balance Sheet.

Once the projected income statement is complete, the pro forma balance sheet can be prepared. The standard procedure followed is to forecast directly all balance sheet accounts except cash and short-term loans. These two accounts then take on whatever residual values are necessary to equate the projection of total assets with the estimate of total liabilities and net worth. In this manner, the cash and short-term loan balances are the final result of the process of constructing the pro forma balance sheet, just as they are the end result of the cash budget shown in Table 21-6. In a cash budget, they are directly calculated. In a pro forma balance sheet, they are indirectly determined by the values assigned to all other balance sheet accounts. The cash and short-term loan balances derived from either approach, however, will be identical. Starting with current assets, we will review the June 30 pro forma balance sheet for Union Garden Products shown in Table 21-9.

Cash. The cash balance of $3,655,000 is a residual (balancing) amount based on the calculations for all other assets, liabilities, and net worth. Thus, we will briefly defer the discussion of its calculation.

Receivables. Accounts receivable are equal to that portion of sales on the income statement for which the firm is awaiting payment. Recall from our discussion of the cash budget that 25% of sales are for cash, 50% are collected one month after the sale, and 25% are collected two months after the sale. Thus, as of June 30, the only months whose sales are represented in the receivables balance are May

Pro Forma and Actual Balance Sheets for Union Garden Products (in Thousands)

TABLE 21-9

	Actual Dec. 31	Calculation	Pro Forma June 30
Cash	$ 500	Balancing item	$ 3,655
Receivables	3,280	75% of June sales and 25% of May sales	3,500
Inventory	2,440	July cost of goods sold	2,800
Other current assets	600	Reduced by real estate and insurance receipts	200
Current assets	6,820		10,155
Net fixed assets	7,680	Add acquisitions; subtract depreciation	6,780
Total assets	$14,500		$16,935
Short-term loans	$ 0	Balancing item	$ 0
Payables	1,190	Purchases paid for in July	1,400
Accruals	1,200	No change	1,200
Current liabilities	2,390		2,600
Long-term debt	4,500	No change	4,500
Common stock	3,500	No change	3,500
Retained earnings	4,110	Add EAT; subtract dividends	6,335
Total liabilities and net worth	$14,500		$16,935

and June. There are 25% of the projected May sales and 50% of June's sales that remain to be collected in July, while another 25% of June's sales will be collected in August. Consequently, the accounts receivable balance on June 30 is:

$$\text{June receivables} = 0.75 \times \$3,000,000 = \$2,250,000$$
$$\text{May receivables} = 0.25 \times \$5,000,000 = \underline{1,250,000}$$
$$\text{Total receivables} \quad \$3,500,000$$

Inventory. The company policy is to produce quantities in any month equal to the next month's projected sales. The inventory on hand at the end of June, therefore, is equal to the cost of goods produced in June to meet expected July sales of $4,000,000:

Direct material	$0.35 \times \$4,000,000 =$	$\$1,400,000$
Direct labor	$0.25 \times 4,000,000 =$	$1,000,000$
Factory overhead	$400,000 =$	$\underline{400,000}$
Cost of goods for July sales	$=$	$\$2,800,000$

Other Current Assets. The $600,000 balance in this account on December 31 is projected to decline during the next six months due to the collection of $100,000 in May for real estate previously sold and $300,000 in February for an insurance claim. The June 30 balance is only $200,000 as shown below:

Other current assets, Dec. 31	$\$600,000$
Less: Receipt of payments	$\underline{(400,000)}$
Other current assets, June 30	$\$200,000$

Net Fixed Assets. Net fixed assets is the difference between gross plant and equipment and accumulated depreciation. In their estimate of the June 30 net fixed assets balance, the financial managers simply added to the December 31 account balance the forecast of spending on new fixed assets and subtracted additions to accumulated depreciation. Union's operating plans for the six-month period require the acquisition of $300,000 in new equipment, while its depreciation expense will total $1,200,000. Its new net fixed asset balance must be:

Net fixed assets, Dec. 31	$\$7,680,000$
Added plant and equipment	$300,000$
Less depreciation	$\underline{(1,200,000)}$
Net fixed assets, June 30	$\$6,780,000$

Since the cash balance is the last calculation performed for the pro forma balance sheet, we cannot yet determine the totals for current assets and total assets. Moving to the other half of the balance sheet, liability and net worth items are determined as follows:

Short-Term Loans. As is true of the cash balance, this is a residual amount whose calculation must be deferred until all other liability and net worth amounts are estimated.

Payables. Accounts payable represent the purchases made by Union that have not as yet been paid. Since June production is based on July sales, materials equal to 35% of July sales were purchased in June. Because payment is expected to be delayed one month, payables on June 30 are equal to

$$\text{Accounts payable} = 0.35 \times \$4,000,000 = \$1,400,000$$

Accruals. These are miscellaneous bills due for payment within a year. Union's financial managers estimate that payment of outstanding bills will be matched by additional accruals over the next six months.

Long-Term Debt and Common Stock. Union's managers foresee no changes in these accounts over the next six months.

Retained Earnings. The change in this balance is equal to forecasted EAT less dividends. Union's pro forma income statement projects EAT for the next six months to be $2,425,000. The firm expects to pay dividends of $200,000 to its stockholders during the same period. The projected retained earnings balance is therefore calculated as follows:

Retained earnings, Dec. 31	$4,110,000
Projected EAT	2,425,000
Less dividends	(200,000)
Retained earnings, June 30	$6,335,000

Cash and Short-Term Loans. The first step in determining the balances for the cash and short-term loan accounts is to sum the other asset accounts and the other liability and net worth accounts and compare the preliminary total assets to the preliminary total liabilities and net worth. The required residual balances can be calculated through the use of the following rules:

1. If the excess of the preliminary liabilities and net worth over the preliminary total assets is larger than the firm's minimum desired cash balance, set the cash balance equal to the excess and the short-term loan balance to zero.
2. If rule number (1) does not apply, set the cash balance equal to the desired minimum and the short-term loan balance at whatever value is necessary for total assets to equal total liabilities and net worth.

The application of these rules to Union Garden Products' balance sheet projections under the assumption of a minimum desired cash balance of $500,000 is shown below.[1]

Assets:	
Receivables	$ 3,500
Inventory	2,800
Other current assets	200
Net fixed assets	6,780
Preliminary Total	$13,280
Liabilities and Net Worth:	
Payables	$ 1,400
Accruals	1,200
Long-term debt	4,500
Common stock	3,500
Retained earnings	6,335
Preliminary Total	$16,935
Preliminary Liabilities and Net Worth	$16,935
Preliminary Assets	(13,280)
Excess	$ 3,655
Minimum desired cash balance	$ 500
Using rule number (1):	
June 30 Cash Balance	$ 3,655
June 30 Short-Term Loan Balance	—

---

[1] As an illustration of the application of rule number (2), let us assume that Union's projected June 30 cash balance is only $200,000, while its minimum desired cash balance remains at $500,000. According to rule number (2), the cash balance should be increased to $500,000. The source of this increase must be a $300,000 short-term loan.

The cash balance of $3,655,000 and the short-term loan balance of $0 are the residual figures that complete the pro forma balance sheet shown in Table 21-9. Notice that the June 30 cash balance shown above is identical to the June 30 balance in the cash budget in Table 21-6. Given consistent assumptions about future operations and sales, the cash balance in these two statements will always be identical. In fact, a discrepancy in these two estimates of the cash balance would be an indication of inconsistent assumptions or incorrect calculations in the construction of the pro forma balance sheet or cash budget.

Projection of Financial Statements Using Ratios

In addition to constructing pro forma financial statements for detailed operating and financial plans, it is possible to project the statements using more general balance sheet and income statement relationships. Although the result is less accurate pro forma statements, the unavailability of detailed operating and financial plans may make the type of forecasting procedure described above infeasible. The use of financial ratios to project financial statements begins with an estimate of sales. The sales forecast, rather than being based on operating plans for specific products and markets, is often derived from management's general estimate of the future growth rate in sales. Next, it is assumed that there are specific percentage relationships between sales and the balance sheet accounts and income statement items. While the percentages are usually based on a study of past financial statements of the firm, a firm's financial managers may use some other benchmark, such as an industry average, if they feel that the past is not likely to be a good indicator of the future.

The Income Statement. As an illustration of projecting an income statement, we will return to Dayton Products, the example from Chapter 2. Table 21-10 includes the income statement and balance sheet for 2000. The income statement is also expressed as a percentage of sales by dividing each income statement item by sales of $110.1 million. This procedure is known as constructing a common size statement.[2]

Dayton's income statement for 2001 can be projected by assuming that the percentages of expenses to sales will equal those of 2000. These percentages can then be multiplied by the 2001 sales projection ($132.1 million) to derive the pro forma income statement. While quick and simple, this procedure may result in significant inaccuracy for some items because it treats all costs as variable. Certain items, such as depreciation and amortization of goodwill, are clearly not related to sales in the short term. Other expenses, such as selling and administrative, are likely to be neither totally variable nor totally fixed. Categorizing all the income statement items as fixed or variable can be difficult, especially if detailed information about the firm's cost structure and operating plans is unavailable. Thus, the use of ratios to construct a pro forma income statement can require considerable judgment on the part of the financial managers.

The pro forma income statement projected by Dayton Products' financial managers is shown in Table 21-11. Sales in 2001 are forecasted to increase by 20% over the $110.1 million figure for 2000. Cost of goods sold are equal to forecasted 2001 sales multiplied by the ratio of cost to sales. Gross profit is simply the difference between sales and the cost of goods sold. Both depreciation and amortization of

---

[2] The common size statement can be a useful tool for the evaluation of past income statements as well as the projection of future statements. By putting all items on a percentage basis, the common size procedure makes it possible to compare the relative composition of different firms' income statements for a given year or one firm's income statements over a number of years.

TABLE 21-10

Historical Financial Statements for Dayton Products, Inc.

Balance Sheet December 31, 2000 (in Thousands)

Cash	$ 2,000	Accounts payable	$ 7,200
Accounts receivable	15,100	Notes payable	5,600
Inventory	27,500	Accruals	8,700
Other	900	Taxes payable	400
Current assets	45,500	Current liabilities	21,900
Plant and equipment	64,500	Long-term debt	28,000
Less accumulated		Common stock ($2 par)	8,000
depreciation	(26,200)	Retained earnings	30,000
Net fixed assets	38,300	Total liabilities and net worth	$87,900
Goodwill	4,100		
Total assets	$ 87,900		

Income Statement for the Year Ending December 31, 2000 (in Thousands)

Sales	$110,100	100.00%
Cost of goods sold	(83,900)	(76.20)
Gross profit	26,200	23.80
Depreciation	(2,300)	(2.09)
Amortization of goodwill	(400)	(0.36)
Selling & administrative	(14,100)	(12.81)
EBIT	9,400	8.54
Interest	(2,800)	(2.54)
EBT	6,600	6.00
Taxes	(3,300)	(3.00)
EAT	$ 3,300	3.00%

goodwill are held constant at their 2000 levels. The common size statement in Table 21-10 indicates that selling and administrative expenses amounted to 12.81% of sales in 2000. The firm's financial managers have determined that $6.1 million of these expenses are fixed. As a result, they have divided them into two components for 2000:

Variable selling and administrative	= $ 8,000,000	7.27%
Fixed selling and administrative	= 6,100,000	5.54%
Total selling and administrative	= $14,100,000	12.81%

The ratio of the variable component to sales (0.0727) was multiplied by 2001 forecasted sales to arrive at the estimated variable selling and administrative expenses. Interest expense is assumed to remain a constant 2.54% of sales because the projected increase in sales is expected to be accompanied by a proportionate expansion in outstanding debt.[3] Finally, application of the firm's expected average income tax rate of 50% yields the projected EAT of $4.80 million. Notice that the

---

[3] The validity of such an assumption depends heavily on the emphasis on debt in the firm's future financing plans relative to its utilization of debt financing in the past. If the firm alters its debt/equity ratio in the future, it may also alter the interest expense/sales ratio. This ratio can also be affected by changes in the interest rate on outstanding debt or on new debt. Since these changes are caused by fluctuations in economic conditions, they can be very difficult to predict.

Dayton Products, Inc. Pro Forma Income Statement for 2001

TABLE 21-11

	Calculation (in Thousands)	Pro Forma 2001
Sales	110,100 × 1.20	$132,100
Cost of goods sold	132,100 × 0.762	100,700
Gross profit	—	31,400
Depreciation	assumed fixed	(2,300)
Goodwill amortization	assumed fixed	(400)
Variable selling and administrative	132,100 × 0.0727	(9,600)
Fixed selling and administrative	fixed	(6,100)
EBIT	—	13,000
Interest	132,100 × 0.0254	(3,400)
EBT	—	9,600
Taxes	9,600 × 0.50	(4,800)
EAT		$ 4,800

net margin (EAT/Sales) for the actual income statement in Table 21-10 and the pro forma income statement in Table 21-11 are significantly different. The ratio for the former is 3.00%, while that for the latter is 3.63% ($4,800/$132,100). This difference points out the danger in projecting net income directly by merely multiplying forecasted sales by a firm's historical net margin. It totally ignores the impact of operating leverage on the response of net income to a change in sales. For a firm with substantial fixed costs in its cost structure, the time saved by estimating EAT in such a manner is not worth the inaccuracy introduced into the forecast.

The Balance Sheet. Dayton Products' pro forma balance sheet shown in Table 21-12 is based on the historical relationship of the balance sheet accounts to sales and the 2000 balance sheet shown in Table 21-10. As in our earlier example of Union Garden Products, the cash and short-term loans (notes payable) accounts are not projected directly but, rather, are calculated as residuals that make the balance sheet balance. The calculations for the other accounts on the balance sheet are described below.

Receivables. Dayton's financial managers expect an average collection period of 50 days. Using the definition of ACP and the sales forecast of $132,100,000, they have calculated expected receivables as:

$$50 = \frac{Receivables}{Daily\ Sales} = \frac{Receivables}{\$132,100,000/360}$$

$$Receivables = (50)(\$132,100,000/360) = \$18,350,000$$

Inventory. Inventory turnover is expected to be 3.2. This figure can be combined with the forecasted cost of goods sold of $100,700,000 to find the expected inventory:

$$3.2 = \frac{Cost\ of\ goods\ sold}{Ending\ inventory} = \frac{\$100,700,000}{Ending\ Inventory}$$

$$Ending\ Inventory = \$31,470,000$$

Other Current Assets. Because they lack detailed information about these assets, the financial managers assume that current assets are proportional to sales. Thus,

http://

Investigate the net worth worksheet link to do your own personal balance sheet.

http://www.e-analytics.com/fp37.htm

TABLE 21-12

Dayton Products' Pro Forma Balance Sheet for 2001 (in Thousands)

	Calculation	Pro Forma Dec. 31, 2001
Cash	Balancing item	$ 2,000
Accounts receivable	50 × 132,100/360	18,350
Inventory	100,700/3.2	31,470
Other	1.20 × 900	1,080
Current assets	—	52,900
Plant and equipment	64,500 + 3,000	67,500
Less: Accumulated depreciation	26,200 + 2,300	(28,500)
Net fixed assets	—	39,000
Goodwill	4,100 − 400	3,700
Total assets	—	$95,600
Accounts payable	1.20 × 7,200	$ 8,640
Notes payable	Balancing item	7,160
Accruals	1.20 × 8,700	10,440
Taxes payable	1.20 × 400	480
Current liabilities	—	26,720
Long-term debt	No change	28,000
Common stock	No change	8,000
Retained earnings	30,000 + 4,800 (1 − 0.4)	32,880
Total liabilities and net worth		$95,600

the expected 20% increase in sales is forecast to lead to an identical increase in other current assets:

$$\text{Other current assets} = 1.20 \times \$900,000 = \$1,080,000$$

Net Fixed Assets. Dayton's investing plans for 2001 call for the acquisition of $3.0 million in new plant and equipment. The change in the firm's accumulated depreciation is equal to the depreciation expense shown on the pro forma income statement in Table 21-11. Taken together, the changes in these two accounts determine the forecast of net fixed assets:

$$\begin{aligned}
\text{Plant and equipment} &= \$64,500,000 + 3,000,000 = \$67,500,000 \\
\text{Less: Accumulated depreciation} &= \$26,200,000 + 2,300,000 = \$28,500,000 \\
\text{Net fixed assets} &= \$38,300,000 + 700,000 = \$39,000,000
\end{aligned}$$

Goodwill. The previous balance in the account is reduced by the amount amortized on the income statement:

$$\text{Goodwill} = \$4,100,000 - 400,000 = \$3,700,000$$

Accounts Payable, Accruals, and Taxes Payable. With the exception of notes payable, which is treated as a residual, current liabilities are assumed to be proportional to sales. Thus, the expected 20% increase in sales should cause current liabilities to increase at the same rate:[4]

---

[4] An alternate calculation that would give the same results would be to multiply the forecasted sales of $132.1 million by the ratio of the actual balance in each account to sales in 2000. For example, the forecast of the balance in accounts payable could be calculated as follows:

$$\text{2000 Accounts Payable/2000 Sales} = \$7,200,000/\$110,100,000 = 0.0654$$
$$\text{2001 Accounts Payable} = 0.0654 \times \$132,100,000 = \$8,640,000$$

This is the same type of calculation that was used to calculate the variable expenses on Dayton's pro forma income statement.

$$\text{Accounts payable} = 1.20 \times \$7,200,000 = \$\ 8,640,000$$
$$\text{Accruals} \qquad\quad = 1.20 \times \$8,700,000 = \$10,440,000$$
$$\text{Taxes payable} \quad\ = 1.20 \times \$\ \ \ 400,000 = \$\ \ \ \ 480,000$$

Long-Term Debt and Common Stock.   Dayton's financing plans call for the acquisition of required funds either from retention of earnings or the issuance of short-term debt (notes payable). Thus, long-term debt and common stock are expected to remain unchanged in 2001.

Retained Earnings.   Dayton's financial managers estimate that the firm will pay out as dividends 40% of the projected 2001 EAT on the pro forma income statement in Table 21-11. This estimate results in the following calculation of 2001 retained earnings:

$$\text{Retained earnings} = \$30,000,000 + (4,800,000)(1 - 0.40)$$
$$= \$30,000,000 + 2,880,000 = \$32,880,000$$

Cash and Notes Payable.   The balances for these two accounts can be projected by using the same procedure that was earlier described in the case of Union Garden Products. Given Dayton's minimum desired cash balance of $2 million, the residual balances required in cash and notes payable accounts are:

Assets:	
Receivables	$18,350
Inventory	31,470
Other current assets	1,080
Net fixed assets	39,000
Goodwill	3,700
Preliminary Total	$93,600
Liabilities and Net Worth:	
Accounts payable	$ 8,640
Accruals	10,440
Taxes payable	480
Long-term debt	28,000
Common stock	8,000
Retained earnings	32,880
Preliminary Total	$88,440
Preliminary Liabilities and Net Worth	$88,440
Preliminary Assets	(93,600)
Deficit	(5,160)
Minimum desired cash balance	$ 2,000
Using rule number (2):	
2001 Cash balance	$ 2,000
2001 Notes payable	$ 7,160

Since preliminary liabilities and net worth are insufficient to finance preliminary assets by $5,160,000, Dayton must borrow that amount in 2001 plus another $2,000,000 to meet its minimum desired cash balance.

The calculations shown above for Dayton Products indicate that the financial ratios introduced in Chapter 2 for analyzing past performance are also useful in forecasting a firm's future performance and financial position. In their application of financial ratios to the construction of pro forma statements, however, a firm's financial managers must use considerable judgment. All the caveats that we mentioned regarding the use of ratios to evaluate past performance certainly apply to their use in predicting future performance. In particular, if the managers feel that the past will not be indicative of the future or that past firm performance was not

■ Financial

ISSUES

THE LINK BETWEEN EMPLOYEE ATTITUDES AND SALES GROWTH AT SEARS ROEBUCK

In our discussion of pro forma financial statements in this chapter, we emphasized the pivotal role of the sales forecast. Without an accurate estimate of future sales, reliable

forecasts of earnings, assets, and liabilities are highly unlikely. In its efforts to improve its financial planning, Sears Roebuck, the nation's second largest retailer after Wal-Mart, has developed a financial model that directly relates the attitudes and behavior of its 300,000 employees to the firm's sales growth.

The starting point for the new model was an executive task force that proposed measurements of employee success at making Sears a "compelling place to work, shop, and invest." Ultimately, the firm's executives identified six measures of success for these three areas that could be used to build a performance index. The firm then collected data on actual customer satisfaction, employee satisfaction, and financial performance.

After analysis of these data, Sears managers concluded that employee attitudes about their jobs and the company predicted their behavior in front of the customer. That behavior, in turn, affected customer retention and recommendations, which ultimately predict financial performance. The firm's management team contends that if a Sears store increases its employee satisfaction score by five measurement units in the current quarter, customer satisfaction will rise by two units

in the next quarter. That increase in customer satisfaction will result in revenue growth in the following quarter that exceeds the national average for all Sears stores by 0.5%.

To implement this planning model, management instituted a series of educational seminars for employees, designed to inform them of the model's basic relationships among employee satisfaction, customer satisfaction, and financial performance. Sears also began to randomly survey customers involved in the 468 million transactions conducted annually through its cash registers. These data will be related to the performance of individual salesclerks whose compensation will be partially influenced by customer satisfaction.

Sears' executives believe that, if they are successful in their employee educational campaign, not only will Sears' financial performance improve, but their model will also remove much of the guesswork traditionally involved in sales forecasts for the firm. They have also decided to put their money where their mouth is by linking 30% to 70% of the pay of the firm's top 200 executives to the results of this innovative financial planning model.

optimal, past financial ratios may be poor forecasting devices. Factors that invalidate past financial ratios include changing competitive or economic conditions.

SUSTAINABLE CORPORATE GROWTH

Pro forma financial statements reveal the financial implications of a firm's operating plans. In the Dayton Products example, the projected 20% growth in sales for 2001 was accompanied by increases in assets and liabilities as well as in earnings. The relationships between asset and liability items and sales may be used to assess both a firm's likely longer-run profitability and its funding requirements. A central concept in this regard is the notion of *sustainable corporate growth*. As we have seen from the Dayton Products case, the rate at which a corporation is able to increase its sales depends upon the asset requirements that accompany each sales increase, the funding it obtains spontaneously through accounts payable and other current liabilities, the borrowing it does based on its decision about how much debt to have in its capital structure, and the retained earnings it generates from profits after paying out dividends. Sufficient funds must be available to have the firm's assets be matched by its liabilities and equity. This fundamental balance sheet requirement holds not only at any given point in time, but also must hold *incrementally* as well: each additional dollar in assets needed to support increased

sales must be matched by an additional dollar in liabilities and equity. Equivalently, incremental *uses* of funds must be equal to incremental *sources*. The availability of such sources is what ultimately constrains the rate at which sales can grow.

If a firm is to grow in a healthy fashion over time, of course, it must do so in a way that does not involve an increasing relative reliance on debt capital. The firm must be able to grow with a stable *debt ratio* that will assure both creditors and stockholders of the firm's financial soundness. If the firm attempts to grow faster, it will eventually encounter financial distress. This was exactly the concern of Dell Computer's management in the mid-1990s as it watched sales skyrocket along with receivables and inventories. The managers felt that the firm's profitability and stock price were suffering due to uncontrolled sales growth and the associated lack of liquidity. Their response was to slow the rate of increase in sales and reduce the level of receivables and inventories required to support each dollar in sales. The firm's earnings and stock price promptly responded positively to these actions. We may examine the growth constraint on a firm by establishing the attributes that link asset needs and funding to sales volumes. We begin our analysis with the following definitions:

CA = current assets (cash, receivables, and inventory) as a percent of the firm's annual sales volume;

FA = net fixed assets (plant and equipment, net of accumulated depreciation) as a percent of sales;

CL = spontaneous current liabilities (payables, accruals, deferred taxes) as a percent of sales. These exclude *negotiated* current liabilities such as short-term debt;

M = the firm's after-tax profit margin on sales (after-tax profits as a percent of sales);

B = borrowed funds (both short- and long-term debt) as a percent of the firm's total capitalization (that is, debt as a percent of the total of debt plus equity);

d = the firm's dividend payout ratio (dividends as a percent of profits);

E = the firm's total common equity (common stock, capital surplus, and accumulated retained earnings);

S = the firm's current annual sales volume.

We can use these variables to express symbolically the requirement that sources and uses of funds must be equal, and to establish the conditions that permit the firm to grow.

Consider, as an example, the situation of Machines Rennes S.A., whose annual sales are currently FF20 million and whose balance sheet appears as follows (in thousands):

Current Assets	FF 6,000	Current Liabilities	FF ,000
Net Fixed Assets	8,000	Debt (Short-Term and Long-Term)	3,000
		Common Equity	7,000
Total	FF14,000		FF14,000

This balance sheet can be summarized in terms of the following variables:

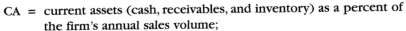

$$CA = 6,000/20,000 \quad = 0.30$$
$$FA = 8,000/20,000 \quad = 0.40$$
$$CL = 4,000/20,000 \quad = 0.20$$
$$B \;\; = 3,000/(3,000 + 7,000) = 0.30$$

and we can reexpress the balance sheet in the equivalent form:

Assets	Liabilities and Equity
(CA)(S)	(CL)(S)
(FA)(S)	(B)(CA + FA − CL)(S)
	E

(CA)(S) is the franc amount of current assets, (FA)(S) the amount of fixed assets, and (CL)(S) the amount of spontaneous current liabilities. Notice the relationship between the firm's debt and its sales volume. The firm's total capitalization (long-term debt and equity) needed to finance its assets comes to (CA + FA − CL)(S). If the *percentage* of this total that consists of debt is B, the *amount* of debt is (B)(CA + FA − CL)(S), as shown. The remainder of the firm's capitalization is equity, in the amount E.

Assume that the indicated balance sheet is for the beginning of a given year. Suppose the firm expects its sales to increase by ΔS to the new annual rate $S + \Delta S$ in the following year. These higher sales will require that the firm have additional assets in place by the end of the current year, in order to support next year's higher sales. At an increased sales volume, of course, additional financing will also be generated so that the firm's year-end balance sheet will look like:

Assets	Liabilities and Equity
(CA)(S + ΔS)	(CL)(S + ΔS)
(FA)(S + ΔS)	(B)(CA + FA − CL)(S + ΔS)
	E + ΔE

A key question for Machines Rennes, therefore, is: how much of an increase in equity is required to make the year-end balance sheet balance?

If all the increase comes from retained earnings (internal equity sources), the additional amount of equity will be

$$\Delta E = \text{profits, less dividends paid} = (M)(S)(1 - d)$$

where (M)(S) is the amount of after-tax profit generated during the current year, and (1 − d) is the proportion of those profits that are retained after paying out the fraction d in dividends. Accordingly, the firm's financing requirement for the coming year can be expressed as follows:

Incremental Uses = Incremental Sources

Asset Increase	=	Spontaneous Liability Increase	+	Debt Increase	+	Equity Increase
(CA + FA)(ΔS) =		(CL)(ΔS)	+	(B)(CA + FA − CL)(ΔS)	+	(M)(S)(1 − d)

When we rearrange and collect terms, this expression becomes:

$$(M)(S)(1 - d) = (1 - B)(CA + FA - CL)(\Delta S) \qquad (1)$$

Notice that the left-hand side of the expression represents the amount of new equity which *will* become available, while the right-hand side represents the amount of new equity which *must* become available, to support the added investment in assets due to higher sales. The right-hand side captures the required increase in the firm's total capitalization that is not provided by debt financing.

To return to our example of Machines Rennes, suppose the firm's dividend payout ratio is 30% of profits (d = 0.30) and its after-tax profit margin on sales is 5% (M = 0.05). From the current year's operations, therefore, the firm will add

$$(FF20 \text{ million})(0.05)(1 - 0.30) = FF700 \text{ thousand}$$

to its retained earnings. If it expects sales in the following year to increase by 10%—to FF22 million—its balance sheet at the end of the current year will turn out to be (again, in thousands):

Current Assets	FF 6,600	Current Liabilities	FF 4,400
Net Fixed Assets	8,800	Debt	3,300
		Common Equity	7,700
	FF15,400		FF15,400

where current assets, fixed assets, and current liabilities will have increased by 10% each, in order to support next year's expected 10% increase in sales. If the firm maintains its target debt ratio of 30% of total capitalization, debt will also increase by 10% from the current year's level. Thus, the FF700 thousand of additional retained earnings will be just sufficient to provide the needed amount of new common equity capital, and the increments in sources and uses of funds will match.

In this circumstance, the firm's projected growth rate in sales is described as "sustainable" because sales can grow at a 10% annual rate while still maintaining a balance in the capital structure that consists of 30% debt and 70% equity. The definition of a firm's **sustainable growth rate** is: *the rate at which a firm's sales can grow without requiring an increasing proportion of debt in its capital structure* to support additional assets.

Notice that, in the Machines Rennes example, if the firm's profit margin on sales were only 4% instead of 5%, it would add only (FF20 million)(0.04)(1 - 0.30) = FF560 thousand to retained earnings in the current year. Hence, year-end equity would amount only to FF7,560,000 rather than FF7,700,000—and the firm would have to raise its debt to FF3,440,000 and the *proportion* of debt to total capitalization. If sales were to continue to increase by 10% each year in subsequent years, the proportion of debt would continue to rise. Eventually, the extra interest costs would begin to lower the firm's profit margin; the debt ratio would have to increase even faster to make up for the lower margin (and lower retained earnings); and the firm would be headed for a financial disaster. A 10% annual growth rate in sales would *not* be sustainable under those circumstances. Either growth would have to slow down, or something else about the firm's situation would have to change, in order to stabilize its debt ratio.

Sustainable Growth Rate The rate at which a firm's sales can grow without requiring an increasing proportion of debt in its capital structure.

http://
Look at the sustainable earnings growth rate in a study of the Nifty Fifty.
http://www.worth.com/articles/Z9602107.html

The Sustainable Growth Formula

We can specify the determinants of sustainable growth by returning to the sources=uses requirement expressed in equation (1). If we divide both sides of that expression by the firm's current sales volume, S, we get:

$$(M)(1 - d) = (1 - B)(CA + FA - CL)(\Delta S/S)$$

The term $\Delta S/S$ in this equation is the ratio of the *increase* in sales volume in the coming year to the *current* sales volume of the firm. Thus, $\Delta S/S$ represents the percentage *rate of growth* (g) in sales, and we can rewrite the equation as:

$$(M)(1 - d) = (1 - B)(CA + FA - CL)(g)$$

This equation can be rearranged to solve for the variable g:

$$g = \frac{(M)(1-d)}{(1-B)(CA+FA-CL)} \tag{2}$$

Equation (2) is the general formula for the firm's sustainable growth rate. The equation specifies the relationship between the firm's profit margin (M), its debt and dividend policies (B and d), its net asset needs (CA + FA − CL), and the growth rate in sales that the firm can support without raising the proportion of debt in its capital structure over the long term. Underlying this expression is the simple requirement that the firm's sources and uses of funds must be equal, as a firm grows.

Equation (2) can be reinterpreted in a slightly different fashion if we multiply both the top and the bottom of the right-hand side of the equation by the firm's current annual sales volume, S:

$$g = \frac{(M)(S)(1-d)}{(1-B)(CA+FA-CL)(S)}$$

(M)(S) is the total after-tax profit earned by the firm in the current year. The product (1 − B)(CA + FA − CL)(S) is the equity portion of the firm's total capitalization at the beginning of the year. Since after-tax profits divided by equity equals a firm's return on equity (ROE), a simpler form of the above expression is:

$$g = (ROE)(1-d) \tag{3}$$

In this form, the requirement for a particular growth rate to be "sustainable" becomes clear. If a firm is to grow without experiencing an increasing debt ratio in its capital structure, its common equity must grow as fast as its debt grows—and both must grow as fast as the firm's *sales* grow. Thus, a firm with a 15% ROE and a 50% dividend payout ratio will add (0.15)(1 − 0.5) = 0.075, or 7.5% each year to its equity base, in the form of retained earnings. With a requirement that debt grow no faster than equity, the firm's long-term sustainable growth rate is simply the same 7.5% annual rate at which its *common equity* is able to grow.

When we talk about sustainable growth, it is important to understand that we are talking about a *long-term* phenomenon. The parameters, CA, FA, CL, B, M, and d in the expressions above are to be interpreted as the long-run "typical" or "normal" relationships between assets, liabilities, profits, dividends, and sales. These will reflect competitive conditions in the firm's product markets as indicated by the level of receivables, inventories, and fixed assets required by its business (the parameters CA and FA). They will also reflect the manner in which the firm deals with its suppliers and has various accruals in the normal course of its operations (the parameter CL). Finally, the firm's debt ratio (B) and its dividend policy (d) define its long-term financial policies.

In any given year, the firm's actual situation may depart from certain of these long-run characteristics. For example, in a year when profits are temporarily depressed, the firm may have a higher-than-normal dividend payout ratio because it does not want to alienate its stockholders by cutting the *amount* of its dividend. Alternatively, the firm may raise funds in the long-term debt market in an unusually large amount because it is planning several years into the future. This may temporarily raise the firm's debt ratio until additional retained earnings accumulate to restore balance to the firm's capital structure. Any firm will experience some variation in its operating and financial characteristics of this sort from year to year. The relationships that are relevant to the concept of sustainable growth, however, are

■ Valuation

ISSUES

WHAT DETERMINES REPORTED EARNINGS— OPERATINGS RESULTS OR ANALYST EXPECTATIONS?

In this chapter, we describe techniques that managers can use to project the results of a firm's future operations. The sequence of financial planning begins with tentative

operating plans whose expected results are then summarized in terms of cash budgets, pro forma statements, and sustainable growth estimates. The goal of the managers should be to produce financial plans that realistically reflect operating plans. Any subsequent deviations of reported firm profit performance should provide some indication of the ability of a firm's executives to *manage operations*. Critics of corporate financial reporting in the 1990s, however, argue that such deviations merely indicate management's inability to *manage reported earnings*.

According to these critics, many investors base their valuation of stocks on the ability of firms to produce quarterly earnings that meet or beat the estimates provided by security analysts. This phenomenon was dramatically illustrated in late 1997 when the software company Oracle announced second quarter earnings of $0.19 per share as opposed to analyst expectations of $0.23 per share. The next day, the firm's stock price plummeted 29% (by over $9 billion in total market value) on trading volume of 172 million shares. Consequently, the ultimate measure of success for many managers is the ability to produce consistent growth in reported earnings. In response to this incentive, managers have reportedly become very adept at hitting earnings targets.

To produce the desired earnings pattern, corporate managers often make use of the discretion granted to them under Generally Accepted Accounting Principles (GAAP) accounting. For example, Microsoft defers

recognition of revenue from software sales under the assumption that customers are also buying the right to discounted upgrades and free customer support in future years. Recently, Microsoft showed $1.1 billion in unearned revenues that could be recognized as needed to produce desired growth in sales and earnings. Manufacturers in the computer industry routinely engage in "stuffing the channel" at the end of a fiscal quarter. This practice involves boosting sales by inducing distributors to accept delivery of excess inventory even if it is likely to be returned in the next quarter. Other earnings management techniques involve either capitalizing cash expenditures as assets to minimize reported expenses or recognizing massive restructuring costs ("big bath accounting") to offset unusual gains from the sale of assets. Increases and decreases in reserves for bad debts, product returns, and insurance losses are another commonly used tool of earnings management.

In response to some of these practices, the Financial Accounting Standards Board (FASB) created a requirement beginning in 1998 that firms report a new measure of earnings called "comprehensive income." In addition to standard earnings, this new measure must include adjustments for foreign exchange rate fluctuations, variation in pension plan liabilities, and fluctuation in the market value of securities owned by firms. Since this new regulation is likely to increase the variability of reported earnings, the reaction of financial managers was predictably less than enthusiastic.

the *permanent*, or "normal" ones dictated by the firm's long-term policies and its operating environment.

Determinants of Sustainable Growth

The underlying influences on a firm's sustainable growth rate can readily be seen from equation (2):

$$g = \frac{(M)(1-d)}{(1-B)(CA + FA - CL)}$$

It is evident that sustainable growth will increase when

1. the firm's profit margin *increases*;
2. its dividend payout ratio *decreases*;
3. its debt ratio *increases*;

4. current assets *decrease* in relation to sales;
5. fixed assets *decrease* in relation to sales;
6. current liabilities *increase* in relation to sales.

The reasoning and intuition are straightforward. The larger the firm's profit margin and the smaller its dividend payout, the more retained earnings it will generate per dollar or franc of sales. A higher debt ratio—within the limits imposed by the avoidance of financial distress—means that each dollar's or franc's worth of retained earnings will be combined with a greater amount of additional debt to support asset growth. Finally, the smaller are asset needs per sales dollar or franc, and the greater the funding from spontaneous liabilities, the easier it is for retained earnings to provide the funding required by sales growth.

We can get a feel for the magnitude of these influences by returning again to the case of Machines Rennes, where:

$$CA = 0.30 \qquad FA = 0.40 \qquad CL = 0.20$$
$$B = 0.30 \qquad d = 0.30$$

If we insert these values into equation (2), we can identify the relationship between the firm's profit margin on sales and its sustainable growth rate:

$$g = \frac{(M)(1 - 0.30)}{(1 - 0.30)(0.30 + 0.40 - 0.20)} = 2M$$

This indicates that the firm can sustain a long-run rate of growth in sales—and of course in assets, liabilities, debt, equity, and dividends—equal to *twice* the profit margin it realizes on its sales. This relationship is tabulated in Part A of Table 21-13.

Now suppose that, due to careful attention to collecting accounts receivable more rapidly, managing inventory more efficiently, investing in fixed assets that support more sales per franc of investment, or stretching accounts payable further, the combined net asset parameter CA + FA − CL declines from 0.50 to 0.40. We will call this the case of *increasing efficiency* in the utilization of (net) assets. Part B of Table 21-13 shows the extent to which sustainable growth is enhanced by this increased efficiency. Each of the growth rates listed is larger than its counterpart in Part A, for any given level of the firm's profit margin.

Alternatively, with CA + FA − CL back at its original value of 0.50, suppose the firm reduces its dividend payout ratio to 20% of profits (d = 0.20) from 30%. The increase in sustainable growth for Machines Rennes is shown in Part C of Table 21-13. Finally, with CA + FA − CL still at 0.50 and dividend payout ratio back again to 0.30, suppose the firm raises its target debt ratio to 40% of total capitalization (B = 0.40) from 30%. The corresponding new sustainable growth rates are listed in Part D of Table 21-13. If we compare each sustainable growth rate in Parts B, C and D of Table 21-13 with the counterpart growth rate in Part A, the comparative effects of all these changes on sustainable growth may be summarized as follows:

If	Then Sustainable Growth Rate Increases by
The Efficiency of Asset Utilization Increases by 20%	25%
Dividend Payout Ratio Is Reduced by 33%	14%
Debt Ratio Is Increased by 33%	17%

While these particular effects are specific to the Machine Rennes example, the general conclusion that *an improvement in the efficiency of asset utilization* is likely to produce the most pronounced gain in long-run sustainable growth *is* valid for most firms.

The Effect of Changes in Operating and Financial Characteristics on Machines Rennes' Sustainable Long-Run Growth Rate

TABLE 21-13

A. With Original Characteristics as Given (CA + FA − CL = 0.5, B = 0.3, d = 0.3):

Profit Margin	Growth Rate
2.5%	5.0%
5.0%	10.0%
7.5%	15.0%
10.0%	20.0%

B. With a 20% Improvement in the Efficiency of Asset Utilization (CA + FA − CL = 0.4):

Profit Margin	Growth Rate
2.5%	6.3%
5.0%	12.5%
7.5%	18.8%
10.0%	25.0%

C. With a 33% Reduction in Dividend Payout Ratio (d = 0.2):

Profit Margin	Growth Rate
2.5%	5.7%
5.0%	11.4%
7.5%	17.1%
10.0%	22.9%

D. With a 33% Increase in the Firm's Debt Ratio (B = 0.4):

Profit Margin	Growth Rate
2.5%	5.8%
5.0%	11.7%
7.5%	17.5%
10.0%	23.3%

External Equity Financing

The conditions in equation (2) and the impacts identified in Table 21-13 apply only to circumstances where the firm's growth is supported solely by retained earnings (internal equity) and the additional debt that can be obtained (in the proportion B) as the firm's common equity base is increased by those retained earnings. If the firm is willing to issue additional shares of common stock (external equity), however, there is essentially *no* constraint on how fast it can grow.

To demonstrate this point, let us expand the basic sources=uses condition stated in equation (1) to allow for external equity financing. If the firm is willing to add the amount (e)(S) from new common stock issues each year, the sources=uses condition becomes:

Incremental Uses = Incremental Sources

Asset Increase = Spontaneous Liability Increase + Debt Increase +
Internal Equity Increase + External Equity Increase

$$(CA + FA)(\Delta S) = (CL)(\Delta S) + (B)(CA + FA - CL)(\Delta S) + (M)(S)(1 - d) + (e)(S)$$

where e is the ratio of the volume of new stock issued to annual sales volume. Rearranging and dividing by S to solve for the implied growth rate g, we find that

$$g_E = \frac{(M)(1 - d)}{(1 - B)(CA + FA - CL)} + \frac{e}{(1 - B)(CA + FA - CL)} \tag{4}$$

where g_E is the sustainable growth rate when external equity can be obtained. Equation (4) states that the firm's sustainable growth will be equal to the sum of two components. The first component (the first term on the right-hand side of the equation) is the rate of sustainable growth *in the absence of external equity financing*. Notice that this component is equal to g in equation (2). The second component (the second term on the right-hand side of the equation) is the extra growth which *is supported by external equity financing*. Given that there is no theoretical limit to the amount of external equity financing a firm may choose to do, the second term on the right-hand side of equation (4) can be made as large as the firm wishes. The only limit the firm faces is that which is set by its opportunities to expand sales in its competitive product market.

As an illustration, take the case of a company that has $200 million of total capitalization and annual sales currently of $500 million. Thus, the combined net asset parameter CA + FA – CL for the firm is

$$\frac{\$200}{\$500} = 0.40$$

Suppose the firm's after-tax profit margin on sales is 4%; its dividend payout ratio is 50%; and its policy is to have debt be 40% of total capitalization.

If the firm elects not to issue common stock to support its growth, retained earnings each year will increase the firm's capitalization by:

$$\frac{(M)(1-d)}{(CA + FA - CL)} = \frac{(0.04)(1 - 0.5)}{0.40} = 0.05 = 5\%$$

It can therefore grow over time at the annual rate that is defined by the first component on the right-hand side of equation (4). With a debt ratio of 40%, the value of this component is

$$\frac{(M)(1-d)}{(1 - B)(CA + FA - CL)} = \frac{(0.04)(0.5)}{(0.6)(0.40)} = 0.0833 = 8.33\%$$

If, however, it wishes to grow at a rate of *15%* per year, the firm will need additional external equity funding. This extra funding must support

$$15.00\% - 8.33\% = 6.67\%$$

of extra annual growth—which must be made possible by the second component of equation (4):

$$\frac{e}{(1 - B)(CA + FA - CL)} = \frac{e}{(1 - 0.4)(0.4)} = 0.0667 = 6.67\%$$

Solving for e, we find that:

$$e = 0.016 = 1.60\%$$

What this means is that the firm will have to issue new common stock each year in an amount equal to 1.6% of its annual sales volume. If it does, it will be able to attain its desired 15% annual growth rate—in sales, assets, dividends, debt, and equity.

Financial managers can use the concept of sustainable growth in the process of financial planning in a number of ways. First, they can identify what growth rate is attainable *given* the firm's current financial policies and asset requirements. Second, they can "turn the analysis around" by asking what sort of *changes* in policies and requirements are necessary to achieve a *different* desired growth rate. Adding external equity, as in the example presented above, is one possible change. Another would be an improvement in the efficiency of asset utilization, or a change in dividend policy. Alternatively, the managers can determine the *combined* changes in each of these various characteristics that would allow a chosen growth rate to be sustained. The process of identifying the changes in policies and asset requirements that are consistent with a target rate of sustainable growth is one form of "sensitivity analysis." Through the use of sensitivity analysis, financial managers can very quickly identify the steps they will have to take to achieve any desired rate of growth.

An Application of Sustainable Growth Analysis

As an illustration of the use of sustainable growth in financial planning, we can return to the Dayton Products example discussed earlier in this chapter. Suppose the firm's financial managers wish to calculate sustainable growth for 2001, based on the firm's 2000 balance sheet shown in Table 21-10 and its projected 2001 dividend policy. As a starting point for their analysis, the managers assume that the actual 2000 values for profit margin, debt ratio, and asset requirements will serve as targets for 2001. When these values are combined with the firm's projected dividend policy for 2001, the managers obtain the results shown in Figure 21-2.

The sustainable growth rate of 5.5% indicated in the figure is considerably smaller than the projected 2001 growth rate of 20%, which was used by the managers to construct the pro forma statements shown in Tables 21-11 and 21-12. This raises the question of how the pro forma statements could have been constructed with such a large discrepancy between projected growth and sustainable growth. The answer is simply that one or more of the six key financial variables in the sustainable growth equation must have deviated from the target values listed in Figure 21-2. In order to evaluate this situation, Dayton Products' managers calculate the projected values for the six variables based on the 2001 pro forma statements. The results are outlined in Figure 21-3.

Figure 21-3 divides the six variables in the sustainable growth equation into two categories: those that reflect *investing* decisions (M, CA, and FA) and those that reflect *financing* decisions (CL, B, and d). The figure indicates that Dayton's excessively rapid growth resulted in substantial deviations of the variables from their targets in the area of investing decisions. Specifically, the profit margin (M) is projected to increase from 3.0% in 2000 to 3.6% in 2001. This increase is due to the operating leverage provided by depreciation, amortization, and fixed selling and administrative expenses. The current asset requirement (CA) is projected to decline from the target of 0.413 to only 0.400 in 2001. Finally, the fixed asset

Dayton Products' Sustainable Growth for 2001

FIGURE 21-2

$$g = \frac{(M)(1 - d)}{(1 - B)(CA + FA - CL)}$$

M = EAT/Sales
d = Dividends/EAT
B = Debt/(Debt + Equity)

CA = Current Assets/Sales
FA = Fixed Assets/Sales
CL = Spontaneous Current Liabilities/Sales

Actual 2000 Values (2001 Targets):

M = \$3,300/\$110,100 = 0.030
CA = \$45,500/\$110,100 = 0.413
FA = \$38,300/\$110,100 = 0.348
CL = (\$7,200 + 8,700 + 400)/\$110,100 = 0.148
B = (\$5,600 + 28,000)/(\$5,600 + 28,000 + 8,000 + 30,000) = 0.469

Projected 2001 Dividend Policy: d = 0.40

$$g = \frac{(0.030)(1 - 0.40)}{(1 - 0.469)(0.413 + 0.348 - 0.148)} = 0.055 = 5.5\%$$

FIGURE 21-3

The Effect of Excessively Rapid Growth on Dayton Products

Projected 2001 Sales Growth = 20.0%   2001 Sustainable Growth = 5.5%

Values of Key Variables:

	2001 Target	2001 Projected
Investing Decisions:		
M	0.030	0.036
CA	0.413	0.400
FA	0.348	0.295
Financing Decisions:		
CL	0.148	0.148
B	0.469	0.462
d	0.400	0.400

requirement (FA) shows a projected decline to 0.295, which is below its target of 0.348.

Dayton Products' managers must now assess the implications of the changed ratio values shown in Figure 21-3. From a purely mathematical standpoint, the 2001 projected variables have corrected for the gap between sustainable growth and projected growth. From a financial viewpoint, however, the managers must decide whether the deviation of the variables from their targets will have a positive or negative effect on the firm's *value*. This judgment will depend on the answers to numerous questions. For example, how realistic are the actual 2000 ratio values as targets for 2001? Are they precise goals or merely rough guidelines? Apparently, the 2000 profit margin of 3.0% was only a rough guide because it ignored the positive effect of operating leverage as sales volume increases. Is there sufficient excess plant capacity to allow sales to grow at a much faster pace than additions to plant and equipment? Can the firm reduce its levels of receivables and inventories relative to sales without alienating customers due to inventory shortages or a tighter credit policy?

Typically, there will be no obvious answers to such questions. Yet the mere process of considering these issues should enable a firm's managers to improve their coordination of investing and financing decisions. One particularly valuable analytical approach is to use a sensitivity analysis that solves for the values of the key ratios that are consistent with a particular target level of sustainable growth. For example, the managers may set targets for the sustainable growth rate (g) as well as for profit margin (M), asset requirements (CA and FA), current liabilities (CL), and dividend policy (d). They can then solve the sustainable growth equation for the associated required debt ratio (B). If this amount of leverage is infeasible, the process can be repeated with different target values until an acceptable joint solution is found.

Suppose Dayton Products' managers determine that all the target ratios that resulted in a sustainable growth rate of 5.5% in Figure 21-2 are appropriate long-term targets. They could then perform an analysis that would indicate how much new common stock (external equity) must be sold each year in order to boost the sustainable growth rate to 20%. Based on equation (4), the requirement for external equity financing would be:

$$g_E = \frac{(M)(1-d)}{(1-B)(CA+FA-CL)} + \frac{e}{(1-B)(CA+FA-CL)}$$

$$20\% = 5.5\% + \frac{e}{(1 - B)(CA + FA - CL)}$$

$$14.5\% = \frac{e}{(1 - B)(CA + FA - CL)}$$

$$e = (0.145)(1 - 0.469)(0.413 + 0.348 - 0.148) = 0.047 = 4.7\%$$

From this calculation, Dayton's managers know that they would have to issue stock each year in an amount equal to 4.7% of the company's annual sales volume in order to achieve a sustainable growth rate of 20%. They must then decide whether that financing strategy is either feasible or desirable.

GROWTH, FINANCIAL POLICIES, AND VALUE

The question of desirability, of course, has to do with the impact of alternative financial policies and growth paths on the price of the firm's common stock and thereby on the wealth of the firm's common stockholders. These impacts can be identified if we combine the concept of sustainable corporate growth with the framework of the Investment Valuation Model.

Recall from Chapter 7 that the current price of a firm's common stock represents the present value of the stock's expected future dividends per share. In a setting where dividends are projected to grow at the long-run average rate g from the coming year's initial amount D_1, and where K_E is the return investors require in order to be willing to purchase the stock, we found that we could express the current share price P_0 as:

$$P_0 = \frac{D_1}{K_E - g}$$

If we multiply P_0 by the number of common shares outstanding for the firm in question, we obtain the *total* market value of the firm's common stock, MV. Similarly, if we multiply D_1 by the number of common shares, we get the aggregate dividends (AD_1) expected to be paid by the firm in the coming year. Thus, we can also write the equation above in the form:

$$MV = \frac{AD_1}{K_E - g} \tag{5}$$

In this equation, the aggregate dividend AD_1 can be expressed as the product of the firm's expected aggregate earnings AE_1 in the coming year times the firm's dividend payout ratio, d. In turn, AE_1 can be expressed as the product of the current book value of the firm's equity, BV, times the firm's return on book equity, ROE. Equation (5) therefore can be rewritten as:

$$MV = \frac{(d)(BV)(ROE)}{K_E - g}$$

or, by dividing both sides of the equation by BV, as:

$$\frac{MV}{BV} = \frac{(d)(ROE)}{K_E - g} \tag{6}$$

where the left-hand side of the equation is the firm's "market-to-book" ratio: the market value of equity divided by the book value.

From equation (3) of this chapter, the compact expression for a firm's sustainable growth rate was found to be:

$$g = (ROE)(1 - d)$$

Equivalently:

$$g = (ROE) - (d)(ROE)$$

and, rearranging:

$$(d)(ROE) = ROE - g \tag{7}$$

If we substitute this expression for (d)(ROE) into equation (6), we get:

$$\frac{MV}{BV} = \frac{ROE - g}{K_E - g} \tag{8}$$

which says that a firm's market-to-book ratio will depend upon the rate of return it earns on its book equity, the expected long-run sustainable growth rate of its earnings and dividends, and the rate of return investors require from owning its common shares. Book equity, of course, represents the funds provided to the company by stockholders, through retained earnings and purchases of new common shares, to invest on their behalf. For a *given* amount of book equity, the greater is the firm's market-to-book ratio, the higher is its stock price. Financial and operating strategies that increase the ratio MV/BV, therefore, are value-enhancing strategies for stockholders.

ROE and Stockholder Wealth

It is evident from equation (8) that the relationship between ROE and K_E is central to the impact of growth on a firm's market-to-book ratio. In particular, firms whose ROEs exceed the market-required return K_E will have market-to-book ratios greater than 1.0 and will be wealth creators for their stockholders. They make the market value of the stockholders' investment in the firm greater than the original amount invested. This is because the firms are taking on investment projects whose rates of return are greater than the cost of capital—projects with positive net present values. Conversely, firms whose ROEs are less than K_E will have market-to-book ratios less than 1.0 because they are investing in poor projects that destroy stockholder wealth.

As examples, consider a firm whose dividends are expected to grow at a 6% annual rate in the future, whose actual return on equity is 15%, and whose required return on equity is 12%. From equation (8), the firm's market-to-book ratio will be:

$$\frac{MV}{BV} = \frac{0.15 - 0.06}{0.12 - 0.06} = 1.50$$

Suppose, instead, we let the firm's ROE be 12% and the RRR on equity be 15%. The market-to-book ratio then becomes:

$$\frac{MV}{BV} = \frac{0.12 - 0.06}{0.15 - 0.06} = 0.67$$

When ROE and K_E are equal, the firm's book and market values are the same and stockholders have neither benefited nor suffered from the investments the firm has made.

In Figure 21-4, we plot the relationship between a firm's market-to-book ratio and the extent to which its ROE either falls short of or exceeds K_E—holding constant the firm's growth rate. For the growth rate not to change, the assumption is

that the firm has a steadily higher dividend payout ratio as ROE increases. It is these higher dividends that cause the firm's market value to rise.[5]

Dividend Policy and Stockholder Wealth

The relationship between a firm's dividend policy and its market-to-book ratio, holding ROE constant, can also be identified. The greater the fraction of its earnings the firm pays out as dividends, the larger will be the current dividend received by stockholders, but the slower will be the firm's growth rate because it will be reinvesting less to sustain growth. The slower growth then means that future dividends will increase at a slower rate as well. It is this trade-off between cash now and cash later that determines the effect of dividend policy on stock value. It should come as no surprise that the outcome of the trade-off depends on whether the ROE earned by the firm when earnings are retained is above or below the rate of return K_E that investors require.

To see the effect, let us return to the case in which ROE is 15% and K_E is 12%. Suppose the firm is paying out 60% of its earnings as dividends. Its sustainable growth rate, therefore, will be:

$$g = (ROE)(1 - d) = (0.15)(1 - 0.60) = 0.06 = 6\%$$

per annum and, from equation (8), we again have:

$$\frac{MV}{BV} = \frac{ROE - g}{K_E - g} = \frac{0.15 - 0.06}{0.12 - 0.06} = 1.50$$

Now assume the firm lowers its dividend payout to just 40% of earnings. As a result, its sustainable growth rate will increase to:

$$g = (ROE)(1 - d) = (0.15)(1 - 0.40) = 0.09 = 9\%$$

per annum and its market-to-book ratio will rise to:

$$\frac{MV}{BV} = \frac{ROE - g}{K_E - g} = \frac{0.15 - 0.09}{0.12 - 0.09} = 2.00$$

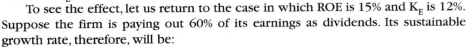

The Impact of the Relationship Between Actual Return on Equity and Required Return on Equity on a Firm's Market-to-Book Ratio When Growth Is Constant

FIGURE 21-4

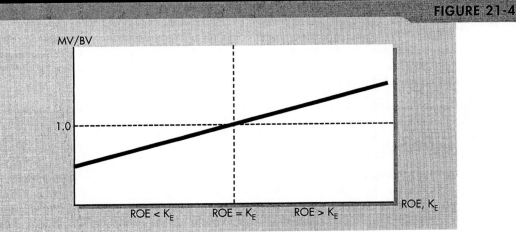

---

[5] We are also assuming the increase in ROE results from improvements in the firm's operations and not an increase in its leverage. If the latter were the cause, the required return K_E would also increase and would thereby lessen the rate at which the firm's market-to-book ratio rises. This would show up as a curved line in Figure 21-4.

The Impact of Changes in the Actual Return on Equity, the Required Return on Equity, and Dividend Payout Ratio on the Ratio of Market Value to Book Value for a Firm

SUMMARY FIGURE 21-5

When	The Ratio MV/BV
ROE Increases	Increases
K_E Increases	Decreases
d Increases and ROE < K_E	Increases
d Increases and ROE = K_E	Is Equal to 1.0
d Increases and ROE > K_E	Decreases

This increase occurs because the firm is investing internally to earn a higher rate of return than investors could earn for themselves externally from other equity investments of comparable risk. For that reason, the decline in value from reduced dividends in the short run (as d drops from 0.60 to 0.40 and the dollar amount of the dividend also drops) is more than made up for by the extra value of the much larger longer-term dividends that the additional growth brings.

It should also be clear that if ROE were *less* than K_E, a reduction in the firm's dividend payout ratio would *lower* rather than raise its market-to-book ratio. The recommendation would be that dividends should be *increased* in such a situation. Indeed, if ROE is expected to remain less than K_E, the firm in question should raise its dividend to the ultimate. It should go out of business, liquidate its assets, pay off its debts, and distribute all the remaining proceeds to stockholders because it is not earning a competitive return for them.

It is interesting to note that if ROE is *equal* to K_E, the firm's dividend policy has *no* effect on its market-to-book ratio. Under that circumstance, earnings are being reinvested to earn a rate of return that is exactly what investors require. Hence, every dollar's worth of retained earnings produces just a dollar's worth of extra stock value, and stockholders break even as compared with receiving the dollar in dividends. A greater percentage of retained earnings will make the firm larger, of course (g will increase), but the extra size brings with it no incremental gain in value for stockholders. We summarize the effects of ROE, K_E, and g on market-to-book ratios in Figure 21-5.

SUMMARY

In this chapter, we turned our attention to the forecasting of future financial performance. Pro forma balance sheets, income statements, and cash budgets are all part of the larger planning system of a firm. Their role is to translate strategic operating plans into projected financial results. These profit plans or budgets can be used internally as benchmarks against which to evaluate actual performance. They can also be used externally as a source of information about the firm for potential creditors and investors. Cash budgets should be prepared frequently enough to enable the financial managers to make an early identification of the investing opportunities and financing needs associated with cash surpluses and deficits. Pro forma balance sheets and income statements can either be prepared directly from detailed operating plans or indirectly through the relationship of past balance sheet accounts and income items to sales. The indirect procedure is generally less time-consuming but less accurate. In either case, the accuracy of the projected statements depends heavily on the accuracy of the firm's sales forecast.

The concept of sustainable growth is a planning tool that can help determine whether proposed financing and investing decisions taken together are consistent and feasible. Sustainable growth is defined as the percentage increase in sales that can be achieved without issuing common stock or altering the historical ratios of assets to sales, profits to sales, dividends to profits, or debt to total capitalization. If a projected sales increase exceeds sustainable growth, the components of the sustainable growth equation can help management judge the feasibility of more rapid growth and determine what steps are necessary to make that growth possible. The equation can also help management identify the valuation effects of alternative financial policies.

chapter equations

1. $(M)(S)(1 - d) = (1 - B)$
   $(CA + FA - CL)(\Delta S)$

2. $g = \dfrac{(M)(1 - d)}{(1 - B)(CA + FA - CL)}$

3. $g = (ROE)(1 - d)$

4. $g_E = \dfrac{(M)(1 - d)}{(1 - B)(CA + FA - CL)}$
   $+ \dfrac{e}{(1 - B)(CA + FA - CL)}$

5. $MV = \dfrac{AD_1}{K_E - g}$

6. $\dfrac{MV}{BV} = \dfrac{(d)(ROE)}{K_E - g}$

7. $(d)(ROE) = ROE - g$

8. $\dfrac{MV}{BV} = \dfrac{ROE - g}{K_E - g}$

CONTENT QUESTIONS

1. Distinguish between a firm's strategic plan and its profit plan.
2. What determines the frequency of preparing cash budgets?
3. Why is the sales forecast important to cash budgets?
4. Briefly explain the relationship between a cash budget and pro forma financial statements. Why must both give the same cash balance at the end of the period?
5. When is it appropriate to use financial ratios in preparing pro forma financial statements?
6. Define sustainable growth in terms of the financial relationships that are held constant.
7. Why is a stable debt ratio important to a firm as it grows over time?
8. What would happen to the value of sustainable growth if unlimited new common stock issues were permitted?
9. Holding other variables constant, what would happen to sustainable growth if asset requirements or dividend payout increased?
10. Holding other variables constant, what would happen to sustainable growth if financial leverage or net profit margin increased?

CONCEPT QUESTIONS

1. A firm's controller has prepared the firm's cash budget for the next six months. The budget shows that the firm will have a cash surplus of $1 million at the end of that period. Thus, the controller informs the firm's financial manager that the firm will not need a bank line of credit during that period. Under what conditions would the controller's conclusion be incorrect?
2. A firm's pro forma balance sheet indicates that notes payable in the coming year will be $7,500,000. Since the notes payable on last year's balance sheet were $4,800,000, the firm's financial manager decides to arrange for a bank

line of credit of $12,300,000 in the coming year. Is the financial manager's conclusion correct?

3. International In late 1997, the Financial Accounting Standards Board passed a requirement that, from 1998 onward, firms must report as part of "comprehensive income" the gains and losses from foreign currency translation adjustments for the assets and liabilities of their overseas operations. The chief financial officer at a major U.S. corporation argued that such information is of limited short-term value because random currency fluctuations even themselves out over an extended period of time. Do you agree or disagree with this statement? Why?

4. The financial manager at a firm determines that the firm's sustainable growth rate is 10% based on the use of equation (2) in the chapter. The firm's pro forma financial statements, however, are based on a projected sales growth rate of 15%. What adjustments can the manager make to investing and financing decisions to boost the sustainable growth rate to 15%?

5. Ethics Should financial managers use the discretion permitted them by GAAP accounting rules to manage earnings so that they meet or exceed security analyst forecasts? Is such a manipulation of earnings in the best interests of a firm's stockholders?

PROBLEMS

1. Stover Mills prepares a monthly cash budget. As a basis for its 2001 cash budget, it has compiled the following information:

   (1) Monthly sales forecast for 2001 as follows:

January	$350,000	June	510,000	October	450,000
February	375,000	July	525,000	November	450,000
March	425,000	August	475,000	December	425,000
April	525,000	September	475,000	January	375,000
May	515,000				

   (2) Eighty percent of sales are on credit terms, and 20% are for cash. Sixty percent of total sales are collected in the first month following the month of sale. The remainder are collected in the second month following the month of sale.

   (3) Materials purchases in each month are equal to 30% of sales forecasted for the next month. The purchases are paid for in the month after purchase.

   (4) Production is scheduled at the level of forecasted sales for the following month. Labor expenses are equal to 45% of forecasted sales and are payable in the month of production.

   (5) Selling and administrative expenses of $40,000 per month are paid in the month incurred.

   (6) Interest expense of $18,500 on long-term debt and bank loans is due on June 30 and December 31.

   (7) Overhead expense of $45,000 per month is paid in the following month.

   (8) Estimated tax payments are:

April 15	$20,000	September 15	35,800
June 15	25,000	December 15	25,000

   (9) No dividends will be paid.

   (10) Actual sales in the last two months of 2000 were:

November	$400,000	December	400,000

   (11) Depreciation expense is $5,000 per month.

a. Prepare a monthly schedule of sales revenues and total cash inflows.

b. Prepare a monthly schedule of operating expenses and a monthly schedule of other expenditures.

c. If the cash balance is $50,000 on Dec. 31, 2000, determine the cash balance each month during 2001 without financing.

2. Given the information on Problem 1, prepare a pro forma income statement for 2001 for Stover Mills.

3. Given the balance sheet on Dec. 31, 2000, (shown below) and the information in Problems 1 and 2, prepare a pro forma balance sheet for Dec. 31, 2001. Stover Mills does not intend to pay dividends. It maintains a $40,000 minimum cash balance and will borrow short-term (notes payable), if necessary, to maintain this minimum.

Stover Mills Balance Sheet Dec. 31, 2000

Cash	$ 50,000	Notes payable	$ 0
Accounts receivable	400,000	Accounts payable	105,000
Inventory	307,500	Accruals	200,000
Current assets	757,500	Current liabilities	305,000
Plant and equipment	885,000	Long-term debt	300,000
Less: Accumulated depreciation	(225,000)	Common stock	500,000
Net fixed assets	660,000	Retained earnings	312,500
Total assets	$1,417,500	Total liabilities and net worth	$1,417,500

4. Given the following added information about Stover Mills' operating and financing plans for 2001, repeat Problems 1, 2 and 3.

a. Dividends of $10,000 are to be paid each quarter in March, June, September, and December.

b. A $100,000 principal payment on long-term debt is due to be paid in July. (Assume interest expense does not change.)

c. An addition to plant and equipment of $250,000 is planned for December.

d. Additional common stock will be sold in November. Proceeds of the sale are expected to be $400,000.

5. Union Garden Products (the example in this chapter) has decided to plan the second half of the fiscal year, July 1 to December 31. Assume that all information regarding Union Garden Products' operations given in the chapter still holds. In addition, you have obtained the following information:

(1) Sales Forecast (in Thousands)

July	$4,000	November	5,000
August	5,000	December	4,000
September	6,000	January	4,000
October	6,000		

(2) In July, $2,000,000 of new machinery will be purchased and paid for in November.

(3) A long-term loan of $500,000 will be received in November.

(4) Dividend payments will be increased to $200,000 payable in September and $400,000 payable in December.

(5) The second interest installment of $225,000 is due in July.

(6) Estimated tax payments of $935,000 each are due in September and in December.

a. Prepare a monthly schedule of sales receipts and total cash inflows for July through December.

b. Prepare a monthly schedule of operating expenses and a monthly schedule of total cash outflows.

c. Determine the end-of-month cash balances for July through December.

6. Prepare a pro forma statement of net income for Union Garden Products for the period July 1 to December 31 and a pro forma balance sheet for December 31.

7. Schiller Machinery is completing its pro forma financial statements. It has estimated all of its accounts except cash and notes payable as follows:

Long-term debt	$ 5,000,000	Inventories	3,000,000
Retained earnings	10,000,000	Accounts receivable	4,000,000
Plant and equipment	15,000,000	Other current assets	1,000,000
Accumulated depreciation	7,000,000	Other current liabilities	1,000,000
Common stock	2,000,000	Accounts payable	2,000,000

Find Schiller's expected cash balance and notes payable, respectively, if it maintains a $2,000,000 minimum cash balance and obtains needed financing through a short-term loan.

8. Construct the pro forma income statement for 1999 for Athens Electric. The firm's management has estimated the following for 1999:

(1) Forecasted sales = $20,000,000

(2) Cost of goods sold = 80% of sales

(3) Depreciation per year = $300,000

(4) Selling and general expense = 5% of sales plus $800,000 per year

(5) Interest expense = $300,000

(6) Tax rate = 50%

9.

ATHENS ELECTRIC
Balance Sheet
December 31, 1998
(in Thousands)

Cash	$ 300	Notes payable	$ 100
Accounts receivable	900	Accounts payable	1,300
Inventories	1,500	Other liabilities	700
Current assets	$2,700	Current liabilities	$2,100
Plant and equipment	$7,000	Long-term debt	$1,500
Less: Depreciation	2,000	Common stock	1,500
Net fixed assets	$5,000	Retained earnings	2,600
Total assets	$7,700	Total liabilities and net worth	$7,700

Given the income statement for Athens Electric that you prepared in Problem 8, the balance sheet shown above, and the following additional information, construct the balance sheet for December 31, 1999:

(1) The ACP is expected to be 18 days.

(2) Inventory turnover is expected to be 8 times.

(3) Additions to plant and equipment are planned to be $700,000.

(4) Accounts payable are expected to be 8% of sales.

(5) Other liabilities are expected to be 6% of sales.

(6) Dividends are planned to be $400,000.

(7) The minimum desired cash balance is $300,000.

10. Prepare a pro forma income statement for 2001 for Duralite Corporation using the following information (round answers to the nearest $1,000):

a. Projected sales: $5,500,000

b. Cost of goods sold: 75% of sales

c. Selling and administrative expense:
Variable = 10% of sales, Fixed = $40,000 per month

d. Depreciation: $6,500 per month
e. Interest expense: $37,000 per year
f. Tax rate: 40%

11. Use the pro forma income statement from Problem 10, the balance sheet for Duralite Corporation for December 31, 2000, (shown below), and the following information to construct a pro forma balance sheet for December 31, 2001 (round answers to the nearest $1,000):
   a. The minimum cash balance desired by the firm is $40,000.
   b. Additions to plant and equipment in 2001 are expected to total $185,000.
   c. The average collection period is projected to be 25 days at year-end.
   d. Inventory turnover is projected to be 11.0.
   e. Accounts payable have been about 2.0% of sales in the past and are expected to remain near that percentage at year-end.
   f. On December 31, 2001, accrued labor expense is expected to be $65,000, taxes payable $55,000, and accrued overhead 1.0% of sales.
   g. No change is expected in either long-term debt or common stock.
   h. Dividends equal to 30% of net income are expected to be paid in 2001.

Duralite Corporation Balance Sheet December 31, 2000

Assets			Liabilities and net worth	
Cash		$ 35,000	Bank loan	$ 100,000
Accounts receivable		350,000	Accounts payable	75,000
Inventory		325,000	Accrued labor	50,000
		710,000	Taxes payable	40,000
			Accrued overhead	25,000
Total current assets			Total current liabilities	$ 290,000
Gross plant and equipment	$1,200,000		Long term debt @ 9%	300,000
Less:			Common stock	300,000
Accumulated depreciation	(700,000)		Retained earnings	320,000
Net plant and equipment		500,000		
Total assets		$1,210,000	Total liabilities and net worth	$1,210,000

12. Maple Lane Academy is a private elementary school with eight primary grades and two teaching stations per grade. The following budget has been prepared by the finance committee of the Maple Lane board of trustees:

Budget—July 1, 1999 to June 30, 2000

Expenses		
Salaries and benefits		
Principal	$ 42,000	
Teachers	480,000	
Staff	60,000	$582,000
Books and equipment		$170,000
Office expense		24,000
Utilities		
Electricity	$ 24,000	
Gas	50,000	74,000
		$850,000
Revenue		
Tuition ($1,500 per student)		$600,000
Book fees ($100 per student)		40,000
Smithson Foundation		100,000
Government grant		150,000
		$890,000

Prepare a monthly cash budget (rounded to the nearest $100) for Maple Lane for the next year beginning with July. Show the net cash flow and the cash balance each month, given the following additional information:

a. Maple Lane does not pay taxes.

b. The cash balance on June 30, 1999 is $50,000.

c. The principal and staff are paid on a 12-month basis. However, teachers are paid over 9 months beginning with September.

d. Books are ordered in July and paid for in September. Equipment, which represents $60,000 of the total books and equipment expense, is expected to be purchased and paid for in December.

e. Book fees are paid at the time of preregistration in May and are nonrefundable.

f. Tuition payments are made twice annually, in September and in January.

g. The school is a beneficiary of the Smithson Foundation. The funds are distributed on January 1 each year.

h. The government grant is received quarterly in July, October, January, and April.

i. The electricity expense is spread evenly over the year.

j. Gas is used primarily for heating the school. The following represents the distribution of heating cost over the heating season:

October	5%	February	20
November	15	March	15
December	20	April	5
January	20		

k. Office expense is spread evenly over the year.

13. Quesada Corporation reported net income of $4 million on sales of $100 million. It retained 50% of its net income. A summary of Quesada's balance sheet (in millions) is:

Current Assets	$20	Current Liabilities	$10
		Debt	20
Fixed Assets	40	Common Stock	30
Total	$60	Total	$60

Based on this information, calculate Quesada's sustainable growth rate.

14. Calculate the sustainable growth rate for Quesada Corporation, given the following changes to the data given in Problem 13.

a. Dividend payout is reduced to 40%

b. Profit margin is increased to 6%.

c. The debt ratio is increased to 50%.

15. Quesada Corporation (Problem 13) is willing to cut its dividend in order to achieve a sustainable growth rate of 12%. What payout ratio is necessary to achieve that growth rate, given the information in Problem 13?

16. Quesada Corporation (Problem 13) is unwilling to cut its dividend payout of 50% but is willing to raise external equity in order to achieve its target of 12% sustainable growth. As a percent of sales, how much external equity must be raised each year to reach this target?

17. Allenwood Company's financial statements for the last year are summarized below:

Sales	£15,750,000
EAT	2,250,000
Dividends	1,350,000
Debt	4,175,000
Equity	5,825,000
Net Assets	10,000,000

The firm's managers have decided to use this information to calculate the firm's sustainable growth rate for the coming year. Calculate Allenwood's sustainable growth rate. (Net assets equals current assets plus fixed assets less current liabilities.)

18. What must the dividend payout ratio become in order for Allenwood to double the sustainable growth rate calculated in Problem 17?

19. As a percent of sales, what amount of external equity would be required each year in order to double the sustainable growth rate calculated in Problem 17?

20. The Cranston Corporation's financial managers are evaluating projected investing and financing decisions for the coming year. They have decided to use the firm's current values of the following ratios as targets for the coming year (Net assets equals current assets plus fixed assets less current liabilities):

| Profit Margin | 4.35% | Net Assets/Sales | 0.34 |
| Debt/Total Capital | 0.46 | Dividend Payout | 45% |

The managers' desire that sales will grow by 20% in the coming year.

a. Based on this information, calculate the firm's sustainable growth rate.

b. If Cranston's managers are willing to reduce the dividend payout ratio to 25%, will the sustainable growth rate be high enough to allow the firm to achieve its desired sales growth?

c. If all ratios except profit margin are held at their original targets, what margin will enable the firm to achieve a sustainable growth rate of 20%?

21. If all ratios for Cranston Corporation (Problem 20) are held at their targets, what amount of external financing as a percent of sales each year will be required to achieve 20% sales growth in the future?

INTERNET EXERCISE

After reading the article "Sometimes Growth Isn't Enough" (www.worth.com/articles/29602I07.html), write a memo to your instructor discussing the impact of dividends on the earnings growth of growth stock. Through the Internet, research three firms with current high growth rates for earnings and comment on their dividend policy and growth rates.

SELF-STUDY QUIZ

1. Raycom Electronics has a target dividend payout ratio of 40% and expects a profit margin of 6%. A summary of Raycom's balance sheet (in millions) is given below:

Current Assets	$200	Current Liabilities	$100
		Debt	150
Net Fixed Assets	300	Common Equity	250
Total	$500	Total	$500

Annual sales are $800 million. Find the sustainable growth rate for Raycom implied by this information.

2. Raycom is targeting a growth rate of 15% and is willing to cut its dividend payout to reach that goal. Find the dividend payout ratio necessary to achieve 10% growth.

3. Raycom is targeting a growth rate of 15% but is unwilling to cut dividends to reach that goal. Instead, it is willing to sell common stock if necessary. Find the amount of external equity as a percent of annual sales that would be required.

Appendix A

Financial Calculator Appendix

INTRODUCTORY COMMENTS

We have structured the problems in the text so they can be solved with a standard four-function (+ − × ÷) calculator. In particular, the time value of money problems can be solved with a basic calculator and the tables of compounding factors and discounting factors contained in the back of the text. Chapter examples and end-of-chapter problems intentionally use interest rates and time periods that can generally be found in those tables. The infrequent exceptions to this rule can be solved using the interpolation techniques described in the chapters.

For those instances in which greater accuracy is required or in which the tables are unavailable or otherwise inadequate, a financial calculator can be very helpful. This appendix contains basic instructions for the use of two specific calculators: the Texas Instruments BAII Plus and the Hewlett-Packard HP-10B. After an initial overview of basic features of these calculators, the appendix describes how to use them to solve some of the time value of money problems contained in the Self-Study Quizzes at the end of various chapters.

KEYSTROKE SYMBOLS

In this appendix, financial function and mathematical operation keystrokes are illustrated by boxes. An unshaded box indicates the function or operation shown on the calculator key itself. For example, the keystroke sequence 4 ÷ 2 = divides the number 4 by the number 2 and displays the answer. Most keys on both calculators also have alternate functions which are shown on the keyboard above the individual keys. These alternate functions are accessed by pressing a special "shift" key followed by the specific function key. The shift key on the BAII Plus is the grey 2nd key, while on the HP-10B, it is the unlabeled solid orange key. In this appendix, a shaded box preceded by either 2nd or ▓ indicates the alternate function. For example, 2nd CLR TVM clears the time value of money memory on the BAII Plus. On the HP-10B, ▓ CLEAR ALL performs a similar function.

BASIC CALCULATOR SETTINGS

1. **Clearing the Calculator**
   Before performing a calculation or making a setting, you need to clear the memory and display.

   BAII Plus: 2nd CLR TVM clears the time value of money memory
   2nd CLR Work clears the memory within the cash flow worksheet
   CE/C CE/C clears the display
   CE/C clears an erroneous numerical entry

HP-10B: ☐ | CLEAR ALL | clears all memories
| C | clears the display and cancels an operation

2. **Number of Decimal Places**

You can set either calculator to display any number of digits to the right of the decimal point. The standard assumption in this appendix is to display two decimal places. To set the calculator for two decimal places:

BAII Plus
1. | 2nd | | Format |
2. 2 | ENTER |
3. | CE/C | | CE/C |

HP-10B
1. ☐ | DISP |
2. 2
3. | C |

3. **Annuity Cash Flows**

For problems that involve a level stream of periodic cash flows (annuities), you need to specify whether the cash flows occur at the beginning or the end of each period. In most problems, the payments are made at the *end of each period*. This is the *default setting* for both calculators. To switch between the "Begin" and "End" modes:

BAII Plus
1. | 2nd | | BGN |
2. | 2nd | | SET |
3. | 2nd | | QUIT |

HP-10B
1. ☐ | BEG/END |

For both calculators, a Begin indicator appears on the display when the calculator is in that mode.

4. **Frequency of Payments and Compounding**

The calculator can be set to accommodate any frequency of payments or compounding per period. The typical problem involves one payment per year and annual compounding. Some bond and loan problems, however, may involve semi-annual, quarterly, or monthly frequency of payments and compounding.

To be consistent with the approach used in the text, *this appendix* will always *assume one payment per each compounding period*. For problems that involve compounding and payments more frequent than once per year, the following adjustments must be made:

a. # periods = # years × frequency of compounding per year
b. periodic interest rate = annual interest rate ÷ frequency of compounding per year

To set the calculators to one payment per compounding period:

BAII Plus
1. | 2nd | | P/Y |
2. 1 | ENTER |
3. | 2nd | | QUIT |

HP-10B
1. 1 ☐ | P/YR |

NOTE: The settings discussed in (2), (3), and (4) above will continue indefinitely (even if the calculator is turned off) unless they are changed. Once they are set, they need to be adjusted only when they are no longer valid for a particular problem. Unless explicitly noted, the calculations in this appendix are based on the following settings:

1. 2 decimal places
2. end-of-period cash flows
3. 1 payment and compounding per period

5. **Signs on Cash Flows**

The cash flows, present values, and future values provided by the calculators will have a + or – sign attached. The convention is that cash inflows are preceded by a + sign and cash outflows are preceded by a – sign. In order to have the correct sign associated with a problem answer, you must enter data with the appropriate sign.

To indicate a cash outflow of $1,000 on either calculator, the following keystrokes should be used:

1,000 $\boxed{+/-}$

BASIC TIME VALUE OF MONEY PROCEDURE

Any time value of money problem that is solved with a financial calculator involves the following five variables:

1. the number of periods: $\boxed{N}$
2. the interest rate per year: $\boxed{I/Y}$
3. the payment amount: $\boxed{PMT}$
4. the future value: $\boxed{FV}$
5. the present value: $\boxed{PV}$

In order to solve a problem, you must enter the value of the four variables that you know and then solve for the unknown value of the fifth variable.

CALCULATION OF TABLE COMPOUNDING AND DISCOUNTING FACTORS

If you wish to solve time value of money problems using the format shown in Chapter 5, you need to calculate the compounding and discounting factors for the following formulas from Chapter 5:

Eq. (2): FV = (Cash Flow) $(CF_{K,N})$
Eq. (4): PV = (Cash Flow) $(DF_{K,N})$
Eq. (7): FV = (Annual Cash Flow) $(ACF_{K,N})$
Eq. (8): PV = (Annual Cash Flow) $(ADF_{K,N})$

Since the table values show three decimal places, the calculator should also be set for three decimal places:

BAII Plus
1. $\boxed{2^{nd}}$ $\boxed{Format}$
2. 3 $\boxed{ENTER}$
3. $\boxed{CE/C}$ $\boxed{CE/C}$

HP-10B
1. $\boxed{}$ $\boxed{DISP}$
2. 3
3. $\boxed{C}$

1. $CF_{K,N}$: Table I

   Problem: $CF_{0.10,5} = ?$

   Keystrokes: **BAII Plus**   **HP-10B**

	BAII Plus	HP-10B
1.	1 +/- PV	1. 1 +/- PV
2.	5 N	2. 5 N
3.	10 I/Y	3. 10 I/YR
4.	0 PMT	4. 0 PMT
5.	CPT FV	5. FV

   Answer: FV = 1.611   1.611

2. $ACF_{K,N}$: Table II

   Problem: $ACF_{0.10,5} = ?$

   Keystrokes: **BAII Plus**   **HP-10B**

	BAII Plus	HP-10B
1.	1 +/- PMT	1. 1 +/- PMT
2.	5 N	2. 5 N
3.	10 I/Y	3. 10 I/YR
4.	0 PV	4. 0 PV
5.	CPT FV	5. FV

   Answer: FV = 6.105   6.105

3. $DF_{K,N}$: Table III

   Problem: $DF_{0.10,5} = ?$

   Keystrokes: **BAII Plus**   **HP-10B**

	BAII Plus	HP-10B
1.	1 +/- FV	1. 1 +/- FV
2.	5 N	2. 5 N
3.	10 I/Y	3. 10 I/YR
4.	0 PMT	4. 0 PMT
5.	CPT PV	5. PV

   Answer: PV = 0.621   0.621

4. $ADF_{K,N}$: Table IV

   Problem: $ADF_{0.10,5} = ?$

   Keystrokes: **BAII Plus**   **HP-10B**

	BAII Plus	HP-10B
1.	1 +/- PMT	1. 1 +/- PMT
2.	5 N	2. 5 N
3.	10 I/Y	3. 10 I/YR
4.	0 FV	4. 0 FV
5.	CPT PV	5. PV

   Answer: PV = 3.791   3.791

SOLUTION OF TIME VALUE OF MONEY PROBLEMS

NOTE: The following problems were taken from various Self-Study Quizzes contained at the end of each chapter in the text. The problem answers obtained from the calculator may differ slightly from those shown in the Self-Study Quiz Solutions due to differences in the rounding of compounding factors and discounting factors.

1. **Future Value of a Lump Sum**

    Problem: Compute the future value in two years of $5,000 deposited into a savings account that pays 12% interest:

    a. compounded annually (Chapter 5, problem 1a)
    b. compounded monthly (Chapter 5, problem 1b)

    a. **Keystrokes:** *BAII Plus*   *HP-10B*

1. 5,000 [+/-] [PV]	1. 5,000 [+/-] [PV]
2. 2 [N]	2. 2 [N]
3. 12 [I/Y]	3. 12 [I/YR]
4. 0 [PMT]	4. 0 [PMT]
5. [CPT] [FV]	5. [FV]

    Answer: FV = $6,272.00 $6,272.00

    b. **Keystrokes:** *BAII Plus*   *HP-10B*

1. 5,000 [+/-] [PV]	1. 5,000 [+/-] [PV]
2. 2 [×] 12 [=] [N]	2. 2 [×] 12 [=] [N]
3. 12 [÷] 12 [=] [I/Y]	3. 12 [÷] 12 [=] [I/YR]
4. 0 [PMT]	4. 0 [PMT]
5. [CPT] [FV]	5. [FV]

    Answer: FV = $6,348.67 $6,348.67

    This problem requires that the number of years be multiplied by 12 (the frequency of compounding) in step 2 and the annual interest rate be divided by 12 in step 3 to adjust for monthly compounding.

2. **Effective Interest Rate**

    Problem: What is the effective interest rate for 12% annual interest compounded monthly? (Chapter 5, problem 2)

    Keystrokes: *BAII Plus*   *HP-10B*

    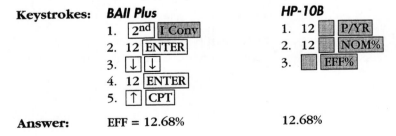

1. [2nd] [I Conv]	1. 12 [P/YR]
2. 12 [ENTER]	2. 12 [NOM%]
3. [↓] [↓]	3. [EFF%]
4. 12 [ENTER]	
5. [↑] [CPT]	

    Answer: EFF = 12.68%   12.68%

3. **Present Value of a Lump Sum**

   Problem: What is the present value of $400,000 to be received in eight years at an opportunity cost of 12% per year? (Chapter 5, problem 3a)

   Keystrokes: **BAII Plus**   **HP-10B**

1.	400,000 FV		1.	400,000 FV
2.	8 N		2.	8 N
3.	12 I/Y		3.	12 I/YR
4.	0 PMT		4.	0 PMT
5.	CPT PV		5.	PV

   Answer: −$161,553.29   −$161,553.29

4. **Present Value of an Annuity**

   Problem: What is the present value of an annuity of $2,000 per year for nine years at an opportunity cost of 10.75% per annum? (Chapter 5, problem 4b)

   Keystrokes: **BAII Plus**   **HP-10B**

1.	2,000 PMT		1.	2,000 PMT
2.	8 N		2.	8 N
3.	10.75 I/Y		3.	10.75 I/YR
4.	0 FV		4.	0 FV
5.	CPT PV		5.	PV

   Answer: PV = −$10,384.65   −$10,384.65

5. **Loan Payments**

   Problem: What is the monthly payment on a $75,000 loan that will be repaid in equal monthly installments over two years if the annual interest rate is 18%? (Chapter 5, problem 5b)

   Keystrokes: **BAII Plus**   **HP-10B**

1.	75,000 PV		1.	75,000 PV
2.	2 × 12 = N		2.	2 × 12 = N
3.	18 ÷ 12 = I/Y		3.	18 ÷ 12 = I/Y
4.	0 FV		4.	0 FV
5.	CPT PMT		5.	PMT

   Answer: PMT = −$3,744.31   −$3,744.31

Notice that both the number of time periods (step 2) and the interest rate per period (step 3) are adjusted for monthly payments and compounding.

6. **Loan Interest Rate**

   Problem: What is the interest rate on a $75,000 two-year loan that requires monthly payments of $3,531? (Chapter 5, problem 5a)

   Keystrokes: **BAII Plus** | **HP-10B**

   BAII Plus
   1. 75,000 [PV]
   2. 2 [×] 12 [=] [N]
   3. 3,531 [+/-] [PMT]
   4. 0 [FV]
   5. [CPT] [I/Y] [×] 12 [=]

   HP-10B
   1. 75,000 [PV]
   2. 2 [×] 12 [=] [N]
   3. 3,531 [+/-] [PMT]
   4. 0 [FV]
   5. [I/YR] [×] 12 [=]

   Answer: I/Y = 12.00   12.01

   The monthly interest rate in step 5 was annualized by multiplying it by 12.

7. **Investment Time Period**

   Problem: If you invest $161,600 today in an investment that earns 12% per year, how long will it take for the investment to accumulate to $400,000? (Chapter 5, problem 3a)

   Keystrokes: **BAII Plus** | **HP-10B**

   BAII Plus
   1. 161,600 [+/-] [PV]
   2. 12 [I/Y]
   3. 400,000 [FV]
   4. 0 [PMT]
   5. [CPT] [N]

   HP-10B
   1. 161,600 [+/-] [PV]
   2. 12 [I/YR]
   3. 400,000 [FV]
   4. 0 [PMT]
   5. [N]

   Answer: N = 8.00 Years   8.00 Years

8. **Bond Valuation**

   Problem: A bond has an 8.5% coupon and a par value of $1,000. Its yield-to-maturity is 10.0%, and its term-to-maturity is 15 years. If the bond pays interest semi-annually, what is its price? (Chapter 7, problem 1)

   Keystrokes: **BAII Plus** | **HP-10B**

   BAII Plus
   1. 1,000 [FV]
   2. 1,000 [×] .085 [÷] 2 [=] [PMT]
   3. 15 [×] 2 [=] [N]
   4. 10 [÷] 2 [=] [I/Y]
   5. [CPT] [PV]

   HP-10B
   1. 1,000 [FV]
   2. 1,000 [×] .085 [÷] 2 [=] [PMT]
   3. 15 [×] 2 [=] [N]
   4. 10 [÷] 2 [=] [I/Y]
   5. [PV]

   Answer: PV = -$884.71   -$884.71

   The size of the coupon interest (step 2), number of periods (step 3), and periodic interest rate (step 4) are all adjusted for semiannual payment of interest.

9. **Bond Yield-To-Maturity**

Problem: A 15-year bond with an 8.5% coupon and a $1,000 per value has a price of $884.31. If the bond pays interest semiannually, what is the bond's yield-to-maturity (YTM)? (Chapter 7, problem 1)

Keystrokes: *BAII Plus*   *HP-10B*

1. 1,000 $\boxed{\text{FV}}$ 1. 1,000 $\boxed{\text{FV}}$
2. 1,000 $\boxed{\times}$.085 $\boxed{\div}$ 2 $\boxed{=}$ $\boxed{\text{PMT}}$ 2. 1,000 $\boxed{\times}$ .085 $\boxed{\div}$ 2 $\boxed{=}$ $\boxed{\text{PMT}}$
3. 15 $\boxed{\times}$ 2 $\boxed{=}$ $\boxed{\text{N}}$ 3. 15 $\boxed{\times}$ 2 $\boxed{=}$ $\boxed{\text{N}}$
4. 884.31 $\boxed{+/-}$ $\boxed{\text{PV}}$ 4. 884.31 $\boxed{+/-}$ $\boxed{\text{PV}}$
5. $\boxed{\text{CPT}}$ $\boxed{\text{I/Y}}$ $\boxed{\times}$ 2 $\boxed{=}$ 5. $\boxed{\text{I/YR}}$ $\boxed{\times}$ 2 $\boxed{=}$

Answer: I/Y = 10.01%   10.01%

Adjustments are made to the interest coupon (step 2), the number of periods (step 3), and the periodic interest rate (step 5) to account for the semiannual payment of interest.

10. **Net Present Value (NPV) and Internal Rate of Return (IRR)**

Problem: Given an RRR of 10% and the following cash flows, what is the investment's NPV and IRR? (Chapter 9, problems 1 and 2)

Year	Cash Flow
0	-$100,000
1	20,000
2	100,000
3	10,000

Keystrokes: *BAII Plus*   *HP-10B*

1. $\boxed{\text{CF}}$ $\boxed{\text{2}^{\text{nd}}}$ $\boxed{\text{CLR Work}}$ 1. $\boxed{\text{CLEAR ALL}}$
2. 100,000 $\boxed{+/-}$ $\boxed{\text{ENTER}}$ $\boxed{\downarrow}$ 2. 100,000 $\boxed{+/-}$ $\boxed{\text{CFj}}$
3. 20,000 $\boxed{\text{ENTER}}$ $\boxed{\downarrow}$ 3. 20,000 $\boxed{\text{CFj}}$
4. 1 $\boxed{\text{ENTER}}$ $\boxed{\downarrow}$ 4. 1 $\boxed{\text{Nj}}$
5. 100,000 $\boxed{\text{ENTER}}$ $\boxed{\downarrow}$ 5. 100,000 $\boxed{\text{CFj}}$
6. 1 $\boxed{\text{ENTER}}$ $\boxed{\downarrow}$ 6. 1 $\boxed{\text{Nj}}$
7. 10,000 $\boxed{\text{ENTER}}$ $\boxed{\downarrow}$ 7. 10,000 $\boxed{\text{CFj}}$
8. 1 $\boxed{\text{ENTER}}$ $\boxed{\downarrow}$ 8. 1 $\boxed{\text{Nj}}$
9. $\boxed{\text{IRR}}$ $\boxed{\text{CPT}}$ 9. $\boxed{\text{IRR/YR}}$

Answer: IRR = 14.74%   14.74%

10. $\boxed{\text{NPV}}$ 10 $\boxed{\text{ENTER}}$ $\boxed{\downarrow}$ 10. 10 $\boxed{\text{I/YR}}$
11. $\boxed{\text{CPT}}$ 11. $\boxed{\text{NPV}}$

Answer: NPV = $8,339.59 $8,339.59

The number 1 shown in steps 4, 6, and 8 is simply the number of periods that the cash flow entered in the previous step (3, 5, or 7) repeats itself. The NPV obtained from the calculator differs from the Self-Study Quiz Solution in the text due to rounding differences.

Appendix B

Answers to Selected Problems

CHAPTER 2

1. Net worth = $18,870,000

3. a. Current liabilities = $18,000,000
   b. Inventories = $9,000,000

5. a. 1996 net income = $6,000,000
   b. 1997 dividends = $2,500,000
   c. 12/98 retained earnings = $84,250,000

7. Dividends in 2000 = $145 million

9. Net cash flow from operating activities = $215
   Net cash flow from operations and investng = $165
   Net cash flow from financing activities = $(160)

11. 1999 Dividends = $160

13.

	1998	1999
Current ratio:	1.04	0.79
Acid-test ratio:	0.61	0.42
Avg. collection period:	25 days	32 days
Inventory turnover:	5.65	4.94
Fixed asset turnover:	2.59	1.95
Total asset turnover	1.64	1.32
Debt ratio:	0.47	0.54
Interest coverage:	15.5	4.2
Gross margin:	0.47	0.42
Net margin:	0.096	0.031
ROA:	0.305	0.095
ROE:	0.296	0.089

15. a. Sources
       Funds from operations = $650,000
       Total = $950,000
    Uses
       Increase in plant + equipment = $150,000
       Dividends paid = $200,000
       Total = $950,000
    b. Major sources: funds from operations
       Major uses: increase in assets, decrease in notes payable, dividends
       Non-normal item: decrease in notes payable

17. a. Net cash flow from operating activities = $600,000
       Net cash flow from operations and investng = $450,000
       Net cash flow from financing activities = $(400,000)
    b. Positive Aspects: Net income and depreciation were a large source of cash. The firm has expanded plant and equipment to maintain its production capacity.
       Negative Aspects: Large investment in receivables and inventories suggests possible overinvestment in current assets. Financing activities have used rather than provided cash.

19. a. Sources
       Funds from operations = $91,400
       Total = $201,000
    Uses
       Increase in plant + equipment = $47,300
       Dividends paid = $53,500
       Total = $201,000
    b. Major sources: large increase in accounts payable and funds from operations. Major uses: large increases in accounts receivable, plant & equipment, and dividends.
    c. dividends, accounts receivable, and accounts payable

21. a.

	1998	1999	Industry Average
Current ratio:	2.0	1.52	2.10
Acid-test ratio:	0.95	0.77	1.10
Avg. collection period:	25 days	34 days	30
Inventory turnover:	4.96	5.29	6.0
Fixed asset turnover:	4.81	4.90	4.0
Total asset turnover:	2.09	2.03	2.0
Debt ratio:	0.56	0.59	0.45
Interest coverage:	6.72	4.94	6.0
Gross margin:	0.30	0.25	0.33
Net margin:	0.06	0.04	0.06
ROA:	0.30	0.19	0.12
ROE:	0.29	0.20	0.22

   b. The primary weakness of Valco is the deterioration of profitability due to a decline in gross and net margins. Liquidity is declining because accounts payable are the primary source of financing. Its debt ratio is high and interest coverage is falling. The main strength of Valco is its fixed and total asset turnovers.

CHAPTER 3

1. a. Investing = 653 of Real Assets   c. Savings deficit
   b. Saving = 519 of Net Worth

3. a. Nominal interest rate = 20%
   b. Expected real interest rate = 10%

5. a. r = 19%   b. actual r_R = 9%

7. a. (15%)(1 − T) = 12%   b. (15%)(1 − 0.60) = 6%

9. a. Default risk premium is 9.38% − 8.95% = 0.43%.
   b. Yield spread between Aaa and Baa bonds of similar maturities is a reflection of investors' perceptions of higher default risk on the Baa bonds.
   c. Yield spread has two components: the longer maturity of the Aaa bonds and the higher risk of default.
      Maturity Risk Premium = 1.40%
      Default Risk Premium = 0.43%
      Total Yield Spread = 1.83%

11. Equivalent Pre-Tax Yield on Municipal Bonds = 9.43%
    They would be rated Baa because 9.43% is close to the Baa
    corporate bond yield of 9.40%.

13. Bond Issue = 526,316 bonds at $1,000 selling price.

15. a. The 1981 yield curve is downward sloping.
    The 1993 yield curve is upward sloping.
    b. In 1981, investors expected short-term rates to decline
    after 1981. In 1993, investors expected short-term rates
    to rise after 1993.

CHAPTER 4

1. a. £7,500 = $12,245.25   c. ¥300,000 = $2,459.10
   b. DM10,000 = $5,658

3. a. $FD_{£/\$}$ = −1.49%   c. $FD_{¥/\$}$ = +5.37%
   b. $FD_{DM/\$}$ = +2.12%

5. a. $IER_{£/\$}$ = £.6125/$ c. $IER_{¥/\$}$ = ¥121.996/$
   b. $IER_{DM/\$}$ = DM1.7674/$

7. a. $DER_{£/DM}$ = £0.3497/DM
   b. $DER_{£/¥}$ = £0.005107/¥
   c. $DER_{DM/¥}$ = DM0.01460/¥

9. Based on the answers to Problem 3, the Japanese yen was
   expected to be the strongest currency because it had the
   largest 90-day forward premium against the U.S. dollar. The
   British pound has a forward discount against both the yen
   and the deutschemark. The deutschemark itself, however,
   has a forward discount against the yen. Since all three currencies have a forward discount against the yen, it must be
   the strongest currency.

11. a. Transaction Risk = −DM19,260
    b. This represents a potential gain for Bosch Industries.
    c. The British firm faces no transaction risk.

13. a. Anticipated Earnings = $9,999,999
    Consolidated Earnings = $8,939,019
    Translation Risk = $1,060,980
    b. Actual Earnings = $9,456,123
    Actual Earnings are less than Anticipated Earnings.

15. a. A150,000 = $151,500   c. Lit1,000,000 = $578.70
    b. DKr7,500 = $1,114.50

17. a. FR = $.7398/SF   b. SF2,027,575

19. a. Amount at Sale = $434,913
    b. Covered Payment Amount = $430,595

CHAPTER 5

1. a. FV_{10} = $1,219   b. FV_{10} = $2,594
3. a. PV = $820   b. PV = $386
5. a. FV_{10} = $1,100   b. FV_{10} = $2,594
7. a. PV = $909   b. PV = $386
9. a. PV = $50,000   b. PV = $10,000
11. FV = $1,270
13. Annual Cash Flow = FF34,514
15. Annuity PV = DM5,650   Lump Sum PV = DM5,152
    Annuity of DM1,000 is more valuable.

17. a. FV = $830.06   b. FV = $1,004.37
19. PV = $16,757
21. Annual Cash Flow = £6,694.34
23. K = 9%

25.
Year	1	5
Amount owed at beginning of year	$10,000	$2,398
PLUS		
Interest @ 10%	1,000	240
EQUALS		
Amount owed at end of year	11,000	2,638
MINUS		
Amount paid at end of year		
EQUALS	(2,638)	(2,638)
Amount owed at beginning of next year	$ 8,362	—

27. PV = $227,460
    Cost of New Machine = $240,000
    Since cost is greater than value of savings, Lane should not
    purchase the new machine.

29. Maximum Annual Payments = $3,600
    Purchase Price = $10,933

31. Since PV of the 20 annual payments is $14,845,600, you
    would accept a lump sum equal to that amount.

33. Indifference Point = $34,586

35. 10 Years

CHAPTER 6

1. PV = FF614.50

3. a. An increase in the estimated inflation by 2% would
    increase the RRR (K) from 10% to 12%.
    b. Revised answer to Problem 1: P = FF565
    Revised answer to Problem 2: PV = FF504.50

5. a. PV = FF33,520   c. PV = FF62,590
   b. PV = FF50,190   d. PV = FF66,667

7. K = 15%

9. σ = $158,114   CV = 0.316

11. Opportunity X
    $\overline{X}$ = 1,000   σ = 774.60   CV = .775
    Opportunity Y
    $\overline{X}$ = 1,000   σ = 154.92   CV = .155

13. Opportunity Y
    $\overline{X}$ = 1,000   σ = 154.92   CV = .155
    Opportunity Z
    $\overline{X}$ = 1,000   σ = 126.49   CV = .126

15. Since the PV of the expected cash flow is only $522,000,
    Macedonia should sell the oil well to Scandia for $900,000.

17. $β_p$ = 1.115

19. b. β = 1.38
    c. For each 1% change in the market return, we expect GF's
    return to change by 1.38%.

21. a. K = .161   b. K = .182   c. K = .212   d. K = .244

23. Market Risk Premium = 10.8%

25. $β_j$ = 1.6

CHAPTER 7

1. a. $V_B = DM865.60$ c. $V_B = DM981.56$
    b. $V_B = DM920.58$
    d. Value approaches par as term-to-maturity decreases.

3. a. $V_B = \$855.40$ c. $V_B = \$851.54$
    b. $V_B = \$852.40$
    d. Since the effective interest rate increases with the frequency of payment, the present value of future cash flows must decline.

5. a. Current Yield = 9%   Capital Gains Yield = 0%
    b. Current Yield = 9.75%   Capital Gains Yield = 0.25%
    c. Current Yield = 8.44%   Capital Gains Yield = –0.44%

7. a. HPY = 18.34%   b. HPY = 11%   c. HPY = 4.4%

9. a. $V_B = \$588.70$ c. $V_B = \$742.90$
    b. $V_B = \$634.45$ d. $V_B = \$1,000$
    e. V_B approaches par as the maturity date approaches because the decrease in term-to-maturity makes the price less sensitive to changes in YTM.

11. Current Yield = 7.82%   Capital Gains Yield = 5.18%

13. Current Yield = 13.76%   Capital Gains Yield = –0.76%

15. a. $V_P = \$58.33$ b. $K_P = 14\%$

17. a. 2,000,000 shares   b. Proceeds = $207,400,000

19. a. $V_E = \$32.00$ b. $K_E = 16\%$

21. a. Capital Gains Yield = 5%   Dividend Yield = 11%
    b. Capital Gains Yield = 10%   Dividend Yield = 6%
    c. Capital Gains Yield = –5%   Dividend Yield = 21%

23. a. $K_E = 16\%$
    b. Capital Gains Yield = 12%   Dividend Yield = 4%

25. $P_0 = \$29.12$

27. a. $V_A = \$7,843$
    b. At the price of $10,675, the YTM of the annuity is 8%. The market is not efficient because the annuity sells to yield less than the RRR.

29. $P_0 = \$3.29$

31. a. $P_0/E_1 = 3.95$ b. "Trailing" P/E = 3.75

CHAPTER 8

1. You could earn arbitrage profits by buying the copper in Chicago and selling it in Zurich.

3. A trader could buy oil in Tokyo for delivery in 6 months and simultaneously sell oil in New York for delivery in 6 months. The profit could be guaranteed by covering this transaction in the currency futures market.

5. a. ESR $(1)_{FIM/DM}$ = FIM 4.155/DM
    b. ESR $(2)_{FIM/DM}$ = FIM 4.317/DM
    c. ESR $(3)_{FIM/DM}$ = FIM 4.484/DM

7. $I_D = 2.7\%$

9. $SR_{DM/\pounds}$ = DM2.175/£ $ASR_{DM/\pounds}$ = DM2.102/£

11. a. $ Rent = $1,500   c. Peso Inflation = 6.3%
    b. $ Rent = $1,787   Dollar Inflation = 19.1%

d. The dollar inflation in the rent exceeded the peso inflation because the dollar weakened against the peso as a result of a U.S. inflation rate of 19.1%.

13. $I_P^* = 10.4\%$

CHAPTER 9

1. Payback Period = 3.3 Years

3. a. Investment I: AROI = 23.3%
       Investment II: AROI = 16.25%
    b. Investment I: Payback = 3.2 years
       Investment II: Payback = 1.82 years

5. $NPV_A = -\$8,322$, $NPV_B = \$5,084$

7. a. NPV = SF38,130   b. IRR = 36.2%

9. NPV = $480,155

11. IRR = 3.8%, Since IRR < RRR, reject project.

13. a. K = 12.42%
    b. According to the NPV criterion, A is preferable to B at any RRR less than 12.42%.

15. a. $NPV_A = \$990$, $NPV_B = -\$645$
       Investment A is preferable at K = 17%.
    b. $NPV_A = \$35,000$, $NPV_B = \$39,000$
       Investment B is preferable at K = 0%.
    c. At K = 10%: $NPV_A = NPV_B$

17. NPV = $481,100, PVI = 2.41

19. a. Should accept Projects ABC.
    b. Increase in firm value associated with ABC is £590,000.
    c. Opportunity Cost = £500,000. This answer is based on acceptance of Project F and rejection of Project A.

CHAPTER 10

1. All figures in millions.

a.		
Sales		$30.0
–Labor		–10.0
–Material		– 8.0
–Other		– 6.0
–Depreciation		– 2.0
EBT		$ 4.0
–Tax (0.4)		– 1.6
EAT		$2.4
+Depreciation		2.0
Cash Flow		$4.4

    b. Cash flow = ($30)(1 – 0.4) – (10)(1 – 0.4)
       – (8)(1 – 0.4) – (6)(1 – 0.4) – (2)(–0.4)
       = $18 – 6 – 4.8 – 3.6 + 0.8 = 4.4

3. a. Building Cost—irrelevant, sunk cost
    b. Depreciation—irrelevant, same for both
    c. Salvage Value—irrelevant, same for both
    d. Lease Payment—relevant, incremental
    e. Property Tax—irrelevant, same for both
    f. Maintenance—relevant, incremental
    g. Rental Expense—relevant, incremental

5. Average Tax Rate = 34%, Marginal Tax Rate = 38%

7. a. After-Tax Proceeds = $12,000
   b. After-Tax Proceeds = $7,200

9. a.

1991	$2,000,000	1996	$1,000,000
1992	0	1997	$2,000,000
1993	$2,500,000	1998	$5,000,000
1994	$1,000,000		

b.

1991	$2,000,000	1996	$1,000,000
1992	0	1997	$2,000,000
1993	0	1998	$5,000,000
1994	$800,000		

c.

1991	$2,000,000	1996	$700,000
1992	0	1997	$2,000,000
1993	0	1998	$5,000,000
1994	0		

d.

1991	$2,000,000	1996	0
1992	0	1997	$1,800,000
1993	0	1998	$5,000,000
1994	0		

11. NPV = $329,050

13. NPV = $3,577,200

15. NPV = $73,522

17. NPV = $52,010

19. a. Initial Period Cash Flow: −$12,500,000
    b. Project Life Annual Cash Flow: $2,600,000
    c. Project Termination Cash Flow: $2,500,000
    d. NPV = $7,179,400

21. NPV = £4,124,400

23. a. NPV = −$78,150   b. Maximum Price = $421,850

25. a. Annual Real Savings = $2,000,000

   b.

Year	Nominal Pre-Tax Savings
1	$2,100,000
2	2,205,000
3	2,315,250
4	2,431,013
5	2,552,563

   c.

Year	Nominal After-Tax Savings
1	$1,260,000
2	1,323,000
3	1,389,150
4	1,458,608
5	1,531,538

   d. NPV = −$345,696

27. NPV = −$11.515 million

29. Annualized PV_X = −$60,209, Annualized PV_Y = −$71,243

31. a. NPV_A = $8,150, NPV_B = $9,840   Both should be accepted since both have positive NPVs.
    b. $NPV_{B,5}$ = −$7,830   Investment A should be chosen since it has a positive and higher NPV than B.
    c. Annualized PV_A = $2,261, Annualized PV_B = $1,847 Investment A should be chosen due to its higher annualized PV.

CHAPTER 11

1. a. EBIT for Q = 180,000: EBIT= −$300,000

   EBIT for Q = 220,000: EBIT = $300,000
   b. Breakeven point = 200,000 units

3. a. Current Q' = 60,000 units, New Process Q' = 50,000 units
   b. Current DOL = 1.67, New Process DOL = 1.50

5. a. Variable CGS = $15.00/ unit, Fixed CGS = $400,000
   b. Variable S&G = $4.00/unit, Fixed S&G = $600,000
   c. DOL = 4.13

7. At Q = 200,000: NPV = $15,000,000
   At Q = 220,000: NPV = $18,755,400
   At Q = 180,000: NPV = $11,244,600

9. a. and b. Optimistic NPV = $5,963,052, Expected NPV = $1,571,280, Pessimistic NPV = −$3,044,562

11. a. and b. Pessimistic NPV = −$215,980, Expected NPV = $153,620 Optimistic NPV = $362,180

13. a. and b. Pessimistic NPV = −$3,853,180, Expected NPV = $7,179,400, Optimistic NPV = $12,962,736

15. a. and b. Pessimistic NPV = −DM6,754,200, Expected NPV = DM2,398,800, Optimistic NPV = DM10,492,425

17.

Outcome	Total NPV	Probability	NPV × Probability
Base Only	−$2,000,000	0.18	−$360,000
Base + D1	−1,000,000	0.12	−120,000
Base + D2	0	0.42	0
Base + D1 + D2	1,000,000	0.28	280,000
		Total 1.00	−$200,000

CHAPTER 12

1.

Market Value	Decision
a. <$1,000 (Par)	Open Market Purchase
b. $1,000	Open Market Purchase
c. $1,085.54	Open Market Purchase
d. $1,294.98	Forced Redemption

3. Since $ADF_{0.15,7}$ = 4.160, the rate of interest is 15%.

5. Loan = $5,000,000

7. a. Annual Interest Payment = $200,000 (Years 1–5), Principal Payment = $2,000,000 (Year 5)
   b. Annual Payment = $1,055,131 (Years 1–5)
   c. Payment Schedule: $1,255,131 (Years 1–4); $3,255,131 (Year 5)

9. Unamortized Portion Payments: Annual Interest = $1,600,000 (Years 1–7), Principal Payment = $20,000,000 (Year 7)
   Amortized Portion Payments: Annual Payment = $3,841,721 (Years 1–7)
   Payment Schedule: $5,441,721 (Years 1–6); $25,441,721 (Year 7)

11. Third payment = $638,000

15. Since $DF_{0.12,6}$ = 0.507, r = 12%.

17. Principal = $1,481,481,400

19. Value of Lease Side Effects = −$45,180

21. Value of Lease Side Effects = $362,400

CHAPTER 13

1. Effective Tax Rate = 12%

3. A marginal tax rate of 40% favors the preferred stock. The 70% dividend exclusion more than offsets the higher pre-tax yield on the bonds.

5. a. $W = P_o = \$48$
   b. $W = P_E + R = 46.67 + 1.33 = \$48$
   c. $W = P_E + (P_E - S)/5 = 46.67 + (46.67 - 40)/5 = \$48$
   d. $W = P_E + R = 46.67 + 1.33 = \$48$
   e. $W = P_E = \$46.67$

7. a.

Before:	700 shares	=	FF42,000
After:	700 shares	=	FF41,650
	700 rights	=	350
			FF42,000

   b.

Before:	700 shares	=	FF42,000
After:	700 shares	=	FF40,250
	700 rights	=	1,750
			FF42,000

9. a. Change = FF5,600 b. Change = FF4,000

11. a. 1) 800,000 shares   3) $P_E = \$148.15$
       2) 12.5 rights per new share   4) $R = \$1.85$
    b. 1) 1,000,000 shares   3) $P_E = \$145.45$
       2) 10 rights per new share   4) $R = \$4.55$

13.

Common Stock at SF100 par value	SF 100,000
Capital-in-excess-of-par	1,400,000
Net Worth	SF1,500,000

15. a. Book value = $9.00 per share
    b. Selling price = $4.00 per share

17. a. $V_C = \$705$ b. $V_C = \$900$

19. a.

Stock Price	V_C	V_B	V_{TC}
$25	$ 750	$900	$ 900
30	900	900	900
35	1,050	900	1,050
40	1,200	900	1,200

   b.

Stock Price	CP
$25	$120
30	150
35	135
40	90

21. a. $V_B = \$937.25$
    b.

Stock Price	V_C	V_B	V_{TC}
$45	$ 900	$937.25	$ 937.25
50	1,000	937.25	1,000
55	1,100	937.25	1,100
60	1,200	937.25	1,200

   c.

Stock Price	CP
$45	$52.75
50	50
55	25
60	10

   d. Minimum Price to Force Conversion = $56

CHAPTER 14

1. a. EBIT = $42,000,000   d. ROE = 34.8%
   b. EAT = $20,880,000   e. EPS = $8.35
   c. ROA = 35%

3.

	Low Leverage	High Leverage
a. ROA = 23.3%		= 23.3%
b. EAT = SF300,000		= SF250,000
ROE = 15%		= 25%
c. EPS = SF3.00		= SF5.00

5. b. Breakeven EPS-EBIT point is EBIT = $300,000 and EPS = $1.00. At that EBIT, ROA is equal to the interest rate on debt (10%). When ROA = K_D, leverage does not affect the magnitude of EPS.

7. EBIT = £6,000,000

9. a. EPS = $3.75, ROE = 7.5%
   b. Increased leverage will increase expected EPS and ROE because the firm's ROA of 15% is greater than the pre-tax cost of debt of 12%.

11. a.

	Bad Year	Good Year
	No Leverage	
EPS	$2.50	$5.00
ROE	5.0%	10.0%
	25% Leverage	
EPS	$2.33	$5.67
ROE	4.67%	11.3%
	50% Leverage	
EPS	$2.00	$7.00
ROE	4%	14%

   b. The breakeven EBIT is the EBIT level at which ROA is equal to the interest rate on debt (12%): EBIT = $1,200,000

13. a. Common Stock Financing: EPS = $0.48, EPS = $1.28, EPS = $2.08: Debt Financing: EPS = $0.12, EPS = $1.32, EPS = $2.52
    b. The rule that the breakeven EBIT corresponds to the EBIT levels at which ROA = interest rate on debt does not hold in problems such as this when there is an old and a new debt issue with different interest rates.

15. a. Personal Leverage:

Government's Share =	$200,000
Lender's Share =	$ 28,000
Owner's Share =	$272,000

   Corporate Leverage:

Government's Share =	$200,000
Lender's Share =	$ 28,000
Owner's Share =	$272,000

   b. Both plans are identical from the shareholders' point of view.

17. Personal Leverage:

Lender's Share =	$20,000
Government's Share =	$40,000
Owner's Share =	$40,000

   Corporate Leverage:

Lender's Share =	$20,000
Government's Share =	$32,000
Owner's Share =	$48,000

   Difference in Owners' Share = $8,000

19. a. Repurchase Price = $65: Shares Repurchased = 230,769, New Stock Price = $73.54

Repurchase Price = $70: Shares Repurchased = 214,286, New Stock Price = $69.30
Repurchase Price = $75: Shares Repurchased = 200,000, New Stock Price = $66.00

b. ΔValue = $4,800,000

Repurchase Price = $65:

Shares Sold	= $1,153,845	(24%)
Shares Kept	= 3,645,388	(76%)
	$4,799,233	

Repurchase Price = $70:

Shares Sold	= $2,142,860	(45%)
Shares Kept	= 2,657,140	(55%)
	$4,800,000	

Repurchase Price = $75:

Shares Sold	= $3,000,000	(63%)
Shares Kept	= 1,800,000	(37%)
	$4,800,000	

21. a. $K_E = 13.2\%$ b. $V_L = \$400,000,000$ c. $K_U = 12\%$

CHAPTER 15

1. $K_A = 13\%$
3. a. $K_D = 5.85\%$ b. $K_D = 6.825\%$ c. $K_D = 8.29\%$
5. $K_P = 14.04\%$
7. $K_E = 12\%$
9. $K_A = 11.91\%$
11. Adjusted Outlay = $52,631,578
    Adjusted NPV = –$631,578
13. a. $K_A = 14\%$ b. $K_U = 12.8\%$
15. a. Current $K_A = 12\%$
    b. Both K_D and K_E have fallen by the same 4% as have market interest rates. The firm's capital structure (W_D and W_E) has remained constant since 1997.
    c. Since McGraw was using a discount rate that was high, the NPV estimates were biased downward. Thus, it is likely that McGraw rejected proposed investments that should have been accepted.
17. Federal Airlines: $P_0 = \$87.50$
    National Airlines: $P_0 = \$116.67$
19. For Jason Electronics: Estimated $K_U = 12.05\%$ (Average K_U of three software companies)
    Estimated $K_E = 12.73\%$, $K_A = 11.05\%$
21. $K_A = 17\%$

CHAPTER 16

1. a. Dividend per Share = $6.00   c. $PV_1 = \$60.00$
   b. $PV_0 = \$60.00$ d. HPY = 10%
3. a. Barnes HPY = 10%   b. Barnes A-T HPY = 6%
   Arnett HPY = 10%   Arnett A-T HPY = 6.2%
5. a. HPY = 15%   b. HPY = 15%
7. a. $HPY_A = 16.5\%$ b. After Tax $HPY_A = 12.75\%$
   $HPY_B = 20.0\%$ After Tax $HPY_B = 11.50\%$

9. a. Common Stock Financing: Dividend Income$_1$ = $400, Market Value$_1$ = $4,000, HPY = 10%
   Retained Earnings Financing: Dividend Income$_1$ = $0, Market Value$_1$ = $4,400, HPY = 10%
   b. To establish a dividend payout ratio of 0% in Year 1, the stockholder could reinvest all dividends in additional shares of stock:

11.

Year	1	2	3	4	5
a. Dividends	$2,000,000	$1,000,000	$2,000,000	$1,000,000	$1,000,000
b. Payout Ratio	67%	25%	50%	14%	33%
c. EPS	$2.00	$2.67	$2.67	$4.67	$2.00
DPS	$1.33	$ .67	$1.33	$ .67	$ .67

13. This Year: Surplus Earnings = SF7 million: Future Years: Surplus Earnings = SF5 million: Luzern should declare a regular dividend of SF5 million and an extra dividend of SF2 million. As an alternative to an extra dividend, Luzern could repurchase SF2 million of its shares.

15.

	Before	After
a. Market Value for Share	¥4,500	¥3,750
b. Total Value of Shares	¥450,000	¥450,000

17.

Year	1	2	3	4	5
a. Required Equity	$60	$60	$ 0	$ 0	$80
b. Debt Ratio	48.2%	46.5%	52.1%	52.1%	50%

19. a. Dividends = $270, Retained Earnings = $150, Common Stock = $100

Year	1	2	3	4	5
b. Dividend	54	54	54	54	54
Retained Earnings	$ 46	$ 26	$ 6	$26	$46
c. Debt			$150		
Retained Earnings	$ 46	$ 26	$ 6	$26	$46
Common Stock		100			
Total Financing	$ 46	$126	$156	$26	$46
Surplus (Deficit) Financing	$(14)	$ 52	$128	$54	$ 0

21.

Year	1	2	3	4
a. Dividend	$ 15	$ 15	$15	$15
Retained Earnings	$ 10	$ 15	$15	$20
b. Surplus (Deficit)	$(10)	$(25)	$ 5	0
c. Debt Ratio	39.6%	39.0%	40.7%	40%

23.

Year	1	2	3	4
a. Dividend	0	$50	$10	$40
b. Surplus	0	$10	0	0
c. Debt Ratio	31.9%	36%	34.3%	33.3%

25.

Year	1	2	3	4
a. Retained Earnings	$ 5	$15	$25	$35
Common Stock	40	0	0	0
b. Surplus (Deficit)	$ 5	$30	$(5)	$ 0
c. Debt Ratio	31.7%	35.3%	34.4%	33.3%

CHAPTER 17

1. a. Permanent Assets = £250,000,000
   b. Maximum Temporary Assets = £30,000,000
3. a. Maximum Temporary Financing = £30,000,000
   Maximum Negotiated Current Liabilities Required = £22,500,000

b. Maximum Temporary Financing Required
= £12,000,000
Maximum Negotiated Current Liabilities Required
= £4,500,000

5. a. Spontaneous Current Liabilities = ¥1.8 billion
b. Temporary Spontaneous Current Liabilities
= ¥1.05 billion
Permanent Spontaneous Current Liabilities
= ¥0.75 billion
c. Negotiated Current Liabilities = ¥5.95 billion

7. a. Long-Term Debt Required = ¥12.75 billion
b. Long-Term Debt Required = ¥8.75 billion

9. a. Permanent Assets = $31,000,000
Maximum Temporary Assets = $14,000,000
b. Permanent Spontaneous Current Liabilities = $3,000,000
c. Permanent Financing = $31,000,000

11. a. Permanent Financing Required = $40,000,000
b. Maximum Temporary Financing Required = $6,000,000

13. a. Permanent Financing Required = $42,000,000
Maximum Temporary Financing Required = $4,000,000
b. Maximum Negotiated Current Liabilities = $2,800,000
c. Maximum Excess Permanent Financing = $2,000,000
This excess will occur in April and November.

15. Excess Financing = $600,000

17. a. Permanent Assets = $103,000,000
Maximum Temporary Assets = $20,000,000
b. Permanent Financing Required = $103,000,000
Long-Term Debt = $48,600,000
c. Temporary Financing Required = $20,000,000
Negotiated Current Liabilities = $14,000,000

CHAPTER 18

1. Cost of Trade Credit = 37.11%

3. a. APR = 55.7%   b. APR = 24.5%   c. APR = 7.3%

5. a. APR = 49.0%   b. APR = 24.5%

7. a. APR = 0% because trade credit is costless during the discount period.
b. APR = 36.7%, EIR = 43.9%
c. APR = 146.9%, EIR = 328.0%

9. a. Loan = DM1,666,667   b. Loan = DM1,764,706
c. Loan = DM2,000,000

11. EIR = APR since the Turnover = 1 for each of the three loans.

13. Bank A: Loan = FF13,333,333, APR = 13.33%
Bank B: Loan = FF11,111,111, APR = 13.33%
The banks are offering identical effective interest rates.

15. a. APR = 12.2%, EIR = 12.2%
b. APR = 12.2%, EIR = 12.2%

17. a. Commercial Paper Issue = $5,288,312
b. APR = 23.1%, EIR = 25.2%

19. Bank Loan: EIR = 14.0%
Commercial Paper: EIR = 22.2%

CHAPTER 19

1. Credit Policy Delay = 37 days

3. a. Accounts Receivable = $1,650,000
b. Accounts Receivable = $1,450,000
c. FA_R = $200,000

5. a. FA_R = DM300,000
b. Maximum Compensating Balance = DM300,000
c. Pretax Fee = DM83,333

7. NPV = £40,000

9. NPV = –$75,000

11. NPV = $140,000

13. Pretax Fee = $393,750

15. NPV = $250,000

17. Individual Bank CB = $100,000

CHAPTER 20

1. ACP = 36 days

3. a. 30 days: A/R = $3,750,000
40 days: A/R = $5,000,000
b. 30 days: A/R = $5,000,000
40 days: A/R = $6,666,667

5. a. EIR = 3.7%   b. EIR = 21.9%   c. EIR = 0%

7.
Risk Category		
A	NPV	DM463,542
B	NPV	DM233,333
C	NPV	DM117,750

9. NPV = $175,000

11. a. Accounts Receivable = FF16,666,667
b. Accounts Receivable = FF35,000,000

13. NPV = DM661,111

15. NPV = $7,923,333

17. NPV = $94,444

19. NPV = FF600,000

CHAPTER 21

1.
	Jan.	Feb.	Mar.	Apr.	May
a. Total Collections	$390,000	$365,000	$380,000	$435,000	$503,000
b. Total Cash Outflows	$358,750	$388,750	$448,750	$494,250	$469,000
c. Ending Cash Balance	$ 81,250	$ 57,500	$–11,250	$–70,500	$–36,500

June	July	Aug.	Sept.	Oct.	Nov.	Dec.
$516,000	$514,000	$512,000	$485,000	$470,000	$455,000	$445,000
$517,750	$456,250	$441,250	$465,800	$422,500	$411,250	$424,750
$–38,250	$ 19,500	$ 90,250	$109,450	$156,950	$200,700	$220,950

3. Preliminary Total Liabilities + Net Worth = $1,577,200
Preliminary Total Assets = $1,356,250
Excess = Liabilities – Assets = $ 220,950

5.

	July	Aug.	Sept.	Oct.	Nov.	Dec.
a. Total Cash Inflows	$3,750	$4,000	$5,000	$5,750	$6,250	$5,000
b. Total Cash Outflows	$3,875	$4,250	$5,735	$4,350	$5,750	$4,735
c. Ending Cash Balance	$3,530	$3,280	$2,545	$3,945	$4,445	$4,710

7. Preliminary Total Assets $16,000,000
Preliminary Total Liabilities and Net Worth $20,000,000

9. Preliminary Liabilities and Net Worth = $8,800
Preliminary Assets = $8,400
Excess = Liabilities − Assets = $ 400

11. Preliminary Liabilities + Net Worth = $1,302,000
Preliminary Assets = $1,364,000
Excess = Liabilities − Assets = −$ 62,000

13. $g = 6.67\%$

15. $d = 10\%$

17. $g = 15.5\%$

19. $e = 5.7\%$

21. $e = 1.3\%$

CHAPTER 22

1. a. Chemikalwerk: EPS_C = DM4.00 per share, P/E_C = 18.00; Elm: EPS_E = DM2.00 per share, P/E_E = 9.00
   b. Post-Merger EPS = DM4.33 per share
   Market Price per share = DM78.00
   c. Value (Post-Merger) = DM468,000,000
   Value (Premerger) = DM414,000,000

3. Market Price per Share = $128.00
Post-Merger Value = $3,200,000,000

5. V_{SB} = $420,000,000

7. a. E = 1.67
   b. E = 1.25
   c. P_C = $61.54/share
   d. Price = $461,550,000
   e. NPV_B = $38,450,000
   NPV_S = $61,550,000

9. a. E = 1.19
   b. P_C = $84/share
   c. Gain of Puritan Shareholders = $4.00 per share
   d. Gain of Russell Shareholders = $20 per share

11. a. V_C = $500,000,000
   b. Maximum Price Acceptable to Buyer = $120,000,000
   c. Minimum Price Acceptable to Seller = $80,000,000
   d. NPV_B = $10,000,000, NPV_S = $30,000,000
   e. NPV_B = −$15,000,000, NPV_S = $55,000,000

13. a. Value to Sampson Shareholders = $100,000,000
   Value to Baxter Shareholders = $400,000,000
   b. Sampson's Proportion = 0.20
   Shares to Sampson's Stockholders = 6,000,000 shares
   Baxter's Proportion = 0.80
   Shares to Baxter's Stockholders = 24,000,000 shares
   c. Sampson Exchange Ratio: E = 6.0
   Baxter Exchange Ratio: E = 2.40

15. Price = $200,000,000 = $\dfrac{\$18,000,000}{0.12 - g}$, g = 3%

17. a.

**Postmerger Balance Sheet
Pooling of Interests Accounting
(in Millions)**

Current assets	$ 300
Fixed assets	1,100
Total Assets	$1,400
Debt	$ 600
Equity	800
Total Debt and Equity	$1,400

b.

**Postmerger Balance Sheet
Purchase of Assets Accounting
(in Millions)**

Current assets	$ 300
Fixed assets	1,160
Goodwill	140
Total Assets	$1,600
Debt	$ 600
Equity	1,000
Total Debt and Equity	$1,600

c. Tax Reduction = $6,133,333 per year

CHAPTER 23

1. NPV = −$80 million

3. ΔV_S = $60 million, ΔV_D = −$140 million

5. NPV = −$20 million

7. X_1 = 0.056, X_2 = 0.194, X_3 = 0.042, X_4 = 0.542, X_5 = 0.083, Z = 0.886

9. X_1 = −0.086, X_2 = 0.389, X_3 = 0.095, X_4 = 1.83, X_5 = 1.32, Z = 3.174

11. a. V = $120 million
   b. Net Going Concern Value = $114 million
   Since its net going concern value is greater than the net liquidation value, Infinity should be reorganized.

13. **Infinity Corp. Pro Forma Balance Sheet After Reorganization**

Current Assets	$ 35	Accounts Payable	$7.50
Net Fixed Assets	91.25	Notes Payable	—
Total Assets	$126.25	Accrued Wages	4
		Accrued Taxes	6
		Current Liabilities	$17.50
		Mortgage Bonds	40
		Debentures	41.25
		Common Stock	27.50
		Total Liabilities and Network	$126.25

15. a. Available to Unsecured Creditors and Common Stockholders $161 million
   b.

	Unsecured Claim	70% Share of $161 Million	Total Payment Received
Mortgage Bonds	$ 30	$ 21	$ 71
Notes Payable	50	35	50
Accounts Payable	30	21	21
Subordinated Debentures	120	84	69
	$230	$161	$211

Since $230 million exceeds $161 million, common stockholders receive $0.

17.

	Claim	85% Share of $238 Million	Final Settlement
Mortgage Bonds	$ 80	$ 68	$ 72
Notes Payable	50	42.5	50
Accounts Payable	30	25.5	25.5
Subordinated			
Debentures	120	102	80.5
Common Stock	195	—	10
	$475	$238	$238

CHAPTER 24

1. a. $r = 20\%$ b. $r_R = 13.21\%$
3. $r_{DM} = 6.45\%$
5. $I_{FF} = 3.07\%$

7. $FR(1)_{DM/SF} = DM1.434/SF$
9. Future Price = $20.97
11. Spot Price = $21.24
13. $ Loan: $r_{SEK} = 9.44\%$, SF Loan: $r_{SEK} = 10.2\%$
15. a. $FR(1)_{\$/DM} = \$0.559/DM$ b. $r_\$ = 13.26\%$
17. a. $r_\$ = 8.66\%$
    b. (1) Convert FF loan proceeds into $ on the spot market:
        Initial Loan = FF152,439,020
        Proceeds = $25,000,000
       (2) Calculate the loan payment required:
        Loan Repayment = FF167,682,920
       (3) Enter into one-year forward contract to exchange
        dollars for francs to repay the loan at the end of one
        year: Dollars Required = $27,164,633
19. a. $K_{A,US} = 14.55\%$ b. $K_{A,I} = 19.6\%$

Appendix C

Future Value and Present Value Tables

TABLE I THE FUTURE VALUE OF $1: $CF_{K,N} = (1 + K)^N$

Opportunity Cost, K

Time (N)	1%	2%	3%	4%	5%	6%	7%	8%	9%	10%	11%	12%	13%	14%	15%	16%	17%	18%	19%	20%
1	1.010	1.020	1.030	1.040	1.050	1.060	1.070	1.080	1.090	1.100	1.110	1.120	1.130	1.140	1.150	1.160	1.170	1.180	1.190	1.200
2	1.020	1.040	1.061	1.082	1.102	1.124	1.145	1.166	1.188	1.210	1.232	1.254	1.277	1.300	1.323	1.346	1.369	1.392	1.416	1.440
3	1.030	1.061	1.093	1.125	1.158	1.191	1.225	1.260	1.295	1.331	1.368	1.405	1.443	1.482	1.521	1.561	1.602	1.643	1.685	1.728
4	1.041	1.082	1.126	1.170	1.216	1.262	1.311	1.360	1.412	1.464	1.518	1.574	1.631	1.689	1.749	1.811	1.874	1.939	2.005	2.074
5	1.051	1.104	1.159	1.217	1.276	1.338	1.403	1.469	1.539	1.611	1.685	1.762	1.842	1.925	2.011	2.100	2.193	2.288	2.386	2.488
6	1.062	1.126	1.194	1.265	1.340	1.419	1.501	1.587	1.677	1.772	1.870	1.974	2.082	2.195	2.313	2.436	2.565	2.700	2.840	2.986
7	1.072	1.149	1.230	1.316	1.407	1.504	1.606	1.714	1.828	1.949	2.076	2.211	2.353	2.502	2.660	2.826	3.001	3.186	3.379	3.583
8	1.083	1.172	1.267	1.369	1.477	1.594	1.718	1.851	1.993	2.144	2.305	2.476	2.658	2.853	3.059	3.278	3.512	3.759	4.021	4.300
9	1.094	1.195	1.305	1.423	1.551	1.689	1.838	1.999	2.172	2.358	2.558	2.773	3.004	3.252	3.518	3.803	4.108	4.436	4.786	5.160
10	1.105	1.219	1.344	1.480	1.629	1.791	1.967	2.159	2.367	2.594	2.839	3.106	3.395	3.707	4.046	4.411	4.807	5.234	5.695	6.192
11	1.116	1.243	1.384	1.540	1.710	1.898	2.105	2.332	2.580	2.853	3.152	3.479	3.836	4.226	4.652	5.117	5.624	6.176	6.777	7.430
12	1.127	1.268	1.426	1.602	1.796	2.012	2.252	2.518	2.813	3.138	3.499	3.896	4.335	4.818	5.350	5.936	6.580	7.288	8.064	8.916
13	1.138	1.294	1.469	1.665	1.886	2.133	2.410	2.720	3.066	3.452	3.883	4.364	4.898	5.492	6.153	6.886	7.699	8.599	9.597	10.699
14	1.150	1.320	1.513	1.732	1.980	2.261	2.579	2.937	3.342	3.798	4.310	4.887	5.535	6.262	7.076	7.988	9.008	10.147	11.420	12.839
15	1.161	1.346	1.558	1.801	2.079	2.397	2.759	3.172	3.643	4.177	4.785	5.474	6.254	7.138	8.137	9.266	10.539	11.974	13.590	15.407
16	1.173	1.373	1.605	1.873	2.183	2.540	2.952	3.426	3.970	4.595	5.311	6.130	7.067	8.137	9.358	10.748	12.330	14.129	16.172	18.488
17	1.184	1.400	1.653	1.948	2.292	2.693	3.159	3.700	4.328	5.054	5.895	6.866	7.986	9.277	10.761	12.468	14.427	16.672	19.244	22.186
18	1.196	1.428	1.702	2.026	2.407	2.854	3.380	3.996	4.717	5.560	6.544	7.690	9.024	10.575	12.376	14.463	16.879	19.673	22.901	26.623
19	1.208	1.457	1.754	2.107	2.527	3.026	3.617	4.316	5.142	6.116	7.263	8.613	10.107	12.056	14.232	16.777	19.748	23.214	27.252	31.948
20	1.220	1.486	1.806	2.191	2.653	3.207	3.870	4.661	5.604	6.728	8.062	9.646	11.523	13.744	16.367	19.461	23.106	27.393	32.429	38.338
21	1.232	1.516	1.860	2.279	2.786	3.400	4.141	5.034	6.109	7.400	8.949	10.804	13.021	15.668	18.822	22.575	27.034	32.324	38.591	46.005
22	1.245	1.546	1.916	2.370	2.925	3.604	4.430	5.437	6.659	8.140	9.934	12.100	14.714	17.861	21.645	26.186	31.629	38.142	45.923	55.206
23	1.257	1.577	1.974	2.465	3.072	3.820	4.741	5.871	7.258	8.954	11.026	13.552	16.627	20.362	24.892	30.376	37.006	45.008	54.649	66.247
24	1.270	1.608	2.033	2.563	3.225	4.049	5.072	6.341	7.911	9.850	12.239	15.179	18.788	23.212	28.625	35.236	43.297	53.109	65.032	79.497
25	1.282	1.641	2.094	2.666	3.386	4.292	5.427	6.849	8.623	10.835	13.586	17.000	21.232	26.462	32.919	40.874	50.658	62.669	77.388	95.396
30	1.348	1.811	2.427	3.243	4.322	5.743	7.612	10.063	13.268	17.449	22.892	29.960	39.116	50.590	66.212	85.850	111.065	143.371	184.675	237.376
35	1.417	2.000	2.813	3.946	5.516	7.686	10.677	14.785	20.414	28.102	38.575	52.780	72.069	98.100	133.176	180.314	243.503	327.997	440.701	590.688
40	1.489	2.208	3.262	4.801	7.040	10.286	14.974	21.725	31.409	45.259	65.001	93.051	132.781	188.884	267.864	378.721	533.869	750.378	1051.668	1469.772
45	1.565	2.438	3.782	5.841	8.985	13.765	21.002	31.920	48.327	72.890	109.530	163.988	244.641	363.679	538.769	795.444	1170.479	1716.684	2509.651	3657.262
50	1.645	2.692	4.384	7.107	11.467	18.420	29.457	46.902	74.357	117.391	184.565	289.002	450.736	700.233	1083.657	1670.704	2566.215	3927.357	5988.914	9100.438

TABLE II THE FUTURE VALUE OF AN ANNUITY OF $1:

$$ACF_{K,N} = \sum_{t=1}^{N} (1+K)^{N-1} = \frac{(1+K)^N - 1}{K}$$

Opportunity Cost, K

Time (N)	1%	2%	3%	4%	5%	6%	7%	8%	9%	10%	11%	12%	13%	14%	15%	16%	17%	18%	19%	20%
1	1.000	1.000	1.000	1.000	1.000	1.000	1.000	1.000	1.000	1.000	1.000	1.000	1.000	1.000	1.000	1.000	1.000	1.000	1.000	1.000
2	2.010	2.020	2.030	2.040	2.050	2.060	2.070	2.080	2.090	2.100	2.110	2.120	2.130	2.140	2.150	2.160	2.170	2.180	2.190	2.200
3	3.030	3.060	3.091	3.122	3.152	3.184	3.214	3.246	3.278	3.310	3.342	3.374	3.401	3.439	3.472	3.501	3.539	3.572	3.606	3.640
4	4.060	4.122	4.184	4.246	4.310	4.375	4.440	4.506	4.573	4.641	4.710	4.779	4.850	4.921	4.993	5.067	5.141	5.216	5.290	5.368
5	5.101	5.204	5.309	5.416	5.526	5.637	5.751	5.867	5.985	6.105	6.229	6.353	6.480	6.610	6.742	6.877	7.015	7.154	7.297	7.442
6	6.152	6.308	6.468	6.633	6.802	6.975	7.153	7.336	7.523	7.716	7.913	8.115	8.324	8.536	8.754	8.978	9.207	9.442	9.683	9.930
7	7.214	7.434	7.662	7.898	8.142	8.393	8.654	8.923	9.200	9.487	9.784	10.089	10.405	10.730	11.067	11.414	11.772	12.142	12.523	12.916
8	8.286	8.583	8.892	9.214	9.549	9.897	10.260	10.637	11.028	11.436	11.859	12.300	12.757	13.233	13.723	14.240	14.774	15.327	15.902	16.499
9	9.368	9.755	10.159	10.583	11.027	11.491	11.978	12.488	13.021	13.579	14.164	14.776	15.415	16.085	16.786	17.518	18.285	19.086	19.924	20.799
10	10.462	10.950	11.464	12.006	12.578	13.181	13.816	14.487	15.193	15.937	16.722	17.549	18.420	19.337	20.304	21.321	22.393	23.521	24.709	25.959
11	11.567	12.169	12.808	13.486	14.207	14.972	15.784	16.645	17.560	18.531	19.562	20.655	21.815	23.044	24.349	25.733	27.200	28.755	30.404	32.150
12	12.683	13.412	14.192	15.026	15.917	16.870	17.888	18.977	20.141	21.384	22.714	24.133	25.650	27.271	29.002	30.850	32.824	34.931	37.180	39.580
13	13.809	14.680	15.618	16.627	17.713	18.882	20.141	21.495	22.953	24.523	26.212	28.029	29.985	32.089	34.352	36.786	39.404	42.219	45.245	48.497
14	14.947	15.974	17.086	18.292	19.599	21.051	22.550	24.215	26.019	27.975	30.095	32.393	34.883	37.581	40.505	43.672	47.103	50.818	54.842	59.196
15	16.097	17.293	18.599	20.024	21.579	23.276	25.129	27.152	29.361	31.772	34.405	37.280	40.418	43.842	47.581	51.659	56.112	60.965	66.263	72.035
16	17.258	18.639	20.156	21.825	23.657	25.673	27.888	30.324	33.003	35.950	39.190	42.753	46.672	50.981	55.717	60.925	66.647	72.939	79.853	87.440
17	18.430	20.012	21.762	23.698	25.840	28.213	30.840	33.750	36.973	40.545	44.501	48.883	53.739	59.118	65.073	71.675	78.984	87.067	96.021	105.931
18	19.615	21.412	23.414	25.645	28.132	30.906	33.999	37.450	41.301	45.599	50.696	55.750	61.725	68.393	75.840	84.144	93.406	103.740	115.266	128.117
19	20.811	22.841	25.117	27.671	30.539	33.760	37.379	41.446	46.019	51.159	56.939	63.440	70.054	78.971	88.213	98.606	110.285	123.414	138.166	154.740
20	22.019	24.297	26.870	29.778	33.066	36.786	40.995	45.762	51.160	57.275	64.203	72.053	80.946	91.029	102.444	115.380	130.033	146.628	165.418	186.688
21	23.239	25.783	28.676	31.969	35.719	39.993	44.865	50.423	56.764	64.002	72.265	81.709	92.469	104.768	118.810	134.841	153.139	174.021	197.847	225.026
22	24.472	27.299	30.537	34.248	38.505	42.392	49.006	55.457	62.873	71.403	81.214	92.500	105.491	120.436	137.632	157.415	180.172	206.345	236.438	271.031
23	25.716	28.845	32.453	36.618	41.430	46.996	53.436	60.893	69.532	79.543	91.145	104.603	120.205	138.297	159.276	183.601	211.801	244.487	282.362	326.237
24	26.973	30.422	34.426	39.083	44.502	50.816	58.177	66.765	76.790	88.497	102.174	118.155	136.831	158.659	184.168	213.978	248.808	289.494	337.010	392.484
25	28.243	32.030	36.459	41.646	47.727	54.865	63.249	73.106	84.701	98.347	114.413	133.334	155.620	181.871	212.793	249.214	292.105	342.603	402.042	471.981
30	34.785	40.568	47.575	56.085	66.439	79.058	94.461	113.283	136.308	164.494	199.021	241.333	293.199	356.787	434.745	530.312	647.439	790.948	966.712	1181.882
35	41.660	49.995	60.462	73.652	90.320	111.435	138.237	172.317	215.711	271.024	341.590	431.664	546.681	693.573	881.170	1120.713	1426.491	1816.652	2314.214	2948.341
40	48.886	60.402	75.401	95.026	120.800	154.762	199.635	259.057	337.882	442.593	581.826	767.091	1013.704	1342.025	1779.090	2360.757	3134.522	4163.213	5529.829	7343.858
45	56.481	71.893	92.720	121.030	159.700	212.744	285.749	386.506	525.859	718.905	986.639	1358.230	1874.165	2590.565	3585.129	4965.274	6879.291	9531.577	13,203.424	18,281.310
50	64.463	84.579	112.797	152.667	209.348	290.336	406.529	573.770	815.084	1163.909	1668.771	2400.018	3459.507	4994.521	7217.716	10,435.649	15,089.502	21,813.093	31,515.336	45,497.191

TABLE III THE PRESENT VALUE OF $1: $DF_{K,N} = 1/(1 + K)^N$

Opportunity Cost, K

Time (N)	1%	2%	3%	4%	5%	6%	7%	8%	9%	10%	11%	12%	13%	14%	15%	16%	17%	18%	19%	20%
1	0.990	0.980	0.971	0.962	0.952	0.943	0.935	0.926	0.917	0.909	0.901	0.893	0.885	0.877	0.870	0.862	0.855	0.848	0.840	0.833
2	0.980	0.961	0.943	0.925	0.907	0.890	0.873	0.857	0.842	0.826	0.812	0.797	0.783	0.769	0.756	0.743	0.731	0.718	0.706	0.694
3	0.971	0.942	0.915	0.889	0.864	0.840	0.816	0.794	0.772	0.751	0.731	0.712	0.693	0.675	0.658	0.641	0.624	0.609	0.593	0.579
4	0.961	0.924	0.889	0.855	0.823	0.792	0.763	0.735	0.708	0.683	0.659	0.636	0.613	0.592	0.572	0.552	0.534	0.516	0.499	0.482
5	0.951	0.906	0.863	0.822	0.784	0.747	0.713	0.681	0.650	0.621	0.593	0.567	0.543	0.519	0.497	0.476	0.456	0.437	0.419	0.402
6	0.942	0.888	0.837	0.790	0.746	0.705	0.666	0.630	0.596	0.565	0.535	0.507	0.480	0.456	0.432	0.410	0.390	0.370	0.352	0.333
7	0.933	0.871	0.813	0.760	0.711	0.665	0.623	0.583	0.547	0.513	0.482	0.452	0.425	0.400	0.376	0.354	0.333	0.314	0.296	0.279
8	0.923	0.853	0.789	0.731	0.677	0.627	0.582	0.540	0.502	0.467	0.434	0.404	0.376	0.351	0.327	0.305	0.285	0.266	0.249	0.233
9	0.914	0.837	0.766	0.703	0.645	0.592	0.544	0.500	0.460	0.424	0.391	0.361	0.333	0.308	0.284	0.263	0.243	0.225	0.209	0.194
10	0.905	0.820	0.744	0.676	0.614	0.558	0.508	0.463	0.422	0.386	0.352	0.322	0.295	0.270	0.247	0.227	0.208	0.191	0.176	0.162
11	0.896	0.804	0.722	0.650	0.585	0.527	0.475	0.429	0.388	0.350	0.317	0.287	0.261	0.237	0.215	0.195	0.178	0.162	0.148	0.135
12	0.887	0.788	0.701	0.625	0.557	0.497	0.444	0.397	0.356	0.319	0.286	0.257	0.231	0.208	0.187	0.168	0.152	0.137	0.124	0.112
13	0.879	0.773	0.681	0.601	0.530	0.469	0.415	0.368	0.326	0.290	0.258	0.229	0.204	0.182	0.163	0.145	0.130	0.116	0.104	0.093
14	0.870	0.758	0.661	0.577	0.505	0.442	0.388	0.341	0.299	0.263	0.232	0.205	0.181	0.160	0.141	0.125	0.111	0.099	0.088	0.078
15	0.861	0.743	0.642	0.555	0.481	0.417	0.362	0.315	0.275	0.239	0.209	0.183	0.160	0.140	0.123	0.108	0.095	0.084	0.074	0.065
16	0.853	0.728	0.623	0.534	0.458	0.394	0.339	0.299	0.252	0.218	0.188	0.163	0.142	0.123	0.107	0.093	0.081	0.071	0.062	0.054
17	0.844	0.714	0.605	0.513	0.436	0.371	0.317	0.270	0.231	0.198	0.170	0.146	0.125	0.108	0.093	0.080	0.069	0.060	0.052	0.045
18	0.836	0.700	0.587	0.494	0.416	0.350	0.296	0.250	0.212	0.180	0.153	0.130	0.111	0.095	0.081	0.069	0.059	0.051	0.044	0.038
19	0.828	0.686	0.570	0.475	0.396	0.331	0.277	0.232	0.195	0.164	0.138	0.116	0.098	0.083	0.070	0.060	0.051	0.043	0.037	0.031
20	0.820	0.673	0.554	0.456	0.377	0.312	0.258	0.215	0.178	0.149	0.124	0.104	0.087	0.073	0.061	0.051	0.043	0.037	0.031	0.026
21	0.811	0.660	0.538	0.439	0.359	0.294	0.242	0.199	0.164	0.135	0.112	0.093	0.077	0.064	0.053	0.044	0.037	0.031	0.026	0.022
22	0.803	0.647	0.522	0.422	0.342	0.278	0.226	0.184	0.150	0.123	0.101	0.083	0.068	0.056	0.046	0.038	0.032	0.026	0.022	0.018
23	0.795	0.634	0.507	0.406	0.326	0.262	0.211	0.170	0.138	0.112	0.091	0.074	0.060	0.049	0.040	0.033	0.027	0.022	0.018	0.015
24	0.788	0.622	0.492	0.390	0.310	0.247	0.197	0.158	0.126	0.102	0.082	0.066	0.053	0.043	0.035	0.028	0.023	0.019	0.015	0.013
25	0.780	0.610	0.478	0.375	0.295	0.233	0.184	0.146	0.116	0.092	0.074	0.059	0.047	0.038	0.030	0.024	0.020	0.016	0.013	0.010
30	0.742	0.552	0.412	0.308	0.231	0.174	0.131	0.099	0.075	0.057	0.044	0.033	0.026	0.020	0.015	0.012	0.009	0.007	0.005	0.004
35	0.706	0.500	0.355	0.253	0.181	0.130	0.094	0.068	0.049	0.036	0.026	0.019	0.014	0.010	0.008	0.006	0.004	0.003	0.002	0.002
40	0.672	0.453	0.307	0.208	0.142	0.097	0.067	0.046	0.032	0.022	0.015	0.011	0.008	0.005	0.004	0.003	0.002	0.001	0.001	0.001
45	0.639	0.410	0.264	0.171	0.111	0.073	0.048	0.031	0.021	0.014	0.009	0.006	0.004	0.003	0.002	0.001	0.001	0.001	*	*
50	0.608	0.372	0.228	0.141	0.087	0.054	0.034	0.021	0.013	0.009	0.005	0.003	0.002	0.001	0.001	0.001	*	*	*	*

TABLE III THE PRESENT VALUE OF $1 (continued)

Opportunity Cost, K

Time (N)	21%	22%	23%	24%	25%	26%	27%	28%	29%	30%	31%	32%	33%	34%	35%	36%	37%	38%	39%	40%	50%
1	0.826	0.820	0.813	0.806	0.800	0.794	0.787	0.781	0.775	0.769	0.763	0.758	0.752	0.746	0.741	0.735	0.730	0.725	0.719	0.714	0.667
2	0.683	0.672	0.661	0.650	0.640	0.630	0.620	0.610	0.601	0.592	0.583	0.574	0.565	0.557	0.549	0.541	0.533	0.525	0.518	0.510	0.444
3	0.564	0.551	0.537	0.524	0.512	0.500	0.488	0.477	0.466	0.455	0.445	0.435	0.425	0.416	0.406	0.398	0.389	0.381	0.372	0.364	0.296
4	0.467	0.451	0.437	0.423	0.410	0.397	0.384	0.373	0.361	0.350	0.340	0.329	0.320	0.310	0.301	0.292	0.284	0.276	0.268	0.260	0.198
5	0.386	0.370	0.355	0.341	0.328	0.315	0.303	0.291	0.280	0.269	0.259	0.250	0.240	0.231	0.223	0.215	0.207	0.200	0.193	0.186	0.132
6	0.319	0.303	0.289	0.275	0.262	0.250	0.238	0.227	0.217	0.207	0.198	0.189	0.181	0.173	0.165	0.158	0.151	0.145	0.139	0.133	0.088
7	0.263	0.249	0.235	0.222	0.210	0.198	0.188	0.178	0.168	0.159	0.151	0.143	0.136	0.129	0.122	0.116	0.110	0.105	0.100	0.095	0.059
8	0.218	0.204	0.191	0.179	0.168	0.157	0.148	0.139	0.130	0.123	0.115	0.108	0.102	0.096	0.091	0.085	0.081	0.076	0.072	0.068	0.039
9	0.180	0.167	0.155	0.144	0.134	0.125	0.116	0.108	0.101	0.094	0.088	0.082	0.077	0.072	0.067	0.063	0.059	0.055	0.052	0.048	0.026
10	0.149	0.137	0.126	0.116	0.107	0.099	0.092	0.085	0.078	0.073	0.067	0.062	0.058	0.054	0.050	0.046	0.043	0.040	0.037	0.035	0.017
11	0.123	0.112	0.103	0.094	0.086	0.079	0.072	0.066	0.061	0.056	0.051	0.047	0.043	0.040	0.037	0.034	0.031	0.029	0.027	0.025	0.012
12	0.102	0.092	0.083	0.076	0.069	0.062	0.057	0.052	0.047	0.043	0.039	0.036	0.033	0.030	0.027	0.025	0.023	0.021	0.019	0.018	0.008
13	0.084	0.075	0.068	0.061	0.055	0.050	0.045	0.040	0.037	0.033	0.030	0.027	0.025	0.022	0.020	0.018	0.017	0.015	0.014	0.013	0.005
14	0.069	0.062	0.055	0.049	0.044	0.039	0.035	0.032	0.028	0.025	0.023	0.021	0.018	0.017	0.015	0.014	0.012	0.011	0.010	0.009	0.003
15	0.057	0.051	0.045	0.040	0.035	0.031	0.028	0.025	0.022	0.020	0.017	0.016	0.014	0.012	0.011	0.010	0.009	0.008	0.007	0.006	0.002
16	0.047	0.042	0.036	0.032	0.028	0.025	0.022	0.019	0.017	0.015	0.013	0.012	0.010	0.009	0.008	0.007	0.006	0.006	0.005	0.005	0.002
17	0.039	0.034	0.030	0.026	0.023	0.020	0.017	0.015	0.013	0.012	0.010	0.009	0.008	0.007	0.006	0.005	0.005	0.004	0.004	0.003	0.001
18	0.032	0.028	0.024	0.021	0.018	0.016	0.014	0.012	0.010	0.009	0.008	0.007	0.006	0.005	0.005	0.004	0.003	0.003	0.003	0.002	0.001
19	0.027	0.023	0.020	0.017	0.014	0.012	0.011	0.009	0.008	0.007	0.006	0.005	0.004	0.004	0.003	0.003	0.002	0.002	0.002	0.002	·
20	0.022	0.019	0.016	0.014	0.012	0.010	0.008	0.007	0.006	0.005	0.005	0.004	0.003	0.003	0.002	0.002	0.002	0.002	0.001	0.001	·
21	0.018	0.015	0.013	0.011	0.009	0.008	0.007	0.006	0.005	0.004	0.003	0.003	0.003	0.002	0.002	0.002	0.001	0.001	0.001	0.001	
22	0.015	0.013	0.011	0.009	0.007	0.006	0.005	0.004	0.004	0.003	0.003	0.002	0.002	0.002	0.001	0.001	0.001	0.001	0.001	0.001	
23	0.012	0.010	0.009	0.007	0.006	0.005	0.004	0.003	0.003	0.002	0.002	0.002	0.001	0.001	0.001	0.001	0.001	0.001	0.001		
24	0.010	0.008	0.007	0.006	0.005	0.004	0.003	0.003	0.002	0.002	0.002	0.001	0.001	0.001	0.001	0.001	·				
25	0.009	0.007	0.006	0.005	0.004	0.003	0.003	0.002	0.002	0.001	0.001	0.001	0.001	0.001	0.001	·	·	·	·	·	
30	0.003	0.003	0.002	0.002	0.001	0.001	0.001	0.001	·	·	·										
35	0.001	0.001	0.001	0.001	·	·	·	·	·	·	·										
40	·	·	·	·	·																

TABLE IV THE PRESENT VALUE OF AN ANNUITY OF $1:

$$ADF_{K,N} = \sum_{t=1}^{N} 1/(1+K)^N = \frac{1-\dfrac{1}{(1+K)^N}}{K}$$

Opportunity Cost, K

Time (N)	1%	2%	3%	4%	5%	6%	7%	8%	9%	10%	11%	12%	13%	14%	15%	16%	17%	18%	19%	20%
1	0.990	0.980	0.971	0.962	0.952	0.943	0.935	0.926	0.917	0.909	0.901	0.893	0.885	0.877	0.870	0.862	0.855	0.848	0.840	0.833
2	1.970	1.942	1.913	1.886	1.859	1.833	1.808	1.783	1.759	1.736	1.713	1.690	1.668	1.647	1.626	1.605	1.585	1.566	1.547	1.528
3	2.941	2.884	2.829	2.775	2.723	2.673	2.624	2.577	2.531	2.487	2.444	2.402	2.361	2.322	2.283	2.246	2.210	2.174	2.140	2.107
4	3.902	3.808	3.717	3.630	3.546	3.465	3.387	3.312	3.240	3.170	3.102	3.037	2.975	2.914	2.855	2.798	2.743	2.690	2.639	2.589
5	4.853	4.713	4.580	4.452	4.329	4.212	4.100	3.993	3.890	3.791	3.696	3.605	3.517	3.433	3.352	3.274	3.199	3.127	3.058	2.991
6	5.795	5.601	5.417	5.242	5.076	4.917	4.767	4.623	4.486	4.355	4.231	4.111	3.998	3.889	3.785	3.685	3.589	3.498	3.410	3.326
7	6.728	6.472	6.230	6.002	5.786	5.582	5.389	5.206	5.033	4.868	4.712	4.564	4.423	4.288	4.160	4.039	3.922	3.812	3.706	3.605
8	7.652	7.326	7.020	6.733	6.463	6.210	5.971	5.747	5.535	5.334	5.146	4.968	4.799	4.639	4.487	4.344	4.207	4.078	3.954	3.837
9	8.566	8.162	7.786	7.435	7.108	6.802	6.515	6.247	5.985	5.759	5.537	5.328	5.132	4.946	4.772	4.607	4.451	4.303	4.163	4.031
10	9.471	8.983	8.530	8.111	7.722	7.360	7.024	6.710	6.418	6.145	5.889	5.650	5.426	5.216	5.019	4.833	4.659	4.494	4.339	4.193
11	10.368	9.787	9.253	8.760	8.306	7.887	7.499	7.139	6.805	6.495	6.207	5.938	5.687	5.453	5.234	5.029	4.836	4.656	4.487	4.327
12	11.255	10.575	9.954	9.385	8.863	8.384	7.943	7.536	7.161	6.814	6.492	6.194	5.918	5.660	5.421	5.197	4.988	4.793	4.611	4.439
13	12.134	11.348	10.635	9.986	9.394	8.853	8.358	7.904	7.487	7.103	6.750	6.424	6.122	5.842	5.583	5.342	5.118	4.910	4.715	4.533
14	13.004	12.106	11.296	10.563	9.899	9.295	8.745	8.244	7.786	7.367	6.982	6.628	6.303	6.002	5.725	5.468	5.229	5.008	4.802	4.611
15	13.865	12.849	11.938	11.118	10.380	9.712	9.108	8.560	8.061	7.606	7.191	6.811	6.462	6.142	5.847	5.576	5.324	5.092	4.876	4.676
16	14.718	13.578	12.561	11.652	10.838	10.106	9.447	8.851	8.313	7.824	7.379	6.974	6.604	6.265	5.954	5.669	5.405	5.162	4.938	4.730
17	15.562	14.292	13.166	12.166	11.274	10.477	9.763	9.122	8.544	8.022	7.549	7.120	6.729	6.373	6.047	5.749	5.475	5.222	4.990	4.775
18	16.398	14.992	13.753	12.659	11.690	10.828	10.059	9.372	8.756	8.201	7.702	7.250	6.840	6.467	6.128	5.818	5.534	5.273	5.033	4.812
19	17.226	15.678	14.324	13.134	12.085	11.158	10.336	9.604	8.950	8.365	7.839	7.366	6.938	6.550	6.198	5.878	5.585	5.316	5.070	4.844
20	18.046	16.351	14.877	13.590	12.462	11.470	10.594	9.818	9.129	8.514	7.963	7.469	7.025	6.623	6.259	5.929	5.628	5.353	5.101	4.870
21	18.857	17.011	15.415	14.029	12.821	11.764	10.836	10.017	9.292	8.649	8.075	7.562	7.102	6.687	6.313	5.973	5.665	5.384	5.127	4.891
22	19.661	17.658	15.937	14.451	13.163	12.042	11.061	10.201	9.442	8.772	8.176	7.645	7.170	6.743	6.359	6.011	5.696	5.410	5.149	4.909
23	20.456	18.292	16.444	14.857	13.489	12.303	11.272	10.371	9.580	8.883	8.266	7.718	7.230	6.792	6.399	6.044	5.723	5.432	5.167	4.925
24	21.244	18.914	16.936	15.247	13.799	12.550	11.469	10.529	9.707	8.985	8.348	7.784	7.283	6.835	6.434	6.073	5.747	5.451	5.182	4.937
25	22.023	19.523	17.413	15.622	14.094	12.783	11.654	10.675	9.823	9.077	8.422	7.843	7.330	6.873	6.464	6.097	5.766	5.467	5.195	4.948
30	25.808	22.396	19.600	17.292	15.372	13.765	12.409	11.258	10.274	9.427	8.694	8.055	7.496	7.003	6.566	6.177	5.829	5.517	5.235	4.979
35	29.409	24.999	21.487	18.665	16.374	14.498	12.948	11.655	10.567	9.644	8.855	8.176	7.586	7.070	6.617	6.215	5.858	5.539	5.251	4.992
40	32.835	27.355	23.115	19.793	17.159	15.046	13.332	11.925	10.757	9.779	8.951	8.244	7.634	7.105	6.642	6.233	5.871	5.548	5.258	4.997
45	36.095	29.490	24.519	20.720	17.774	15.456	13.606	12.108	10.881	9.863	9.008	8.283	7.661	7.123	6.654	6.242	5.877	5.552	5.261	4.999
50	39.196	31.424	25.730	21.482	18.256	15.762	13.801	12.233	10.962	9.915	9.042	8.304	7.675	7.133	6.661	6.246	5.880	5.554	5.262	4.999

TABLE IV THE PRESENT VALUE OF AN ANNUITY OF $1 (continued)

Opportunity Cost, K

Time (N)	21%	22%	23%	24%	25%	26%	27%	28%	29%	30%	31%	32%	33%	34%	35%	36%	37%	38%	39%	40%	50%
1	0.826	0.820	0.813	0.807	0.800	0.794	0.787	0.781	0.775	0.769	0.763	0.758	0.752	0.746	0.741	0.735	0.730	0.725	0.719	0.714	0.667
2	1.510	1.492	1.474	1.457	1.440	1.424	1.407	1.392	1.376	1.361	1.346	1.332	1.317	1.303	1.289	1.276	1.263	1.250	1.237	1.225	1.111
3	2.074	2.042	2.011	1.981	1.952	1.923	1.896	1.868	1.842	1.816	1.791	1.766	1.742	1.719	1.696	1.674	1.652	1.630	1.609	1.589	1.407
4	2.540	2.494	2.448	2.404	2.362	2.320	2.280	2.241	2.203	2.166	2.131	2.096	2.062	2.029	1.997	1.966	1.936	1.906	1.877	1.849	1.605
5	2.926	2.864	2.804	2.745	2.689	2.635	2.583	2.532	2.483	2.436	2.390	2.345	2.302	2.260	2.220	2.181	2.143	2.106	2.070	2.035	1.737
6	3.245	3.167	3.092	3.021	2.951	2.885	2.821	2.759	2.700	2.643	2.588	2.534	2.483	2.433	2.386	2.339	2.294	2.251	2.209	2.168	1.824
7	3.508	3.416	3.327	3.242	3.161	3.083	3.009	2.937	2.868	2.802	2.739	2.678	2.619	2.562	2.508	2.455	2.404	2.356	2.308	2.263	1.883
8	3.726	3.619	3.518	3.421	3.329	3.241	3.156	3.076	2.999	2.925	2.854	2.786	2.721	2.658	2.598	2.540	2.485	2.432	2.380	2.331	1.922
9	3.905	3.786	3.673	3.566	3.463	3.366	3.273	3.184	3.100	3.019	2.942	2.868	2.798	2.730	2.665	2.603	2.544	2.487	2.432	2.379	1.948
10	4.054	3.923	3.799	3.682	3.571	3.465	3.364	3.269	3.178	3.092	3.009	2.930	2.855	2.784	2.715	2.650	2.587	2.527	2.469	2.414	1.965
11	4.177	4.035	3.902	3.776	3.656	3.544	3.437	3.335	3.239	3.147	3.060	2.978	2.899	2.824	2.752	2.683	2.618	2.556	2.496	2.438	1.977
12	4.279	4.127	3.985	3.851	3.725	3.606	3.493	3.387	3.286	3.190	3.100	3.013	2.931	2.853	2.779	2.708	2.641	2.576	2.515	2.456	1.985
13	4.362	4.203	4.053	3.912	3.780	3.656	3.638	3.427	3.322	3.223	3.129	3.040	2.956	2.876	2.799	2.727	2.658	2.592	2.529	2.469	1.990
14	4.432	4.265	4.108	3.962	3.824	3.695	3.573	3.459	3.351	3.249	3.152	3.061	2.974	2.892	2.814	2.740	2.670	2.603	2.539	2.478	1.993
15	4.489	4.315	4.153	4.001	3.859	3.726	3.601	3.483	3.373	3.268	3.170	3.076	2.988	2.905	2.826	2.750	2.679	2.611	2.546	2.484	1.995
16	4.536	4.357	4.189	4.033	3.887	3.751	3.623	3.503	3.390	3.283	3.183	3.088	2.999	2.914	2.834	2.758	2.685	2.616	2.551	2.489	1.997
17	4.576	4.391	4.219	4.059	3.910	3.771	3.640	3.518	3.403	3.295	3.193	3.097	3.007	2.921	2.840	2.763	2.690	2.621	2.555	2.492	1.998
18	4.608	4.419	4.243	4.080	3.928	3.786	3.654	3.529	3.413	3.304	3.201	3.104	3.012	2.926	2.844	2.767	2.693	2.624	2.557	2.494	1.999
19	4.635	4.442	4.263	4.097	3.942	3.799	3.664	3.539	3.421	3.311	3.207	3.109	3.017	2.930	2.848	2.770	2.696	2.626	2.559	2.496	1.999
20	4.657	4.460	4.279	4.110	3.954	3.808	3.673	3.546	3.427	3.316	3.211	3.113	3.020	2.933	2.850	2.772	2.698	2.627	2.561	2.497	1.999
21	4.675	4.476	4.292	4.121	3.963	3.816	3.679	3.551	3.432	3.320	3.215	3.116	3.023	2.935	2.852	2.773	2.699	2.629	2.562	2.498	2.000
22	4.690	4.488	4.302	4.130	3.971	3.822	3.684	3.556	3.436	3.323	3.217	3.118	3.025	2.937	2.853	2.775	2.700	2.629	2.562	2.499	2.000
23	4.703	4.499	4.311	4.137	3.976	3.827	3.689	3.559	3.438	3.325	3.219	3.120	3.026	2.938	2.854	2.775	2.701	2.630	2.563	2.499	2.000
24	4.713	4.507	4.318	4.143	3.981	3.831	3.692	3.562	3.441	3.327	3.221	3.121	3.027	2.939	2.855	2.776	2.701	2.630	2.563	2.499	2.000
25	4.721	4.514	4.323	4.147	3.985	3.834	3.694	3.564	3.442	3.329	3.222	3.122	3.028	2.939	2.856	2.777	2.702	2.631	2.563	2.499	2.000
30	4.746	4.534	4.339	4.160	3.995	3.842	3.701	3.569	3.447	3.332	3.225	3.124	3.030	2.941	2.857	2.778	2.702	2.631	2.564	2.500	2.000
35	4.756	4.541	4.345	4.164	3.998	3.845	3.703	3.571	3.448	3.333	3.226	3.125	3.030	2.941	2.857	2.778	2.702	2.632	2.564	2.500	2.000
40	4.760	4.544	4.347	4.166	3.999	3.846	3.703	3.571	3.448	3.333	3.226	3.125	3.030	2.941	2.857	2.778	2.702	2.632	2.564	2.500	2.000
45	4.761	4.545	4.347	4.166	4.000	3.846	3.704	3.571	3.448	3.333	3.226	3.125	3.030	2.941	2.857	2.778	2.702	2.632	2.564	2.500	2.000
50	4.762	4.545	4.348	4.167	4.000	3.846	3.704	3.571	3.448	3.333	3.226	3.125	3.030	2.941	2.857	2.778	2.702	2.632	2.564	2.500	2.000

Appendix D

Answers to Self-Study Quizzes

CHAPTER 2

1. Dividends = Net Income − Change in Retained Earnings
   = 300 − (800 − 700) = $200

2. Investment in plant and equipment =
   Change in Net Fixed Assets + Depreciation
   = (1,400 − 1,200) + 75 = 275

3.
Statement of Sources and Uses of Funds
Roundnumber Corporation
Dec. 31, 1999 to Dec. 31, 2000
(in Millions)

Sources of Funds

Increase in current liabilities		$ 50
Increase in long-term debt		90
Increase in common stock		60
Funds for operations		
Net income	300	
Depreciation	75	375
		$575

Uses of Funds

Increase in cash	$ 40
Increase in other current assets	60
Increase in plant and equipment	275
Dividends paid	200
	$575

4.
Statement of Cash Flows
Roundnumber Corporation
Dec. 31, 1999 to Dec. 31, 2000
(in Millions)

Cash Flows from Operating Activities:

Net income	$300
Additions:	
Depreciation	75
Interest expense	70
Increase in current liabilities	50
Deductions:	
Increase in other current assets	(60)
Net cash flows from operating activities	435

Cash Flows from Investing Activities:

Increase in plant and equipment	(275)
Net cash flows from operations and investing	160

Cash Flows from Financing Activities:

Increase in long-term debt	90
Interest expense	(70)
Increase in common stock	60
Dividend paid	(200)
Net cash from financing activities	(120)
Net cash flow for 2000	40
Cash balance Dec. 31, 1999	60
Cash balance Dec. 31, 2000	$100

5.

	1999	2000
Current ratio	$\frac{600}{500} = 1.20$	$\frac{700}{550} = 1.27$
Debt ratio	$\frac{900}{1,800} = 0.50$	$\frac{1,040}{2,100} = 0.495$
Interest coverage		$\frac{570}{70} = 8.14$
Return on assets		$\frac{570}{2,100} = 0.271$
Return on equity		$\frac{300}{1,060} = 0.283$

CHAPTER 3

1.

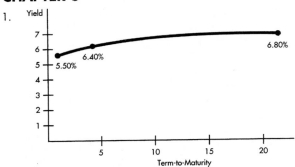

It is an upward sloping yield curve.

2. Default Risk Premium =
    Corporate Bond Yield – Treasury Bond Yield
    Default Risk Premium Aaa = 7.60% – 6.80% = 0.80%
    Default Risk Premium Baa = 8.30% – 6.80% = 1.50%

3. Yield Spread = Yield on Baa – Yield on Aaa
    = 8.30% – 7.60% = 0.70%
    Investors require high yields on Baa bonds to compensate for the higher default risk.

4. Municipal bonds are exempt from federal income taxes. A taxable corporate bond would have to yield 5.70%/ (1 – 0.30) = 8.14% to offer the same after-tax yield as the municipal.

5. a. Nominal rate of return =
    $$\frac{\text{Repayment} - \text{Investment}}{\text{Investment}} = \frac{\$70,000 - 50,000}{\$50,000} = 40\%$$

    b. Real Rate of Return = Nominal Rate – Inflation Rate
    $$r_R = r - p = 40\% - 4\% = 36\%$$

CHAPTER 4

1. a. Dollars received = (Francs Exchanged)(DER $/FF) =
    10,000 (0.1679) = $1,679

    b. $\text{IER FF}/\$ = \dfrac{1}{\text{DER}_{\$/FF}} = \dfrac{1}{\$0.1679/FF} = (FF5.9559)$

    c. Francs Received = (Dollars Exchanged)(IER$_{FF/\$}$) =
    (1,000)(5.9559) = FF 5,955.90

2. $FD_{FF/\$} = \left(\dfrac{\text{ForwardRate} - \text{SpotRate}}{\text{SpotRate}}\right)\left(\dfrac{12}{MF}\right)(100)$
    $= \left(\dfrac{0.1696 - 0.1679}{0.1679}\right)\left(\dfrac{12}{6}\right)(100) = 2.025\%$

3. $DER_{FF/DM} = \dfrac{\text{IER}_{FF/\$}}{\text{IER}_{DM/\$}} = \dfrac{\text{FF } 0.1680/\$}{\text{DM } 0.5660/\$} = \text{FF } 0.2968/DM$

4. a. Amount at Sale =
    (500 cases)(25,000 pesos/case)($0.002410) =
    (12,500,000 pesos)($0.002410) = $30,125

    b. Amount at Payment =
    (500 cases)(25,000 pesos/case)($0.002400) =
    (12,500,000 pesos)($0.002400) = $30,000

CHAPTER 5

1. a. FV = $5,000 $(1 + 0.12)^2$ = 5,000 (1.254) = $6,270

    b. Because of monthly compounding
    $$N = 12 \times 2 = 24 \quad \text{and} \quad K = \frac{0.12}{12} = 0.01$$
    FV = ($5,000)$(1 + 0.01)^{24}$ = (5,000)(1.270) = $6,350

2. a. For annual compounding; the effective interest (EIR) rate is the stated rate.

    b. $\text{EIR} = \left(1 + \dfrac{0.12}{12}\right)^{12} = 12.7\%$

3. PV = (Cash flow)($DF_{K,N}$)

    a. PV = ($400,000)($DF_{0.12,8}$)
    Using table or formula: $DF_{0.12,8} = 0.404$
    PV = ($400,000)(0.404) = $161,600

    b. PV = $400,000 ($DF_{0.1075,8}$)
    $$DF_{0.12,8} = \frac{1}{(1+K)^N} = \frac{1}{(1.1075)^8} = 0.442$$
    PV = ($400,000)(0.442) = $176,800

4. PV = (Annual Cash Flow)($ADF_{K,N}$)

    a. PV = ($2,000)($ADF_{0.12,8}$)
    Using table or formula: $ADF_{0.12,8} = 4.968$
    PV = ($2,000)(4.968) = $9,936

    b. PV = (2,000)($ADF_{0.1075,8}$)
    $$ADF_{0.1075,8} = \left(\frac{1 - \dfrac{1}{1.1075^8}}{0.1075}\right) = \left(\frac{1 - 0.4418}{0.1075}\right) = 5.1926$$
    PV = ($2,000)(5.1926) = $10,385

5. The amount of the loan is the present value of an annuity consisting of the monthly payments:
    75,000 = (Payment)($ADF_{K,N}$)

    a. Since payments are monthly $K = \dfrac{0.12}{12} = 0.01$ and
    $N = 2 \times 12 = 24$
    75,000 = (Payment)($ADF_{0.01,24}$)
    Using tables or formula: $ADF_{0.01,24} = 21.243$
    $75,000 = (Payment)(21.243)$
    $$\text{Payment} = \frac{\$75,000}{21.243} = \$3,531$$

    b. Since payments are monthly
    $K = \dfrac{0.18}{12} = 0.015 \quad N = 24$
    $$ADF_{0.015,24} = \left(\frac{1 - \dfrac{1}{(1.015)^{24}}}{0.015}\right) = 20.030$$
    $75,000 = (Payment)(20.030)$
    $$\text{Payment} = \frac{75,000}{20.030} = \$3,744$$

CHAPTER 6

1. $V = \sum_{t=1}^{N} \dfrac{C_t}{(1+K)^t}$

   a. $V = (10,000)(ADF_{0.08,15})$
   $V = (10,000)(8.560) = \$85,600$
   b. $V = (10,000)(ADF_{0.12,15})$
   $V = (10,000)(6.811) = \$68,110$

2. $\overline{X} = (-\$20)(0.4) + (\$30)(0.3) + (\$50)(0.3) = \$16$

   $\sigma = \sqrt{(-20-16)^2(0.4) + (30-16)^2(0.3) + (50-16)^2(0.3)}$

   $\sigma = \sqrt{518.4 + 58.8 + 346.8} = \sqrt{924} = \$30.40$

   $CV = \dfrac{30.40}{16} = 1.90$

3. Firm betas: Merrill Lynch = 1.95, General Motors = 1.10, McDonald's = 0.80, Homestake Mining = 0.55
   Given equal proportions, the portfolio beta is:
   $\beta = (1.95)(0.25) + (1.10)(0.25) + (0.80)(0.25) + (0.55)(0.25)$
   $\beta = 1.10$

4. a. Market Risk Premium = $(K_M - i) = (0.12 - 0.05) = 0.07$
   b. SML: $K_j = 0.05 + (0.07)(\beta_j)$
   c. Slope of characteristic line = beta = 1.15
      RRR for Samson: $K = 0.05 + (0.07)(1.15) = 0.1305$
   d. Increase in inflation expectations of 2% should increase both the risk-free rate and market return by 2%: SML:
      $K_j = 0.07 + (0.14 - 0.07)(\beta_j)$
      $K_j = 0.07 + (0.07)(\beta_j)$

CHAPTER 7

1. $Price = \left(\dfrac{\$85}{2}\right)(ADF_{0.05,30}) + (1,000)(DF_{0.05,30})$

   $= (\$42.50)(15.372) + (\$1,000)(0.231)$

   $= \$653.31 + 231.00 = \$844.31$

2. $Current\ Yield = \dfrac{\$85}{\$884.31} = 0.096 = 9.6\%$

   Capital Gains Yield = $0.10 - 0.096 = 0.004 = 0.4\%$

3. $HPY = \dfrac{Current\ Income + (Ending\ Price - Beginning\ Price)}{Beginning\ Price}$

   $= \dfrac{\$92.50 + (\$1,050 - \$995)}{\$995}$

   $= \dfrac{\$147.50}{\$995} = 0.1482 = 14.82\%$

4. $V_E = \dfrac{D_1}{K_E - g} = \dfrac{\$0.75(1 + 0.11)}{(0.16 - 0.11)}$

   $V_E = \dfrac{\$0.83}{0.05} = \$16.65$

5. K_E = Dividend Yield + Capital Gains Yield

   $K_E = \dfrac{D_1}{P_0} + g = \dfrac{\$0.83}{16.65} + 0.11$

   $K_E = 0.05 + 0.11 = 0.16$

CHAPTER 8

1. a. $SR_{\$/C\$} = \dfrac{\$\ Spot\ Price\ of\ One\ lb.\ of\ Coffee}{C\$\ Spot\ Price\ of\ One\ lb.\ of\ Coffee}$

   $SR_{\$/C\$} = \dfrac{\$1.75\ /\ lb.}{C\$\ 2.50\ /\ lb.} = \dfrac{1.75}{2.50} = \$0.700\ /\ C\$$

   b. Buy coffee in New York for \$1.75/lb.
   Sell coffee in Toronto for C\$2.50/lb.
   Exchange C\$ for \$ = (\$0.75/C\$)(C\$2.50) = \$1.875
   Trading profit per lb. of coffee = \$1.875 - \$1.750
   = \$0.125

2. a. $ESR(1)_{\$/ATS} = \left(SR_{\$/ATS}\right)\left(\dfrac{1 + I_\$}{1 + I_{ATS}}\right)$

   $= (0.08150)\left(\dfrac{1 + 0.04}{1 + 0.06}\right) = \$0.07996\ /\ ATS$

   b. $ESR(3)_{\$/ATS} = (0.08150)\left(\dfrac{1 + 0.04}{1 + 0.06}\right)^3 = \$0.07697\ /\ ATS$

3. $ASR(1)_{\$/RS} = \left(SR_{\$/RS}\right)\left(\dfrac{1 + I_\$^*}{1 + I_{RS}^*}\right)$

   $0.260 = (0.0280)\left(\dfrac{1.09}{1 + I_{RS}^*}\right)$ $I_{RS}^* = 1.17 - 1 = 0.17 = 17\%$

CHAPTER 9

1. NPV = $-100,000 + (20,000)(DF_{0.10,1}) + (100,000)(DF_{0.10,2})$
   $+ (10,000)(DF_{0.10,3})$
   = $-100,000 + (20,000)(0.909) + (100,000)(0.826) +$
   $(10,000)(0.751)$
   = $-100,000 + 108,290 = \$8,290$
   Since NPV > 0, the investment should be made.

2.
Year	Cash Flow	$DF_{0.14,N}$	PV	$DF_{0.15,N}$	PV
1	\$ 20,000	0.877	\$ 17,540	0.870	\$17,400
2	100,000	0.769	76,900	0.756	75,600
3	10,000	0.675	6,750	0.658	6,580
	\$130,000		\$101,190		\$99,580

14% Discount Rate: NPV = \$101,190 - 100,000 = \$1,190
15% Discount Rate: NPV = \$99,580 - 100,000 = -\$420
14% < IRR < 15%
Based on Footnote #5: Approximate IRR =

$0.14 + \dfrac{\$1,190}{\$1,190 - (-420)}\ (0.15 - 0.14)$

$= 0.14 + 0.74 = 14.74\%$
Since IRR = 14.74% > RRR = 10%, the investment should be made.

3. NPV = $-400,000 - (100,000)(ADF_{0.16,10})$
   = $-400,000 - (100,000)(4.833)$
   = $-400,000 + 483,000 = \$83,300$

   $PVI = \dfrac{NPV}{Initial\ Outlay} = \dfrac{\$83,300}{\$400,000} = 0.208$

CHAPTER 10

1.

	Pretax	After-tax Equipment	Year
a.	$12,000	($12,000)(1 − 0.40) = $7,200	
b.	−$200,000	−$200,000	
c.	−$25,000	(−$25,000)(1 − 0.40) = −$15,000	
d.	$10,000	$10,000 − (10,000 − 6,000)(0.40) = $8,400	
e.	$6,000	6,000 − (6,000 − 10,000)(0.4) = $7,600	
f.	−$500,000	− $500,000	0
		$+\dfrac{500,000}{5}(0.4) = \$40,000$	1 to 5
g.	−$500,000	−$500,000	0
		+($500,000)(0.20)(0.4) = +$40,000	1
		+($500,000)(0.32)(0.4) = +$64,000	2
		+($500,000)(0.192)(0.4) = +$38,400	3
		+($500,000)(0.1152)(0.4) = +$23,040	4
		+($500,000)(0.1152)(0.4) = +$23,040	5
		+($500,000)(0.0576)(0.4) = +$11,520	6

2. Net Outlay = −$750,000

Annual Operating Cash Flows

		Years 1–5
Savings (1 − T)	($160,000)(1 − 0.40) =	$96,000
Depreciation (T)	$\dfrac{750,000}{10}(0.4) =$	$30,000
Annual Operation Cash Flow		$126,000

		Years 6–10
Savings (1 − T)	($80,000)(1 − 0.40) =	$48,000
Depreciation (T)		$30,000
Annual Operation Cash Flow		$78,000

Termination Cash Flow = $60,000 − (60,000 − 0)(0.4) = $36,000

NPV = −$750,000 + (126,000)(ADF$_{0.08,5}$) + (78,000)(ADF$_{0.08,10}$ − ADF$_{0.08,5}$) + (36,000)(DF$_{0.08,10}$)
NPV = −750,000 + (126,000)(3.993) + (78,000)(6.710 − 3.993) + (36,000)(0.463) = −$18,228
Since NPV < 0, the machine should not be purchased.

3. Depreciation of Old Machine = $\dfrac{\$300,000}{10}$ = $30,000 per year
Book Value Now = $300,000 (−5)(30,000) = $150,000

Relevant Cash Flow from the Replacement of the Old Machine

Initial Period Cash Flow =
After-Tax Proceeds from Sale of Old Machine =
+$120,000 − (120,000 − 150,000)(0.4) = $132,000
Operating Life Cash Flows =
Lost Depreciation Tax Shield on Old Machine =
(−$30,000)(0.4) = −12,000 (Years 1–5 only)
Termination Cash Flow =
Lost Salvage in year 10 because the old machine is sold
now = −$40,000 + (40,000 − 0)(0.4) = −$24,000

Recalculation of Cash Flow for New Machine Including the Replacement of Old Machine

Net Outlay = −750,000 + 132,000 = $618,000

Annual Operating Cash Flows

	Years 1–5	Years 6–10
Savings (1 − T)	$ 96,000	$48,000
Depreciation (T)		
New Machine	30,000	30,000
Old Machine	−12,000	0
	$114,000	$78,000

Termination Cash Flows = $36,000 − 24,000 = $12,000
NPV = −$618,000 + (114,000)(3.993) + (78,000)(6.710 − 3.993) + (12,000)(0.463) = $54,684
Since NPV > 0, the machine should be purchased.

CHAPTER 11

1. Since we know the project's NPV, we can calculate the incremental effect of the changes in sales and add or subtract them from the project's NPV of $6,000,000.
Incremental Effect = (100)(0.10)(100,000)(ADF$_{0.16,15}$)
= ($1,000,000)(5.576) = $5,576,000
10% Increase: NPV = $6,000,000 + 5,576,000
= $11,576,000
10% Decrease: NPV = $6,000,000 − 5,576,000
= $424,000

2. Incremental Effect
= (−$500,000)(0.10) + (500,000)(0.10)(DF$_{0.14,10}$)
= −50,000 + (50,000)(0.270) = −36,500
10% Increase = NPV = $2,400,000 − 36,500
= $2,363,500
10% Decrease = NPV = $2,400,000 + 36,500
= $2,436,500

3. a. EBIT = P(Q) − (VC)Q − FC   0 = 19Q − 15Q − 2,600,000
= (19 − 15)(Q) − 2,600,000
$Q = \dfrac{2,600,000}{4}$ = 650,000 units

b. Assume a 10% change in Q from 900,000
EBIT (900,000) = (19 − 15)(900,000) − 2,600,000
= $1,000,000
EBIT (990,000) = (19 − 15)(990,000) − 2,600,000
= $1,360,000
% Change in EBIT = $\dfrac{1,360,000 − 1,000.000}{1,000,000} \times 100 = 36\%$

% Change in Q = $\dfrac{990,000 − 900,000}{900,000} \times 100 = 10\%$

DOL = $\dfrac{\% \text{ Change in EBIT}}{\% \text{ Change in Q}} = \dfrac{36\%}{10\%} = 3.6$

The following equation can also be used:
DOL = $\dfrac{(P − VC)(Q)}{(P − VC)(Q) − FC} = \dfrac{(19 − 15)(900,000)}{(19 − 15)(900,000) − 2,600,000}$

DOL = $\dfrac{3,600,000}{3,600,000 − 2,600,000} = \dfrac{3,600,000}{1,000,000} = 3.6$

CHAPTER 12

1. This problem is solved by working through a 3-year amortization schedule with the first two payments given as $100,000 and $200,000, respectively. The last payment is the amount that decreases the remaining balance to zero.

Year	Payment	Interest 12%	Payment of Principal	Remaining Principal
0	—	—	—	400,000
1	100,000	48,000	52,000	348,000
2	200,000	41,760	158,240	189,760
3	X	22,771	189,760	0

X = Interest on Last Year's Principal + Remaining Principal
X = (0.12)(189,760) + 189,760
X = $22,771 + 189,760 = $212,531

2. a. V_B = (Interest) $(ADF_{0.10,15})$ + (Par) $(DF_{0.10,15})$
   V_B = 0 + 1,000(0.2394) = $239.40

   b. Number of Bonds = $\dfrac{\text{Funds Required}}{\text{Price per Bond}}$ = $\dfrac{100,000,000}{\$239.40}$
   = 418,410 bonds

   c. The total to be repaid at maturity is the Face Value of the total bond issue.
   Face Value = Number of Bonds × Par Value per bond
   = (418,410)($1,000) = $418,410,000

3. a. Value of Lease Side Effect = VBL – PV (Residual)
   VBL = Purchase Price – PV (Lease Cash Flow)
   After-Tax Lease Payment = ($25,000)(1 – 0.40)
   = $15,000

   Depreciation Tax Shield Lost = $\left(\dfrac{\$100,000}{5}\right)$(0.40)
   = $8,000

	t = 0	t = 1	t = 2	t = 3	t = 4	t = 5
After-Tax Payment	$15,000	$15,000	$15,000	$15,000	$15,000	
Lost Tax Shield		8,000	8,000	8,000	8,000	8,000
LCF	$15,000	$23,000	$23,000	$23,000	$23,000	$8,000

RRR = (0.10)(1 – 0.40) = 0.06
PV(LCF) = $15,000 + (23,000)$(ADF_{0.06,4})$ + (8,000)$(DF_{0.06,5})$
PV(LCF) = $15,000 + (23,000)(3.465) + (8,000)(0.747)
= $100,671
VBL = Purchase Price – PV(LCF) = $100,000 – 100,671
= –$671
Residual After-Tax = $20,000 – (20,000 – 0)(0.40)
= $12,000
PV (Residual) = ($12,000)$(DF_{0.12,5})$ = ($12,000)(0.567)
= $6,804
PV (Maintenance) = ($5,000)(1 – 0.40)$(ADF_{0.06,5})$
= ($3,000)(4.212) = $12,636
Value of Lease Side Effects = VBL – PV(Residual) + PV(Maintenance) = –$671 – 6,804 + 12,636 = $5,161
Because the Value of Lease Side Effect is positive, the asset should be leased.

   b. NPV (Leased Asset) = NPV (Base) + Value of Lease Side Effects

NPV (Leased Asset) = –$4,000 + 5,161 = $1,161
Because the NPV is positive, the asset should be leased.

CHAPTER 13

1. a. Number of New Shares = $\dfrac{\text{Financing Required}}{\text{Subscription Price}}$

   = $\dfrac{\$100\text{ million}}{\$50}$ = 2 million shares

   b. Number of Rights for One New Share = $\dfrac{\text{Number of Outstanding Shares}}{\text{Number of New Shares}}$

   N = $\dfrac{8\text{ million}}{2\text{ million}}$ = 4

   c. $P_E = \dfrac{(P_0)(N) + S}{N + 1} = \dfrac{(75)(4) + 50}{4 + 1} = \dfrac{350}{5} = \$70$

   d. R = $\dfrac{P_E - S}{N}$ $\dfrac{\$70 - \$50}{4}$ = $5.00
   or   R = $P_0 - P_E$ = $75 – $70 = $5.00

2. a. Wealth Before = Value of Common Stock
   = ($75)(100) = $7,500
   Wealth After = Value of Common Stock + Proceeds from Rights Sale = ($70)(100) + (5)(100) = $7,500
   Investment Change = Investment After – Investment Before
   = $7,000 – 7,500 = –$500
   Note: Investment Change = Proceeds from Sale of Rights

   b. Wealth Before = $7,500
   Wealth After = Value of Common Stock – Cash Paid for New Stock
   = (P_E)(New Shares + Old Shares) – (S)(New Shares)
   = $(\$70)\left(\dfrac{100}{4} + 100\right) - (50)\left(\dfrac{100}{4}\right)$
   = ($70)(125) – (50)(25) = $8,750 – 1,250 = $7,500
   Investment Change = Investment After – Investment Before
   = (70)(125) – 75(100) = $1,250
   Note: Investment Change equals cash paid for new stock.

3. a. $V_B = \left(\dfrac{\$100}{2}\right)(ADF_{0.06,50}) + (\$1,000)(DF_{0.06,50})$

   = ($50)(15.762) + ($1,000)(0.054)

   = $788.10 + 54.00 = $842.10

   b. Conversion Ratio = $1,000/$25 = 40
   V_C = Conversion Ratio × Market Price per Share
   = (40)($19) = $760.00

   c. V_{TC} = Higher of V_B or V_C = $842.10
   CP = $V_{MC} - V_{TC}$ = $1,100 – 842.10 = $257.90

   d. Minimum Stock Price = Call Price/Conversion Ratio
   = $1,060/40 = $26.50

CHAPTER 14

1. a. Personal Leverage:
   Lenders' Share = rD = (0.12)($400,000) = $48,000
   Government's Share = (EBIT)(T) = ($1,500,000)(0.40)
   = $600,000

Owners' Share = EBIT − Lenders' Share − Government's
Share = $1,500,000 − 48,000 − 600,000 = $852,000
Corporate Leverage:
Lenders' Share = rD = (0.12)($400,000) = $48,000
Government's Share = (EBIT)(T) = (0.40)($1,500,000)
= $600,000
Owners' Share = EBIT − Lenders' Share − Government's
Share = $1,500,000 − 48,000 − 600,000 = $852,000

b. Personal Leverage:
Lenders' Share = rD = (0.12)($400,000) = $48,000
Government's Share = (EBIT)(T) = (0.40)($1,500,000)
= $600,000
Owners' Share = EBIT − Lenders' Share − Government's
Share = $1,500,000 − 48,000 − 600,000 = $852,000
Corporate Leverage:
Lender's Share = rD = (0.12)($400,000) = $48,000
Government's Share = (EBIT−rD) T
= ($1,500,000 − 48,000)(0.40) = $580,800
Owner's Share = EBIT − Lender's Share − Government's
Share = $1,500,000 − 48,000 − 580,800 = $871,200

c. Cash Flow Advantage = $871,200 − 852,000
= +$19,200/year to Owners
Cash Flow Disadvantage = $580,800 − $600,000
= −$19,200 to Government
Tax Savings from Corporate Debt = rTD
= (0.12)(400,000)(0.40) = $19,200

$$\text{Value} = \sum_{t=1}^{\infty} \frac{rTD}{(1+K_U)^t} = \frac{rTD}{K_U} = \frac{\$19,200}{0.15} = \$128,000$$

2. a. Without Leverage: $V_S = V_U$ and $K_E = K_U$
$V_S = V_U$ = Number of shares × price per share
$V_U = (10,000,000)(\$15) = \$150,000,000$
Dividends = (EBIT) (1 − T) = ($25,000,000)(1 − 0.40)
= $15,000,000

$$\text{Since } V_U = \sum_{t=1}^{\infty} \frac{(EBIT)(1-T)}{(1+K_U)^t} = \frac{(EBIT)(1-T)}{K_U},$$

$$K_U = \frac{(EBIT)(1-T)}{V_U} = \frac{\$15,000,000}{\$150,000,000} = 0.10$$

b. $V_L = V_U + \theta D = V_U + \left(\frac{rT}{K_U}\right)(D)$

$$V_L = \$150,000,000 + \left(\frac{0.075}{0.10}\right)(0.40)(50,000,000)$$

$V_L = \$150,000,000 + \$15,000,000 = \$165,000,000$
and: $V_L = V_S + D$
165,000,000 = V_S + 50,000,000
$V_S = \$115,000,000$

c. Dividends = (EBIT − rD)(1 − T)
= [$25,000,000 − (0.075)(50,000,000)](1 − 0.40)
= $12,750,000

$$K_E = \frac{(EBIT - rD)(1-T)}{V_S} = \frac{\$12,750,000}{\$115,000,000} = 0.111 = 11.1\%$$

or

$$K_E = \frac{K_U - rL}{1-L} = \frac{0.10 - (0.075)\left(\dfrac{50}{165}\right)}{1 - \left(\dfrac{50}{165}\right)} = 11.1\%$$

d. Shares after Recapitalization
= Original Shares − Shares Repurchased
= Original Shares − $\dfrac{\text{Debt}}{\text{Repurchase Price}}$

$$= 10,000,000 - \frac{50,000,000}{\$16.50} = 6,969,696$$

$$\text{Price / Share} = \frac{V_S}{\text{Shares}} = \frac{115,000,000}{6,969,696} = \$16.50$$

Those stockholders who sold received $16.50 per share,
while those who held have stock worth $16.50. All
stockholders shared equally in the $15 million increase in
firm value due to the recapitalization: θD =
$15,000,000 = (10,000,000 \text{ shares})(\$16.50 - 15.00)$

CHAPTER 15

1. Estimate the dividend growth rate from EPS data:
$(EPS_{1989})(1 + g)^9 = EPS_{1998}$ $(2.25)(1 + g)^9 = 4.50$

$$(1+g)^9 = \frac{4.50}{2.25} = 2.00$$

$g = (2.00)^{1/9} - 1 = 1.08 - 1 = 0.08$

$$K_E = \frac{(D_0)(1+g)}{P} + g = \frac{(\$4.50)(1.08)(0.40)}{\$21.34} + 0.08$$

$= 0.09 + 0.08 = 0.17 = 17\%$

2. First, find the cost of each component:
Equity: $K_E = i + (K_M - i)(\beta) = 0.05 + (0.08)(1.75) = 0.19$
Preferred Stock: $r_P = \dfrac{D}{P_0} = \dfrac{4.50}{30.00} = 0.15$

Debt: $K_D = (YTM)(1 - T) = (0.12)(1 - 0.40) = 0.072$
Second, calculate the weighted average cost of capital:
$K_A = (W_D)(K_D) + (W_P)(K_P) + (W_E)(K_E)$
$K_A = (0.072)(0.40) + (0.15)(0.10) + (0.19)(0.50)$
$K_A = 0.0288 + 0.015 + 0.095 = 0.1388 = 13.88\%$

3. a. With no debt in the capital structure:
$K_A = (W_D)(K_D) + (W_E)(K_E)$
$K_A = (0.00)(0.10)(1 - 0.40) + (1.00)(0.13)$
$K_A = 0.00 + 0.13 = 13\%$
b. From (a), $K_U = 13\%$:
$$K_E = \frac{K_U - rL}{1-L} = \frac{0.13 - (0.10)(0.15)}{(1 - 0.15)} = 0.1353 = 13.53\%$$

$K_A = (W_D)(K_D) + (W_E)(K_E)$
$K_A = (0.15)(0.10)(1 - 0.40) + (0.85)(0.1353)$
$K_A = 0.009 + 0.1150 = 0.1240 = 12.40\%$

c. $K_E = \dfrac{0.13 - (0.10)(0.30)}{(1 - 0.30)} = 0.1429 = 14.29\%$

$K_A = (W_D)(K_D) + (W_E)(K_E)$

$K_A = (0.30)(0.10)(1 - 0.40) + (0.70)(0.1429)$
$K_A = 0.018 + 0.100 = 0.118 = 11.8\%$

CHAPTER 16

1. Because dividends are constant indefinitely:

$$P_0 = \frac{D}{K_E} \text{ and } K_E = \frac{D}{P_0} = \frac{\$3.60}{\$30} = 0.12 = 12\%$$

2. a. New Shares $= \dfrac{\text{Required Financing}}{\text{Market Price}} = \dfrac{\$3,600,000}{\$30}$

   $= 120,000$ shares

   b. EAT $= (\$3.60)(1,000,000) + \$432,000 = \$4,032,000$

   $$EPS = \frac{\$4,032,000}{1,000,000 + 120,000} = \$3.60$$

   DPS = EPS (with 100% payout) = $3.60

   c. $P_1 = \dfrac{D}{K_E} = \dfrac{3.60}{0.12} = \$30.00 / \text{share}$

3. a. EAT = \$4,032,000 $EPS = \dfrac{\$4,032,000}{1,000,000} = \$4.032$

   DPS = EPS (with 100% payout) = $4.032

   b. $P_1 = \dfrac{D_2}{K_E} = \dfrac{\$4.032}{0.12} = \$33.60$

4. a. HPY = Current Yield + Capital Gain Yield

   $= \dfrac{D_1}{P_0} + \dfrac{P_1 - P_0}{P_0} = \dfrac{\$3.60}{\$30} + \dfrac{\$30 - 30}{\$30} = 0.12 + 0 = 12\%$

   b. $HPY = \dfrac{D_1}{P_0} + \dfrac{P_1 - P_0}{P_0} = \dfrac{\$0}{\$30} + \dfrac{\$33.60 - 30.00}{\$30.00}$

   $= 0 + 0.12 = 12\%$

5. a. $HPY = \left(\dfrac{D_1}{P_0}\right)(1 - T_D) + \left(\dfrac{P_1 - P_0}{P_0}\right)(1 - T_{CG})$

   $HPY = (0.12)(1 - 0.50) + (0)(1 - 0.30) = 0.06 = 6\%$

   b. $HPY = (0)(1 - 0.50) + 0.12(1 - 0.30) = 0.084 = 8.4\%$

CHAPTER 17

1. Minimum Current Assets = Permanent Current Assets
   = $40 (Feb.)   Maximum Current Assets = $100 (July)
   Maximum Temporary Assets = $100 − 40 = $60 (July)

2. Permanent Assets = Fixed Assets + Permanent Current Assets
   = $200 + 40 = $240
   Permanent Financing = Permanent Assets + Permanent
   Financing of Temporary Assets = $240 + (0.40)(60) = $264

3. Maximum Temporary Financing = Maximum Temporary
   Assets − Permanent Financing of Temporary Assets
   = $60 − 24 = $36

4. a. Long-Term Debt = Permanent Financing − Owners' Equity
      − Permanent Spontaneous Liabilities
      = $264 − 100 − (0.25)(40) = $154
   b. Maximum Negotiated Current Liabilities
      = Maximum Temporary Financing − Maximum Temporary
      Spontaneous Liabilities = $36 − (0.25)(60) = $21
   c. Maximum Excess Financing
      = Permanent Financing − Permanent Assets
      = $264 − 240 = $24

CHAPTER 18

1. a. $APR = \dfrac{0.03}{100 - 0.03} \times \dfrac{360}{30 - 10} = (0.0309)(18) = 55.62\%$

   $EIR = (1.0309)^{18} - 1 = 1.7294 - 1 = 72.94\%$

   b. $APR = (0.0309) \times \dfrac{360}{30 - 20} = (0.0309)(36) = 111.24\%$

   $EIR = (1.0309)^{36} - 1 = 2.9909 - 1 = 199.09\%$

2. a. Loan − Compensating Balance = Cash Available
      Loan − (0.10)(Loan) = 100,000

   $Loan = \dfrac{100,000}{0.90} = \$111,111$

   Cash Paid = (111,111)(0.15) = $16,667

   $APR = \dfrac{\$16,607}{\$100,000} = 16.67\%$

   b. Loan − Compensating Balance − Discount
      = Cash Available
      Loan − (0.10)(Loan) − (0.15)(Loan) = 100,000

   $Loan = \dfrac{100,000}{0.75} = \$133,333$

   Cash Paid = (133,333)(0.15) = $20,000

   $APR = \dfrac{\$20,000}{\$100,000} = 20\%$

3. a. Loan − Discount − Other Prepaid Fees = Cash Available

   $Loan - (0.12)\left(\dfrac{120}{360}\right)(Loan) - (60,000 + 40,000)$

   $= \$10,000,000$
   Loan − (0.04)(Loan) − 100,000 = $10,000,000
   Loan (0.96) = $10,100,000

   $Loan = \dfrac{\$10,100,000}{0.96} = \$10,520,833$

   b. Cash Paid = ($10,520,833)(0.04) + 100,000
      = $520,833

   $APR = \dfrac{\$520,833}{\$10,000,000} \times \dfrac{360}{120} = 0.052 \times 3 = 15.62\%$

   c. $EIR = (1.052)^3 - 1 = 1.1643 - 1 = 16.43\%$

CHAPTER 19

1. a. Funds Available = Reduction in Collection Delay × Daily
      Credit Sales $FA_R = (3 + 2)(200,000) = \$1,000,000$
   b. NPV = FA_R − Compensating Balance − PV of After-Tax Fees

   $NPV = \$1,000,000 - 500,000 - \dfrac{(100,000)(1 - 0.40)}{0.10}$

   = $1,000,000 − 500,000 − 600,000 = −$100,000
   Since NPV < 0, the system should *not* be implemented.

2. Funds Available = Reduction in Collection Delay × Daily
   Credit Sales $FA_R = (2)(1,000 \text{ Checks} \times \$400 \text{ per check})$
   = (2)(400,000) = $800,000
   NPV = FA_R + PV Operating Savings − Compensating
   Balance − PV Fees

   $NPV = \$800,000 + \dfrac{(200,000)(1 - 0.4)}{0.10} - 300,000 -$

$$\frac{[220,000 + (0.10)(1,000)(360)](1 - 0.4)}{0.10}$$

$$= 800,000 + 1,200,000 - 300,000 - 1,536,000$$
$$= \$164,000$$

Since NPV > 0, the bank's proposal should be accepted.

CHAPTER 20

1. Incremental Cash Flow = $[(\Delta S)(1 - VC)$
   $- (\Delta S)(BD) - \Delta CE](1 - T)$
   Moderate Risk: $C = [(\$2,000,000)(1 - 0.7)$
   $- (2,000,000)(0.05) - 10,000](1-0.4) = \$294,000$
   High Risk: $C = [(\$1,000,000)(1-0.7) - (1,000,000)(0.20) -$
   $25,000](1-0.4) = \$45,000$
   Incremental Investment = (ACP)(Sales/Day)(VC)

   Moderate Risk: $I = (45)\left(\frac{\$2,000,000}{360}\right)(0.7) = \$175,000$

   High Risk: $I = (80)\left(\frac{\$1,000,000}{360}\right)(0.7) = \$155,555$

   NPV = PV of Cash Flow − Investment
   Moderate Risk:

   $$NPV = \frac{\$294,000}{0.20} - \$175,000 = \$1,295,000$$

   High Risk: $NPV = \dfrac{\$45,000}{0.30} - \$155,555 = -\$5,555$

   Credit should be granted to moderate risk (NPV > 0).
   Credit should be denied to high risk (NPV < 0).

2. Incremental Cash Flow = $[(\Delta S)(1 - VC) - (\Delta S)(BD)](1 - T)$
   $C = [(\$50,000,000)(1 - 0.75)$
   $- (50,000,000)(0.02)](1 - 0.40) = \$6,900,000$
   Incremental Investment:
   New Customers I_N = (ACP) (Sales per day) (VC)

   $$= (40)\left(\frac{\$50,000,000}{360}\right)(0.75)$$

   $$= \$4,166,667$$

   Old Customers $I_O = (\Delta ACP)$ (Sales per day)

   $$= (40 - 20)\left(\frac{\$300,000,000}{360}\right)$$

   $$= \$16,666,667$$

   $I = I_N + I_O = \$4,166,667 + 16,666,667 = \$20,833,334$
   NPV = PV of cash flow − I

   $$NPV = \frac{\$6,900,000}{0.20} - 20,833,334 = \$13,666,666$$

   The credit period should be extended because NPV > 0.

3. Determine the changes:

Policy	Δ Inventory	Δ Carry Cost	Δ Lost Sales	RRR
A	$200,000 − 100,000 = 100,000	$5,000	$200,000	20%
B	300,000 − 200,000 = 100,000	5,000	150,000	25
C	400,000 − 300,000 = 100,000	5,000	50,000	30

   Incremental Cash Flow = $[(\Delta S)(1 - VC) - \Delta CC](1 - T)$
   Policy A: $C = [(\$200,000)(1 - 0.7) - 5,000](1 - 0.4)$
   $= \$33,000$
   Policy B: $C = [(\$150,000)(1 - 0.7) - 5,000](1 - 0.4)$
   $= \$24,000$

Policy C: $C = [(\$50,000)(1 - 0.7) - 5,000](1 - 0.4)$
$= \$6,000$
NPV = PV cash flow − Investment in Investory

Policy A: $NPV = \dfrac{\$33,000}{0.20} - 100,000 = \$65,000$

Policy B: $NPV = \dfrac{\$24,000}{0.25} - 100,000 = -\$4,000$

Policy C: $NPV = \dfrac{\$6,000}{0.30} - 100,000 = -\$80,000$

The best policy for Talbert is Policy A because NPV > 0. For both Policy B and Policy C, NPV < 0.

CHAPTER 21

1. $CA = \dfrac{\$200}{\$800} = 0.25 \quad FA = \dfrac{\$300}{\$800} = 0.375 \quad d = 0.40$

   $CL = \dfrac{\$100}{\$800} = 0.125 \quad B = \dfrac{\$150}{\$400} = 0.375 \quad M = 0.06$

   $$g = \frac{(M)(1 - d)}{(1 - B)(CA + FA - CL)} = \frac{(0.06)(1 - 0.4)}{(1 - 0.375)(0.25 + 0.375 - 0.125)}$$

   $$= \frac{0.036}{0.3125} = 0.1152 = 11.52\%$$

2. $0.15 = \dfrac{(0.06)(1 - d)}{0.3125}$

   $1 - d = \dfrac{(0.15)(0.3125)}{0.06} = \dfrac{0.0469}{0.06} = 0.78$

   $d = 1 - 0.78 = 0.22;$ Reducing the payout ratio from 40% to 22% will increase sustainable growth to 15%.

3. $g_E = \dfrac{(M)(1 - d)}{(1 - B)(CA + FA - CL)} + \dfrac{e}{(1 - B)(CA + FA - CL)}$

   $0.15 = \dfrac{(0.06)(1 - 0.4)}{(1 - 0.375)(0.25 + 0.375 - 0.125)}$

   $\qquad + \dfrac{e}{(1 - 0.375)(0.25 + 0.375 - 0.125)}$

   $0.15 = 0.1152 + \dfrac{e}{0.3125}$

   $\dfrac{e}{0.3125} = 0.15 - 0.1152 = 0.0348$

   $e = (0.3125)(0.0348) = 1.09\%$

CHAPTER 22

1. a. $V_C = V_B + V_S + V_{SB}$
   $V_C = (\$45)(7,000,000) + (\$60)(1,000,000) + 25,000,000$
   $V_C = \$315,000,000 + \$60,000,000 + \$25,000,000$
   $= \$400,000,000$
   b. Maximum price for Starway gives 100% of value created to Starway stockholders:
   Maximum Price = $V_S + V_{SB}$
   $= \$60,000,000 + \$25,000,000 = \$85,000,000$
   c. Minimum Price for Starway gives 100% of value created to Bridgeton stockholders:
   Minimum Price = $V_S = \$60,000,000$
   d. NPV_S = Price − V_S = Premium
   $= \$75,000,000 - 60,000,000 = \$15,000,000$

$NPV_B = V_S + V_{SB} - Price = V_{SB} - Premium$
$= \$60,000,000 + \$25,000,000 - 75,000,000$
$= \$25,000,000 - 15,000,000 = \$10,000,000$

2. a. Highest exchange rate (E) implies the maximum purchase price of $85,000,000 from (1b):

Price = Post-merger Share Price × Shares to Starway

$$= \left[\frac{V_C}{N_B + (E)(N_S)} \right](E)(N_S)$$

$$\$85,000,000 =$$

$$\left[\frac{400,000,000}{7,000,000 + (E)(1,000,000)} \right](E)(1,000,000)$$

E = 1.889 shares of Bridgeton for one Starway

b. Lowest exchange rate implies the minimum price of $60,000,000 from (1c): $60,000,000 =

$$\left[\frac{400,000,000}{7,000,000 + (E)(1,000,000)} \right](E)(1,000,000) \quad E = 1.235$$

c. $P_C = \dfrac{V_C}{N_B + (E)(N_S)} = \dfrac{400,000,000}{7,000,000 + (1.6)(1,000,000)}$
$= \$46.51$

d. Price = $(P_C)(E)(N_S)$ = ($46.51)(1.6)(1,000,000)
$= \$74,416,000$

e. $NPV_S = Price - V_S = Premium$
$= \$74,416,000 - \$60,000,000 = \$14,416,000$
$NPV_B = V_S + V_{SB} - Price = V_{SB} - Premium$
$NPV_B = 60,000,000 + 25,000,000 - 74,416,000$
$= 25,000,000 - 14,416,000 = \$10,584,000$

3. a. Value to Bridgeton = $V_B + (0.40)(V_{SB})$
$= \$315,000,000 + (0.40)(25,000,000)$
$= \$325,000,000$

Value to Starway = $V_S + (0.60)(V_{SB})$
$= \$60,000,000 + (0.60)(25,000,000) = \$75,000,000$

b. Proportion of shares to Bridgeton =

$$\frac{\$325,000,000}{\$325,000,000 + 75,000,000} = 81.25\%$$

Proportion of shares to Starway =

$$\frac{\$75,000,000}{\$325,000,000 + 75,000,000} = 18.75\%$$

Shares to Bridgeton = (10,000,000)(0.8125)
= 8,125,000 shares
Shares to Starway = (10,000,000)(0.1875)
= 1,875,000 shares

c. Bridgeton: Exchange Ratio = $\dfrac{8,125,000}{7,000,000}$

= 1.16 shares of Bridgestar for each share of Bridgeton

Starway: Exchange Ratio = $\dfrac{1,875,000}{1,000,000}$

= 1.875 shares of Bridgestar for each share of Starway

CHAPTER 23

1. $NPV = (600)\left(\dfrac{3}{10}\right) - (300)\left(\dfrac{7}{10}\right) = -\$30$ million

2. a. Since the common stock has no value, the stockholders do not experience the downside of the risky investment. On the other hand, they expect to gain $500 out of the $600 million of the value created on the upside, sharing $100 million with creditors as the market value of debt rises to face value.

$$\Delta V_S = \left(\frac{3}{10}\right)(\$500) - \left(\frac{7}{10}\right)(0) = \$150$$

b. Creditors stand to gain $100 on the upside but lose $300 on the downside:

$$\Delta V_D = \left(\frac{3}{10}\right)(\$100) - \left(\frac{7}{10}\right)(300)$$

$$= 30 - 210 = -\$180 \text{ million}$$

c. $NPV = \Delta V_S + \Delta V_D = \$150 - \$180 = -\$30$ million

3. a. $X_1 = \dfrac{\text{Net Working Capital}}{\text{Total Assets}} = \dfrac{300 - 100}{800} = 0.250$

$X_2 = \dfrac{\text{Retained Earnings}}{\text{Total Assets}} = \dfrac{350}{800} = 0.438$

$X_3 = \dfrac{\text{EBIT}}{\text{Total Assets}} = \dfrac{240}{800} = 0.300$

$X_4 = \dfrac{\text{Market Value Equity}}{\text{Book Value Total Liabilities}} = \dfrac{93}{100 + 200} = 0.310$

$X_5 = \dfrac{\text{Sales}}{\text{Total Assets}} = \dfrac{500}{800} = 0.625$

$Z = 1.2X_1 + 1.4 X_2 + 3.3X_3 + 0.6X_4 + 1.0X_5$
$= (1.2)(0.250) + (1.4)(0.438) + (3.3)(0.300) + (0.6)(0.310) + (1.0)(0.625)$
$= 0.300 + 0.6132 + 0.990 + 0.186 + 0.625 = 2.7142$

b. A Z-score above 2.99 is associated with non-bankruptcy. A Z-score below 1.81 is associated with bankruptcy. Since Calidad's Z-score is between these two values, no firm prediction can be made.

CHAPTER 24

1. $\dfrac{1 + r_{DM}}{1 + r_{FF}} = \dfrac{1 + I_{DM}}{1 + I_{FF}}$ $1 + r_{DM} = (1 + 0.06)\left(\dfrac{1 + 0.03}{1 + 0.04}\right)$

$r_{DM} = 1.0498 - 1 = 0.0498 = 4.98\%$

2. $ESR(1)_{\$/DM} = (SR_{\$/DM})\left(\dfrac{1 + r_{\$}}{1 + r_{DM}}\right)$

$= (0.55)\left(\dfrac{1 + 0.08}{1 + 0.06}\right) = 0.5604$

3. Find the rate in dollars of the investment in Japan:

$1 + r_{\$} = (1 + r_{¥})\left(\dfrac{FR_{\$/¥}}{SR_{\$/¥}}\right)$ $1 + r_{\$} = (1 + 0.12)\left(\dfrac{0.0078}{0.0080}\right)$

$r_{\$} = 1.092 - 1 = 9.2\%$ per year in dollars.
The U.S. investment yielding 10% per annum in dollars is preferred.

Glossary

A

Absolute Physical Life The time period after which an asset has deteriorated to such an extent that it can no longer be used. (Ch. 10, p. 324)

Accrual Accounting Convention An accounting system that tries to match the recognition of revenues earned with the expenses incurred in generating those revenues. An accrual accounting system ignores the timing of the cash flows associated with revenues and expenses. (Ch. 2, p. 32)

Accruals A source of spontaneous credit that represents expenses for which the firm is currently liable but has not yet paid. (Ch. 18, p. 579)

Activity Ratios Ratios that measure how effectively management is utilizing its resources by relating the magnitude of various assets to revenues or expenses. (Ch. 2, p. 41)

Actual Future Spot Rate The spot rate between two currencies on a given future date. It will differ from the current spot rate by the extent to which actual inflation rates in the two currencies differ in the meantime. (Ch. 8, p. 253)

Adverse Investment Decisions Acceptance of high risk, negative NPV projects and rejection of low risk, positive NPV projects. (Ch. 23, p. 724)

Adverse Liquidity Decisions The sale of needed assets in order to generate cash or the failure to make necessary expenditures in order to conserve cash. (Ch. 23, p. 726)

Agency The principle that decisions should not be based on the needs and desires of the agents (corporate managers) but rather on the interests of those individuals whom the agents represent (shareholders). (Ch. 1, p. 4)

Agency Costs The expenses associated with stockholder efforts to monitor the actions of managers to minimize the agency problem. (Ch. 1, p. 6)

Agency Problem The conflict of interest between the welfare of a firm's owners and its managers due to the small ownership position of the managers. (Ch. 1, p. 5)

Amortized An amortized loan provides for periodic payments throughout the life of the loan that serve both to pay interest and reduce the principal. (Ch. 12, p. 384)

Annualized Present Value The annual cash flow from an annuity with the same life and present value as a specific investment under evaluation. (Ch. 10, p. 329)

Annuity A series of cash flows for which the amount of payment or receipt is the same each period. (Ch. 5, p. 141)

Arbitrage The simultaneous purchase and sale of a given commodity or financial instrument on two different markets in order to take advantage of discrepancies in the trading prices on those markets. (Ch. 8, p. 243)

Authorized Shares The maximum number of shares a firm may issue. Present stockholders must authorize the sale of any additional stock. (Ch. 13, p. 426)

B

Backup Line of Credit A bank line of credit obtained by an issuer of commercial paper to protect the investor from default. The issuer pays a commitment fee to the bank. (Ch. 18, p. 583)

Balloon Payment In a partially amortized or unamortized loan, it is the last large payment that repays all the remaining principal and interest. (Ch. 12, p. 384)

Banking Delay Time required for processing, clearing, and collecting a check through the banking system. (Ch. 19, p. 602)

Basis Point A quotation for interest rates and loan spreads that is equal to 1/100 of one percent. (Ch. 24, p. 760)

Best Efforts Basis An alternative to underwriting a security issue whereby an investment banker agrees only to attempt to sell the securities at the best available price. (Ch. 3, p. 82)

Beta A measure of investment risk that assesses only the undiversifiable risk associated with an investment. (Ch. 6, p. 183)

Bond A long-term promissory note that is issued by a corporation or government. It represents a loan agreement in which the issuer (the borrower) is contractually obligated to make specific cash payments to the bond's owner (the lender) over a fixed period of time. (Ch. 7, p. 207)

Bond Indenture A contract drawn up by the issuer prior to the issuance of the bond. The agreement contains the essential covenants of the bond issue. (Ch. 12, p. 388)

Book Value Common shareholder's equity divided by the total number of common shares outstanding. (Ch. 13, p. 427)

Bootstrapping The increase in the EPS of a high P/E firm that results from the acquisition of a lower P/E firm. (Ch. 22, p. 690)

Brokers They specialize in bringing borrowers and lenders together, act as go-betweens, or actually purchase the direct claims from the deficit unit before reselling them to the surplus unit. (Ch. 3, p. 65)

C

Call Option This provision of the bond indenture gives the issuing firm the right to repurchase the bond prior to maturity at a set price. (Ch. 12, p. 392)

Call Price The price at which the issuing firm can redeem its bonds prior to their maturity. (Ch. 13, p. 434)

Call Protection A restriction put on the ability of the issuing firm to call its bonds prior to maturity. Usually stated as a specific number of years before the bond is callable. (Ch. 12, p. 392)

Callability The right of the issuer of a security to redeem the security prior to maturity by "calling it in," or forcing the holder to sell it back. (Ch. 3, p. 77)

Capital Asset Pricing Model (CAPM) The theoretical model that quantifies the risk/return trade-off associated with an investment in terms of the Security Market Line. The CAPM enables an individual to specify an investment's RRR once one estimates its beta. (Ch. 6, p. 194)

Capital Budgeting The process of analyzing potential investing decisions in long-lived assets to determine whether they should be selected and how they will be implemented. (Ch. 9, p. 264)

Capital Investment An expenditure of funds made in the hope of realizing benefits that are expected to occur over the future. (Ch. 9, p. 264)

Capital Market Its role is to facilitate long-term financial arrangements between savers and users of funds to allocate capital to its most productive uses. (Ch. 3, p. 72)

Capital Rationing A situation in which a firm is forced to reject investment proposals with positive NPVs due to lack of sufficient financial or personnel resources. (Ch. 9, p. 282)

Carrying Costs Costs associated with maintaining an inventory that increase as the level of inventory increases. (Ch. 20, p. 632)

Cash Discount A reduction in the purchase price granted the buying firm if it pays its account within a specified discount period. (Ch. 18, p. 578)

Certificate of Deposit (CD) Documentation of a bank deposit. It specifies the amount of the deposit, the duration of the deposit, and the interest rate to be earned. (Ch. 24, p. 764)

Chapter 7 Proceedings The provisions of the Bankruptcy Reform Act under which the debtor firm's assets are liquidated by a court because reorganization would fail to establish a profitable business. (Ch. 23, p. 733)

Chapter 11 Proceedings The provisions of the Bankruptcy Reform Act under which the debtor firm is reorganized by a court because the estimated value of the reorganized firm exceeds the expected proceeds from its liquidation. (Ch. 23, p. 731)

Characteristic Line (CL) A line that represents the rate at which changes in the return on the market portfolio are accompanied by changes in the return on a specific firm's common stock. The slope of this line is the beta of the firm's common stock. (Ch. 6, p. 190)

Chattel Mortgage A loan agreement that grants to the lender a lien on property other than real estate. (Ch. 12, p. 384)

Clean-up Period A period of time during the year when a firm must repay all borrowings under a line of credit. (Ch. 18, p. 582)

Clientele Effect The notion that different dividend policies attract different types of investors so that a stable dividend policy will attract and hold a certain clientele. (Ch. 16, p. 529)

Coefficient of Variation A measure of investment risk that defines risk as the standard deviation per unit of expected return. (Ch. 6, p. 181)

Coinsurance Effect The process by which the business units of a diversified company pool their earnings to meet the company's debt obligations. (Ch. 15, p. 511)

Collateral Trust Bond A bond that is secured by other bonds or stock owned by the issuing firm. (Ch. 12, p. 391)

Commercial Paper A short-term (270 days or less) unsecured IOU of a firm sold in the money market. (Ch. 18, p. 582)

Commercial Risk The fundamental risk that any investment in a market economy will turn out to be unprofitable because the good or service involved will not gain customer acceptance. (Ch. 4, p. 103)

Commitment Fee A fee paid by a firm to a commercial bank for the guaranteed access to funds provided by a revolving credit agreement. (Ch. 18, p. 582)

Commodity Bundle One unit of the collection of the complete set of goods produced and sold in the world market. (Ch. 8, p. 246)

Common Stock A financial instrument that represents equity financing of a firm and grants a residual claim on the firm's earnings and assets. (Ch. 7, p. 218; Ch. 13, p. 422)

Compensating Balances Non-interest-bearing deposits that a firm must maintain with a bank as required by a line of credit or revolving credit agreement. (Ch. 18, p. 582)

Competitive Bidding An auction procedure used to sell a new security issue to the investment banking syndicate that submits the highest bid for the securities. (Ch. 3, p. 82)

Composition Cancellation of all of a nonviable debtor's firm's outstanding debt by its creditors in exchange for immediate partial repayment. (Ch. 23, p. 731)

Compounding The process of determining how rapidly a sum of money will grow over time when it is continually invested to earn a return. (Ch. 5, p. 133)

Concentration Banks A small number of large banks used by a firm to periodically collect the firm's deposit balances from a network of smaller banks. (Ch. 19, p. 604)

Conglomerate Merger A combination of two firms that operate in unrelated industries. (Ch. 22, p. 687)

Consolidation A transaction in which both firms that combine cease to exist as separate corporations. (Ch. 22, p. 686)

Contingent Voting Power Enables preferred stockholders to vote with their shares when the company fails to satisfy the agreement between itself and the preferred stockholders. (Ch. 13, p. 420)

Contractual Claim Specifies an amount that must be paid periodically to the buyer of a security as well as the time at which the principal must be repaid. (Ch. 3, p. 71)

Contractual Intermediary Issues an indirect claim in the form of a contract that specifies that the individual saver will make periodic, fixed payments to the intermediary in exchange for the right to receive payments from the intermediary in the future. (Ch. 3, p. 69)

Control Limits The upper and lower limits on the acceptable level of cash that minimizes the sum of the opportunity cost of excessive cash and the cost of marketable security transactions. (Ch. 19, p. 598)

Conversion Period The time period during which an investor can exchange a convertible security for common stock. (Ch. 13, p. 433)

Conversion Premium The excess of the market value of a convertible bond over its theoretical value. (Ch. 13, p. 434)

Conversion Price The effective price per share at which a convertible bond can be converted into common stock. (Ch. 13, p. 433)

Conversion Ratio The number of shares of common stock for which a convertible bond can be exchanged. (Ch. 13, p. 433)

Conversion Value The current total market value of the common stock into which a convertible bond can be converted. (Ch. 13, p. 434)

Corporate Restructuring A major change in the size, capital structure, or ownership of a firm. (Ch. 22, p. 683)

Cost of Capital The minimum rate of return an investment project must earn in order not to diminish stockholder wealth. (Ch. 15, p. 489)

Cost Recovery Period The number of years it takes to fully depreciate a capital asset. This time period is based on the specific classification of the depreciable life of an asset. (Ch. 10, p. 310)

Country Risk The component of the risk of foreign operations, which depends on the general state of the economy of the foreign country. (Ch. 4, p. 104)

Coupon The nominal annual rate of interest that the bond issuer is obligated to pay on its bonds. The coupon is normally fixed over the life of the bond. (Ch. 7, p. 207)

Coupon Bond Requires that the lender remove a coupon, which is attached to the bond certificate, and send it to the issuer's paying agent in order to receive the interest payment. (Ch. 12, p. 393)

Covered Foreign Currency Loan A loan denominated in a currency other than that of the borrower's home currency, for which repayment terms are prearranged through the use of a forward currency contract. (Ch. 24, p. 21)

Covered Interest Rate Parity The principle that the yields from interest-bearing foreign and domestic investments should be equal when the forward currency market is used to predetermine the domestic currency payoff from a foreign investment. (Ch. 24, p. 756)

Covering The process of using forward currency contracts to predetermine the domestic currency amount of an expected future foreign receipt or payment. (Ch. 24, p. 755)

Credit Policy Delay The time lag between the sale of goods on a credit basis and the payment for those goods. This lag is determined largely by the selling firm's credit policy. (Ch. 19, p. 602)

Credit Rating Agencies Firms that compile information on and establish credit ratings for a large number of companies. (Ch. 20, p. 621)

Credit Standards The guidelines followed in determining whether a credit applicant is creditworthy. (Ch. 20, p. 618)

Credit Terms The conditions under which credit will be extended to a customer. The components of credit terms are: cash discount, credit period, net period. (Ch. 20, p. 620)

Cross-Section Ratio Analysis A method of analysis that compares a current value of the firm's ratios with some chosen industry benchmark. The benchmark usually chosen is the average ratio value for all firms in an industry for the time period under study. (Ch. 2, p. 39)

Cumulative Preferred Stock All missed dividends on this type of preferred stock must be paid before any dividend can be paid on noncumulative preferred or common stock. The dividends accumulate. (Ch. 13, p. 419)

Currency Exchange Risk Uncertainty about the rate at which revenues or costs denominated in one currency can be converted into another currency. (Ch. 4, p. 106)

Current Coupon Bond Bonds on which the coupon is set approximately equal to the bonds' yield-to-maturity at the time of their issuance. (Ch. 12, p. 395)

Current Liability A category of debt that must be repaid within one year. (Ch. 2, p. 28)

D

Date of Record Persons owning a stock as of this date are entitled to a specific subsequent benefit associated with the stock, such as the receipt of a dividend or a right. (Ch. 13, p. 428)

Debenture A bond that specifies no collateral but rather rests on the general creditworthiness of the issuer. (Ch. 12, p. 390)

Debt Capacity The level of financial leverage at which adding debt to the financial structure of a corporation would cause problems with servicing the debt. (Ch. 14, p. 476)

Debtor-in-Possession (DIP) Loans Loans that take priority over all of a firm's prior debt because they are made after it has filed for bankruptcy. (Ch. 23, p.735)

Decision Break-Point Analysis A type of sensitivity analysis that indicates the value at which a key variable will result in a negative NPV for an investment project. (Ch. 11, p. 355)

Default The failure to make the principal and interest payments required on debt financing. (Ch. 2, p. 43)

Default Risk Uncertainty regarding a borrower's ability to meet the scheduled interest payments and to pay the principal at maturity. (Ch. 3, p. 74)

Deficit Unit An economic unit (individual, business firm) whose investment spending on real assets exceeds its saving. (Ch. 3, p. 62)

Depository Intermediaries These institutions raise funds by issuing indirect claims in the form of deposits, which can be classified into two basic categories: transaction and time. (Ch. 3, p. 68)

Depository Transfer Check A method of transferring funds collected at local and regional banks to concentration banks in a concentration banking system. (Ch. 19, p. 604)

Dilution Lowering the proportional voting power and earnings of a given number of shares by issuing new shares of common stock. (Ch. 13, p. 423)

Direct Claim A financial claim issued by a deficit unit to acquire funds for investment in real assets. (Ch. 3, p. 64)

Direct Exchange Rate The home-currency price of one unit of a foreign currency. (Ch. 4, p. 110)

Direct Lease A lease in which the lessor acquires an asset from its manufacturer or from a vendor in order to lease it to the lessee. (Ch. 12, p. 399)

Discount Interest Under this form of loan agreement, all the interest is paid at the beginning of the loan. (Ch. 18, p. 590)

Discount Period The maximum number of days within which a cash discount is granted to the buying firm. (Ch. 18, p. 578)

Discount Rate The investment opportunity cost used to compute the present value of a future cash flow. (Ch. 5, p. 135)

Discounting The computation of the present value of a future cash flow, recognizing the opportunity to earn a return in the meantime. (Ch. 5, p. 135)

Distribution Cost Advantage A source of competitive advantage that depends on the efficient delivery of a product or service to customers. (Ch. 4, p. 99)

Diversification A strategy of spreading available funds across a number of different investments. (Ch. 6, p. 182)

Divestiture The sale of a portion of a corporation's assets to another corporation. (Ch. 22, p. 703)

Dividend Payout Ratio The percentage of a firm's earnings that are paid out to shareholders as dividends. (Ch. 7, p. 224)

Double Taxation A system of taxation that applies to corporate income under which corporate taxes are assessed against the corporation's earnings and personal taxes are assessed against cash dividends paid to stockholders. (Ch. 1, p. 17)

Draft A financial instrument similar to a check except that it must be accepted by the person by whom it is written before the bank will pay out any funds. (Ch. 19, p. 605)

Duration An alternative to term-to-maturity as a measure of the remaining life of a

bond. It identifies how far in the future the average cash flow from the bond is scheduled to be received. (Ch. 7, p. 237)

E

Economic Life The time period over which an asset's NPV is maximized. Economic life can be less than absolute physical life due to: technological obsolescence, physical deterioration, and product life cycle. (Ch. 10. p. 324)

Economic Risk Exposure The risk that changes in currency exchange rates will affect the home-currency value of foreign operations. (Ch. 4, p. 108)

Effective Interest Rate The annual rate at which an investment grows in value when interest is credited more often than once a year. (Ch. 5, p. 148)

Efficient Market A market in which the current market price of an asset is the best estimate of its value. (Ch. 7, p. 215)

Eurobond A bond denominated in a currency that is different from that of the country in which it is issued. (Ch. 4, p. 119)

Eurocredit A short-term Eurocurrency loan from an international bank. (Ch. 4, p. 118)

Eurocurrency A currency that is on deposit in a bank located outside the country of origin of the currency. (Ch. 4, p. 117)

Ex-Dividend Date The date on which the right to the current dividend no longer accompanies the stock. (Ch. 16, p. 533)

Ex-Rights Date The date on which a right no longer accompanies a stock. It is usually two business days prior to the date of record. (Ch. 13, p. 428)

Exchange Rate Mechanism A formal system for the stabilization of EU currency values according to a set of target exchange rates among the currencies. (Ch. 4, p. 114)

Exchange Ratio The number of new shares in an acquiring firm that are traded for each outstanding share of an acquired firm. (Ch. 22, p. 693)

Expected Spot Rate The exchange rate between two currencies, which is expected to prevail in the spot market on a given future date. It differs from the current spot rate by the extent to which inflation expectations in the two currencies differ. (Ch. 8, p. 247)

Expected Value The weighted average of the possible cash flows associated with an investment. The weights are equal to the probability of each potential cash flow. (Ch. 6, p. 173)

Explicit Bankruptcy Costs Costs incurred during the bankruptcy process such as legal fees, court costs, consultants' fees, and document preparation expenses. (Ch. 23, p. 727)

Expropriation The seizure of all or part of a foreign company's assets by the host country's government without compensation. (Ch. 4, p. 106)

Extension Voluntary alteration of a debtor firm's loan agreements by creditors because they believe that the firm's financial distress is only temporary. (Ch. 23, p. 730)

Extra Dividend A temporary increase in a firm's dividends beyond its normal level. (Ch. 16, p. 532)

F

Factor The lending institution that buys accounts receivable under a factoring agreement. (Ch. 18, p. 584)

Factoring Selling accounts receivable to a lending institution in order to receive the cash more quickly. (Ch. 18, p. 584)

Finance Companies Companies that raise funds by selling their own debt instruments to surplus units and by borrowing from other financial intermediaries. (Ch. 3, p. 70)

Financial Distress 1. Inability of a firm to meet its cash flow commitments without seriously disrupting operations. (Ch. 11, p. 347; Ch. 14, p. 470) 2. An unexpected and persistent shortage of cash due to the weakness of a firm or its business environment. (Ch. 23, p. 721)

Financial Intermediaries Institutions that produce mutually agreeable terms between borrower and lender by reaching separate agreements with the borrower and the lender. (Ch. 3, p. 65)

Financial Lease A lease that has payments that provide the lessor with reimbursement for the cost of the leased asset net of any residual value plus a return on investment. In addition, the lessee may have the option to purchase the asset at the termination of the lease. (Ch. 12, p. 398)

Financial Leverage The presence of fixed financing costs in a firm's cost structure. (Ch. 14, p. 446)

Financial Risk The variability in the firm's earnings after taxes not due to operating leverage. It is affected by the amount of financial leverage present in a firm. (Ch. 14, p. 450)

Financing Cost Savings A source of competitive advantage that depends on access to differentially lower-cost sources of capital. (Ch. 4, p. 100)

Floating Exchange Rates A system of currency exchange in which currencies trade freely in value against each other in response to market supply and demand, rather than at exchange rates that are fixed by government policies. (Ch. 4, p. 107)

Floating Lien A loan agreement that grants the lender a general claim on a borrower's entire inventory rather than some specific part of it. (Ch. 18, p. 586)

Floor Planning A term used to describe the use of trust receipts by manufacturers or banks to finance inventories of autos at auto dealerships. (Ch. 18, p. 586)

Flotation Costs The costs incurred by the issuer of securities during the process of issuance. (Ch. 3, p. 83; Ch. 16, p. 526)

Foreign Bond A bond issued by a foreign borrower and denominated in the currency of the country in which it is sold. (Ch. 4, p. 119)

Forward Contract A commitment to buy or sell a currency in the future at the forward exchange rate. (Ch. 4, p. 111; Ch. 8, p. 249)

Forward Cover A technique to predetermine the home-currency value of a future foreign currency receipt or expenditure, by using the forward currency exchange market. (Ch. 4, p. 116)

Forward Differential A measure of the extent to which one currency is expected to strengthen or weaken against another currency. It is calculated by comparing spot and forward exchange rates. (Ch. 4, p. 112)

Forward Discount A negative forward differential, which indicates that the foreign currency is expected to weaken against the home currency. (Ch. 4, p. 113)

Forward Exchange Rate The transaction price for the future delivery of a currency. (Ch. 4, p. 111; Ch. 8, p. 249)

Forward Premium A positive forward differential, which indicates that the foreign currency is expected to strengthen against the home currency. (Ch. 4, p. 113)

Free Cash Flow The net cash flow from a firm's operating and investing activities during a given period of time. (Ch. 2, p. 51)

Free Cash Flows The after-tax operating cash flow of a firm less investments in working capital and fixed assets. (Ch. 22, p. 692)

Friendly Merger A business combination that the management of both firms believes will be beneficial to stockholders. (Ch. 22, p. 698)

Funded Liability A source of funds that a firm must take overt action to arrange and that carries an interest cost. (Ch. 2, p. 28)

Funds Any form of financing that allows assets to be acquired, liabilities to be reduced, or dividends to be paid. (Ch. 2, p. 49)

Futures Market Transactions for the future delivery of commodities at specified prices. (Ch. 8, p. 251)

G

General Covenants Provisions in a loan agreement that are designed to assure that management follows the most basic concepts of efficient business management. (Ch. 12, p. 380)

General Partnership A contractual relationship in which two or more people combine their capital, skills, and knowledge to carry on a business and each party possesses unlimited liability. (Ch. 1, p. 15)

Global Firm A company whose international operations are designed to seek business opportunities in any country where it can gain a competitive advantage in selling, producing, or financing. Ch. 4, p. 102)

Going-Concern Value The present value of forecasted free cash flow that is expected from a reorganized firm. (Ch. 23, p. 739)

H

Historical Cost Accounting Convention An accounting technique that values an asset for balance sheet purposes on the basis of the price paid for the asset at the time of its acquisition. (Ch. 2, p. 29)

Holding Period Yield (HPY) The annual rate of return actually realized on an investment in a bond. (Ch. 7, p. 213)

Horizontal Merger A combination in which the two firms are competitors in the same line of business. (Ch. 22, p. 686)

Host Country The name commonly used to refer to the foreign country in which a company has operations. (Ch. 4, p. 100)

Hostile Merger (Takeover) A business combination in which the acquiring firm overcomes the resistance of the acquired firm's management by gaining control of the target firm's shares. (Ch. 22, p. 698)

Hurdle Rate The minimum acceptable annual rate of return for a given investment. (Ch. 9, p. 266)

I

Implicit Bankruptcy Costs Opportunity costs incurred prior to the bankruptcy process such as the loss of sales or financing. (Ch. 23, p. 727)

Income Bond This type of bond requires the payment of interest only when the firm generates enough earnings to cover the interest payment. (Ch. 12, p. 394)

Incremental Cash Flows The net impact of a proposed investment on a firm's cash flows. Only incremental cash flows are relevant to the evaluation of an investment. (Ch. 10, p. 304)

Independent Investments Investments available to a firm that may be selected individually or in groups because each investment is different in its nature and purpose. (Ch. 9, p. 266)

Indirect Claim Claims issued by a financial intermediary are indirect claims because the intermediary relends the funds to the deficit unit to enable it to acquire real assets. (Ch. 3, p. 65)

Indirect Exchange Rate The foreign-currency price of one unit of the home currency. (Ch. 4, p. 110)

Information Signaling The idea that a firm's dividend policy provide signals to investors concerning the value of that firm's stock. (Ch. 16, p. 526)

Initial Public Offering (IPO) The sale of common stock to the public by a corporation that was previously privately owned. (Ch. 22, p. 710)

Insolvency-in-Bankruptcy When a firm has both negative net worth and negative net cash inflows that reflect both liquidity and profitability problems. (Ch. 23, p. 729)

Interest in Arrears Under this form of loan agreement, the borrower pays all interest due at the maturity date rather than paying it out periodically over the life of the loan. (Ch. 18, p. 590)

Interest Rate Risk The uncertainty in the holding period yield on a bond when its holding period is shorter than its term-to-maturity and its yield-to-maturity fluctuates over time. (Ch. 7, p. 214)

Intermediation The process whereby a surplus unit channels funds through the financial intermediary before they reach a deficit unit. (Ch. 3, p. 65)

Internal Rate of Return (IRR) The discount rate that equates the cost or price of an asset with the present value of its anticipated cash flows. The IRR on a bond is called its yield-to-maturity. (Ch. 9, p. 273)

Investment The commitment of a known amount today for a specific period of time in return for a series of anticipated future benefits. (Ch. 6, p. 165)

Investment Banker A financial institution that facilitates the sale of securities by the issuing firm to investors. (Ch. 3, p. 81)

Investment Companies These companies sell their own stock to small surplus units to raise funds for the purchase of direct claims issued by larger deficit units. (Ch. 3, p. 70)

Investment Risk The uncertainty about the future benefits to be realized from an investment. (Ch. 6, p. 167)

Investment Tax Credit (ITC) A system of investment tax incentives that serves as a direct reduction in a corporation's tax liability as opposed to a tax deductible expense, which reduces taxable income. (Ch. 10, p. 313)

Investment Valuation Model (IVM) The basic mathematical technique of finance that calculates the value of an investment as the present value of all future cash flows expected to be generated by the investment. (Ch. 6, p. 168)

L

Lender Liability Lawsuits Legal action filed against creditors by a debtor firm that alleges unfair enforcement of loan covenants or violation of implied terms of a loan agreement. (Ch. 23, p. 735)

Lessee A person or firm that enters into a lease agreement promising to pay installments in return for the use of plant or equipment. (Ch. 12, p. 396)

Lessor A person or firm that enters into a lease agreement promising to supply plant or equipment for use by another in return for installment payments. (Ch. 12, p. 396)

Letter of Credit A bank guarantee of payment for the sales price of goods shipped to a foreign customer. (Ch. 4, p. 116)

Leverage The presence of fixed costs in a firm's cost structure. (Ch. 14, p. 445)

Leverage Ratios Ratios concerned with measuring the extent and effect of debt financing. (Ch. 2, p. 43)

Leveraged Buyout (LBO) A transaction in which a group of investors takes a firm private by using primarily borrowed funds to acquire its public shares of stock. (Ch. 22, p. 705)

Leveraged Lease Under this type of lease, the lessor borrows money to pay for some percentage of the asset. The lease agreement and a mortgage on the asset itself serve as the only collateral for the loan. (Ch. 12, p. 399)

Leveraged Recapitalization A transaction that significantly increases a firm's financial leverage and management ownership through a debt-financed cash payment to stockholders and issuance of new shares to managers. (Ch. 22, p. 708)

Limited Liability A form of liability that exists in corporations and limited partnerships whereby the liability of the owners for financial obligations of the firm is limited to the amount of capital they have invested in the business. (Ch. 1, p. 16)

Limited Partnership A form of business ownership in which the liability of one or more of the partners is legally limited to their initial investment in the firm. A limited partnership must have at least one general partner with unlimited liability. (Ch. 1, p. 15)

Line of Credit An agreement with a commercial bank that allows a borrower to borrow any amount up to a specified limit at any time prior to the termination of the agreement. (Ch. 18, p. 581)

Liquidation by Assignment A liquidation of a debtor firm's assets voluntarily agreed to by its creditors who estimate that the firm's liquidation value exceeds its going-concern value. (Ch. 23, p. 731)

Liquidity The ability of a firm to meet its current cash flow obligations. Liquidity also refers to the rapidity and certainty with which a specific asset can be converted into cash. (Ch. 19, p. 608)

Liquidity Ratios Ratios that examine the firm's ability to meet its short-term cash outflows in terms of the relationship between current assets and current liabilities. (Ch. 2, p. 39)

Loan Preference Principle If a covered loan is less expensive when its cost is calculated in one currency, it will also be less expensive in all other currencies. (Ch. 24, p. 763)

Lock Box System A collection of locally or regionally centered post office boxes from which a local bank collects funds and transfers them to a firm's regular bank account. (Ch. 19, p. 605)

London Inter-Bank Offered Rate (LIBOR) The interest rate that large international banks in London charge each other for Eurocurrency loans. It is used as the benchmark rate for pricing Eurocurrency loans to nonbank borrowers. (Ch. 4, p. 118; Ch. 24, p. 749)

Long-Term Liability Debt financing that need not be repaid until one year or more in the future. (Ch. 2, p. 28)

Loss Carry-Back (Forward) A tax relief that allows operating losses to be used as a tax shield to reduce taxable income in prior and future years. Losses can be carried backward for 3 years and forward up to 15 years under current tax codes. (Ch. 10, p. 314)

M

Mail Delay Time required by the postal service to deliver to the selling firm checks put in the mail by a credit customer. (Ch. 19, p. 602)

Market Portfolio A diversified portfolio used to measure the returns realized on an investment of average risk. In practice, the S&P 500 is the most widely used version of the market portfolio. (Ch. 6, p. 186)

Market Risk The extent to which an investment's outcomes are sensitive to movements in the general level of securities prices. It is another name for systematic risk. (Ch. 6, p. 185)

Market RRR Schedule A line that indicates the minimum return required by investors at each level of investment risk. The schedule begins at the risk-free interest rate and rises as risk increases. (Ch. 6, p. 177)

Marketability The ease and speed with which an investor can resell a security on the secondary market. (Ch. 3, p. 77)

Maturity Date The date on which a bond's issuer is obligated to pay to the bond's owner an amount equal to the bond's par value. (Ch. 7, p. 207)

Merger A transaction in which one of two combined firms ceases to exist as a separate corporation after the combination. (Ch. 22, p. 685)

Modern Portfolio Theory A framework for investment valuation, which recognizes that investment risk must be viewed according to how an investment affects the risk of an investor's total portfolio. (Ch. 6, p. 189)

Money Market Short-term securities traded on the money market are used by economic units to adjust their balance sheets for temporary cash surpluses and deficits. (Ch. 3, p. 71)

Mortgage Bond A bond that has some specific piece of real property (land, building, etc.) pledged as collateral against it. (Ch. 12, p. 390)

Mutually Exclusive Investments Alternative investments available to a firm that represent different approaches to a single goal or task. A firm can accept only one investment out of a group of mutually exclusive investments. (Ch. 9, p. 266)

N

Negotiated Current Liabilities That part of current liabilities that does not respond automatically to financing needs, such as bank loans. (Ch. 17, p. 564)

Negotiated Offering A procedure for issuing new securities whereby the issuing firm hires an investment banker to assist in designing the terms of the security issue. (Ch. 3, p. 83)

Net Period The maximum number of days granted to the buying firm before its accounts payable are considered overdue. (Ch. 18, p. 578)

Net Present Value (NPV) The difference between the present value of an investment's anticipated future cash flows and its initial cost. (Ch. 9, p. 271)

Net Working Capital The difference between current assets and current liabilities. (Ch. 17, p. 558)

Nominal Currency The actual amount of a cash flow at some time in the future. (Ch. 10, p. 330)

Nominal Interest Rate The total percentage return from investing in debt securities. This return can be observed in financial markets. (Ch. 3, p. 80)

Normative A form of financial analysis that dictates how decisions should be made rather than merely describing how they are made. (Ch. 1, p. 4)

NPV Profile A graph that indicates possible NPVs at different discount rates. (Ch. 9, p. 276)

O

Open Account A form of trade credit in which there is no formal loan agreement and the invoice is the only evidence of the loan. (Ch. 18, p. 578)

Operating Assets Another term for working capital. (Ch. 17, p. 558)

Operating Lease A lease whose duration is much shorter than the useful life of the leased asset. (Ch. 12, p. 398)

Operating Leverage The presence of fixed operating costs in a firm's cost structure. (Ch. 14, p. 446)

Operating Risk 1. The combined effect of sales variability and operating cost structure on variability in NPV. (Ch. 11, p. 350) 2. The variability in a firm's EBIT. Operating risk is positively related to both the variability in a firm's sales and to the level of the firm's operating leverage. (Ch. 14, p. 449)

Opportunity Cost The rate of return that can be earned from alternative investments. It measures the cost of waiting to receive cash flows. (Ch. 5, p. 130)

Optimum Leverage Ratio The leverage ratio that maximizes the value of the firm. The cost of capital to the firm is minimized at that same leverage ratio. (Ch. 15, p. 504)

Ordering Costs Costs associated with placing orders that are fixed regardless of the size of the order. (Ch. 20, p. 632)

Original Issue Discount Securities (OIDS) Bonds on which the coupon rate is set considerably below their yield-to-maturity at the time of issuance so that the bonds are issued at a discount from a par value. (Ch. 12, p. 395)

Outstanding Shares The differences between the number of shares of issued stock and the number of shares of Treasury stock. In other words, the number of shares held by investors. (Ch. 13, p. 426)

Overcapitalization A situation in which a firm cannot service its debt even though its debt/equity ratio is not excessive. (Ch. 23, p. 722)

Overhanging Bond Issue A convertible bond issue that is not converted by investors into common stock because the stock doesn't appreciate in value. (Ch. 13, p. 437)

P

P/E Ratio The ratio of the market price of a share of stock to the firm's earnings per share. (Ch. 7, p. 223)

Par Value The face value of a financial instrument. The par value of a bond represents the size of the loan that the bond's issuer must repay at maturity. (Ch. 7, p. 207) (Ch. 13, p. 427)

Payout Ratio The percentage of earnings after taxes paid out to stockholders in the form of dividends. (Ch. 16, p. 520)

Permanent Assets Fixed assets (plant and equipment) and permanent current assets. (Ch. 17, p. 562)

Permanent Current Assets The minimum level of current assets needed by the firm to continue operation. Because some level is always maintained, they are called permanent current assets. (Ch. 17, p. 562)

Permanent Financing Any long-term source of funds. It has three components: long-term debt, equity, and permanent spontaneous current liabilities. (Ch. 17, p. 563)

Permanent Spontaneous Current Liabilities The minimum level of spontaneous current liabilities that is continuously maintained by a firm. (Ch. 17, p. 564)

Perpetuity An annuity that is expected to continue forever. (Ch 5, p. 151)

Placement Fees A fee paid by issuers of commercial paper to commercial paper dealers in return for their services in selling that paper. (Ch. 18, p. 590)

Political Risk Governmental actions that specify the conditions under which foreign companies are permitted to operate in the host country. (Ch. 4, p. 106)

Post-Audit The process of comparing the actual operating results of an implemented investment proposal to those forecasted by the sponsoring manager. (Ch. 11, p. 369)

Preemptive Right Gives present stockholders the right to buy a proportion of a new stock issue equal to the proportion of the present stock they own. (Ch. 13, p. 424)

Preferred Stock A source of equity financing on which the issuing firm promises to pay a specific periodic dividend. While preferred stock's residual claim on a firm's income and assets is subordinate to that of debt, it is superior to that of common stock. (Ch. 7, p. 215; Ch. 13, p. 417)

Prepackaged Bankruptcy A hybrid form of bankruptcy in which a reorganization plan is developed by a firm and its creditors before the firm files for bankruptcy. (Ch. 23, p. 733)

Present Value Components Analysis An analytical tool that establishes a base NPV for a project which can then be adjusted for the incremental NPV effect of separate components of the project's overall potential sales. (Ch. 11, p. 357)

Present Value Index (PVI) The ratio of the NPV of a project to the initial outlay required for it. The index is an efficiency measure for investment decisions under capital rationing. (Ch. 9, p. 287)

Price Elasticity A measure of the sensitivity of a bond's price to changes in its required yield to maturity. It is calculated by dividing the percentage change in price by the percentage change in YTM. (Ch. 7, p. 236)

Primary Market The issuance or original sale of a financial claim by a deficit unit takes place on the primary market. (Ch. 3, p. 66)

Primary Offering An IPO that raises additional cash for investment in a corporation through the sale of previously unissued stock. (Ch. 22, p. 710)

Prime Rate The interest rate set by banks in the United States that indicates the general cost of bank credit and serves as the index rate for variable interest rate loans. (Ch. 18, p. 582)

Private Placement Bonds issued through personal negotiations between the issuer and the buyer. (Ch. 12, p. 388)

Probability Distribution A statistical tool that specifies all the possible outcomes associated with an action and assigns probabilities to each of those outcomes. (Ch. 6, p. 173)

Processing Delay Time required by the selling firm to record receipt of the check and deposit it in its bank after it has been received. (Ch. 19, p. 602)

Product Differentiation A source of competitive advantage that depends on a product having or being regarded as having unique and valuable characteristics. (Ch. 4, p. 99)

Production Cost Advantage A source of competitive advantage that depends upon becoming the low-cost producer of a product or service. (Ch. 4, p. 99)

Production Costs Costs associated with shutting down a production line and then restarting it. (Ch. 20, p. 633)

Profitability Ratios Ratios that measure the firm's overall financial performance on a relative basis by relating various measures of profits to either sales or investment. (Ch. 2, p. 44)

Promissory Note A form of trade credit used when the customer has a poor or inadequate credit history. A written IOU serves as the evidence of the loan. (Ch. 18, p. 578)

Prospectus A summary of the vital information contained in the registration statement filed with the SEC. Copies of the prospectus must be made available to the public. (Ch. 3, p. 85)

Protective Covenants Provisions of long-term debt agreements designed to protect the lenders from events that might lead the borrower to default. (Ch. 12, p. 380)

Proxy Fight Occasionally an outside group will compete with present management for the stockholders' proxies in order to generate enough votes to elect a new board of directors. (Ch. 13, p. 424)

Proxy Statement A document that assigns the voting power of one person's stock to another. (Ch. 13, p. 423)

Public Offering The issuance of securities to the general public through a network of investment bankers and brokers. (Ch. 12, p. 388)

Purchasing Power Parity (PPP) The concept that a given commodity or financial instrument cannot simultaneously trade at different prices in different markets if investors are behaving rationally. It is also called the "law of one price." (Ch. 8, p. 242)

Pure Play A firm that operates in a single line of business. (Ch. 15, p. 509)

R

Real Currency The purchasing power in today's currency of future nominal currency to be disbursed or received. (Ch. 10, p. 330)

Real Interest Rate A measure of the rate of increase in an investor's consumption opportunities after inflation is deducted from the nominal interest rate. The effective yield on a loan in constant purchasing power after adjusting the stated interest rate for inflation. (Ch. 3, p. 80; Ch. 24, p. 751)

Recourse The right of a factor to demand payment from the selling firm for accounts receivable that are uncollectible. (Ch. 18, p. 585)

Registration Statement A statement that must be filed with and verified by the SEC before a firm may issue securities. The statement contains a variety of information concerning the firm and the security issue. (Ch. 3, p. 85)

Repatriation The process of transferring profits earned in a foreign country to the firm's home country. (Ch. 4, p. 106)

Replacement Chain A concept that views a capital investment as an indefinite commitment to a specific type of technology. The replacement chain concept can be used to allow the comparison of mutually exclusive investments with unequal lives. (Ch. 10, p. 327)

Required Rate of Return (RRR) The minimum annual percentage rate of return required by investors to induce them to select a particular investment. (Ch. 6, p. 170)

Residual Claim A claim on a firm's assets and earnings that is associated with equity financing. Residual claims do not specify the amount that must be paid periodically or a fixed date for repayment of principal. (Ch. 3, p. 71)

Restrictive Covenants Provisions in a loan agreement that will restrict management's financing and investing decisions. (Ch. 12, p. 380)

Return on Investment (ROI) The ratio of the after-tax operating profits of a firm's business unit to the firm's investment in that business unit. It is a measure of the unit's performance during a specified time period. (Ch. 9, p. 290)

Revolving Credit Agreement A loan agreement that guarantees a firm's access to a specified maximum amount of funds. This usually covers a longer period than a line of credit and involves the paying of a commitment fee by the borrower. (Ch. 18, p. 582)

Right A negotiable instrument that allows its holder to buy newly issued common stock during a rights offering. Initially issued to stockholders by the corporation, but they can be sold to others who wish to exercise them to obtain stock. (Ch. 13, p. 428)

Rights Offering (Privileged Subscription) When new common stock is offered first to existing stockholders in accordance with their preemptive right. (Ch. 13, p. 428)

Risk Investor uncertainty about the size or timing of the forecasted returns on an investment. (Ch. 1, p. 9)

Risk Aversion The preference of investors for certain investment benefits over uncertain benefits of equal expected size. (Ch. 6, p. 167)

Risk Premium The portion of an investment's RRR that is a combination of the effects of investment risk and investor risk aversion. Mathematically, the risk premium equals the excess of an investment's RRR over the risk-free interest rate. (Ch. 6, p. 176)

Risk-Free Interest Rate The return available to an investor in a risk-free security. The risk-free interest rate compensates the investor for the temporary sacrifice of consumption. (Ch. 6, p. 167)

Risk/Return Trade-off The principle that financial decisions which increase a firm's anticipated returns also increase the riskiness of those returns. The trade-off involves the positive effect on firm value of larger expected returns versus the negative effect of greater uncertainty of returns. Ch. 1, p. 9)

Rule of Absolute Priority A condition of bankruptcy proceedings under which junior claim holders can receive no payment until senior claim holders are paid in full. (Ch. 23, p. 736)

S

Sale and Leaseback An agreement under which the lessee sells the asset to the lessor and then immediately leases it back. (Ch. 12, p. 399)

Scenario Analysis A form of sensitivity analysis that recognizes the interdependence of variables by calculating a project's NPV for different assumptions about the combined value of all major variables. (Ch. 11, p. 354)

Secondary Market The resale of an outstanding security by one surplus unit to another takes place on the secondary market. (Ch. 3, p. 66)

Secondary Offering An IPO in which existing privately held shares in a corporation are sold to the public. (Ch. 22, p. 710)

Security Market Line (SML) The line that establishes a specific relationship between an investment's RRR and its systematic risk as measured by its beta. (Ch. 6, p. 193)

Segmented Market A market in which there are impediments to the free flow of labor, capital, and information. (Ch. 4, p. 101)

Selling Group Brokerage firms that purchase newly issued securities from investment bankers in relatively large blocks and resell them to individual investors. (Ch. 3, p. 82)

Selling Syndicate A group of investment bankers that underwrites and issues a firm's securities by buying them from the issuing firm and reselling them to a group of smaller brokerage firms for eventual sale to individual investors. (Ch. 3, p. 81)

Sensitivity Analysis Analysis done to determine the responsiveness of a project's NPV or IRR to changes in the values of the variables that go into its calculation. (Ch. 11, p. 348)

Serial Bonds A bond issue divided into maturity segments that are scheduled to be retired at specific intervals over the life of the issue. (Ch. 12, p. 392)

Share Repurchase An alternative to paying cash dividends. The company repurchases shares from the stockholders with an accompanying capital gain equal to the dividend the firm could have paid. (Ch. 16, p. 536)

Shelf Registration A procedure whereby a firm files a general two-year financing plan with the SEC that allows it to sell registered securities at any time during that period without filing additional registration forms or prospectuses. (Ch. 3, p. 85)

Short-Form Registration A procedure that allows a firm to reduce the size of its registration statement and prospectus by referencing financial data already on file with the SEC. (Ch. 3, p. 85)

Sinking Fund A fund that is established by the bond issuer to retire the issue over its life. (Ch. 12, p. 392)

Spin-Off The distribution to a firm's stockholders of separate ownership rights to a portion of the corporation. (Ch. 22, p. 703)

Spontaneous Current Liabilities Short-term obligations that automatically increase and decrease in response to financing needs, such as accounts payable. (Ch. 17, p. 563)

Spontaneous Liability A source of funds that arises automatically in the course of operating a business, when a firm buys goods and services on credit. (Ch. 2, p. 27)

Spot Exchange Rate The transaction price for the immediate delivery of a currency. (Ch. 4, p. 111; Ch. 8, p. 243)

Spot Market Transactions for the immediate delivery of a commodity. (Ch. 8, p. 243)

Spread The interest rate premium that is added to LIBOR to arrive at the final price for a loan. It reflects an appraisal of the borrower's credit risk and the lender's desired interest profit margin. (Ch. 24, p. 760)

Standard Deviation A measure of investment risk that examines the dispersion of the potential cash flows of an investment around their expected value. (Ch. 6, p. 179)

Statement of Cash Flows An analysis of the size and composition of a firm's cash-generating power. (Ch. 2, p. 49)

Stock Dividend The distribution of additional shares of stock to the firm's current stockholders at no additional cost. (Ch. 16, p. 533)

Stock Split A process by which each current share of stock is split into some greater number. (Ch. 16, p. 533)

Stretching Payables Delaying the payments of accounts payable beyond the seller's maximum credit period. (Ch. 18, p. 578)

Strong Currency One whose value relative to other currencies is improving, as indicated by a decrease in the direct exchange rates for the currency. (Ch. 4, p. 110)

Subordinated A claim ranked lower in priority than other claims. Common stock is always subordinated to debt. (Ch. 12, p. 380)

Subscription Price The price at which stock is offered to the holders of rights during a rights offering. (Ch. 13, p. 429)

Sunk Cost A historical cost to the firm that cannot be altered by a firm's future investing decisions. A sunk cost is irrelevant to the evaluation of a capital investment proposal. (Ch. 10, p. 306)

Surplus Unit An economic unit (individual, business firm) whose saving exceeds its investment spending for real assets. (Ch. 3, p. 62)

Sustainable Growth Rate The rate at which a firm's sales can grow without requiring an increasing proportion of debt in its capital structure. (Ch. 21, p. 663)

Sweetener A feature of a preferred stock or bond issue that makes it more attractive. Sweeteners are used to reduce the RRR of investors on the security issue. (Ch. 13, p. 438)

Syndicated Loan A large Eurocurrency loan from a group of international banks. (Ch. 4, p. 118)

Systematic Risk The variability in the returns from an investment that is determined by general market factors. (Ch. 6, p. 183)

T

Takedown The act of borrowing funds available under a line of credit. (Ch. 18, p. 581)

Target Leverage Ratio The ratio of the market value of debt to the total market value of the firm that management seeks to maintain. (Ch. 15, p. 496)

Tax Reduction Strategy A source of competitive advantage that depends on differences in the tax rates imposed in different locations. (Ch. 4, p. 100)

Tax Shield A term that refers to any tax-deductible expense of a firm. The expense shields the firm's earnings from taxation by reducing taxable income. The size of the tax shield equals the tax-deductible expense. (Ch. 10, p. 311)

Technical Insolvency When a firm has positive net worth and negative net cash inflows that reflect liquidity but not necessarily profitability problems. (Ch. 23, p. 729)

Temporary Assets That portion of a firm's current assets that fluctuates in response to seasonal variations in sales. (Ch. 17, p. 563)

Temporary Financing The sum of negotiated current liabilities and temporary spontaneous current liabilities. (Ch. 17, p. 564)

Tender Offer A formal public offer to buy stock at a specified price from a target firm's stockholders. (Ch. 22, p. 698)

Term Structure of Interest Rates Expresses the relationship between the yield and the term-to-maturity of securities that differ only in their term-to-maturity. (Ch. 3, p. 75)

Term-to-Maturity The number of periods remaining until the maturity of a debt instrument. (Ch. 7, p. 207)

Time Value of Money The principle that the value of any cash flow depends both on its amount and its timing. (Ch. 5, p. 137)

Timeliness A source of competitive advantage that depends on being the first to enter a given market with a product or service. (Ch. 4, p. 99)

Total Market Capitalization The total market value of all the firm's outstanding securities. (Ch. 15, p. 496)

Transaction Risk The risk of changes in the home-currency value of a specific future foreign-currency cash flow. (Ch. 4, p. 107)

Transactions Costs The costs associated with buying or selling financial instruments in established markets. (Ch. 16, p. 526)

Translation Risk The risk of changes in the reported home-currency accounting results of foreign operations due to changes in currency exchange rates. (Ch. 4, p. 107)

Treasury Stock Shares of stock that were originally issued to the public but are subsequently bought back by the issuing firm. (Ch. 13, p. 426)

Trend Ratio Analysis The comparison of the successive values of each ratio for a single firm over a number of years. (Ch. 2, p. 39)

Trust Receipt A loan agreement that grants a lender legal title to some identified pieces of the borrower's inventory. (Ch. 18, p. 586)

Trustee Hired by a bond issuer to handle the administrative aspects of a loan and to insure that the borrower complies with the terms of the bond indenture. (Ch. 12, p. 388)

U

Underpricing Pricing new securities in the primary market below the price of outstanding securities prevailing in the secondary market to ensure the success of the issue. (Ch. 3, p. 83)

Underwriting The process carried out by an investment banker in buying a stock or bond issue and then reselling it. The investment banker takes the risk of price changes during this time. (Ch. 3, p. 81)

Underwriting Commission The fee charged by investment bankers for underwriting a security issue. (Ch. 3, p. 82)

Unique Diversification Benefit The reduction in the likelihood of financial distress for a conglomerate firm, due to its diversified investments. (Ch. 15, p. 511)

Unlimited Liability The liability that applies to both general partnerships and proprietorships whereby no legal distinction is made between personal and business activities or assets and liabilities. (Ch. 1, p. 15)

Unsystematic Risk The variability in the returns from an investment that is caused by factors specific to the investment. (Ch. 6, p. 183)

V

Valuation Opportunity Cost The potential increase in firm value associated with investments that are foregone due to capital rationing. (Ch. 9, p. 284)

Value Additivity Principle The value of a given investment is independent of the firm making the investment. (Ch. 15, p. 508)

Value Maximization The maximization of owners' wealth achieved by the maximization of the value of a firm's common stock. (Ch. 1, p. 6)

Vertical Merger A merger involving firms in different stages of the production process in the same industry. (Ch. 22, p. 686)

W

Warehouse Receipt A document issued by a warehousing company that identifies the specific items of a borrowing firm's inventory that serve as collateral for a loan. A warehouse receipt grants the lender both physical and legal control over the inventory. (Ch. 18, p. 586)

Weak Currency One whose value relative to other currencies is declining, as indicated by an increase in the direct exchange rates for the currency. (Ch. 4, p. 110)

Weighted Average Cost of Capital The discount rate used to calculate the present value of an investment project. It is calculated by weighing the cost of each form of capital by the proportion that the form comprises of the firm's total capitalization. (Ch. 15, p. 497)

Wire Transfer A method of transferring funds collected at local and regional banks to concentration banks that utilizes electronic systems. (Ch. 19, p. 604)

Working Capital The sum of a firm's current assets. (Ch. 17, p. 558)

Worst Case Scenario Analysis Evaluation of the effect of a project on a firm's cash flows under the most unfavorable economic conditions for the firm. (Ch. 11, p. 359)

Y

Yield The annual percentage return available to an investor. (Ch. 3, p. 73)

Yield Curve The graphical representation of the term structure of interest rates that plots term-to-maturity on one axis against yield-to-maturity on the other axis. (Ch. 3, p. 75)

Yield Spread The difference in yields between two securities, also known as the yield differential. (Ch. 3, p. 73)

Yield-to-Maturity (YTM) The interest rate that equates the present value of all future cash flows over a bond's remaining life to its current market price. The YTM represents both the RRR and the anticipated annual rate of return on a bond. (Ch. 7, p. 211)

Z

Zero Coupon Bonds Bonds on which the coupon rate is zero. Since no interest is paid, the bonds are issued at a price well below par value. (Ch. 12, p. 395)

Index

A

Absolute physical life, 324–325
Accelerated cost recovery depreciation, 311–312
Accounts payable, 577–579
Accounts receivable
  affecting firm value, 617
  aging schedule, 628
  average collection period, 628
  and credit collection agencies, 620
  credit standards, 618–619
  credit terms, 619–621
  factoring, 584–586
  pledging, 583–584
  sales variability affecting, 628–630
  uncollected balance profile, 630
  and using credit information, 621–622
Accruals/accrual accounting, 32, 579–580
Acid-test ratio, 40
Activity ratio, 40–42
Actual future spot rate, 253–257
Adverse investment decisions, 724–726
Adverse liquidity decisions, 726–727
Agency, 4–6
Agency costs, 6, 473–474
Agency problem, 5–6
Amortization, 384, 385–387
Announcement date, 428, 429
Annualized present value, 329
Annuities, 141–146, 149–150, 153
Arbitrage, 242–243, 245
Assets
  Capital Asset Pricing Model, 194, 494, 509–510
  common stock claim on, 422–423
  fixed asset turnover ratio, 42
  operating, 558
  permanent, 562, 566–567
  preferred stock claim on, 417–420
  real versus financial, 6
  sale of, affecting taxes, 313–314
  sale of depreciable, 313–314
  stock affected by write-off of, 38

  temporary, 563, 567–568
  total asset turnover ratio, 42
  valuation of, 30, 38
Authorized shares, 426
Average collection period ratio, 41
Average payment period ratio, 41–42
Average return on investment, 265–267

B

Backup line of credit, 583
Balance sheet
  debt and equity financing on, 27–29
  historical cost accounting, 29–30
  pro forma, 652–655
  relationship to income statement, 32, 33
  role of, 27
  using ratios to project, 657–660
Balloon payments, 384
Bankers' acceptances, 611
Banking delay, 602
Bank loans, 580–582, 589–590
Bankruptcy. *See* Financial distress
Bankruptcy Reform Act of 1978, 731–733
Bartering, 581
Basis point, 760
Best efforts basis, 82
Beta
  characteristic line, 189–193
  common stock estimated, 190
  definition and interpretation, 186–187
  examples, 188–189
  market portfolio, 185–186
  market risk, 184–185
  overview, 182–183
  security market line, 193–194
  systematic and unsystematic risk, 183–184, 192–193
Board of Directors, 5–6, 16, 19
Bond indenture, 388
Bonds
  call provisions on, 216
  convertible to common stock
    features of, 432–434
    motives for issuing, 437–438
    valuation of, 434–437
  corporate
    classification methods, 390
    features, 387–390

    interest payment methods, 393–394
    principle repayment methods, 391–393
    refunding, 410–413
    types of security and priority of claim, 390–391
  definition, 207
  duration and interest rate risk, 235–238
  features of, 207–208
  IVM calculation example, 208–209
  and market efficiency, 214–215
  rating agencies, 77
  reducing cost of capital, 491
  required rate of return components, 212–213
  semiannual interest payments, 209–210
  yield-to-maturity calculation, 210–215
Book value, 427
Bootstrapping, 690
Bridge loan, 418
Brokers, 65
Budgeting, cash, 646–649
Business organization, 12–18
Buyouts. *See* Corporate restructuring; Mergers

C

Callability, 77–78
Call options, 392–393, 538
Call price, 434, 437
Call protection, 392–393
Capital, 61–62
Capital Appropriations Control System, 369
Capital Asset Pricing Model
  in estimating RRR, 494
  and security market line, 194
  simulated approach, 509–510
Capital budgeting
  definition, 264
  and estimating product demand, 362
  and inflation, 329–332
  method survey results, 277
  steps in
    corporate strategy compatibility, 363, 364–366
    financial evaluation, 363, 366–367
    overview, 361–362, 363, 364
    post-audit, 363, 369–370

    project evaluation, 363, 364–368
    project implementation, 363, 368–369
    proposal generation, 362–364, 365
    strategic financial plan compatibility, 363, 367–368
Capital investments
  definition, 264
  measuring business unit performance, 289–292
  and project abandonment, 356
  proposal types, 304
  return on investment versus net present value, 292
  valuation of, versus securities valuation, 263
Capital market, 72, 73, 119–120
Capital rationing
  and liquidation proceeds, 285–287
  overview, 282–285
  and present value index, 287–288
Carrying costs, 632
Cash accounting, 32
Cash discounts, 578, 619–621
Cash flow equivalence, 131–133
Cash flows
  capital investment analysis depreciation, 310–312, 313–314
  discounted, 283
  economic life determination, 324–325
  embedded real options, 307
  expansion estimation example, 316–320
  and income tax, 305–306, 308–310
  incremental, 304
  interest expense and dividends, 306, 314
  investment tax credits, 313
  loss carry-backs and carry-forwards, 314–315
  and multiple internal rates of return, 299–301
  non-discounted, 265–269
  perceived accuracy of, 352
  replacement estimation example, 320–324

sale of depreciable assets, 313–314
sample form, 366, 367
special financing, 306–307
timing of, 291–292
value of lost opportunities, 306
contractual, 171–172
discounted, 283
factors negatively affecting, 721–723
forecasting, 321, 646–649, 766
investor use of, 309
in leasing, 403–404
management of
accelerating collections, 603–605
affecting firm value, 596
collection process, 601–603
optimal level of, 596–597, 598, 599, 601
reengineering, 606
slowing disbursements, 605
system evaluation, 605–608
nominal versus real, 330–332
non-contractual, 172–175
overview, 48–49
purpose of, 27
random versus known, 597–598
Certificates of deposit, 610–611, 764–766
Changes in state of incorporation, 701
Chapter 7 Proceedings, 730, 732–733
Chapter 11 Proceedings, 730, 731–732
Characteristic line, 189–193
Chattel mortgage, 384
Cheat sheets, 418
Clayton Act of 1914, 687, 698
Clean-up period, 582
Clientele effect, 529
Coefficient of variation, 181–182
Coinsurance effect, 511
Collateralized mortgage obligations, 397
Collateral trust bonds, 391
Collections, 41, 601–605, 621
Commercial paper, 582–583, 590–591, 610
Commercial risk, 103–104, 108
Commitment fee, 582
Commodity bundles, 245–246
Common stock
accounting for, 426–428
advantages and disadvantages of, 426

bonds convertible to, 431–438
characteristics, 423
claim on income and assets, 422–423
cost of
CAPM in estimating, 494
dividend growth model, 492–493
issuance expense, 494–496
overview, 490–491
definition, 218, 422
evaluating
level and timing of financing with, 543–545
P/E ratios and IVM on, 223–226
required rate of return components, 221–223
value calculation, 218–221
variable growth rate calculation, 226–229
yield calculation, 221–223
financing capital investments, 521
other rights for holders of, 424–425
rights offering issue, 428–431
voting power, 423–424
Compensating balances, 582
Competitive bidding, 82
Composition, 730, 731
Compounding, 133–134, 157, 162–163
Comprehensive income requirement, 665
Concentration banks, 604
Conglomerate merger, 687
Contingent voting power, 420
Continuous distribution, 173–175
Contractual claims, 71, 73
Contractual intermediaries, 69–70
Control limits, 598, 599
Conversion period, 433
Conversion premium, 434, 435–437
Conversion price, 433
Conversion ratio, 433
Conversion value, 434, 435
Corporate divestitures, 289, 703–705
Corporate growth
application of, 669–671
determinants of sustainable, 665–666
dividend policy and stockholder wealth, 520–522, 673–674
external equity financing, 667–669

formula, 663–665
link to employee attitudes, 660
market-to-book ratio, 671–672
overview, 660–663
Corporate restructuring
definition, 682, 683
divestitures, 289, 703–705
leveraged buyouts, 701, 705–708
leveraged recapitalizations, 701, 708–710
methods overview, 683, 684
rationales for, 683–685
spin-offs, 703–705
Cost of capital
common equity, 490–496
debt, 489–490
definition, 489
implications of changes in, 506–507
preferred stock, 490
weighted average
book and market weights, 499–501
calculating cost, 496–497
capitalization targets, 496
changes in operations, 504
financial planning strategy, 497–499
in international investing, 767–768
leverage ratio changes, 501–503
market environment changes, 504–506, 507
optimum degree of leverage, 43–44, 504, 505
Cost recovery period, 310
Country risk, 104–105, 108
Coupon, 207, 208
Coupon bonds, 393–394, 395
Covered foreign currency loans, 763–764
Covered interest rate parity, 753, 755–757, 759
Covering, 755–757
Credit collection agencies, 621–622
Credit policies
collection decision, 626–628
and credit granting decision-making, 623–625
credit terms decision, 625–626
evaluation procedure, 622–623
letters of credit, 116–117
lines of credit, 581–582
Credit policy delay, 602
Credit rating agencies, 621–622

Credit standards, 618–619, 623–625
Credit terms, 619–621, 625–626
Cross-section ratio analysis, 39, 46
Cumulative preferred stock, 419
Currency exchange risk, 106–108
Currency market
chart of currency by country, 115
direct and indirect exchange rates, 110
European monetary system, 113–114, 117
exchange risk, 106–108
foreign currency borrowing, 760–762
foreign currency investing, 764–766
forward differentials, 112–113
forward exchange rates, 111–112, 249–253
nominal versus real currency, 330–332
traders affecting, 250
trading in, 114–115
Current coupon bonds, 395
Current liabilities, 28
Current ratio, 39–40
Current value, 29

D
Date of record, 428, 429
Debentures, 390
Debt capacity, 476
Debt instruments. See Contractual claims
Debtor-in-possession loans, 735
Debt ratio, 43
Decision break-point analysis, 355–356
Default, 43
Default risk, 74–75
Default risk premium, 78
Deficit unit, 62
Denomination intermediation, 67
Depository intermediaries, 68–69
Depository transfer checks, 604
Depreciation, 310–312, 313–314
Dilution, 423
Direct claims, 64, 73
Direct exchange rates, 110
Direct lease, 399
Disbursements, 605
Discounted cash flows, 283

Discounting
  analysis from present value, 153–156
  annual, 134–137
  continuous, 162–163
  deferred annuities, 149–150
  key symbols used in, 157
  non-annual, 146–149
  perpetuities, 151–153
Discount period, 578
Discount rates, 135, 766–767
Discrete distribution, 173, 174
Disequilibrium, 269–270
Distribution cost advantage, 99
Diversification
  definition, 182
  and estimating required rate of return, 507–512
Divestitures, 703–705
Dividend capture, 610
Dividend payout ratio, 224
Dividends
  affecting taxes, 314
  extra, 532
  growth model, 492–493
  policy on
    affecting firm's value, 519
    affecting stockholder returns, 520–522, 673–674
    dividends as a priority, 526
    dividends as a residual, 524–526, 530
    establishing, 528–532
    payment procedure, 532–533
    share repurchase, 533, 536–537, 538
    stock dividends and splits, 533–536
    stockholder preferences, 523–528
Double taxation, 17
Drafts, 605
Dual class recapitalization, 701
Duration, 237–238

E

Earnings per share, 45–46
Economic life, 324–325
Economic risk exposure, 108
Economies of scale, 67–68
Efficient market, 214–215, 238–240
Equity carve-out, 703
Equity financing. See Long-term financing
Equity instruments. See Residual claims
Ethics
  affecting stakeholders, 20
  between company and franchisees, 650
  in company environment, 18–19
  in corporate divestitures, 289
  and corporate responsibility for factory employees, 370
  and corporate social responsibility, 330
  corporate training programs in, 172
  environmental impact and cost of capital, 498
  European illegal practices crackdown, 764
  and financial reporting, 52
  and golden parachute clauses, 7
  in initial public offerings, 418, 712
  and insider information, 84
  of lottery prize brokers, 151
  of outside directors, 19
  and prime rate discounts, 584
  and trading blocs, 103
  of unequal voting rights, 432
  and working capital management issues, 565
Eurobonds, 119, 120
Eurocredits, 118, 120
Eurocurrency, 117
European monetary system, 113–114
European Union, 103, 113, 754
Exchange Rate Mechanism, 114
Exchange rates, 754–755
Exchange ratio, 693–696
Ex-dividend date, 533
Executive compensation, 2, 5–6, 7, 293
Expected spot rate, 246–249, 257
Expected value, 173–174
Expiration date, 428, 429
Explicit bankruptcy costs, 727–728
Expropriation, 106
Ex-rights date, 428–429
Extension, 730–731
Extra dividends, 532

F

Face value. See Par value
Factor, 584–586
Factoring accounts receivable, 584–586
Federal Trade Commission deregulation, 684, 687, 698
Finance companies, 70
Financial Accounting Standards Board, 401, 665
Financial analysis, 27, 48–49, 52
Financial assets, 6

Financial distress
  Bankruptcy Reform Act of 1978, 731–733
  causes of, 721–723
  cost of, 723–728
  court-administered settlements of, 730, 731–732
  from creditors' perspective, 734–736
  definition, 721
  and leverage, 470–474
  and liquidation, 736–739
  predicting, 728–729
  and prepackaged bankruptcies, 730, 733–734
  and private negotiated settlements, 730–731
  recovery example, 732
  and reorganization, 736–737, 739–742
  in risk analysis, 347–348
  technical insolvency versus insolvency-in-bankruptcy, 729
Financial intermediaries, 65, 67–68
Financial leases, 398–399
Financial management, 2–4, 26, 61
Financial managers, 12–14, 525
Financial planning
  and cash budget, 646–649
  and comprehensive income requirement, 665
  cost of capital strategy, 497–499
  as duty of financial manager, 13–14
  financial statement projection using ratios, 655–660
  financial structure and firm value, 537
  level and timing of common stock financing in, 543–545
  level and timing of debt financing in, 540–542
  level and timing of retained earnings in, 542–543
  in not-for-profit organizations, 544
  overview, 645–646
  relative costs of long-term financing, 538–539
  sequence of long-term financing, 539–540
  strategic operating plan, 540, 541, 542
  temporary delay of proposed investments in, 541, 545–546
  using pro forma financial statements, 649–655

Financial risk, 450–451
Financial statements
  pro forma, 649–655
  unethical, 52
  using ratios to project, 655–660
Financial system, external
  economic efficiency, 63–64
  financial instrument and market types, 70–72
  overview, 60–61
  role of financial markets in, 62–63
  role of intermediaries in, 65, 67–70
  simple and complex, 64–66
Financing. See Long-term financing; Short-term financing
Financing cost savings, 99–100
Fixed asset turnover ratio, 42
Fixed charge coverage ratio, 43–44
Floating exchange rates, 107
Floating lien, 586
Floor planning, 586, 588
Flotation costs, 83, 526
Forecasting. See Financial planning
Foreign bonds, 119, 120
Forward contracts, 111–112, 249
Forward covers, 116
Forward differentials, 112–113
Forward discounts, 113
Forward exchange rates, 111–112, 249–253, 257
Forward premiums, 113
Fourth market, 95
Free cash flows, 51, 692
Friendly mergers, 698
Funded liabilities, 28
Funds, 49
Futures market, 251–252
Future value
  of annuities, 141–143
  interpretation of, 156–157
  overview, 138–139
  and present value, 140–141

G

General covenants, 380, 381
General partnerships, 15–16
Global firm, 101–102
Going-concern value, 737, 739–740
Golden parachute clauses, 7
Goodwill, 32
Greenmail, 701
Gross margin, 44

H

Historical cost accounting convention, 29–30

Holding period yield, 213–214, 215
Horizontal merger, 686
Host country, 100
Hostile mergers, 698
Hot-money traders, 121
Hurdle rate, 266

I

Implicit bankruptcy costs, 727–728
Income bonds, 394–395
Income statements, 30–33, 650–652, 655–657
Income taxes. *See* Taxes
Incremental cash flows, 304
Independent investments, 266, 276–278, 326
Indirect claims, 65, 73
Indirect exchange rate, 110
Inflation, 329–332, 752–753
Inflation premium, 79–80
Information signaling, 526, 527
Initial public offerings
   ethical issues in, 418, 712
   and insider information, 84
   overview, 710–712
   web site, 80
Insolvency-in-bankruptcy, 729
Installment loans, 145–146
Integrated financial analysis, 52
Interest
   affecting taxes, 314, 458–461
   expense in calculating cash flows, 306
   payment of, on term loans, 384–385
   semi-annual, on bonds, 209–210
Interest coverage ratio, 43
Interest rate risk, 214–215
Interest rates
   behavior of, over time, 78–80
   and bonds, 213–214, 215, 235–238
   definition, 72
   determinants of, on securities, 73–78
   and international financial market
      basis point, 760
      covered interest rate parity, 753, 755–757
      inflation affecting, 752–753
      real interest rate, 749–752
      relationship to exchange rates, 754–755
      spread, 760
   risk-free, 175–176, 177, 178
Intermediation, 65
Internal rate of return
   analyzing multiple, 299–301
   in evaluating independent in-

vestments, 276–278
   in evaluating mutually exclusive investments, 278–282
   versus net present value, 276–282
   overview, 273–276
   rationale for using, 282
   role of, in capital analysis, 269–271
   using free cash flows, 340–344
International financial market
   affecting stock valuation, 227
   investing in
      cost of capital approximation, 768
      debt financing, 463
      discount rates, 766–767
      exchange rate insurance, 757
      foreign capital markets, 389
      key relationships, 750
      loan preference principle, 763–764
      securities trading, 95
      weighted average cost of capital, 767–768
   marginal tax rates, 23
   operating in
      advantages, 120
      capital market, 119–120
      cultural issues, 629
      and deregulation, 87
      and ethical behavior, 764
      Eurocurrency, 117
      hot-money traders, 121
      money market, 117–119
      motives for international operations, 98–102
      overview, 96–98
   price comparisons, 256
   relationship overview, 758–759
   risk in (*see* Risk)
   valuation
      current exchange rates, 243–246
      key relationships, 242, 249, 254, 255
      purchasing power parity, 242–243, 244
Internet commerce, 569
Inventories
   affecting firm value, 617
   components of, 631
   Internet commerce affecting, 569
   just-in-time policy, 632
   lender control over, 588
   policy evaluation, 632–635, 636
   and seasonal sales, 636–637
   securing loans with, 586–587

Inventory turnover ratio, 41
Investment bankers, 81–83
Investment companies, 70
Investment risk, 167, 348
Investments, 165
Investment tax credits, 313
Investment Valuation Model
   application of, to security valuation, 206
   benefits component, 169–170
   bond valuation, 208–212
   common stock valuation, 218–221, 226–229
   estimating anticipated benefits, 171–175
   future exchange rates, 248
   overview, 166, 168–171
   and P/E ratios, 223–226
   preferred stock, 215–218

J

Junk bonds, 391

L

Law of one price. *See* Purchasing power parity
Leasing
   acquisition methods, 399–400
   evaluating choices, 402–405
   financial motives for, 400–402
   operating versus financial, 397–399
   overview, 396
Legal issues
   affecting value maximization, 18–19
   Bankruptcy Reform Act of 1978, 731–733
   causing financial distress, 723
   Clayton Act of 1914, 687, 698
   common stock, 425
   corporate bonds, 388–389
   covenants, 380–382
   equity financing overview, 415–416
   forms of business ownership, 14–18
   FTC deregulation, 684, 687, 698
   litigation by the target, 701
   in mergers, 698–699
   preferred stock, 418
   reorganization tests, 737
   securities regulations, 84–87
   Sherman Antitrust Act of 1890, 698
   subordinated claims, 380
   term loans, 383
   Williams Act of 1968, 698–699
Lender liability lawsuits, 735–736

Lessee, 396
Lessor, 396
Letters of credit, 116–117
Leverage
   affecting cost of capital, 501–504, 505
   affecting firm value
      corporate taxes, 457–461
      growing firm, 467–470
      no-growth firm, 462–467
      in tax-free environment, 456–457
   affecting profitability
      EBIT-EPS breakeven chart, 453–455
      magnitude of return, 451–453
      variability of return, 455–456
   and financial distress, 470–474
   financial versus operating, 446–447
   in financing sports stadiums, 457
   fixed versus variable financing costs, 447–448
   operating versus financial, 446–451
   optimal level of, 474–476
   optimum leverage ratio, 43–44, 504, 505
   overview, 445
Leveraged buyouts, 701, 705–708
Leveraged leases, 399–400
Leveraged recapitalizations, 701, 708–710
Leverage ratio, 43–44, 504–505
Liabilities, 27–28, 563, 564
Limited liability, 15–16
Limited partnerships, 15–16
Line of credit, 581–582
Liquidation, 736–739
Liquidation by assignment, 730, 731
Liquidation proceeds, 285–287
Liquidity, 608
Liquidity ratio, 39–40
Litigation by the target, 701
Loan preference principle, 763–764
Lock box system, 604–605
London Inter-Bank Offered Rate, 118–119, 749
Long-term financing
   choosing between debt and equity, 450
   debt
      contractual claim of lender, 380

cost of, 489–490
definition, 27
maturity composition, 565–566
optimal level and timing of, 540–542
primary versus secondary market transactions, 382
protective covenants, 380–382
term loans, 382–387
equity
characteristics of, 415–417
definition, 27
external, 667–669
off-balance sheet, 401–402
100% financing, 401–402
relative costs of, 538–539
retained earnings versus common stock, 520–522
risk/return trade-off, 379
sequence of, 539–540
Long-term liabilities, 28
Loss carry-backs, 314–315
Loss carry-forwards, 314–315
Lottery prizes, 145, 151

M

Mail delay, 602
Marketability, 77, 383, 389, 608–609
Marketable securities. *See* Securities
Market efficiency, 214–215, 238–240
Market risk, 184–185
Market RRR schedule, 176–177
Market stabilization, 82
Maturity
of corporate bonds, 387–388
in determining yield, 75
and risk/return trade-off, 565–570
of term loans, 382
terms-to-maturity, 207, 208, 235–238
yield-to-maturity, 210–215, 273
Maturity date, 207, 208
Maturity intermediation, 67
Mergers
accounting environment, 699–700
cash purchase, 691–693
cautions in evaluating, 697
consolidations, 696–697
definition, 685
exchange of stock, 693–696
legal environment of, 698–699
motives for, 687–690
success rate of hostile, 702

takeover defenses, 700–702
types of, 685–687
Modern portfolio theory, 189
Money market, 71–72, 73
Mortgage bonds, 390–391
Mutually exclusive investments, 266, 278–282, 326–329

N

National Association of Securities Dealers Automatic Quotations, 94
National Association of Security Dealers, 418, 712
Negotiable certificates of deposit. *See* Certificates of deposit
Negotiated current liabilities, 564
Negotiated offering, 83
Net margin, 44–45
Net period, 578, 619–621
Net present value
in evaluating independent investments, 276–278, 326
in evaluating mutually exclusive investments, 278–282, 326–329
versus internal rate of return, 276–282
NPV profile, 276
overview, 271–273, 276
and present value index, 287–288
versus return on investment, 292
role of, in capital analysis, 269–271
using free cash flows, 340–344
and valuation opportunity cost, 284–285
Net working capital, 558
New York Stock Exchange, 61
No-growth model, 218–219, 221
Nominal currency, 330–332
Nominal interest rates, 80
Noncumulative preferred stock, 419
Non-discounted cash flows, 265–269
Normative analysis, 4
North American Free Trade Agreement, 103
Not-for-profit organizations, 17, 544
NPV profile, 276

O

Offshore financing, 117–119
Open account, 578
Operating assets, 558
Operating leases, 398
Operating leverage, 446–447

Operating risk, 350–354, 448–451
Opportunity cost, 130–131
Optimum leverage ratio, 43–44, 504, 505
Ordering costs, 632–633
Organizational chart, financial managers on, 12–13
Original issue discount securities, 395
Outstanding shares, 426
Overcapitalization, 722–723
Overhanging bond issue, 437
Over-the-counter market, 94

P

Partnerships, 15–16, 18
Par value, 207, 208, 427
Payback period method, 267–269
Payout ratio, 520–522
Permanent assets, 562, 566–567
Permanent current assets, 562
Permanent financing, 563
Permanent spontaneous current liabilities, 564
Perpetuities, 151–153
Placement fees, 590–591
Poison pills, 701
Political risk, 105–106, 108
Pooling of interests accounting, 699, 700
Post-audit, 363, 369–370
Preference stock. *See* Preferred stock
Preferred stock
adjustable-rate, 610
advantages and disadvantages of, 420–422
calculating value of, 216–217
calculating yield on, 217–218
characteristics of, 417
claim on income and assets, 417–420
convertible into common stock, 421
cost of, 490
exchangeable, 421
overview, 215–216
retirement of, 420
step-down, 421
voting power, 420
Prepackaged bankruptcies, 730, 733–734
Present value component analysis, 356–358
Present value index, 287–288
Present value
analysis, 153–156
annualized, 329
of annuities, 143–145
component analysis, 356–358
and future value, 140–141

index, 287–288
interpretation of, 156–157
overview, 135, 140
Price/earnings ratio, 223–226
Price elasticity, 236
Price pegging, 82
Price quotations, 93–94
Primary market. *See* Securities
Primary offerings, 710
Prime rate, 118, 582, 584
Private placement, 388
Privileged subscription, 428–431
Probability distributions, 173–175
Processing delay, 602
Product differentiation, 99
Production cost advantages, 99
Production costs, 633
Profitability ratio, 44–46
Profit maximization, 10–11
Promissory note, 578
Prospectus, 85, 86
Protective covenants, 380–382
Proxy fights, 424, 425
Proxy statement, 423–424
Public offerings, 80–81, 388
Purchase of assets accounting, 699, 700
Purchasing power parity, 242–243, 244, 754, 759
Pure play, 509, 510

Q

Quick ratio, 40

R

Ratio analysis
implementing, 46–48
in projecting financial statements, 655–660
purpose of, 27
summary of uses, 40
types of
acid-test ratio, 40
activity ratio, 40–42
average collection period ratio, 41
average payment period ratio, 41–42
average return on investment, 265–267
conversion ratio, 433
current ratio, 39–40
debt ratio, 43
exchange ratio, 693–696
fixed asset turnover ratio, 42
fixed charge coverage ratio, 43–44
interest coverage ratio, 43
inventory turnover ratio, 41
leverage ratio, 43–44, 504–505
liquidity ratio, 39–40